*A History of East Central Europe*

VOLUMES IN THE SERIES

* Forthcoming

VOLUME VII

# The Lands of Partitioned Poland, 1795-1918

*A HISTORY OF EAST CENTRAL EUROPE*

*VOLUME VII*

EDITORS

PETER F. SUGAR
*University of Washington*

DONALD W. TREADGOLD
*University of Washington*

# The Lands of Partitioned Poland, 1795-1918

BY PIOTR S. WANDYCZ

UNIVERSITY OF WASHINGTON PRESS
*Seattle and London*

Library of Congress Cataloging-in-Publication Data
Wandycz, Piotr S. 1923–
    The lands of partitioned Poland, 1795–1918
    (A history of East Central Europe, P.F. Sugar and D.W. Treadgold, editors, v.7)
    Bibliography: p.
    1. Poland—History—1795–1864. 2. Poland—History—1864–1918. I. Title.
II. Series: Sugar, Peter F. A history of East Central Europe, v. 7.
DR36.S88 vol. 7 [DK434.9]  914.9s  [914.38′03′3]    74–8312
ISBN 0–295–95358–6 (pbk.)

*For my sister Anna Maria Mars*

# Foreword to the 1993 Printing

THE systematic study of the history of East Central Europe outside the region itself began only in the last generation or two. For the most part historians in the region have preferred to write about the past of only their own countries. Hitherto no comprehensive history of the area as a whole has appeared in any language.

This series was conceived as a means of providing the scholar who does not specialize in East Central European history and the student who is considering such specialization with an introduction to the subject and a survey of knowledge deriving from previous publications. In some cases it has been necessary to carry out new research simply to be able to survey certain topics and periods. Common objectives and the procedures appropriate to attain them have been discussed by the authors of the individual volumes and by the coeditors. It is hoped that a certain commensurability will be the result, so that the ten volumes will constitute a unit and not merely an assemblage of writings. However, matters of interpretation and point of view have remained entirely the responsibility of the individual authors.

No volume deals with a single country. The aim has been to identify geographical or political units that were significant during the period in question, rather than to interpret the past in accordance with latter-day sentiments or aspirations.

The limits of "East Central Europe," for the purposes of this series, are the eastern linguistic frontier of German- and Italian-speaking peoples on the west, and the political borders of Russia/the former USSR on the east. Those limits are not precise, even within the period covered by any given volume of the series. The appropriateness of including the Finns, Estonians, Latvians, Lithuanians, Belorussians, and Ukrainians was considered, and it was decided not to attempt to cover them systematically, though they appear in these books. Treated in depth are the Poles, Czechs,

Slovaks, Hungarians, Romanians, Yugoslav peoples, Albanians, Bulgarians, and Greeks.

There has been an effort to apportion attention equitably among the regions and periods. Three volumes deal with the area north of the Danube-Sava line, three with the area south of it, and three with both areas. Three treat premodern history, six modern times. Volume I consists of an historical atlas. Each volume is supplied with a bibliographical essay of its own, but we all have attempted to keep the scholarly apparatus at a minimum in order to make the text of the volumes more readable and accessible to the broader audience sought.

The coeditors wish to express their thanks to the Ford Foundation for the financial support it gave this venture, and to the Henry M. Jackson School of International Studies (formerly Far Eastern and Russian Institute) and its five successive directors, George E. Taylor, George M. Beckmann, Herbert J. Ellison, Kenneth Pyle, and Nicholas Lardy, under whose encouragement the project has moved close to being realized.

The whole undertaking has been longer in the making than originally planned. Two of the original list of projected authors died before they could finish their volumes and have been replaced. Volumes of the series are being published as the manuscripts are received. We hope that the usefulness of the series justifies the long agony of its conception and birth, that it will increase knowledge of and interest in the rich past and the many-sided present of East Central Europe among those everywhere who read English, and that it will serve to stimulate further study and research on the numerous aspects of this area's history that still await scholarly investigators.

PETER F. SUGAR
DONALD W. TREADGOLD

# *Preface*

THIS volume tells the story of a large area of East Central Europe that until 1772 had been a single although a multinational and a heterogeneous state. Partitioned between Russia, Austria, and Prussia, the Polish-Lithuanian Commonwealth *(Res Publica)* retained some common identity throughout a good part of the nineteenth century and appeared as a reality to Poles and non-Poles alike. This common identity began to wane gradually not only as a result of the threefold division, but also because of the rise of modern nationalism of the Poles, Lithuanians, Ukrainians, and Belorussians who had composed the old commonwealth.

As conceived this book is both more and less than a history of the Polish nation in the nineteenth century. Its emphasis on the state territory of the commonwealth explains why such predominantly ethnic Polish lands as parts of Teschen (Cieszyn, Těšín), East Prussia, or Upper Silesia are only barely touched upon. At the same time predominantly Lithuanian, Ukrainian, and Belorussian areas are included, although the histories of these nations could not be treated here in a comprehensive fashion. Lithuanian, Ukrainian, and Belorussian developments are mainly discussed from the point of view of their interaction with Polish trends, as well as in terms of the gradual departures of these nations from the common historic tradition of the commonwealth. While the Germans and the Jews, who constituted sizable groups in the historic *Res Publica*, are discussed, the stress once more is on their relations with the Poles. Given the crucial importance of Polish culture as a link between the partitioned lands, short chapters have been added which survey cultural developments. The relatively cursory treatment of the Polish question in its international setting in no way implies that the author underestimates the great importance of international factors for Polish struggles for independence and for Poland's eventual rebirth in 1918.

Meant to serve as a bridge between the volume that deals with the Polish-Lithuanian Commonwealth and the one concerned with interwar East Central Europe, this study attempts to explore the nineteenth-century processes and to indicate how they affected the Polish lands. Their heritage for the reborn Poland was in many instances crucial.

Although this is mainly a chronological survey and a reference work for students of East Central Europe, it does raise, or at least implies, certain basic questions that the reader ought to keep in mind while using it. The history of this region is obviously part of a broader European history, and the nineteenth century was an age of rapid change connected, to put it in the simplest terms, with the effects of the French and Industrial Revolutions. The great currents going from west to east moved in the direction of parliamentary democracy and economic and social modernization. How did they affect the people of the area under discussion? How did the Poles and the other nations of the old commonwealth react to these challenges?

In the field of politics one must look not only at the impact of the partitioning powers, but also at the local institutions and at the growth of modern nationalism. It is evident that autocratic Russia, the centralized and bureaucratic Prussia, and the traditionally conservative Austria resisted changes coming from the more advanced West. Their political structures imposed severe limitations on the evolution of the Polish lands in the direction of parliamentarism and liberalism. At the same time the Poles were not completely deprived of possibilities to engage in politics or denied a parliamentary experience. They were in charge of the political machinery of the Duchy of Warsaw (1807–13) and to a large extent of that of the Congress Kingdom (1815–31). The Republic of Cracow (1815–46) was virtually self-governing, and Galicia was autonomous after the 1860s. The existence of native sejms (diets) of the duchy and of the kingdom, Polish participation in the Galician diet, the Viennese Reichsrat, the Poznanian diet, the Prussian Landtag, the German Reichstag, and finally even the Russian Duma must not be ignored. Nor should one forget completely some participation of Ukrainian deputies in the parliamentary bodies of the Habsburg monarchy or a more token Lithuanian, Belorussian, and Ukrainian representation in the Russian Dumas.

The existing conditions of a partitioned country shaped and distorted the character of local political trends and parties. Some of them could only operate in the underground, others acquired specific forms and characteristics. To give but one example, the virtual absence of a conservative party from Polish politics after 1918 was largely due to nineteenth-century Triple Loyalism and the emergence of modern nationalism. Polish nationalism in its liberal form had long identified with progressive trends coming from the West: the Enlightenment, the French Revolution, liberalism, radicalism, and, finally, socialism. Toward the end of the nineteenth century, however, a different type of nationalism emerged; based on ethnic masses rather than on the historic "noble nation," it defied the past and the heterogeneous tradition of the commonwealth. Polish integral nationalism necessarily collided with the intense nationalism of the Lithuanians and Ukrainians. This was a development not unique at the time, but what made it particularly acute was the ethnically mixed area in which it operated, the intensity of the struggle waged by the underdog, and the peculiar socioeconomic evolution of this region.

The old commonwealth possessed a unique social group, the numerous and ethnically heterogeneous *szlachta*. The partitions destroyed its *raison d'être*, but in turn they accelerated the emergence of another peculiar elite, the intelligentsia. In the case of the Poles, the latter carried over some of the *szlachta* tradition; in that of the Ukrainians and Lithuanians, the intelligentsia rose from the bottom ranks of their societies. The liquidation of serfdom in large part ended the "two nations" phenomenon and gave rise to an integrated modern class society; but since social consciousness could not be divorced from national consciousness, the "new" Polish nation found itself in direct confrontation with the similarly evolving Lithuanians and Ukrainians.

The modern society that developed in Polish lands took largely the form of a conglomerate of gentry, peasants, and plebeians, in contrast to the West where the chief components were the middle class and the proletariat. This too had been largely an effect of the partitions. In economic terms, Poland as a unit "missed" the nineteenth century. A native middle class came into existence late, slowly, and on a small scale. The pauperization of Galicia, the transformation of Congress Poland—the only region that really went through an industrial revolution—all stemmed from the threefold divisions and the policies pursued by the partitioning powers. With this integration of Polish lands into three different economic structures, the very question of economic viability of the future reborn Poland occasioned bitter debates and dissensions. They were not the only disputes, for in the course of the nineteenth century virtually every generation of Poles which sought national independence was confronted with vital and agonizing questions. Would violent resistance or slow socioeconomic and cultural improvement better advance the national cause? Insurrection versus "organic work," "realism" versus "ideal-

ism," native efforts versus outside support—these were the big issues
which divided contemporaries and which subsequent historiography
has often appraised in an emotionally or ideologically involved
manner.

Overawed by the magnitude of the task of sketching a broad yet
reasonably full picture, confronted with a vast body of historical
literature, and attempting a difficult approach that is neither a history
of the nation nor of the state, the author has sought advice, information, and criticism from colleagues and friends. He wishes to thank
here Dr. Adam Ciołkosz of London, Professors Witold Jakóbczyk and
Lech Trzeciakowski of the Poznań University, Professor Wacław
Jędrzejewicz of the Piłsudski Institute of America, and Dr. Wojciech
Wasiutyński of New York.

The author owes a special debt of gratitude to two scholars:
Professors Henryk Wereszycki of the Jagiellonian University of Cracow and Wiktor Weintraub of Harvard University. The former read
with unwavering patience and understanding the entire manuscript
and offered most valuable and constructive criticism. The latter read
the four cultural chapters, pointed out the shortcomings, and gave
counsel and encouragement. The volume is dedicated to my sister
Anna Maria Mars, who received a Ph.D. in art history at the
Jagiellonian University and whose interest in my work has been a
great stimulus over many years.

P.S.W.

New Haven

# Contents

14.  *The Rise of Mass Movements*                          275

15.  *From Revolution to World War*                        308

16.  *The First World War and the Rebirth of Poland*       331

17.  **The Era of "Young Poland"**                         371

     *Bibliographical Essay*                               381

     *Index*                                               413

# Maps

# GUIDE TO POLISH PRONUNCIATION

| | | | | |
|---|---|---|---|---|
| ą | as in French bon | ś | soft as in sure |
| c | ts | u | oo as in roof |
| ć | soft ts | w | v as in van |
| ę | as in French main | y | as in yield |
| h | roughly as in loch | ź | soft zi |
| i | ee as in beet | ż | zh as in measure |
| j | y as in yield | dż | dj as in journey |
| ł | w as in war | ch | h as in loch |
| ń | soft n as in cañon | cz | ch as in church |
| ó | u as in true | rz | zh as in measure |
| s | as in sister | sz | sh as in ship |

## NOTE ON LITHUANIAN AND UKRAINIAN PRONUNCIATION

Lithuanian unlike Polish is not a phonetic language. The reader's attention is drawn to the existence of a number of diacritical marks that lengthen the e (é, e), a (ą), i (i), and u (ų), as well as to č which equals ch, š which equals sh, and ž which equals zh. There are several systems of transliterating Ukrainian from the Cyrillic alphabet, and in addition Ukrainians living in Galicia often spelled their names using Polish and German spelling. This may explain the seeming inconsistency in rendering Ukrainian names in the text.

*Part One*

THE AFTERMATH OF THE PARTITIONS,
1795–1815

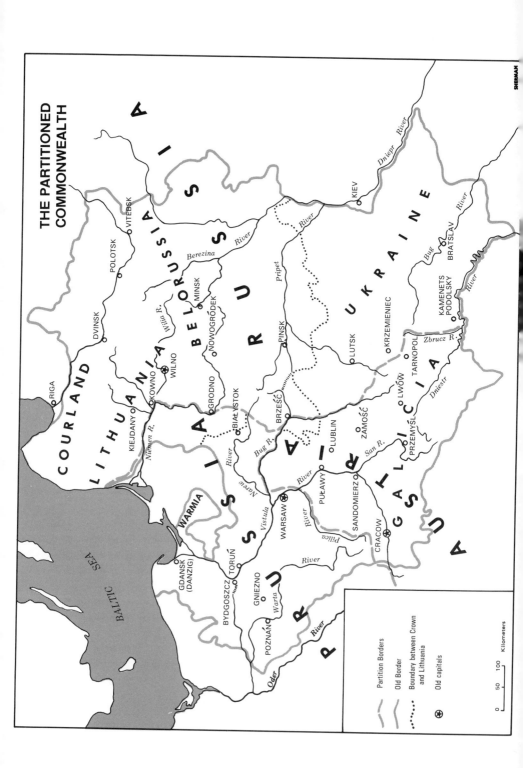

# THE PARTITIONED COMMONWEALTH

SHERMAN

RUSSIA

UKRAINE

GALICIA

AUSTRIA

PRUSSIA

LITHUANIA

BELORUSSIA

COURLAND

WARMIA

BALTIC SEA

RIGA

DVINSK

POLOTSK

VITEBSK

MINSK

NOWOGRÓDEK

WILNO

KOWNO

KIEJDANY

GRODNO

BIAŁYSTOK

BRZEŚĆ

PINSK

LUTSK

KRZEMIENIEC

KIEV

BRATSLAV

KAMENETS PODOLSKY

TARNOPOL

LWÓW

PRZEMYŚL

ZAMOŚĆ

LUBLIN

SANDOMIERZ

PUŁAWY

CRACOW

WARSAW

TORUŃ

BYDGOSZCZ

GDANSK (DANZIG)

GNIEZNO

POZNAŃ

Berezina River

Wilia R.

Niemen R.

Narew River

Bug R.

Vistula

Pilica River

Warta

Oder River

River

San R.

Pripet River

Dniepr River

Bug River

Dniestr River

Zbrucz R.

Niemen R.

River

River

Partition Borders

Old Border

Boundary between Crown and Lithuania

⊕ Old capitals

0    50    100
Kilometers

# CHAPTER 1

# The Country and the People

I. THE OLD COMMONWEALTH

EFFACED from the political map of Europe by the third and last partition in 1795, the Polish *Res Publica* had been a large and a heterogeneous state. Stretching from the Baltic to the Carpathian Mountains and across the northeastern European plain from the borders of Prussia to the Dnieper River, it occupied an area of some 730,000 square kilometers. On the eve of the partitions its population was around eleven million, and by 1795 it was almost fourteen.[1] This made Poland the fourth most populous country in Europe after France, the Holy Roman Empire, and Russia. The density of population has been calculated at from fourteen to nineteen persons per square kilometer, and in that respect Poland occupied the ninth place in Europe. The population was unevenly distributed; the greatest density was in the southern provinces and Poznania, the lowest in the northeastern borderlands.

The Kingdom of Poland, generally known as *Res Publica,* i.e. a commonwealth, was highly diversified. Not only did the Polish nation contain ethnic mixtures, the usual result of cohabitation of different groups within the same state, but the country comprised several peoples whose mother tongue was not Polish. Few if any of them had as yet a clear consciousness of national identity. The Polish-speaking group probably had a slight over-all majority, but Lithuanians, Ruthenians, and Belorussians predominated in several areas, and Germans and Jews constituted sizable segments of the population. The smaller groups comprised Russians (mainly Old Believers), Tatars, Walachians, Gypsies, Karaites, and Latvians. Some of these nationalities were native to the area, others were descended from

1. These figures are only approximations, and historians differ in their estimates.

immigrants who had settled there in the course of history. The religious picture of the commonwealth also reflected a large degree of heterogeneity. The Catholics were the biggest and in a sense the privileged group; they were followed by Uniates, Orthodox, Jews, and Protestants. The remaining denominations comprised 2 to 3 percent of the total population. This ethnic and religious diversity was not exceptional by eighteenth-century standards. Most large states were composed of many linguistic and religious groups, and prior to the birth of modern nationalism this was not regarded as a handicap to the state. Thus, while noting the multinational and multireligious character of the commonwealth, one needs to turn to the more directly significant constitutional and socioeconomic characteristics of old Poland.

The state consisted of two principal units: the Crown (korona) which comprised Polish and Ruthenian (Ukrainian) areas, and the Grand Duchy of Lithuania encompassing Lithuanian and Belorussian lands. The city of Gdańsk (Danzig) enjoyed autonomy under the direct jurisdiction of the king. The Duchy of Courland was a vassal state, and Livonia was placed under both the Crown and Lithuania. In addition, there were special autonomous regimes in certain parts of the country. Polish-Lithuanian dualism, expressed in the phrase "Res Publica of two nations," was reflected in separate administrations, armies, treasuries, and legal codes. Common executive organs appeared only at the end of the eighteenth century; a basic change embodied in the 1791 constitution—four years before the last partition—occurred too late to affect the country.

The old commonwealth recognized estates as social groups or classes, but in a different manner than, for instance, the ancien régime in France. Although people spoke of the gentry, Jews, burghers, and peasants as estates, formally and in a political sense the term was applied to the king, the senate, and the chamber of deputies (the last two known collectively as the diet or Sejm). The diet comprised only representatives of the gentry (szlachta), unlike the Etats Généraux which consisted of three estates. Hence, politically speaking, the gentry was the only estate that really mattered. In the course of centuries Poland developed a parliamentary republic of the szlachta. The word szlachta defies translation because everyone who had a noble status was a member of it, irrespective of his wealth or social position. A "nobleman" enjoyed rights that were both anachronistic and progressive. Unlike many a European counterpart, he was free from arbitrary arrest and need not fear confiscation of his land, which he held in full ownership. He participated in the election of the king and of the deputies to the diet; he had a virtual monopoly of all offices in the state; and however poor he might be he could boast of a status of legal equality with the most powerful magnate of the land. Neither race nor creed— except for a relatively brief period of discrimination against the Orthodox and Protestants—was an obstacle to his exercise of rights and liberties. In actual practice there were, of course, great distinctions within the body of the *szlachta*, based on wealth and tradition. A magnate may well have addressed a well-to-do squire by the appellation "brother," but the two were not equals. A petty nobleman who owned a peasant-like plot of land or no land at all was usually a client of a magnate whose favors he courted. But his status as a member of the *szlachta* was important all the same.

The nobility of the commonwealth was a melting pot of its nationalities. When the Grand Duchy of Lithuania joined Poland, first in a dynastic and later in a real union, the Lithuanian boyars became members of the *szlachta*. Many a nobleman had a Ruthenian, Belorussian, or German name. Jews who embraced Christianity were traditionally ennobled. There were cases of ennoblement of entire villages as reward for their military exploits. Consequently, the commonwealth developed a leading class that was more numerous than in most European countries. The gentry constituted roughly 8 to 10 percent of the entire population; the figures were somewhat higher for Lithuania and lower for the Crown. According to recent calculations, a quarter of all Polish-speaking inhabitants of the commonwealth belonged to the *szlachta*. Most noblemen in Lithuania, the Ukraine, or Belorussia became "Polish" in the sense of embracing a higher form of state nationality. They did not become denationalized, as witnessed by the expression *gente Rutheni natione Poloni* (of Ruthenian race and Polish nation). Being a good Lithuanian in no way interfered with being a Pole. This notion of a state and of a regional nationality survived the partitions of Poland. In a sense the *szlachta* was *the* nation, and it could rightly claim that it had achieved a degree of liberty and of participation in state affairs unsurpassed by any other nation in Europe.

The predominance of the *szlachta* was closely connected with the agrarian socioeconomic structure of the commonwealth, which had relegated the towns and the burghers to a position of inferiority. There were few large towns in eighteenth-century Poland, and many formerly important centers were in decay. From the 1760s Warsaw (Warszawa) began to grow rapidly and had two hundred thousand inhabitants on the eve of the last partition, but Wilno (Vilnius, Vilna), the capital of Lithuania, had only a little over twenty thousand. Only 17 percent of the population lived in towns, many of which were hardly more than large agricultural agglomerations. The burghers, who constituted around 7 percent of all inhabitants, had no representation in the diet, and their former rights and privileges were seriously curtailed. The Jews, who amounted to roughly 10 percent, were often referred to as an estate but distinct from that of the burghers. They were a majority in many a town, especially in the eastern part of the country, and engaged in trade and crafts or acted as middlemen. Until 1764 they enjoyed a self-governing autonomy under their diet (Vaad) based on the Kahals. Restrictions imposed on their commercial activities and on settlement in certain towns, as well as attempts by the state to integrate them, awakened Jewish fears. The Hassidic movement with its emotional and social overtones contributed to a strengthening of Jewish separateness and isolation from outside influences. It competed with the Haskalah Enlightenment which later contributed to assimilation trends. In contrast to the above two movements, the small Frankist phenomenon produced a number of Christian converts who became absorbed by the *szlachta*. The middle class as a whole, composed of an isolated Jewish community and the Christian burghers, had great difficulties in asserting itself. Besides, the most lucrative foreign trade (chiefly in grains) was not in its hands but in those of the noble landowners who controlled the bulk of the land.[2]

Polish agriculture specialized in the production of grains for export. It was based on manor farms that relied on serf labor *(corvée, Robot)*. The Germans call it *Gutsherrschaft*, the Poles *folwark pańszczyźniany*. The prevailing serfdom had three distinct, although closely related, features: a personal-legal relationship between the serf and the lord, a public-legal relationship, and an economic relationship. The first amounted to the peasant's lack of freedom as a person (for instance, his attachment to the soil). The second was the peasant's dependence on the lord as administrator and judge, and there was no appeal from the seigneurial justice. The third had to do with the peasant's right to the plot he cultivated without a legal deed of ownership, and the compulsory labor he performed on the lord's estate. The situation of the peasants in the commonwealth was not uniform. Roughly 64 percent lived on land controlled by the nobility; 17 percent, on church property; about 19 percent, on estates belonging to the crown. The last group had more firmly established rights to the soil it cultivated. It had lighter labor obligations or paid rents in lieu of *corvée*. It could also appeal to special royal courts. The position of peasants on church and noble lands was far worse. Then there were certain exceptions in different parts of the commonwealth. For instance, in some western and northwestern parts of Poland there were peasant farms that were altogether free from labor

2. Taking *dym* (hearth) as a unit, the nobles controlled 78 percent of the total, the crown 13 percent, and the church 9 percent.

obligations; and in heavily forested or mountainous regions peasants were only subject to small payments in cash or kind. This shows that sometimes both very advanced and very backward economic conditions could operate to the advantage of the peasantry. In areas that had too many peasants the peasants could occasionally buy themselves out from labor obligations. There were certain groups such as the German settlers in Pomerania (Olędrzy—Dutchmen) and some Ukrainians who had no labor duties at all. In the eighteenth century the process of commutation of labor obligations to rents intensified, although in some royal estates the reverse was also true. But although there were peasant-tenants (some of them virtually permanent tenants) and other categories of farmers, the *folwark* system prevailed throughout the country, and it placed the peasantry at the mercy of the noble class.

By the eighteenth century, the constitutional and socioeconomic system of the old commonwealth was in full decay. Devastated by wars and invasions, the country registered a decline in the volume of production, a diminishing productivity of agriculture, a rise in prices, and a general economic regression. With the agricultural revolution beginning in the West, the *folwark* system entered the phase of structural crisis. The limitation of the domestic market, increasing poverty of the peasantry, and the decline of cities were all part of the same general phenomenon.

The republic of the nobles could not effectively cope with these problems, especially as a constitutional crisis began to paralyze the functioning of the state. Under the pretense of safeguarding the rights of the "nation," the magnates were in fact running the country and catering to their own vested interests. The notorious *liberum veto*—the unanimity rule in the diet—together with elections of kings *viritim* (by all *szlachta*) opened the way to all kinds of abuses. The magnates and the foreign powers, using corruption and intimidation, exploited the Polish constitutional system. Prussia and Russia especially were determined to prevent any meaningful reform. While most European powers had adopted absolutism, Poland had been moving in the opposite direction. At a time when other monarchs were creating bureaucracies, effective systems of taxation, and large armies, the kings of Poland had no bureaucracy, an inadequate budget, and a small army. In 1780 the revenues of Poland were allegedly forty times smaller than those of France and ten times smaller than those of Russia. The "noble nation," which had won impressive personal liberties and political rights for itself and had been in the forefront of constitutionalism in Europe, had finally used its position to disrupt the state and to undermine its power and economic stability.

The first partition of Poland in 1772 came as a rude awakening to realities. A period of intense national revival followed, culminating in the adoption of the remarkable constitution of May 3, 1791. The reformers sought to transform Poland into a constitutional monarchy of an advanced type. The state was to enter the era of "enlightened liberty," bypassing the stages of absolutism and enlightened despotism. Drawing on Montesquieu's interpretation of the English constitution, on elements of the Austrian and Prussian Enlightenment, and on the new ideas of the American and French revolutions, the constitutional document of May 3, 1791, had its roots in the best native tradition. The constitution strengthened royal power, notably by substituting elections of dynasties for those of individual kings; it also stipulated that every royal act must be countersigned by a minister. The latter could be removed by a two-thirds majority of the diet. A strict separation between executive, legislative, and judiciary powers was introduced. The constitution abolished the *liberum veto* and laid foundations for an efficient functioning of the diet. Emphasizing the will of the nation as the source of power in the state, the constitution broke with the concept of the "noble nation." According to articles 4 and 11, the nation was understood as comprising the whole population. The rights and privileges of the *szlachta*, except for its poorest segment, were not curtailed, but the Polish equivalent of habeas corpus *(neminem captivabimus)* was extended to the burghers and the Jews. The reformers had plans of a new autonomy for the latter but did not include them in the constitution. The status of the burghers improved with the reestablishment of town autonomy in the royal cities. The burghers could acquire land and received some representation in the diet. The way was open to their fuller participation in the affairs of the country.

Provisions concerning the peasants were purposely vague. The reformers could not afford to change too much too quickly; as it was they were antagonizing the die-hard conservatives. But the articles that spoke of the peasantry as the "most numerous part of the nation" and promised it state protection were a token of more to come. Concrete projects of subsequent reforms were discussed and elaborated.

The May 3 Constitution, which Edmund Burke described in glowing terms and which was toasted in Philadelphia and Richmond, was a bold and sweeping reform. Trying to strengthen the state without making it absolute and preserve constitutionalism while eliminating its abuses, the constitution sought to extend gradually the rights and privileges of the gentry to the burghers. At the same time it was depriving the poorest stratum of the *szlachta*—a dangerous instrument in the hands of the magnates—of its voting powers. This was a step in the direction of associating political rights with property qualifications rather than with noble status. Future improvements in the position of the peasantry were also regarded as part of a general transformation of society.

The constitution amounted to a bloodless revolution and was accomplished amidst changing economic and cultural relations. In the eighteenth century the magnates' latifundia entered the road of industrialization. The early type of factories based mostly on serf labor appeared on the lands of the magnates and began to produce for a larger market. Magnates established ironworks and factories of textiles, glass, and luxury articles. This process received new stimulus in the 1760s with a general improvement in economic opportunities. Some order was put in the financial field, weights and measures standardized, and customs regulations improved. The magnates and the king took the initiative in canal building and the creation of new workshops. A network of royal factories was planned and partly realized in Lithuania; joint stock companies appeared in textile industries (wool and linen). The capital was largely that of the magnates and of the state, but later the gentry and burghers invested in joint stock companies. The first private banks came into existence. Much of the burden of this early type of industrialization was put on the shoulders of the peasantry and involved, in some cases, a switch from rents to compulsory labor.

In the countryside there was progress in farming techniques and experimentation with new crops. Agricultural production increased. The landlords' need of money as well as the feeling that serfdom deprived the peasantry of economic incentives led to a movement that advocated redemption of labor obligations and transformation of serfs into rent-paying tenants. In certain areas of the country labor obligations were converted to rents. Several economists and reformers argued that the growth of towns and industries was essential to increase the volume of exchange between town and country. Industrialization was encouraged as a panacea, and much of it was planned in a somewhat bureaucratic way. There was much waste, and the new factories needed the type of protection possible only in an absolute monarchy. External factors such as the first partition greatly interfered with foreign trade and led to its partial reorientation to the Black Sea. But, among the positive achievements, one can mention modernization of ironworks—the introduction of blast furnaces—and the beginnings of hard-coal mining. The textile industry in western Poland continued to develop satisfactorily. Warsaw grew as an important trading, banking, and industrial center.

The cultural and intellectual life of the country underwent important changes. The dissolution of the Jesuit Order enabled the state to launch a major program of educational reform and to establish the Commission of National Education, the first ministry of education in Europe. The commission supervised a thorough revision of school curricula, modernized education, and established a coordinated network of schools. Polish replaced Latin as the language of instruction, and textbooks departed from the scholastic tradition. A special Knights' School (Szkoła Rycerska) was founded by the last king, Stanislas Augustus; there the country's elite was educated with emphasis on civic virtues. Learning marked new achievements in the humanities and sciences; critical historical writing appeared. The ancient University of Cracow (Kraków) became truly a modern school.

New ideas, largely from the West, contributed to an intellectual ferment, and a literary and artistic milieu patronized by the king grew in Warsaw. Freemasonry, which spread rapidly in the 1770s, had its part in influencing the elite. It was characteristic of the changing society that several burghers appeared among the prominent leaders of the reformist movement, for example, Stanisław Staszic (1755-1826). Political literature reached impressive heights, and the term "Kołłątaj's Forge," denoting a group of radical reformers led by the priest Hugo Kołłątaj (1750-1812), was particularly appropriate to describe their efforts. There were notable developments in architecture (particularly in Warsaw), some in painting (although here foreigners predominated), and in music. A Polish opera appeared. The literature of the Stanislas Augustus period reached new heights; the Polish Enlightenment, with its emphasis on education and politics, was in full swing.

Unlike the first partition, the last two came at a moment when Poland was emerging from its previous state of decline and apathy. In spite of the vocal opposition of die-hard conservatives, the country was moving in a direction that opened before it large vistas and possibilities. The neighboring great powers grew alarmed by such signs of vitality. Exploiting the opposition of a handful of magnates who created a union in defense of the old order—the Targowica Confederation—Catherine II of Russia intervened militarily. The country was partitioned once again, in 1793, and the insurrection led by Tadeusz Kościuszko (1746-1817), a participant in the American Revolutionary War, could not prevent the final collapse. Affecting a large part of central Poland, Lithuania, and the Prussian-occupied lands, the insurrection showed socially radical features not yet apparent in the May 3 Constitution. In his Połaniec Manifesto, Kościuszko promised personal freedom to the peasantry and a reduction of labor obligations. There was hope of more to come and the peasants responded favorably. In Warsaw Polish Jacobins attempted to imitate Parisian terror, although Kościuszko disapproved of it. The insurrection fell to the overwhelming might of the three neighboring powers;

and in 1795 independent Poland disappeared from the map of Europe.

The commonwealth was split into three parts. Russia annexed around 62 percent of the area and 45 percent of the population. Prussia took 20 percent of the land and 23 percent of the people. The respective figures for the Austrian share were 18 and 32 percent. The newly drawn borders corresponded to neither historical, ethnic, economic, nor geographical criteria. Although the courts of St. Petersburg, Berlin, and Vienna had invoked dynastic or other claims to justify their actions, the determining factor was the balance of power which by the eighteenth century had degenerated into the *système copartageant* as Albert Sorel called it. Poland was not the first country to experience it, but she was the first big and ancient state to be completely wiped out as a result of its application. It was no wonder that the partitions of Poland produced a revolutionary change on the map of Europe and had far-reaching repercussions for East Central Europe and the continent as a whole.

II. UNDER THE HABSBURG RULE

Since the Habsburg monarchy did not participate in the second partition, the Austrian share consisted of territories acquired at two different times: in 1772 and in 1795. These comprised several provinces of so-called Little Poland and Great Poland. The new boundaries cut across old divisions; on the whole they followed the course of rivers: the Zbrucz and Bug in the east, the Pilica and part of the Vistula in the west. The part acquired in 1772 was called the Kingdom of Galicia and Lodomeria, a latinized version of Vladimir and Halich, two medieval duchies to which the Habsburgs unearthed an old Hungarian claim. In fact, Halich formed only a small part of the acquisition and the town of Vladimir lay outside the region. The area added in 1795 received the name of New (or Western) Galicia. All these lands belonged to the most densely populated territories of the former commonwealth. Their northern and western parts were ethnically Polish; in the eastern part the population was largely Ruthenian in speech and Uniate in religion. Although population figures are only approximations, especially in view of the natural increase that occurred between the dates of various partitions, Galicia (New and Old) had between three and three-quarters to four million inhabitants in 1795, of which roughly a quarter of a million were Jews.

The province had the important salt mines of Bochnia and Wieliczka, was a producer of meat and grains, and provided a good market for Austrian textiles, agricultural implements, and investments. Old Galicia was not affected by the fighting of the Kościuszko Insurrection and so escaped the devastations that accompanied and followed it elsewhere. Nevertheless, Galicia did not fare well under the Habsburg rule. State boundaries cut the old trade routes and contributed to the decline of towns; separated from its natural markets, Galicia stagnated. After a brief period of investments, Vienna, uncertain whether it would retain the province for good, began a fiscal exploitation of the province and drained it of manpower conscripted to service in the imperial army. The introduction of tobacco and salt monopolies, new taxes, the neglect of factories, and the use of depreciated banknotes marked the beginning of a course that was to make Galicia one of the poorest and most backward provinces of the Habsburg monarchy. The Napoleonic wars, which generally exhausted Austria, also had adverse effects on the Galician economy.

The lands annexed to Austria found themselves under a regime that was totally different from that of the Polish Commonwealth. Under Maria Theresa and Joseph, the monarchy was undergoing a thorough reform; and Josephinism went counter both to the old Polish tradition and to the reformist efforts of the May 3 Constitution. From 1786 Austrian codes replaced Polish laws. A complex bureaucratic machine was installed, which included the Galician Court Chancellery and a gubernium office in Lwów (Lviv, Lvov), renamed Lemberg. The Austrian bureaucracy assumed control over the province, which was subdivided into administrative units under nominated officials. The old elected towns' councils survived for a while but were later placed under the officials' rule. The provincial diets (dietines, sejmiki) which had elected deputies to the Polish diet and exercised some local functions disappeared. So did the elected Polish officials of various types. A new Assembly of Estates was set up in Galicia, although not in New Galicia; it was composed of the clergy, the magnates, and the gentry. Comparable to similar assemblies in other Habsburg lands, it could petition the monarch but had no real powers of its own. The conversion of the ancient royal castle (Wawel) in Cracow to Austrian army barracks was symbolic of the demise of Polish political and state traditions.

The new regime meant the end of the former position of the *szlachta*. The Austrian government destroyed its egalitarian character by splitting it into two estates: the magnates and the gentry. The government ended the nobles' exemption from taxation, freed them from military service, and subjected them to Austrian laws which provided for no personal and property guarantees comparable to those the *szlachta* had enjoyed in the commonwealth.

The Josephine reforms in the agrarian sphere affected both the nobles and the peasantry. Inspired in part by fiscal and demographic and in part by humanitarian motives, Josephinism sought to regulate landlord-peasant relations under the control of the state. In 1782 personal subjection of the peasant was abolished and a moderate serfdom *(gemässigte Untertänigkeit)* introduced. The peasant was free to marry, to change his occupation, and to leave the land provided he could find a replacement. Protected by the law, he could sue his landlord in courts. At the same time he became subject to a highly complicated system of justice and taxation in which both the administration and the lord participated. All the land, including the crown estates, most of which were sold to private individuals, was divided into dominical (demesne) and rustical (peasant) land, and none of the latter could be added to the former except through administrative process. Thus, the peasants' rights to the plots they cultivated became more firmly established; formally, the peasants became hereditary users of their land.

The law of 1786 lowered and regulated in detail the labor obligations *(Robot)*, but, as in other cases, the theory of the Josephine legislation did not always accord with the prevalent practice. The socioeconomic position of the nobility was sufficiently strong to restrict the benefits of the reforms. Some laws were modified, others bypassed. Although less arbitrary and more moderate than in the commonwealth, serfdom remained in the form of labor obligations and of the peasant's dependence on the noble landowner. Moreover, under the Austrian system the peasantry became subject to new obligations: payment of heavier taxes, and compulsory military service which was at first for life and then for a twenty-year period. These additional hardships may explain why peasants seemingly did not try to escape from the Polish lands (after the first partition) and come to Galicia.

The Josephine reforms contributed to tension in landlord-peasant relations. By making the lord responsible for levying taxes, partially administering justice, and furnishing recruits for the army, the administration identified him with most of the measures that were particularly disliked by the peasantry. In the peasant's eyes the oppressive lord offered a contrast to the benevolent emperor who cared for his peasants and tried to improve their lot. The Austrian authorities cultivated these beliefs which were likely to assist the government in its conflicts with the Polish nobility.

The Austrian regime also affected the towns and burghers in Galicia, and not only in the administrative sense mentioned above. The burghers were obliged to pay much heavier taxes than in the commonwealth, and the Jews were mercilessly exploited. While Joseph's policies, notably his toleration decree, greatly improved the status of Jews in the Habsburg monarchy, the benefits for Galician Jews were more doubtful. Unaccustomed to dealing with such a large and distinct Jewish group, Joseph attempted to break its separateness by subjecting Jews to military service, imposing secular schools on them, and forcing them to accept German surnames. These were unwelcome novelties for Galician Jews, although they appealed to the Haskalah which saw in German culture a vehicle for modernization and progress. In the specific Galician conditions many of these reforms proved to be a fiasco. A superficial germanization of the Jews, however, was achieved, and heavy taxes as well as small but vexing restrictions effectively maintained.

The state interference so typical of Enlightened Despotism and noticeable in all spheres of life in Galicia—political, economic, and educational—was even felt in the religious life of the province. The state carefully watched the relations between the Polish clergy and Rome. Meddling reached ridiculous heights when the zealous gubernium ordered that the words "Queen of the Polish Crown pray for us" be changed in a litany to "Queen of the Kingdom of Galicia and Lodomeria pray for us." The establishment of a ministry of police with wide powers of censorship added to the oppressive atmosphere that characterized the province under the Austrian rule.

III. PRUSSIAN POLAND

The Prussian share in the partitions of Poland was larger in size but smaller in population than that of Austria. In the first partition Prussia annexed so-called Royal Prussia (Pomorze) and Warmia (Ermland), and thus joined Brandenburg with her eastern possessions. In the remaining two, she obtained large areas of Great Poland, including Warsaw, and a slice of the Grand Duchy of Lithuania up to the Niemen (Nemunas) River. All these areas were rather densely populated and were predominently Polish ethnically. Through these acquisitions the Kingdom of Prussia increased by nearly one-half. Roughly three out of her eight million inhabitants were now former subjects of the commonwealth.

The Prussian regime as introduced in the Polish territories bore some resemblance to Austrian Enlightened Despotism. In both cases the government sought to render the new provinces similar in outlook and organization to the bulk of its possessions. The relatively small size of Prussia imposed some limits on a policy of complete absorption and uniformity. Thus, at first only Prussian legal procedure was introduced, and Polish law survived, although in the long run it was restricted to such matters as inheritance and marital contracts. In 1794-97, the *Allgemeines Landrecht* brought Prussian codes of law into the former Polish territories. Administrative changes came more rapidly, and Prussian bureaucracy took over effective control. The new provinces, which were called West Prussia, Southern Prussia, and New East Prussia, were divided into departments and districts. Old Polish provinces, dietines, and elected officials disappeared, as did town autonomy. Relations between Prussian officialdom and the *szlachta* had some peculiar features. Used to elected officials drawn from their own social class, the nobles were contemptuous of the German bureaucrats. The latter, while seeming to show deference toward the Polish nobility, looked down upon them as representatives of a culturally and politically inferior nation. The *szlachta* soon became the object of heavy Prussian sarcasm.

Seeking to obtain a firm hold over the newly acquired provinces, the Prussian government took over the former royal lands and confiscated the estates belonging to the leaders of the Kościuszko Insurrection. Fiscal motives played an important part in these moves, and much of the land was subsequently sold to Prussian Junkers and Berlin bankers, providing additional revenue to the state. German settlers were encouraged to come to the annexed provinces to develop them economically.

The Prussian socioeconomic system affected the existing class structure. Only nobles were allowed to own landed estates; the burghers who had gained this right under the May 3 Constitution were now deprived of it. Having virtually no town autonomy left, the burghers were worse off than in the last years of the Polish Commonwealth. The development of towns was also affected by the Prussian rule. While Poznań, now called Posen, grew and attracted a large number of Germans, Warsaw, reduced to the category of a provincial town, dwindled rapidly, and its population shrank to roughly sixty thousand. The position of the Jews changed. Like the other partitioning powers, Prussia was faced for the first time with the question of how to deal with a large and totally distinct religious and national group. In an attempt to diminish the size of this group, the government sought to expel the poorest Jews and divided those who remained into "protected" and "tolerated," depending on their wealth. The *Judenreglement* of 1797 was meant to "europeanize" the Jews by destroying their autonomy and germanizing them. The first objective was somewhat modified on fiscal grounds; policies of germanization, however, remained in force and corresponded to the Berlin-oriented Haskalah's efforts. The Poles considered that Prussia was, on the whole, favoring the Jews, and a certain Polish animosity toward them increased.

The economic situation under Prussia was temporarily favorable to agriculture. There was a great demand for grains, and the grain-growing estates went through a period of boom. Farming methods had been more advanced in this part of Poland than elsewhere, and technical progress continued. Attempts were made to abandon the traditional three-field system and introduce rotation of crops. Sheep breeding proved profitable. The cultivation of potatoes, a relative novelty, became more widespread, especially on peasant plots. Some estates began to use hired labor. All this prepared the way for a gradual transition to a new and more advanced stage in agriculture. The seeming prosperity, however, was not without its shadows. The Prussians established land-record offices which, by appraising the estates on the basis of their maximum profits, overstated their real value. Profiting from easy credit which Prussia extended them, the landowning gentry mortgaged their estates beyond their capacity to pay. This accumulation of debts eventually proved fatal to the *szlachta* and caused the loss of many a Polish estate in Prussia.

Although the government promoted easy credit in agriculture, it did not invest much in other branches of the economy. In some respects it even exploited the new provinces. The woolen textile industry of Great Poland—the largest of the commonwealth—suffered from a prohibition to export to other Prussian territories, while duty-free Prussian products were allowed into the Polish lands. The local industry became endangered. Mining fared better, although in Prussia as in Austria the landowner had no right to underground deposits on his estates. These were part of the royal monopoly of mining (*regale*).

Prussian laws determined relations between noble landlords and peasant serfs in the spirit of Enlightened Despotism. As compared with Josephinism, the Prussian system was more advantageous to the nobility. True, the state took the peasants under its protection and granted them recourse to royal courts, but seigneurial justice was administered through mixed state-landlord procedures similar to those in Austria. Evictions of peasants from the plots they cultivated were forbidden; this strengthened the peasants' right to the land, but evictions still took place in practice. Only in the former royal estates was there a marked improvement in the position of the peasants, who gradually became rent-paying tenants. Still, the peasantry had to carry new burdens in the form of taxes and a twenty-year-long military service. The dominant position of the landowning nobility was not undermined.

In spite of beliefs, widely held in Berlin, that the Prussian rule meant uniform progress for the acquired Polish provinces, this was certainly not true in the field of education. As compared with the reforms carried out by the Polish Commission of National Education, the Prussian system appeared inferior in several respects. In the annexed territories the number of schools was diminished; some of them were germanized. Students seeking higher education were advised to obtain it at the existing Prussian and German universities, where the instruction was in a language foreign to them.

IV. UNDER THE SCEPTER OF THE TSARS

The share of Russia in the partitions was by far the largest: more than one-half of the old commonwealth and nearly one-half of its population. The annexed territories comprised almost all of the Grand Duchy of Lithuania, the Ukraine, and several other provinces of the Crown east of the Bug River. While Austria and Prussia had attempted to justify their acquisitions by invoking dubious historical and dynastic claims, Catherine II went much further; after the second partition she ordered a medal struck with the inscription: "I recovered what had been torn away" *(ottorzhennaia vozvratikh).* Thus, the tsaritsa took the position that she had merely reunited lands that had once been part of the Kievan patrimony. This view was not shared by most of her contemporaries, and the sons and grandsons of Catherine considered that the partitions of Poland had been a crime and only Russian *raison d'état* and exigencies of the balance of power justified the need to retain the annexed areas. For a long time these lands were called the "provinces detached from Poland and united with Russia" *(ot Pol'shi prisoedinennye gubernii)* or simply the "Polish provinces" or "Polish guberniias." The expression "western guberniias" began to appear sporadically only a quarter of a century after the last partition. Many Russians assumed that these lands which had never belonged to the state of Muscovy were primarily inhabited by Poles and Lithuanians. Even an early nineteenth-century geography textbook by I. A. Arsenevich referred to the Poles as a "nation constituting the major part of the population in the Kingdom of Poland and in the guberniias [taken] from Poland and united [with Russia]."[3]

The "Polish provinces" were mainly inhabited by Ukrainians, Belorussians, and Lithuanians, but the Poles represented a significant group there. The Grand Duchy of Lithuania had been the most heterogeneous part of the old commonwealth, and while modern notions of nationality were hardly existent in the late eighteenth century, the duchy's linguistic and religious composition is of interest. According to Polish studies, Belorussians constituted nearly 40 percent of the total, Poles around 26 percent, Lithuanians 20 percent, Jews around 10 percent, and Russians 3.6 percent. In terms of denominations, the Uniates numbered about 40 percent, the Catholics 38 percent, the Orthodox 6.5 percent, and the Jews 10 percent. Apart from numerous *szlachta* (about 10 percent in the Grand

3. Cited in I. I. Lappo, *Zapadnaiia Rossiia i eia soiedienie s' Pol'sheiu* (Prague: "Plamia," 1929), p. 59.

Duchy), the Polish-speaking group included a large part of the clergy, most of the burghers, the polonized Tatars, and even a sizable part of the peasantry. The classes that really mattered in eighteenth-century society were almost exclusively Polish, although not necessarily of ethnic Polish origin. The picture was somewhat different in the Ukraine, where the bulk of the population, including many burghers, was Ukrainian (Ruthenian); but even here the *szlachta* was almost entirely Polish.

Russia divided her acquisitions into provinces (guberniias) placed under appointed governors and their administrative staffs. These guberniias were grouped together in three larger units: the Lithuanian, the Belorussian, and the Ukrainian general guberniias. The Russian administration, however, did not eliminate all of the previously existing institutions. Thus, the Lithuanian Statute—the old code of laws prevailing in Lithuanian and Ukrainian lands—remained in force. Dietines, local courts, and some elected officials continued to function, although their powers were restricted. Polish remained the language used in courts, but the Polish system of taxation was somewhat altered and higher taxes introduced. Unlike their compatriots in Prussia and Austria, the *szlachta* retained at least some means of participation in public life on the local level.

The magnates and the well-to-do nobility fared well, and the economic prosperity of the landowning *szlachta*, especially in the Ukraine, continued or even increased. One reason was the lucrative export of grains through the Black Sea ports, which was now easier than before. The small gentry, which was unknown in Russia, fell victim to chicaneries. The government often refused to recognize the noble status of the poorest, peasant-like *szlachta* and deported them in large numbers to the Black Sea guberniias (especially Kherson and Ekaterinoslav). The relations between the landowning nobles and the peasantry altered to the disadvantage of the latter. Russian serfdom was even harsher than that which had prevailed in Poland; there had been mass escapes of Russian serfs to the commonwealth, about which the Russian government protested to Warsaw in 1793. While in both countries the peasant was attached to the soil, in Russia he was more the personal property of his lord; he could be sold separately from the land he cultivated, he could be given away, rented, or sent as a punishment to Siberia. Complaints against the lords were forbidden and punishable by law. In the commonwealth compulsory labor obligations were calculated on the basis of the size of the peasant plot; in Russia the determinant was the number of peasant "souls." A landlord paid a tax on each "male soul" and obliged each serf to perform compulsory labor. An increase in population meant a proportionate increase in the labor force.[4]

Although these provisions were not officially introduced into the annexed provinces, the Russian usage spread fairly rapidly. All former Polish crown lands were taken over by the state and a large number of private estates confiscated. Consequently, masses of peasants came into direct contact with Russian proprietors. What is more, according to some estimates Catherine II granted about 650,000 "souls" to her favorites and officials who, in turn, arbitrarily increased the number of days of compulsory labor. The practice proved contagious and some Polish nobles imitated it. They knew that their rule over the peasants was now backed by a state whose machinery was stronger than that of the old commonwealth and that in doubtful cases the tsarist administration was not immune to bribery. In contrast to the situation in Prussia and Austria, the new peasant obligation to pay higher taxes and serve twenty-five years in the army was not compensated by reforms that alleviated his lot in other respects.

Factories, cut off from their sources of raw material in central Poland —mainly wool and iron—decayed rapidly. At first towns retained their municipal organization but not the new improvements brought under the May 3 Constitution. Later they were affected by Russian administrative measures. The burghers were divided into several categories, depending on their financial status, and had to pay higher taxes than in the commonwealth. The large Jewish population, roughly half a million people, presented a novel problem for the Russian administration. The tsars had never let in Jews before, and Catherine II established a sphere of settlement, the "pale," whose eastern boundary corresponded to the prepartition Polish frontier. The Jews were divided into several categories, and the government sought to move them into larger towns. The reasons were in part fiscal, in part political. In an attempt to russify the Jews, the administration admitted them to municipal councils and even made some efforts to convert them to Eastern Orthodoxy.

The traditional Russian view of the church as subordinate to the state found its expression in the religious policies pursued in the annexed provinces. The regime introduced there proved particularly oppressive for the Uniates. Regarded as the main link with Poland and an obstacle to a full merger of the "Polish guberniias" with Russia, the Uniate church saw all but one of its bishops deposed and replaced with a consistory which had little chance of resisting governmental policies. Using such means of pressure as the confisca-

4. The above remarks refer to serfs, not to state peasants.

tion of their land and the takeover of Uniate churches, the state sought to return the Uniates to the fold of Orthodoxy. Mass conversions, often forcible, took place, especially in the Ukraine. The Catholic clergy in turn became subject to stricter controls. Dioceses were reorganized, contact with Rome limited, and papal bulls published only with the approval of St. Petersburg. Thus, for instance, Russia ignored the dissolution of the Jesuit order and used the latter's services in the educational sphere.

## V. THE IMPACT OF THE PARTITIONS

To draw some general conclusions from the survey presented thus far, one must stress the fact that the lands of partitioned Poland found themselves under three monarchies whose character and outlook differed sharply from that of the old *Res Publica*. Two of these monarchies were passing through the stage of enlightened absolutism, the third had a despotic regime with a thin veneer of enlightenment. While the nobility occupied a leading position in Austria, Prussia, and Russia, its importance stemmed from the functions it performed in the political and socioeconomic structures of the states concerned, and not from genuine constitutional safeguards. For the egalitarian in spirit and politically active Polish nobility the partitions meant a loss of legislative, administrative, and partial judiciary powers. They legalized a breaking up of the *szlachta* into categories ranging from aristocracy down to the poorest group to which Russia denied a noble status and against which Austria discriminated. Only a small portion of the *szlachta* came to form the new landowning estate; the rest gradually drifted into other social classes.

In the partitioned Polish lands administrative and judiciary functions were concentrated in the hands of a largely alien administration. The real political power rested with the monarch. Under the socioeconomic system of the partitioning powers, the landowning nobility retained and in some cases improved its superior status. But if it became more secure, backed as it was by the might of the absolute monarchies, it was also less secure because of the arbitrariness of absolute government. The nobles were helpless when confronted with confiscations and enforced sales of their land. In 1797 the partitioning powers abolished the category of "mixed subjects" and forced the nobles to choose a single citizenship and sell lands held in other parts of old Poland. Only by special favors of the monarchs could the nobles be exempt from these regulations. Many magnates compromised in the Kościuszko Insurrection lost their estates; others were deprived of Polish crown lands that they had leased for generations. These losses also affected the clientele of the magnates, the poorest gentry, whom they had financed and employed on their estates. On purely economic grounds, many a Polish aristocrat felt he had to seek favors from the partitioning courts, and these considerations largely explain the address of the nobles from Lithuania which thanked Catherine II for taking over their country. Fear of "Jacobinism" accounts for the declaration of the municipality of Warsaw, which called the Russian conqueror, Field Marshal Aleksandr Suvorov, a "liberator." In general, while the average wealthy nobleman who was disinterested in politics may have found that the partitions interfered little with his way of life, his class as a whole was significantly affected.

The burden of heavy taxes and standing armies fell largely on the shoulders of the middle class and the peasantry. These burdens lessened the advantages derived from the regulation of the peasant's status in Austria and Prussia. The burghers registered few if any gains. The Jews, used to extensive autonomy which had disappeared only a short time before the partitions, became the object of new fiscal exploitation. Their freedom of settlement in Russia was restricted, and whether politics of modernization and germanization in Austria and Prussia brought unmitigated advantage to Jewry is, at best, debatable. Virtually all the Belorussians and the bulk of the Ukrainians found themselves under Russia and became the subject of russification, yet their specific experiences under the old commonwealth made their absorption into Russia difficult. Whether the partitions advanced or slowed down the growth of Ukrainian and Belorussian national self-determination is a question to which there is no easy answer.

The Catholic church had lost a good part of its land and became more strictly dependent on the state. In both Prussia and Russia it had to function under a monarch of a different faith. In Austria, even though the ruler belonged to the Catholic denomination, contemporary trends were not favorable to the church. The endangered ecclesiastical hierarchy found it prudent to be pliable vis-à-vis the governments, but it was not always successful. In contrast to the plight of the Uniates in Russia, those in Galicia fared far better, and Maria Theresa showed some interest in the Uniates as a potential ally against the Catholic Poles.

The partitions interrupted an important process of reform in the commonwealth, which sought to transform the country into a constitutional monarchy that rested on a gradually widening social base. By doing away with all parliamentary experiments and enforcing a traditional division into estates, the partitions set the country on a different course. Even if in the economic field some crafts, mining, iron works, and agriculture registered progress, most of the new factories folded. State borders destroyed the economic unity of the country and linked the three parts with the economies of the partitioning powers. The possibility of a gradual evolution of serfdom in the direction of rent-paying tenantry was largely denied. The splendid cultural revival, especially striking in the educational sphere, suffered a setback. The intellectual milieu of Warsaw disintegrated. The network of schools established by the Commission of National Education, the lively press, and artistic and scholarly activities deprived of royal and magnate patronage were among the first victims. The great Załuski library with its 160,000 volumes and 5,000 manuscripts went to St. Petersburg to become the nucleus of the university library there. The destinies of the Poles were taken out of their hands, and one can only speculate what might have been the evolution of the commonwealth within the new Europe born out of the French and Industrial Revolutions. As it was, the Polish lands became part of three conservative bulwarks that opposed the new trends. But the Polish nation only superficially merged with the Hohenzollern, Romanov, and Habsburg monarchies: it began to live its own peculiar life as a partitioned nation.

The possibility of survival of a nation without a state was not immediately apparent to the Polish elite. The very term "nation" lacked a precise meaning and was used in different ways. One could speak of the traditional "noble nation," which to a large degree was identical with the state, and of the rising "nation of property-owners," which was likely to assume a clearer shape after the May 3 reforms. Finally, there was the budding concept of the nation as including all the people (lud), to which the French Revolution gave an important stimulus. To most contemporaries, nation and state were identical, and the disappearance of the latter meant the end of the former. The words attributed to the defeated Kościuszko, Finis Poloniae, were most likely apocryphal, but not the sentiments expressed by the prominent radical reformer Kołłątaj or the learned and enlightened Tadeusz Czacki (1765-1813). The former wrote that Poland had "ceased to belong to nations actually existing"; the latter echoed this sentiment by saying that Poland was "erased from the number of nations."[5] The collapse of Poland was likened to the finality of the fall of Carthage and of Troy.

Feelings of despair were mingled with attempts to forget the past and enjoy the present. While the leaders of the Kościuszko Insurrection languished in Russian, Austrian, and Prussian prisons, the conservative magnate Szczęsny Potocki (1751-1805) wrote his friend that he was destined to become "Russian for ever." Frightened for their

5. Cited in Marian Kukiel, *Dzieje Polski porozbiorowe 1795–1921* (London: B. Świderski, 1961), p. 53.

positions or simply wishing to escape the atmosphere of collapse and gloom, many aristocrats and wealthy nobles plunged into a gay social life. The unquestionably patriotic nephew of the last king of Poland, Prince Józef Poniatowski (1763-1813), presided over revelries in the half-deserted Warsaw. Rich nobles eagerly sought Austrian and Prussian titles and orders. It seemed as if the partitions had not only destroyed the state but also the morale of its leading class. But this "danse macabre" on the ruins of the commonwealth proved but a brief episode.

Having bargained for nearly two years after the last partition over the final division of spoils, the three powers solemnly agreed in 1797 never to revive the name of Poland in any form or fashion. Yet, the same year a deputation of the *szlachta* petitioned the new tsar, Paul I, to reestablish Polish as the official language in the "Polish guberniias," appoint at least one-half of all officials from among the Poles, return the church lands, stop the persecution of the Uniates, and reopen the Wilno academy and Polish schools. In 1797 the Prussian government learned from a confidential report from Posen (Poznań) that nobles, priests, burghers, Jews, and peasants in South Prussia were dissatisfied with the new regime. The Austrian government was closely watching the small gentry and the ex-Polish officers in Galicia who seemed to adopt an attitude of total opposition to the new order and had little to lose from an armed uprising. Finally, in the course of the same year, 1797, news came that a Polish legion had been formed in Lombardy under the aegis of revolutionary France. The first lines of their marching song, later to become the Polish national anthem, proudly announced to the world that, "Poland is not yet lost as long as we live."

# CHAPTER 2

# *"Poland Is Not Yet Lost"*

THE commonwealth succumbed at a time when all of Europe was shaken by the French Revolution and by the War of the First Coalition. The revolution represented a challenge to the old regime, of which the three partitioning powers were the strongest pillars. The war absorbed Austria and to some extent Prussia, leaving Russia a much freer land in East Central Europe. In 1795 Prussia left the anti-French coalition to attend to her more immediate interests in Poland. This provoked the wrath of Catherine and added new fuel to the burning disagreements connected with the final delimitation of Polish spoils. The three courts intrigued against one another, and the possibility of reopening the Polish question appeared. Momentarily stunned by the seeming finality of the partitions, the Poles began to think and act in political terms.

Active groups represented a wide range of views. They comprised moderates and radicals, evolutionists and revolutionaries, people who believed in work at home and those who went abroad. Means for furthering Poland's independence varied, depending on the political outlook of the given milieu. Among the existing trends, two need to be mentioned. The first pointed to the possibility of working for Poland's reconstruction in cooperation with one of the partitioning powers against the others. This approach appealed to the conservative magnates, who were socially and economically committed to the old regime and fearful of the slogans of the French Revolution. The second pinned its hope on France, whose revolutionary declarations offering aid to oppressed nations could reinforce traditional French interest in Poland. Consequently, many of the former May 3 leaders (magnates and gentry alike) as well as the Kościuszko insurgents turned their eyes toward Paris.

The solidarity of the three courts vis-à-vis the Polish question was not as real as it may have appeared at first. Catherine II threatened to free the imprisoned Kościuszko and turn him loose on Prussia, should Prussia try to use the Polish card against her. Russian fears were not groundless because Berlin was listening to Polish suggestions that the king of Prussia recreate the Polish state and assume the Polish crown. A pro-Austrian trend had emerged in Galicia as early as 1790, when the leading nobles had put forward the project of a "Carta Leopoldina" bestowing constitutional privileges on the Poles of that province. The actual release of Kościuszko, together with many other Polish prisoners, by Tsar Paul I in 1796 alarmed the Germanic powers. They were also worried about some of the concessions that the new tsar had made to his Polish subjects. In these circumstances the supplementary treaty of January 26, 1797, which forbade the use of any title with the word Polish in it, was directed against plans any of the three courts might have for reviving Poland, as much as it was against the Poles. The treaty notwithstanding, Berlin, St. Petersburg, and Vienna proved unwilling to dispense altogether with the Polish card, which could well prove a trump in the involved and uncertain diplomatic game of the 1790s.

The potential partner of the partitioning powers was by and large the Polish aristocracy. Long used to conducting a foreign policy of their own and linked by family ties and connections to the three courts, the magnates were quick to engage in political schemes. Berlin, St. Petersburg, and Vienna attempted to use them to further their own political aims. Even a nonaristocrat such as General Jan Henryk Dąbrowski (1755-1818) received offers to enter both the Russian and Prussian military services. Prince Józef Poniatowski was placed high on the military lists of all three partitioning powers. Using a method of stick and carrot, threats of confiscation of estates or promises of court and military advancement, the tsar, the emperor, and the king tried to keep Poland's aristocracy in tow.

As for France, Paris treated the Polish question largely as a useful diversion against its enemies. By tying down Prussia and Russia, the Poles had played an important part in assisting the French war effort in 1793-95. It was no wonder Kościuszko was made an honorary citizen of France, and the president of the Convention embraced a Polish delegate as a brother-fighter against monarchic reaction. Whether France would be willing to go beyond these gestures, at a time when revolutionary slogans of national liberation sounded more and more hollow, remained to be seen.

There were few important figures among the Polish émigrés who had left the country after the breakdown of the Kościuszko Insurrection; most of the leaders were imprisoned or remained at home. The émigrés were scattered. Some went to Venice, Dresden, Leipzig, or Constantinople. Paris, as the revolutionary capital, naturally attracted only certain groups of emigrants, and Polish political activities there centered around an envoy of Kościuszko, Franciszek Barss (1760-1812), whom the French recognized as a representative of Poland. His group, which was called the Agency (Agencja), included Józef Wybicki (1747-1822), a deputy to the last Polish Diet and an important writer and politician. In late summer of 1795 a small group of émigrés established another center in Paris known as the Polish Deputation (Deputacja), in which the learned radical priest Franciszek K. Dmochowski (1762-1808) was a principal figure. The Agency and the Deputation soon became rivals, each claiming to speak on behalf of the Polish nation. Both cultivated contacts with people at home; the former mainly with the reformist magnates, the latter with the more radical elements. Real cooperation, however, was not easy given the influence of the conservative magnates, the cautious and evolutionist outlook of the May 3 reformers, and a certain spirit of parochialism on the part of the Polish patriots, who distrusted influences coming from abroad.

The Agency, which regarded itself as a diplomatic representation of Poland rather than a fighting ideological organization, pursued moderately liberal aims. It opposed armed uprisings and revolutionary activity in the homeland. The Deputation early adopted a more doctrinaire approach. Dmochowski believed that the loss of political independence could not be permanent so long as the nation survived, and he viewed the latter in a broad sense, i.e., to include all citizens. He wrote that the Polish nobility had realized that it could not preserve its own freedom unless it shared it with all its countrymen. While this was the view of the reformers, Dmochowski oversimplified the picture for the benefit of the French by ascribing it to all the *szlachta*. The Deputation leaders professed equality of all the estates and personal freedom for the peasants: some of them adopted Jacobin-sounding slogans. This was in keeping with the outlook of the left wing of the Kościuszko camp and with the ideas of the French Revolution, but it went beyond the May 3 Constitution. The Deputation used ruthless methods when dealing with its Polish opponents, whom it tried to discredit. Its policies were often inconsistent and improvised.

The Deputation favored conspiracies at home, which were unlikely to achieve concrete results. In Galicia the organization that had backed the Kościuszko Insurrection survived, and out of it there emerged a secret General Assembly with its headquarters in Lemberg. Called the Centralization (Centralizacja), it espoused a pro-Austrian policy based on the assumption that the Habsburg monarchy would conclude peace with France and turn against its Russian rival. At the same time the group believed in a Polish uprising in Galicia, which by necessity would have had an anti-Austrian edge and would have been irreconcilable with policies aimed at bringing Vienna over to Poland's side. Consisting mainly of well-to-do nobility, the Centralization eventually became involved in the rash venture of a former Polish brigadier, Joachim Denisko (1756–1812).

Tolerated by the Turks and the Moldavian prince, Denisko had concentrated a small Polish troop in Bukovina. At first he hoped to provoke Russo-Turkish hostilities, but in mid-July, 1797, he launched an attack against the Austrians and was easily defeated. The whole episode was connected at this point with a larger plan of action in which the victorious campaign of Bonaparte against the Austrians and the presence of Polish legions in Italy all played a part. Uncoordinated with Franco-Austrian developments—Bonaparte had already signed the preliminary peace of Leoben—the Denisko venture could only be a fiasco. It provided, however, the first Polish martyrs in Galicia, and it sealed the fate of the Centralization by exposing that organization's inner inconsistencies. The Austrian police launched investigations and arrests, and the half-hearted Galician conspiracy broke up.

A similar fate befell other underground attempts. The activity of Franciszek Gorzkowski (1760-1830), a radical of poor gentry background, who called on the peasants to fight for Poland, freedom, and equality against national and social oppressors, collapsed with his arrest by the Austrians in 1797. So did patriotic conspiracies in Lithuania, Podolia, and Volhynia when discovered by Russian authorities. Most of these movements had some contacts with the Deputation in Paris and with other Polish émigrés. The exact extent of the domestic conspiracies is hard to determine. Probably only small segments of the population were involved, and the majority of the *szlachta* remained aloof from secret activities. The Gorzkowski movement was plebeian. The involvement of small gentry, burghers, and ex-officers was understandable for several reasons. These groups, patriotic reasons aside, fared worse under the new regime than did the aristocracy or the wealthy nobility, and they stood less to lose from opposing the partitioning powers. They were also more receptive to revolutionary appeals. But the police could fairly easily identify them as a potential opposition and keep them under surveillance; chances of major uprisings were slender indeed.

In 1798 a new secret organization arose in Prussian-held Warsaw. It had links with the Deputation in Paris and was strongly influenced by French revolutionary ideas. Called the Society of Polish Republicans (Towarzystwo Republikantów Polskich), it firmly believed in the Declaration of the Rights of Man and of Citizen and favored the drafting of a new constitution for Poland, modeled on that of the Directory (of Year III). Among the few hundred members of the society there were also Poles from Galicia, particularly from Cracow. The membership was mainly of small gentry and burgher background. The Republicans established some contact with the peasants, but on the whole they were the Polish equivalent of a middle-class Western European revolutionary group. The society viewed Kościuszko, then an émigré in Paris, as its moral leader, although later a breach between them occurred. The activities of the society were largely propagandistic—preparation of the ground for an uprising—and involved some military intelligence and aid to Poles who were leaving the country to fight for the national cause abroad.

II. THE LEGIONS

The idea of carrying on an armed struggle from abroad had appeared in the last phases of the Kościuszko Insurrection. There were various projects that resulted in hasty and uncoordinated action, such as the above-mentioned Denisko episode. More serious were the attempts to interest France in the creation of a Polish fighting force on her soil, but the Directory, in power since 1795, handled the question with caution. Paris considered it highly inadvisable to unite its enemies, Austria and Prussia, and to antagonize Russia by supporting the Poles and challenging the verdict of the partitions. The Polish circles in exile were not discouraged, and they tried to find a powerful French protector. In September, 1796, one of the more prominent émigrés, Michał Ogiński (1765–1833), addressed a letter to the rising military star of France, General Bonaparte, in which he appealed for French support. Bonaparte answered orally through his aide-de-camp, the brilliant young Polish aristocrat by birth and Jacobin by conviction, Józef Sułkowski (1773-98). According to Sułkowski, Bonaparte said that he had a high opinion of the Poles and considered the partitions an iniquity. He cautioned the Poles against listening to deceptive promises; a nation oppressed by its neighbors could only rise with arms in hand. Bonaparte added that after a victorious campaign in Italy he himself would lead the French troops against Russia to force her to grant independence to Poland.

While Napoleon was expressing these views, the Agency in Paris was busy preparing concrete plans for the creation of a Polish armed force. From Poland it brought General Dąbrowski, whose exploits during the Kościuszko Insurrection had earned him military fame. Dąbrowski's arrival in Paris coincided with developments in Italy, which made the Directory interested in creating a Polish auxiliary legion. Worried by Napoleon's ambitious plans, the Directors preferred a Polish contingent to a large Italian army which could interfere with Franco-Austrian negotiations and commit France too deeply to Italy. A Polish legion that was attached not to France but to the newly created Republic of Lombardy would not place Paris under any direct and undesirable obligation to the Poles.

Dąbrowski appeared in Bonaparte's headquarters in Milan in December, 1796, and at first met with a cool reception. Napoleon suspected an intrigue on the part of the Directory, and Sułkowski, linked with the radical émigrés, regarded Dąbrowski as a creature of the Agency. The Polish general's eventual success in obtaining Bonaparte's blessing for a military agreement with Lombardy was due to more than his frank approach and engaging personality. Dąbrowski's argument that the Austrian army comprised a large Polish contingent which could become the basis of a legion was confirmed by the facts. As mentioned above, Vienna had been draining Galicia of manpower, and many of the recruits, when taken prisoners by the French, reacted favorably to Dąbrowski's appeal issued on January 20, 1797.

By virtue of Dąbrowski's convention with Lombardy a Polish auxiliary legion was formed. It received Polish-type uniforms, the French tricolor, and an Italian inscription, *Gli uomini liberi sono fratelli* (free men are brothers). In his appeal to the Poles, Dąbrowski spoke of a struggle against tyranny, of striving, under the gallant Bonaparte, for the freedom of nations, and he added that perhaps "you as victors will rebuild your fatherland." When in April, 1797, the French army marched north in the direction of Vienna, a six-thousand-strong Polish legion was getting ready to fight. Hopes ran high, and it seemed as if a simultaneous drive of the legion, the action by Denisko, and an armed uprising against the Austrians in Galicia would result in the partial liberation of Polish territory. All these calculations collapsed with the news of the preliminary peace concluded by Napoleon with the Austrians at Leoben on April 18, 1797.

Leoben was a terrible blow to the Poles, but Dąbrowski was not a person who gave in easily. The build-up of the legion proceeded, and Wybicki, on his arrival from Paris, was cheered by the sight of Polish troops, the symbol of Poland's will to fight against the verdict of the partitions. In Dąbrowski's headquarters he composed and sang the march of the legions. Its tune was a traditional Polish mazurka (*mazurek*); its opening lines, "Poland is not yet lost" ("dead" in the original version), rang out like a challenge. The song alluded to past victories, prophesied Dąbrowski's march to Poland and his entry into Poznań—although Prussia was not then a member of the anti-French coalition—and invoked Kościuszko's name and the spirit of the last insurrection.

Although the preliminaries of Leoben had led to the final peace treaty of Campo Formio in October, 1797, hostilities began again in 1799. In addition to Dąbrowski's legion, another unit was formed in Italy under the ambitious and quarrelsome General Józef Zajączek (1752-1826), a former soldier of Kościuszko and a Jacobin. General Karol Kniaziewicz (1762-1842) organized a Danubian legion which fought on the German front. All of these units distinguished themselves in combat. Kościuszko's arrival in Paris from America in 1798 increased Polish hopes. The legionnaires at once recognized the moral authority of Kościuszko. Polish generals addressed reports to him, and although he made no move to take actual command, he reinforced Dąbrowski's authority. In his letters and manifestoes to the Polish soldiers, Kościuszko professed republican sentiments and a hatred of kings and tyrants. He insisted that Polish legionnaires be educated in a republican spirit. After a rift with Barss and the Agency, Kościuszko lent his support to the Society of Republicans in Warsaw. In spite of differences between Kościuszko and some émigré centers, and despite his deep-seated distrust of the Directory and Bonaparte, émigré Poles and the French continued to regard Kościuszko as the supreme chief of the legions and a semiofficial minister of Poland.

The peace of Luneville in 1801, which made no mention of the Polish question, was a severe disappointment to the legions. Their sustained military effort appeared to have been in vain, and a profound crisis affected officers and men. The legions had gone through many hardships, only in the end to be transformed into an auxiliary corps attached to the Kingdom of Etruria and entrusted with police duties in Italy. Protesting against the role of a mercenary, General Kniaziewicz resigned, and many officers and soldiers followed his example. Dąbrowski, who believed in the necessity of preserving a Polish military force even at the cost of a breach with France, considered fantastic schemes of moving his troops to Corfu or landing them on the coast of Greece. A new French decision to integrate the legions with the armies of the republic appeared to some Poles as the best possible solution, but when the remnants of the legions, transformed into French-type half brigades, were sent to fight to San Domingo, they saw in it a Machiavellian scheme to eliminate the Polish troops altogether.

The use of Poles in the San Domingo expedition, in which many of them perished, need not be regarded as an intentional death sentence passed on cumbersome allies. True, the new Consular

Republic did not fail to notice the growth of Jacobin tendencies among the legionnaires, which made them suspect to Napoleon. Still, the expedition did not appear at first to be condemned to failure, and the decision to remove Polish troops from Italy was not tantamount to a desire to see them perish on the far-off island. Certain units did remain on Italian soil, and some officers found service in the French armies. Although deprived of his former command, Dąbrowski received an honorary post in the Italian army, was awarded the Golden Eagle of the Legion of Honor, and attended the crowning of Napoleon in Nôtre Dame. Subjected to unceasing attacks and calumnies by Polish radical opponents, the general kept waiting for new opportunities to serve the Polish cause.

Should the Treaty of Luneville in 1801 be regarded as the end of the legionary epic? Given the continuing, albeit greatly reduced, activities of Polish soldiers after that time, some historians reject 1801 as the closing date. There is no disagreement, however, on the years between 1797 and 1801 as being the heyday of the legionary idea and activity. What was its significance for Poland?

During that period several hundred officers and twenty-five to thirty thousand soldiers passed through the ranks of the legions. This was a considerable figure, given the size of the armies involved in the Italian campaign. Their battle losses were high, and both contemporary and later critics blamed Dąbrowski for sacrificing Polish lives in a forlorn struggle. Taken in a broader context, this criticism is not justified. The number of Poles conscripted in the armies of the partitioning powers was undoubtedly much higher, and more people perished fighting under the enemy flag than under the standards of the legions. Austria had formed a Galician noble guard and filled her lancer regiments with Poles. In Russia the "noble Belorussian standards" were composed of small Polish gentry. Prussia organized a "Bosnian" regiment of Polish lancers, and many infantrymen were Polish draftees. In the course of the Revolutionary and Napoleonic wars, Austria allegedly recruited a hundred thousand Poles for her armies, and the blood they spilled was of no advantage to the Polish nation.

The Dąbrowski legions were predominantly composed of Polish prisoners of war who had formerly served with the Austrian troops. Only some 20 percent were Poles who either lived abroad, escaped the country, or deserted from foreign armies. As for the social composition of the legions, officers and men included, about 65 percent were peasants, 25 percent were burghers, and 10 percent were gentry. There were hardly any aristocrats among them, and the general character of the troops was democratic. Kościuszko and Dąbrowski stressed the soldiers' education and encouraged advancement based on merit. Following the French practice, the usual form of address was "citizen"; no corporal punishment was used.

The significance of the legions for Polish history is threefold. First, the legions were an armed protest against the partitions. Second, they were a school of civic virtues and democracy for the mass of the soldiers. Third, they formed a cadre of officers and men trained in modern warfare, a cadre that proved indispensable for the organization of the army of the future Duchy of Warsaw. On political, ideological, and practical grounds the efforts of Dąbrowski and his men were far from wasted, but in 1801 the Poles could hardly appreciate this fact.

The apparent collapse of the legions and of the ideology that had produced them contributed to the rise of new attitudes and trends. These attitudes and trends were noticeable abroad, but they were especially marked at home. Kościuszko, considered the spiritual father of Polish resistance, was no longer a genuine leader. Surrounded by intrigues, suspicious of the authoritarian trends in France, he was in many ways a lonely figure. At the same time he was not inactive, and he inspired his secretary, Józef Pawlikowski (1768-1829), to compose a political tract which was published anonymously in Paris in 1800. Entitled *Can the Poles Regain Their Independence? (Czy Polacy mogą się wybić na niepodległość?)*, the booklet developed, for the first time, a Polish theory of insurrectionary warfare. It rejected the idea that Poles could count on effective foreign aid. They had to mobilize their own forces, and the only way to do this was to draw on the main reservoir of manpower, namely, the peasantry. Rejecting the argument that peasants had to be educated before they were emancipated, Kościuszko asserted that "in order to educate the people one has to set them free." In keeping with some of the contemporary military views, notably those of Suvorov, Kościuszko believed that hand to hand combat rather than firearms decided battles. A million peasants armed with scythes could defeat the armies of the partitioning powers. Kościuszko's prescription for a Polish armed effort was a general guerilla-type warfare under the leadership of a commander with dictatorial powers. This in turn implied a war of liberation, both national and social, and the author of *Can the Poles?* predicted that peasants in Russia and the Ukraine would rise to help a mass Polish movement.

The booklet met with criticism from the legionnaires and from the members of the Agency. The Society of Republicans in Warsaw considered that by openly advocating an insurrection Kościuszko had violated the secrecy rule of the society. A formal breach followed. In spite of disappointments in France, Polish public opinion was not prepared to face the idea of mass insurrection. It was only much later that Kościuszko's and Pawlikowski's views inspired Polish revolutionary leaders, and the booklet became an important precursor of populist insurgent theory.

III. THE POLICIES OF CZARTORYSKI

After 1801 the center of Polish political activity shifted to the homeland. The legions had not fulfilled their expectations, and the planned political center abroad, composed of leading Polish representatives from the Polish lands, did not materialize. The prevalent trend in the homeland was reformist and evolutionary, with an emphasis on cultural and economic revival. The returning émigrés, who included such generals as Kniaziewicz and such radical politicians as Dmochowski, found that conditions in partitioned Poland offered some possibilities for constructive work. Intellectual life in Warsaw was reviving, and although in Galicia there was no appreciable relaxation of the regime, the Puławy home of the powerful Czartoryski family was a cultural and intellectual center. The greatest opportunities, however, appeared under the Russian rule.

The brief reign of Paul, followed by that of the youthful Alexander, created a new atmosphere in Russia. Paul's concessions to the Poles, as well as a relaxation of religious measures directed against the Uniates, prepared the ground for a Russo-Polish dialogue. The nobility could and did engage in activities that appeared both patriotic and profitable. Even the former Republicans joined in. A trading company that facilitated exchanges between Warsaw and Odessa came into existence. The Beresina and the Dnieper-Dvina canals were constructed. Export of grain from the great Polish latifundia in the Ukraine through the Black Sea ports stimulated agriculture. But the most grandiose plans, cultural and political, became identified with the person of Prince Adam Jerzy Czartoryski (1770-1861).

Prince Adam was sent to St. Petersburg in 1775 as a pledge of good behavior of the Czartoryskis, who were threatened with the sequestration of their estates by Russia. Scion of a great aristocratic family related to the last king of Poland, the young prince became imbued with ideas of the English Whigs and French republican thinking. Establishing close friendship with Alexander, prior to the latter's accession to the throne, he became part of the grand duke's intimate circle of liberal-minded Russians which included Pavel Stroganov and Nikolai Novosiltsov. Alexander assured Czartoryski of his disapproval of the partitions of Poland. He also told him of his plans to modernize Russia. A complex relationship between the two men developed (in which Alexander's wife, whom Czartoryski loved, also figured), and historians still disagree on whether it was the prince who influenced the tsar or the tsar who influenced the prince. When Alexander became tsar in 1801 he made Czartoryski the minister of foreign affairs (first under the old chancellor Aleksandr Vorontsov and then independently), a member of the Council on Education and later of the Council of State, and a senator.

Czartoryski's position was paradoxical. A Pole who came to Russia as a semihostage, distrusted and disliked by many leading Russians, he now became a prominent figure in the government of the most powerful among the partitioning states. In some ways he was a liability to the tsar; in others the tsar's friendship limited his freedom of action. Although the prince wished to see his country regain freedom and independence, as a Russian statesman he had to be extremely circumspect. It seems that he succeeded in reconciling in his own mind the greatness of Russia with the eventual rebirth of Poland. He sought to modernize and liberalize Russia and hoped that this new Russia would then force the other partitioning powers to give up their shares of Poland. A reconstituted Polish state in close alliance with Russia, possibly ruled by a Romanov, could satisfy both Polish and Russian interests. By attempting to resolve the traditional antagonism, Czartoryski became the first postpartition exponent of a pro-Russian Polish policy.

Czartoryski was deeply involved in the process of modernizing Russia through education. As the curator of the Wilno educational district he played both a cultural and political role. The Wilno district, which encompassed most of the lands Russia had obtained in the partitions, achieved a high degree of Polish cultural self-government. Ably assisted by a number of leading Polish educators, Czartoryski sought to regenerate the leading class, educate it in the spirit of the May 3 reforms, and promote a general program of religious toleration and social progress. Politically speaking, he saw the Wilno educational district as a bridge between Russia and Poland, the nucleus of a reconstructed Polish state. By raising the area intellectually and socially, the prince was forging links between the district and a future united Poland.

These were long-range objectives that could hardly be openly stated, and for the time being the policy of Alexander and Czartoryski worked to the advantage of the Polish *szlachta* in these guberniias. No wonder the nobles could say that they were better off than in the prepartition days, for "although without Poland we are in Poland and we are Poles."[1] A feeling of self-satisfaction mingled with increasing loyalty to the tsar. Later Russian historians saw other aspects of the

1. Cited in Bolesław Limanowski, *Historia demokracji polskiej* (4th ed.; Warszawa: Książka i Wiedza, 1957), 1: 114.

process and spoke with bitterness about the polonization of the western guberniias under Alexander's rule. Czartoryski's policies delayed the russification of Lithuanians, Belorussians, and Ukrainians and thus indirectly aided their subsequent national reawakening. From the Polish point of view, the blossoming of Polish culture in the former eastern lands had a great impact on the territories under Austrian and Prussian rule. As Staszic expressed it: "If light had not shone in Wilno it would have gone out all over Poland."[2]

Czartoryski's activities as curator of the Wilno district formed the domestic Russian side of his long-range policies. The international aspect was linked to a broad program of a general reconstruction of Europe, based on collaboration between Russia and England. Adapting his ideas to the traditional goals of Russia's foreign policy, Czartoryski advocated active diplomacy in the Balkans and the extension of Russian influence in East Central Europe. The prince also pointed to a broader vision of European reconstruction. He believed that only an inspiring program that took into account national aspirations and the desire for liberty could successfully compete with the goals of the French Revolution and those of Napoleon. Unification of the West German and Italian states figured in his program, as well as an international system of cooperation among states. The prince was undismayed by the seeming vagueness of such goals, and he said that, "If we wish to progress we must have an object we have not yet attained. And in order to be always in progress we must be capable of conceiving an object that will never be attained."[3]

Seen in the context of a day-to-day diplomacy, Czartoryski's plans pointed to cooperation with England and were principally directed against Prussia. Prussia was internationally vulnerable because of her policy of maneuvering between the coalition and Paris. Novosiltsov's mission in 1804 to London accomplished its objective, an alliance between Russia and England, even though London was not interested in the long-range goals and implications of Czartoryski's policy. Nor was Novosiltsov himself, and the tsar was equivocal about the adoption of an anti-Prussian policy. As early as 1802 Alexander had established close personal contact with the Prussian royal couple, and there were strong pro-Prussian currents in St. Petersburg. Czartoryski's plans only heightened the feeling of suspicion that constantly surrounded the Polish outsider in charge of Russia's diplomacy.

In 1805 Czartoryski felt that he came closer to the realization of his goals. The War of the Third Coalition began, and the prince

2. Cited in W. J. Rose, *Poland Old and New* (London: G. Bell and Sons, 1948), p. 81.
3. Cited in Marian Kukiel, *Czartoryski and European Unity 1770–1861* (Princeton: Princeton University Press, 1955), title page.

sought to link Russo-Austrian cooperation with action against neutral Prussia. Prussian refusal to let the Russian army cross the Hohenzollern lands was to be used as a pretext for a campaign against Berlin. Czartoryski began to work feverishly to promote a policy that was to culminate in the re-creation of a Polish kingdom under Alexander. He established contacts with leading magnates in the "Polish guberniias" and went on to prepare the scene in Warsaw and among the Galician Poles. When Alexander stopped at the Puławy residence of the Czartoryskis, the plan for destroying Prussia (*Mordplan gegen Preussen*, the Prussian historians have called it) seemed practically ready. Did Alexander ever see in it anything more than a means of pressuring Berlin? If not his calculations and the hopes of Czartoryski were far apart. Receiving last minute assurances from Berlin that Prussia would let Russian armies through, the tsar rushed to Berlin. Bypassing Warsaw, which was ready to acclaim him as king of Poland, Alexander swore eternal friendship to the Hohenzolern over the tomb of Frederick the Great. But, if Russo-Prussian reconciliation destroyed Czartoryski's hopes, those of Alexander were shattered at the battle of Austerlitz (Slavkov). Prostrate Austria signed a peace with Napoleon, and the dispirited tsar returned to St. Petersburg. The hostilities that had come so close to Polish lands were not yet over, and a few months later, in the autumn of 1806, they would be resumed with Poland in the center of the stage.

IV. THE ORIGINS OF THE DUCHY OF WARSAW

In early October, 1806, the Franco-Prussian war began, and in a lightning campaign the Grande Armée won its victories of Jena and Auerstadt which delivered Berlin to the French. Shortly thereafter Napoleon's troops crossed the former boundary between Prussia and Poland. The French were now on Polish soil, and Napoleon expected a general insurrection to assist his military effort. Prior to the campaign he had authorized General Zajączek to form a Polish troop under the neutral name of the "Northern Legion." After entering Berlin the emperor summond Dąbrowski and Wybicki. He ordered that efforts be made to induce Kościuszko to lend his name and prestige to an uprising in Prussian Poland. He declared that France had never recognized the partitions. It was up to the Poles whether they would prove "worthy to be a nation" once again, and he demanded from them a serious military effort. At the same time he made no binding political promises to the Poles. The reasons were obvious: a commitment to Poland would strengthen Russia's determination to fight, and it might provoke an Austria smarting from defeat and the Treaty of Pressburg (Pozsony, Bratislava). The last thing Napoleon wanted to do was to unite all three partitioning powers against France.

In spite of the absence of political guarantees, Wybicki and Dąbrowski decided to follow Napoleon's lead. Wybicki appealed to his countrymen, and quoting Napoleon's words that he would have to see whether the Poles were worthy of being a nation, sounded a call to arms. He recalled the efforts of the legions and promised that Kościuszko himself would soon address the Poles. Emissaries were dispatched to Warsaw and to the provinces that were still occupied, inciting them to revolt. On November 6, 1806, Dąbrowski and Wybicki entered the liberated Poznań where the enthusiastic crowds greeted them by singing the march of the legions. Three weeks later the advance guard of the Grande Armée, led by Napoleon's brother-in-law Marshal Joachim Murat, reached Warsaw.

The political response of the Poles to Napoleon's victorious advance was more equivocal than the emperor had expected. True, in Poznania anti-Prussian feelings had preceded the entry of the French troops. The atmosphere was tense. On the eve of the Franco-Prussian War, banks suspended payment of mortgage rates, and silver disappeared from circulation; the specter of an economic crisis was haunting the land. French revolutionary slogans appealed to the small gentry, burghers, and peasants, and these strongly anti-Prussian groups were in a state of excitement. Conscripted or threatened with conscription in the Prussian army, the Polish Jews were in ferment. The magnates pressed Berlin for concessions, and Prince Antoni Radziwiłł (1775-1833) suggested that the king of Prussia assume the Polish crown. This idea, incidentally, was briefly considered by Napoleon himself at a later stage. But the Polish-Prussian exchanges proved inconclusive. As the great reformer Baron Karl von Stein put it, in retrospective, the Prussian policies lacked imagination. Polish national will was a fact, and constitutional concessions were needed to satisfy the national pride of the Poles and to assure the distinctiveness of the Polish provinces. Yet nothing had been done.

The entry of the French and the activity of Dąbrowski led to a quick Polish takeover of the western parts of Prussian Poland. Prussian troops were disarmed, officials driven out. Prompted by Napoleon, former Polish dignitaries addressed manifestoes to the *szlachta*, urging them to organize noble cavalry units. Dąbrowski proceeded to transform these units into regular army regiments.

The situation was different in Warsaw and in "South Prussia." The memory of San Domingo was alive, and France was far from popular. The Polish émigrés who had returned to Warsaw were connected with the French republicans and distrusted Napoleon.

Economic and even some educational achievements under Prussia contrasted with the apparent failure of Polish military efforts in Italy and Germany. Thinking of their estates in the lands held by Prussia and Austria, the magnates were unwilling to risk everything by openly siding with the French. The aristocratic Warsaw in which Louis XVIII and the Bourbon princes had found refuge after 1801 was suspicious of the radical slogans of Napoleonic France. The proximity of Russia also acted as a brake on any rash moves.

Conservative and moderate political leaders waited for French commitments and guarantees: they were hardly encouraged by Napoleon's statement in the thirty-sixth bulletin of the Grande Armée (December 1, 1806), that only God knew if Poland would recover her statehood. Consequently, there was no insurrection in Warsaw. Acting at the request of the king of Prussia, Prince Poniatowski assumed control over the city and sought to preserve order. While the Warsaw population warmly welcomed the arriving French detachments, Poniatowski wore his Prussian orders when he greeted Murat. Remaining in contact with Czartoryski, who urged a policy of collaboration with Russia, and involved in Radziwiłł's wooing of the Hohenzollerns, the prince was not prepared to switch overnight to Napoleon.

During the first weeks after liberation, Franco-Polish relations presented a complex picture. Dąbrowski and Zajączek were busy organizing a Polish army—Dąbrowski true to his long-standing pro-French policy, Zajączek largely because of an almost servile devotion to Napoleon. Kościuszko was still in Paris. He responded to French overtures by naming three conditions for his cooperation: introduction of an English-type government in Poland, emancipation of the peasantry, and the re-creation of a state stretching from Riga to Odessa and from Danzig to the Carpathian Mountains. Such demands were unlikely to be accepted. Kościuszko's preference for the English parliamentary system could hardly appeal to Napoleon. It was up to the Poles themselves to resolve the peasant question. As for frontiers, France could not afford to antagonize all three partitioning powers, particularly Austria whose neutrality mattered a great deal at that time.

Kościuszko's stand has given rise to historical controversies. Some Polish historians condemn him, others consider his attitude as fully justified. There is general agreement that Kościuszko's republicanism played a large part in his decision to remain aloof. Did the oath that Kościuszko took after his release by Tsar Paul, namely, not to take up arms against Russia, paralyze his will to act? Joseph Fouché, entrusted by Napoleon to negotiate with Kościuszko, undoubtedly antagonized the latter by such underhanded procedures as forging

Kościuszko's name on the appeal to the Poles. Perhaps the minister of police, considering that Kościuszko's presence in Poland would only complicate France's policy, wished for negotiations to fail. Kościuszko's poor health and the prolonged stay abroad which weakened his contacts with Poland also entered into the picture. Be that as it may, his absence from Poland at this critical juncture was keenly felt. It deprived the progressive movement of a popular and universally respected leader.

Overcoming their initial distrust of Napoleon and his regime, the former radical groups in Poland declared in favor of cooperation with France. Napoleon's victories over the partitioning powers appealed to popular imagination and surrounded him with a halo of heroism. The ex-Jacobin Zajączek advised immediate abolition of noble privileges in Poland and the creation of a government led by Kościuszko and Kołłątaj. Conscious of the decisive part played in the old commonwealth by the magnates and the gentry, Napoleon did not want to base his Polish policy on support of the masses. He kept telling Wybicki that it was essential for the *szlachta* to take up arms and provide the leadership in collaboration with the French. Napoleon also had other reasons. Tsar Alexander and even the king of Prussia were likely to exploit radicalism in Poland to their advantage. Czartoryski's orientation had many adherents among the nobles, who were worried about the social implications of French victories. Napoleon had no wish to provide his enemies with political tools they could use to win the hesitant aristocracy to their side. He played a cautious game, trying to gain the support of influential Poles while avoiding any firm political commitments to their goals.

It seemed logical that the command of the nascent Polish army should fall to Dabrowski, an excellent organizer, an experienced soldier, and a man endowed with great perseverance. Dąbrowski was ready to assume the responsibility, and after his arrival in Warsaw in early December, 1806, behaved as the *de facto* commander in chief. At that point Poniatowski decided to throw in his lot with Napoleon. Telling Murat that the emperor ought to put more trust in those who joined him after mature reflection than in hotheaded enthusiasts, Poniatowski clearly wished to have the command of the army. He wanted to redeem the Poniatowski name and efface the memory of his previous indecisiveness and political indolence. For the French, the adhesion of Poniatowski meant winning over the Polish aristocracy, i.e., achieving the goals pursued in Warsaw by Murat and Talleyrand.

The Polish upper classes used Napoleon's stay in Warsaw in mid-December to dispel his displeasure with their formerly lukewarm attitude. Even the church hierarchy spoke out; in an address it referred to "broken fetters" and to liberty under Napoleon's protection. The emperor could not fail to be impressed by the rapid growth of the Polish army; nor was he insensible to the charm of Polish ladies, as witnessed by his love affair with Maria Walewska (1789-1817). He authorized the setting up of a civilian Polish administration in the country, an implicit if not an explicit commitment to Polish statehood. Rejecting proposals to recall the last Polish diet to proclaim the rebirth of the *Res Publica*, Napoleon named a seven-man Governing Commission (Komisja Rządząca) as the highest legislative and administrative Polish organ. The commission operated through five departments: justice, treasury, police, interior, and war. Except for Wybicki, its members came from aristocratic families and represented the former adherents of the May 3 Constitution.[4] All five directors of the departments were aristocrats.[5] The left had no representatives in the governmental structure. The proposal to make a hero of the Kościuszko Insurrection, Jan Kiliński (1760-1819) the shoemaker, mayor of Warsaw was not carried out.

The nomination of Poniatowski as director of the war department was a bitter disappointment to Dąbrowski, but he did not indulge in recriminations. Zajączek, who always had to hate someone, did his best to complicate Poniatowski's work. The first measures taken by the prince were, in fact, unfortunate. Poniatowski singled out the officers of prepartition Poland to the detriment of the legionnaires; in a decree reestablishing old army regulations he restored corporal punishment. Legionary officers headed by Dąbrowski reacted violently, and the decree was never applied.

During the winter of 1806–1807 the situation in former Prussian Poland was not easy. French armies were living off the land; French officials had the final say in civilian matters. The Polish war effort was considerable, and the magnates showed a largesse in forming and equipping whole regiments at their own expense. By 1807 nearly forty thousand Polish troops were under arms, many of them engaged in bitter fighting against the combined Russian and Prussian armies. Politically, there was uncertainty about the final solution of the Polish question, and the great powers devoted a good deal of attention to it in their behind-the-scenes diplomacy.

Berlin and St. Petersburg continued their efforts to play the Polish card, and Czartoryski's activity reached new heights. In several memoranda the prince urged Alexander to recreate Poland in order to forestall Napoleon. He insisted on prepartition boundaries and suggested a union between Russia and Poland on the Austro-Hungarian

4. They were: Stanisław Małachowski, Ludwik Gutakowski, Stanisław Kostka Potocki, Józef Wybicki, Ksawery Działyński, Piotr Bieliński, and Walenty Sobolewski.
5. They were respectively Feliks Łubieński, Jan Małachowski, Aleksander Potocki, Stanisław Breza, and Józef Poniatowski.

pattern. It is possible that Czartoryski's program affected Kościuszko's stand, but Alexander was not convinced, although he did give serious thought to the Polish question. The tsar authorized Czartoryski to bring General Kniaziewicz for a talk concerning the creation of a Polish army in Russia, but the talk was inconclusive. The general did not wish to be part of a situation in which two rival Polish armies would oppose each other. Alexander worried about scattered Polish insurrectionary movements in Volhynia and about the possibility of an uprising in Lithuania. The latter Napoleon regarded as a useful pro-French diversion. But the Polish leaders in Russia were doing their best to calm hotheads in the "Polish guberniias." The Governing Commission in Warsaw was unwilling to provoke an uprising in the absence of Napoleon's proclamation of an independent Poland. Napoleon himself tried to sound out Russia and Prussia about an acceptable compromise.

The victorious French campaign that culminated in the battle of Friedland on June 14, in which Dąbrowski's troops performed exceedingly well, led to the famous encounter between Napoleon and Alexander at Tilsit. On a raft on the River Niemen the two sovereigns discussed peace and the division of Europe into spheres of influence. The Polish issue naturally figured in the conversations, and just as historians disagree in their appraisals of Tilsit so they differ in their interpretation of the respective attitudes of Napoleon and Alexander toward Poland. Most Polish historians credit Napoleon, and not Alexander, with the initiative of creating the Duchy of Warsaw. Napoleon could not easily ignore the Poles, but his main concern was to weaken Prussia by depriving her of the Polish territories. He was conscious, however, of the effect a Polish state might have on the partitioning powers. The Duchy of Warsaw—this name was chosen to avoid offending the sensibilities of the three courts—could easily become a source of embarrassment to its protector. Hence, Napoleon, who knew of Czartoryski's plans and sought to turn them to his advantage, suggested that the duchy be placed under Alexander as king of Poland. The tsar refused. It is likely that he found this offer not only embarrassing vis-à-vis his Prussian ally, but also identifying him too closely with Poland. He realized that Napoleon wished a *quid pro quo:* the acquisition of Prussian Silesia, which was to be given to Jerome Bonaparte. Such an arrangement would put Prussia at the mercy of France. In his turn the tsar proposed that Jerome become duke of Warsaw and ruler of Saxony, but Napoleon turned this down, fearing direct Franco-Russian friction over the Polish problem. Finally, a compromise was reached. The Duchy of Warsaw would go to the king of Saxony, a neutral ruler sympathetic to Napoleon. It would be endowed with a constitution that would guarantee its freedom but not endanger the neighboring powers. This solution became part of the final agreement at Tilsit concluded in July, 1807.

The Poles greeted the news of the accord with silence and disappointment. They had hoped to receive East Prussia and Silesia, and possibly Galicia. They had had no means of influencing the decisions at Tilsit, nor had they been consulted in the course of the negotiations. Galician Poles, whose deputies visited Napoleon, were told to be patient; delegates from Lithuania were sent home. The Tilsit decision seemed a poor reward for Polish military efforts and the adherence of the Poles to France. Poland's name did not reappear on the map, and once again new borders cut across Polish territories. And yet, the history of the twelve years after 1795 showed that the verdict of the partitions need not be the last word on the subject. The Polish state was gone, but the Polish question came to assume an important place in European diplomacy. Legionnaires who had fought in Italy, San Domingo, Hohenlinden, and Friedland returned home. Dąbrowski did enter Poznań, and the song of the legions proved not to be divorced from reality. At the same time, everyday life in the vast areas of the old commonwealth kept on posing new questions and undergoing new processes. Under Russia's rule educational and religious issues began to come to the forefront; under Prussia, economic and administrative-judiciary matters acquired increasing importance; in the Habsburg monarchy one had a foretaste of later national-social and administrative questions. The individual lands of partitioned Poland began to be marked by distinctive and centrifugal tendencies.

# CHAPTER 3

# The Duchy of Warsaw

I. THE CONSTITUTION AND ITS APPLICATION

ESTABLISHED in accord with the Treaty of Tilsit, the Duchy of Warsaw was placed under the hereditary rule of Frederick August, king of Saxony. With an area of 102,744 square kilometers, and nearly 2.6 million inhabitants, the duchy comprised territories taken by Prussia in the last two partitions (Danzig and the Białystok districts excluded) and a small area taken in the first partition. The borders corresponded neither to prepartition divisions nor to Prussian administrative boundaries. Danzig became a free city under the joint protection of Saxony and Prussia, but in reality it was under French military control and made a part of the imperial economic system. The Napoleonic code was introduced in the city. The district of Białystok went to Russia, which had insisted on territorial compensation. Since the duchy and Saxony were not territorially contiguous, the Treaty of Tilsit granted them the use of a military road through Silesia. There were no provisions for free communications between the duchy and Danzig. After the victorious war against Austria in 1809 the territory of the Duchy of Warsaw increased to 155,430 square kilometers and its population reached 4.3 million people. A population census conducted a year later showed that the Poles constituted 79 percent of the people, Jews 7 percent, Germans 6 percent, Lithuanians 4 percent, and Ruthenians (Ukrainians) 4 percent.

Although the wording of the treaty avoided explicit references to Poland and the Polish nation, the duchy was clearly a Polish state. The language of administration was Polish, and only citizens of the duchy could exercise public functions. Poles from other parts of the country who served in the French or the duchy's army automatically acquired citizenship. Traditional Polish coats of arms and orders were revived, as well as some titles and constitutional terms. Including within its borders Warsaw, the old historic capital Cracow, and Poznań, the state constituted the core of ethnic Poland.

The Treaty of Tilsit provided for an amnesty to all Poles involved in the last conflict, and it stipulated that the duchy would receive a constitution that "by securing freedoms and privileges of the peoples of this duchy would insure the peace of the neighboring states." The Poles differed in their views about the nature of such a constitution. The governing circles favored the model of May 3, 1791, although with some modifications; the radicals opposed it, but their projects lacked clarity. It fell to old Staszic to offer concrete suggestions in a pamphlet on Poland's statistics, which bore the telling subtitle "A brief outline of information needed by those who want to liberate this country, and those who want to rule it." Staszic's analysis, based on an antiaristocratic approach, pointed to the need of a strong government and a progressive social program. Napoleon cut short the controversies by imposing a *Statut constitutionnel du duché de Varsovie* (the original was in French), signed on July 22, 1807.

Comparable to other Napoleonic constitutions, the document took into account specific Polish conditions, as the emperor understood them. This was reflected in the retention of some traditional Polish procedural rules in the parliament, a division of deputies into noble and non-noble (a modified version of the May 3 provisions), and the adoption of the elective principle on the level of departmental and district councils. The constitution provided for a near absolute monarchy and vested the king with full executive powers and exclusive initiative in legislation. The king could delegate his powers to a viceroy (if and when one would be needed) and to ministers who were solely responsible to him. In spite of the existence of a council and a president, the ministers did not act collectively. From 1810 on they could carry out decisions agreed upon in the council without prior authorization of the king. In 1812, on the eve of the war against Russia, Frederick August delegated full royal power to the ministers. The five ministers were in charge of justice, internal and religious affairs, war, treasury, and police; the sixth, called secretary of state, resided in Dresden and acted as a liaison between the ruler and Warsaw.

The constitution established a Council of State which comprised ministers and other officials and acted as a court of appeal, a supreme administrative tribunal, and an organ that prepared new legislation. Differing somewhat from its French model, the council was chiefly important in judicial matters. Its relationship to the

Council of Ministers was ambiguous and led to friction between the two bodies.

Legislative powers, although greatly circumscribed, were vested in a bicameral Sejm. The upper chamber, the Senate, was composed of a fixed number of appointed lay and ecclesiastical dignitaries (first eighteen, then thirty) with the State Council members participating *ex officio*. The Senate's special function was to watch over the electoral system and the political rights of the citizens. The Chamber of Deputies consisted of sixty representatives elected by the noble sejmiki and forty deputies chosen by the communal assemblies (later one hundred and sixty-six, respectively). Whether noble representatives or deputies, all members of the Sejm had equal rights. All electors had to satisfy property qualifications except for some voters in communal assemblies whose rights could also be derived from educational criteria or recognized merit. The king had the exclusive right to call the Sejm, the sejmiki, and the communal assemblies and to prorogue or to dissolve them.

The Sejm voted on tax legislation, although it had no say in drawing up the budget, and approved changes in matters of civil and criminal law. If the senate refused its sanction, the king could override it. Only the members of the three parliamentary commisions on treasury, civil law, and criminal law had the right to participate in the discussion of governmental projects; the rest of the Sejm could only vote on the measures presented. This provision stemmed from Napoleon's distrust of "Polish anarchy" and his fear of tumultous parliamentary debates. Unofficial sessions of the Sejm, in which lively discussions took place, were tolerated by the king and provided a safety valve. Regular sessions were biennial and limited to a fifteen-day period.

According to the constitution the duchy was divided into six (later ten) departments headed by nominated prefects (Warsaw, Kalisz, Poznań, Bydgoszcz, Płock, Łomża, plus Cracow, Lublin, Radom, and Siedlce). These were subdivided into districts *(powiaty)* under subprefects. The system was highly centralized and involved a large bureaucratic machine with some 4,700 officials in 1808, and 9,000 after the duchy's expansion in 1809. The Polish principle of elected self-government operated in the case of departmental and district councils, whose ill-defined duties were mainly advisory. The sejmiki elected twice as many candidates for councilors as there were vacancies, and the king chose the councilors from among that number.

The constitution provided for an independent judiciary (with judges named for life), open civil and criminal procedures, and a hierarchy of courts, from justices of the peace up to a court of appeals. After the introduction of the Napoleonic code in 1808 and of the commercial code a year later, French laws formed the basis of the judiciary system in the duchy.

The opening articles of the constitution guaranteed freedom of worship for all religions, although the Catholic denomination was called the state religion. The all-important Article 4 stated that "all citizens are equal before the law" and protected by the courts of justice. The constitution did not, however, expressly guarantee the civil rights of citizens (for instance, freedom of speech, of press, of assembly, or immunity from search and arbitrary arrest). Nor did it contain any provisions for constitutional amendments and revisions. The document could only be altered from above. These lacunae were not keenly felt. Open parliamentary sessions and court proceedings militated against arbitrary acts of the government. Furthermore, the king used his powers with a good deal of discretion, censorship was mild, and no political trials ever took place. Still, the constitution was an imported product reflecting a certain stage, political and socioeconomic, reached by Napoleonic France, and the members of the Governing Commission (except for Wybicki) received it with a mixture of surprise and shock. They felt that under the specific Polish conditions it could hardly be effective.

The discrepancy between the constitutional provisions and socioeconomic realities was especially evident in Article 4 which abolished serfdom (*esclavage* in the text). Though the constitution made the peasant legally free, and liberated him from compulsory labor, it said nothing about his right to the land he cultivated. When the revolution had abolished feudalism in France it freed the peasant-owned land from seigneurial burdens. The Napoleonic code did not foresee a type of conditional ownership. The situation in Poland was entirely different and one could interpret Article 4 in two ways. The Polish conservatives argued that the peasants were users of the land and stock solely in exchange for labor obligations or rents. Once they ceased to discharge their obligations, they had no legal right to their strips. The progressive circles, including some members of the government, favored a guaranteed tenure system that would allow the peasant eventually to buy out the land he cultivated. In economic terms the issue was very real for the landowners. The peasants provided not only free labor but they also worked on the lord's land with their own oxen and horses (they owned three-fourths of the total) and their tools. While the peasantry was not a uniform mass and there were enough hands to work for wages, the landlords still had to be assisted to make the transition from the *corvée*-operated estates to farms that possessed their own farming equipment and relied on paid labor.

The minister of justice, Feliks Łubieński (1758-1848), adopted the more conservative interpretation, which served as a basis for the royal decree of December 21, 1807. The decree provided that the peasants who would fulfill their traditional obligations could stay on the land for a year, after which time they were free to move if they complied with minor formalities. The land they cultivated and their dwellings, livestock, seeds, and farming equipment would then become the property of the landowner. While the decree provided for freely negotiated contracts, under the protection of the law, between the lord and the peasants, this provision immediately became a dead letter.

Under these conditions the peasants, in the words of contemporaries, became "free as birds" and lost "their chains together with their boots." In practice the peasants could either stay and perform compulsory labor, which was now extra-legal and gave rise to abuses, or they could leave everything and migrate to another estate or to the cities. The latter were not flourishing (Warsaw had only 78,000 inhabitants in 1810), and often the army became the sole refuge that gave the peasant a sense of full citizenship. Relatively few peasants could become landowners, and relatively few were forcibly evicted when the lord enlarged his domain at their expense. In most cases a *de facto* economic serfdom survived, and the French resident in Warsaw, Louis Bignon, commented that it would take a long time before the lords got used to treating their peasants as human beings.

Another group that did not enjoy full equality was the Jewish community. In 1808 a royal decree suspended the political rights of Jews for ten years on the grounds that they were as yet unassimilated in the society. They were disfranchised, barred from holding offices, and forbidden to buy estates, the ownership of which conferred voting privileges. The decree provided for exceptions in the case of assimilated Jews—the often quoted example was the famous cavalry colonel, Berek Joselewicz (1764-1809); it also tended to favor the richer Jewish burghers, who in practice were able to buy real estate in towns. Naturally, converts to Christianity were not affected by these restrictions, and several Poles of Jewish origin served in the administration and in the judiciary.

The constitution blurred but did not abolish the traditional division between estates.[1] The *szlachta* retained a monopoly in the sejmiki and as representatives at the Sejm. Since a nobleman could also be, and often was, elected a deputy by the communal assembly, this further altered the ratio in the diet between nobles and non-nobles to the advantage of the former. In 1809 non-nobles consti-

1. It is worth noting that the Napoleonic constitutions of Spain, Naples, or Westphalia also recognized the existence of the nobility as a separate class.

tuted only 29 percent of Sejm. Although nearly 40 percent of the *szlachta* was landless and lived in towns, the nobles were still the dominant element in the countryside (economically and administratively) and controlled the lesser towns. At the same time, the bourgeoisie began to emerge as a junior partner of the nobility. Burghers could and did buy land and were strongly represented in the army, the administration, and the judiciary. The protection of property rights by the *Code Napoléon*, as well as property voting qualifications operated to the advantage of the burghers and even of some richer peasants who qualified as voters in the communal assemblies.

The Napoleonic code strongly affected the church and state-church relations. The introduction of civil marriage, and the divorce question led to friction. The leading circles in the duchy were imbued with secularism, and freemasonry, to which many of the leading politicians and soldiers belonged, contributed to a laicization of society. The lodges, like the army, attracted the bourgeois element which could thus assert itself in the evolving social structure.

The army occupied a particularly important position, and it is arguable that the military rather than the noble element *per se* predominated in the state. The Duchy of Warsaw was the product of war, and it had increased its size through war; on the eve of the 1812 invasion of Russia it was regarded as the nucleus of a large Poland to be achieved after the victory. The constitution established a thirty-thousand-strong army (doubled after 1809), thus imposing a disproportionately heavy financial burden on the state. To alleviate this burden, France took several regiments on her pay roll—the Vistula legion and the light horse guards—which fought in Spain but had to rely on replacements coming from the duchy. Probably some 180,000 to 200,000 men went through the military service, which lasted for six years. After 1808 it was based on conscription, which was greatly repugnant to gentry conservatives. They had an equal dislike for the democratic character of the army characterized by the absence of mechanical drill and corporal punishment. The officers' corps largely consisted of former legionary or French army officers. The army of the Duchy of Warsaw, often described by French experts as superb, was the center of the Napoleonic cult which so strongly affected Polish mentality during the period.

II. ECONOMIC AND POLITICAL PROBLEMS

Throughout its existence the duchy experienced severe economic difficulties. The point of departure was an economy devastated by war; a traveler gave the following description of the land between Warsaw and Poznań in the spring of 1807: "Empty manors, broken windows, sheaves thrown out of barns . . . here and there a peasant in rags wandering about and begging in the roads; no signs of restoration or cultivation anywhere, no cattle in the whole area."[2] Heavily mortgaged estates could only hope to survive through moratoria on payments and the continued use of free peasant labor. Since Napoleon had taken over the Prussian state mortgages, the duchy appealed to him to help resolve the problem. France agreed to sell the mortgages, calculated by the French negotiators at 43 million francs, for 20 million payable in installments over a four-year period at a low rate of interest. The arrangement was not an economically sound one for the duchy. Warsaw had little chance of collecting from the landowners unless it auctioned their estates, and it had to pay large sums to France, which were believed to have been unfairly calculated. The "Bayonne sums"—the Franco-Polish agreement was signed in Bayonne in 1808—became proverbial and entered the Polish language. The duchy was unable to pay on time and extensions had to be arranged. Beginning with a deficit of some 35 million francs in 1807, burdened with the French debt, and spending two-thirds of its budget on the army, the treasury of the duchy was in constant trouble.

The duchy's main sources of revenue were the crown lands (and after 1809 one-half of the income from the Wieliczka salt mines), monopolies, and direct and indirect taxes voted by the Sejm. Income from the crown lands declined significantly since Napoleon had distributed one-fifth of them as tax-exempt donations. Treated as "imperial fiefs," they went to French marshals and dignitaries, although Poniatowski, Dąbrowski, and Zajączek were also among the recipients. Presumably intended to bind the French elite more closely with the whole system of Napoleonic Europe, the donations are considered by some economic historians as equally harmful to the duchy's economy as were the Bayonne debts. In these conditions, the bulk of the revenue came from taxes, and the government sought at first to increase direct taxes and follow a policy of inflation. In 1811 the treasury introduced an almost balanced budget which diminished direct taxes and raised indirect taxation. In an attempt to improve the position of the landowners, the government permitted them to pay their share in kind; it also imposed greater burdens on the masses, already reduced to a near subsistence level. When in 1812 the half-million-strong Grande Armée had to be housed and fed by the duchy, the country was on the verge of bankruptcy.

Napoleon's Continental System, which closed off the traditional markets for Polish grain, adversely affected the duchy's economy.

2. Cited in Polska Akademia Nauk, Instytut Historii, *Historia Polski* (Warszawa: Państwowe Wydawnictwo Naukowe, 1958-), vol. 2, pt. 2, p. 112.

Recent research, however, has questioned the long-accepted thesis of total commercial stagnation by pointing to a favorable balance of trade in 1810 and 1811 (the balance of payments remained unfavorable) and to the growth of a domestic market. Still, customs regulations that accorded preferential treatment to French and Saxon goods and permitted free entry of Russian imports while prohibiting exports to Russia rendered trade most difficult. The tariff of 1810 made trade with Prussia impossible. Internal commerce suffered from bad communications and too small a market. Attempts to secure foreign, mainly French, loans against the security of the Wieliczka mines proved unsuccessful.

Industrial development was in its infancy. Breweries and water mills, small brick works, iron works, and coal mines—some of them situated in the lands given to Marshal Lannes—glass works, paper mills were among the most important branches of production. The need for cloth for army uniforms provided incentives for sheep breeding and helped the Poznania weaving industry, which actually increased its production. In spite of their gradual decline, the guilds were acting as a brake on the transition from crafts to factories. Credit was scarce. Having no currency of its own until 1810, when a mint producing gold, silver, and brass coins was established, the duchy used devalued Prussian currency, and this added to the rampant inflation.

Operating in adverse and somewhat peculiar economic circumstances, the duchy lived under a political system that had many odd features. The ruler, Frederick August, was an absentee monarch who visited his state only four times. Orderly and conscientious, if somewhat slow, the king insisted on approving all the decisions of his ministers; this naturally caused considerable delays. His scrupulous observance of Napoleon's wishes diminished his own initiative. Although he knew Polish and two of his ancestors had been kings of Poland, he was looked upon as a foreigner. Respected, even liked in some quarters, he did not win the hearts of the Poles.

The Council of Ministers, which on October 5, 1807, succeeded the Governing Commission, had few outstanding personalities. The respective presidents of the council and of the State Council never became real leaders. The two successive ministers of the interior were competent but not brilliant, and the same was true for the finance ministers, with the exception of Tadeusz Matuszewicz (1765-1819), who entered the government in 1811. The second minister of police was a distinct improvement on the first. Only Łubieński and Poniatowski, respectively in charge of justice and war, and the state secretary residing in Dresden, Stanisław Breza (1752-1847), kept their posts during this entire period. The controversial Łubieński combined the qualities of an excellent organizer, indefatigable worker, and a good judge of men, with a penchant for intrigue, opportunism, and ruthlessness. Although an aristocrat, he did not always represent the interests of his social class. Except in military matters, Łubieński's influence was felt in all spheres of life in the duchy. The dashing Poniatowski, appealing to the imagination of his countrymen, came to personify the army of the duchy. After a brief episode in 1807, he succeeded in dispelling the distrust of Napoleon and of all the all-powerful commander of French and Polish troops in the duchy, the impetuous Marshal Louis-Nicholas Davout, who recommended the prince as his successor. Poniatowski's relations with his two potential rivals, Dąbrowski and Zajączek, also improved after 1809.

Formally dependent solely on the king, Polish ministers were subject to constant controls by Davout and the French residents in Warsaw: the youthful and dictatorial Etienne Vincent up to 1807; the able though over-bearing Genoese, Jean C. Serra, to 1810; and the moderate Louis Bignon until 1812. Both Serra and Bignon were well versed in the politics of the duchy. The former maintained contacts with the radical opposition and on occasion interfered in governmental matters. A protagonist of Łubieński, he became more popular with the government during his last year in Warsaw. Bignon possessed more tact and moderation and stood closer to the governing circles; his reports showed a genuine understanding of, and a sympathy for, the Poles.

The constitution of the Duchy of Warsaw was authoritarian, centralized, and individualistic, as well as democratic and at the same time antiliberal, and it did not really satisfy the major political groups in the country. The ruling circle, composed largely of the May 3 reformers, adapted itself to the new political and social conditions, although many of its members preferred the native tradition. The radicals, although greatly disappointed, were willing to accept the system but only as a starting point of an evolutionary process, and their moral leader Kołłątaj, writing under the telling *nom de plume* "Nil Desperandum," advocated a pro-Napoleonic stand. But, except for minor positions, the leaders of the Polish "Jacobins" were kept out of the government and remained opposed to it. In turn, the die-hard conservatives objected to the new regime and the new ideas. Disliking the Napoleonic code and legal equality, they looked toward Russia, where the nobles still enjoyed the benefits of the Lithuanian statute. Occasionally they and the radicals—who considered linking the Polish question with Russo-English cooperation—met on the common ground of opposition to the government. Thus, only the army, the bureaucracy, the small gentry, and most of the burghers identified themselves fully with the duchy and Napoleon.

A dichotomy between the state and the nation existed, and the latter, unable to express itself fully in the Sejm and in the censored press, used as its political media the unofficial meetings of the diet and political pamphlets. In 1809 the departmental councils largely succeeded in becoming "the real and only representatives of the nation" but could not effectively maintain this position. A contemporary satire which reflected the critical view of the duchy shared by many conservatives and radicals points to its obvious peculiarities. It spoke of the duchy as being ruled by "a German king, a Polish soldier, Prussian money, and the French government, law, and code." It singled out such novelties as "a nobleman made a recruit" and Jews, peasants, and burghers put on a footing of equality; it also mentioned the "free but naked cultivator" and "the soldier, unpaid but gay."[3]

### III. THE WAR OF 1809 AND ITS AFTERMATH

In April, 1809, war began between France and Austria which immediately involved the Duchy of Warsaw. Six months earlier, at the Erfurt meeting, Napoleon had attempted to make Tsar Alexander a protector of the duchy, and in order to reassure him, withdrew Davout's army corps to Germany. But Alexander had no intention of becoming embroiled with the Habsburg monarchy over the duchy, whose existence all the partitioning powers resented. He let Vienna know that his troops would delay intervention and avoid clashes with the Austrians.

On April 15, a thirty-thousand-strong Austrian army moved on Warsaw. Poniatowski could oppose its advance with only half of the Polish forces; the remainder was outside the country or locked in fortresses. Facing great odds, the Polish troops fought the bloody battle of Raszyn and undefeated retreated to Warsaw. Then the high command devised an excellent operational plan which tradition ascribes to Dąbrowski. Abandoning, through a formal convention, Warsaw to the Austrians, and immobilizing a large number of their troops in the capital, Poniatowski's army began a liberation campaign in Galicia. In turn, the Austrians, hoping to conquer all of the duchy and use it as bait to bring Prussia into the war, concentrated their efforts west of the Vistula.

A strange situation developed. While the Austrian armies fought Polish military detachments and hastily organized levies in the western part of the duchy, Poniatowski's troops liberated Zamość and Sandomierz and reached Lemberg. Uncertain of the final out-

3. Cited in Adam Skałkowski, *Książę Józef* (Bytom: Nakład Katolika, 1913), p. 310.

come of the war, Poniatowski discouraged a popular insurrection in Galicia and prudently occupied it on behalf of Napoleon. He accepted, however, the cooperation of Galician magnates who speedily formed and equipped regiments, called, for the sake of appearances, Franco-Galician and put on the French pay roll. The authority of Warsaw was not extended to Galicia; instead, a Provisional Central Government was set up in the province.

From the beginning of the campaign the Poles had awaited Russian assistance, but when the Russian troops finally marched in they behaved in an ominous fashion. In the areas of Galicia they occupied they were restoring local Austrian authorities and interfering with the conduct of Polish military operations. In July they reached Cracow and vainly tried to prevent Poniatowski from entering the city. But meanwhile the war was being decided on other battlefields, and after the Wagram defeat Vienna asked for peace.

The Polish question in the Treaty of Schönbrunn, which Austria had to accept, presented difficulties. The Poles had played an important part in the war—about fifty-two thousand had been mobilized and fought in the campaign—and they could not be denied Galicia. At the same time, Napoleon could ill-afford to antagonize Russia who had shown an implacable enmity toward the Duchy of Warsaw. Complaining that the actions of his Russian ally were hurting his feelings, Napoleon sought Alexander's blessing for an enlargement of the duchy. To reassure the tsar he declared through diplomatic channels and the Corps Législatif that he had no intention of recreating Poland. He agreed that Russia receive as compensation the Tarnopol district of Eastern Galicia. At the same time the Treaty of Schönbrunn transferred to the duchy the whole of New or Western Galicia, including Cracow, as well as some areas taken in the first partition. The important salt mines of Wieliczka were placed under joint Austro-Polish control.

The campaign of 1809 had far-reaching repercussions on the Polish political situation. The French resident, Serra, had forced the State Council to issue a mobilization decree that led to the constitution of a revolutionary directorate in Warsaw. In the provinces, departmental councils assumed new powers and competed with special governmental delegates. All this was a definite shift to the left, and the "Jacobins" rose to prominence. The government, which had moved twice to provincial towns, lost some power and prestige, and Serra, returning to Warsaw from Berlin, tried to push the ministers further into the background. The political moves of Poniatowski and the Provisional Government in Galicia largely escaped the control of the government. What is more, both the Galician magnates and the radicals, seeking to alter constitutional arrangements, opposed an immediate incorporation of Galicia into the duchy. While Napoleon's decision on incorporation ended all the discussion, the addition of the Galician provinces strengthened the opposition.

The War of 1809 greatly affected Polish national consciousness. All social classes in Galicia had welcomed the entry of Polish troops, and they were shocked that almost all of "old" Galicia was left with Austria. Polish volunteers from Lithuania, Volhynia, and Podolia had participated in the war and suffered the reprisals of the tsarist authorities. More than ever the government of the Duchy of Warsaw was conscious of representing only a fraction of old Poland. In 1809 it spoke of the future restoration of the entire country, but this, it said, required time, effort, and virtue. Still the unification of ex-Prussian Polish lands (the duchy) with ex-Austrian provinces (New Galicia) seemed to augur well for the future. The Poles no longer had any doubts about national survival, and a poem celebrating the return of the troops to Warsaw expressed this feeling by saying that "a nation always remains a nation."

International and domestic difficulties which had beset the duchy since its inception became more acute after 1809. Tsar Alexander sought to discredit Napoleon in the eyes of the Poles and to win the governing circles in the duchy over to a pro-Russian policy. He succeeded in signing a convention with the French ambassador, Louis de Caulaincourt, which, among other things, said that "the Polish Kingdom will never be restored" and provided for the elimination of the term "Polish" in titles, for the abolition of Polish orders in the duchy, and the liquidation of "mixed subjects." Napoleon saw the trap and failed to ratify the convention, but the fact that it could have been signed cast doubts on France's Polish policy.

Could Russia be trusted to be more understanding toward the Poles? Unable to choose between his old loyalty to Alexander and loyalty to the Duchy of Warsaw, in which his brother commanded a Galician regiment, Czartoryski took a leave of absence in 1810. He explained that he could no longer develop the former Polish guberniias as a rival to the duchy for fear of a fratricidal strife. In early 1811, Alexander revealed to the prince a war plan against France which would involve a lightning invasion of Prussia. The participation of the duchy was crucial for its success, and the tsar assured Czartoryski that he proposed to restore under his scepter a Kingdom of Poland with a favorable eastern border (Dvina-Beresina-Dnieper). When Czartoryski suggested that the May 3 Constitution be revived, Alexander seemingly agreed. Although dubious of the results, Czartoryski sounded out Poniatowski who not only refused to go along with Alexander's schemes, but first conveyed a discreet

warning to the French and then informed Napoleon. Czartoryski
had to explain to the tsar that Polish loyalty and gratitude to Napoleon,
as well as the fear of a break, made Warsaw unwilling to consider
his overtures. Instead, the prince counseled that Alexander and
Napoleon settle the Polish question amicably and he recalled
Napoleon's willingness at Tilsit to see Alexander assume the crown
of Poland.

Did Alexander sincerely wish to rebuild a Polish state? He
realized the tremendous Russian opposition to such plans, as expressed by Nikolai Karamzin's urgent plea, "that there be no Poland
under any shape or name." Undoubtedly he wished to drive a wedge
between the Poles and the French. He sounded out both, as
evidenced by a new proposal to Paris that France compensate
Russia for the seizure of Oldenburg with concessions in the Duchy
of Warsaw. Napoleon rejected the idea, and in the summer of 1811
he openly denounced the aggressive designs of the tsar. Should
it come to war, he said, he himself would rebuild Poland.

Alexander was more successful in his negotiations with a number
of Lithuanian magnates headed by the ex-émigré Ogiński. To them
he proposed the establishment of a Lithuanian Grand Duchy,
composed of the eight former Polish guberniias, with its own constitution and government. Ogiński found the idea attractive and
suggested an arrangement similar to that prepared for Finland.
While displaying a certain amount of Lithuanian separatism, Ogiński
and his collaborators did not intend to replace permanently the
old Polish-Lithuanian commonwealth with a Russian-Lithuanian
union. For them, a revived historic Lithuania would be a step toward
unification with the Duchy of Warsaw and lead eventually to the
recreation of the old *Res Publica*. Their pro-Alexander stand also
reflected the class interest of the Lithuanian magnates, which the
tsar seemed to satisfy better than Napoleon. Not that they were all
narrow-minded reactionaries. One of them, Prince Ksawery Drucki-
Lubecki (1779-1846), who was later destined to play a great role
in Polish politics, favored a gradual liberation of the Lithuanian
peasantry. He felt that the May 3 ideas had to be further developed,
and he also realized that the abolition of serfdom in the duchy
could not be simply ignored. Similar suggestions had been made
earlier by the gentry of the Białystok district after it was handed
over to Russia in 1807.

All these moves behind the scenes were but imperfectly known
in the political circles in the Duchy of Warsaw. The radical and
liberal-conservative opposition sharply criticized the enlarged army
budget, unaware that war with Russia was a distinct possibility
in 1811. Huge military expenditure seemed unnecessary and

contrary to the economic interests of the duchy. The opposition continued to attack the Bayonne arrangement and the donations for French generals. It was indignant that Polish blood was being spilled in Spain, where the light horse guards had won fame by their charge at Somosierra. The poorer gentry resented the costly and involved judicial procedure under the Napoleonic code. Ministers, especially Łubieński, were attacked for their slavish imitation of French models.

To alleviate the criticism of a large and expensive bureaucratic machinery, the treasury proposed budget cuts, and even a return to the Polish tradition of elected and unpaid officials. This was hardly possible, but under the influence of the new French resident, Bignon, a series of ministerial changes took place. Matuszewicz became finance minister. By introducing higher taxes, he succeeded in balancing the budget, but due to another decline of grain prices and a virtual end of wool export, he could not radically alter the economic situation in the duchy.

The opposition in the Sejm was reinforced by increased activity of the departmental councils and by some clandestine plots. Since 1809 the councils had been allowed to deliberate on the welfare of the departments and permitted to voice complaints and recommend improvements in the administrative apparatus, and in 1811 and 1812 they petitioned for greater participation in the government. As for "Jacobin" conspiracies, their extent has never been fully established, but they allegedly had contacts with Dąbrowski, French republicans, and the German Tugenbund. Were there plans for an armed "Jacobin" coup in 1811? Definite proof is lacking. With the coming of the war of 1812, which carried hopes of the re-creation of Poland, a political truce prevailed in the country.

IV. THE WAR OF 1812

The Second Polish War, as Napoleon called it in his army bulletin, began in June, 1812, and a half-million-strong Grande Armée decended on the duchy. The national elation of the Poles was real enough, but the mass invasion created immense difficulties. Requisitions and confiscations carried out by the French military paralyzed the Polish administration, and on Poniatowski's initiative the ministers offered to resign and entrust the country directly to Napoleon. They wished to show the emperor that the duchy could hardly stand on its own feet and that France had to assume the ultimate responsibility. There has been much controversy concerning Napoleon's objectives in 1812 and his intentions vis-à-vis Poland. It seems likely that he wanted to force Alexander's return to the French alliance system against England, rather than to destroy the Russian Empire. As for

Poland, Napoleon's spokesman, the Duke de Bassano, probably summed up fairly accurately his emperor's thinking when he said that "a complete restoration of Poland" was "one of the possible ways of terminating the conflict."[4]

Napoleon had no blueprint, and it was only at St. Helena that he called a large Polish state the key stone of the European edifice. In 1812 he weighed various alternatives. He explored the possibility of exchanging the Illyrian provinces for Galicia and alarmed the Austrians, who, fearful of a spontaneous Polish movement, promptly introduced martial law there. Rather than annexing the Polish guberniias to the Duchy of Warsaw, he played with the idea of setting up a confederated state in the east. Bassano told the Poles that independence was a political fact which Napoleon could not fail to recognize, and intimated that it was up to them to show that they could exist on their own. While he seemed to leave the initiative to the Poles, the emperor did not give them a free hand. He thought of replacing Frederick August with his brother Jerome, but dropped the idea when the latter antagonized the Warsaw government and the Polish army. He did appoint, however, a full-fledged French ambassador, and his unwise choice for that post was the vain, ambitious, and intriguing Archbishop Dominique de Pradt. The latter meddled in everything, at first weakening the Polish élan and then becoming an instrument in the hands of the ruling circles in the duchy. Napoleon later blamed him bitterly for wasting the Polish opportunities.

At Matuszewicz' suggestion, Napoleon decided to use the old Polish device of calling a "confederation" of the *szlachta* to serve as a rallying point of an all-Polish movement. Presided over by the aged father of Czartoryski and led by a number of magnates, the confederation gave a strongly conservative tone to the movement. Perhaps a more revolutionary body, suggested by Serra, that harked back to the Kościuszko Insurrection might have antagonized the conservative Lithuanian nobility, but the confederation with its appeal to the *szlachta* was anachronistic. Nor was the precise task of the confederation ever defined. Patriotic exaltation among the Poles was undeniable, even though Pradt weakened and delayed its manifestations by careful staging. The Sejm of the duchy met on June 28, and after Matuszewicz's stirring words, "Poland will be, why Poland is already," transformed itself into a confederation and declared that "the Kingdom of Poland is restored and the Polish nation reunited in one body." A delegation led by Wybicki appeared before Napoleon in Wilno but the emperor addressed it in generalities. On July 1, he

4. Cited in Juliusz Willaume, *Fryderyk August jako książę warszawski* (Poznań: Towarzystwo Przyjaciół Nauk, 1939), p. 280.

established a Provisional Governing Commission of Lithuania which for two weeks delayed Lithuanian accession to the confederation. Since the latter had no real powers either in the duchy or in Lithuania, it remained a somewhat ineffectual symbol of commonwealth unity.

Other opportunities were wasted. Nearly a hundred thousand Polish soldiers participated in the campaign, but instead of operating as a unit they were dispersed among several army corps. The Fifth Army Corps, which was called the Polish Corps and was commanded by Poniatowski, comprised only a part of the Polish forces. The Poles suspected that this arrangement was designed to deprive them of their own distinct contribution to the struggle. Poniatowski suggested an offensive of the Polish troops in the Ukraine in order to liberate the former provinces of the commonwealth. His proposal was not accepted. Unable to appreciate the complexities of the Lithuanian and Ukrainian guberniias, Napoleon complained that the local Poles were different from those who in 1806 had risen to follow his lead. The situation in 1806 and 1812 was, of course, hardly comparable. In 1812 the Polish guberniias were politically disoriented. Unable to persuade the tsar to release him from his oath of allegiance, Czartoryski had gone abroad. Ogiński and his friends, who had awakened hopes of a fruitful collaboration with Alexander, had been ordered out of Lithuania by the tsar. Although emotionally patriotic, the nobility feared Napoleonic social reforms, his rigid administrative system, and the economic strains they had observed in the Duchy of Warsaw. Russian influence was strong among the magnates of the Ukraine, and some of them raised Cossack regiments for the tsar, not for Napoleon.

Admonishing the Poles that love of country was the highest virtue and that national unity was indispensable for success— remarks really addressed to the absent Czartoryski and the Ogiński group—Napoleon appointed as military governor of Lithuania a Dutchman, General Count Dirk von Hogendorp, and later promoted him to the presidency of the Governing Commission. The general had no knowledge of local conditions, and although the imperial commissar, the former resident in the duchy, Bignon, tried to improve matters, there were constant frictions and difficulties. The commission consisted of former Kościuszko insurgents; most of these men were of aristocratic background, and while they were well-meaning they were old and without standing in local politics. There was urgent need for a leader. Kościuszko, who had refused to join the confederation, was again approached but without success. Dąbrowski, serving as a divisional commander under Poniatowski, was wasting his real organizational and political talents.

The French established four departments (Wilno, Grodno, Minsk, and Białystok) run by three-member administrative commissions, thirty-six subprefects, military governors, and intendants. The pre-partition provinces of Vitebsk and Mohilev were not included in the Lithuanian administration. The officials were careful not to antagonize the *szlachta*. Only vague references were made to the social conditions in the duchy, which were represented as satisfying the peasants while not injuring the interests of the landowners. The Lithuanian peasants, who at first had shown greater enthusiasm for the French liberators than had the gentry, became lukewarm. They soon suffered from oppressive measures of a huge army that lived off the land, and from marauders who soon infested the country-side. Peasant uprisings, sometimes directed against the manors, took place in Lithuania and Belorussia and were ruthlessly suppressed. In Samogitia, where the Lithuanian language predominated, the Governing Commission made the mistake of addressing the people in Polish, while already during the Kościuszko Insurrection appeals had been issued in Lithuanian. This harmed a united pro-Napoleonic front more visible in Samogitia than elsewhere. The Catholic clergy cautiously welcomed the Grande Armée; the Uniates were more enthusiastic; the Eastern Orthodox clergy was negative. While the burghers adopted a generally pro-French attitude, the Jews, especially the Orthodox leaders, were less sympathetic. They viewed Napoleon as a godless man and objected to the Jewish policies pursued in the duchy.

Napoleon insisted that the population show its will for national freedom through a massive war effort, but the organization of a Lithuanian army proceeded fairly slowly. There was a shortage of funds and of horses, and the oppressive regime of military com-manders impoverished the country. Officers were lacking, and the old method of naming aristocratic officers who would raise and equip their troops worked only moderately well. The unpopular Russian recruiting system was retained, and a universal levy of the *szlachta* was not decreed until December. The formation of a light horse guards' regiment attracted the Lithuanian elite and thereby weakened other units. A Lithuanian Tatar squadron was organized. The goal of five infantry and four cavalry regiments was not attained. Given a uniform similar to that of the Duchy of Warsaw (but with the Lithuanian coat of arms *Pogoń, Vytis*) and numbers consecutive to the duchy regiments, the Lithuanian units were directly under Napoleon's command. After much effort more than ten thousand troops were organized in the course of the winter, full strength to be reached by January, 1813. The collapse of the Grande Armée permitted only a minor participation of these troops in the campaign. The Lithuanian Governing Commission and some units withdrew together with the Poles to share the ultimate fate of the duchy's government and army. The war was lost, and the Poles and Lithuanians felt that their interests had not received priority among Napoleon's goals.

The Polish army had fought well and suffered severe casualties. Almost all the commanding generals had been wounded, the chief of staff killed. The remnants had saved all the artillery pieces and their regimental flags. Although Poniatowski had not been allowed to leave reserves or training cadres in the duchy, he rapidly reconstructed an army of sixteen thousand men. But Austrian and Prussian defections opened the duchy to the Russian armies which in February, 1813, occupied Warsaw. Except for the garrisons that resisted in fortresses, Polish troops concentrated in Cracow where Poniatowski was torn between conflicting orders and pressures. The king authorized him to save the army through an armistice; Napoleon belatedly ordered an offensive in the duchy which was impossible. Considering Napoleon's defeat final, several Polish ministers attempted to bargain with Alexander and persuade him to restore a Polish kingdom comprising the duchy and Lithuania either under a revised May 3 Constitution or a modified constitution of the duchy. Surrounded by intrigues and on the verge of suicide, Poniatowski decided to march west and join with Napoleon's armies. During this time of treason and desertion, his main preoccupation was that the Poles maintain their reputation of loyalty. The last odyssey of the Polish troops had its finale at Leipzig (October, 1813) where Poniatowski was killed. His death marked the birth of the Napoleonic legend in Poland.

Historians disagree in their appraisal of Poniatowski's decision. Some blame him for a lack of realism and for his romantic notion of soldierly honor. Others consider that his decision preserved the Polish question as an international issue. Saxony was not saved at the Congress of Vienna by her desertion of Napoleon, and had the Poles imitated Dresden they would have lost not only in moral but also in political stature. In his final surrender act, Napoleon remembered the Polish troops and recommended them to the tsar. The latter allowed their return to Poland and praised their "honorable services."

V. FROM 1813 TO THE CONGRESS OF VIENNA

For roughly two years the Duchy of Warsaw lived under a provisional regime. Alexander assured his allies (Treaty of Kalisz and the Quadruple Alliance) that he would respect their interests in Poland and that the duchy would be liquidated. But he failed to respond to Prussia's demand for a return of territories up to the so-called Knesebeck Line,[5] and indicated to the Poles his interest in a restored Poland under his scepter. Although bitter toward the Poles and especially toward the Lithuanians who had sided with France, the tsar did not seek revenge. In the occupied duchy he tolerated the existence of the Senate, local administration, and courts. He even permitted the creation of a Central Committee with advisory and informative functions. It was composed of the delegates of the former departmental councils which were reestablished. The returning Polish troops were placed under the command of the tsar's brother, Grand Duke Constantine Pavlovich, assisted by a military committee in which Dąbrowski had a leading role. Later a civilian committee was added. In a short time there was an army of twenty thousand men as well as a sizable national guard. The *Code Napoléon* and the remaining French reforms became the object of much discussion. The unresolved peasant question was submitted to an inquiry in 1814, which revealed a diversity of views ranging from the support of labor obligations to the advocacy of a system of rent tenure. For the time being no decisions were taken.

In March, 1813, the duchy received an interim government, called the Provisional Supreme Council (Tymczasowa Rada Najwyż-sza) and presided over by a Russian, Senator Vasilli S. Lanskoi. It comprised Novosiltsov, a former Prussian-Saxon administrator, and two Poles from Lithuania, of whom Drucki-Lubecki was one. Virtually an occupation regime, it used Russian as the official language and had the final authority in the duchy. Czartoryski, who once again returned to active politics, received permmission to communicate directly with the tsar and formulate recommendations. He used his position to complain about the arbitrary acts of the Russian police, and army requisitions which were ruining the exhausted country. Seeking to strengthen the tsar in his pro-Polish intentions, the prince tried to win England over to the cause of Poland's restoration. In working toward this end, however, he acted independently of Alexander and aroused the tsar's suspicion and anger.

The final settlement of the Polish question was reserved to the congress of the victorious powers which met in Vienna in September, 1814. Reduced to its bare essentials, the problem was whether Alexander would be allowed to retain the duchy and, by linking it with other Polish lands, set up a kingdom of Poland under his scepter. Prussia was willing to be bought off by some minor territorial concessions in Poznania and the annexation of Saxony. Paying lip service to an independent Polish state within its prepartition boundaries, Lord Castlereagh of England opposed an undue exten-

5. Following Przemsza, Pilica, Vistula, Bug, Narew, and Niemen rivers to East Prussia.

sion of Russian might. Vienna was against a Prussian annexation of Saxony which would strengthen the Hohenzollerns in Germany. An Anglo-Austrian coalition reinforced by France and directed against Russia emerged. Alexander posed the threat of *faits accomplis*, and the Polish troops in the duchy were alerted for another war for Poland, this time under the Russian aegis. In October, 1814, Dąbrowski urged that Polish troops occupy areas claimed by Austria and even Prussia. The Polish-Saxon question led to a deadlock in Vienna, and eventually Alexander agreed to a compromise. Although ably assisted by Czartoryski, he could not defy the other powers, and his own diplomats considered a reconstitution of Poland under the tsar's scepter a folly. A new redistribution of Polish lands took place. The tsar retained most of the duchy but Prussia received its western portions as well as Danzig, which vainly sought to remain a free city. Contested Cracow became a free city under the joint protectorate of the three powers.

Largely thanks to Alexander, the Congress of Vienna recognized the special position of the Polish nation. Article 14 of the Final Act provided for the maintenance of free navigation, circulation of agrarian and industrial products, and free transit within the prepartition borders of the commonwealth. Article 1 promised that Poles subject to the three monarchies would receive national representations and institutions in so far as compatible with the interests of the partitioning powers. While the Congress sanctioned the western borders of the new Kingdom of Poland linked with Russia through a constitution and the person of the tsar-king, it said nothing about the eastern boundaries, leaving an eventual union of the kingdom with the Polish guberniias an open question. Those Poles who had hoped for a sizable Poland under the scepter of the tsar were greatly disappointed. Kościuszko, who had favored the idea of a Polish-Russian relationship resembling that between Austria and Hungary, remained in exile. Alexander, in turn, was deeply hurt that his liberal notions regarding Poland were not appreciated by the Congress. The opposition of the allies and even the threat of war came to him as a shock; his ambition of being the maker of a new Europe suffered.

The Congress of Vienna both reaffirmed the partitions and recognized the existence of the Polish nation. This seeming paradox was due in no small degree to the fact that the powers could not altogether ignore Polish political vitality as shown in the first decade of the nineteenth century. The period of the Duchy of Warsaw mattered a great deal in this respect. The duchy lasted nominally for eight years, *de facto* for six, and enjoyed only three years of peace. Never fully a master of its own destiny, it was nevertheless a Polish state, a phenomenon which had a great moral and political significance for the entire nation. Its existence contradicted the verdict of the partitions; its army not only revolutionized the Polish military tradition but also served to educate the masses in a patriotic and liberal sense. It was impossible to dismiss these facts and return to the year 1797 when the very name Poland had been obliterated. The Kingdom of Poland—commonly known as the Congress Kingdom—was the logical sequel to the duchy and was unimaginable without the latter.

The period of the Duchy of Warsaw saw the beginnings of a special kind of modernization. Judicial and political reforms coming from above preceded the spontaneous process of social and economic transformation; people who had not yet lost "feudal" habits began to enjoy rights of a more advanced type of society. There were glaring discrepancies as, for instance, the *de facto* maintenance of compulsory peasant labor in spite of the abolition of serfdom. Institutional changes, which the social elite attempted to interpret in a conservative spirit, stimulated structural changes. Increased social mobility, largely the result of wars, contributed to long-range developments in line with the evolution of Europe as a whole. Insurmountable difficulties allowed for only modest improvements in the economic sphere, but even here the trend was toward modernization. The Napoleonic civil code, which protected property and contracts, and the commercial code created favorable conditions for the growth of a more advanced economy. Some banking activity and the establishment of the mint, as well as increased production of textiles and metallurgical works, belied theories of a complete stagnation.

The gentry and the burghers were especially affected. Deprived of their land monopoly, awakened from the lethargy into which they had fallen under the Prussian rule, drawn into a centralized bureaucratic system, and made subject to the same law and courts as all other classes, the gentry became deeply involved in the general process of change. Tradesmen and early bankers came to the foreground of the rising middle class whose source of wealth was liquid rather than industrial capital. Buying estates and intermarrying with the gentry, the leading burghers helped to blur the distinction between urban and rural upper classes. Participating in the administration, diet, departmental councils, army, national guard, and masonic lodges, the townsmen advanced socially, politically, and economically. Among the fifteen members of the Sejm commissions, four were non-noble, and there was widespread criticism when no burghers were included in the deputation sent to Napoleon in 1812. Modernization and a certain laicization of society was reflected in education and culture, but this aspect will be treated separately. Here, as elsewhere, the gentry was still the dominant class, but the beginnings of a bourgeois emancipation were visible.

The Duchy of Warsaw was a creation of Napoleon and it went down with his fall. But the Napoleonic legend remained and gained a sway over Polish thinking and imagination. Napoleon and France became identified with progress, glory, and the national struggle for independence. If the legend engendered illusions it also strengthened the faith in the value of military efforts—not since the late seventeenth century had the Polish soldier tasted victory. Changes that took place in the duchy outlived its existence and affected both its inhabitants and the Poles who lived outside of its borders. The basic reforms in the political and military spheres remained in force until 1831; in the administrative field until 1863 and 1867; in the judicial area till 1876. Notions of civil law derived from the Napleonic code endured until the middle of the twentieth century.

# CHAPTER 4

# From the Congress of Vienna to 1830

I. THE SITUATION IN 1815

THE new division of Polish territories brought about by the Congress of Vienna survived, by and large, until the First World War. From the point of view of internal status and organization, the lands of the old commonwealth now fell into six categories: (1) West Prussia and (2) the Grand Duchy of Posen (Poznań) under Prussia, (3) Galicia under Austria, (4) Cracow, (5) the Kingdom of Poland, and (6) the former Polish guberniias of the Russian Empire. The Kingdom of Poland was the focal point of national activities. As the nineteenth century progressed, it came to be increasingly regarded, especially in the West, as identical with Poland, although it comprised roughly one-seventh of the territory and one-fifth of the population of prepartition Poland. In 1815 the idea of the old commonwealth was still very much alive, as witnessed by the Congress' articles on Polish nationality and free trade and communications within the 1772 frontiers.

The greatest possibilities for a genuine Polish political life existed in the kingdom. It seemed that a policy of cooperation with Russia could preserve the kingdom's constitutional identity and create a means of unification with the former Polish guberniias. Political activities here ranged from collaboration through constitutional opposition to conspiracies. Under Prussia the Poles sought to preserve and enlarge the autonomy granted to the Grand Duchy of Posen; in the Habsburg monarchy, where the Metternich regime did not go beyond minor institutional concessions, chances for political acitivity were slender.

The economic provisions of the Congress remained for the most part a dead letter, although the city republic of Cracow did become a center of Polish trade. But no all-Polish market could operate

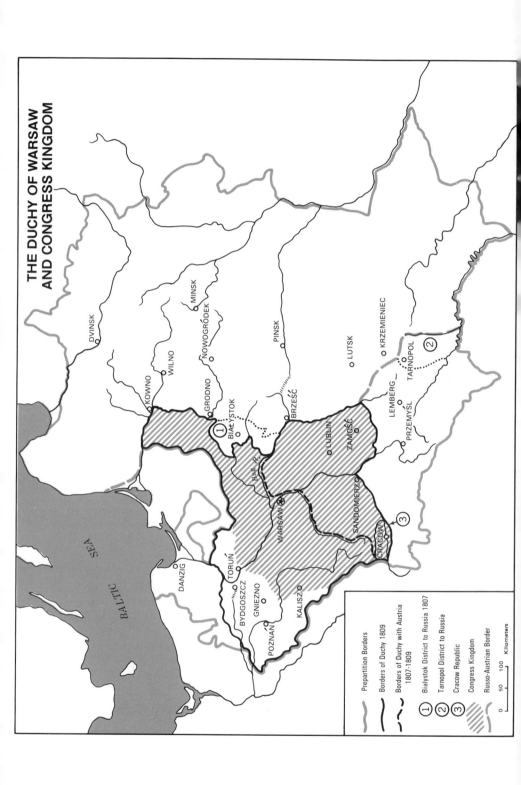

# THE DUCHY OF WARSAW AND CONGRESS KINGDOM

BALTIC SEA

DANZIG

DVINSK

MINSK

NOWOGRÓDEK

PINSK

WILNO

KOWNO

GRODNO

BIAŁYSTOK

BRZEŚĆ

LUTSK

KRZEMIENIEC

TARNOPOL

LEMBERG

PRZEMYSL

LUBLIN

ZAMOŚĆ

SANDOMIERZ

WARSAW

CRACOW

KALISZ

POZNAN

GNIEZNO

BYDGOSZCZ

TORUŃ

Bug R.

① ② ③

Prepartition Borders

Borders of Duchy 1809

Borders of Duchy with Austria 1807–1809

① Białystok District to Russia 1807

② Tarnopol District to Russia

③ Cracow Republic

Congress Kingdom

Russo-Austrian Border

0    50    100
Kilometers

after 1815, and some of the industrial activities noticeable in the Duchy of Warsaw were interrupted by border changes. The Austrian and Prussian parts had to adjust to the economies of the ruling countries; it was only in the Congress Kingdom that one could speak of *Polish* economic policies. Affected by the destructions of the Napoleonic wars, the predominantly agrarian economy had to operate under unfavorable postwar conditions of falling grain prices in the West. The landowning class was naturally hard hit, and the whole agrarian question was in the forefront of discussions. The socioeconomic structure varied greatly, of course, from one part of old Poland to the other. In the kingdom the peasant was free but without legal rights to the land. He was a serf in the ex-Polish guberniias, and a semiserf protected by the state in Galicia. Under Prussia he was a free man with some guaranteed land tenure, although there were differences between West Prussia, which was affected by the emancipation decree of 1807, and the Duchy of Posen. The peasant question demanded a solution on economic, social, and humanitarian grounds, and it was pregnant with political meaning. Depending on the kind of solution, the peasant could either become a loyal subject of the partitioning powers or a politically conscious member of the Polish nation. A struggle for the peasant's allegiance filled much of the history of the nineteenth century.

The developments of the post-1815 period did not threaten the political and social predominance of the Polish gentry. The chances of the bourgeoisie seemed brightest in the kingdom, although a new wave of German immigration posed some competition. The status of the Jews was not affected by the creation of the kingdom; there they continued to be temporarily deprived of political and civic rights. Nor did the Prussian emancipation decree of 1812 apply immediately to the Jews of Poznania. In the religious sphere, the partitioning powers sought to prevent the Catholic church from being an all-Polish institution and tried to establish some control over it. The centralized ecclesiastical hierarchy received a blow with the elevation of the archbishops of Warsaw, Lemberg (Lwów, Lviv), and Gniezno-Poznań (Gnesen-Posen) to positions of primates. A single primate of all Poland no longer existed.

Although in 1815 the various parts of the old commonwealth entered on divergent paths of development, one must not picture them as completely isolated from one another. Their politically conscious classes were able to interact, and Polish culture and learning continued to transcend political borders. None of the partitioning powers could conduct its Polish policy in isolation, and developments in one area, especially in the kingdom, affected the Polish situation everywhere.

II. PRUSSIAN POLAND

The Polish provinces of Prussia consisted in 1815 of West Prussia—held uninterruptedly since the partitions and now enlarged by the addition of Thorn (Toruń) and two districts—and of the newly established Grand Duchy of Posen. Only the latter, which had an area of nearly 29,000 square kilometers and 776,00 inhabitants, enjoyed an autonomous regime in accord with the recommendations of the Congress of Vienna. Upon taking over the province the king of Prussia assured the inhabitants that they were not obliged to renounce their own nationality. The oath of loyalty required of the nobility said that they recognized "that part of Poland which returned to the King of Prussia" as their fatherland.[1]

The grand duchy received as its viceroy (Statthalter) Prince Antoni Radziwiłł; a liberal Prussian, Josef von Zerboni di Sposetti, became governor (Oberpräsident). Although Radziwiłł was weak and absolutely loyal to Prussia, Zerboni was an influential politician with pro-Polish tendencies and enjoyed the support of liberal dignitaries in Berlin. The Prussian government declared that Polish would rank beside German as the official language of the duchy, and the Poles had every right to use their mother tongue in educational and judiciary fields. They could also serve as administrators and officers, although few of them did so hoping for an eventual reunion with the Kingdom of Poland.

Poznania was divided into two regencies (Regierungsbezirk) which were subdivided into districts presided over (until 1832) by elected officials. The duchy had its provincial diet composed of three estates: noble landowners, towns, and rural communes. Suffrage was indirect, and high property qualifications limited the number of electors. The Poles commanded a majority only in the first estate and had no representatives in the third. Even so, during the first decades they had an over-all majority in the Poznanian diet. The diet was triennial, and the king determined the length of its sessions. It could only advise, petition, and submit complaints to the crown. In 1828 municipal government was introduced, and a year later local district dietines. Only landowning gentry and wealthier peasants could participate in the latter. In 1827 the Poles proposed equality for the Jews—to take effect in ten years' time—but nothing came of it during the period in question. In 1821 a papal bull regulated state-church relations, and although the church had a great deal of independence, the government had a voice in the nomination of bishops. The archbishopric of Gniezno became in 1821 the

1. Leonard Chodźko (Comte d'Angeberg), *Recueil des traités, conventions et actes diplomatiques concernant la Pologne 1762–1862* (Paris: Amyot, 1862), p. 690.

Gniezno-Poznań archbishopric and lost control over the Breslau (Wrocław) diocese.

The Prussian system favored the nobility without granting it genuine legislative powers. In educational and judicial fields concessions to the Poles were tempered by zealous local officials who identified germanization with progress and higher culture. Although sharply reprimanded by the liberal minister of education in 1822, the local administration continued to discriminate against the Poles. After 1824 attempts to promote the use of German in schools gained momentum, and the government flatly refused to establish a Polish university in Posen. Liberal Polish deputies led by Andrzej Niegolewski (1786-1857) combined their protests against Prussian policies with demands for wider powers of the diet and urged self-government of the grand duchy. Polish conservatives were more cautious in their requests. There is little doubt that the moderately liberal Prussian policies in the grand duchy reflected not only differences within the administration, but also developments in the Kingdom of Poland. Berlin realized that, as a Polish general put it, the Poles would follow the partitioning power that most effectively recognized the principle of nationality, "this deity of the present times which the Poles worship no less than other nations of Europe."[2] It was important that Tsar Alexander not have a monopoly on a pro-Polish policy, and it was also important to guard against the periodic tensions in Congress Poland, which could grow into an all-Polish insurrection. Poznanian Poles took some part in Warsaw's secret societies, and they set up one of their own called the Society of Scythemen (Towarzystwo Kosynierów). A Polish student organization at Breslau—where a chair of Polish language existed—served as a meeting ground with students from Congress Poland. Prussian investigations of Poznanian links with Warsaw's secret societies resulted in a trial held in 1827. Only light sentences were imposed; the Polish policy of Berlin was still characterized by caution and moderation.

The situation was vastly different in West Prussia. Although in 1815 the Poles constituted roughly one-half of the population there, they had no special rights or privileges. Systematic germanization was the rule rather than the exception in this efficiently administered province. In 1824 West Prussia was administratively joined with East Prussia; this meant a further diluting of the Polish element in the German mass. The landed estates, which at first were predominantly held by the Poles, were changing hands, and the same was true for Polish farms in that part of East Prussia which had once belonged to the commonwealth.

2. Cited in Bolesław Limanowski, *Historia demokracji polskiej*, 1:180.

The emancipation of the peasantry in Prussia began in 1807, and it differed sharply from peasant reforms in other Polish lands. In 1808 peasants on crown lands were enfranchised, but it took several years and the decrees of 1811, 1816, and 1821 before the principle of emancipation was applied to private estates. The estates of West Prussia were affected in 1821, and those of the Grand Duchy of Posen two years later. The Prussian reforms were accomplished gradually and favored the landlords and the wealthier strata of the peasantry. The peasants acquired full property rights to the land they cultivated, but they had to compensate the lords either by ceding a portion of their land or by rent payments stretched out over a long period of time. In lieu of payment the landlord could exact some compulsory labor over the next twenty-five years, or he could contract the peasant for compulsory hire.

Without entering into all the complex technicalities of the Prussian reform, one needs to review the major stages, particularly as they operated in Poznania. In 1816 the Napoleonic code was replaced by the old Landrecht minus provisions for seigneurial justice. Three years later the government prohibited evictions of the peasantry, and in 1823 it introduced the final emancipation decree, which repeated the prohibition of eviction in stricter terms than in other Prussian provinces. In the process of emancipation the "regulated" peasants, i.e., those to whom the decrees applied, gave up one-sixth of their land to the lords in West Prussia, one-seventh in Poznania, and one-fifth in East Prussia. By way of comparison the predominantly Polish peasants in Upper Silesia gave up one-third of the land. The smaller the amount of peasant land ceded, the higher were the capital payments or rents exacted from the peasantry.

The effects of the reform, which began in 1830, were manifold. From the point of view of the landowners the system enabled a transition to more advanced forms of agriculture based largely on hired labor and assisted financially by credit operations. A credit society called the Landschaft came into being in Poznania in 1821; land credit organizations in West Prussia had already been in existence for over thirty years. Bankrupt estates in Poznania were forcibly sold in 1815, and consequently one-sixth of all estates changed hands. This significantly lowered the amount of land held by the Polish gentry. The same was true for West Prussia, where Polish landowners were frequently denied credit. The wealthier peasants were able to own farms that were economically efficient; the poorest strata became landless. Poznania and West Prussia gradually became a land of large estates and of sizable peasant farms. As an agrarian *Hinterland* of the Prussian state, the two provinces had the incentive to move in the direction of a "capitalist-type" agriculture.

The surplus agrarian population could not be absorbed by local industry, which was minimal, and had to seek means of livelihood outside of the provinces. A steady emigration began. Industrial development in Prussian Poland suffered from competition with the more developed German provinces and from the loss of former Polish markets. The textile industry declined; glass works, paper mills, and brick factories fared poorly. Beet sugar refineries appeared in 1820 in Poznania, but due to the primitive methods used they were unable to survive beyond the 1860s. Breweries and food-processing industries did a little better, but Polish craftsmen were losing ground to the growing German element. The city of Danzig was stagnating; and in the early 1820s there was some social unrest and strikes in the area.

III. GALICIA AND CRACOW

In 1815 Austrian Poland comprised Galicia within its 1809 borders, plus the eastern district of Tarnopol, which had been returned by the Russians. The Kingdom of Galicia and Lodomeria covered an area of 77,300 square kilometers, and its population numbered three and a half million in 1817. According to 1822 figures, Poles constituted 47.5 percent of the population; Ruthenians, 45.5 percent; Jews, 6 percent; and Germans, 1 percent. The density of population, especially in Western Galicia, was among the highest in Europe and roughly twice that of Prussian Poland or the Congress Kingdom. During the period 1816–30 the population grew to 4 million inhabitants which the backward Galicia could hardly support. The largest city, Lemberg, had only forty thousand inhabitants. There were a few primitive industries in the country, such as textiles, glass works, breweries, and the first beet sugar refineries which collapsed by the 1850s. The Galician economy suffered from lack of capital, fiscal exploitation, and competition of the more advanced provinces of the Habsburg monarchy. In 1817 only about one-sixth of the taxes collected in Galicia was used for expenditure in the province; a large part of this sum paid for the large bureaucracy. Roads were bad, sanitary conditions deplorable. Around 1821 the province had only seventy-eight physicians. In agriculture the three-field system and antiquated methods of farming predominated. Serfdom proved wasteful and uneconomical. Credit was scarce and interest rates high; the authorities did not permit the establishment of land credit institutions comparable to the Prussian Landschaft.

The political and social regime was Metternich's absolute government tinged with feudal elements. The state relied on the Catholic church, particularly the Jesuits who had been expelled from Russia in 1820, and on the Uniate church, which was separated from that in Russia and endowed with a metropolitan see in Lemberg. The Uniate hierarchy nurtured a certain antagonism toward the Poles and had taken an anti-Polish stand during the War of 1809. The contemptuous attitude displayed by the Polish nobility toward the Uniate clergy and their offspring—the nucleus of the Ruthenian elite—helped to keep this antagonism alive. Political concessions granted to Galicia in the spirit of the Congress of Vienna were limited to the establishment of an Assembly of Estates (Stände) in Lemberg. Set up in 1817 and based on four estates—clergy, magnates, knights, and towns—this diet was merely a token representative body. Without a building of its own, with even narrower prerogatives than the Poznanian diet, in theory the assembly was supposed to meet once a year. It had an executive organ of its own (Landesauschuss or Wydział Krajowy) but no administrative machinery.

Suspicious of the attraction exercised on Galician Poles by the Congress Kingdom—in 1817 a Polish delegate presented a secret memorandum to the viceroy in Warsaw, pleading that Galicia be unified with the kingdom—the Viennese government paid close attention to Russo-Polish developments. During the Russo-Turkish war of 1828–29 Vienna decided on pro-Polish gestures. The new governor of Galicia, Prince August Lobkowicz, opened the diet in Polish and sought to court the nobility. Austrian officials were instructed to learn the language of the province. Although some Galician-Polish circles again made advances to the tsar, Vienna dealt leniently with Poles active in secret societies which had branched out from the kingdom to Galicia. The Austrians probably knew that their impact was negligible and, in fact, the Patriotic Society in Warsaw could not find a representative for the Lemberg region. Even though some of the Polish magnates were active in Vienna, Galicia stagnated politically, and the local diet was hardly conducive to the growth of native political life.

The "free, independent, strictly neutral city of Cracow with its district" was the result of a compromise reached by the great powers at Vienna. With an area of 1,164 square kilometers and a population of 88,000, which by 1827 increased to over 120,000, the Cracow Republic comprised, apart from the city itself, three towns and over two hundred villages. Its constitution, hastily drawn up by Adam Czartoryski, was completed in 1818. It provided for a Senate, headed by a president, vested with full executive powers and initiative in legislation. The Senate was elected by the Assembly of Representatives, but the university and the cathedral chapter also chose a few senators. More than half of the members of the Assembly of Representatives were elected by communal assemblies; the remainder were appointed by the Senate, the university, and the cathedral chapter. In addition six judges sat in the assembly. The size of the electorate was limited by property, educational, and age qualifications as well as by the exclusion of Jews. However, richer peasants could vote and larger villages had indirect suffrage rights; this was something of a novelty.

Cracow retained the Napoleonic code, and its citizens were equal in the eyes of the law. Courts were independent, and all official acts were drawn up in Polish. The three partitioning powers, acting through their residents, exercised a protectorate over the republic, and although they did not always act in unison, several times the residents jointly intervened in the internal affairs of Cracow.

The bulk of the population of the tiny republic lived in the country-side, and a Peasant Commission was set up early to carry out agrarian reforms. The commission sought to commute all peasant labor obligations to rents, and although the latter were calculated at too high a level, a gradual transformation of peasants into rent-paying farmers was well underway by 1830. The reforms affected first the crown and church land, i.e., four-fifths of the estates. In the process the peasants did not lose any of the land they had traditionally cultivated. Their emancipation thus followed a different pattern than in Poznania, and was in fact the only peasant reform sponsored and executed by Poles in the nineteenth century.

The Congress of Vienna made Cracow a free trade area in the sense that it could import duty-free goods from other parts of Poland, but it had to pay duties on exports. While this policy harmed local industries, it did promote trade. Although the Senate failed to provide imaginative leadership, Cracow became an important center, especially of transit (and of smuggling), and contributed to the semblance of an all-Polish trading area. Cracow's industries comprised some textile factories and numerous crafts. An adjoining district had iron ore and coal mines, and zinc foundries; for a while it also produced marble. The mines and factories were operated in fairly primitive ways, although in 1817 the first steam engine—the first in Poland—was used in a mine belonging to the Potocki family. In mines and factories hired labor was gradually replacing serfs.

The sociopolitical structure had certain unique features. Cracow had a large group of intelligentsia, professors, lawyers, and representatives of the free professions, as well as an urban oligarchy. A sizable student body produced an intellectual ferment with radical overtones which affected the artisans and the lesser bourgeoisie. Hence, while the aristocracy and the gentry played a leading part, urban elements were important, and the university gave a special stamp to local developments. Russian influences were strongest in the Senate—originally appointed by the three powers—which relied on the urban and rural oligarchy and the upper clergy. The Austrians and Prussians were influential in the more liberal Assembly of Representatives, in which the middle class and the university predominated. The conservatives and the liberals clashed over such issues as the autonomy of the university, prerogatives of the assembly, independence of the judiciary, and the peasant question. On occasion the foreign residents interfered jointly, as in 1823 when they applied pressure through a committee composed of pro-Russian senators, or in 1828 when they annulled the decisions of the assembly and kept the defeated president of the Senate in power.

The University of Cracow enjoyed a position that went beyond that of a local institution of higher learning. It was permitted to admit students from all parts of the former commonwealth, and its official protector was the tsar in his capacity as King of Poland. Naturally the university became a focus of student political activity, and in 1821 the authorities ended its autonomy. Five years later the Russian senator Novosiltsov became the curator of Cracow university, which event, taken together with the political interference of the three residents, cast a shadow over the seemingly independent and neutral republic.

IV. THE KINGDOM OF POLAND: ITS CONSTITUTION AND CHARACTER

The Congress Kingdom occupied a smaller area than the Duchy of Warsaw (120,000 square kilometers) but its population rose from 3,300,000 in 1815 to over 4 million in 1827. In comparison to the duchy, its ethnic composition changed slightly, the percentages of Jewish and German population rising a little. The size of Warsaw increased, and by 1827 the city had over 130,000 inhabitants. Lublin was the next largest town with only 13,000. Some 80 percent of the total population lived from agriculture.

The status of the kingdom was first outlined in the Constitutional Bases drafted by Czartoryski and announced together with the proclamation of the kingdom on July 20, 1815. A provisional government was set up with Czartoryski as vice-president. The final constitution, promulgated on November 27, 1815, was called the Constitutional Charter. The document said that, "the Kingdom of Poland is forever united with the Empire of Russia" through the tsar, a hereditary king of Poland. So, the statement made in the Constitutional Bases and at the Congress of Vienna, that it was *the constitution* that formed the principal link uniting Poland to Russia, was not repeated. The separate character of the kingdom, however, was spelled out clearly. Thus, it had its own borders and separate citizenship and passports. A distinction was made between Polish subjects and those Poles who served in the army and only took a military oath. Polish was the language of the administration, and only native or naturalized Polish citizens could hold public functions. While the foreign affairs of the two states were common, the Polish army could not be used outside Europe, and the tsar-king determined Poland's participation in wars waged by Russia. The charter recognized Catholicism as the religion of the majority of the inhabitants but without prejudice to other Christian denominations.

The political structure of the kingdom was largely modeled on that of the Duchy of Warsaw. The position of the ruler was similar, except that before being crowned kings of Poland Alexander's successors had to swear to observe the charter. Again there were five ministers and a secretary of state, but they were grouped in an Administrative Council, and presided over collective commissions or boards. The former Ministry of the Interior and Religion now became that of the Interior and Police. A separate Ministry of Police was abolished, and a new Commission of Religion and Public Education added. The relations of ministers with the king and with the parliament remained on the whole unchanged. Two men were named to the Administrative Council *ad personam*: Novosiltsov and Czartoryski. The large Council of State pretty much retained its former character. The lower chamber of the Sejm consisted of representatives and deputies, but now all of them had to be landowners. The ratio between the two groups was set at seventy-seven to fifty-one. The Senate was composed of royal nominees with very high property qualifications and princes belonging to the Russian imperial family. The number of senators could not exceed one-half the number of the representatives of the lower chamber. The two chambers had equal prerogatives in legislative matters; the Senate also served as a high tribunal dealing with political and administrative cases referred to it by the ruler. The Sejm acted through commissions, but all members could participate in discussions provided they spoke from memory. The biennial sessions lasted twice as long as under the duchy.

The collegiate principle introduced on the ministerial level also operated in the provincial administration. Commissions headed by appointed presidents governed the eight voievodships (Cracow, Sandomierz, Lublin, Kalisz, Płock, Podlasie, and Augustów). The system tended to weaken the personal responsibility of presidents as well as of ministers. Towns had municipal councils from 1816; rural communes were governed by officials called *wójt*, and a decree provided that local landowners exercise these functions. Only landowners were eligible to voievodship commissions and could be made presidents of certain courts of law. Mainly, though not exclusively, noble, the upper class occupied a privileged position in the government of the country.

The Constitutional Charter had an impressive sounding section on civil liberties, which guaranteed freedom of the press, personal and religious freedom, equality before the law, and freedom from arbitrary arrest and punishment. Private property was declared inviolable. These guarantees were more of a statement of intention than actual safeguards. According to a contemporary saying, the constitution of the Duchy of Warsaw had no guarantees of civil liberties but nobody noticed it, that of the kingdom did and nobody noticed it either. It was also said that the Constitutional Charter was on the table and the whip under it, and one better be careful lest the positions be reversed. Indeed, theory and practice soon drew apart, but one has to admit that the charter itself was an impressive document. In some ways more liberal than Napoleon's constitution, it was also less democratic. Articles that figured in the Czartoryski draft, promising universal education and holding out some hope to the peasantry, were not included in the constitution. Even if the electorate was larger than that of contemporary France (one hundred thousand electors in the small kingdom) effective power was in the hands of the propertied classes.

The charter, which Alexander granted and presumably could revoke, contained loopholes. The old Polish version of habeas corpus *(neminem captivabimus)* was changed to a formula *neminem captivari permittemus* which could justify arbitrary arrest. The king could, in exceptional cases, appoint non-Poles to public office. In budgetary matters he could bypass the Sejm.

The problems facing the country were unusually complex. First, there was the question of the constitution and its part in the relations between Russia and Poland. Would the constitutional kingdom be a step toward liberalization of the empire, or would Russia strive to extend its autocracy to Warsaw? Second, there was the issue of the former Polish guberniias. Would they become a bridge between Warsaw and St. Petersburg or a rock on which cooperation would founder? Third, there were the large economic issues arising out of the destitute position of Poland. If the kingdom was to survive as a show place of Alexander's liberalism, it would need to prove that it was economically viable, capable of resolving its agrarian difficulties, and able to develop its trade and industries. What were the best ways of tackling these problems and creating a *modus vivendi* between Russia and Poland? A good deal depended on the personalities of the leaders on both sides.

The maker of the kingdom and its ruler, Tsar Alexander I, has baffled contemporaries and historians. A liberal by education and sentiment, an autocrat by temperament and in virtue of his position, Alexander seemed genuinely interested in the liberal experiment in the kingdom. He visited Warsaw almost annually and wanted to use the Poles as an element to transform his empire. He never forgot the fate of Tsar Paul, and Poland and the ex-Polish provinces seemed a trump card to be played against his conservative opponents at home. What is more, Alexander's Polish policy was part of a larger scheme of manipulating liberal elements throughout Europe for purposes of Russian foreign policy in Italy, Germany, and Eastern Europe. Alexander was determined to maintain his brother, Grand Duke Constantine, as commander in chief of the Polish army, partly because he preferred not to have him in Russia, partly because the presence of the grand duke in Warsaw was a pledge of the seriousness of the tsar's Polish policy.

An autocrat and disciplinarian, capricious, high-strung, cruel and affectionate at the same time, Constantine was a tragic figure, a split personality, who could do great harm in politics. He came to Poland detesting the country and the people. He left it fifteen years later having become genuinely attached to Poland and feeling at home in Warsaw. But during all those years he did not cease to maltreat Poland as he maltreated all whom he loved. From the beginning his position was extraconstitutional, and indicated that Alexander refused to be bound by the charter if it did not suit his purposes.

If Constantine was the unpredictable force in the kingdom, Novosiltsov was its evil spirit. His position as special representative of the tsar was not foreseen by the constitution, and Novosiltsov never became a citizen of the kingdom. Brilliant, lazy, corrupt, and utterly unscrupulous, Novosiltsov made himself indispensable to Alexander by fanning the tsar's suspicions of the Poles and especially of Czartoryski. Linked to a powerful court camarilla at St. Petersburg, which viewed the kingdom as a hotbed of Jacobinism and a threat to Russian rule over the "western guberniias," Novosiltsov excelled in techniques of provocation and denunciation. He intrigued against Constantine, who in turn disliked and despised him openly.

The logical candidate for the post of viceroy, Czartoryski, had already lost much of Alexander's confidence. By criticizing Constantine, he made the latter a personal enemy. Cooperating at first with his former protegé Novosiltsov, he slowly awakened to the senator's sinister role in the kingdom. Although he enjoyed wide support in the country and was permitted to communicate directly with Alexander, Czartoryski had limited influence. The position of viceroy went unexpectedly to the old general Zajączek, whose Jacobin complex made him suspicious of the Polish upper classes, and whose jealous disposition made him a docile tool of Alexander and Constantine. Zajączek showed a contempt for his countrymen, the Sejm, and all signs of opposition. After his death no viceroy was named, and the powers of the office devolved on the Administrative Council. Supreme power continued to be exercised by Constantine and Novosiltsov. After 1821 Prince Drucki-Lubecki was named minister of the treasury and rose to a position of great influence in Polish public life.

Among the ministries, the Commission of War shortly became leaderless; the army was the domain of Constantine and he suffered no interference. Financed at first by the imperial treasury, later absorbing a large part of the kingdom's budget, the Polish army (it was not commonly called the army of the kingdom) occupied an important place in the country. Excellently trained and well administered, it was the pride of the Poles and the arena of bitter conflicts with Constantine. Organized in accord with the Russian model, subject to a Prussian-type drill and the despotism of the grand duke, the army differed radically from the democratically oriented troops of the Duchy of Warsaw. Constant inspections and parades and an intensive use of corporal punishment drove the soldiers to despair. Some officers who had been insulted by Constantine committed suicide; several older generals resigned their commissions. Secret police filled the army with spies. The bulk of the soldiers came from the peasant class, a system of substitution making it possible for townspeople and richer peasants to avoid the draft. The service lasted for ten years. The officers' corps was chiefly composed of gentry and burghers. As a result of constitutional provisions and the policy of Constantine the army had certain inherent weaknesses. It lacked its own supplies because the kingdom was not allowed to build arms factories. Enamored with drill, Constantine neglected the operational training of staff officers and commanders.

A political contest between liberals (May 3 reformers, moderates of the Duchy of Warsaw, and freemasons) and reactionary conservatives, who enjoyed support from the church hierarchy and the Jesuits, affected several ministries. This was true particularly for the Commission of Education and Religious Cult, and for that of Justice. The former under the presidency of Stanisław Kostka Potocki (1755-1821), an old reformer and the master of the Grand Orient, accomplished a great deal in the educational field. Under his reactionary successor, Stanisław Grabowski (1780–1845), education declined. The achievements of the Commission of Justice, which also passed from the reformers to the reactionaries, were small. The Commission of Interior and Police saw no personal changes and fared well under its original minister. Through its Department of Industry and Trade it had an important part in economic affairs until the Commission of the Treasury under Drucki-Lubecki gained virtual control over the Polish economy.

## V. ATTEMPTED INDUSTRIALIZATION OF THE KINGDOM

After 1815 the economic picture of the Congress Kingdom was grim. In spite of renewed efforts to balance the budget there was a large deficit by 1820. The problem of debts to Austria and Prussia was resolved only after several years of negotiations, and an adverse balance of trade continued. Agriculture, the main source of wealth, was in dire difficulties. The heavily mortgaged private estates, with their uneconomical serf labor and primitive farming methods, could not increase yields per acre. Only 34 percent of the land was under plow. Prices for grains were low and credit facilities unavailable. Yet, it was essential for the state to save the big landed estates from debt and encourage their productivity. The peasantry, 29 percent of which was landless, faced threats of eviction and expropriation by landowners trying to enlarge their holdings. Crushed by direct and indirect taxes and forced to consume their own products, the peasantry, which amounted to nearly 80 percent of the population, was virtually eliminated from the market. Attempts to make the peasants proprietors, for example, Staszic's measures of enfranchisement and the creation of peasant-run cooperative farms in his Hrubieszów estate, were exceptional. Only in the crown lands was there a marked move toward making the peasants tenant farmers.

The state was the largest landowner in the kingdom; it possessed about one-fifth of all cultivated land and a large part of the forests. It was on the crown lands that the so-called Old Polish Basin was situated, which had the biggest ferrous and nonferrous ore mines, most of the high furnaces, and an ample supply of timber and water energy. Iron and zinc were already under exploitation, but charcoal was used in furnaces and water served as power. Old methods of smelting and forging iron prevailed. Coal discovered at the end of the eighteenth century was not yet a market commodity, and only forges and smithies could use the semifinished metal products for the manufacture of agricultural tools. Building industries did not as yet use iron structures, and it seemed that there was no real incentive to modernize or to expand operations in the Old Polish Basin, in spite of the importance of that basin from the point of view of the treasury.

Staszic, however, who headed the Department of Industry and Trade, was a man of vision. He promoted plans for expansion of the basin. In 1816 a Mining Directorate was set up. There was prospecting for new deposits, zinc mills were built (one of them working on coke), and the first rolling mill constructed. Already in 1817 the state prohibited export of iron ores and imposed duties on imports. Staszic created a special Miners' Corps, which was organized along semimilitary lines and provided old-age pensions and sickness benefits to its members. This was the first organized industrial labor force in Poland. Staszic's policy came under attack from the gentry who feared that the new center would draw away their laborers and give rise to new taxes. The newly appointed minister of the treasury, Drucki-Lubecki, felt that the basin was not bringing in enough revenue, and he succeeded in taking the management of industrial affairs away from Staszic. In a short time, however, Drucki-Lubecki returned to Staszic's ideas and launched a large-scale plan of industrialization and transformation of the entire Polish economy.

Drucki-Lubecki took over the treasury in 1821, at a moment of severe economic crisis which threatened the very existence of the kingdom. Trusted by the tsar, successful in getting around Zajączek and in establishing a temporary working cooperation with Novosiltsov, and able to use the reactionary politicians, Drucki-Lubecki achieved a position of unusual power which he used wisely if ruthlessly. He first succeeded in balancing the budget by obtaining part of the taxes in advance, borrowing money from bankers, and increasing direct and indirect taxes, especially on salt and tobacco which were state monopolies. When in 1822 Russia granted commercial autonomy to the kingdom, which since 1819 had been part of her customs area, Drucki-Lubecki introduced a protectionist policy vis-à-vis Austria and Prussia and brought a tariff war with the latter to successful conclusion. Aware that Poland had lost part of her western markets for grain, he sought to reorient her trade toward Russia. As a result of an advantageous trade agreement with St. Petersburg Poland could export goods that were manufactured in the country from domestic or foreign materials, subject to very low Russian entry duties. Over-all export to Russia, which consisted mainly of textiles, foodstuffs, and, for a few years, of zinc, increased threefold. This was a significant departure from the previously prevailing trade patterns.

Drucki-Lubecki sought to transform the kingdom into a modern industrial state linked with the empire and its markets but remaining autonomous and self-sustaining. By necessity the capital had to come from the state, and a policy of direct intervention followed. This was a novelty in Poland, a land that had never really experienced mercantilism. Drucki-Lubecki's program of large investments in industry was also designed to assist agriculture, and through urbanization, road building, and credit facilities he sought to create an internal market. Capital expenditure was covered by budgetary means and by foreign loans. In 1828, Drucki-Lubecki established the Bank of Poland to service the country's public debt, finance industry, and assure trade credits. The funding capital was collected through money transfers from governmental institutions and by attracting state and individuals' deposits. The bank issued notes that did not, however, become a compulsory legal tender. It advanced money to investors and engaged in investments of its own. It also controlled the Exchange. The saying attributed to Drucki-Lubecki, that Poland needed three things: schools, industry and trade, and arms's factories, indicated that he sought to modernize the country and make it more independent of Russia. Although he was unwilling to submit his model budgets to the Sejm's scrutiny and was often disrespectful of the constitution, which earned him the ire of the liberals, Drucki-Lubecki was anything but a blind tool of Alexander and Nicholas.

Drucki-Lubecki's favorite field of investment was the Old Polish Basin, which relied mainly on water power and charcoal. Here four blast furnaces were built together with sixteen puddling-process furnaces and casting and rolling mills. The production of iron, copper, and zinc increased. The output of hard coal mining, where small steam engines were applied for pumping out the water, doubled in the years 1824–36. Workers' houses and roads were built in the area, and the state acted as investor, producer, and seller of iron, zinc, and coal. The eventual collapse of the ambitious program of Drucki-Lubecki may have been due to overinvestment and a relative neglect of the more promising Dąbrowa Basin.

In the textile and food-processing industries, the state assisted private enterprises with protection and credit. Łódź, the future Polish Manchester, was built on crown lands. A small village with some eight hundred inhabitants in 1821, its population grew to over four thousand people in nine years. The wool industry developed and tripled its production in the period from 1823 to 1829; the cotton industry which grew in the 1820s increased production five-fold between 1825 and 1830. The chief customers for cloth were the Polish army and later Russia. At first weaving was done individually, but centralized factories soon appeared, and that of Krusche in Pabianice was one of the largest capitalist-type enterprises in East Central Europe. The growth of weaving industries was signally assisted by a large immigration of artisans from Poznania and Germany. The introduction of machinery was slow, but steam-driven mechanical spinning appeared in the late 1820s.

The growth of Warsaw, whose budget increased eightfold from 1816 to 1830, was intimately connected with the city's varied industries. Apart from being an important communication center, the city was a producer of textiles, luxury items, and metal articles. The first power loom appeared in Warsaw in 1821. Steam engines were used for spinning processes, and a small engine was in operation in a factory, owned by the Englishmen Evans and Morris, that made metal machinery and instruments. A network of modern roads was designed to link Warsaw with the chief centers in the kingdom and with the other Polish lands. Canal building progressed, notably with the opening of the Augustów Canal in 1829.

The recovery of agriculture during the period of Drucki-Lubecki resulted from several factors. The state assisted the landowners, especially by the creation of the Land Credit Society in 1825, and made it possible for the great estates to clear themselves of debt. Improved sheep breeding, which doubled the number of sheep between 1822 and 1830, proved advantageous to the landlords. So did the cultivation of potatoes, which also enabled the peasants to survive on the diminishing plots that resulted from landlords' pastures encroaching on peasant land. A new industry, the distillation of vodka from potatoes, arose, and landlords found it more profitable than the export of grains. They quickly established a monopoly of distillery and sale of spirits on their estates (so-called *propinacja*). Finally, the cultivation of beets led to the emergence of the first sugar beet refinery in 1826 and opened new possibilities for agricultural industry. Observing an accumulation of private capital, Drucki-Lubecki sought to obtain additional funds for the state by selling the crown lands to individuals. The plan announced in 1828 was not realized because of the outbreak of the November Insurrection in 1830.

Although the extent to which Drucki-Lubecki's reforms laid the foundations for the late nineteenth-century industrialization of the kingdom is subject to controversy, his policy produced a balanced budget and a reorientation of trade, and meant significant progress in both light and heavy industries. But the price paid for such achievements was an oppressive system of taxation which fell on the shoulders of the poorest classes, the failure to create a genuine domestic market in the absence of measures improving the lot of the peasantry, and an increased liberal opposition to the high-handed methods of Drucki-Lubecki and the government.

VI. THE RULE OF ALEXANDER: FROM COOPERATION TO SECRET SOCIETIES

The first Sejm of the kingdom opened in 1818 in an atmosphere of mutual trust between Alexander and the Poles. Alexander was regarded as the legitimate ruler. People assumed the permanency of constitutionalism and showed no fear of becoming subordinated to autocratic Russia. Clashes between the reformist and conservative factions and criticism of the government were not directed against the king. Alexander confirmed Polish hopes for a liberalization of Russia and for a closer association between the kingdom and the Polish guberniias. "I am resolved to accomplish my intentions," he said, "They are well known to you."[3]

In the fields of education and administration the Polish guberniias continued along the path fixed by Czartoryski. In 1817 the tsar created a special Lithuanian army corps that was recruited from the Grodno, Wilno, Minsk, Volhynian, and Podolian provinces and wore a uniform similar to that of the Polish troops. He placed it under the command of Grand Duke Constantine. Even such a level-headed politician as Drucki-Lubecki considered this was a token of more to come, and people recalled the unification of "Old Finland" with the Grand Duchy of Finland in 1811. True, there were some shadows. Delegates of Podolia and Volhynia had not been allowed to come to Warsaw to greet Alexander in 1815, although those from the Lithuanian provinces had come. The Julian calendar introduced in 1800 remained unchanged, and there were disquieting police pressures in the ex-Polish provinces. But hopes for unification remained. In the kingdom itself infringements of the constitution had taken place, and Czartoryski warned the tsar repeatedly about the unconstitutional behavior of Zajączek and several ministers. He also complained about the unclarified position of Constantine. The tsar was annoyed, and Czartoryski withdrew from political life; the ultraconservative forces in the kingdom were on the offensive. In 1819 Zajączek imposed censorship; this was a severe blow at the flourishing press in the kingdom. The church gained more influence over schools, and the Polotsk Jesuits battled against the Wilno university. Their expulsion from Russia in 1820 marked only a temporary victory of the reformist group. Economic and financial difficulties plagued the kingdom, and Matuszewicz, who headed the treasury, was forced to resign, largely because of Novosiltsov's opposition. His successor considered continued Russian aid of two million rubles essential to balance the budget, an unrealistic assumption given the empire's own deficit.

The Sejm that met in 1820 must be viewed against this background of economic difficulties as well as signs of political dissatisfaction in the kingdom. Alexander came to Warsaw on his way to the Troppau (Opava) Congress, and he needed a docile Sejm to prove that his constitutionalism was not undermining the Holy Alliance. He was already growing disenchanted with liberalism and was annoyed with the mounting obstacles to the realization of his great projects. Freemasonry and secret societies in Russia were

3. Chodźko, *Recueil*, p. 738.

showing an independent and even an antitsarist spirit. Not only Russian conservatives but liberals as well rejected the idea of linking the Congress Kingdom with the "western guberniias." In 1819 the tsar had extended Constantine's jurisdiction to the five "western guberniias," but this may have been just a concession to his brother to speed up the negotiations concerning imperial succession. Constantine, who was morganatically married to a Pole, was willing to cede his rights to his younger brother Nicholas, but his price apparently was a viceroyalty in Poland and in the ex-Polish guberniias.

The second Sejm was much stormier than the first. A liberal opposition composed mainly of representatives from Kalisz (hence the name "Kalisz opposition") and led by the two Niemojowski brothers sought to expose the arbitrariness of the government and its attempts to muzzle the Sejm. Although inspired by Polish parliamentary tradition, the liberals were directly influenced by French liberalism and Benjamin Constant. Wincenty Niemojowski (1784–1834), the theorist of the group, regarded the king as the source of power. He could do no wrong but the ministers who countersigned royal decrees could, and their infringements of the constitution had to be exposed. Niemojowski set great store by public opinion, hence his dogma of a free press, but he had no real social program. Neither he nor his supporters were in any sense revolutionaries; they were merely members of a legal opposition. In the Sejm they fought against censorship and limitations of the public character of Sejm debates. They insisted on the right to impeach ministers. Alexander, who for the first time saw parliamentary opposition in action, viewed it as an attack upon the monarchy. He was indignant and gave a virtual *carte blanche* to Constantine to disregard the constitution. Reprisals followed immediately. The Niemojowski brothers lost their mandates; the Kalisz voievodship commission was dissolved; no Sejm would be called for the next four years.

A wave of conservative reaction swept away Potocki, who was dismissed from the Commission of Education and Religious Cult in 1820 and deposed as grand master of Polish freemasonry. The latter position went to the chief of police, a personal friend of Novosiltsov. The impending economic crisis, which Novosiltsov and anti-Polish cricles in St. Petersburg sought to use as an argument that a separate kingdom was nonviable, was averted by the appointment of Drucki-Lubecki. Meanwhile Constantine's position grew stronger, especially after his oral promise in 1822 to make room for Nicholas. The grand duke became the commander in chief in the "western guberniias," and the Austrian, Prussian, and French consuls in Warsaw were informally accredited to him. The atmosphere in the kingdom was changing, making people either more subservient to the pressures and arbitrariness of the government or pushing them in the direction of a political underground.

Secret societies of various types were a general European phenomenon after 1815. Alexander at first tolerated, or perhaps even encouraged, freemasonry, and the Poles were very active in it. The Grand Orient had about thirty-two lodges and some four thousand members in the kingdom, and about fifteen lodges and one thousand members in Lithuania and Podolia. The Lodge of United Slavs in Kiev was headed by a Pole. On the fringes of freemasonry, often borrowing their ritual and name for cover, there operated several secret societies composed of army officers, students, and members of the intelligentsia. Dissatisfied with the Kalisz liberal program, the younger generation combined their individualistic outlook and love of liberty with Napoleonic cult. They worshipped universal humanist principles together with a liberally conceived nationalism. Inspired by the German Tugenbund and the French Amis de la Verité, societies such as Panta Koina in Warsaw in 1817, Polonia at the universities of Berlin and Breslau, the Association of Free Poles, and the Wilno Philomats, later called Philarets and Philadelphists, subscribed to a lofty moral and political theory of freedom of nations, republicanism, and power of the people. The Wilno society, operating in the Lithuanian-Belorussian area, showed sympathy and understanding for the masses of the native population. Youthful exaltation and a romantic outlook were fairly characteristic of the students.

The National Freemasonry, founded in 1819, operated in a different milieu. Invoking Dąbrowski as its ideological father, the National Freemasons came predominantly from the army and were strongly influenced by their grand master, Major Walerian Łukasiński (1786-1868), a man of great integrity, patriotism, and iron will. Łukasiński was not a revolutionary dreamer. He was a liberal who preferred the kingdom's constitution to that of May 3, 1791, and who wished to alleviate the lot of peasants and the Jews. Revolution was to him a far-off contingency that might occur in the midst of a general European crisis. He wanted to preserve and build the strength of the nation, not to dissipate it in an insurrection. He envisaged his organization as a pressure group influencing Polish public opinion and the government. Given this ideology, which was not contrary to the early ideas of Alexander, it cannot be ruled out that the National Freemasonry was formed with Alexander's knowledge. After a while, Łukasiński dissolved his organization to have it reemerge in 1821 as the National Patriotic Society. The society discarded the masonic ritual—in 1821-22 freemasonry was outlawed in Russia—and adopted an organization which seemed to indicate carbonari influences. It comprised several sections: the kingdom, Lithuania, Volhynia, Galicia, Poznania, Cracow, and the army. The membership was small, a few hundred, and Łukasiński's own section, the army, was probably the most active. The aim of the society was the preservation of national spirit and of Polish unity. Political independence was conceived as the ultimate goal.

Łukasiński and several of his collaborators were arrested in 1822. Constantine was reluctant to admit that conspiracies could exist in his army, and he suspected at first a provocation on the part of Novosiltsov. Determined to nip the whole affair in the bud, he ordered unconstitutional proceedings. To make an example of Łukasiński, he had him sentenced to nine years in fortress, a sentence that eventually became one of life imprisonment. Buried alive in the gloomy fortress of Schlüsselburg, Łukasiński died in 1868. The survivors of the Patriotic Society showed some activity in the late 1820s and established contacts with clandestine Russian organizations, the future Decembrists.

Largely responsible for the destruction of secret societies in the kingdom, Novosiltsov led the attack on the students' organizations in Wilno. He wished not only to strengthen Alexander's suspicion of liberalism, but also to discredit Czartoryski as curator of the university. Investigations failed to reveal the existence of the Patriotic Society, or of Philadelphists and carbonari (headed by the historian Joachim Lelewel, 1786–1861). Neither the tsar nor Constantine desired the affair to be blown out of all proportion, but there was enough incriminating evidence to dismiss the rector of the university and Lelewel, and to arrest and administratively deport many students. The young poet Adam Mickiewicz (1798–1855) was among those sent to Russia. Several high school students were also imprisoned, and their schools, especially in Kiejdany (Kédainiai) and Kroże (Kražiai) closed. Czartoryski, who had pleaded with Alexander to grant complete control over Lithuania to the less dangerous Constantine, had to resign his Wilno curatorship. Shortly thereafter Novosiltsov became the new curator as well as the curator of Cracow university.

Arrests and sentences in the Wilno affair marked the beginning of an offensive against the Polish cultural program in the "western guberniias." The chances of their future unification with the kingdom were dim. As the verdict justifying the deportation of students put it, the reason behind it was "not to leave [them] in the Polish guberniias where they sought to extend by means of education the unreasonable Polish nationality."[4]

Reprisals against secret societies enhanced their importance and produced martyrs for the Polish national cause. These small societies, operating as they did on the margins of political life, provided an outlet

4. Cited in Szymon Askenazy, *Łukasiński* (Warszawa: E. Wende, 1908), 2:196.

for self-expression that was missing under the existing regime. Many rose and disappeared unknown to the wider public, and Łukasiński himself compared them to a straw fire. On the whole, the conspirators did not question the right of the monarch to judge and to sentence them. Their original inspirators had not been revolutionaries; rather they were leaders who sought to create nuclei of national public opinion, or pressure groups that would preserve and develop the national spirit and a sense of national unity. Secret societies were supposed to lead to the eventual formation of a clandestine all-Polish party representing the best national elements and having a common policy of long-range goals. The target of unification of all Polish lands around the kingdom was not far removed from the original thinking of Alexander, as expressed in Vienna and in conversations with the Polish leaders.

The last Sejm of Alexander's reign met in 1825 in a quieter atmosphere, and the tsar seemed to court the Poles once again. True, debates were no longer public and opposition was silenced. Niemojowski was forcibly prevented from entering the capital and taking his seat. A lonely voice was raised to advocate peasant ownership of land, but the conservative majority did not take up the question. For all practical purposes the Chamber of Representatives had abdicated its leadership of national and constitutional causes, and henceforth this role would pass to the Senate. If there were chances of a new phase in the relations between Alexander and the Poles they never materialized, for on December 1, 1825, the tsar suddenly died in Taganrog.

VII. NICHOLAS I: FROM THE SEJM TRIBUNAL TO THE INSURRECTION

The new tsar-king was very different from his brothers. An autocrat without the vacillations and dreams of Alexander, a soldier and a disciplinarian without the neurotic personality of Constantine, Nicholas deserved his nickname of the "gendarme of Europe." His accession to the throne brought a realignment of political forces in the Congress Kingdom. Released from his obligations to Alexander, Czartoryski, who was on bad terms with Nicholas, proceeded to mount an opposition in the Senate. Constantine, feeling that his position was more than ever linked with the kingdom and the "western guberniias," advised Nicholas to pursue the unfulfilled plans of Alexander. After Zajączek's death in 1826 the tsar named no viceroy. Drucki-Lubecki, whose economic achievements impressed the tsar, fortified his position and came into open conflict with Novosiltsov. There appeared the dim possibility of a Czartoryski-Constantine *rapprochement*, but there was too much bad blood between the two men to allow its realization.

In his first manifesto Nicholas assured the Poles that he would observe the constitution and would not change his predecessor's policies. The assurance was misleading as far as the "western guberniias" were concerned, for Nicholas regarded them as an inalienable part of Russia. The Lithuanian army corps became more Russian; Russians, not Poles, were nominated to vacant administrative posts; Novosiltsov was busy bringing the Wilno educational district in line with the rest of Russia. There were discriminatory measures against the small gentry; the Catholic diocese of Łuck (Lutsk) was abolished, and in 1828 a secret committee formed in St. Petersburg to deal with Uniate affairs, a harbinger of renewed pressures to win them over to Orthodoxy.

The immediate political issue confronting Nicholas, Constantine, and the Poles concerned Polish complicity in the Decembrist uprising in Russia. Ties between the Decembrists and the remnants of the Patriotic Society existed, but cooperation between the groups had been tenuous and full of mutual reservations. The Polish side was mainly interested in national goals, the Russians in sociopolitical objectives. Few Decembrists were willing to recognize Polish territorial demands in the "western guberniias," and only individual members of the Patriotic Society participated in the Decembrists' uprising in the Ukraine.

Aware of Polish contacts with the Decembrists, Nicholas ordered an investigation by means of a mixed Russo-Polish commission, which gathered its evidence through brutal methods and recommended a trial of eight members of the Patriotic Society. Constantine and Novosiltsov, although acting for different reasons, demanded a court martial. Inspired by Drucki-Lubecki, Nicholas ordered the Senate, acting as the highest tribunal, to try the accused. This was a challenge to that body, which had publicly to define its position on the question of whether plans for rebuilding Poland could be classified as high treason. After conducting its own investigation and running into procedural delays, the tribunal, presided over by the old but courageous Piotr Bieliński (1754-1829), gave its verdict in 1828, opposed only by two senators. The verdict was that no high treason had been committed and that consequently only relatively minor sentences were in order. Constantine immediately suspended the verdict and forebade the senators to leave Warsaw. Nicholas wanted to have the senators tried, but there was no court of law in the kingdom that had the competence to do it. Consequently, the tsar resorted to asking the Administrative Council for an opinion on whether ill-will on the part of the senators or a faulty statute of the tribunal were responsible for the verdict. Led by Drucki-Lubecki, the council blamed the statute thereby striking a blow at its author, Novosiltsov, and allowing the tsar to preserve face. A year later the verdict, with one exception, was upheld, and the Poles understood it to mean that a union with Russia did not exclude their right to seek Poland's rebirth. The young saw in the verdict an implicit sanctioning of secret societies.

Nicholas' restraint stemmed largely from the Russian involvement in the Turkish war, foreshadowing likely complications with Austria. Constantine ordered one of the imprisoned Polish staff officers to prepare plans for a campaign against Austria. He showed keen interest in developments in Austrian and Prussian Poland, and in 1827 was heard to refer openly to the partitions as shameful robbery. Identifying himself more and more with Poland, Constantine made advances to Czartoryski. He also urged Nicholas to hasten his coronation in Warsaw and to take up Alexander's pro-Polish policies. Novosiltsov pursued an opposite approach. He kept pointing to the separate status and the constitution of the kingdom as the source of all evils, and went on arousing Russian fears of Polish designs on the "western guberniias." He also fanned Russian resentment against Polish economic competition on the imperial market. In reality, the economic situation in the kingdom worsened during 1829 and 1830. Hard winters and bad harvests produced a slump in agriculture; cloth exports to Russia declined; there was unemployment in the mining industries, and some unrest. Prices went up and a plague in Russia prevented imports of Russian cattle.

By 1829 most of the country was in opposition to the existing regime, although there were varying shades of opposition, which at times canceled each other out. Constantine secretly opposed Nicholas; Czartoryski encouraged a constitutional opposition of the Senate; the Kalisz liberals led a center or a left-center opposition. In 1828 a conspiracy began in the Warsaw cadet-officers' school, directed by lieutenants Piotr Wysocki (1797-1874) and Józef Zaliwski (1797–1855). By 1830 there were conspiratorial civilian groups among writers, journalists, and students. The talented publicist Maurycy Mochnacki (1804–1834) was a leading figure among those young radicals who advocated a national and social revolution, including emancipation of the peasantry, but had no very coherent program of action.

The rallying point of the various political groups was a defense of the constitution, which had been systematically violated almost since its inception. The list of governmental transgressions was long: censorship and restrictions of personal freedom, the dissolution of the Kalisz commission, the curtailment of public sessions of the Sejm, annulment of elections, interference with courts, irregularities in the Łukasiński trial, and an increasing activity of the secret police. By 1830 three different networks of secret police and spies operated in the kingdom, contributing to an atmosphere of fear and uncertainty. When in May, 1829, Nicholas came to Warsaw to be crowned, he listened to numerous complaints about the arbitrariness of Constantine, Novosiltsov, and the ministers. Seemingly friendly, he indulged in the gestures of an understanding constitutional monarch. Tradition speaks of a "coronation plot" against Nicholas being frustrated by the older generation which condemned regicide. If such a plot existed it showed the growing exasperation of the younger radical elements.

Nicholas opened the Sejm of 1830, in which Constantine served as an elected deputy. The chamber presented a hundred petitions to the throne and showed a critical attitude toward new laws and actions of the Administrative Council. The Senate offered recommendations that advocated greater control over the Administrative Council, the submission of budgets to the Sejm, reglementation of courts, and a discussion of the peasant and Jewish questions. The upper chamber also criticized educational policies and censorship.

Was it possible to satisfy Polish grievances under the existing regime? It has been argued that the period from 1815 to 1830 saw the bankruptcy of the political programs of Czartoryski and the liberal Kalisz opposition. Even the largely successful policy of Drucki-Lubecki greatly depended on cooperation with Russia, and by 1829–30 there were signs of difficulties. Did Nicholas and the Russian reactionary forces actually welcome a showdown to end the separate and autonomous status of the kingdom? Could the Poles have found a way out of the deadlock by pursuing a cautious policy, one that kept strictly within the limits of legality and exploited internal Russian dissensions? The answer will never be known, because on November 29, 1830, a revolution began in Warsaw opening a new chapter in Russo-Polish relations, and indeed in Polish history.

What was the socioeconomic balance sheet of the fifteen years in Russian Poland? Thanks to processes initiated before 1830, there appeared a more advanced type of agricultural estates, some commutation of labor to rents, the early stages of an industrial revolution in textiles, and a gradual transition from charcoal to hard coal and from water energy to steam power in heavy industries. The position of the landlords, especially those engaged in food-processing industries, breeding, and distilleries, improved; that of the peasantry did not. Although some emancipation of the peasantry took place in the Baltic provinces of Russia, the tsarist regime was opposed to changes in the former Polish guberniias even when the nobility advocated them. But, on the whole, the landowners in the "western guberniias" and in the kingdom did not favor peasant emancipation. Except for the crown lands, where by 1830 around one-half of the peasants paid rents (this figure is questioned by some historians as being too high), there was no visible progress. The lot of the oppressed and fiscally exploited peasantry was of little concern to the public.

The bourgeoisie continued to make some gains. Big traders and bankers, to a large extent of Jewish origin, such as the Fraenkels and Koniars, too weak to contest the leadership of the nobility, moved closer to the landowners. Some of them became baptized and fully assimilated. An intelligentsia, mainly of gentry and middle class background, gradually assumed a more important role in Warsaw, more so than in Galicia or Poznania. The working class was tiny (about seven thousand workers in iron works and mines), and town "plebeians," consisting of small craftsmen and laborers rather than an industrial proletariat, were characteristic for the kingdom.

The position of Jews did not improve, although it underwent some changes. Discriminatory measures in the countryside (exclusion from inn-keeping) and greater opportunities in the cities resulted in a rapid increase of the Jewish urban population. This in turn led to housing restrictions and separate Jewish quarters in certain towns *(rewiry)*. The Jewish bourgeoisie fought vainly for full political equality; the masses, differing in religion, speech, dress, and habits from the surrounding population, wished to preserve their separate identity and strict orthodoxy. Their pro-Russian sympathies suffered a blow when in 1827 Nicholas extended military service to the Jews and sought to "europeanize" or even convert them to Eastern Orthodoxy. As a result many Jews adopted a pro-Polish stand during the November Insurrection.

# CHAPTER 5

# The Era of Late Classicism
# and Early Romanticism

THE partitions interrupted the Polish Enlightenment of the Stanislas
Augustus era. Deprived of the patronage of the king and his circle,
Warsaw lost its position as a leading cultural center. Magnates
retired from their city palaces to their country seats but only that of
Puławy continued to radiate its cultural influence on an all-Polish
scale. Princess Izabella Czartoryska (1746-1835) established there a
museum of national memorabilia—the Temple of Sybil—and set an
example for others who sought to preserve and collect monuments
of Polish history and culture.

These early efforts were synchronized and formalized with the
creation in 1800 in Prussian-occupied Warsaw of the Society of
Friends of Learning (Towarzystwo Przyjaciół Nauk). The society, a
kind of academy of arts and sciences, was divided into scholarly
sections and emphasized the Polish language and Polish history; it
took an active interest in other disciplines. It sought to popularize
learning and shape intellectual and artistic trends in the country.
Dilettantes mingled with men of learning, and the society's varied
membership of aristocrats, priests, generals, burghers, writers,
journalists, and genuine scholars was flexible enough to include a
poor Jewish scientist, Abraham Stern (1769–1842). For the first time
scholarship emancipated itself from court patronage and operated
through a "republic of scholars" who shouldered the burden of
national leadership in the intellectual sphere. Under the successive
chairmanship of Staszic—who endowed it with a building used today
by the Polish Academy of Science—and Julian Ursyn Niemcewicz
(1758–1841), the society played an important role in Polish life and
enjoyed the support of the Duchy of Warsaw and the Congress
Kingdom.

Under the auspices of the society or through efforts of individuals who stood close to it, valuable works appeared. Fully aware of the role of language for the national survival of a partitioned people, the society sponsored the first monumental dictionary of the Polish language, compiled by Samuel Bogumił Linde (1771–1847), which appeared from 1806 to 1814. In elaborating Polish terminology of natural sciences, the astronomer, mathematician, geographer, and philosopher Jan Śniadecki (1756–1830) and his brother Jędrzej (1768-1838), a natural scientist, doctor, and philosopher, enriched and modernized the language. In the field of philosophy, Kołłątaj published in 1811 his *Philosophical-Moral Order (Porządek Filozoficzno-moralny)*, containing theories of evolution. Staszic, who was deservedly called the father of Polish geology but worked in many other fields as well, contributed his treatise in blank verse, *Mankind (Ród ludzki)*. Published in 1819 it was banned by the censors in the Congress Kingdom. The versatile Niemcewicz popularized Polish history in his *Historic Chants (Śpiewy historyczne)*, which appeared with accompanying music in 1816. Although the volume was at one point banned under the Congress Kingdom, successive generations of youth learned from it about the highlights of the Polish past. Fryderyk Skarbek (1792–1866), a scholar and administrator under the Duchy of Warsaw, was a pioneer in the field of economic theory. Following Adam Smith and the laissez-faire school, he put emphasis on labor as a source of wealth and strongly opposed the peasant *corvée*.

Several enlightened Polish aristocrats rendered great services to national culture by financial contributions and patronage. In Lemberg Józef Maksymilian Ossoliński (1748-1826) began to collect old Polish manuscripts and documents. In 1817 the Austrian government permitted the creation of the Ossoliński Institute, which became an archive, a museum, and a center of scholarly publications; the institute survived in part the two World Wars. In Prussian Poland, Tytus Działyński (1796-1861) and Edward Raczyński (1786-1845) founded the great libraries and archival centers of the region.

Emphasis on history as the preserver of national values was natural in a partitioned country. Yet, at first only popular works (those of Niemcewicz) and textbooks written by mediocre historians appeared. The real turning point in historiography came toward the end of the period under discussion (1795-1830). Scientific history, as developed in Europe in the course of the nineteenth century, began with Joachim Lelewel (1786-1861), who was associated with Wilno and Warsaw universities. His study on methodology of history came out in 1815, and his popular synthesis of Polish history appeared in 1829; but his greatest works belong to a later period. Lelewel rejected the concept of history as mere narrative and insisted on criticism of sources, causal relationships, and the didactic role of history. He became the founder of a school that viewed the historical process in Poland as a corruption of the original self-governing and egalitarian Slav society by princely, lordly, and ecclesiastical power. In his view the subject of history was the people, not the rulers, and he placed Polish history in the broad context of the Slav past. Lelewel's contribution transcended the limits of his discipline and affected ideological and political trends in the country and in the post-1831 emigration. Some of his views influenced Russian radicals and their historical views.

Intellectual efforts of individuals, the activity of the Society of Friends of Learning, and the patronage of enlightened magnates were of tremendous importance in the early years after the partitions which had destroyed the Polish educational system. Under Prussia the number of Polish high schools was cut by half, although that of elementary schools was increased. Both became subject to gradual germanization; Polish teachers were sent to Germany to complete their education. Some Polish and Latin continued to be taught at the Posen lycée. The Piarist schools, which had played a leading part in the Polish educational reform, were slowly closed down, the college of Rydzyna surviving until 1820. Galicia, which except for "New Galicia" had not benefited from the reforms of the Commission of Education, fared even worse. Cracow university was germanized, Zamość Academy abolished. High schools remained backward, and nothing was done for elementary education. Under the Duchy of Warsaw, Cracow university was revived as a Central School (Szkoła Główna), but plans for a complete restoration of the ancient Jagiellonian University were interrupted by the collapse of the duchy. They were finally realized after the establishment of the Cracow Republic in 1815, and for several years the university fulfilled the role of a genuinely all-Polish school of higher learning. In 1816 Jews were allowed to enroll as students, and the university reorganized the educational system of the entire tiny republic. Reprisals by the three powers and the appointment of Novosiltsov as curator put a virtual end to the university's autonomy and importance. In 1817 the Austrians transformed the old college at Lemberg from a lycée into a full-fledged university with Latin, and later German, as the language of instruction. By 1826 the University of Lemberg had at least a chair in Polish language and literature.

The first university to revive after the partitions was that of Wilno, and its importance for Polish culture transcended the borders of the Russian-ruled lands. The Wilno educational district came into existence by virtue of Alexander's educational reform in Russia which in turn had been influenced by the Polish model of the Commission of Education. The district—one of six into which the empire was divided—comprised the guberniias of Wilno, Grodno, Minsk, Vitebsk, Mohilev, Kiev, Volhynia, and Podolia. Czartoryski became its curator and was instrumental in bringing Jan Śniadecki to the University of Wilno as its rector (president). The university consisted of four departments, including divinity and education, and enjoyed a wide range of autonomy in matters of teaching and research. It occupied a supervisory and guiding role in the district. It prepared curricula and textbooks for schools, and set as a goal the creation of at least one high school as well as several elementary schools in every district *(uezd)*. Given the geographical remoteness of Wilno and its traditional orientation toward the Lithuanian and Belorussian provinces, it became necessary to establish another center for the Ukrainian provinces (Kiev, Podolia, and Volhynia). Here Tadeusz Czacki (1765-1813), well-known for his cultural activities, deputized by Czartoryski and ably assisted by Kołłątaj, founded in 1804-1805 the Krzemieniec school which eventually became a lycée or a junior college. Reaching a high educational level, the school created around it a cultural milieu second only to Wilno. Its professors, as those in Wilno, included many who came from other parts of partitioned Poland or even from abroad.

After 1815 the Wilno educational district could boast one university, one lycée, and some 430 schools of various levels with 1,000 instructors and 21,000 students. Using Polish as the language of instruction, Wilno university and its circle showed a great interest in the Lithuanian and Belorussian languages, folklore, and history. Slavic studies arose, contributing to the linguistic and cultural nationalism of Poles and Lithuanians. Lelewel's contribution to Slav history has already been mentioned, but one can add here that of Zorian Dołęga-Chodakowski (1784–1825). Chodakowski viewed folk culture as remnants of a civilization that predated the Christian era, and he was an eager student of Belorussian, Ukrainian, and Russian folklore and ethnography.

The creation of the Wilno educational district was a blow to the Jesuit academy in Polotsk. Favored by Catherine II and Paul, the academy sought to encompass all of Lithuania within the network of its scholastic-type education which was combined with a conservative servilism toward the Russian rulers. Wilno won the battle when the Jesuits were expelled from Russia in 1820, but its triumph was short-lived. The fruitful decade 1813–23 ended with political reprisals against the professors and university students at Wilno as well as against high school students. Following Czartoryski's resignation, Novosiltsov came to preside over the liquidation of Wilno university. Purged of outstanding scholars and active students, the university was finally closed in 1830. The Krzemieniec lycée survived it by only two years.

While the Wilno educational district was preserving Polish culture and learning in the eastern lands of the former commonwealth, the central Polish provinces went through an educational revival following the creation of the Duchy of Warsaw. Under the experienced leadership of the former members of the Commission of Education, the duchy adopted in 1808 legislation providing for educational reforms. These reforms became applicable to the ex-Austrian provinces acquired by the duchy in 1809. Since Cracow university lay within the new borders, the Ministry of Education took only preliminary steps toward the creation of a second university in Warsaw. A school of law and administration, a school of medicine, and three lycées were established in the capital; a school of artillery and engineering and a school of education were set up outside of Warsaw. The government achieved its aim of one high school in every department, and by 1811 the duchy also had some 35 technical or artisan high schools and over 1,200 elementary schools (486 in towns and 803 in villages) with more than 50,000 students. This was an impressive achievement. Schools were predominantly secular, and the high schools were on the whole better than the elementary coeducational schools. There was some pressure on the parents to send their children, even though there was no compulsory education as such.

The educational system of the duchy continued during the first years of the Congress Kingdom. Under the ministry of Potocki the number of schools increased. New Sunday schools for craftsmen and secular Jewish schools were created; teaching methods were modernized. In response to attacks from clerical and conservative forces, Potocki wrote a biting satire under the telling title *Travels to a City of Darkness (Podróż do Ciemnogrodu)*, in which in a Voltairean spirit he derided his opponents. Forced to resign in 1820, he had to make room for ultraconservative forces that greatly harmed the educational structure of the kingdom. Schools declined in quality and in actual numbers. While in 1819 there were some 45,000 students the number dwindled to 29,000 in 1828. Still, students in the kingdom outnumbered those in the much larger Wilno educational district.

The Congress Kingdom registered an important gain in the sphere of higher education with the creation in 1816 of the Alexander University in Warsaw. Absorbing the previously existing schools of higher learning in the capital and receiving new departments including that of fine arts, the university granted over twelve hundred diplomas by 1830. A music conservatory was established in 1821; Warsaw was once again the educational and cultural center of Poland.

The absolutist regimes that controlled the Polish lands naturally interfered with the development of a press. Hardly any existed in Galicia or Prussian Poland. There was only an official and colorless press in the Duchy of Warsaw. In 1818 the first uncensored political daily, the *Gazeta Codzienna Narodowa i Obca* (Daily National and Foreign Gazette), appeared but quickly succumbed when censorship was introduced in 1819. Such journals as the *Orzeł Biały* (White Eagle), *Polska Dekada* (Polish Decade), or *Minerwa* were short-lived. Editors operated under constant pressures including arrest; only a few strictly conformist papers vegetated.

Polish fine arts, music, theater, and literature during the period from 1795 to 1830 were under the strong influence of neoclassicism, which during the last decade was challenged by romanticism. In the early years the epigoni of the Polish Enlightenment continued to dominate the cultural and artistic life of the divided country. There were few outstanding successors to the Stanislas Augustus school of painting as represented by Marcello Bacciarelli (1731–1818)—whose last canvases appeared under the duchy—or Jean Pierre Norblin (1745–1830). A gifted pupil of the former, Franciszek Smuglewicz (1745–1807), painted mainly in Wilno; Norblin's pupil Aleksander Orłowski (1777–1832) lived and worked in St. Petersburg. Alongside portraits, classical and historical themes predominated in their works. A new group of artists appeared in Warsaw during the 1820s—so-called Warsaw classicism—of whom Antoni Brodowski (1784–1832) was the most gifted, especially as a portrait painter. But even though there were few if any outstanding artists, there was increased interest in art, as evidenced by exhibitions, art criticism, and the departments of fine arts at Warsaw, Cracow, and Wilno universities.

Neoclassicism reigned supreme in architecture. During the early years of the Congress Kingdom urban construction was significantly affected by planning and the destruction of ancient city fortifications in Warsaw. The fortifications of Cracow were also largely demolished during this period. While the façades of many country palaces and manors were rebuilt in the classical "Empire" style, Warsaw saw the construction of several new public buildings, including the Belweder Palace, the Bank of Poland, and the Great Theater of Antonio Corazzi.

In music the *polonaises* of the gifted magnate Michał Ogiński (1765-1833) continued the Stanislas Augustus tradition. The somewhat naive Polish opera of Józef Elsner (1769-1854) inspired imitators.

Elsner's school, which was transformed into a conservatory, produced toward the end of the period the greatest name in Polish music, Frederyk Chopin (1810–49), whose star rose in Warsaw shortly before the Insurrection of 1830.

The prepartition theater of Wojciech Bugusławski (1757–1829) was revived in Warsaw in 1799, although it also staged productions in Austrian and Prussian Poland. It became *the* theater of the Duchy of Warsaw. State-supported, it produced classical French dramas as well as plays by Polish authors, and also began to introduce Shakespeare and Lessing. Under the duchy, melodrama (in the original sense of the term) predominated over tragedy, although classical rules of the theater were not questioned. Alojzy Feliński's (1771–1820) historical drama *Barbara Radziwiłłówna* and a few plays by the versatile old Niemcewicz rose above the general level of mediocrity.

In Galicia, the German theater in Lemberg occasionally staged plays in Polish, and it was actually a Galician playwright, Aleksander Fredro (1793–1876), who became one of the great names of the Polish theater and the father of Polish comedy. In the early 1820s his first plays appeared on the Warsaw stage and appealed to a wide public. Fredro was satirical without being bitter and ridiculed human foibles with a *grand seigneur*'s indulgence. A keen observer, he created a superb gallery of human types firmly set in and almost inseparable from contemporary Polish (Galician) reality.

In the first three and a half decades after the partitions, the classical tradition reigned supreme in Polish literature. Late classicism, however, which was closely linked with the propertied classes, had more pronounced conservative features than in the Stanislas Augustus period. Revering the models of antiquity and the great French literature, such authors as Kajetan Koźmian (1771–1856), Ludwik Osiński (1775–1838), and Jan Paweł Woronicz (1757–1829) largely ignored German writings, even those of Lessing. They rejected the possibility of introducing new literary genres in addition to those sanctified by tradition: odes, descriptive poems, and tragedies. Written in an elegant and polished language, their works, as for instance, odes addressed to Napoleon the liberator or glorifying the army of the Duchy of Warsaw, lacked spontaneity and power of expression. They tended to become somewhat stilted products of an "academic" character. Under the Polish conditions in which notions of patriotic sacrifice and national tragedy were ever present, there was need for a more emotional type of expression. Individual classicists such as Woronicz in an ardent early poem or Niemcewicz in his historical themes were themselves willing to disregard some of the literary canons and include elements that were not recognized by official literature. The writings of a legionary officer killed in action, Cyprian Godebski (1765–1809), had touching spontaneity. The rising novel sought to express reality and pay heed to the senses. The novel *Malwina*, published in 1816 by Princess Maria of Würtemberg (the sister of Adam Czartoryski), did, in spite of its sentimentality, show some feeling for real life. So did the early novels of Klementyna Tańska-Hoffmanowa (1798–1845), a pioneer of women's education. The most important and original novel of the period, written in French and published outside of Poland, *Manuscript trouvé à Saragosse* by Jan Potocki (1761–1815), was not in the mainstream of nineteenth-century Polish literature. "Discovered" a century later, the novel has been highly appreciated for its construction, fantasy, and originality.

Romanticism, in the form it affected Polish intellectuals, combined the influences of Schiller and Goethe, Schelling and Herder, the historicism of Walter Scott, Shakespeare, and above all Rousseau and Byron. Rousseau's *Nouvelle Heloïse* led to a veritable Rousseau cult. Herder's thesis that literature ought to express the national character of the people was taken up by Kazimierz Brodziński (1791–1835). In an essay on classicism and romanticism he advocated the idyllic as the characteristically Polish literary form. His principal poem *Wiesław*, an idyll on peasant life, did indeed show sentimentality and awareness of Slavic folklore, but it lacked the passion, imagination, and love of the mysterious and irrational that were so typical for the rising romantic school. In that sense Brodziński stood half-way between the classicists and the romanticists.

Romanticism in Poland exhibited features which predestined it to have a long-lasting and powerful influence on the Polish mind. As Mochnacki put it in his essay on Polish literature, which appeared in 1830, one of romanticism's main tasks was the awakening of national consciousness. The divided Polish nation proved particularly susceptible to this task. The revolt of the romanticists in Poland was also a conflict of generations. The young intelligentsia, dynamic and impatient, felt politically fettered by the conditions in the kingdom and the eastern lands; intellectually they felt confined by the rationalist and static rules of the classicists. Often coming from impoverished homes, the romanticist leaders combined patriotism with a certain contempt for the rich and established. They attacked rationalism in the name of feeling, criticized tepid sentimentality, and demanded the recognition of passion. In the name of freedom of expression they rejected literary canons. Their answer to cosmopolitan rationalism was the cult of the nation and the people *(lud)*.

It was hardly a coincidence that most of the romantic poets came from the eastern lands of the former commonwealth. The interest in folklore and native antiquities, which characterized the Wilno circle, combined with the tradition of the exuberant, free, and often violent life of the eastern plains and steppes. Poets from Lithuania and the Ukrainian lands brought with them a freshness of breath and outlook which contrasted with Warsaw's classicism.

The year 1822 represented a turning point with the publication of the first volume of Adam Mickiewicz's (1798–1855) *Ballads and Romances (Ballady i romanse)*. Mickiewicz's credo expressed in the poem "Romanticism" *(Romantyczność)*: "Faith and love are more discerning than lenses or learning"[1] was a challenge to the rational classicists. The author was born in Nowogródek, in the mainly Belorussian district of Lithuania, and belonged to the small gentry whose strong Polish patriotism was intermixed with deep attachment to the Grand Duchy of Lithuania. A student of literature at Wilno university, Mickiewicz was active in patriotic youth organizations. Arrested in 1823 and a year later banned to Russia, he spent some time in Moscow, St. Petersburg, and Odessa. In 1829 he received a passport which permitted him to travel to Western Europe.

Warsaw literary critics showed interest in Mickiewicz in 1823 when his second volume appeared, containing parts of *The Forefathers' Eve (Dziady)* and a historic Lithuanian tale, *Grażyna*. The former, centering around a supposedly ancient religious peasant ceremony, expressed all the romanticists' fascination with the weird and the supernatural, as well as a preoccupation with the tormented human soul. *Grażyna*, with its mysterious aura of medieval knighthood, spoke of treason and patriotic sacrifice and introduced pagan Lithuania into Polish literature. During his stay in Russia, Mickiewicz published, among other works, the *Crimean Sonnets* and the historic tale *Konrad Wallenrod*. The latter glorified patriotism to the point of self-abnegation and exercised a powerful and long-lasting influence on the Poles. Attacked by the classicists for his unorthodox style and form, his use of local dialect, and his vulgarization of the literary language, Mickiewicz quickly became the idol of the younger generation. Acclaimed by Pushkin, the young poet was on his way to becoming a giant of Polish poetry. He reached the heights of his talent and glory as an émigré, never able to return to his native land.

The impact of the Lithuanian surroundings on Mickiewicz's writing was undeniable, and it constituted a novelty in Polish literature. The same was true for a trio of lesser poets who came from the southeastern borderlands and were generally called "the Ukrainian

1. Translation of W. H. Auden, cited in Czesław Miłosz, *The History of Polish Literature* (New York: Macmillan, 1969), p. 213.

school." In his long poem *Maria*, Antoni Malczewski (1793–1826) described a lovers' drama set against the background of the seventeenth-century Ukraine. His mood was one of sadness and melancholy, in contrast to Józef Bohdan Zaleski (1802–86) whose idyllic and melodic poems about the Ukraine earned him the nickname "nightingale." Very different from the gloomy Malczewski and the dreamy Zaleski was Seweryn Goszczyński (1801–76), a radical conspirator, who in his *Kanev Castle (Zamek kaniowski)* painted a horrifying picture of a Cossack rebellion against the Polish oppressors. His poem was comparable in its weird character to some of Byron's poems, or the Ossian tale. The Polish literature of the eastern borderlands exercised a great influence on the nascent romantic poetry in the Lithuanian and Ukrainian languages, and in a sense Polish poets constituted a link between the two.

Modernized during the Enlightenment period and by its epigoni and rendered more vigorous and closer to life by the romanticists, the Polish language was the strongest link between the various parts of the partitioned commonwealth. An all-Polish cultural life continued almost uninterruptedly and gained new momentum after 1815. The three Polish universities of Cracow, Warsaw, and Wilno gathered professors and students from all parts of the country. The historian Lelewel taught at Warsaw and Wilno, influencing the younger generation in both cities. Staszic, who originally came from western Poland, was chiefly active in Warsaw. The "Galician" Fredro found his first audiences in Warsaw. Mickiewicz, Goszczyński, and Zaleski looked to Warsaw's literary critics. Intellectual *salons* and the new coffee houses attracted poets and writers who moved freely between various parts of the old commonwealth. The great controversy between the classicists and the romanticists cut across state borders and was echoed in all Polish intellectual circles. Publications appearing in Congress Poland were avidly read and discussed in the provinces ruled by Austria and Prussia. This cultural unity was a crucial factor in the national strivings of the Polish people. Gone were the early days after the partitions when the very survival of the nation seemed at stake. In 1831 Brodziński could assert that "the nation is an inborn idea, which its members, fused into one, strive to realize."[2]

Cultural nationalism was a powerful weapon of the subjugated and divided nation. Czartoryski saw it clearly when he had attracted Śniadecki to Wilno and Czacki to Krzemieniec and strove to maintain a cultural unity of the lands of the old commonwealth. Slavophilism to which Czartoryski, Woronicz, Staszic, Brodziński, and

2. Cited by Peter Brock in Peter F. Sugar and Ivo J. Lederer, eds., *Nationalism in Eastern Europe* (Seattle and London: University of Washington Press, 1969), p. 317.

others subscribed, and which appealed to the romanticists, was not only the reflection of a political desire for a *modus vivendi* with Russia. It also embodied a spirit of competition and a bid for primacy among Slavs. In ideological and cultural terms, prepartition Poland continued her existence.

*Part Two*

THE AGE OF INSURRECTIONS, 1830-64

# CHAPTER 6

# The November Insurrection

# and Its Aftermath

## I. REVOLUTION OR INSURRECTION?

DURING the night of November 29, 1830, a small band of civilian conspirators attacked Belweder Palace, in an attempt to kill Constantine. Simultaneously, the cadet-officers' school marched toward Warsaw's old city, skirmishing on its way with Russian troops. It was a night filled with confusion. The prearranged signal for coordinated action had failed; the grand duke escaped unharmed. The cadets begged several generals whom they encountered to assume the leadership of the revolutionary movement; some who refused and tried to stop what they regarded as a mutiny were killed. Many of the Polish troops in the capital failed to realize the nature of the uprising, and obeying the orders of their commanders joined the Russian regiments that concentrated around Constantine's residence. The wealthy quarters of Warsaw answered with frightened silence the cries: "to arms" and "the Moscovites are killing our people." The populace of the old city, however, joined the attack on the arsenal, and the terrified grand duke refused to order his troops to attack the revolutionaries. After relatively minor struggles the youthful conspirators were *de facto* masters of Warsaw.

The uprising of November 29 can only be understood when related to the revolutionary year of 1830 and to the atmosphere prevailing in Warsaw on the eve of the event. The July Revolution in Paris and the Belgian Revolution had acted as catalysts, although historians still dispute their exact impact on the Warsaw events. Nicholas' preparations for a crusade against the Western revolutionaries raised anxieties in Paris and Brussels, and there is circumstantial evidence that the French carbonari and leftist elements inspired the uprising in Warsaw to paralyze the strong arm of

Russia. Nicholas' decision to mobilize several Russian armies, including the Lithuanian corps and the Polish army, may well have been a decisive factor. It was known that Constantine had opposed the use of Polish troops as a vanguard of intervention, and the appearance of mobilization orders in the Polish press on November 18 and 19 could have been understood as marking the end of the grand duke's resistance. If the Polish army were effectively mobilized and the Russian troops entered the kingdom, all chances of a revolutionary coup would have been nullified. There were also other reasons for hastening the uprising. Constantine's police already had lists of conspirators, and although the grand duke supported by Czartoryski attempted to delay arrests so as not to precipitate a showdown, St. Petersburg demanded action. This too was known among the plotters.

Even if the events on November 29 came largely as a surprise, there was widespread feeling that a revolution was around the corner. The hated Novosiltsov deemed it prudent to leave Warsaw. Czartoryski and other highly placed Poles knew that something was afoot. The leaders of the conspiracy, Zaliwski, Wysocki, and Mochnacki, were trying to establish contact with prominent national figures, and they approached Lelewel. Lelewel, who was hardly a man of action, gave equivocal counsels, but he led the revolutionaries to believe that the nation and its political leaders could not fail to follow the example of the army and the people. After a final talk with Lelewel, the decision was reached to begin on November 29; fear of arrests played a large part in the decision to hasten the date of a revolutionary outbreak. Only Mochnacki thought that the revolutionaries ought to seize power themselves. Wysocki looked upon the movement as an instrument to be placed in the hands of the nation and its leaders. The conspirators were to kindle the revolutionary fire by killing the grand duke, disarming the Russian troops in Warsaw, taking over the arsenal and the gun powder stores in the suburb of Prague, and securing the bridge over the Vistula. Then they would submit to a truly national and representative Polish government.

Thus, the chaotic night of November 29 was not an accidental event, and it must be viewed in the context of the Western revolutions, contacts with French carbonari, tension in Warsaw, fear of a counter-revolutionary crusade led by Nicholas, and the danger of arrests which could have destroyed the conspiracy. If the handful of youth had not been backed by the people of Warsaw and had not reflected deep-seated aspirations of many Poles, the movement would have never gotten off the ground.

The man who saw that clearly was Drucki-Lubecki. Upon hearing that the revolutionaries had not created a government of their own and that the grand duke was refusing to use the troops, the minister seized the initiative. Constantine kept telling Czartoryski, Drucki-Lubecki, and other Polish leaders that this was an affair started by the Poles and that it was up to them to settle it. This position of seeming neutrality reflected probably not only a genuine disinclination on Constantine's part to involve his regiments (all of which belonged to the Lithuanian corps) in city fighting, but also a personal fear of a revolutionary situation. Drucki-Lubecki decided then to assert the power of the Administrative Council and to achieve two objectives: one, to curb any revolutionary tendencies that threatened the social order, and two, to exploit the outbreak to obtain concessions from Nicholas. Dealing from a position of relative strength, Drucki-Lubecki sought to transform the revolution into a political manifestation in defense of the constitution and the unfulfilled plans of Alexander regarding the "western guberniias."

The situation bordered on paradox. The grand duke had withdrawn with his troops, which also included some Polish units, to the nearby Wierzbno. The Administrative Council, having shed a few of its most unpopular members, presided over a city in the midst of revolutionary and patriotic fervor and tried to steer a moderate and conservative course. But in turn it was not immune to the general atmosphere. The first proclamation of the council, which was still issued in the name of the king, condemned the "sad" and "un-expected" events of the night of November 29, but it bore the signatures of such respected and trusted men as Czartoryski and Niemcewicz. Changes in the composition of the Administrative Council, which for a while included Lelewel, reflected concern with public opinion. Eventually, both Drucki-Lubecki and Lelewel were dropped from the council. In order to act as a pressure group, the revolutionaries organized themselves in a club called the Patriotic Society under the nominal chairmanship of Lelewel. But when Mochnacki, who misjudged the situation, made a bid for power he was nearly lynched, and the Patriotic Society went to pieces.

The government made a deal with Constantine, which embodied a policy of not burning the bridges to St. Petersburg. The grand duke promised not to call in the Lithuanian army corps or attack Warsaw. He vaguely promised to intercede with the tsar, although he had no wish to be played by the Poles against Nicholas. He acknowledged demands for the observance of the kingdom's constitution and for concessions in the former Polish guberniias. Finally, he agreed to send back the Polish regiments, which were already in a state of ferment and unlikely to stay with him much longer. In return, the grand duke was allowed to leave the kingdom unmolested, together with his Russian troops. Thus, the plan advocated by the revolutionaries to make Constantine a prisoner and disarm his regiments fell through. The Poles lost the opportunity to neutralize some five to six thousand soldiers and to capture arms which included forty artillery pieces. On December 13 Constantine crossed the border, stealthily taking with him the luckless prisoner Łukasiński.

A week prior to Constantine's departure, General Józef Chłopicki (1771–1854) proclaimed himself dictator, possibly at Drucki-Lubecki's instigation. The dictator was enthusiastically received by the revolutionaries and the army. Their trust was entirely misplaced. Chłopicki regarded the November 29 outbreak as a senseless riot and sought to curb the revolution and to negotiate an honorable surrender with St. Petersburg. While prepared to argue the Polish case on the grounds of legitimate defense of national rights violated by arbitrary government, as a professional soldier he saw no chance of winning a regular war with Russia. He thus differed from Czartoryski, who also favored negotiations but was not ready to give in if they failed. Czartoryski wished to negotiate to gain time to prepare the country militarily and diplomatically, and he dispatched envoys to France and England. Chłopicki did strengthen the army on a small scale, but only to enhance his negotiating position, not in preparation for war. He nominated ministers, endorsed summons of the Sejm, and legalized the spontaneous organization of national militia, all the while attempting to preserve a fiction of legality. No wonder that the tsar thought that Chłopicki had brought the revolution to a standstill and might end up by shooting the perpetrators of the November 29 uprising.

Negotiations with St. Petersburg, undertaken by Drucki-Lubecki and two other envoys, could produce no result. The tsar ordered military preparations and demanded that the Poles throw themselves at his mercy. St. Petersburg regarded the events of November 29 as the work of irresponsible and childlike rebels. An independent Poland was but a dangerous illusion. Nicholas told Constantine that as a result of the November revolution either Russia or Poland would have to perish.

Meanwhile the Sejm met on December 18, and, acting under the pressure of public opinion, recognized the uprising of November 29 as an "act of the nation." This meant, as Lelewel later put it, that while at first the Polish leaders saw only a revolution that they did not dare call a national insurrection, they subsequently saw only a national insurrection to which they denied a revolutionary content. The Sejm justified the uprising on two grounds. The union of a constitutional king's crown with that of a despot was a "political monstrosity." The failure to reunite the former Polish provinces, which were denied even the privileges mentioned at the Congress of Vienna, was a breach of faith. The stand of the Sejm went against Chłopicki's policy; the general resigned but soon resumed his office (the so-called second dictatorship) on the condition that the Sejm be dissolved. But under increased pressure of the Left—the "party of action"—and public opinion, Chłopicki could not ignore the government and the Sejm. After St. Petersburg's demands for surrender became known, the "dictator of deceived hopes," isolated in his desire to submit and no longer viewed as being indispensable, resigned on February 18, 1831. The Sejm appointed a new commander in chief, a colorless old aristocrat whom Chłopicki promised to assist in directing military operations.

Chłopicki's fall reactivated the Patriotic Society. Threatening manifestoes issued by the commander of the Russian army, Field Marshal Ivan Diebitsch, reached Warsaw on January 23 and added fuel to revolutionary flames. Two days later the Sejm openly challenged Russia by depriving Nicholas of the Polish throne. Presumably inspired by the "party of action," the motion passed without the observance of usual parliamentary procedures in a tense atmosphere to which the Patriotic Society contributed by a public manifestation honoring the Russian Decembrists. The act of dethronement carried with it tremendous implications. It transformed a revolution of the tsar's subjects into a national struggle for independence, and corresponded to the Belgian Revolution's dethronement of the house of Orange-Nassau. It showed that the Polish-Russian struggle went beyond a constitutional conflict, and excluded the possibility of negotiations with the tsar. Finally, it hastened a polarization of political groups in the kingdom and showed an increase of leftist, even republican, influences in the Sejm.

The act of dethronement of January 25 struck at the Vienna system and weakened the Polish case diplomatically. Indeed, it launched the insurrection upon a new and largely uncharted course.

II. WAR AND POLITICS

The dictatorship of Chłopicki had greatly harmed the course of the insurrection. By undermining confidence in a strong individual leadership, it contributed to the adoption toward the end of January of a weak form of government. Power was divided between the Sejm which remained in permanent session, the National Government elected by the Sejm, the ministers who headed their respective departments, and the commander in chief appointed and recalled by the Sejm to which he was only responsible. The commander was in charge of military operations and could negotiate an armistice. He participated in governmental sessions with a "decisive voice" on broadly defined military matters. He issued directives to administrative organs and had jurisdiction over cases pertaining to military security.

The National Government constituted under the presidency of Czartoryski was internally divided. Two members, including Czartoryski himself, represented the conservative or aristocratic faction; two, including the former leader of the Kalisz group, W. Niemojowski, were of the liberal faction; the fifth member, Lelewel, distrusted by all his colleagues, occupied a somewhat awkward position. He was both in the government, and, as nominal head of the Patriotic Society, a leader of the left opposition to the government.

Czartoryski had been rightly described as the central but not the leading figure of the insurrection. He did not seek power. He assumed the presidency in part because he felt a sense of duty toward his countrymen and his name attracted the support of the nobility, and in part because his life-long experience in diplomacy uniquely qualified him to conduct his country's foreign policy. The prince was not a born leader of men, and he was often unfortunate in his choice of associates. Obstinate in matters of foreign policy, he was conciliatory in domestic affairs and willing to make compromises which he personally disliked. Starting with his appeal to the Poles and Europe on January 30, 1831, Czartoryski adopted the position that the insurrection was a national movement, not a social upheaval. Stressing Alexander's unfulfilled promises and subsequent violations on the part of Russia, he tried to adhere as much as possible to constitutional legality. He sought to reassure the powers that the kingdom was neither Jacobin nor anarchic.

The liberals in the government had all the merits and faults of a group which had always been in opposition; they now had to learn the art of government. Strongly legalistic and suspicious of revolutionary changes, they defended the Sejm against the attacks of the Left without being able to provide real leadership themselves. In most ways they were closer to Czartoryski than to the lonely Lelewel, who wavered from the beginning, neither a man of the revolution nor its opponent. His frequent references to "social revolution" frightened the conservatives and the liberals, although in reality Lelewel sought merely to preserve and develop moderate demands for social change. A republican at heart, he voiced no objection to the officially retained monarchial form. Having been elected by fewer votes than his colleagues, he had to cede his place to the commander in chief if the latter wished to participate in governmental meetings. This humiliating arrangement brought out Lelewel's native sarcasm, sensitivity to criticism, and stubbornness.

He was less of a genuine leader of the Left than Mochnacki or the fiery Tadeusz Krępowiecki (1798-1847).

The real center of power in the kingdom was in the Sejm, which took over many of the former prerogatives of the king, including the oath of allegiance. A large and unwieldy body, it was composed of deputies elected before the November events, that is, of people who had no experience in governing a country.[1] Prior to the insurrection the Sejm had only debated the bills submitted to it by the government; after November 29 it largely followed the trends of public opinion. Although jealous of its newly won status, at first the Sejm did not attempt to impose its will on the commander in chief or to interfere with the weak government. Still, it was in the Sejm that the great issues had to be resolved: first that of defense of the constitution versus independence, and later the character and the course of the insurrection. On the whole, the Sejm sought to guard the country against a social revolution. As a predominantly conservative body it was under constant pressure from the Left.

There were no real political parties in the Sejm, although one can speak of three main trends in Polish politics in 1831: the aristocratic, the liberal, and the revolutionary. Political parties would have been a healthier phenomenon than the often ill-defined factions which had no clear programs or strong social basis. The Czartoryski group was mainly based on the nobility, many of whom did not believe in victory but felt it their duty to remain with the fighting nation. Only a few chose neutrality or St. Petersburg. The liberals had their supporters among the gentry, and they made no real effort to court the masses. The "party of action" was largely composed of lesser gentry and some townspeople. In its Patriotic Society, which had only a couple of hundred members, the intelligentsia predominated, but the influence of the "party of action," exercised mainly through the press, penetrated wider circles and affected Warsaw artisans and laborers.

The wealthy bourgeoisie was not in the forefront of Polish national politics. The Jews were divided; some pursued a policy of neutrality, others tried to participate actively in the insurrection. There was some friction over Jewish participation in the national guard, but individual Jews fought in the army, achieving officers' ranks and gaining military decorations. Most Germans took an unfriendly or even an openly inimical stand. The most important question, however, was the attitude of the peasant masses who constituted the bulk of the nation.

1. The only additions were fifteen deputies, four of whom represented Białystok; six, Wilno; and five, Minsk.

At first, the peasants did not resist the army draft and fought well in the ranks. At a later stage of the Russo-Polish war, some resistance manifested itself, and voices were heard that the peasants had nothing to do with a war fought by the lords against the tsar. The Left advocated a peasant reform, and some of its spokesmen asked that land be given to the peasantry. Such demands were part of a general, though vague, program that also stressed the international brotherhood of revolutionaries, as exemplified by the slogan ascribed to Lelewel, "for our freedom and for yours." It was argued that concessions to the peasants would produce a patriotic élan in the masses, an argument based in part on wishful thinking. A much more cogent argument for the emancipation of the peasantry was that a free Polish government had a unique chance to fuse its struggle for national independence with the cause of social reform at home. The peasant question, as raised in the leftist press and by the deputy Jan Olrych Szaniecki (1783-1840) in the Sejm, failed to receive the attention it merited. Timidity on the part of the government, class egoism of the landowners, and fear of splitting national ranks and weakening the Polish cause abroad by adoption of "revolutionary" decrees made the Sejm reject even modest proposals submitted by the minister of finance.

In the forthcoming military showdown with Russia, Poland's chances of victory looked dim. The ratio between the two armies was one to ten, and the kingdom had no arms or munition factories. Although there was a surplus budget for 1831, the actual financial resources were considerably cut by the freezing of large sums in St. Petersburg and Berlin and by extraordinary expenditures. There was the problem of food supplies for the army as well as for the city of Warsaw, especially after the Russian troops occupied the eastern parts of the country. Due to a concerted Polish effort the 38,000 strong army rose to nearly 57,000 by February, 1831, and to 68,000 front troops (out of a total of 85,000) by March. If one adds to them the twenty to thirty thousand partisans in Lithuania and a few thousand in the Ukraine, the actual ratio between the Polish and Russian armies in the field was reduced to one to two. In many respects the Polish troops proved superior to the Russians; their chief weaknesses were on the high command level. Only two divisional commanders fought in the campaign, and most of the junior generals lacked training in more complex operations. A few outstanding officers achieved the rank of general in the last stages of the campaign: for instance, Józef Bem (1794-1850) and Ignacy Prądzyński (1792-1850). They could not decisively influence the course of military events. None of the successive commanders in chief believed in victory, and each, partly for political reasons, wasted the existing military possibilities.

Chłopicki had opposed a quick build-up of the army, and by refusing to seize military initiative imposed a purely defensive strategy on the country. He rejected Prądzyński's plan to disarm Constantine's troops and to carry out an offensive into Lithuania. Even though the latter was a risky undertaking, it held out some promise of success. The Russians greatly feared a Polish incursion into Lithuania, and in early December the province was placed under martial law. Since Constantine was in command of the Lithuanian corps but still bodily in Warsaw, an effective defense of that province would have been greatly complicated. Chłopicki also rejected the notion of large-scale partisan warfare which was likely to reduce the disparity between the Russian and Polish forces. His strategy exposed the kingdom to an early Russian invasion, reduced the theater of operations, and on several occasions forced the Polish troops to fall back on Warsaw, thus impairing the national morale.

The economic and logistic difficulties were hard to overcome, but efforts in that direction were made. Small arms' and munition factories were set up and began to produce. Some of the magnates made large donations for the purpose of raising new regiments. Although trade came to a standstill, taxes were difficult to collect, and forced requisitions became a burden on the poorer strata of the population, the Bank of Poland survived the war with its deposits intact.

In spite of all the efforts, the kingdom could not gain its independence from Russia without the assistance of the great powers. Warsaw made repeated approaches to Paris, London, and Vienna. The French government refused to go beyond expressions of sympathy. Britain was unwilling to become embroiled with Russia. By paralyzing Russia, the November Insurrection contributed to the preservation of peace on the continent, and none of the powers was willing to disturb the precarious balance by espousing the Polish cause. In order not to antagonize Austria and Prussia, Chłopicki forbade the creation of units made up of Galician or Poznanian volunteers. Czartoryski engaged in exchanges with Vienna, using the bait of the Polish crown. Vienna was undecided. Metternich wished for a speedy collapse of the insurrection; other Austrian politicians took a friendlier position that bordered on benevolent neutrality. Galicia later became an auxiliary base for the insurrection—volunteers and arms coming across the frontier. Czartoryski was aware that London and Paris might come out in support of a victorious Poland, and he repeated to the government and the commander in chief that Polish diplomacy could only succeed if backed by genuine military success. Thus, the prince has been rather unjustly blamed for a blind faith in diplomacy. His opponents were on surer grounds when they criticized his belief that the insurrection had a greater chance of foreign aid if it were "legitimized" by a rejection of its revolutionary content and explained in terms of a breach of the Vienna settlement of 1815.

Lelewel bitterly clashed with Czartoryski and insisted that history knew of no national insurrection that was not simultaneously a revolution. The Polish insurrection had been started by revolutionaries and would collapse without their activity. Lelewel and his supporters considered that aid was more likely to come from the liberals and radicals in Europe than from the cabinets. Undoubtedly there were strong pro-Polish feelings among the liberal circles in France and England, and among the Hungarians, Czechs, Slovaks, and Italians. The trust put in Russian liberals proved to be, on the whole, misplaced. The Sejm rejected Lelewel's proposed appeal to the "Russian Brethren," and even the radical Mochnacki considered the struggle as one between Poles and Russians and not between the abstract notions of constitutionalism and autocracy.

Russo-Polish hostilities began with Diebitsch's offensive in early February, 1831. Stubborn Polish resistance and a sudden thaw defeated the Russian plan for a rapid victory. The Poles won an engagement at Stoczek, and after several skirmishes fought a bloody battle at Grochów on February 25. Chłopicki, who *de facto* directed the battle, was severely wounded, and the Poles withdrew to Warsaw. In spite of what amounted to a defeat, the Polish troops had shown fine fighting qualities. Having suffered heavy losses, the Russian army was unable to advance on the capital.

After Grochów the Sejm appointed a new commander in chief, General Jan Skrzynecki (1787–1860), who had distinguished himself by great bravery. An arch-conservative, Skrzynecki did not believe in victory. He sought to preserve the army and taking advantage of his broadly defined prerogatives, engaged in negotiations with Diebitsch. These proved futile and only recalled the early days of Chłopicki's indecision. Vain and jealous of his power, Skrzynecki made little use of the newly appointed chief of staff and the quartermaster general—Prądzyński held the latter position—who advocated offensive strategy. His prudence had an unfortunate impact on revolutionary developments in Lithuania.

An armed uprising in the Lithuanian provinces began in late March. In Samogitia the movement acquired a broad social base with mass participation of the peasants, who in some instances showed more resolution than the gentry. The Samogitian partisans sang "Poland is not yet lost while the Samogitians live" *(Dabar lenkai naprapule kol Žemaitiai gyvi)*; the leaders promised, in appeals written in three languages, that the peasants would no longer be *muzhiks* but "genuine free Poles." Badly armed and waiting in vain for military assistance from the kingdom, the Lithuanian partisans succeeded in taking control over most of Lithuania, with the exception of Kowno (Kaunas) and Wilno. By cutting the St. Petersburg-Tilsit and the Dvinsk (Dünaburg, Daugavpils)—Kowno roads, they greatly interfered with Russian lines of communications. They also immobilized about thirty thousand Russian troops.

In early April the Polish troops began a well-planned offensive and won the battles of Wawer, Dębe Wielkie, and Iganie. But Skrzynecki was fearful of advancing too far—"we conduct this war like cowards," lamented his chief of staff. Polish victories were not properly exploited. A favorable impression created in the West and a feeling of discouragement which arose in Russia proved to be passing phenomena. By the end of April the unassisted Lithuanian insurrection was being crushed, and an uprising in the Ukrainian provinces did not fare well.

The struggle in the Ukrainian provinces appeared as a "war of the gentry"; it received no support from the Orthodox clergy and the towns. The few peasants and Cossacks from the latifundia who participated did so out of personal loyalty to some of the Polish magnates and not from patriotic feelings. In spite of promises to abolish serfdom, the insurrection found no response in the masses which on the whole were anti-Polish. A relief force sent from the kingdom was forced, after a few minor battles, to cross over into Galicia. This was a blow to Polish prestige and pride.

Polish regular troops appeared in Lithuania in May, as part of a new offensive operation. First a small detachment arrived, followed by a several-thousand-strong corps, which had been cut off from the main Polish forces. The insurrection was revived and gained control over a large area including Kowno; a provisional government came into existence. But the Lithuanians and Poles proved unable to capture two crucial centers: Wilno and the harbor of Połąga (Palanga) which was needed for communications with the outside world. The leadership proved inept and committed political and military mistakes. Bitterness and resentment accompanied the last stages of the Lithuanian insurrection.

In May a boldly conceived attack against the Russian guards failed because of Skrzynecki's timidity, and after a series of faulty maneuvers the Polish army confronted the main Russian forces at Ostrołęka. In spite of Skrzynecki's personal bravery and the exploits of his troops the battle was lost on May 26. "We have fought a most shameful battle,"

Skrzynecki reported to Warsaw, *finis Poloniae*. The commander in chief, however, soon recovered and sought to minimize the defeat which had shaken his prestige and position. Facing pressure from Czartoryski, the general turned to the liberals and exploited internal divisions in the government. After another badly timed and executed military operation, Skrzynecki tried to shift the blame onto the generals who were in actual field command. Several of them were arrested, together with a number of civilians accused of an antigovernment plot. The background of the entire affair which led to a riot in Warsaw in late June is still obscure. Was it a plot, a denunciation stemming from the Patriotic Society, a provocation by the Russian secret service, or Skrzynecki's deliberate attempt to deflect the anger of public opinion from his person? The capital was seething, and the radical elements were gaining control of the street. The cry of "treason" was heard in Warsaw.

A general Russian offensive under the new commander, Ivan F. Paskevich, met with no effective Polish countermeasures. Although the Sejm finally deprived the compromised Skrzynecki of supreme command, it found no worthy successor. In an atmosphere of partisan strife the leadership of the insurrection was disintegrating, and radical groups openly preached terror against the conservatives. On August 15 Warsaw mobs stormed the royal castle and murdered a number of political prisoners and the luckless generals still awaiting their trial. The government was in danger, and Czartoryski left the capital to join one of the army corps. A belated move by the Sejm to create a strong government that could control the commander in chief led to the emergence of General Jan Krukowiecki (1772–1850). Krukowiecki became the head of the government and the *de facto* commander in chief endowed with dictatorial powers. Deeply involved in political intrigues, he was not the man to save the disintegrating insurrection.

By a well-conceived and executed maneuver, Paskevich attacked Warsaw from the west, and Krukowiecki ended the raging battle by negotiating, in early September, the surrender of the city. The Sejm wanted no part in it; a new government and a new commander in chief were named. But in spite of the fact that the Polish army outside of Warsaw was almost as large as at the beginning of the war, its morale was broken. The fall of the capital had a symbolic meaning which even isolated examples of heroism could not obliterate. The insurrection was over; a new phase in Polish history began.

What was the balance sheet of the November Insurrection? It had begun as a revolutionary coup and was at first represented as a national manifestation against an autocracy that had violated the constitution and the promises of Alexander I. After the dethronement of Nicholas, the uprising became a national struggle for independence with revolutionary elements inherent in it. Resulting in the loss of the semi-independent status of the kingdom, the insurrection has often been condemned as a foolhardy undertaking. Having failed to resolve the peasant question, it lost a great opportunity of integrating the masses into the socioeconomic and political fabric of the nation. At the same time, the insurrection strengthened Polish national consciousness, translated the aspirations for full independence into political and military action, and marked an important stage in the national liberation struggle so characteristic of oppressed peoples throughout nineteenth-century Europe.

III. THE GREAT EMIGRATION

After the collapse of the insurrection the Polish political, ideological, and cultural center shifted abroad. Plans for an emigration *en masse* existed already in the last stages of the war and resulted in the departure of most members of the government, ministers, many Sejm deputies, generals, junior officers, and common soldiers. A large number of the leaders of the Left went abroad hoping to achieve, in cooperation with Western revolutionaries, the political ascendency that had eluded them in the kingdom. The émigrés numbered some nine thousand people. Two-thirds of them were of noble background—although few were magnates—and one-third were of urban-plebeian or peasant origin. Officers outnumbered common soldiers. As a result of this exodus, Paris, where many of the émigrés settled, became a veritable headquarters of Polish national life. The emigration represented an elite of the nation and counted among its members some of the greatest names in Polish literature, history, music, and political thought. Cultural achievements will be discussed elsewhere, but given the intimate connection between culture and politics in exile, ideological aspects need to be mentioned here.

Polish romanticism rose to its full stature in the emigration. Given the natural limitations of practical politics abroad, the great poet, the "bard" *(wieszcz)*, assumed a position of spiritual and ideological leadership. The romanticists put the concept of the nation above that of the state, and their more radical wing placed the people *(lud)* on a pedestal. Inspired by Lelewel's historical interpretation of original Slav democracy, the idealized people (in fact, the peasantry) was seen as the embodiment of the nation to which selfish noble interests had to be subordinated. No wonder that Karl Marx, who remained in close touch with Lelewel, viewed the emphasis placed by the Polish emigration on agrarian democracy as one of its great contributions. The notion of revolution was in turn presented in lofty moral terms, and the emigration was conceived as a pilgrimage, a purifying process in the search for freedom and justice. The Polish messianic creed, especially in its more mystic form, represented Poland as the Christ of nations who redeemed through her national Golgotha not only herself but all mankind.

Influencing the milieu in which they operated, the Polish émigrés were in turn influenced by the ideas of Mazzini, Buonarotti, Saint Simon, and Lamennais, to mention but a few of the leading radical figures in the West. The emigration became a great school for political thought, and ideological debates transcended local partisan conflicts. The three main trends of Polish politics in 1830 and 1831 continued abroad, but two of them soon became of lasting significance: the constitutional-monarchical camp of Czartoryski and the predominantly republican democratic Left. The two differed fundamentally in their appraisal of the causes of the defeat and in their formulation of a program of Poland's liberation.

The democrats blamed the defeat on Czartoryski's "diplomatic faction" which, by relying on the aid of the great powers, had deprived the nation of its revolutionary élan. Their more radical representatives accused the nobility of having played a counter-revolutionary part; out of class egoism it had sacrified the real nation, the peasantry. One of the November conspirators wrote Mochnacki that "the whole question of future existence consisted in . . . making the [national] cause attractive to the Polish people . . . awakening the whole national might against the enemy."[2] This had not been done in 1830-31, and the insurrection had to perish. Hence, the emancipation of the peasantry would occupy a central place in a future revolution not only because victory was unthinkable without peasant participation, but because without repairing social injustice Poland had no moral right to demand independence.

A national revolution was part of a general revolutionary process. When crossing Germany on their way to France, the émigrés were greeted enthusiastically as fighters of freedom and comrades in a common cause; many of them acquired an exaggerated notion of international solidarity among peoples. Lelewel viewed the emigration as the vanguard of a European revolutionary army, and when in 1832 the Democratic Society was founded in France its program spoke of a "Holy Alliance of Peoples." In 1836 the society issued its famous Poitiers Manifesto which defined its program for Poland's salvation. The manifesto promised to do away with the past by abolishing all privileges. It threatened with the people's wrath those who stood in the way of the happiness of millions. The two

2. Nabielak to Mochnacki, November 28, 1834, cited in Bolesław Limanowski, *Historia demokracji polskiej*, 1:288.

separate and inimical nations—the nobility and the peasantry—would have to merge into one under the watchword "all for the people through the people." According to the manifesto the road to the future led "through the [Democratic] Society to Poland, through Poland to humanity." Only a reunited, independent, and free Poland could fulfill its great mission, "to break the alliance of absolutism, to destroy its pernicious influence on Western civilization, to spread democratic ideas among the Slavs today used as tools of subjugation . . . and by her virtues, by her purity and strength of spirit give rise to the universal emancipation of the European peoples."[3]

The program of the Democratic Society provided for peasant emancipation without compensation to the landlords, but it did not provide for a division of the estates or for land for the landless. Extreme leftist groups, which subscribed to utopian socialism and rejected private property, broke away from the society. In some ways they may be regarded as forerunners of Polish socialism or communism. These groups, which were composed mainly of common soldiers, set up communes in England; Krepowiecki and Stanisław Worcell (1799-1857), who temporarily seceded from the Democratic Society, were among the leaders of these Polish People (Lud Polski) communes.

The revolutionary program of the Left implied participation in revolutions in the West and conspiratorial-revolutionary activity in the homeland. Indeed, the democrats were conspicuous in both movements. At first, action was not coordinated and adherents of the carbonari, Young Poland, and of Lelewel's Vengeance of the People (Zemsta Ludu) competed with one another. The first partisan expedition led by Zaliwski from Cracow into the Congress Kingdom in 1833 ended in utter failure. A more serious conspiracy led by an émigré emissary, Captain Szymon Konarski (1808–39), branched out from Cracow into Galicia and then into the kingdom and the Ukrainian and Lithuanian guberniias. Konarski created a sizable underground network, and his arrest and execution in 1839 led to numerous arrests and property confiscations. Many Poles who were later to become prominent political and literary figures were involved. Apart from its heroic and inspiring features, the Konarski conspiracy exposed the very dilemma of conspiracies that were directed from abroad but brought hardship to people living in the homeland.

Committed to a policy of conspiracy and insurrection at home, the Democratic Society debated the question of organization and tactics. In 1840 a highly centralized leadership, called the Centralizacja,

3. Manfred Kridl, Władysław Malinowski, and Józef Wittlin, eds., *'For Your Freedom and Ours': Polish Progressive Spirit through the Centuries* (New York: Frederic Ungar, 1943), p. 82.

was set up in Versailles to direct all revolutionary activities. There
was disagreement, however, on the type of warfare to be promoted.
Some, such as Henryk Kamieński (1813-65), formulated a theory
of partisan warfare, in which even poorly armed masses (mainly
peasants) using terrorist tactics could overcome regular armies of
the partitioning powers. Ludwik Mierosławski (1814-78), on the other
hand, accepted guerrilla-type action as only the first stage, to be
followed by a rapid transformation of the uprising into regular war.
In the various plans the figure of twenty-eight million Poles was
frequently contrasted with the relatively small professional armies
of Russia, Austria, and Prussia. Little heed was paid to the population
reservoir and resources of the three powers.

While the democrats saw Poland's salvation through a national
and social revolution at home and cooperation with European
revolutionaries abroad, the Czartoryski camp held completely different
views. It saw the causes of the 1831 defeat in Poland's international
isolation and in the paralysis of a government that was subject to
conflicting pressures. Consequently, Czartoryski engaged in a gigantic
diplomatic effort, directed from his Paris residence, Hôtel Lambert,
to gain allies for Poland and to weaken the international position
of Russia. As he put it: "We want to have the rights of Poland
engraved on the walls of the parliaments,"[4] and he concentrated on
winning the Western liberal powers to Poland's cause. He opposed
revolutions in the West not only out of his conservative, moderate
convictions, but because they were likely to weaken Poland's
potential allies. To Czartoryski the emigration was a political center,
not a revolutionary crusade. In order to be treated as a partner by
London and Paris he had to make full use of his own as well as
Poland's political assets. Able to contribute his profound knowledge
of Russian and indeed European diplomacy, disposing of an entire
network of agents, Czartoryski fought a great diplomatic duel with
St. Petersburg. In cooperation with the West he influenced the
course of events in the Balkans where he sought to reconcile South
Slav national aspirations and Turkish interests. To Russian Panslavism he opposed a Polish version of Slavism based on complete
equality of all Slav nations, big and small. He propagated the Slav
cause in the West where he was instrumental in the creation of a
chair of Slavic literature, at the Collège de France, which was
given to Mickiewicz. Regarding the Polish émigré soldiers as the
cadre of a future national army, he promoted the idea of a Polish
legion which he was willing to see in active cooperation with the
West. This last move earned him new enmity of the Left which
accused him of wishing to turn Polish soldiers into mercenaries.

4. Cited in M. Kukiel, *Czartoryski*, p. 203.

Just as his international program stood in opposition to that of the democrats, so did his policy toward the homeland. Czartoryski rejected a revolutionary creed and subscribed to a moderate constitutional-monarchic ideology in which nationalism, Slavism, and Catholicism occupied a large place. The program of his camp (1833) spoke of equality before the law, religious freedom, personal liberty, freedom of the press, and maintenance of private property and guaranteed tenure of land to the peasants. Czartoryski himself believed in peasant emancipation along the lines of the Prussian reform, and he tried to persuade the landowners to make voluntary concessions lest the peasants succumb to revolutionary propaganda or manipulations by the partitioning governments. But he did not advertise his position for fear of alienating the more conservative Polish nobles. Seeking to strengthen national resistance, Czartoryski advocated a sustained effort in the cultural and economic spheres, a program which would later be given the name "organic work."

The prince did not oppose a national insurrection, but he wanted it to take place under the most favorable international conditions and with a united front at home. Much of his activity was aimed at preparing such conditions. As for the character of such an insurrection, it might at the outset take the form of a partisan-type struggle— as one of the pro-Czartoryski generals was the first to point out— but to succeed it would have to become a regular war.

Although for obvious tactical reasons Czartroyski emphasized the illegality of Russian conduct in Congress Poland, both his camp and the democrats always thought of Poland in its prepartition boundaries. They believed that once the social grievances of the Lithuanian, Ukrainian, or Belorussian masses were satisfied, these peoples would naturally merge in an all-embracing Polish political nation. The Hôtel Lambert and the democrats were in fairly constant touch with all of the former Polish lands, inspiring and influencing their elite and even the emerging elite of the non-Polish nationalities. The Czartoryski camp had its long-standing political and family connections; the Democratic Society was in contact with people at home through its emissaries and conspiratorial networks. Even if the contacts of the former were usually on a higher social level, both groups operated through the landowning gentry, which alone could shelter and protect the emissaries. The nature of the relations between the two émigré camps and the homeland largely stemmed from their respective programs. Czartoryski sought to inspire and to guide rather than to direct the developments at home. His concept of "organic work" corresponded to a major trend in the country after the insurrection. His views on peasant reform, however, ran counter to the vested interests of the landowners. The Democratic

Society sought to lead domestic conspiracies—also an important trend in the Polish lands after 1831—but in the long run its leadership was challenged by revolutionaries at home who demanded a bigger share in decision making.

IV. CONGRESS POLAND AND THE "WESTERN GUBERNIIAS" AFTER 1831

The Russian victory in 1831 changed drastically the situation in the Congress Kingdom. The constitution of 1815 was suspended; the Sejm and separate army abolished. Many common soldiers were incorporated in the Russian army to serve a twenty-five-year term and fight the tsar's battles in the Caucasus. After a transition period of a Russian-dominated provisional government, the tsar granted the Organic Statute in 1832; this statute was subsequently modified or ignored. Under Viceroy Paskevich the State Council existed until 1841. Then the Russian Senate took over its functions. The Administrative Council was limited to three departments: the Interior together with Religious and Cultural Affairs, Treasury, and Justice. Its competence was gradually restricted.

By 1839 educational matters were transferred to the Russian Ministry of Education which assumed control over the "Warsaw educational district." The University of Warsaw and the Society of Friends of Learning were closed; many libraries, museum collections, and art treasurers were taken to Russia. The number of high schools was cut, and children of non-nobles, viewed as potential revolutionaries, faced discriminatory admission policies. In the religious field, the regime made use of the 1832 Papal breve "Cum Primum," which had condemned the insurrection and ordered submission to the monarch, to oppress the Catholics and to promote Eastern Orthodoxy. The office of primate disappeared, and for lengthy periods the Warsaw archbishopric was administered by suffragan bishops. A Warsaw Orthodox diocese came into being, and new regulations governing mixed Catholic-Orthodox marriages discriminated against the Catholics.

From the administrative point of view the Congress Kingdom was brought more in line with the empire. First the voievodships were changed into guberniias, and then the ten guberniias were consolidated into five to make for more efficient control by the governors. While the Polish language remained in the administration and in courts, the increased use of Russian as well as the introduction of the Russian criminal code in 1847 opened the gates to russification. But whatever the external forms of government were, it was clear that Nicholas intended to rule Poland through fear. As he put it in 1835: "If you persist in nursing your dreams of a distinct nationality, of an independent Poland . . . you can only draw the greatest of misfortunes upon yourselves." Pointing to the new citadel constructed in Warsaw, he told the Poles that in case of an uprising he would destroy the capital and "I certainly will not be the one to rebuild it."[5] Reinforced by the new fortresses of Dęblin and Modlin (renamed Ivangorod and Novogeorgevsk), the oppressive regime of Paskevich established an iron grip on the country.

The postinsurrection period saw important changes in the economic life of the kingdom. State intervention reached its high point in the policies of investment and management of heavy industry. A tariff barrier between the kingdom and the empire, introduced in 1831 and followed by the abolition of transit to China, struck a blow at the woolen industries. Having lost their chief domestic consumer, the army, and being virtually denied access to the Russian market, woolen factories declined or moved across the border to Białystok. Thus, Białystok became the chief cloth-producing center for the "western guberniias." Cotton mills, which had been producing for the home market and competing with Russian imports, significantly increased their production. The industry became technically more advanced with the mechanization of spinning; consequently it was able to produce cheaper textiles. The budding Polish Manchester, Łódź, grew to twenty thousand inhabitants by 1840. Linen production was concentrated in a large factory at Żyrardów, established in 1833.

Mining in the kingdom had been largely in the hands of the state; iron was produced chiefly by private owners. State-owned mining and metal industries had received much capital under the Lubecki administration, but the new regime refused to continue his policies. Consequently, the Bank of Poland, which was the largest creditor, was allowed in 1833 to take these industries under its direct control. During the next decade the bank was the prime mover of Polish economic development. Planning eventually to lease the government works and mines to private entrepreneurs, the bank concentrated on developing iron works in the Dąbrowa Basin. New plants were constructed, particularly the Huta Bankowa, one of the largest in Europe. Using coke as fuel and equipped with steam engines, the Huta produced pig and rolled iron mechanically through puddling and rolling processes. As compared with the 1820s, the output of iron increased tenfold. But the relatively primitive economy of the kingdom had no real need for such large works, which proved expensive to operate. Iron prices fell, stockpiles of iron and zinc accumulated. The bank had overinvested in iron and neglected other industries. There were other difficulties connected with the construction and operation of the ironworks: technical

5. Leonard Chodźko (Comte d'Angeberg), *Recueil*, p. 937.

problems, inadequacy of the Dąbrowa coking coal, financial irregularities, and the red tape of the Paskevich administration ever suspicious of the bank's autonomy. By 1842, iron and zinc mills that had been briefly leased out to private capitalists came back under the treasury's control. In the next few years they vegetated; the big Huta Bankowa stood idle. Coal mining fared better and did not experience a similar crisis during this period. As for transport, in 1845 the first railroad line in the kingdom was opened. Called the Warsaw-Vienna railroad, it was started by private capitalists but then completed and taken over by the state.

In spite of the above activities in the industrial field, the kingdom retained its predominantly agrarian character. Developments in agriculture itself were fairly slow. True, yields per acre and the over-all output increased due to better farming methods, a gradual transition from the three-field system to a rotation of crops, and a greater amount of land under cultivation. This was particularly noticeable in the case of potatoes. Sheep breeding, mainly on the estates, and pig raising, chiefly on peasant strips, led to a sharp increase in the number of cattle and pigs. The earlier mentioned new crop—white beet—was becoming more popular; sugar refineries continued to be constructed. But, the whole problem of modernization of agriculture was closely linked with the difficult and controversial peasant question.

The government gradually commuted labor to rent in the state lands, former church lands, and estates confiscated after the insurrection and given in entail to Russian owners. A number of Polish magnates attempted to resolve the question of peasant *corvée* on their estates. On the huge Zamoyski entail regulations consisted in the introduction of quarterly peasant ransoms. If the peasants were unable to pay they would revert to compulsory labor. In the lands of another magnate (Wielopolski) the peasants could buy out their labor obligations and become tenants. The lesser landowners found these experiments costly, and only the richer peasants fared well under these new arrangements. Many of the poorer peasants were evicted and their land added to the demesne. Still, the whole peasant structure continued to evolve, and by 1848 the divisions were as follows: *corvée* peasants, 1,355,800; tenants, 459,000; colonists, 141,200; and landless peasants, 848,200. With various other processes taking place, the countryside was slowly moving toward a more modern "capitalist" farming system.

The oppressive regime in the kingdom prevented any genuine political activity. The collapse of the Zaliwski expedition, the smashing of student conspiracies in the late 1830s, and the failure in 1844 of a purely peasant uprising prepared by Father Piotr Ściegienny

(1800-90) demonstrated the near impossibility of clandestine revolutionary action. Only the "organic work" policy, namely, the seeking of economic improvement and modest social reform, seemed to stand any chance of success. An example of this policy was a reformist movement centered on Andrzej Zamoyski's (1800- 74) model estate, which was run without *corvée* at Klemensów. At annual meetings, landowners discussed the technical and social aspects of modernizing agriculture, and the methods by which the economic level of the country could be raised. Another manifestation of the "organic work" spirit was a temperance movement in the mid-1840s, which sought to combat alcoholism among the peasants. Led by the clergy, it spread to most of the former Polish lands and registered impressive, although temporary, results.

Tsarist policies toward the kingdom were directed at assuring full control over Congress Poland. Those pursued in the Lithuanian, Belorussian, and Ukrainian guberniias sought to speed up their absorption into Russia. Although after the insurrection Nicholas granted an amnesty with important exceptions, none applied to the "western guberniias." The tsar personally saw to it that Prince Roman Sanguszko (1800-81), one of the Polish magnates in the Ukraine, traveled on foot to his exile in Siberia. A special Committee for the Western Guberniias, set up in 1831, prepared plans to sever insofar as possible all the ties that had linked these lands with the old commonwealth.

The abolition of the old Lithuanian Statute in 1840 put an end to elected officials and municipal self-government. Administrative and judicial posts were henceforth reserved for Russians, and the Polish language was eliminated from offices and courts. The tsar ordered the introduction of a new name, the Northwestern Land *(severo-zapadnyi krai)*, to replace that of the Lithuanian-Belorussian guberniias. The government concentrated its attack on Polish cultural centers and on the Uniate church, which stood in the way of total integration with Russia. The University of Wilno was abolished, and the number of schools in Lithuania drastically cut. The Krzemieniec lycée was closed. Cultural russification went hand in hand with a campaign against the Uniate church. This campaign reached its high point with the apostasy of Metropolitan Iosif Semasho (Siemaszko, 1798-1868), who in 1839 took his church over to Eastern Orthodoxy. Resistance of the Belorussian peasantry was suppressed; the only organized Uniate diocese survived in the Congress Kingdom, in Chełm.

The anti-Polish policy raised serious questions in the social sphere. Should the government try to foster animosity between the peasantry and the Polish nobles, or should it assume that the vested interests of the latter would preclude their alignment with a revolutionary Polish program? At the time of the Konarski trial some Russians expressed fears lest Polish propagandists convince the peasantry that its emancipation depended on the reemergence of Poland. But reliance on the peasants against the lords was a highly dangerous social policy to adopt for a state such as Russia. The suggestion that all state lands in Lithuania be transferred to Russians, in the hope that "within twenty-five years the entire Polish nationality would perish for ever,"[6] seemed too drastic a measure. Hence, except for the confiscation of some three thousand estates of people involved in the November Insurrection, the government did not tamper with the social status of the big Polish landowners. Such was not the case with the lesser gentry who constituted about two-thirds of the Polish noble class in the Ukraine and were the backbone of Polishness in the "western guberniias." New regulations passed in 1836, which required proofs of nobility, allowed the government to deprive many of the small gentry of their traditional rights. Treated as peasants, some 54,000 of them were deported between 1832 and 1849 from Lithuania, Podolia, and Volhynia to the Caucasus, Siberia, or beyond the Volga. Yet in spite of these reprisals Polish conspiratorial networks continued to exist in the "western guberniias," particularly in the Lithuanian and Belorussian areas.

There were few changes in the socioeconomic life during the post-1831 period. Developments in agriculture followed a pattern fairly similar to that of the kingdom, even though farming methods were more antiquated. Budding industries were mainly linked to agriculture. The sale of peasants separately from the land became illegal only in 1841; a primitive and harsh serfdom continued to prevail. The town population was small and heavily Jewish. The government sought to achieve the russification of Jews, whose status, especially among the richer groups, was perhaps in some ways more advantageous than that enjoyed by their coreligionaries in the kingdom. Still, most of them could not move freely beyond the Pale of Settlement and were restricted to special quarters in some cities. On the whole, Jews in the "western guberniias" were beginning to lose their links with the old Polish tradition.

V. GALICIA, CRACOW, AND PRUSSIAN POLAND AFTER 1831

The November Insurrection awakened Galicia from the political apathy and economic stagnation that had prevailed during the first fifteen years after the Congress of Vienna. Thousands of volunteers

6. Cited in Dawid Fajnhauz, *Ruch konspiracyjny na Litwie i Białorusi 1846–1848* (Warszawa: Państwowe Wydawnictwo Naukowe, 1965), p. 19.

fought in the insurrection; many exiles settled in the province. A new patriotic spirit manifested itself through political activity of a conspiratorial nature, on the one hand, and attempts at socio-economic reform, on the other. Galician conspiracies went through several stages and involved people from the gentry, the lower clergy, and the intelligentsia. Between 1831 and 1835 secret organizations inspired by the Polish carbonari, Young Poland, and other radical émigré groups came into existence and branched out to other parts of Poland. Konarski's Association of the Polish People (Związek Ludu Polskiego), for instance, originated in Cracow at the initiative of Young Poland and of Lelewelists.

Galician conspiracies operated under conditions of growing tension between the peasants and the landlords and between the Poles and Ruthenians. The country continued to be backward. In 1843 Galicia comprised nearly 29 percent of the total population of Austria (without Hungary), but its share in industry amounted to only 10 percent, and in terms of industrial establishments, to 3.4 percent. The agrarian situation was deplorable. Landlord-peasant relations continued to be regulated by the antiquated and often bypassed Josephine laws. In 1830 the Galician diet was still reluctant to investigate actual peasant obligations and defended the manorial monopoly of the production and sale of spirits *(propinacja)*. Only 8 percent of peasant holdings were converted to tenantry before 1842, and the authorities made rent reforms so difficult that the landowners hardly cared to attempt them. Subdivisions of peasant holdings, while forbidden by the authorities, were condoned by landlords and resulted in tiny plots of land which were utterly uneconomical. Democratic gentry agitators preaching emancipation of the peasantry found it difficult to reach the villagers' ears. A suspicion of landowners, even those who realized the need for social change and were involved in conspiracies, was too deep-rooted and prevented conspiracies from extending to the villages.

Antagonism between the Latin and Uniate rites, which had its social aspects since most Uniates belonged to the peasantry, was beginning to acquire national (Polish versus Ruthenian) overtones. The rising Ruthenian intelligentsia, which was mainly composed of seminary students, was in some instances willing to cooperate with the Polish conspirators, but its emphasis on Ruthenian national revival created difficulties. The nascent movement also had its own problems. The Austrian police and the Uniate church hierarchy viewed a linguistic revival with suspicion. Attempts by the young seminarians to influence the peasantry were sporadic and unsuccessful.

The entire situation in Galicia was discouraging. A report written to the Versailles Centralizacja in 1838 estimated that: the aristocracy preferred foreign rule to a native radical regime; the Polish peasantry manipulated by Austrian authorities hardly considered itself Polish; and the Ruthenians detested the Poles on religious, linguistic, and social grounds. Only the gentry, the poorer groups of the middle class, and the youth were willing to participate in patriotic and socially progressive movements. By 1840 the Galician conspiracies had been crushed by the police, and their leaders imprisoned at Kufstein and Spielberg (Špilberk). Hopes of gaining the masses, both Polish and Ruthenian, remained unfulfilled, and Austrian reprisals frightened the upper classes.

The reformist trend in Galicia, which rejected conspiracy and sought to preserve and strengthen the nation by cultural and socio-economic improvement, had to fight an uphill battle against the reluctant administration and conservative nobility. Due to the persistent efforts of Prince Leon Sapieha (1803–78)—a one-time collaborator of Drucki-Lubecki—and his supporters, in the period between 1841 and 1845 the administration allowed the creation of the Land Credit Society, the Savings Bank, the Technical Academy, and an Economic Society. Urged by Czartoryski, Sapieha advocated peasant reform on the grounds that it could save Galician agriculture, undercut revolutionary agitation, and limit Austrian machinations in the villages. The argument that serf labor was uneconomical was used together with appeals to the patriotic sentiments of the landowning class. Attention was also drawn to the danger of a social upheaval. In 1843 the diet raised the question of commutation of corvée (Robot) to rents and asked Vienna's permission to study the manor-village relations. A year later, in order to dispel the government's fears that a radical change in the agrarian structure could affect other provinces of the monarchy, the diet excluded from the debates the issue of serfdom. Only in 1845 did it authorize its commission to study the question of peasant emancipation, but by then it was already too late.

To turn from Galicia to Cracow, the tiny republic was politically active during and after the November Insurrection. It contributed volunteers, provided shelter for émigrés, and became a center of conspiratorial activities. Its continued survival was due to jealousies between the partitioning powers, but the days of the republic were numbered. In 1832 Cracow was temporarily occupied, and a year later a new president was imposed, unreliable senators purged, and civil liberties restricted. By the Münchengrätz (Mnichovo Hradiště) Agreement of 1833 the three powers provided for the liquidation of Cracow's independence should the senate prove unable to control it effectively. Two years later, Russia and Austria agreed that Cracow be incorporated in Austria; only a pretext for such action was needed. In 1836 Austrian troops occupied Cracow in reprisal for the murder of a secret agent and initiated a period of repression. The local militia was disbanded, strict censorship imposed, and a special court established to deal with political offenses. The troops remained in the city for the next four years.

Economically, the republic fared reasonably well. The construction of the Cracow-Mysłowice railroad began in 1844. The population continued to grow. An advantageous trade convention with the kingdom, however, was not renewed, and a Russo-Austrian trade agreement of 1836 ruined part of Cracow's trade. In the social field the process of commuting *corvée* obligations to rents was nearing completion, a fact that had important consequences for the peasantry's attitude toward patriotic Polish activities in the years to come.

What was the situation in the Polish lands under Prussia? The collapse of the November Insurrection and the suspension of the kingdom's constitution had a direct impact on this part of Poland as well. The government no longer had to vie with the attraction a constitutional Polish kingdom held for Prussian Poles; it could tighten the reins of its regime in Poznania. Numerous volunteers from the province who had fought against Russia were heavily fined. The office of viceroy (Statthalter) was abolished, and the gentry was deprived of the right to elect the province captains (Landraten). The German language virtually became the official language of the province, and the judicial system was more strictly subordinated to Berlin. The new governor (Oberpräsident) of Poznania, Edward Flottwell, strove to destroy all that could prevent a total merger of the Grand Duchy of Posen with the rest of the monarchy. This implied a policy of weakening the position of the leading Polish groups: the nobility, by economic means, and the clergy, by making it more dependent on the state. As for the masses, they were educated in the Prussian spirit through the army and schools where the teaching of German increased. The Jews paid for their emancipation with the acceptance of germanization, and the authorities encouraged settlements of German colonists in Poznania.

Prussian policies achieved some of their objectives. In 1832 there were over 1,000 Polish landed estates as compared to 288 in German hands. Ten years later the figures were, respectively, 950 and 400. In 1840 the city of Posen was half Polish, but two-thirds of the land and most of the trades and crafts were in German and Jewish hands. Yet, conditions prevailing in Poznania made it possible for the Poles to resort successfully to "organic work." Berlin and the local authorities were interested in the progress and well-being of the province within the general framework of the Prussian economy.

The emancipation of the peasantry was creating a fairly healthy economic and social structure, and it greatly mitigated the manor-village antagonism. Thus, "organic work" fitted well into the process of economic modernization and could be pursued more effectively here than by Zamoyski in the kingdom or by Sapieha in Galicia. Prussia's stress on education, even if viewed as a means of germanization, helped to raise the cultural level of the people. And, priding itself on being a law abiding state (Rechtsstaat), Prussia could not easily resort to overt arbitrary acts. The Poles had more room for legal maneuver, especially after 1840 with the liberalizing King Frederick William IV on the throne.

The reformist movement in Poznania made important strides. In 1835 the first Kasyno, a landowners' society for the promotion of culture and better economy, was set up in Gostyń. Enlightened landowners such as Dezydery Chłapowski (1788-1879), who rotated crops and engaged in diversified farming on his estates (dairy, sugar-beet cultivation, brewing, and sheep breeding), showed the way toward better exploitation and higher productivity of the soil. In Posen itself, Dr. Karol Marcinkowski (1800–46), who had returned from the emigration where he had been closely associated with Czartoryski, became a leading propagator of "organic work." Using the opportunities provided by the post-1840 liberalization of Prussian policies—notably linguistic concessions and relaxation of censorship—Marcinkowski became instrumental in the creation in 1841 of the Society of Educational Aid (Towarzystwo Naukowej Pomocy) and the Poznań Bazar. The former gave scholarships to poor students; the latter consisted of a hotel and shops that served as a center of Polish crafts and trade and as a meeting place for the progressive gentry and townsmen. Marcinkowski and his supporters sought to strengthen the native middle class so that it could successfully compete with the dominant German and Jewish bourgeoisie.

The Prussian government vetoed other projects of Marcinkowski— a Polish national theater and a school of agriculture—but progress was noticeable. A conflict between the state and the Catholic church over mixed marriages made Archbishop Marcin Dunin (1774-1842) a national martyr and enhanced the influence of the clergy as defenders of the "Polish faith." With a freer press, an impressive intellectual life in which new exiles from the kingdom participated, and close contacts with the emigration, Poznania was moving toward a position of all-Polish primacy. Czartoryski came to believe that it would even assume the place that the kingdom had held prior to 1830.

The Poznanian version of "organic work" appealed mainly to the middle-of-the-road groups. The ultraconservative nobility was somewhat aloof because they disliked the bourgeois and liberal, egalitarian tendencies of the reformers. The democrats objected that channeling Polish efforts in the direction of economic betterment and cultural progress turned the nation's attention away from the political goal of Poland's independence. By 1840 the Poznania democrats had established close ties with the Centralizacja in Versailles. A committee presided over by the philosopher and educator of humble social origin, Karol Libelt (1807–75), was set up in Posen. A moderate and an ex-volunteer in 1830–31, Libelt did not follow blindly the dictates of Versailles, but even so his leadership was challenged by the younger extremists who sought to emancipate the democratic camp from émigré tutelage. This was understandable. With the passage of time conflicts between the émigrés and the people at home grew sharper. The former thought in all-Polish terms, the latter were necessarily affected by the existing conditions in the kingdom, Galicia, or Prussian Poland. The émigrés counted on Russo-English enmity as a condition for the realization of long-range Polish political goals. But a Russo-English *détente* was advantageous for the economy of the kingdom which exported agricultural products to England. It was easy to be a radical agrarian democrat in Paris; it was much harder to reach the masses at home. A leader of the Centralizacja who secretly spent two years in Poland discovered this fact; during that time he had only one serious talk with a peasant. Not unnaturally, most Russian, Prussian, or Austrian Poles gave their first thought to the province in which they lived. Just as "organic work" was inextricably linked with local conditions, so patriotic conspiracies, despite their all-Polish goal, could not be divorced from circumstances prevailing in the various parts of the partitioned country. The subsequent revolutionary years showed this all too clearly.

# CHAPTER 7

# The Decade of Hope and

# Despair, 1846–56

IN THE mid-1840s the democratic camp in Poland began to move toward a national and social revolution. The Centralizacja had been rebuilding its network since 1840, and two committees connected with Versailles came into existence: the Polish National Association in Warsaw and Libelt's group in Posen. The latter was recognized as the central committee of the Democratic Society for the homeland, and it led rather than followed the headquarters in France. Within the democratic movement radical individuals and groups were coming to the fore. In Posen the emergence of the Society of Plebeians (Związek Plebejuszy), founded by a bookseller, indicated the widening of the social basis of the conspiracy. The Plebeians also agitated in Pomerania, the most germanized Polish province of Prussia, in which the passage of the 1831 exiles had left traces. The writings of a landowner from Congress Poland, Henryk Kamieński, notably his *Democratic Catechism* which was published under a pseudonym in the West, showed a radicalization of social thinking among the younger Polish democrats. The great émigré poet Zygmunt Krasiński (1812–59) answered Kamieński's pamphlet with an impassioned warning about the horrors of a class war and a plea for national solidarity under the leadership of the nobles. Another émigré literary giant, Juliusz Słowacki (1809–49), in turn challenged Krasiński by accusing him of expressing the typical nobleman's fear of the almighty people *(lud)*.

Kamieński's cousin and also a scion of a noble family, Edward Dembowski (1822–46), who escaped from the kingdom to Poznania, became a brilliant theorist of agrarian revolution. Influenced by Hegel's dialectics, the youthful Dembowski combined great intellectual qualities with the talents of a tireless organizer and a fearless agitator. He epitomized Kamieński's dictum "I act therefore I exist" and became an almost legendary figure of a revolutionary traveling in disguise through the Polish lands. Another emerging leader, Ludwik Mierosławski, impressed the Versailles group and the conspirators at home with his military concepts and his oratorial gifts. Mierosławski's self-confidence, however, bordered on conceit. Brilliant and erratic, he was destined to become "a general of defeat."

In the spring of 1845 the Posen Central Committee decided in favor of an early revolution; Mierosławski and Dembowski bore a large part of the responsibility for this decision. The conspirators feared that delays would either bring about a spontaneous social upheaval which the great powers would crush, or produce government-sponsored reforms which would cut the ground out from under their feet. The plan was to begin action in Poznania and Galicia where small Prussian and Austrian garrisons (respectively four and thirty thousand) could easily be overcome. Once in possession of these provinces, the main revolutionary thrust would be eastward toward Congress Poland. The final goal was the reestablishment of Poland's prepartition frontiers. Mierosławski imposed his idea of quickly going beyond a partisan stage and beginning a regular war even without adequate military equipment. As for the social program, it announced immediate emancipation of the peasantry and called on the nobles to rehabilitate themselves by joining unreservedly a social and national revolution. At this point the importance of the social issue was recognized by all the Polish political movements, even by those that opposed the terrorist phraseology of Kamieński, Dembowski, and Mierosławski. In 1845 Czartoryski came out openly in favor of peasant emancipation and urged his supporters to follow his example lest they lose all political initiative to the democrats.

At a meeting in Cracow in January, 1846, agreement was reached on the composition of the National Government to be presided over by Libelt. Among those present were Jan Tyssowski (1811–57) and two representatives of the Versailles Centralizacja. Revolutionary governors were appointed for various Polish provinces, including the kingdom and Lithuania, and the date of the outbreak was set for the night of February 21–22, 1846. Although skeptical about the success of an insurrection, the moderate gentry began to favor it. The entire plan, however, collapsed when a conspirator decided to prevent the revolution by denouncing its leadership to the Prussian police. Libelt, Mierosławski, and most of the Posen leaders were arrested. On February 18, a small Austrian troop occupied Cracow; arrests also began in Lemberg. The members of the National Government who were in Cracow lost their heads. Orders were issued to call off the revolution. One of the émigré members left hastily, calling on others to return to France. Then orders were changed, and a series of largely uncoordinated acts followed. They included outbreaks in Poznania and even in Pomerania, a nine-day revolution in Cracow, and an attempted insurrection in Western Galicia, which collapsed in the face of a peasant *jacquerie* turned by the Austrian authorities against the revolutionaries and the gentry.

After brief skirmishes with Austrian troops Cracow was free; a Polish National Government proclaimed itself and gained the support of townsmen, neighboring peasants, and miners from the Wieliczka salt mines. The more lukewarm propertied classes could not resist the magic name of a "National Government," and the same was true for the emigration. Czartoryski and his camp declared that they recognized its authority. On February 22, the National Government issued its manifesto, the credo of the democratic Polish patriots. After decreeing an all-Polish insurrection, the document announced the abolition of privileges and the emancipation of the peasantry without compensation to the landlords. It promised land from the crown estates to the landless revolutionaries and formulated the principle that everyone was entitled to the use of land in accord with his capacity and merits. The poor were to be granted special protection, and national workshops were anticipated. A special appeal to the Jews assured them complete equality with the Christians.

Under the weak dictator Tyssowski, Dembowski was the soul of the Cracow revolution. He strove to organize an army—nearly six thousand volunteers joined within three days—and attempted to rouse the peasantry in nearby Galicia. To the horror of the revolutionaries, however, the peasants started a *jacquerie* directed against the manors. In a skirmish with the advancing Austrian troops the insurgents were defeated and then massacred by peasant bands which had been mobilized and paid by the Austrian commander. In a desperate move to stop their drive on Cracow, Dembowski led a procession with church flags and was killed when the Austrian troops fired their first volley. Tyssowski broke down, abandoned the city without a fight, and crossed the Prussian border with over a thousand insurrectionists. The revolution was over, and on March 4, Russian and Austrian troops occupied Cracow. On November 16 the city was incorporated into Austria, and its fate was sealed.

If the speedy collapse of the Cracow revolution, murdered, in Karl Marx's words, "with the bloody hands of mercenary ruffians," was somewhat inglorious, the story of events in Western Galicia was particularly tragic. The insurrection began there with an unsuccessful attack on Tarnów on February 18. It was then drowned in the blood of the mainly gentry insurgents who were massacred by the peasantry. Unwilling to struggle against the peasants, whom they sought to liberate, the revolutionaries were doomed. The *jacquerie* spread, and bands attacked manors, killing, burning, and looting as they went. In the Tarnów district almost 90 percent of the manors were devastated and their owners killed. In all, about two thousand landowners including their families and estate officials perished. Finally the Austrian army suppressed the social upheaval, fearing that it would spread to other provinces in the monarchy. But while ordinary peasants were punished and forced to return to *corvée* obligations, one of the ringleaders, Jakub Szela (1787–1866), received a medal and was discreetly removed to Bukovina where he obtained a freehold farm.

Most contemporaries condemned the Austrian authorities for their perfidious use of the peasantry for counter-revolutionary ends. It is obvious that the Galician peasants lived under an oppressive regime that bred hatred against the landowners. Moreover, 1845 and 1846 were particularly bad years economically. It is equally clear that the government had done nothing to improve the existing system, nor had it permitted others to do so. Local officials played on the backward peasants' fears of the gentry conspirators—"the Poles"— and encouraged the peasant's notion of himself as an "imperial man." The Galician administration, which had taken no preventive measures against the approaching revolution, fostered the peasants' antagonism toward the revolutionary nobles and connived at or in some cases engineered the peasant outbreaks. The notorious administrator of the Tarnów district skillfully used the "divide and rule" principle and in a moment of crisis drove a wedge between the masses and the insurrectionists. No wonder that the revolution never got off the ground! True, in the Tatra Mountains the highlanders, who had never been subjected to real serfdom, rose at Chochołów; but their isolated uprising was put down by Austrians aided by neighboring peasants.

In the Congress Kingdom the Russians took precautions and massed seventy thousand troops in Warsaw. At the news of the Posen arrests, the designated leader of the insurrection fled the country. Only a few isolated coups took place, and although the peasants remained on the whole loyal to the government some did join guerrilla groups. In Prussian Poland, the Plebeians planned a coup against the Posen citadel; in Pomerania, Kashubian peasants under a local leader, Florian Ceynowa (1817–81), moved against Starogard. All these attempts ended disastrously.

The Revolution of 1846 reverberated throughout the emigration and Poland. On its credit side was the Cracow manifesto, which was heartily endorsed by the Versailles Centralizacja and viewed as an ideological turning point in Polish revolutionary history.

Both Marx and Lelewel regarded the Cracow uprising as the first social revolution on Polish soil, and they greeted it as the birth of a new Poland. Among the debits was the obvious failure of the revolution, as well as the peasant *jacquerie* which shook both the democrats and the conservatives. The former were bitterly deceived in their hopes; the latter did not fail to point out that the democrats themselves had contributed in part to the harvest of hate. The leadership of the Democratic Society came under attack; Czartoryski was criticized for his hasty recognition of the National Government in Cracow. The prestige of the emigration had suffered; at home there were gestures akin to despair. In a famous open letter to Metternich, Margrave Aleksander Wielopolski (1803–77) wrote that after such a lesson at Austrian hands Polish nobles would rather be with the Russians at the head of the Slav civilization than be dragged in the dust by the degenerate and self-centered civilization of the West.

There was tension throughout the Polish lands. Events in Galicia and a wave of social discontent that passed through the Lithuanian and Belorussian provinces and the kingdom—caused in part by hunger and poor harvests—made the tsar issue a regulation decree in June, 1846. It banned peasant evictions by landlords, permitted peasant appeals to administration officials, and announced the preparation of procedures for conversion of compulsory labor to rent on private estates. Although the Russian government was intervening in the relations between village and manor, it had no thought-out peasant policy. There were still divisions between those who wished to rely on the peasantry against the Polish gentry and those who abhorred the thought of any radical departure from the prevailing social order. In any case, the administration was not prepared to grant the more progressive landowners an initiative in agrarian reforms, and it stopped such attempts by the gubernial dietines in Lithuania. All rent reforms had to originate from the state, and the state behaved with utmost caution.

In Poznania a state of siege lasted until March, 1848, and the clergy took the lead in opposing harsh government measures, thereby strengthening their position as spokesmen for Prussian Poles. The great trial of the Posen conspirators involved around two hundred people of different social backgrounds (five landowners, forty-two peasants, nine tenants, one officer, and five non-commissioned officers, two soldiers, forty-five artisans, ten clergymen, thirty-seven students, five physicians, five teachers, and seven tradesmen). It lasted for several months. Held in Berlin and given much publicity by the liberal German counsels for the defense, the trial became a link in the chain binding the 1846 revolution with the Spring of Nations of

1848. In his fighting and somewhat theatrical speech, Mierosławski prepared the ground for future German-Polish revolutionary cooperation. Following the trial, Marx, Engels, and other German radicals affirmed that German freedom was unthinkable without Poland's liberty. The Russian revolutionary Mikhail Bakunin spoke of solidarity between the Russian and Polish peoples. No wonder that the Poles linked their hopes more closely than ever with a general revolution in Europe. The accused of the Berlin trial, condemned to death but not yet executed, could await their deliverance only from the hands of the people.

II. THE SPRING OF NATIONS AND PRUSSIAN POLAND

Beginning with the outbreak in Sicily in January, 1848, a revolutionary wave swept over France in February and over Prussia and Austria in mid-March. Throughout Central Europe the established order was crumbling; it seemed that its restoration could only come through an intervention on the part of Russia, the bastion of European reaction. Polish hopes suddenly ran high. When the Italian national revolution began, Mickiewicz launched the idea of a Polish legion in Italy. The change of regime in France opened new perspectives, and the high point was reached with the revolutions in Austria and Germany. Czartoryski considered that the Polish question would occupy a central place in the forthcoming conflict between Russia and the Germanic states. Berlin and Vienna appeared as potential Polish allies. Anticipating the outbreak of war, General Prądzyński prepared a plan for a Prussian offensive in the north to be assisted by an Austrian, or more exactly Hungarian and Polish, advance from the south. Polish insurgents based in Poznania would strike at Warsaw.

Czartoryski rushed to Berlin to confer with the new liberal ministers of Prussia and to establish contact with Polish leaders from the homeland. He instructed the Galician Poles to gain *de facto* independence and await its confirmation from Vienna. The Prussian Poles were to achieve a similar status for Poznania and prepare for an armed conflict with Russia. Czartoryski urged the nobility to abolish serfdom in Galicia—already in 1847 the prince had said that the peasant question was a matter of "life or death"—and assume leadership over the masses. He warned against any revolutionary acts against, or violent clashes with, the Austrian or Prussian administrations.

The Galician and Poznanian gentry was reluctant to follow the lead of the Hôtel Lambert. They felt that they knew the local situation better and resented dictates from outside. Nor were the émigré democrats, who were returning home *en masse*, likely to be accepted as leaders of the democratic forces in the Prussian and Austrian provinces. Their influence, which was often exercised from behind the scenes, clashed with local interests and the plans of Poznanian and Galician Poles.

News of the Berlin revolution electrified Poznania. The Poles learned that the liberated Libelt, Mierosławski, and other condemned conspirators had been saluted by the king and fêted by the Berlin crowds as heroes of a common German-Polish cause. Reckoning with the possibility of war with Russia, the minister of war viewed the Poles as a natural shield against the eastern invader. The president of the Frankfurt Vorparlament asserted that Germany's future was inextricably linked with Poland's freedom. The liberal and radical German press echoed these sentiments.

The Poznanian Poles faced two basic questions: first, should they attempt to seize the province and confront the government with *faits accomplis*; second, what attitude were they to adopt toward German unification? Although the Left wanted immediate action, a compromise was reached, and a joint and fairly representative National Committee appeared in Posen. It prepared an address to the king and issued manifestoes to the people in the province: Poles, Germans, and Jews. The Poznanian delegation that went to Berlin decided to depart from its original demand for independence and limited its request to that of provincial autonomy. Apparently the king anticipated more far-reaching demands because he took pains to explain to the delegates why he could not countenance a separation of Poznania from Prussia. This would be an open provocation of Russia; a province with a million and a half inhabitants stood no chance of separate existence. He agreed, however, to proceed to a "national reorganization" of Poznania. This could mean a return to 1815, but given the developments in the province, it could also be the first step toward a *de facto* independence. The royal decree of March 24 made reorganization dependent on the maintenance of law and order and respect for the existing authorities.

In fact, a semilegal revolution was already underway in Poznania. In anticipation of an approaching war with Russia, a Polish volunteer militia armed with scythes, pikes, and hunting rifles was being organized as a nucleus of a Polish national army. When on March 27 Tsar Nicholas threateningly said "tremble nations, for God is with us," a Polish armed force seemed a natural and necessary product of the situation. In the countryside Prussian officers even helped to train the volunteers, or at least showed a sympathetic attitude toward their new comrades in arms. In Posen itself, after attempting a coup against the Bazar, the Prussian army withdrew to its barracks.

The Posen committee urged calm and announced the abolition of remnants of feudal privileges and burdens as well as full equality for the Jews. The committee's representatives in the provinces were attempting to establish a Polish administration. The Prussian officials sought to oppose them by organizing the local Germans to resist Polish encroachments. Clashes occurred; the German and Jewish population assumed an inimical attitude, and the Polish crowds retaliated. The National Committee was unable to control these nationalistic outbursts in the countryside, and while there were some 800,000 Poles in Poznania as compared with 450,000 Germans and 81,000 Jews, an uneven distribution of the nationalities made certain districts almost exclusively Polish and others heavily German. The attitude of the German population was thus of great importance during the early stages of the promised reorganization.

At first, German democrats and indeed most Germans in Posen showed solidarity with the Poles. A delegation assured the king that it would be impossible to retain the province for Prussia, and declared itself in opposition to a German rule based on Prussian bayonets. They were told in Berlin that even the Poles did not go that far in their demands. The increasing number of clashes in the province and, above all, the changing international situation shortly put an end to the German-Polish honeymoon. Even though the Poles had made the mistake of not inviting some Germans and Jews to the National Committee, nationalist feelings were almost bound to get out of hand under the circumstances. The Russian foreign office quickly realized that once the fear of Russian intervention subsided internal conflicts between liberalism and reaction and between Germans and non-Germans would come into the open. Consequently, St. Petersburg adopted a policy of passivity.

The Frankfurt Parliament proved to be a good barometer of the changing German attitudes toward the Poles. The Posen committee's declaration of March 20, that "we as Poles cannot and will not join the German Reich," met with the understanding of the Vor-parlament. The latter condemned the partitioning of Poland and put off the question of Poznania's representation in an all-German parliament, pending a solution to the Polish problem. Even after the Prussians suppressed Poznania, the Frankfurt Parliament was not unanimous about admitting German deputies from that province. Eventually, however, the pro-Polish sentiments changed, and the Prussian way of resolving the Polish issue gained endorsement, except by the radicals. Faced with the choice between liberalism and nationalism, the Germans opted, in the words of Wilhelm Jordan, for "healthy national egoism."

Frederick William IV obviously had no desire to be involved in a war with Russia, nor did he wish to lose Poznania. He attempted to make the promised "national reorganization" of the province as meaningless as possible; without the knowledge of his liberal ministers, he ordered the army to repress the Poles at the first opportunity.

On their side, Mierosławski and the Polish leaders had no desire to burn their bridges to Berlin. They had created a substitute administration and a military force based on wide social participation, even if it was led by the gentry. The Polish troops had been formed to fight against Russia, not against the Prussians, and their actual use was made dependent on general war. Mierosławski did not believe that he could initiate a partisan warfare in the kingdom with his six or seven thousand badly armed troops. He foresaw nothing but a massacre of the Poznanian volunteers. Was he in a position to force the hand of the cabinets by attempting an invasion of the kingdom? Did he waste the opportunity to launch a "people's war" because he feared a repetition of the 1846 events? Although the Poznanian leadership was essentially "nonrevolutionary," such an interpretation would be misleading. There is no doubt that the Polish masses thought primarily of liberating the province from Prussian rule and viewed war with Russia as a less immediate contingency. The Left had favored a policy of *faits accomplis*, and it may well be that in the initial stages even the small troop of Mierosławski could have gained control of the province. But the leaders could hardly view the Poznanian situation in isolation from the general international situation. Only in the event of war with Russia could Poznanian Poles obtain real political concessions.

Meanwhile, the promised reorganization of Poznania was restricted to the "purely Polish" parts of the province, and the government in Berlin changed the demarcation lines several times, until the Polish section was reduced to a few western districts around Gnesen. The major part including Posen itself was declared German. Such a division was clearly a travesty of justice and could form no basis for a Polish-Prussian understanding. Armed Polish resistance became unavoidable, although it could hardly produce any results. Already on April 4, the Prussian commanding general declared martial law in the province, and bloodshed was averted only by the arrival of a special envjoy from Berlin, General Wilhelm von Willisen. Although a partisan of war against Russia and sympathetic toward the Poles, Willisen could hardly act as a *bona fide* mediator. He demanded disarmament and the dissolution of Polish armed units in exchange for wide autonomy, although he knew that the autonomy promised would only apply to a small fraction of the province.

Willisen was an unwelcome guest to the Prussian army commanders and to the Germans of Poznania. The army felt that it could speedily suppress the Polish movement and was annoyed by delays and new talks with the Poles. Willisen himself thought of a Poznanian Polish division within the Prussian army and induced the Poles to agree to a compromise convention at Jarosławiec (April 11). The convention provided for the dismissal of some Polish volunteers but preserved the nucleus of an armed force grouped in four camps. The National Committee signed the convention reluctantly. Mierosławski avoided doing so, on the grounds that he was merely a military commander, but he saw it as a necessary concession that gave some respite to his remaining troops. He also hoped that a change in the international situation might make the sacrifice worthwhile. The soldiers violently protested against the Jarosławiec "betrayal." A cleavage appeared between the more pliable gentry and the uncompromising masses. Fearing social unrest, the National Committee promised grants of land to the landless members of the militia.

Neither Mierosławski nor the Prussian command viewed the arrangement as permanent. The former sought to evade it; the latter, after Willisen's departure, pressed for a showdown. On April 29, the Prussian troops attacked one of the camps and massacred the militia and the townsmen. Having concentrated the remaining units, Mierosławski fought two engagements in which he defeated the Prussians but suffered heavy casualties. The National Committee dissolved itself, and the militia began to melt away. Its gentry members felt that they had done enough by not capitulating without a battle; the peasant soldiers, who had fought well, were disoriented and discouraged. After a series of quarrels with his officers Mierosławski gave up his command. By the beginning of May, 1848, Poznania was once again under firm Prussian control.

III. THE SPRING OF NATIONS: GALICIA

Early events in Galicia ran parallel to the developments in Poznania and showed similarities as well as important differences. Like Prussian Poland, Galicia appeared to Czartoryski and to the Democratic Society as a center from which an insurrection could spread to the Congress Kingdom. The likelihood of an Austro-Russian clash, however, was smaller than that of a Russian intervention in Germany, and the Galician Poles were hardly prepared to spearhead an offensive against the empire of the tsars. The impact of the 1846 events weighed heavily on Galician society. Fearful of the gentry's revenge and ravaged by hunger and epidemics, the peasantry was passive and suspicious even of the authorities, not to mention the landowners. The democratic camp was decimated and weak. The conservative nobility and gentry were unwilling to come in conflict with the government. A national movement could only draw its support from liberal groups composed largely of bourgeois intelligentsia and some gentry, but even these elements were wary of new revolutionary gambles.

The Italian and French revolutions as well as the propaganda coming from the Democratic Society encouraged the Galician liberals to believe that the Polish question would reappear on the international agenda. Then came the startling news of the March 13-15 revolution in Vienna and the fall of Metternich. The Habsburg monarchy suddenly lost its bearings, and the imperial administration in Galicia was left to cope the best it could with a novel situation. Crowds demonstrated in the streets of Lemberg and acclaimed a Viennese regiment and Hungarian husars as brothers in a common cause against autocracy. On March 18, leading liberals in the city, including such former inmates of Austrian prisons as Franciszek Smolka (1810-99) and Florian Ziemiałkowski (1817-1900), drew up a petition to the emperor which immediately gained some twelve thousand signatures of Poles, Ruthenians, and Jews. The petition demanded guarantees for the Polish nationality in the form of a national army, a separate and native administration, and a diet (Sejm) representative of all classes. It demanded Polish as the language of instruction in schools, political amnesty, abolition of censorship, equality of rights for all citizens, and complete abolition of serfdom. It stated that the landowners were willing to give up their seigneurial rights.

The governor of Galicia, Count Franz Stadion, decided to meet some of the Polish demands. Acting on his own, he abolished censorship, released political prisoners, and agreed to the formation of a National Guard on the Viennese model. In other matters he temporized, awaiting the outcome of events in the monarchy. Meanwhile, he sought ways and means to weaken the united Polish front.

The politically active elements in Galicia were strengthened by the arrival of émigrés, even through the newcomers were not united in their approach; the democrats among them sought *faits accomplis*, while the Czartoryski supporters counseled adherence to the law and coordination of the Polish movements in Austria and Prussia. In Cracow the nascent National Committee, which kept in touch with Mierosławski, entrusted home, army, and police affairs to the émigrés. Indeed, Cracow appeared more revolutionary and determined than did Lemberg and its mood influenced the stand of the Polish delegation that carried a Galician petition to Vienna. The delegation was large and included two peasants and a rabbi. Carrying a Polish flag, the delegates, some of whom were dressed in national costumes, met with an enthusiastic reception from the Viennese crowds. Breathing a new atmosphere of freedom and brotherhood of nations, the Poles became self-confident and bold.

The delegation was received by Emperor Ferdinand. It presented an amended address dated April 6, which contained additional demands for an autonomous regime in Galicia. This was seen as a first step toward a reunification of the province with an independent Poland. The address ascribed to the emperor a willingness to undo the partitions and to take the Polish cause under his protection. Public and private pronouncements that were then being uttered in Vienna made the Poles believe that their demands and hopes corresponded to reality. The emperor's uncle Archduke John spoke of the partitions as a great sin; the government contemplated war against Russia "in cooperation with Poland"; the Austrian diet (Stände) calmly listened to remarks about the separation of the illegally acquired Galicia. Viennese papers wrote that Austria would bring freedom to the Poles and, fortified by a union with Poland and the sympathy of Europe, struggle with Russia to achieve such a "great aim." No wonder that within a short time Galician newspapers would report news from Austria under the heading "news from abroad"!

Appearances notwithstanding, Polish expectations proved vain. None of the Austrian ministers really wanted war with Russia, and St. Petersburg intimated to Vienna that a separation of Galicia from the Habsburg monarchy would be understood as a direct challenge. Mierosławski's hopes that by gaining delays in Poznania— the date of Willisen's arrival coincided with the visit of the Polish delegation to Emperor Ferdinand—he would let Austrian and Galician developments influence Prussian Poland were ill-founded. Vienna was in turmoil, and in Galicia Stadion was doing his best not to lose control over the situation. His main weapons were the peasant and the Ruthenian issues.

Urged by the democrats and the Hôtel Lambert, the committee in Cracow and the council in Lemberg appealed to the landowners to abandon the *corvée*. The committee's date for peasant emancipation was set for April 23, 1848, Easter Sunday. Under the pressure of public opinion some landowners had already begun to free the peasantry; others hesitated. The whole operation was bound to have complex economic effects, and the thorniest question was that of gentry-owned woods and pastures which were traditionally used by the peasants. If these "servitudes" were maintained emancipation would be advantageous to the peasantry. If not, the landlords would have means of pressuring the peasants to procure cheap labor necessary for the estates. Whatever might have happened on April

23, Stadion was determined to deprive the landowners of their initiative. Already on April 5, an administration circular, designed to discourage any spontaneous move, spelled out all the difficult legal aspects of emancipation. On April 22 Stadion announced, on the basis of an imperial decree, the abolition of all the obligations of serfdom. In fact he received the document post factum, antedated April 17. Thus, for purely local political reasons the Galician peasantry was emancipated several months ahead of the peasantry in the rest of the Habsburg monarchy.

Having neutralized the peasants as potential allies of the Galician democrats, Stadion moved against the democratic émigrés. Orders were issued forbidding their arrival and stay in Galicia, and an embargo was placed on the import or production of arms and munitions. On April 26, Austrian troops clashed with the émigrés and the populace in Cracow and then proceeded to bombard the city. Since moderate groups in Cracow were unwilling to engage in a mass struggle, the National Committee capitulated. Analyzing the events in Cracow, Marxist historians have generally blamed the passive gentry; conservative historians have condemned the émigré radicals for their foolhardy action which played into the hands of the reaction.

Having subdued Cracow, the Austrians concentrated on Lemberg. Stadion had already tried to undermine the National Council, first by attempting to call the old diet and then by grouping conservative elements in an advisory body (Beirat). In this part of Galicia, however, the government disposed of a powerful weapon which could be used to checkmate the Poles—namely, the Ruthenians. The strength of the national movement in Galicia lay in the fact that the Poles spoke for the entire province; they were supported at first by Ruthenians and Jews. Many of the Jews continued to side with the Poles and addressed admonititions to the pro-German Poznanian Jews, but the Ruthenians soon questioned the right of Poles to act as spokesmen for the entire province. Although the Ruthenian national revival was still in its infancy, the Austrian administration was well aware of the latent antagonism of the Ruthenians toward the Poles. The Ruthenians, nicknamed the Tyrolians of the East because of their loyalty to the Habsburgs during the Napoleonic wars, were regarded as reliable Austrian subjects. In 1847 Galicia was nominally divided into Western and Eastern Galicia, and in the eastern part Austrian decrees appeared in German and in Ruthenian written in Cyrillic script. As an Austrian historian put it, nascent Ruthenian patriotism "was valuable for the government [but] only insofar as it assured tranquility in Galicia."[1]

1. Cited in Piotr S. Wandycz, "The Poles in the Habsburg Monarchy," *Austrian History Yearbook*, vol. 3, pt. 2 (1967), p. 272n.

As early as March 19, 1848, Stadion had encouraged the Ruthenians to send a separate petition to Vienna, expressing their demand for a real division of Galicia with a separate administration and cultural identity for the Ruthenian part. In early May the small but vocal group centered around the Uniate St. George Cathedral—whence the name St. Georgians *(svetojurcy)*—established, with Stadion's blessings, a Central Ruthenian Council presided over by Bishop Hryhorij Jachymovych (1792-1863). Stadion explained to Vienna that he was using the Ruthenians "for the benefit of the government to paralyze the Polish strivings."[2] The Poles were incensed and accused the governor of having "invented" the Ruthenian question. What Stadion was really doing was pushing the Ruthenian leaders in a clerical, conservative direction, in much the same way in which the Austrians were exploiting Southern Slav grievances for counter-revolutionary ends. The Ruthenian council had no real program of socioeconomic reforms, and its demands were local. By ignoring the Ukrainians under the Russian rule it showed no awareness of the all-Ukrainian issue.

The Galician Poles showed little understanding and sympathy for the Ruthenian cause and responded by organizing a rival Ruthenian Council (Sobor). It represented largely the tradition-oriented "gente Rutheni natione Poloni" circles. Only a few of the Galician magnates and some democrats made efforts to bring about a Ruthenian-Polish reconciliation at the Slav Congress which met in June, 1848, in Prague.

During the spring and summer Polish activity in the Habsburg monarchy was conducted on three levels: in Galicia, at the short-lived Slav Congress, and at the new Reichstag in Vienna. In Galicia, the Lemberg council acted as the supreme Polish center for the province. There was a Polish press, associations—although no mass political parties—and a National Guard of twenty thousand well-equipped, even if only fairly armed, men. To the democrats the National Guard was the nucleus of a Polish army; to the council it was protection against the encroachments of the Austrian administration; and to the conservative upper classes it was a guarantee against social unrest or revolutionary outbreaks. The province was calm and looked to Vienna to bring about desired changes. In June the Poles demanded that the Reichstag call a Galician Sejm organized along modern, representative lines, endowed with legislative powers and control over the executive. They demanded elections and a reorganization of the provincial administration. Finally, they demanded a home army and Polish schools and courts. Their program indicated that Galicia wished to adhere to legality and left the final

2. *Ibid.*

say to the central parliament. But the parliament's ability to act depended on the general situation in the Habsburg monarchy and in Europe, and the outlook was not favorable. By June conservative elements had triumphed in France. In July the Austrians won victories over the Italians. All the hopes of the reaction rested on the imperial armies of Radetzky in Italy, Jelačić who threatened Hungary, and Windischgrätz who on June 11 bombarded Prague.

The bombardment of Prague put an end to the Slav Congress, which was attended by Galician and Poznanian Poles. While the idea of the congress had simultaneously originated in Czech, Polish, and South Slav quarters, Prague was chosen as the site of the meeting. It was not a revolutionary gathering. In fact, its Austro-Slav orientation together with its anti-Hungarian overtones made Marx and Engels condemn the congress as counter-revolutionary. Polish participation was bound to introduce elements that went beyond Austro-Slav issues, and it was bound to promote some pro-Hungarian attitudes. Working together with Czech democrats, the most prominent Polish representative, Libelt, succeeded in having the congress adopt a general manifesto to the nations of Europe. The manifesto stressed national rights to freedom and voiced opposition to oppression by foreign powers. At the congress the Poles attempted a reconciliation with the Ruthenian delegates. Czartoryski, who believed that awakening Ruthenian nationalism should be encouraged to develop into a Ukrainian nationalism that would confront Russia, urged his supporters to work for an agreement. An understanding that provided for equality of the two nationalities in an undivided Galicia was reached, but neither the Polish nor the Ruthenian councils in Lemberg were willing to endorse it.

Austrian military authorities in Prague disbanded the congress, leaving the Poles with ever diminishing chances of linking their cause with a broader program of change. Their last hopes now centered on the Reichstag in Vienna, which met on July 10 to elaborate a constitution for the Habsburg monarchy. The Reichstag was chosen by universal manhood suffrage, and for the first time seventeen Polish and fourteen Ruthenian peasants—many of them elected with the support of the administration—appeared in such an assembly. The peasant deputies generally followed the government and the Right; most of the other representatives from Galicia were in opposition. Even when their respective positions were reversed in the debate on serfdom indemnities, the two groups remained at opposite poles. The leading Galician figure, Smolka, rose to be vice-president and then briefly president of the constituent parliament. He worked for Galician autonomy within a federalized Austrian monarchy, hoping that such a status would one day allow the province to become a Polish Piedmont.

In October a revolution in defense of Hungary and popular liberties swept Vienna, and the Reichstag found itself in the eye of a political storm. The Polish deputies chose noninvolvement, but émigrés with General Bem at their head fought at the barricades. The reaction triumphed, and soon thereafter Galicia became its easy prey. In November, following incidents in Lemberg, the head of the Austrian garrison ordered a bombardment of the city. The weak resistance speedily collapsed, and Galicia was returned to strict Austrian control. As for the Reichstag, it was first moved to Kremsier (Kroměříž) and then dissolved before completing its work on a new constitution.

While in 1848 Polish plans had been tied to German and Austrian events and the perspective of a war against Russia, in early 1849 they were centered on Hungary. True, the Poles identified with and fought for virtually every contemporary revolution. Not only democratic generals such as Mierosławski but also those close to the Hôtel Lambert commanded revolutionary troops in Italy, Germany, and Hungary. The fiery *Tribune des Peuples*, edited by Mickiewicz in Paris, enjoyed the secret support of Czartoryski. Polish involvement in Hungary, however, stemmed not only from a feeling of solidarity with an oppressed nation but also from political calculations. Desirous of seeing a liberal revolution succeed in a country contiguous to Galicia, the democrats thought of rekindling a revolutionary fire in that province. The Hungarians were cautious. The Poles were useful allies, and Bem became a legendary figure of the Hungarian revolution. But to support a Polish coup in Galicia would be a direct challenge to Russia. Even without any such overt provocation, St. Petersburg favored a speedy suppression of the Hungarians at least in part because of the Polish aspects.

The kingdom and the "western guberniias" had been calm during the 1848 revolution, but conspiratorial networks had come into existence. A conspiracy under the leadership of Henryk Krajewski (1826-97) appeared in Warsaw and branched out through the kingdom. Although greatly excited by the Poznanian events, the plotters did not dare start an uprising and awaited an outbreak of a Russo-Prussian war. Later, many individuals escaped from the kingdom to fight in Hungary and in the West. In Lithuania and Belorussia, a conspiratorial Brotherly Union of Lithuanian Youth reached its height during the Hungarian revolutionary war and was in contact with émigré emissaries and with Poles in Kiev. While attempting to gather arms in preparation for an uprising, the organization was discovered by the police and its participants imprisoned or executed. Thus, the tsarist government knew that there were dangerous currents under the calm surface of Russian Poland, and it also worried about the prominent place occupied by Poles in the Hungarian army. After the Russian intervention in Hungary in August, 1849, tsarist authorities sought in vain the extradition of Bem and other Polish émigrés who escaped and found refuge in Turkey.

IV. THE BALANCE SHEET OF 1848

Although Poznania and Galicia were the centers of Polish developments in 1848, the Spring of Nations echoed in other parts of the old commonwealth and even beyond its borders. Each of the provinces involved was largely concerned with its specific problems, and one can agree with the opinion that in 1848 Polish *questions* dominated the Polish question. The revolution in Poznania was really part of the Prussian and German upheaval; the fortunes of Galicia were linked with the course of events in the Habsburg monarchy. Czartoryski's plans for establishing a central "Polish Delegation," which would speak on behalf of the whole partitioned nation, failed largely because Polish leaders could not agree to subordinate immediate local interests to such an agency. True, Poles from Galicia and Poznania regarded the rebirth of a Polish state as their ultimate goal, but in practice they acted within the framework of the state to which they happened to belong.

What did the Poles mean when they spoke of a resurrected and reunited Poland? The manifesto of the Democratic Society spoke of a Poland that stretched "from the Oder and the Carpathian Mountains to the Borysthenes and the Dvina—from the Baltic to the Black Sea." The vision of such a vast Polish state seemed reasonable not only to most Poles but also to Engels; on August 20, 1848, he wrote in the *Neue Rheinische Zeitung* that Poland "must have at least the area it had in 1772" and "not only the watershed but the mouths of its great rivers" and "a considerable stretch of the Baltic sea coast." A sincere democrat such as Lelewel firmly believed that the "Ukrainian, Kashubian, Ruthenian, Great or Little Pole, Lithuanian . . . or the son of whatever land of the old *Rzeczpospolita*" was a Pole.[3] Although the conservatives were for traditional federalist arrangements and the democrats leaned toward the concept of a centralist state, the pre-1772 commonwealth was the only living reality to all of them.

Viewing nation and state in historical terms, in 1848 the Poles

3. Manfred Kridl, Władysław Malinowski, and Józef Wittlin, eds., *"Za waszą i naszą wolność": Polska myśl demokratyczna w ciągu wieków* (New York: "Polish Labor Group," 1945), p. 109.

were brought face to face with new realities. Their belief that popular revolutions and national strivings were fully compatible received a rude shock in Galicia and Poznania. In Galicia they began to perceive that the Ruthenians were an awakening nation that demanded recognition of its separate rights and denied the historical unity of Poland. In Poznania Polish nationalism clashed with German nationalism. Whereas prior to 1848 the contest in Poznania had been between the Poles and Prussian officialdom, it began to turn now into a Polish-German confrontation. In some cases these new developments operated to the advantage of the Poles. The year 1848 marked a Polish awakening in Silesia (Austrian and Prussian) and in the Masurian area, that is, in lands that had been outside the 1772 borders.

In Pomerania, where the Poles had no legal rights to national representation, there were manifestations of solidarity with Poznania. In the town of Kulm (Chełmno), for example, where a Polish high school had existed since 1837, Polish journals appeared and addressed themselves to the people. Since the church hierarchy and most of the landowners in the province were German, the Polish national movement here was democratic and plebeian. In the Masurian area—only a part of which had belonged to prepartition Poland— there was a Polish linguistic, though not yet a widespread political, revival. Such protestant ministers as Gustaw Gizewiusz (1810-48) and Krzysztof Mrongowiusz (1774–1855) defended the rights of the Polish language and stressed the existence of Prussian Polish lands outside of Poznania. There were similar developments in the more economically advanced Silesia, where the Prussian authorities reestablished Polish as the language of instruction in elementary schools as a means of winning over the population. Polish deputies from Pomerania and Silesia were elected to the Prussian National Assembly. Polish associations and newspapers appeared in Austrian Teschen (Cieszyn, Tĕšin) Silesia. Its representatives participated as Polish delegates in the Slav Congress in Prague and demanded political ties with Galicia.

Observing these developments and becoming better acquainted with nationality problems at the Slav Congress, Libelt concluded that Poland could no longer be revived "as a unitary state with a national government which would rule as in the past over Lithuanians, Ruthenians, and Prussians," but it would be revived "as a federation of all these racially distinct lands."[4] This was a novel idea which would later dominate the thinking of the Polish Left.

The social problems in East Central Europe in 1848 were of a

4. Cited in Wilhelm Feldman, *Dzieje polskiej myśli politycznej w okresie porozbiorowym* (Kraków and Warszawa: F. Hoesick, 1913-20), 1:205.

different nature than those in the West, but they were of importance nevertheless. The agrarian question provided the focal point, and it significantly affected the developments. Fears of a new *jacquerie* proved unjustified, and the emancipated peasantry of Poznania showed that it was already part of the nation. The emancipation of the Galician peasants, the most important and lasting achievement of 1848, was the first step toward an eventual integration of the masses into the political and social fabric of the nation. After 1848 only the peasantry under Russia remained unaffected by change. No wonder that the peasant question there assumed a new importance.

The revolution of 1848 deepened the division between the emigration and the homeland. The émigrés' attempts to set the pace of revolutionary events bred resentment. Mierosławski's difficulties in Poznania were at least in part due to the antagonism toward an outsider who in case of defeat could always return to Paris. The Polish Left, both émigré and domestic, was proved wrong in its estimates and policies. True, their failure was only part of the larger failure of the liberal cause. Even if the Poles had acted with greater determination and revolutionary élan they could not have reversed the general trend. But they did fail, and this fact was bound to have important repercussions. Convinced that conspiracies and uprisings brought no advantages to the Polish cause, conservative and moderate circles at home concentrated their efforts on economic and cultural betterment. In the mounting reaction, a policy of *modus vivendi* with the Prussian and Austrian administrations seemed the only sensible approach, and the conservatives appeared to be the only group that could pursue it.

V. FROM 1849 TO THE CRIMEAN WAR

Having crushed the revolution, the Habsburg monarchy went through a decade of neoabsolutism and political oppression. In Galicia martial law remained until 1854, and even the conservative leaders found it impossible to cooperate with Vienna. One of them, Count Adam Potocki (1822-72), was put in jail. Prince Leon Sapieha devoted himself exclusively to economic affairs and was instrumental in initiating a railroad from Cracow to Lemberg, which finally opened in 1861.

Two central issues agitated the province: implementation of the peasant emancipation decree and Polish-Ruthenian relations. The former concerned mainly the "servitudes," i.e., the traditional peasant use of manorial woods (which constituted 90 percent of all woods) and pastures, as well as indemnities. The emancipation reform did not resolve the matter of "servitudes," which remained a constant irritant in the relations between the manor and the village. It also became a powerful weapon in the hands of the Austrian administration. The emancipation provisions included even the poorest strata of peasantry (unlike the provisions in Prussian Poland), and the result was a perpetuation of tiny peasant holdings which operated on near subsistence level. As for indemnity to landlords, Galicia, unlike the rest of the monarchy where the burden was shared by the state, the province, and the peasants, was charged with the whole amount. It was only able to meet these obligations by means of loans advanced by Vienna, an arrangement that made the province completely dependent on financial assistance from the monarchy. The landowners began to receive their indemnity in 1857 in the form of negotiable interest bonds; to cover the interest and amortization a special indemnification tax was added to other Galician taxes.

The Austrian government kept the Ruthenian question open, in part as a means of putting pressure on the Galician Poles. The Ruthenian Council dissolved itself in 1851, but its demand for a division of Galicia was merely shelved. The authorities made minor educational concessions to the Ruthenians, facilitated by the latter's agreement to keep German language instruction in their schools. The evolution of the Ruthenian movement in a Russophile-Slavist direction, however, alarmed Vienna and was cleverly exploited by the Poles. In its position as arbiter of Polish-Ruthenian difficulties, the central government continued its *divide et impera* policy.

During the decade when even the Polish conservatives stood aloof from Vienna, a lonely Polish aristocrat of somewhat newer vintage, Count Agenor Gołuchowski (1812-75), ran Galicia as its governor. Yet, in spite of his unwavering loyalty to the Habsburgs and his conservative pro-Austrian policy, Gołuchowski cannot be described as a mere instrument of Vienna. In his own way he had Polish interests at heart. By his ability to appeal directly to the emperor, whose confidence he enjoyed, he prepared the way for the later Austro-Polish deal. By encouraging his countrymen to join the administration he was forming a cadre of Polish officials. By transferring police powers from the landowners to the bureaucracy (part of the separation of the manorial demesne from the peasant commune in 1855) he freed the gentry from an onerous duty that was greatly resented by the peasantry. With respect to the Ruthenian question, Gołuchowski attempted to promote the use of the Latin alphabet by the Ruthenians, and exposed any Russophile sentiments among them. Needless to say, the Ruthenian circles cordially disliked his regime, which strove to keep Galicia undivided and pushed them into the background. The long-range implications of Gołuchowski's rule became clearer later. For the time being his servility toward Vienna and his acceptance of Austrian neoabsolutism bred the resentment of patriotic Poles.

The victory of the reaction in Prussia resulted in the gradual disappearance in the 1850s of a separate Grand Duchy of Posen together with its 1815 emblem which had displayed a small Polish eagle. The term "Provinz Posen" was substituted in practice. But in spite of preparations for a division of the province into a German and a Polish part, Poznania remained unified. Administrative, political, and economic considerations favored its unity. Although the government had declared an amnesty for all illegal political acts perpetrated in 1848, Polish officers, priests, officials, and teachers were liable to administrative punishment for revolutionary activity. Many Poles thus lost public jobs and were obliged to turn to trade and crafts. This fact, together with the growing belief that "organic work" was the most important and worthwhile field of activity, brought a revival of cultural and economic endeavors.

On the initiative of the philosopher and economist August Cieszkowski (1814-94), a Polish League (Liga Polska) was founded in the summer of 1848. Its object was to work legally and openly for the strengthening of the material and moral forces of Polish nationality. The league, which conservatives and democrats joined somewhat reluctantly, rapidly grew to a membership of forty thousand and even spread out to Pomerania. Its leadership was more conservative than its rank and file, which included many peasants. Most of its successes were in the educational field. The activity of the league and its slogan of defense of land, nationality, and religion made the organization suspect to the authorities. In 1850 the Prussian government dissolved its directorate; local organizations survived a little longer.

The new Prussian constitution with its highly undemocratic electoral law greatly reduced Polish representation in the Poznanian diet. In the Prussian Landtag, however, Polish deputies organized themselves into a Polish Circle (Koło) which was eventually recognized as the leading political organ of Poznania. Although it kept aloof from Pomerania and Silesia, the Circle was naturally bound to become a representation of all Prussian Poles. Administrative measures could and did reduce the number of Polish deputies—which during this period fell from sixteen to six—but could not interfere with the circle itself. Composed mainly of gentry landowners and priests, it also included burghers and peasants. This last group, having suffered Prussian reprisals together with the other social classes, continued its cooperation in a broad Polish front.

The year 1850 saw the completion of the long process of Jewish and, except for some feudal remnants, peasant emancipation. The

Poles voted in favor of granting full civil rights to the Jews but could not reverse the continuing trend of Jewish assimilation into the German nation. As for the peasants, the evolving socioeconomic structure of Poznania made them more akin to Western European farmers than to the socially and culturally retarded Galician peasantry, the *corvée*-burdened peasants of the kingdom, or the serfs of the "western guberniias" of Russia.

In 1854 the outbreak of the Crimean War created the international situation long awaited by Czartoryski. Both England and France, on whom the Hôtel Lambert had relied, were fighting Russia. The Balkans, where Czartoryski's emissaries had battled tsarist diplomacy for years, became the center of attention; the prince's contacts could be invaluable for London and Paris. If Austria could be drawn into the anti-Russian coalition, the Polish question would become internationalized to an extent unknown since the Congress of Vienna. The octagenarian prince displayed great energy. With his blessings, a Polish general proposed a plan for an allied offensive in the direction of the lower Danube and the Crimea, combined with landings in Lithuania. These operations would be reinforced by Polish uprisings in the Ukraine and in Lithuanian lands. Czartoryski explored diplomatic combinations that could result in the re-creation of Poland. A defeated Russia, he felt, would have to relinquish her Polish provinces; Austria could be induced to give up Galicia in exchange for the Danubian principalities, and Prussia compensated for her cession of Poznania by territories in Germany. But London and Paris were unwilling to contemplate such a redrafting of the map of Europe with all the complications and risks it involved. Besides, Austria's temporary occupation of the Danubian principalities not only separated the combatants in the Balkans but also cut off approaches to Galicia and the Ukraine. The war was reduced to a narrow theater of operations on the Crimean peninsula. Thus, the international configuration that seemed so advantageous to Poland proved to be but a mirage.

The domestic ingredients of Czartoryski's plan—anticipated uprisings—although clearly dependent on international factors, were unrealistic. The Crimean War came at a time when the emigration was more divided than ever before and the country exhausted by the events of 1848. The émigré Left was split on several issues, including the appraisal of Napoleon III and his role in European affairs. It was only unanimous in its opposition to the Hôtel Lambert. New emissaries sent to Poland found little response in the homeland. In Poznania the leaders felt that they had at least some representation in the Prussian Landtag and had avoided mass persecutions. The war created a demand for grain, and Poznanian agriculture was booming. The upper classes in the kingdom shared in the general excitement created by the war but were unwilling to run any risks. Although industry was still in a period of crisis, the abolition of the Russo-Polish tariff border in 1851 created new opportunities for Polish eastern exports. A growing bourgeoisie, in which industrialists were joining the great merchants and bankers, was almost pro-Russian in its attitude. Legalism in Poznania, loyalism and class interests in Russian Poland, and neoabsolutism in Galicia militated against actions that could only bring new hardships. Some conspiratorial activity in the kingdom and a few peasant outbreaks in the Ukraine, which under more propitious circumstances the Poles might possibly have exploited to their advantage, could not change the general picture.

Cooperation between the emigration and Turkey—both émigré camps were represented even if Czartoryski's group had the upper hand—resulted in the sultan's permission to organize a Polish division financed by England and placed under supreme Ottoman command. Units of "Ottoman Cossacks" led for the most part by Polish officers appeared. All these efforts proved of no avail, and Czartoryski, who in 1854 assumed the title, last used by Kościuszko, "Chief" (Naczelnik), could not succeed against the odds. From the Polish point of view the Crimean War lasted too long and not long enough. It awakened new hopes but it ended before the allies found it necessary to play the Polish card against Russia. The death of Mickiewicz in Istanbul and the signing of the Treaty of Paris in 1856 marked the virtual end of the Great Emigration.

The period from 1846 to 1856 had been a tumultuous decade. Beginning with revolutionary hopes so devastatingly crushed in 1846, it witnessed a high tide of expectations and illusions during the Spring of Nations. Defeated by the neoabsolutist reaction, the Poles saw a new chance of reopening their question during the Crimean War. They were unsuccessful. "Poor Poland," the English ambassador in Turkey commented. "Her revival is a regular flying Dutchman. Never is—always to be."[5] And indeed the Polish question would soon reappear in all its magnitude in the area that had been largely dormant during the past decade—Russian Poland.

<hr />

5. Cited in M. Kukiel, *Czartoryski*, p. 302.

# CHAPTER 8

# At the Crossroads—the
# January Insurrection

## I. THE POST-CRIMEAN "THAW"

THE Crimean War revealed the inner weakness of Russia and emphasized her backwardness. The new tsar, Alexander II, realized that important changes were needed to forestall a revolutionary upheaval, and in his manifesto of March, 1856, he announced a program of reforms to be accomplished by joint efforts of the government and the nation. Such a liberal-sounding pronouncement aroused hopes and expectations. The term "thaw" was coined for the new era coming after the hard winter of Nicholas' reign.

A major issue that required urgent attention was the agrarian question, and the tsar, wishing to abolish serfdom, sought to do it in cooperation with the landowning gentry. The landowners of the economically more advanced "western guberniias," most of whom where Polish, were willing to entertain the idea of change. Encouraged by the governor general of Wilno, the nobility of Kowno and Grodno presented petitions for the abolition of serfdom and conversion to rents. In response, the tsar ordered the creation of special landowners' committees. In the "western guberniias" those of Kowno, Grodno, Minsk, and Mohilev favored commutation of labor to rents; those of Wilno and Kiev even advocated peasant freeholds. Only Podolia and Volhynia opposed reforms. Then the conservative elements everywhere began to apply the brakes; neither they nor the government wished the reforms to go too far or too fast.

The same was true in other spheres of life. In 1857 Poles began to be readmitted to administrative posts in the "western guberniias." A year later Polish was restored in high schools in Lithuania. Jewish guild merchants were permitted to leave the pale, and university graduates could enter Russian civil service. At the same time the tsar and his officials sharply reminded the nobles that they must not behave as if Lithuania or the Ukraine were Polish lands. Alexander II had no intention of reverting to the early policies of Alexander I.

In the Congress Kingdom the death of Paskevich in 1856 symbolized the passing of an era, and his successor, the old prince Mikhail Gorchakov, introduced a new style in politics. But again the tsar quickly dampened Polish hopes for radical change. Visiting Warsaw in 1856, he voiced approval of the policies of his father and used the words: "no daydreaming, gentlemen." The government was not prepared to implement in full the stillborn Organic Statute of 1832, not to mention the constitution of 1815. But St. Petersburg was willing to make some concessions. The government was undertaking a vast program of reforms in the empire and desired a *rapprochement* with France, and so it wished to keep the kingdom calm by reaching a *modus vivendi* with the Polish upper classes. A political amnesty was decreed, and in 1857 Polish demands for higher academic institutions were partly satisfied by the creation of the Medical-Surgical Academy in Warsaw. The same year permission was granted to establish the Agricultural Society (Towarzystwo Rolnicze), an outgrowth of the Klemensów meetings of the progressive landowners. The society soon became an important factor in the life of the kingdom. Its original membership of twelve hundred rose to four thousand within a short period. Organized in seventy-seven districts and having large funds from membership dues, the society comprised the most influential strata of Polish society. Its sessions, at which public affairs of the country were discussed, began to resemble a substitute diet, and its president, Andrzej Zamoyski, a favorite of the gentry and upper class bourgeoisie, became virtually the spokesman of the Poles in the kingdom.

What was the current situation in Congress Poland? Although the population increase was proportionately smaller than in Prussian Poland, in 1860 the country had over 4.8 million inhabitants. Warsaw with its 230,000 was at least three times larger than Lemberg or Wilno and almost six times larger than Cracow or Posen. But the thirty years of Paskevich's regime had left their imprint on Congress Poland. Virtually all the administration was in non-Polish hands, and it exercised strict controls over the church as well as over educational and cultural spheres. There were no more than seven strictly censored newspapers in Warsaw. The educational system was in ruins: most of the school inspectors knew no Polish. Only thirty-odd schools had more than two grades, and the level of instruction was low. Illiteracy was widespread. No wonder that demands for a radical reform of the education system were high on the list of Polish grievances. As for religious matters, the long years of Russian interference with the Catholic church gave the latter a halo of martyrdom and enhanced its standing among the people. St. Petersburg realized this, and after Alexander II's accession to the throne, the long vacant archiepiscopal seat of Warsaw was finally given to a respected and worthy priest, Antoni Fijałkowski (1778-1861).

In the 1850s the Jewish question in the kingdom assumed a new importance. While Polish-Jewish tensions and frictions existed—on both religious and economic grounds—a movement favoring Jewish emancipation and assimilation gained momentum. To many Poles such a process appeared both necessary and desirable. Many younger Jews showed Polish patriotic sentiments and actively supported assimilationist trends. The patriotic High Rabbi of Warsaw, Dow Ber Meisels (1798-1870), and members of the assimilated bourgeoisie, such as the financiers Mathias Rosen (1804-65) and Henryk Wohl (1842-1905), were active in the movement. Former converts to Catholicism—the greatest Warsaw banker, Leopold Kronenberg (1812-78), and the wealthy Epsteins—promoted Polish-Jewish understanding. So did one of the principal newspapers in the capital, owned by Kronenberg and edited by the prominent Polish novelist Józef Ignacy Kraszewski (1812-87). True, some conservative Jewish elders placed their hopes on Alexander to improve the position of the Jews, and the Hassidic masses remained politically indifferent, but the pro-Polish assimilation movement was a significant and striking phenomenon of the period.

The economy of the kingdom continued to evolve in a capitalist direction. The Paskevich regime had burdened the country with a national debt that was more than the sum of three annual budgets, and there was vocal criticism of state interference and demands for economic liberalism. After the abolition of the tariff barrier in 1851, and especially during the Crimean War, the kingdom's trade rose sharply, and the Poles began to recapture the Russian markets. An influx of German and Polish capital in industry was noticeable as well as the accumulation of capital. The Warsaw bankers who had shared in financing of the Warsaw-St. Petersburg railroad made large profits. In 1855, private joint-stock capital took over the Warsaw-Vienna railroad. A new line was extended in 1859 to the Dąbrowa Basin, and the building of railroads created new incentives for coal mining and iron industries. Prices went up; with lower bank rates credit became easier. Since the output of state-owned mines and iron works reached only the 1842 level, Alexander II endorsed in 1862 the sale of government-owned industrial establishments. Only the outbreak of the 1863 Insurrection prevented its immediate realization. Modernization of the textile industry continued, and diverse light industries developed in Warsaw. Sugar production increased threefold between 1853 and 1860. Much of the industrial establishment in the kingdom was in the hands of the Germans, many of whom were gradually polonized; trade was dominated by the Jews; craftsmen and workers were principally Polish. In the late 1850s there were around 75,000 workers in the country, 15,000 of whom were employed in factories using steam power.

The real center of attention in the kingdom was agriculture. Agricultural production, especially that of the principal grains, increased during this period. This was due in part to the extension of land under cultivation, in part to technical improvements in farming, and in part to continuing conversion of labor obligations to rents. By 1859 more than half of peasant holdings (above four acres) had been commuted to rent—91 percent on state lands, 41 percent on private estates. The status of the peasantry had improved after the 1846 decree which forbade evictions, provided for official ratification of private regulations, and more clearly defined the peasants' obligations toward the landowners. This was, however, only a partial reform which sharply accentuated the need for real change. The complete liquidation of the antiquated *corvée* seemed essential for the continued economic development of the kingdom, but proposals for doing away with it varied greatly. Zamoyski, who not only presided over the Agricultural Society but also chaired the Land Credit Society and was one of the chief initiators and shareholders of the Steamboat Company on the Vistula, advocated freely negotiated conversion to rents. Indeed, in December, 1858, a Russian decree appeared allowing commutation of labor to perpetual tenancy. The procedure, however, was very complex. A large part of the Agricultural Society followed Zamoyski's lead and favored a combination of Prussian-type reforms and English tenancy farming. A minority believed that peasants should be granted full ownership rights in exchange for an indemnity to the landlords to be paid by a central bank. But the establishment of such a bank obviously depended on the consent of the government.

The debate transcended purely economic issues. The reform discussions going on in Russia created a situation in which the government and the Polish landowners were competing for the allegiance of the peasantry. Would reforms in the former Polish lands and the kingdom be credited to the tsar and Russia or to the Polish nobles? This was a question loaded with political and national significance.

In 1859 the Russian government asked the Agricultural Society to prepare a land reform project. The request enhanced the position of the society and was naturally accepted. Only Margrave Aleksander Wielopolski (full title: Count Wielopolski, Margrave Gonzaga-

Myszkowski) voiced opposition. He felt that the question should have been submitted to the Provincial Estates, which had been foreseen by the Organic Statute but had never been called. Wielopolski, mentioned above in connection with his letter to Metternich in 1846, was a lonely and impressive figure. His involvement in the November Insurrection of 1830 and his stay abroad made him reject policies of armed struggle and émigré diplomacy. Events in Galicia in 1846 added to his disillusionment and made him voice the idea of cooperation with Russia, although he had no pro-Russian sympathies. An aristocrat, who was contemptuous of public opinion, and a hard-boiled realist, Wielopolski voiced unpopular views and displayed haughty manners which antagonized even members of his own class. If he belonged to any nineteenth-century Polish trend, he stood closest to the Drucki-Lubecki tradition. His program of reform comprised the emancipation of Jews, whom he regarded as Poland's "third estate," a thorough overhaul of the educational system, and commutation of labor to rents but without an eventual creation of peasant freeholds. In the political field he aimed at the implementation of the Organic Statute, which he regarded as the limit of possible Russian concessions.

In the unfolding drama it was inevitable that Wielopolski and Zamoyski became the main protagonists. Zamoyski too was a magnate and a conservative reformer, but he was highly sensitive to public opinion. Although standing aloof of the Hôtel Lambert led by his uncle and his brother, he feared above all the stigma of collaborating with Russia. He was willing to work with Russia but not in the face of Polish opposition. A man of lesser individuality than Wielopolski, Zamoyski was torn between his belief in economic progress and capitalist *laissez-faire* and a grand seigneur's attachment to the past and the greatness of his class and family. Though he attempted to restrict the activity of the Agricultural Society to the economic sphere, he was being inexorably drawn into the whirlpool of politics.

In the late 1850s there was a revival of political activities in the kingdom. The potentially revolutionary situation in Russia, the peasant question in the kingdom, and events on the international scene roused new expectations. The watchword of national liberation came to the forefront in Italy and in Romania, and Napoleon III appeared as the new champion of subject nationalities. His name held magic for many Poles. Polish students at the universities of St. Petersburg, Moscow, Dorpat (Tartu), and Kiev—in Kiev they constituted four-fifths of the student body—began to organize themselves into revolutionary circles. Imbued with the romantic outlook in which sacrifice for a just cause was the greatest virtue, the students displayed a highly idealistic and emotionally charged attitude toward political and social problems. In the Kievan Triune Association (Związek Trojnicki) they cooperated with Ukrainian students, but their attempts to polonize the university met with the opposition of their Ukrainian colleagues. Nor were their efforts to propagandize the Ukrainian peasantry successful at a time when relations between the Polish manor and the Ukrainian village were deteriorating considerably. Although largely ineffective in its Ukrainian surroundings, the Polish group in Kiev proved an important ideological training ground for the future leaders of the January Insurrection of 1863.

Another circle that emerged at this time in the General Staff Academy in St. Petersburg was composed of Polish, Russian, and Ukrainian officers united in revolutionary solidarity against tsarist autocracy. A friend of Taras Shevchenko and Nikolai Chernyshevsky, Lieutenant Zygmunt Sierakowski (1827-63), was the chief organizer. Captain Jarosław Dąbrowski (1836-71), whom destiny would lead eventually to a generalship in the Paris Commune, belonged to the more prominent members.

In Warsaw revolutionary conspiracy began to center at the School of Fine Arts and the Medical-Surgical Academy, and it was there that the terms Reds (radicals) and Whites (moderates) originated. The numerous conspiratorial groups and circles, including the first Secret Committee led by Karol Majewski (1833-97), often changed their character and composition and they are not easy to identify. But out of them came many of the leaders of the insurrection. Some of the revolutionaries looked up to the emigration where Mierosławski's star was rising again. They established contact with the general, who advocated armed insurrection and regarded himself as its natural leader. The pro-Mierosławski group was challenged by others; the lines between the Whies and the Reds were at times sharp, at other times blurred. A more moderate group which Mierosławski contemputuously called the Millennaries, to imply that their program would put off the attainment of national independence for a thousand years, favored a broad national front achieved through peasant emancipation and integration of the largely nonethnically Polish bourgeoisie. Their contacts were with the middle class rather than with students; their leaders included a minor state employee, Edward Jurgens (1827-63), and such recently released Siberian exiles as Agaton Giller (1831-87) and Karol Ruprecht (1821-75).

Political trends thus represented a wide spectrum in the years 1858–60, ranging as they did from conspiratorial insurrectionist Reds to essential reformist Millennaries and the gentry-based Agricultural Society. The Hôtel Lambert, where Czartoryski was reaching the end of his long career (he died in 1861), lent its support to policies based on working within the legal framework. The leading figures in Galicia and in Prussian Poland also believed that the kingdom could accomplish a great deal through legal means. Such attitudes corresponded to changes then taking place in the Habsburg monarchy, which were marking the beginnings of an evolution from absolutism to constitutionalism, from centralism to decentralization, and from germanization to limited recognition of national rights. Gołuchowski, the principal author of the stillborn October Diploma of 1860 which sought to federalize the empire in a conservative spirit, had to wait a few more years before being able to demonstrate the advantages of loyalism to the Habsburgs. But the provincial statute of 1861 provided the basis for future autonomy. Changes in the monarchy and in Galicia included also the Jews who in 1859 received the right to enter the administration and the teaching profession. In Prussian Poland no concessions were in sight, but the Poles used all available legal means to improve their position. As evidenced by a project of an address to the king of Prussia, which stressed the solidarity of Poznanian Poles with their countrymen under foreign rule, the Polish spirit in Poznania was very much alive. The police were shocked to hear the hymn "God protect Poland" *(Boże coś Polskę)* sung in the streets, and they were stunned by patriotic manifestations which took place even in the germanized Pomerania. Would the Congress Kingdom follow a path of gaining concessions by legally exerted pressures? This was the great question that preoccupied the Polish upper classes in the course of the next two years.

II. THE FATEFUL YEAR 1861

Inspired by radical circles and finding wide response among the populace of Warsaw, patriotic manifestations began in the kingdom in 1858. Such events in the capital as the visit of Prince Napoleon, the funeral of the widow of a general who fell in the defense of Warsaw in 1831, and the meeting between Tsar Alexander, Emperor Franz Joseph, and Wilhelm of Prussia in 1860 provided the opportunity for crowds to demonstrate in the streets. The same year the hymn "God protect Poland" was sung with the lines "freedom and Fatherland restore to us, O Lord." Mounting excitement and displays of exalted patriotic feelings created an atmosphere conducive to a formulation of Polish demands of autonomy; the Hôtel Lambert and several members of the Agricultural Society began to urge Zamoyski to present a petition to the tsar. Wielopolski also felt the time was ripe and prepared his own project.

The annual meeting of the society, scheduled for February, 1861, promised to provide a focal point for political activity. Not only was the domestic atmosphere tense, but the imperial decree abolishing serfdom in Russia was ready for promulgation and its contents were known. Issued on March 3, 1861, the document declared the peasants free and their holdings guaranteed, but it provided at the same time for two more years of *corvée* after which the "temporarily obligated" peasants were to redeem their ownership titles by rent payments or labor. For the time being ownership of the soil remained in the hands of the lords. While individual peasants would eventually have some property rights, the time-honored Russian principle of collective ownership through communes was to be maintained. The implementation of the reform would differ somewhat in the "western guberniias" and in the Białystok district. There the regulation decree of 1846 which recorded peasant obligations to the lords would be the basis for calculating redemption payments; the lord could retain one-third of the cultivated land, provided the peasant plots were not cut by more than one-sixth. Ownership rights would be vested in individual peasants in Lithuania and Belorussia, and in peasant families in the Ukraine.

Even though the decree introduced a radical change in the Russian agrarian structure, it could hardly appeal to the peasants who awaited immediate abolition of *corvée* and hoped for full ownership of their plots. Consequently, a wave of rural unrest swept over Russia. In these circumstances it was particularly important that the Poles in the kingdom propose a comprehensive reform that would not only satisfy the local peasants but also appear attractive to the former Polish eastern lands.

The Agricultural Society had two main questions on its agenda: land reform and the kingdom's autonomy. Zamoyski opposed raising the latter issue on the grounds that it would compromise the society which, strictly speaking, was not entitled to raise political demands. Besides, he felt that the Poles would gain nothing if they *demanded* autonomy, and they ought not to beg the tsar for what was their due. The younger members of the society disagreed. Delegations of students from the "western guberniias" began to arrive in Warsaw to voice demands for Polish rights in these provinces. The society could not ignore what public opinion still regarded as "annexed territories." Nor could the society remain aloof from politics without antagonizing various sectors of Polish society.

The February meeting took place in an atmosphere of excitement. A large manifestation on February 25, commemorating the battle of Grochów, was intended as a means of putting pressure on the society to resolve the peasant question and to demand autonomy. Zamoyski asked for military protection, saying that he could only be held responsible for orderly sessions inside the building, and both the crowds and some of the participants disliked the idea of Russian troops standing between the people and the assembled delegates. After lengthy deliberations the society adopted a resolution favoring a two-stage reform: first, conversion of *corvée* to rents through negotiated contracts; second, an eventual transition to freeholds *(uwłaszczenie)* through redemption of rents by the peasants. It was a compromise and an unhappy one. Although Zamoyski and his supporters believed that the first stage could be accomplished through voluntary contracts, the experience of the last two years had shown that few such contracts had been signed. Nor was it possible to imagine that the peasants could redeem rents without a government subsidy. Hence, the resolution lacked the determination badly needed at this point. Zamoyski and the society had not provided the kind of leadership that was expected of them.

Meanwhile the demonstrators were clashing with the police. A member of the Agricultural Society rushed into a meeting, crying "here we deliberate about manure while our people are being murdered." Black cockades appeared in the streets, and on February 27 Russian troops opened fire on the crowds. Five people were killed, including two bystanders from the Agricultural Society; the town was on the threshold of a revolution. A group of nobles led by Zamoyski and the archbishop, and a city delegation went to protest to Gorchakov. The badly shaken viceroy promised concessions. He was overawed by a united Polish front ranging from Red students and workers to the bourgeoisie, the Catholic, Protestant, and Jewish clergy, and the conservative nobility. Troops withdrew from the streets, and order was maintained by a civic guard controlled by the City Delegation, a new body composed of Warsaw notables in which Kronenberg played a major part.

Under these circumstances Zamoyski could no longer reject the idea of a petition to the tsar. But the text, which followed his notion that the Poles could not demand and must not beg, was vague and open to all kinds of interpretations. It described the unhappy situation of the Poles and listed general grievances, but it was not clear whether the petition referred only to the kingdom or also to the "western guberniias." A much more concrete project of Wielopolski, urging autonomy for the kingdom, was not seriously considered by the Agricultural Society.

The events of February and early March, 1861, constitute a controversial chapter in Polish history. Did the City Delegation and Zamoyski, fearful of a social revolution, prevent by their policies an uprising that might have had greater chances of success than the January Insurrection of 1863? There is no doubt that circumstances favored the Poles at this point. The empire was undermined by peasant resistance to the emancipation decree. Russian forces in the kingdom were fairly weak (around 45,000), and when they were massed near Warsaw unrest spread to the countryside. Not only Polish revolutionaries but the Austrian consul in Warsaw as well believed that a determined revolutionary drive could have expelled the Russian army from the kingdom. But there was really no organized revolutionary force that could have assumed leadership, conquered Warsaw, and emancipated the peasantry. Nor is it certain that a ready-made plan for an insurrection existed. True, the events of February and March had shown the importance of the townspeople of Warsaw, a force to be reckoned with, but it is also clear that the united Polish stand worried Gorchakov more than did the threat of barricades.

The viceroy and his cousin, the chancellor, resisted Alexander's pressure to use reprisals. In their view a contented Poland was needed for a successful implementation of reforms in Russia. A showdown in Warsaw could also interfere with the policy of *rapprochement* with France. Hence, the government sought contact with Zamoyski, the acknowledged spokesman of the Polish upper classes and a popular figure in the country.

Zamoyski, however, could not become a real partner for the Russians. Desiring to accept concessions and avert a revolution, and fearful of being regarded as a collaborationist, he fell back on Rosen's *mot*, "take what they give you and sign no receipt." He believed that Russia would be forced to make concessions in the kingdom and in the "western guberniias," and that Franco-Russian cooperation would assist the recognition of Polish rights. But he had no answer to such questions as: would the Russians be willing to make unilateral concessions, would the Poles take such concessions at face value, and would St. Petersburg tolerate Western interference? Hence, Zamoyski could only support "moral resistance" or a "moral revolution" in the kingdom, try to prevent a real revolution, and sound out discretely the Western powers.

Realizing all this, the Russians turned their attention to Zamoyski's rival, Wielopolski. Negotations with the margrave produced results. Wielopolski knew exactly what he wanted, and having a low opinion of his countrymen, he favored subjecting them to iron discipline and educating them in a spirit of loyal citizenship. The tragedy of Wielopolski, an able lawyer and administrator, lay in the fact that he attached far too much weight to legal and administrative solutions and badly underestimated the national *imponderabilia*. He kept on antagonizing his countrymen and was seemingly blind to the fact that his reforms would have to be backed by the Russian police and army, both of which were an anathema to the Poles.

In the course of negotiations, Wielopolski obtained important concessions from the government. He was allowed to create and chair a Commission (ministry) of Education and Religious Cult and to undertake a basic reform of education which included the organization of a university in Warsaw. In order not to hurt Russian susceptibilities—the Universty of Warsaw had been officially abolished—it was called the Main School (Szkoła Główna). Wielopolski accepted a compromise solution regarding the State Council, which was revived but appointed by the government, and became one of its members. Finally, he obtained the restoration of local self-government and was entrusted with the preparation of reform projects affecting the peasants and the Jews.

Zamoyski and his friends were not opposed to these developments, but they were unwilling to participate. They strongly objected to Wielopolski's condemnation of the "moral revolution" as anarchy and rejected his view that the church hierarchy and the Agricultural Society were undermining the state. When the margrave admonished the clergy that he would not suffer a government within a government and then dissolved the City Delegation and on April 6 the Agricultural Society, the breach between Wielopolski and the Zamoyski camp became final.

The "moral revolution" which was then going on in the country had taken the form of general fraternization within the kingdom and defiance vis-à-vis Russia. Guilds, artisans' associations, and merchants' unions accepted Jews as full-fledged members. A famous Jewish preacher told his coreligionaries that they were all children of the same land although they had looked upon themselves as aliens. Christian-Jewish fraternization corresponded to similar manifestations among social classes. The Hôtel Lambert blessed this movement which would unite all the inhabitants of the kingdom against Russian intrigues. It advised the Poles to maintain pressure on the government to achieve concessions in the "western guberniias" and a satisfactory land reform. A "moral revolution" could easily transform itself into riots, and neither the government nor the Reds were averse to a showdown.

Wielopolski was among the few who truly wished to preserve law and order, and it is ironical that his dissolution of the Agricultural Society and his subsequent introduction of a new procedure for dispersing crowds were responsible for the bloody events on April 8, 1861. On that day huge crowds demonstrating on Warsaw's Castle Square in front of Gorchakov's residence were summoned to disperse, misunderstood the orders, and were then exposed to several salvoes fired by the Russian troops. Unarmed men, women, and children were killed, and although Wielopolski stopped the massacre at the peril of his own life, the event created a chasm between him and the nation. Wielopolski did nothing to conciliate public opinion. He assumed full responsibility for the preservation of law and order and took over the Commission of Justice. To the Reds, Wielopolski was now a traitor worse than the Russian viceroy who died shortly after the massacre of April 8, supposedly from shock.

The temporary successor of Gorchakov tried to bypass Wielopolski and instituted a military regime in the kingdom. If the country was to be governed by bullets the Russians could do it without the margrave. The latter's contribution was the announcement on May 16, 1861, of commutation of compulsory labor—to take place after the harvest—for a heavy ransom (okup). This was a temporary arrangement pending a more comprehensive reform. Most peasants accepted it as a means of ending the hated corvée but not as a real solution since it did not mention freeholds, which Wielopolski was known to oppose.

The new viceroy, Count Charles Lambert, realized Wielopolski's isolation in the kingdom but could not find another man or a group to lean upon. The Zamoyski camp, caught as it was between the Red underground and the brutally behaving Russian army, had little freedom to maneuver. It decided to participate, together with the bourgeois groups, in the elections (to municipalities and local councils) introduced by Wielopolski and attacked by the democrats as being highly unrepresentative. But it could not remain indifferent to the widening conflict between the Poles and the Russian government, which was involving the church and the "western guberniias."

Driven off the streets after the April 8 massacre, supporters of the "moral revolution" took to holding patriotic manifestations in the churches. Various associations ordered special masses to be said; these masses invariably ended with the singing of national hymns. Even non-Catholics participated in this new form of the "moral revolution." The movement spread to Lithuania and Volhynia. In August, 1861, manifestations in Wilno resulted in clashes with the army. In spite of police and Cossack interference, a symbolic meeting of hymn-singing Poles and Lithuanians took place on a bridge across the Niemen River. There was another mass gathering in Horodło, where a Polish-Lithuanian act of union had been signed in 1413. The crowds sang "God protect Poland" in Lithuanian and Belorussian translations. In the autumn of 1861 a state of emergency was introduced in the guberniias of Wilno, Kowno, and Grodno. A huge manifestation in Warsaw accompanied the funeral of Archbishop Fijałkowski; and St. Petersburg urged Lambert to impose martial law on the kingdom.

On October 15, two churches in Warsaw were surrounded by

troops and broken into; thousands of people were arrested and imprisoned in the citadel. Lambert clashed with the commanding general over the unnecessarily brutal fashion in which the orders were carried out. A new Russian commander, General Nikolai Sukhozanet, began to rule by military laws. The administrator of the Warsaw archdiocese, who ordered the closing of all churches in protest against the behavior of the troops, was deported to Russia. Since Protestant churches and Jewish synagogues were also closed in solidarity with the Catholics, the government expelled Rabbi Meisels and severely admonished other ecclesiastical leaders.

Claiming that the worsening of the situation in the kingdom was a result of constant interference by the military, Wielopolski came into conflict with Sukhozanet and tendered his resignation. St. Petersburg ordered the margrave to report to the capital. He was now under a cloud, and the orders provided that he be sent under military escort if he refused to come on his own. With Wielopolski's departure for Russia in December, the year 1861 closed on a note of uncertainty regarding the future. The gulf between Poles and Russians was widening.

III. THE WHITES, THE REDS, AND WIELOPOLSKI

The autumn of 1861 and winter of 1861-62 saw a radicalization of Polish political trends. Although still unable to opt for either collaboration or insurrection, the Whites were forced to depart from a policy of strict legality. In December, partly to counterbalance the Red underground, they founded their own secret organization headed by the Directory. Andrzej Zamoyski's son and two other nobles sat on it together with Kronenberg, Jurgens, and Majewski. The organization relied largely on the younger members of the dissolved Agricultural Society and on the Millennaries. Hoping for reforms, which the "moral revolution" was to accelerate, the Whites tried to restrain revolutionary circles and waited for the results of Wielopolski's stay in St. Petersburg. They remained in contact with other Polish provinces including the "western guberniias."

The Red organization developed from various conspiratorial groups, and in the autumn of 1861 set up a central organ known as the City Committee (Komitet Miejski) or Committee of Action (Komitet Ruchu). Among its founders were such people as Apollo Korzeniowski (1820-69), the father of Joseph Conrad, and the advocate of revolutionary terror Ignacy Chmieleński (1837-70). On lower echelons the lines separating the Whites from the Reds were often blurred, and even on a higher level Majewski cooperated with the Reds—to create a united Polish front, according to some historians, to dull the revolutionary ardor of the Reds, according to others. Adherents of Mierosławski promoted their own aims within the Red organization. There were contacts between the Reds and Russian officers and soldiers stationed in the kingdom who were influenced by Herzen's writings and the nascent underground group Zemlia i volia. A little later a secret officers' circle came into existence. Even part of the clergy was influenced by Red propaganda. The country as a whole was coming closer to a revolutionary situation.

Wielopolski remained in St. Petersburg for several months. He impressed the Russian court with his air of a *grand seigneur* and his conservative views on the agrarian question. The liberals liked his other reform projects, and the diplomatic corps on the whole lent him discreet support. The tsar hesitated. He did not trust the Poles and told Bismarck that all of them strove to recreate a pre-partition Poland. But he also felt that prudence might dictate a conciliatory policy. His final decision came suddenly in May, 1862. He named his brother Constantine the viceroy of Poland and Wielopolski the head of the civilian administration, *de facto* prime minister. He instructed his brother, who had the reputation of being a Slavophile and an opponent of Austria, to stabilize the Polish situation and to secure the loyalty of the kingdom, which was important as a link with the rest of Europe. The tsar expressed his conviction that extreme Polish patriots would never be satisfied even with maximum Russian concessions. A restoration of the kingdom's constitution and its former army was out of the question; far-reaching concessions could only endanger Russian rule in the "western guberniias." Alexander II cautioned Constantine against succumbing to the forceful personality of Wielopolski, whose iron will and determination the tsar correctly appraised.

Wielopolski secured the tsar's approval for a separate Polish administration, the Main School (with departments of history and philosophy, law, natural sciences, and medicine), equality for the Jews, and a land reform which was officially announced in June. Opposed by liberal Russian reformers as being too conservative, the land reform provided for compulsory rents (somewhat more advantageous than the ransom) and only vaguely mentioned future conversion to freeholds *(uwłaszczenie)*. Thus it fell short even of the proposals of the Agricultural Society and could not satisfy the peasants. The conflict with the church was to be settled through the appointment of an ultramontane priest, Zygmunt Szczęsny Feliński (1822–95), to the archbishopric of Warsaw.

St. Petersburg may have viewed the agreement with Wielopolski as a means of splitting the Polish front, gaining the conservative upper classes, and using the margrave himself as an instrument of Russian policy. Wielopolski saw matters in a different light. He felt that he was bringing far-reaching concessions which satisfied legitimate—in his view—Polish demands. A born autocrat, he told some of the Whites, who were willing to assist him in the implementation of the reforms, that while one could do something *for* the Poles one could do nothing *with* the Poles. When he ordered a public hanging of the youthful Red terrorists, he quickly lost the sympathy gained after unsuccessful attempts on his and Constantine's life. His actions played into the hands of the Reds who now had martyrs of their own cause. Wielopolski moved in a political void, and the Grand Duke Constantine decided to talk to the White leaders. As a Russian general told the new archbishop, the Russians worried more about the rich and influential Whites than about the revolutionary Reds.

A conversation between Constantine and Zamoyski proved a total failure. The incensed viceroy described Zamoyski as "a madman, a dreamer, a utopian."[1] Believing that he had to express the feelings of the nation, Zamoyski spoke of a constitution and an army, and he even mentioned the former Polish eastern lands. He refused to collaborate with the government unless these grievances were satisfied. Did Zamoyski take this stand because he wished to retain influence in the country and prevent a revolution, or because he felt that only a constitutional government, backed by a Polish army, could prevent a provocation on the part of the Russian government? Undoubtedly the fear of being branded a Russian collaborator haunted Zamoyski and the other Polish magnates who wished to make it clear that they would never voluntarily endorse Poland's partitions.

The rejection of an offer to collaborate was a turning point in the history of the Whites. They had entered a road that would ultimately lead them to participation in the January Insurrection. Zamoyski himself was called to St. Petersburg; after an audience with the tsar, he was given a passport and ordered to leave the country. While continuing to work in the elected local administration, the Whites moved closer to the Reds. A good part of the gentry subordinated itself to the newly organized National Central Committee, and from November, 1862, began to pay the secretly collected national tax designed to finance the insurrection. The same was true for the lower clergy including the Uniates of Chełm province.

In the course of 1862 the Red organization underwent a transformation, coordinated its activities, and extended them beyond the borders of Congress Poland. In the spring of 1862 Captain Dąbrowski came to Warsaw where he took over the city organization, became the head of the officers' conspiracy, as well as the chief liaison man between the Reds and the Russian revolutionaries in the army. He

---

1. Cited in Stefan Kieniewicz, *Między ugodą a rewolucją: Andrzej Zamoyski w latach 1861–1862* (Warszawa: Państwowe Wydawnictwo Naukowe, 1962), p. 256n.

advocated the bold plan of a surprise attack on the Novogeorgevsk (Modlin) fortress which would provide the insurrection with arms and munitions.

In the late spring of 1862 the City or Action Committee became transformed into the above-mentioned National Central Committee (KCN) which presented itself to the Poles in a proclamation of September 1, as a *de facto* national government. Between the summer of 1862 and January, 1863, the membership of the central committee changed several times, and the committee went through heated debates regarding the forthcoming revolution. It formulated its program of peasant emancipation, established command over an organization comprising some twenty thousand members, created an underground state apparatus, and introduced taxes. Among its more outstanding figures were: such radicals as the engineer Bronisław Szwarce (1834-1904) and Dąbrowski, both of whom were arrested in 1862, and Captain Zygmunt Padlewski (1835-63); and the more equivocal Oskar Awejde (1837-97) and Giller who gravitated to the Whites. Obliged to preserve the anonymity of its members, the central committee was only known by its seal, which appeared on proclamations and commanded the recognition and respect of the Poles.

The supporters of an insurrection envisaged for the spring of 1863, especially Szwarce and Padlewski, argued that revolution was unavoidable for social and national reasons. Poland's fate was bound with that of the masses, i.e., the peasantry which had to be completely emancipated and made into full-fledged citizens. The experiments of Wielopolski and of the tsarist government were bound to perpetuate a division between Poles into two potentially inimical camps. An agrarian revolution and a national insurrection were thus inseparable. Both were necessary to lay foundations for the future greatness of the nation.

A major weakness on the part of the central committee was the absence, especially after the rejection of Dąbrowski's and then Padlewski's proposals, of concrete military plans. The committee sought allies among the Russian revolutionaries, and an agreement was reached with Herzen and the Kolokol group in London and with representatives of Zemlia i volia. Naturally, there were difficulties about the future of the Lithuanian and Ukrainian lands, and Padlewski accepted the principle of national self-determination for the borderlands. This elicited an outburst from Mierosławski against Poles who were abandoning their historical patrimony. But Russian assistance could not be very effective, given the weakness of Zemlia i volia. The Russian military conspiracy, which had shown some strength in the spring of 1862, was badly hurt by arrests and changes of garrison units. In December, 1862, envoys of the central committee—sent to

France to buy arms and munitions—fell into the hands of the French police. As a result their mission was wrecked, and the Russians learned via Paris about the extent of the conspiracy in their own army. The contacts of the Reds with Italian and Hungarian exile leaders raised hopes for a coordinated revolutionary action, but could not bring an assurance of a major diversion that would hurt Russia. Thus, prospects for a successful insurrection were not bright. Furthermore, the central committee was denied the chance to choose a propitious moment for its outbreak by the actions of Wielopolski.

During the summer and autumn of 1862 the margrave carried out his reforms. He polonized the administration, to the annoyance of the Russians, and tried to show that he was the real master of the country. His regime clearly favored the propertied classes and held no prospects of constitutional liberties, not to speak of national independence. Attempting to preserve order, Archbishop Feliński forbade the holding of patriotic masses in the churches; this created a good deal of dissatisfaction. Obviously, the chief obstacle to Wielopolski's policies was the Red underground, and as the conservative Polish historian Bobrzyński rightly observed, the margrave, instead of "curbing it, decided to break it." The method he chose was particularly objectionable. After an interval of several years, the government again introduced a military conscription in the kingdom. Some twenty thousand people were to be included in the draft, and out of this figure twelve thousand were to be drawn by lot for actual service. Wielopolski decided to use the draft to smash the Red organization. He replaced the lottery with a system of lists from which landowners, colonists, and farm laborers were excluded. The youth of Warsaw, which constituted the kernel of the Red organization, was to become the main object of the draft, and as Wielopolski put it to the grand duke, who opposed the scheme, the conscription would amount to proscription.

The National Central Committee had to take up the challenge and oppose the draft. A leaflet bearing the committee's seal (apparently without authorization) declared that the conscription would be resisted by force. The members of the committee were fully aware of the dangers involved in beginning an insurrection in the midst of winter—the draft was to take effect in early January. Means for starting an action in Warsaw were lacking, hence fighting was to begin in the countryside. Hardly anyone or anything was ready for it. Giller, supported by several members of the committee, urged delays, but Padlewski argued for immediate action and he had the backing of several provincial commissars who threatened to disobey the committee if it failed to take a determined stand. Giller resigned, and Stefan Bobrowski (1841-63), a student active in the Ukraine who had just arrived in Warsaw, joined the committee. A dynamic and forceful personality, he strongly supported his friend Padlewski and succeeded in swaying the other members. Hasty preparations began to be made to evacuate the youth threatened with the military conscription.

IV. THE JANUARY INSURRECTION OF 1863

On January 16 the committee took the final decision to begin an insurrection on January 22 and issue a manifesto calling to arms the nations of Poland, Lithuania, and Ruś (Ukraine). The document also called on the Russians not to support the oppressors and threatened them, if they did, with a life and death struggle between European civilization and the savage barbarism of Asia. The last phrase was not well chosen; nevertheless, an appeal of Zemlia i volia of March, 1863, repeated it. The manifesto signed by the committee, acting as a Provisional National Government, announced freedom and equality to all citizens irrespective of religion and descent. It declared peasants full owners of the land they cultivated, and promised plots (from estates of the crown) to landless peasants who joined the insurrection. Landlords were to be eventually indemnified from state funds. A separate decree on peasant emancipation (in the form of *uwłaszczenie*) including "servitude" rights was issued on January 22, and insurrectionist leaders and priests were ordered to read it to the peasantry. Among several other manifestoes and appeals issued by the National Government were two proclamations, one calling on Ruthenians and one on the Jews, to participate in the insurrection. The former document promised full emancipation and land to the peasants. The latter was addressed to "Brethren Poles of Mosaic Faith" and emphasized that a separate appeal was not meant to point to any differences between Jews and other Poles but on the contrary to stress brotherly love for them.

Thousands of people responded to the orders of the anonymous National Government. Since none of the major district commanders was yet at his post, some five to six thousand badly armed insurgents struck in improvised actions against the hundred-thousand-strong Russian army. Eighteen garrisons were attacked, and some thirty-odd skirmishes were fought but no larger town captured. Still, the insurgents forced Russian troops to evacuate three-fourths of the localities they had occupied. This gave the Poles a breathing period of ten days to consolidate their operations. The authorities were clearly taken by surprise; there were no traitors on the side of the revolutionaries. The insurrection, however, had no chance to transform itself into regular warfare. There was no coordinated strategy and no supreme command. On the eve of the outbreak the majority of the National Central Committee had invited Mierosławski to assume military command and the dictatorship, but the luckless general lost a skirmish at the Prusso-Polish border and did not succeed in entering the kingdom. His subsequent attempts to claim the dictatorship proved fruitless, and his role became marginal. By not launching any attacks in Warsaw, which could have immobilized large Russian forces, the insurgents may have committed a serious error. On the political side, the National Government could not openly establish itself because the town of Płock, which it had foreseen as its capital, had not been captured. After leaving Warsaw the government had to wander around the country, unable to assume effective control. Bobrowski as the underground commander in Warsaw acted as the government, and the boundless energy and determination of this youthful leader kept the struggle going.

During March and April the insurrection entered a crucial stage. On the international scene, France, Britain, and Austria made their first *démarche*, and largely to counter it, St. Petersburg offered an amnesty to the insurgents provided they laid down arms. The Whites joined the insurrection and succeeded in asserting their leadership. In late April the insurrection reached beyond the limits of the Congress Kingdom, and it also gained participants from Austrian and Prussian Poland. The originally lukewarm attitude of the peasantry underwent some changes in favor of the revolutionary movement. Finally, by late spring the first heroic phase of the struggle came to its end; many of the original units and their commanders met with death on the battlefield, on gallows, or before firing squads.

The initial reaction of France, England, and Austria to the insurrection was one of embarrassment. Complications arose when Bismarck, desirous of a *rapprochement* with Russia and wishing to drive a wedge between the latter and France, signed the so-called Alvensleben Convention with St. Petersburg. Providing for cooperation against the insurgents, the convention remained largely a dead letter, but it internationalized the Polish question and created a tense diplomatic situation. Napoleon III wanted to escalate the Polish crisis but was unwilling to risk a war against Russia and Prussia without the support of England and Austria. London was glad to see Paris and St. Petersburg drift apart but did not wish to upset the balance of powers. Vienna was not averse to applying pressure on Russia but was not inclined to risk an open conflict. The first result of these hesitant and complex policies was a tripartite diplomatic intervention of the powers in St. Petersburg protesting violations of the Vienna settlement of 1815.

The intervention of April 17 encouraged the Poles. French ministers talking to the Hôtel Lambert representatives had used the word *durez* (keep going). But it would be an oversimplification to say that the prospect of assistance from the great powers was the sole reason for the decision of the Whites to join the insurrection. At first the Whites had opposed what appeared to them a hopeless and anarchic movement, but this attitude could not last. Many of the Whites had been paying the national tax and were involved in preparing an insurrection in Lithuania. Some of the younger and more ardent members had already been drawn into the fighting. The White leadership was seeking a pretext to justify their participation; they were also searching for means of influencing the course of the insurrection. They found the former in the diplomatic action of the powers; they sought to achieve the latter in a series of moves in March and April. In cooperation with some members of the National Government, the Whites arranged for the proclamation, on March 10, of the dictatorship of Marian Langiewicz (1827-87), a successful guerilla leader. His nine-day dictatorship was an episode, but the whole intrigue enmeshed Bobrowski who perished in a duel with a White sympathizer and political adventurer. The insurrection was deprived of one of its most dynamic and devoted leaders.

Having dissolved their Directory, the Whites formally ceased to be a separate party, but they gained great influence over the insurrection by contributing to it their financial resources and political experience. At first artisans, workers, students, intelligentsia, and gentry had filled the insurgents' ranks, but now the upper classes, especially the landowners, came to the fore. The Provisional Government resumed its powers on March 21—following the end of Langiewicz's dictatorship—and a little later dropped the word "provisional." Dominated by the Whites it fell twice, as a result of internal coups, into the hands of the Reds—once toward the end of May and once in September. The Reds tried to further the insurrection by more radical means: increased use of revolutionary tribunals, terror, and attempts at mobilization of the peasantry.

In the summer of 1863 the civilian side of the insurrection, which had been well prepared by Bobrowski, reached its peak of efficiency. The National Government headed a veritable underground state and could use, through its trusted men, the railroads and postal communications. Finances were in good shape, especially after an internal loan was launched to which the Zamoyskis and Kronenberg contributed huge sums. A special police force controlled by the Reds enforced the decrees of the government, although some of the acts of these "stiletto men" have been differently appraised by historians. The anonymous National Government operating from a Warsaw filled with Russian troops and police was really the master of life and death of the kingdom's inhabitants. As General Fedor Berg, whom the viceroy ordered to investigate the degree of penetration of the insurrectionist networks, put it: "I have come to one conclusion, namely, that I don't belong to it." And he added as an afterthought, "nor does Your Imperial Highness."[2]

The military side of the insurrection, prepared and conducted as it was by revolutionaries rather than professional soldiers, suffered from many weaknesses. Lacking proper training of military cadres, the insurgent soldiers had to learn their trade on the battlefields. By late spring, partisan troops fought with greater experience and better equipment—although many of the arms bought by the National Government failed to reach the fighting units—but without the initial élan which had cost the life of many a leader and a soldier. Their actions were still largely uncoordinated. They harassed the enemy, fought hit-and-run engagements, and kept the Russian army off balance.

The National Government was committed to spreading the insurrection to Lithuania, Belorussia, and the Ukraine, but the character of the insurrection in the former eastern borderlands differed from that in the kingdom. In turn, the brief struggle in the Ukraine differed from the prolonged and bitter fighting in Lithuania. In the Ukraine, youthful revolutionary democrats armed with an emancipation manifesto written in Ukrainian—the "Golden Letter"—were massacred by the peasantry. Class, religious, and national antagonism made the Ukrainian masses suspicious of a Polish "gentry rebellion." A short guerilla campaign ended with a catastrophe; the Russian government imposed a huge contribution of five million rubles on the Polish propertied classes.

In Lithuania and Belorussia numerous poor gentry villages proved fertile ground for revolutionary propaganda, and the insurgents succeeded in making contact with the peasantry. The White leader Jakub Gieysztor (1827–97) proclaimed insurrection on April 30, but already the Red organization led by Konstanty Kalinowski (1838–64) had scored successes with its radical social policy and a successful identification with the Lithuanian-Belorussian peasantry. Although an ethnic Pole and a nobleman, Kalinowski, who had propagandized the peasantry with his paper called *Mužyckaia Prauda* (Peasants' Truth), was destined to become a Belorussian national and populist hero. In spite of differences between the Reds and the Whites, insurrection in Lithuania gained a wide social basis. Sierakowski was particularly successful in attracting peasants to his units, and so was Father Antoni Mackiewicz (1826–63), whose detachment struggled in Samogitia. In May and June the fighting in Lithuania reached its

2. Cited in Walentyna Rudzka, "Studies on the Polish Insurrectionary Government in 1863–64," *Antemurale*, 7-8 (1963):429.

peak, and Herzen admitted that Lithuania had declared herself for Poland. Harsh Russian reprisals and the death of many a leader— Kalinowski was hanged in Feburary, 1864—gradually destroyed the insurrection. The last action of a partisan detachment took place as late as October, 1864, but the general movement had collapsed much earlier.

The geographic spread of the January Insurrection was wide. Paris had hinted that the blood of the insurgents would mark the boundaries of future Poland, and indeed insurgents' blood was spilled from the Ukraine, through Belorussia up to the prepartition province of Legalia (in modern Latvia). The insurrection received assistance from Prussian Poland and from Galicia in the form of financial aid and participation of entire volunteer units. Those from Poznania fought well. Galician detachments found it more difficult to adjust to guerrilla fighting and either suffered very heavy casualties—for instance, the loss of an elite troop comprising many young nobles— or hastily retreated, abandoning valuable modern equipment to the Russians. Branches of the National Government existed in both Galicia and Poznania, although there was friction between the local Reds and Whites, the latter being more influential in both provinces.

In mid-May, 1863, "citizen" Czartoryski (Prince Adam's son Władysław, 1828-94) was recognized by the National Government as the Polish diplomatic representative abroad, but the Reds and the Whites differed in their approaches to diplomacy. The former placed their hopes on cooperation with revolutionaries, and, in fact, Herzen, Bakunin, Marx, Engels, Garibaldi, and others declared themselves unreservedly in favor of the insurrection. Many foreign volunteers, including Frenchmen, Italians, Czechs, and Germans, fought and died in the insurgent ranks; the Russian contingent was the largest. But if Russian radicals stood by the Poles, Russian liberals turned against them. A wave of nationalist reaction swept Russia; the Poles were accused of fomenting a Western plot against the tsarist empire. It is doubtful that Russia was ever in real danger of a military intervention by the great powers. A major, six-point démarche made on June 17, 1863, by France, Austria, and England fell short of the insurgents' aims. Russia rejected it, claiming that limited concessions had already been given through Wielopolski but had failed to satisfy the Poles. Vienna and London did not back Napoleon's suggestion for an international conference; Russia had a relatively free hand to deal with the insurrection.

In the summer of 1863 the rule of Constantine and Wielopolski came formally to an end, and both men left Congress Poland. In fact, even before their departure General Fedor Berg had ruled the kingdom as an occupied country, and his regime resembled that of

Lithuania's governor general, Mikhail Muraview, the "hangman." In the autumn, the Reds seized power, having blamed the National Government for reducing the insurrection to an armed demonstration calculated to attract the great powers' intervention. Their regime was short-lived. Intensified terror, including an unsuccessful attempt on Berg's life, provoked harsh retaliations and all but destroyed the Warsaw organization. Red leaders had to leave the capital, and in October Romuald Traugutt (1826-64) took over the National Government as a virtual dictator.

A former tsarist army colonel and a native of the Polish eastern borderlands, Traugutt was closer in outlook to the Whites but he executed an essentially Red policy. A deeply religious man and a pragmatist rather than a doctrinaire, he was more interested in the goal of national independence than in a social revolution. An excellent organizer, he strove to rebuild the shattered forces of the insurrection. He considered, however, that to prolong resistance merely in the hope of foreign intervention was an insufficient reason and indeed demoralized the soldiers. But he did not ignore diplomacy altogether. Until April, 1864, when he was arrested, Traugutt reorganized partisan units into lārger formations, insisted on discipline and cohesion, and put stress on peasant participation. Able commanders appeared in the field, for example, another former tsarist colonel, Józef Hauke "Bosak" (1843-71); they breathed new life into the movement.

Although Berg announced that the campaign in Poland was completed in May, 1864, the real end came with Traugutt's execution in the autumn. Still, sporadic fighting continued even beyond that date, one of the last skirmishes being fought by a peasant detachment in Podlachia.

It was symbolic of the importance of the peasant issue in the January Insurrection that the insurrection had begun with the emancipation decree and ended with Polish peasants fighting the last battle. The National Government offered the peasants more than they received through any of the reforms of the partitioning powers. Still, at first the peasantry was lukewarm and in some cases collaborated with the Russian authorities. By April, 1863, the situation began to change. The peasants refused to pay their rent installments. They saw that several of the partisan commanders were punishing landlords who refused to accept the emancipation decree, and they adopted a friendlier attitude toward the insurrection. While evidence of peasant behavior is sometimes contradictory, more peasants took part in fighting than in any previous uprising including the Kościuszko Insurrection. Soon after the insurrection began the Russian authorities in the "western guberniias" decided to offset its appeal by offering concessions to the local peasantry. A decree of March 1/13, 1863, granted full ownership rights and other privileges to Lithuanian peasants. These benefits were extended to the Ukrainian and Belorussian provinces during the summer and the autumn. In the kingdom itself the viceroy and Wielopolski were at first unwilling to alienate the landowners by encouraging the peasants against the gentry. During the summer of 1863 St. Petersburg hesitated, but by early autumn Alexander II decided that it was necessary to rely on the peasantry, all other means having failed. The chief author of the Russian land reform, Nikolai Miliutin, was entrusted with elaborating recommendations. The outcome of his work was the emancipation decree of February 19/March 2, 1864, but its scope, character, and impact on Congress Poland will be discussed in a subsequent chapter.

What was the balance sheet of the January Insurrection? Polish losses were undoubtedly great. Although the total number of casualties on the battlefield was lower than in 1830-31, the consequences of the uprising affected directly or indirectly a much vaster group of people. The insurrection contributed to a profound socioeconomic transformation of the kingdom; it hastened the parting of the ways between ethnically Polish territories and the former eastern lands of the commonwealth. Russian retribution, which posed a threat to the survival of the nation, made many contemporaries and historians consider the insurrection a folly for which the nation had to pay an exorbitant price. These critics argued that had the Wielopolski experiment received backing from the Poles this tragedy could have been avoided.

Wielopolski's reforms undoubtedly had their merits. They would have raised the cultural and educational levels of the country and given the Poles a chance to gain experience in the political-administrative field. They could have brought greater respect for law and order and perhaps could have assisted the Prussian Poles, because Berlin could not easily afford to see Russia become a potential center of attraction for the Polish nation. But there were clear limits to what Wielopolski could have accomplished under the best of circumstances. Satisfying some Polish aspirations, his reforms would have encouraged the Poles, particularly the upper strata, to become more dependent on Russia. National strivings for self-assertion would have receded into the background; independent Polish political thought would have stagnated. The price to be paid for Wielopolski's achievements also included a postponement of a real solution of the peasant question, a deepening of antagonism between the propertied classes and the masses, and a delay in socioeconomic modernization of the country.

The insurrection could never have assumed such wide proportions and lasted so long if the orders of a few men, acting behind the anonymous National Government, had not corresponded to the real sentiments of the Poles. While, at any given moment, there were never more than twenty or thirty thousand insurgents in the field, about two hundred thousand had voluntarily taken part in the insurrection—a very large number for a population of over four million people. Although they were divided on political strategy and tactics, and although they subscribed to differing ideologies, most Poles strove for the independence of their country. The limited concessions offered by the Russians could not satisfy this goal. Finally, one must not forget that every revolution contains an element of irrationality, and the January Insurrection was no exception. Its participants did not cooly weigh and calculate their chances. Neither the Reds nor the Whites were entirely free agents, and both were often driven by forces largely outside their control.

In spite of the terrible consequences, the insurrection played a crucial role in the emancipation of the peasantry, and it marked another stage in the decline of the landed aristocracy as the leading factor in the nation. It accelerated the evolution of the country toward a modern society and reinforced national bonds among the Poles. Controversy about the insurrection is far from dead, and each generation of Polish historians adds its own interpretation. But there is no disagreement on the important place it occupied in nineteenth-century Polish history; it was a virtual watershed separating the past from the contemporary stage.

# CHAPTER 9

# The Era of Romanticism

THE Age of Romanticism began in Poland before the November Insurrection of 1830 and reached its zenith in the Great Emigration. The fact that the leadership of Polish intellectual life was in the hands of an élite that lived abroad gave Polish romanticism its specific characteristics. There was no preventive censorship in France, and émigré writers could create freely. Although literary, artistic, philosophical, and scholarly life in Paris—the main émigré center—affected the exiles, yet they lived a life of their own, creating in Polish for Poland. In a sense the emigration was isolated both from the milieu in which it operated and from home. Not unnaturally, this was bound to create special problems that a cultural élite active in its own country would not have encountered.

The intellectual émigrés looked upon themselves as the leaders of a nation deprived of its freedom of expression and fettered in its cultural development. Theirs was a mission to continue the struggle that began on that November night in Warsaw, but through other means: pen replaced the broken sword; artists took the place of generals and politicians. It was up to the emigration to cultivate and to broaden national values and to show the way not only to contemporaries but to future generations. Under these conditions art for art's sake was almost meaningless, and already Mickiewicz's *Konrad Wallenrod* indicated that the arts had to be attached to the national chariot. The artist's mission was to give spiritual leadership to the nation, and, to paraphrase the words of one of the greatest émigré poets, the emigration made of Poland's name a prayer addressed to God and a lightning piercing the darkness of oppression and injustice.

Romantic literature elevated sacrifice and sorrow to sublime heights. Poland was compared to the Christ among nations, redeeming through suffering not only the Polish nation but mankind. Poland had a sacred mission to fulfill: to break the chains of absolutism and bring about universal freedom. This belief in large part explains the close ties between Polish romanticism and a liberal, revolutionary outlook; it also does much to explain the weakness of Polish romantic conservatism. In the writings of the romanticists, the November Insurrection became more of a heroic epic than it ever was, and this glorified vision of struggle against tremendous odds deeply affected the Polish *Weltanschauung*. The romantic heritage became an insoluble part of Poland's national inheritance, which although negated and contested many a time never completely disappeared. It shaped the outlook of the 1863 insurgents and was visible in the national and social struggles of the early twentieth century.

The literary and artistic harvest of Polish romanticism was rich and diversified. An accumulation of talent made this period one of the most important in Polish cultural history. Profound divergences among the leading figures explain why certain writers and their works were appreciated at different times and invoked by different groups.

Except for the towering figure of Chopin in music, the greatest contribution of Polish romanticism was in the field of literature, mainly poetry. Mickiewicz was the recognized "national bard" *(wieszcz)*, although he stopped writing before 1840. His *Books of the Polish Nation and the Polish Pilgrims (Księgi Narodu i Pielgrzymstwa)* written in 1832 presented his mystical philosophy of the Polish nation. Poland had sacrificed herself for others, and she was partitioned because she had not followed policies of violence and balance of power; but Poland would eventually resuscitate. The émigrés as pilgrims had to contribute to this resurrection by perfecting themselves and the society. Mickiewicz saw the way to national rebirth and independence through moral regeneration, and his beliefs, as well as those of several other romantic exiles, were later on affected by a mystic from Lithuania, Andrzej Towiański (1799-1878). Towiański saw himself as the prophet of a new era of Christendom, an era divorced from the established church, an era in which politics, thanks to the chosen nations (French, Polish, and Jewish), could become truly Christian. At one point Towiański planned an attempt to "convert" the tsar.

Mickiewicz produced his two principal masterpieces in the early 1830s: the third part of *The Forefathers' Eve (Dziady)* and *Pan Tadeusz*. The former, which was intended for the theater but was never staged during the poet's lifetime, centered on the Russian persecutions at Wilno university in 1823-24, and depicted life in Poland under Grand Duke Constantine. Fragmentary, powerful in parts, and very bold in its technical innovations, the drama influenced several generations of Poles. *Pan Tadeusz*, perhaps the best known and beloved of Mickiewicz's works, was a national epos, with lyric and mock-heroic notes. It was an expression of the émigré's nostalgia for his fatherland, the lost paradise of childhood, as well as a vast and realistic panorama of a world that no longer existed—the rural Lithuania of 1812. The numerous themes of love, hate, and national feelings, all blend in a harmonious whole. With its highly lyrical descriptions of nature and its majestic yet simple style, *Pan Tadeusz* ranks as one of the masterpieces of Polish, indeed Slav, romantic poetry.

More than other leading émigré poets, Mickiewicz was deeply involved in politics. One has to mention his tenure at the Collège de France, and especially the years 1848-49 when he strove to organize a Polish legion in Italy and edited *La Tribune des Peuples* in Paris. His influence and contacts went far beyond the Polish milieu, as witnessed by his relations with Mazzini, Lamennais, and Michelet, among others. He died in 1855, in the midst of the Crimean War, attempting to create a Polish legion against Russia.

Mickiewicz's great rival was Juliusz Słowacki (1809-49), although no contemporaries and not all literary critics considered him his equal. Słowacki appeared as a telling contrast both as an individual and as a poet. Born in an intellectual family, frail—he died prematurely of tuberculosis—Słowacki looked like a figure drawn in pastel colors, unlike the virile and full-blooded Mickiewicz. Yet this contrast was only partly true. Although his lyrical poetry, of which he was a master, and the refined beauty of his language made Słowacki seem an artist who was writing for art's sake, his power of expression and his political passions were not inferior to Mickiewicz's. His epic talents and his vision of the theater put Słowacki among the precursors and masters of modern Polish drama.

Słowacki's philosophy of life and history, which permeated his writings, was difficult to grasp and in a sense ahead of his time. It appealed more to subsequent generations than to the Paris émigrés and led to a veritable cult of Słowacki during the symbolist period of the early twentieth century. His concept of a spirit wandering through centuries and becoming incarnated in leading individuals and nations drew on the idea of reincarnation and the notion of perfection through evolution. It was strongly expressed in Słowacki's gigantic and unfinished epic *The King Spirit (Król Duch)*. Several of Słowacki's works in a way paralleled Mickiewicz's masterpieces. The beautifully cadenced poem in prose *Anhelli* (1838), directed to the emigration, presented a vision comparable to the *Books of the Polish Nation. Kordian*, a national drama centered on the alleged coronation plot against Nicholas I, was Słowacki's counterpart of *Forefathers' Eve*. His great work *Beniowski*, a digressive poem not unlike Byron's *Don Juan*, which gained Słowacki great fame, was an attempt to rival *Pan Tadeusz*. Although vastly different in style and conception, *Beniowski* was also a true portrayal of his historic setting. Though it never achieved the popularity of *Pan Tadeusz*, it ranked as one of the great achievements of Polish romanticism.

As a political radical, Słowacki saw Poland's rebirth and salvation in the people *(lud)*. Bitter in his criticism of the past, he once called his Fatherland a "peacock" and a "parrot of other nations." As he himself expressed it, he was saying those harsh things because "he was sad and full of guilt." Słowacki's impact on Polish literature and outlook was comparable to that of Mickiewicz. As a homage to the two great poets, their remains were eventually brought to Poland and buried in a chapel of the royal castle in Cracow.

Zygmunt Krasiński (1812–59) was sometimes called the third national bard, although he was hardly the equal of Mickiewicz and Słowacki. Krasiński was the scion of an old aristocratic family; although he lived abroad he was not strictly speaking a political émigré. His long-range influence, while important, was never as profound as that of his two great contemporaries. Apart from many poems in which he expressed his creed—messianic but anti-Towiań-ski—Krasiński's fame rested mainly on two dramas: the *Un-divine Comedy (Nieboska Komedia)* and *Irydion*. Both works addressed themselves to the problem of social revolution, a subject which haunted Krasiński. The *Un-divine Comedy* dealt with a forthcoming revolution that would destroy the existing order. Its main characters had symbolic dimensions, and their psychological motivation was presented in almost dialectical terms. The historical drama *Irydion* was set against the background of the decaying Roman Empire. The revolution of the oppressed failed largely because of the refusal of the Christians to use violent means. Krasiński's conservative and Christian philosophy made him reject violence—social violence—as a means of achieving national goals. Poland as the Christ of Nations had to keep her "unsullied garment."

In the *Psalms of the Future (Psalmy Przyszłości)*, Krasiński opposed the radicals' plans of a national and social revolution and called on them to throw away the robbers' knives *(hajdamackie rzućcie noże)*. His poems led to the literary duel mentioned briefly earlier with Słowacki who rebuked Krasiński for his fears of "your father" the people. After the Galician *jacquerie* of 1846, Krasiński penned a bitter reply in another well-known poem.

Preoccupied with Poland's past, present, and future, each of the great poets had his own vision and tried to show his own path leading toward national salvation. Mickiewicz saw it chiefly in moral perfection. Słowacki sought to overcome the noble-dominated past and placed the people *(lud)* on a pedestal. Krasiński strove to win the people over to the traditional values of the Christian and noble Polish culture. Creating in an intellectually active and stimulating environment, the three bards were surrounded by other poets and writers; here only one name will be mentioned, that of Cyprian Kamil Norwid (1821–83). A latecomer to the emigration, Norwid had a highly original and powerful talent. His reflective poetry was written in a purposefully complex and difficult language. His pragmatical *Promethidion* (1851) expressed the idea that the source of art was not inspiration but work conquered through love. His main achievement was a cycle of lyrical and reflective poems, *Vade mecum*. Norwid's novel views of art, philosophy, and history found little understanding at the time, and he exercised no influence on his contemporaries. He was to be "discovered" in the twentieth century as a great literary figure and a forerunner of modern literary trends.

During the first two decades after the November Insurrection, the leadership of the emigration in letters as well as in politics was undisputed. This stemmed from the accumulation of talent abroad and from the impediments to a normal cultural development in the homeland. Russian reprisals after 1831 included the sequestration of Czartoryski's Puławy, mass confiscation of libraries and museums, the closing of the University of Warsaw, the Society of Friends of Learning, and of the Krzemieniec lycée. Although Raczyński and Działyński were still active in Poznania, the magnate protectorate of culture came to a virtual end. Intellectual and cultural activities concentrated in the big cities. Due to relaxation of censorship, Posen in the mid-1840s and Cracow and Lemberg in 1848 went through periods of intense intellectual activity.

Higher learning was in decline. Both the germanized University of Lemberg and the University of Cracow vegetated. The latter became inaccessible to Poles from other parts of the country after 1830 and was germanized between 1847 and 1860. In 1848 the university building and the library of Lemberg were burnt. As substitutes for higher learning there remained privately organized courses in Posen, and the School of Fine Arts, the Agricultural Institute, and some law and medicine courses in Warsaw. The library and collections of the Krzemieniec lycée were transferred to Kiev to become the foundation of the new Russian St. Vladimir University, established in 1834. In these conditions learned societies acquired a special importance. The emigration led the way with its Society of Friends of Learning, the Historical-Literary Society, and the Bibliothèque Polonaise—the last two surviving until today. The closing of the Warsaw Society of Friends of Learning, after more than twenty-five years of active existence, was only in part balanced by the creation of similar societies in Posen and Cracow (1850).

Still, Polish scholarship continued to survive. In historiography the primacy of Lelewel, working in solitude in Brussels, was recognized nationally as well as internationally. His contributions to historical geography and numismatics were of greatest importance. His interpretation of Polish history as a struggle between Slav, democratic, and republican forces on the one hand, and monarchy, church, and feudalism on the other, was not seriously challenged prior to the 1860s. Lelewel's tradition was continued at home by Karol Szajnocha (1818-68). The first significant collections of primary sources appeared, and attention began to be paid to auxiliary historical sciences. From the emigration came the first, and important, history of the November Insurrection, written by Mochnacki.

In philosophy the Polish messianic school, using Hegelian methods, formulated a personalist, theistic, and spiritualistic concept that strongly relied on will and emphasized national and social elements. August Cieszkowski (1814-94), Bronisław Trentowski (1808-69), and Józef Maria Hoene-Wroński (1776-1853) were the most representative and original thinkers. In economics Józef Supiński (1804-93), whose *Polish School of Social Economy* appeared in 1862, prepared the ground for the subsequent "positivist" trend. Other branches of learning were advancing, such as classics, geology, medicine, and hygienics. Oskar Kolberg (1814-90) began to systematize a new discipline, ethnography. Toward the end of this period, the first Polish encyclopedia—Orgelbrands'—started to appear.

In spite of all these achievements, it was clear that education had suffered a severe setback. The situation was alarming under the Russian rule. Deprived of its autonomy in education and controlled by a corrupt system, the kingdom had 2,800 high-school students in 1855 as compared with over 6,000 in 1829. The number of elementary schools did increase but their levels were low. Children of nongentry birth were discriminated against on every educational level. The result was a staggering illiteracy figure of 79 percent in Congress Poland. After the closing of the old Collegium Nobilium and other piarist schools known for their excellence, no bright points remained in the over-all bleak picture. It was no wonder that Wielopolski's first efforts went in the direction of a complete school reform, including the creation of the Surgical-Medical Academy and later a university in all but the name (Szkoła Główna) in Warsaw.

In the "western guberniias" the tsarist educational policy was aimed at the eradication of Polish cultural influences. Russian became the language of instruction in most schools, and Polish was eliminated even as a subject. It was restored only in 1858. The number of high schools in Lithuania dropped catastrophically. The Russians saw a close connection between Catholicism and Polish culture, and they took steps to promote Eastern Orthodoxy to the extent of creating an Orthodox diocese in the kingdom itself. Strong measures were taken against the church and ecclesiastical schools. An attempt by the Papacy to mollify the tsar by issuing the breve "Cum Primum" in 1832 produced little result, but it embittered the Poles. Mickiewicz and Słowacki made harsh references to Rome. In the emigration a religious crisis that opposed Christianity to the established church was largely a reaction to papal policies of conciliation with Russia.

In Galicia high schools were for the main part germanized. Elementary education made some progress after the emancipation of the peasantry in 1848, but village schools remained alarmingly few and their level was low. The Polish provinces under Prussia had, on the whole, a better educational system. In Pomerania it was almost entirely germanized, except for a Polish high school in Kulm. Polish was used in some classes in most elementary schools in Poznania, which were run by the local clergy under the supervision of the government. After 1848 Polish instruction was restored in schools in Silesia, i.e., the province that had been outside the commonwealth's 1772 borders. It was believed that the children would be more easily absorbed in the Prussian state through instruction in a language they could better understand. Polish educators, for example, Józef Lompa (1797–1863) in Upper Silesia and the protestant ministers in the Masurian region of East Prussia—the old Mrongowiusz and Gizewiusz—agitated in defense of the Polish language in areas outside of Poznania. The Prussian government, however, while keenly interested in promoting education, regarded it as means of making Prussian Poles loyal citizens of the state. Concessions to Polish language were regarded as temporary measures.

Polish cultural life in the period between the two insurrections must be seen against this general background. While romanticism predominated in *belles lettres* and the arts, and the primacy of the emigration was evident, local conditions accounted for specific developments in the homeland. Lyrical poetry found its main exponent in Teofil Lenartowicz (1822-93), who together with Norwid was active in Warsaw's bohemian community until driven to emigration in Italy. Wincenty Pol (1807–72) from Galicia specialized in sentimental, often quite charming, patriotic verses lauding the beauty of the Polish countryside; he also made use of a genre popular at the time, namely, a tale with an old-fashioned narrator *(gawęda)*. To the latter belongs his poem about a borderland knight, *Mohort*. Another native of Galicia, Kornel Ujejski (1823–97), acquired the reputation of a lesser national bard, mainly through such poems as "Marathon"—a transparent allusion to the Polish struggle for freedom—and the "Chorale" *(Choral)*, a lamentation for the 1846 revolution. The latter was destined to enter as a song into the Polish national repertory. Władysław Syrokomla—the pseudonym of Ludwik Kondratowicz (1823-62)—was a poet from Lithuania who combined a melancholic romanticism with a passionate concern for the common people. A clandestine revolutionary poem, known much better as a song, which blamed the defeat of the November Insurrection on the nobility "When the nation took to the field" *(Gdy naród . . . )*—came from the pen of the youthful conspirator Gustaw Ehrenberg (1818-95).

Polish prose turned to the past, seeking to enhance national collective identity through history. The favorite form was first the tale *(gawęda)* and then the historical novel. Henryk Rzewuski (1791-1866) and Ignacy Chodźko (1794-1891) excelled in the former. Ignacy Józef Kraszewski (1812-87) became a master of the latter. The voluminous output of Kraszewski—more than two hundred books—reminds one of Walter Scott. His cycle of historical novels, which began with pagan times in *The Old Tale (Stara baśń)* and went up to the eighteenth-century Saxon times, was highly uneven in quality. Certain volumes, however, showed good insight into the past and provided the reader with well-written and easy-to-read stories. Kraszewski's novels left a definite imprint on Polish literature. The author himself, a journalist, essayist, and novelist, ended his life abroad as an émigré.

The Polish theater reached its heights with the production, during this period, of some of the best comedies of Fredro, notably *Vengeance (Zemsta)* and *Pan Jowialski*. Criticized for writing mere comedies without a national or patriotic message, Fredro took offense and stopped producing. The episode was perhaps fairly illustrative of the romantic exaltation of the patriotic circles at the time. Among other playwrights, Józef Korzeniowski (1797–1863) deserves to be mentioned as the author of dramas and comedies, as well as novels, based on keen observation of contemporary society. In that sense his works may be treated as forerunners of the "social novel."

Strict censorship naturally affected journalism. During the course of the November Insurrection some seventy papers and journals appeared, but the press was completely muzzled after 1831. During the first decade after the insurrection the main journals were published abroad, and they ranged from conservative to radical papers and even included a satirical publication. In the early 1840s learned journals were permitted in Warsaw, and literary and scientific reviews also appeared in Prussian Poland. They provided an important forum for literary criticism as well as for discussions of social issues. Kraszewski, Dembowski, and most contemporary writers contributed to the polemics. Among them were also women writers, for example, the novelist Narcyza Żmichowska (1819-76), a pioneer of the women's emancipation movement. The 1848 revolution contributed signally to the rise of great daily newspapers, which by the 1850s assumed an important role in the country. The conservative Cracow *Czas* (Time), the *Dziennik Warszawski* (Warsaw Daily), and the *Dziennik Poznański* (Poznań Daily) appeared in a modern form with telegrams from abroad, foreign correspondents' reports, and *feuilletons*. Although their editions were rather small— few had more than a couple of thousand subscribers—they were read in the cafés by a much wider public.

In contrast to *belles lettres* and writing in general, music and plastic arts produced only a handful of names that deserve recognition. Chopin, of course, was universally admired, and Norwid viewed his music as a perfect example of art expressing and embodying the genius of his nation. But in spite of Chopin's special place in Polish music his influence on musicians at home was limited. Stanisław Moniuszko (1819-72), the only noted composer in Poland, went back to older traditions. His greatly admired opera *Halka* (produced in 1858) dipped into folklore, but its music had little of the innovative and imaginative qualities of Chopin.

Among painters the truly great talent of Piotr Michałowski (1800-55) left little imprint on his contemporaries. Educated in Paris, a prosperous landowner, Michałowski neither exhibited nor sold his pictures. His style resembled Gericault's and he became fully appreciated much later. The portrait painter Henryk Rodakowski (1823-94) and artists who were fascinated by landscape and nature, such as Wojciech Gerson (1831-1901), Juliusz Kossak (1824-99), and others, gained a good deal of popularity. A historical school that cultivated realism was developing in the mid-nineteenth century; later it would have a great impact on Polish society. During this period, the painter who reflected most accurately the exalted and romantic outlook of the Poles was Artur Grottger (1837–67). His moving cycles *Polonia* and *Lithuania*, which dwelt on the January Insurrection, became part of the Polish heritage. Their artistic value was inferior to their appeal to national sentiments, and it is for the latter reason that they deserve emphasis.

Architecture and sculpture of the period between the insurrections was rather mediocre. Neogothic and neorenaissance styles, then fashionable in Berlin and Vienna, affected some building in Prussian

Poland and Galicia. There were hardly any new and interesting native buildings to improve Warsaw's skyline.

As during the pre-1830 decades, Polish culture continued to be the most effective force preserving the unity and identity of the partitioned nation. The Age of Romanticism, however, exhibited certain novel and important features. First, an émigré center influenced Polish culture more decisively than ever before or after. Second, Polish cultural and national consciousness began to awaken in such areas as Upper Silesia, Teschen Silesia, and the regions of East Prussia. Third, this era witnessed the beginnings of native Ukrainian and Lithuanian literature which was influenced to no small degree by Polish romanticism. Barely noticed by contemporaries, this national revival proved to be of great importance in the life of the Lithuanian and Ukrainian nations.

The physical outlook of the lands of the old commonwealth continued to change during the interinsurrection years, although processes of modernization and industrialization were incomparably slower and less far-reaching than in Western Europe. A railroad network was constructed and best developed in Prussian Poland; it linked the Polish provinces with their respective states rather than with each other. From 1851 telegraphic communication existed throughout Polish lands, and postal stamps came into use. In the 1840s the daguerreotype, a forerunner of photography, appeared. Big cities such as Warsaw, Cracow, and Posen acquired running water, sewers, and were lighted by gas. In Galicia Ignacy Łukasiewicz (1822–82) succeeded in distilling crude oil, and in 1853 he built what was probably the first kerosene lamp in the world. Outward signs of changing conditions included the increasing popularity of a universal European "bourgeois" dress. Polish national costumes were worn prior to and for a short time after the January Insurrection; later they became relegated to certain festivities. Only the peasantry and the Jews continued to adhere to their traditional and distinctive dresses.

*Part Three*

TOWARD A MODERN SOCIETY:
THE AGE OF ORGANIC WORK, 1864-90

# CHAPTER 10

# Russian Poland and the
# Industrial Revolution

I. THE AFTERMATH OF THE JANUARY INSURRECTION

THE decades following the January Insurrection constituted a turning point in the history of the partitioned commonwealth. Reduced to a tsarist province, Congress Poland saw its very identity endangered. Prussian Poland, integrated into the new German Empire, became the scene of a German-Polish struggle in which the survival of a separate Polish nationality was at stake. By way of contrast, Galicia gained its local autonomy within the Habsburg monarchy but the price was a perpetuation of conservative loyalism and socioeconomic backwardness. The Polish question, so long an important item on the international agenda, was relegated to near oblivion. In the eastern borderlands, Lithuanian and Ukrainian nationalism awakened and largely directed its thrust against the Poles and the tradition of the historic commonwealth. No wonder that a wave of political pessimism engulfed the leading Polish circles. The heritage of conspiracy and armed struggle was rejected as suicidal. Seeking to preserve at least the cultural and material advancement of the divided Polish lands, a philosophy of "Triple Loyalism" arose. It produced some results in Austria where the loyalty of Polish conservatives to the Habsburgs was appreciated and needed. It was bound to degenerate into servility under Prussia and Russia.

In the socioeconomic field the emancipation of the peasantry in Russian Poland, with all the consequences it entailed, opened a new chapter in Polish history. Congress Poland entered the stage of the industrial revolution which was affected by and in turn affected antiromantic positivism, and indicated new avenues for national development. By the late 1880s and 1890s rising capitalism, Triple Loyalism, and positivism engendered new forces that challenged their supremacy. These were: socialism in both its "internationalist" and "national" form;[1] modern nationalism; and agrarian populism. The appearance of these forces heralded the beginning of a new stage which found its full expression in the twentieth century.

The international context from 1863 to 1890 needs only to be briefly sketched. The course of international events did not favor Polish interests and aspirations. Hopes tied to a Franco-Austrian *rapprochement* directed against Prussia were shattered on the battlefields of Sadova (1866) and Sedan (1870). The possibility of a pro-Polish front of Catholic powers did not materalize; Bismarck's Prussia, inimical to the Poles, became the decisive factor in the new German Empire. The latter in turn rose to the position of the greatest power on the continent. A defeated France looked toward Russia and assured her that the Poles—now doubly suspicious to the French middle classes because of their active role in the Paris Commune—would not be an obstacle to Franco-Russian amity. No major power had any real interest in the Polish question, although most chancelleries secretly recognized its potential usefulness as a diplomatic weapon. The League of Three Emperors of 1873 was a reaffirmation of the partitioners' solidarity vis-à-vis a Polish irredenta.

Persistent Russo-Austrian rivalry kept some Polish hopes alive. During the Balkan crisis of 1875-78 they were briefly encouraged by the formation of an ephemeral Polish "government," secretly set up with Austrian and English blessings in Vienna. But this was only a minor move on the diplomatic chessboard, and the Congress of Berlin ignored Polish petitions altogether. The subsequent German-Austrian alliance of 1879, the new Three Emperors' League of 1881, and Bismarck's Reinsurance Treaty with Russia of 1887 showed that in spite of existing differences between Vienna, St. Petersburg, and Berlin one could not expect a conflict that would reopen the Polish question. Though these intricate diplomatic maneuvers had some relevance for the Poles under Prussia and Austria, they had little effect on the lands under the rule of the tsar. A *modus vivendi* between Russia and the Papacy in 1882 indicated that the Poles could not expect assistance from Leo XIII.

Russian victory over the January Insurrection was followed by a series of measures designed to solve the Polish issue once and for all. Strong anti-Polish feelings pervaded all the leading groups in Russia. Alexander II fulminated against Polish ingratitude; liberals

1. The terms "national" and "internationalist" may be misleading and require an explanation. Both trends were internationalist, but the first put emphasis on national independence as inextricably linked with social revolution. Although the expression "national socialist" was used by some early groups, normally the trend was called "independence-oriented" (*niepodległościowy*), in contrast to the one that rejected or at best ignored demands for independence as being contrary to socialist revolutionary goals.

blamed the Poles for having provoked a conservative reaction in Russia; to the Slavophiles and Panslavists the Poles were "Judases of Slavdom." Poland, the Slavophiles argued, had to be cleansed of the alien Western "Catholic and noble" tradition and restored to Slavdom. Standard bearers of Panslavism advocated a complete eradication of Polish influence in the borderlands, the absorption of Eastern Galicia by Russia, and the retention of a reconstructed ethnic Poland in an all-Slav federation under Russian leadership. An independent Poland, they said, would fall victim to German might and influence. Thus, she had to be saved even in spite of herself.

In its policy toward the Poles the Russian government proceeded on the assumption that the Polish nation consisted of two groups: the inimical clergy and nobility, and the potentially friendly peasantry. As a Russian journalist put it: "There will be no Polish question from the moment the Polish nationality loses not only its material but also its moral authority over the Ruthenian and Lithuanian nationalities in the Western Land, and when the enduring might of the peasant communes in the Kingdom of Poland smashes . . . the old ideals of the Polish gentry."[2]

Retribution against persons involved in the insurrection was harsh. About four hundred people were executed after judicial procedures; the number of those shot or hanged after summary justice is difficult to establish. Thousands were deported to Siberia, others went there as forced laborers or settlers. Some 1,600 estates were confiscated in Congress Poland and 1,800 in the "western guberniias." Most of these lands were given to tsarist officials. Following the example set by Governor Muraviev in Lithuania, the government imposed a contribution of twenty million rubles on landed estates in Congress Poland. The very name Kingdom of Poland was abolished and unofficially replaced by "Vistula Land" *(Privislinsky Krai)*. Names of several towns were russified; for instance, Brześć became Brest-Litovsk, Chelm was changed to Kholm, Jędrzejów was renamed Andreiv. After Berg's death the title of viceroy was discontinued. The governor generals of Warsaw (P. E. Kotzebue, 1874-80; P. O. Albedynsky, 1880-83; and I. V. Gurko 1883-94) received broad powers. From 1875 on they could issue decrees affecting security and administrative penalties, and after 1879 they could order that civilians be tried by military courts or deported without a court verdict. All separate administrative institutions were gradually eliminated—the Council of State and the Administrative Council, the governing commissions (ministries), and the secretary of state in St.

2. Cited in Henryk Wereszycki, *Historia polityczna Polski w dobie popowstaniowej 1864-1918* (Warszawa: Instytut Pamięci Narodowej, 1948), p. 69.

Petersburg. The "Vistula Land" was divided into ten guberniias administered by Russians with Russian as the official language. Attracting the least desirable and competent individuals from the empire, the administration ruled by fear and with bayonets; a "Chinese wall" separated it from the population and the population from it. Such practices were hardly calculated to regain the Poles for Slavdom, and even on the level of districts and communes Russian administrators antagonized the peasants, the supposed ally of the regime.

The abolition of a separate treasury and separate budgets of the former kingdom led in 1886 to the transformation of the Polish Bank into a subsidiary branch of the Imperial Bank. Except for the Napoleonic code which remained, the judiciary became russified. At the same time the Poles were denied some of the advantages of the Russian legal reforms. Thus, Congress Poland had neither elected justices of the peace nor trial by jury. Nor was it allowed to have municipal self-government or zemstvos. The law of 1870 that facilitated the creation of cultural institutions and organizations did not apply to the "Vistula Land."

Russification was particularly striking in education. The Main School, whose students had abstained from the insurrection so as not to endanger their institution, survived only until 1869. It was then replaced by the Russian University of Warsaw. Schools and their curricula were completely russified.

The government took strong measures against the Catholic church which was regarded as the pillar of Polish national resistance, and subordinated it to the Catholic College in St. Petersburg. Although attempts to force the clergy and the faithful to use Russian in sermons, prayers, and hymns were abandoned, constant harassment of the church hierarchy was not. By 1870 not a single bishop remained at the head of his diocese. The destruction of the Uniate church in the Kholm and Podlachia regions was accomplished through an administrator brought over from Galicia. The old union with Rome was officially abolished in 1875, and resisting villagers were converted with the help of troops who flogged the recalcitrants and deported their leaders to Russia. Alexander II announced that he would not tolerate converts to Orthodoxy returning to Catholicism, and his policy was stricly enforced. In spite of such measures, most of the Uniates went underground and preserved their faith until an early twentieth-century toleration law made their reconversion possible. While protesting these abuses, the Papacy attempted to mollify Russia and tried to obtain concessions through the agreement of 1882. Little was achieved, but Leo XIII persisted in admonishing the bishops to submit to the authority of the ruler and his laws.

II. PEASANT EMANCIPATION AND ITS CONSEQUENCES

The emancipation decrees of February 19/March 2, 1864, were issued in the final stages of the insurrection and were clearly designed to deprive it of peasant support. The viceroy's appeal to the peasantry spoke of the realization of "your [peasant] expectations and their fulfillment in such a way that the lords who had oppressed you would have no further possibility or opportunity of doing so in the future."[3] The tsarist government, however, was not unanimous on how to win the masses at the expense of the landlords without endangering the prevailing social structure. Berg wanted to manage the great landowners; the emancipation committee led by Miliutin felt that the Polish peasants were sufficiently advanced to become a reliable pillar of the regime; some of the commissars for peasant affairs wished to bring about the complete ruin of the Polish landlords as a class. It was clear that the government could not offer the peasants less than the insurgent National Government had offered, i.e., full property rights and some land to the landless. It was also necessary to indemnify the landlords.

The Russian reform had to resolve three principal issues: it had to liquidate all labor obligations which had been officially abolished by Wielopolski and then by the National Government but which persisted in about one-third of the villages; it had to put an end to rents established by Wielopolski but no longer paid; and it had to tackle the question of the landless peasantry. Finally, there was the all-important matter of transforming the communal administration in such a way as to end the landowners' control over the villages.

The emancipation decrees liquidated all peasant obligations to the manor (labor or rents) and deprived the landowners of their monopoly of the production and sale of spirits. The peasants received as freeholds the land they used; in addition, they obtained some land in compensation for what they had lost since the 1846 regulations. The landless peasants were given little land. Due to the uneconomical size of their plots the number of landless villagers decreased only temporarily and then rose sharply again. The practical realization of the reform was extremely complex. It was not easy to distinguish between "peasant land" properly speaking and plots that were cultivated by farmhands and were not covered by the reform. Various criteria were used and decisions adopted favoring on the whole the largest estates and the crown lands. From this last category only 27 percent of the land passed into peasant hands; 60 percent was

3. Cited in Polska Akademia Nauk, Instytut Historii, *Historia Polski* (Warszawa: Państwowe Wydawnictwo Naukowe, 1963), 3, pt. 1, p. 372.

given in entail to Russian dignitaries. Estates belonging to the gentry were especially hard hit, and the smaller gentry was rarely given the benefit of a doubt. Occasionally, humane or patriotic landowners suffered more than those with connections who had been guilty of peasant evictions in the past.

The question of "servitudes" was solved slowly in a haphazard fashion that failed to satisfy either side and created a good deal of friction in subsequent years. In principle, "servitudes" remained in force but in varying degrees. Thus, about 65 percent of farms had the right to graze their cattle in manorial pastures; 59 percent could gather wood for burning, and 39 percent could cut timber in the forests. In crown estates "servitudes" were abolished, but the peasants were indemnified by additional land.

The compensation paid to the landlords was calculated in a fashion less advantageous to them than to landlords in Galician or Prussian Poland. It took the form of negotiable bonds which carried a 4 percent interest and were to be amortized in forty-two years. The bonds quickly depreciated. A new land tax added to the hardship of estate owners. Unlike the situation in Russia, the peasants were not required to make payments toward the indemnification costs of emancipation. At the same time, they had to pay a fairly high land tax. It has been calculated that the tsarist government paid a total of 64 million rubles to the landlords and up to 1914 collected 110 million rubles through land taxes. Hence the whole reform became financially profitable to the regime.

The administrative reform in the countryside which established a communal self-government—clearly a misnomer—was part of the emancipation bill. Its objective was to deprive the manor of its influence in the villages and subordinate the latter to Russian administration. A purely peasant commons (gromada), presided over by an elected elder (sołtys), was established. Several commons made a commune (gmina), which was under an elected headman (wójt). Unlike the situation in Prussia and Austria, the manorial demesne was included in the commune, but the landowners were excluded from commons' and communal meetings which elected the elder and the headman. The headman exercised minor police, administrative, and judicial functions under the strict supervision of the Russian district official.

The socioeconomic and political effects of the 1864 peasant emancipation were manifold and in the long run rather different from what the Russians sought to accomplish. By and large, the great latifundia remained little affected. The magnates had the necessary capital to hire farm workers and to invest in machinery.

Prior to 1864 most large estates already had machines for threshing grain and cutting chaff; some had broadcasters and mechanical rakes, reapers, mowing machines, or locomobiles. They could defend themselves in court litigations over woods and pastures. They also could and did bribe the corrupt tsarist bureaucracy. The landowning gentry, which had been singled out as the group to be weakened politically and economically, fared far worse. Many were driven from the land as the result of confiscations or burdensome contributions they could not meet. Many an owner of a smaller estate lacked horses and tools, having relied in the past on the *corvée* performed with peasants' horses. Often the only way out was mortgaging the estate, parceling it out and selling portions of the land, or cutting and selling timber. This last remedy usually led to conflicts with the village which claimed its "servitudes," and resulted in lengthy and costly litigation. A sizable group of former landowners moved to towns, seeking there employment in free professions, industry, or trade. As mentioned above, all the administrative posts in Russian Poland were reserved for Russians only. The ex-gentry element greatly reinforced the intelligentsia and gave it its special outlook. The radical intelligentsia, which despised the magnates and the bourgeois, gradually became the principal force that aspired to awaken and lead the masses. Women played an important part in the movement, and demands for the emancipation of women were early formulated.

Peasant property increased by over 8 percent between 1864 and 1890, a novel phenomenon in Polish conditions. While around 1870 private estates in the kingdom accounted for 46 percent of all land, and peasant holdings for 40 percent, the respective figures by 1890 were 30 and 43 percent. In terms of arable land the percentage of peasant holdings was higher. While the standard of living of the peasantry improved, a clearer division between the village rich and the village poor became noticeable. There were several reasons for this development as well as for the fourfold increase in the number of landless between 1870 and 1891. The emancipation reform did not provide for consolidation of peasant strips; strips remained scattered, producing the "chessboard" effect that was a typical feature of the countryside and survived until the twentieth century. Affected by subdivisions, small and scattered farms could not survive and passed into the hands of more affluent peasants. Only two-thirds of all the landless received allotments, which many of them subsequently lost. The parceling out of manorial estates which proceeded in a highly unorganized fashion until 1890—when the government began to supervise it through credit institutions—did not keep pace with the demand for land. In turn, due to the rapid growth of the population (100 percent during the second half of the nineteenth century) it was impossible to absorb the surplus rural population.

The mass of the landless became a vast reservoir of a labor force. Some of its members were drawn into the developing industries, but many had to seek means of livelihood elsewhere. The result was either seasonal or permanent emigration. A Polish labor market arose which cut across the political boundaries. Laborers from the kingdom went as seasonal workers to Poznania or Silesia; labor hands from Galicia worked on Poznanian farms or in the industries of the Dąbrowa Basin, Łódź, or Warsaw. There was a flow of Polish workers to western Germany, and, finally, an emigration overseas which involved millions of people.

Economic conditions favored the wealthier land proprietors. Up to the 1880s grain prices were rising, and the landowners had little incentive to engage in costly methods of intensive farming. The impressive increase in agricultural production during these years was mainly due to additional land brought under cultivation. By 1865 some 50 percent of the land was under plow, as compared with only 34 percent in 1822. The three-field system still prevailed on peasant farms but it began to be gradually abandoned. The agricultural slump of the 1880s hit the large landed estates and contributed to the parceling out of land. Usually the wealthier peasants benefited from this development.

Seen in a broad context, the emancipation reforms produced important changes in the countryside which benefited a large stratum of the peasantry, weakened the gentry, and contributed to the growth of a landless village population. Social conflicts between the landowners and the peasantry remained, and so did the land hunger of the villagers. But the Russian policies did not result in a confrontation between the defeated Polish upper classes and a peasant mass supposedly grateful to the tsarist regime. Irritated by the russified elementary schools which brought them no real instruction, antagonized by the attacks on the Catholic church to which they were devoted, and annoyed by such chicaneries as the attempt to forbid the wearing of national costumes, the peasants could hardly identify themselves with the tsarist regime. The anti-Polish and essentially conservative Russian system could not truly become a friend and protector of the peasant. As an English historian put it, the developments of 1864 "destroyed the one justification which might have been advanced, that the Russian bureaucracy protected the Polish peasants from the manor. In future the peasants would seek relief from the pressure of Russian officialdom."[4] Eventually they would

4. R. F. Leslie, *Reform and Insurrection in Russian Poland* (London: University of London, Athlone Press, 1963), p. 249.

find it on their own, inspired and led by the radical intelligentsia whose position the Russian policies unwittingly strengthened.

III. THE INDUSTRIAL REVOLUTION

The question of the industrial revolution in Polish lands has given rise to many controversies. When did it begin? Did state intervention, especially during the Drucki-Lubecki period, establish the bases for a continuous industrialization process which reached its peak in the last quarter of the nineteenth century? What were the characteristics of the industrial revolution in Poland?

The thesis of uninterrupted growth has been in part invalidated by Polish historians. State financing in the 1820s proved costly to the country and to the taxpayer and did not prevent the collapse of state-owned heavy industry. Trading conditions prior to the 1850s were not conducive to increased exchanges with foreign countries. The agrarian structure of the Congress Kingdom undoubtedly delayed the evolution and emergence of a larger market A transformation of this structure, culminating with the 1864 reforms, as well as a liberalization of international trade, contributed to an agricultural boom. Producing both for the domestic market and for export to the West—Russia's share in the turnover was only one-third before 1880—agriculture accumulated a good deal of capital. Most of it, however, was not invested in industry, except for food-processing plants; rather it was used for improvements in the agrarian sector.

The growth of an internal market and technological changes, facilitated by England's lifting the embargo on export of machinery in 1842, contributed to the growth of light industries, mainly textiles. Up to 1870 the basis of the kingdom's economic progress was the domestic market, but a radical change occurred in the 1870s and 1880s. During that period Russia switched to protectionist policies, and a slump in agriculture diminished returns from the land. Railroad construction in the Russian Empire created a new demand for iron and coal, whose output grew rapidly. In turn, railroad lines linked the major mining and industrial centers in the kingdom and accelerated their production. A combination of all these factors produced, in the decades following the January Insurrection, a veritable industrial revolution in Congress Poland. To all practical purposes this revolution was completed by 1890.[5]

Increasing mechanization of production and the growth of modern factories may be illustrated by a few figures. In 1865 the kingdom

5. Polish economic historians now define the culminating point of industrial revolution by calculating the output of mechanized enterprises in percentages of total output (measured in quantity or value). When it exceeds 50 percent they consider that a given branch of industry has reached the culminating point. According to this calculation the sugar industry reached this point roughly by 1850, cotton by 1875, and metallurgy by 1890.

had 180 plants using 375 steam engines developing 3,746 horsepower. In 1878 it had 674 plants with 807 engines of a total capacity of 14,627 horsepower. It has been calculated that the use of steam-driven engines, between 1853 and 1888, increased twenty-five times. Concentration of industries, in terms of both region and larger plants, was particularly noticeable in textiles, but big firms also dominated sugar-refining industries and to a great extent iron works and mines. Large industrial areas arose, notably the Warsaw center (in the 1890s the city itself reached over 600,000 inhabitants), the Łódź region (the town's population grew sixfold), and the Dąbrowa mining and metallurgical basin. The total value of industrial production increased over six times between 1864 and 1885 (from 30 to 190 million rubles). In 1892 it reached the figure of 228 million. By the end of the nineteenth century the value of industrial production exceeded that of agriculture. In the years 1864 to 1880s the number of industrial workers rose from some 80,000 to 150,000. In comparison, Galicia and Prussian Poland had respectively about 25,000 and 28,000 workers. Those employed in big industry constituted in the kingdom, Poznania, and Galicia respectively 0.7, 0.1, and 0.3 percent of the total population.

Trade increased significantly in volume, and its general pattern changed. For the first time in four centuries Poland ceased to be an exporter of wheat. In the place of the Western market with its demands for foodstuff and raw material exports which had accounted for the bulk of Polish exportations, vast Russian and Far Eastern markets opened up to penetration of the kingdom's industry. From 1880 to 1890 Russia's part in Polish trade rose to 70 percent, and the export of finished products took the lead over raw materials. This close association of Polish industry, mainly textiles, with the "Eastern markets" gave rise to the theory that the kingdom's economy was inextricably bound with that of Russia and derived great advantages from this association. Although Poland had to import cotton and wool from Russia and was later to face the competition of Russian textiles on its internal market, the balance of trade was distinctly favorable to the kingdom. But this privileged position of Polish industry was likely to last only as long as the empire did not complete its own industrial revolution and did not seriously protect its rising industrial complex from Polish competition. Ominous signs to that effect began to appear after 1890, but prior to that time Russian protectionist policies assisted Poland's industrial development.

The state did not directly finance the industrialization of Congress Poland. In the 1870s it divested itself of its mines and iron works, and in 1892 its zinc works passed into private hands. French and

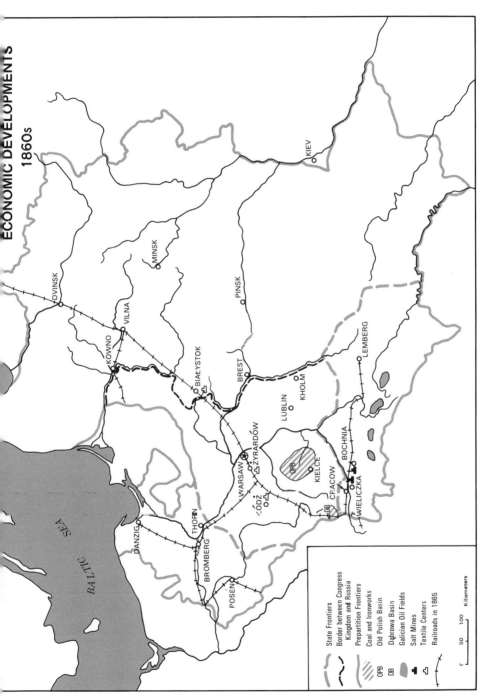

ECONOMIC DEVELOPMENTS

1860s

BALTIC SEA

DVINSK

MINSK

VILNA

KOWNO

PINSK

BIAŁYSTOK

BREST

KIEV

LEMBERG

KHOLM

LUBLIN

ŻYRARDÓW

WARSAW

OPB

KIELCE

BOCHNIA

CRACOW

WIELICZKA

ŁÓDŹ

DB

THORN

DANZIG

BROMBERG

POSEN

State Frontiers
Border between Congress
Kingdom and Russia
Prepartition Frontiers
Coal and Ironworks

OPB     Old Polish Basin
DB      Dąbrowa Basin
        Galician Oil Fields
        Salt Mines
        Textile Centers
        Railroads in 1865

0   50   100
Kilometers

Map 3

Italian capital took over the collieries and iron works of the Dąbrowa Basin. French, German, and Belgian capital came into banking.

The question of foreign capital in the kingdom gave rise to some disputes. It seems to have entered the country largely after 1877 to penetrate the Russian market. According to various calculations, at the turn of the century it amounted to 39 percent of the entire industrial capital and to 60 percent in terms of value of industrial production. At the same time a distinction must be made between foreign capital that was brought into the kingdom by the investors who settled there, foreign capital invested in joint stock and locally controlled, and foreign investments that brought profits to outside concerns. It appears that the first two forms of foreign capital predominated in the kingdom and are hard to distinguish from locally raised funds. Most of the industrial development was financed by banks with their headquarters in Poland and by local joint stock companies. The Commercial Bank (Bank Handlowy), established in 1870 by Kronenberg, had French (Crédit Lyonnais) and native agrarian capital. The Discount Bank (Bank Dyskontowy), which was set up a year later by H. Epstein, disposed of some German capital, mainly from the Deutsche Bank. An urban credit association came into existence at this time; the Land Credit Association which had survived the 1863 insurrection continued to operate. Kronenberg and Jan Bloch (1836–1902), the two greatest bankers in Congress Poland, financed the building of railroads through joint stock operations. From the 1870s on, joint stock controlled most sugar refining industries, collieries, iron and steel works, as well as the cotton industry. It was also important in the machine-building enterprises.

Railroad building, which everywhere played such a crucial part in the industrial revolution, assumed major proportions in the 1860s and 1870s. In 1862 the kingdom had 635 kilometers of tracks; by 1887 it had 2,084. Warsaw had rail communications with Kiev and Moscow; the two other industrial centers, Łódź and Dąbrowa, became accessible by railroad. The kingdom had four lines connecting it with Prussia and one with Austria.

The railroads provide a good example of the specific features of the industrial revolution in Polish lands. The partition borders, which in the age of protectionism became effective economic barriers, naturally prevented the emergence of an all-Polish market and made coordinated development of the various parts of the old commonwealth impossible. Railroads connected the parts of Poland not so much with each other as with the empires to which they belonged. In Congress Poland the network was small; calculated per inhabitant and the size of the country, it exceeded only those of Bulgaria, Greece, and Turkey.

Separated by frontiers, the kingdom had to import coke from the Donets Basin rather than from neighboring Silesia, and oil from Baku instead of Galicia. Due to the different evolutions of the three partitioning empires, Galicia was barely affected by the industrial revolution, and Prussian Poland evolved in the direction of a highly developed agrarian region, a granary of the German Reich. To all practical purposes the industrial revolution was limited to Congress Poland. Reaching the country in the late nineteenth century, it profited from Western technology. On the whole, new foreign techniques preceded foreign investments. Importation of up-to-date English or Belgian machinery permitted a virtually simultaneous rapid growth in several branches of the economy, but interfered with the development of a native machine industry. Technological progress contrasted with local socioeconomic retardation. Old forms of production coexisted with the new. While Cort's puddling processes had been used in Polish lands since the mid-1830s, ancient methods of smelting and forging iron continued for a long time after the advent of the industrial revolution. In agriculture, such "feudal" practices as paying the laborers in kind or exacting labor in lieu of money survived after 1864.

To turn now to a brief survey of the main branches of industry in Congress Poland, textiles undoubtedly occupied the leading place. Concentrated in the Łódź area, where about 90 percent of production took place in large factories, the textile industry employed more than one-third of all industrial workers. Cotton spinning was already done in factories and was mechanized; weaving, in spite of the fact that some machines had been used early, did not become fully mechanized until the 1880s. From 1865 to 1879 the number of power looms increased twenty times; that of spinning machines, three times. The value of the production of cotton, which occupied the first place among Polish textiles, rose from 5 million rubles in 1869 to 25 million in 1889. By the 1880s three-fourths of the cotton goods produced were exported to Russia. The boom gave rise not only to a spectacular growth of Łódź but also to wide speculations in the course of which the great manufacturing families (Scheiblers, Poznańskis, Geyers) made their fortunes. Woollen industries developed less rapidly, and by the 1880s their production was valued at 75 percent of that of cotton. Mechanization as well as the emergence of big factories was slower here. At first local wool was used; later it had to be imported from abroad. Outside of the Łódź region, the Białystok woollen district—incorporated into Russia—registered great progress. In the linen industries, which were third in importance, the decades after 1864 saw a fourfold increase in production, both in terms of value and the number of workers. The old factory of Żyrardów, which was the largest in Congress Poland and employed eight thousand workers in the 1880s, accounted for most of the linen produced.

Prior to the 1870s, coal mining and the iron industry stagnated. Then, railroad construction in Russia and Congress Poland acted as a catalyst, and the kingdom, having a large enough group of trained engineers and qualified workers, could accept and handle big orders for rails and rolling stock. In the 1870s and 1880s heavy industry went through a technical revolution. New open-hearth furnaces, Bessemer converters, and Siemens-Martin installations modernized iron and steel production and increased the demand for coal. Between 1870 and 1890 the output of coal went up from 312,000 tons to over 3 million. Production of iron rose from 18,000 tons in 1877 to 69,000 in 1890. By 1895 the production of steel reached 153,000 tons, i.e., around three times the production of iron. The bulk of it came from modern or modernized plants. Metallurgical industry in Warsaw and in the Old Polish Basin went through a boom between 1870 and 1897, multiplying its production nearly thirty times. The Lilpop, Rau, and Loewenstein works in Warsaw specializing in the construction of freight cars, machinery, and rails became the largest factory of this type in the whole Russian Empire. Shareholders in this new branch of industry were receiving up to 40 percent interest dividends.

The third major branch of industries in the kingdom was represented by the beet sugar refining factories. After 1865 diffusion processes replaced pressing techniques, and the production of sugar rose from thirteen thousand tons in the 1860s to seventy thousand in the 1870s. In the thirty years between 1853 and 1885 there was a ninefold increase in the volume of sugar production. It was no wonder that sugar-refining plants belonged to the most lucrative enterprises and their owners to the wealthiest class in the kingdom.

The industrial revolution transformed the "Vistula Land" into the most advanced part of the Russian Empire. Though the profile of the land was profoundly changed, the country was still not a highly industrialized region by Western standards. The primacy of the agrarian sector was obvious, and by 1897 around 68.5 percent of the population still lived in the countryside, as compared to 76.5 percent in 1857. Crafts, small enterprises, and cottage-type production continued to exist to satisfy the demands of the nonurban population. At the same time, the industrialization of the kingdom was greatly affecting the socioeconomic structure of the country. An industrial proletariat appeared and grew in the typical conditions of nineteenth-century capitalism. Real wages in industry were on the whole higher than in Russia but lower than in Western Europe. Long working hours, bad housing, unsanitary and unsafe conditions in factories, fear of unemployment—all bred resentment and discontent. Although trade unions were forbidden in the tsarist empire—they already existed in Austria and Germany—spontaneous and unorganized strikes began to take place in the 1870s.

Industrialization naturally assisted the growth of a big bourgeoisie in which nonethnically Polish elements were fairly strong. Families of German or Jewish descent—the Kronenbergs, Epsteins, Natansons, Wawelbergs, Rotwands, Lilpops, and others—were rapidly assimilated. They often cooperated with the old aristocracy or took over from them such agricultural industries as, for instance, sugar refineries. A certain amount of intermarriage took place. But if the upper classes of the industrial age became polonized, the non-Polish masses in the kingdom did not. This was particularly true for the bulk of the Jewish population which rapidly increased in size. In Warsaw their percentage rose during this period from 26 to 33 percent; in Łódź from 12 to 30 percent. Policies of assimilation promoted at the time of the January Insurrection gave way to new antagonism, often on economic grounds. True, the anti-Jewish riot in Warsaw in 1881, following the assassination of Alexander II, was provoked and tolerated by the Russian authorities, and no pogroms comparable to those in Russia occurred in Congress Poland, but anti-Semitism was rampant. By the end of the century Zionism on the one hand and Jewish Socialism on the other interfered with any assimilation trends that survived.

IV. WARSAW POSITIVISM AND THE RISE OF NEW POLITICAL FORCES

Economic and social progress in Congress Poland contrasted with political stagnation. Crushed by the magnitude of the defeat, some pessimists came to question the chances of national survival and believed in complete amalgamation with Russia, even if it involved the loss of Polish identity. These, however, were isolated voices, and on the whole Polish outlook was shaped by a new program known as positivism. Its philosophical foundations, broad implications, and specific forms in the different parts of Poland will be discussed in a separate chapter. What concerns us here is the impact of Warsaw positivism on Polish reality. Rejecting romanticism and the tradition of armed uprisings, a Warsaw review asserted that, "we have learned how to die magnificently but we never knew how to live rationally," and it praised the "heroism of a reasonable life."[6] Developing the program of "organic work" which had already been put to practice in Poznania and other parts of Poland in the period between the insurrections, the positivists emphasized the importance of cultural and economic progress. Observing the socioeconomic trans-

6. Cited in *Historia Polski*, 3, pt. 1, p. 437.

formation of the kingdom and Russia, a standard bearer of positivism, Aleksander Świętochowski (1849–1938), spoke of a destiny which "has opened before us wide fields for conquests in business and industry." The positivists put their faith in universal education, technological progress, and above all intense work; external national and political forms mattered less to them than Polish participation in the European march toward progress. Świętochowski summed up well their major objectives when he wrote in 1882: "We desire life and happiness. . . . We discovered in the course of many experiences that neither a game of warlike lottery nor favors from abroad would give us one or the other." It could only come "through hard, calm, and persevering work." Świętochowski spoke of giving up dreams of "external independence" in favor of efforts for "internal independence" which required heroism and sacrifice.[7]

Originally, the Warsaw positivists were anticlerical, antiaristocratic, and scholarly in their orientation. Characterized by abstention from politics and reflecting the nineteenth-century materialism, their program appealed to the rising bourgeoisie which could clothe its slogan of *enrichissez vous* in a socially positive or even patriotic garb. Politically, positivism could be and was gradually exploited by Triple Loyalism, which connected the possibilities of material progress with loyal behavior toward the partitioning governments.

It is obvious that any kind of political activity in the kingdom was narrowly circumscribed. Continuing in his father's footsteps, Count Zygmunt Wielopolski (1833–1902) attempted a reconciliation with Russia on the grounds of Slav solidarity. Yet neither the homage to the tsar rendered in 1876 nor the almost servile address of the nobility four years later produced any response. After the accession to the throne of Alexander III, Polish attempts at reconciliation—in the spirit of narrowly conceived positivism—reached their height. Russian authorities, however, continued to show their neglect of and even contempt for Polish national values. The harsh administrative and educational policies pursued by Governor Iosif Gurko and Curator Aleksandr Apukhtin demonstrated this plainly. Loyalty of the conservative upper classes, strengthened by their fears of rising socialism and nihilism, paid no political dividends.

The epigoni of the Zamoyski camp also favored reconciliation with Russia but could not ignore the oppressive measures in Lithuania and the Ukraine. Though they opposed insurrections, they did not exclude the possibility of a future conflict between the partitioning powers which could reopen the Polish question. Hence, they advocated a kind of "national moral government" which could guide

7. Cited in Feliks Perl (Res), *Dzieje ruchu socjalistycznego w zaborze rosyjskim do powstania PPS* (reedition, Warszawa: Książka i Wiedza, 1958), p. 46.

Polish moves in the partitioned commonwealth and be ready to take political actions when necessary. The possibilities for political maneuvering on the part of the ex-Zamoyski group were minimal.

Another approach to the central Polish-Russian issue was represented by the weekly *Kraj* (Homeland), printed from 1882 in St. Petersburg where censorship was less strict than in the kingdom. Its chief publishers were Włodzimierz Spasowicz (1829-1906), a typical representative of the enlightened intelligentsia, and Erazm Piltz (1851-1929), a moderate close to the bourgeoisie and the landowners. The *Kraj* attempted a dialogue with the Russians and argued the Polish case for separate national, ethnic, and cultural identity in rational terms. Pleading for the same treatment of Poles as of all other subjects of the tsar, it promised, in exchange, loyalty to the empire and a conscientious fulfillment of civic duties. Critical of Polish shortcomings, it advocated moral, intellectual, and economic rebirth of Poland. But it also voiced criticism of Russia. Violently attacked by Russian nationalists and often rebuked by Galician and Poznanian Poles, the *Kraj* could do little more than serve as a weak link between the Polish and the Russian liberal intelligentsia.

Polish conciliatory trends received no encouragement from Russia, but even some nonpolitical goals of the positivists proved hard to achieve. Economic expansion to the east was accompanied by a draining from Poland of engineers and professionals who, unable to find employment in the kingdom, had to seek livelihood in the empire. The ranks of the intelligentsia and middle classes were being depleted. Education, the great panacea of the positivists, continued to be fettered. In 1889 Świętochowski himself had to admit that, "we must live under an arbitrary rule," which is bound to limit seriously the efficacy of the positivist program. What finally remained of it was a sterile criticism of the Polish past, and a middle-class ideology increasingly challenged by forces which rejected the capitalist foundations of society and the authoritarian foreign regime.

The post-January emigration provided an important link between the insurrectionist tradition and the new radicalism. Although a pale shadow of the Great Emigration, the exiles, scattered through France, England, Switzerland, and Italy, cooperated with the First Socialist International as well as with democratic and republican organizations. Among their leading figures were Jarosław Dąbrowski and General Hauke-"Bosak" (the former was killed in the Paris Commune and the later in the Franco-Prussian War), General Walery Wróblewski (1836-1908), and Colonel Zygmunt Miłkowski (1824-1915), who wrote under the pseudonym of T. T. Jeż. In contrast to the positivists at home, the exiles argued that conspiracy and insurrections had, after all, preserved the national heritage, prevented the "digestion" of Poland by the partitioning powers, and kept the Polish question on the international agenda. Even the recent insurrection had produced peasant emancipation, a national organization, and a Polish government, and thus it had continued the socially progressive trend that had been associated with uprisings ever since the partitions of Poland.

Stressing the need for a continuous struggle for independence—even though some émigrés were willing to recognize the usefulness of "organic work" in the eastern borderlands and in Silesia—the radical democrats abroad formulated their ideas of a democratic federation of Poland in which the Lithuanians and Ruthenians would have the right of national self-determination. An evolution of émigré leaders in the direction of socialism may be illustrated by Wróblewski's saying that the concepts of socialism were "clearer and encompassed a wider horizon than the old democratic and republican principles."[8]

In 1886 Miłkowski established contact with the homeland through Zygmunt Balicki (1858–1916), who had been active in clandestine socialist circles. Current Russo-Austrian tension could lead to war, and it was essential that the Poles be prepared for such an emergency. Balicki organized a secret Association of Polish Youth known as Zet. Composed chiefly of students grouped in three grades following the freemasonic pattern—in all likelihood Balicki himself was a free-mason—Zet was to propagate the goal of an independent Poland based on social, national, and political justice. Its members underwent rigorous self-education and became dedicated political workers.

Balicki's return to Poland coincided with the publication of a Warsaw weekly called the *Głos* (the Voice). Taking a firm stand against positivism, "organic work," and bourgeois progressivism on the one hand, and conservative loyalism on the other, the *Głos* expressed the aspirations of the younger generation. As its spokesman and the principal editor, Jan Popławski (1854–1908), put it: " . . . we who are full of life and health do not want to die [politically] and especially to die so stupidly and so basely."[9] Popławski's gesture of sending a wreath to be placed on Mickiewicz's tomb in Cracow, which bore a romantic motto, "measure your strength by your purpose," was a challenge to the positivist creed. Popławski put his faith in the people *(lud)* who had better preserved the national tradition than had the upper classes; a new kind of populism was on the rise.

In 1887 Miłkowski published a booklet entitled *About Active Defense and National Treasury (Rzecz o obronie czynnej i skarbie*

8. Cited in Felicja Romaniukowa, ed., *Radykalni demokraci polscy. Wybór pism i dokumentów 1863–1785* (Warszawa: Państwowe Wydawnictwo Naukowe, 1960), p. xxxv.
9. Cited in Wereszycki, *Historia polityczna Polski*, p. 97.

*narodowym)* which argued against passive resistance and condemned deliberate rejection of all insurrections. He advocated raising funds for national needs and preparing for action at a favorable moment. The same year he was instrumental in the creation of the Polish League in Geneva, a revived version of the old Democratic Society. Envisaged as a center for political activity, the league strove to unite and consolidate all national elements bent on recovery of Poland's independence. It emphasized all-Polish goals in contrast to Triple Loyalism, which by its very acceptance of the *status quo* tended to deepen divisions between different Polish lands. Future Poland was seen as a federation of equal nationalities. At that stage the Polish League together with Zet, which recognized its leadership, and the *Głos* stood for a national, democratic, and populist program. While the league was to give impetus to the modern doctrine of Polish nationalism, it did not yet oppose the nascent Polish socialism.

Drawing their inspiration from Marx and Engels and strongly affected by the Russian *narodniki* and revolutionaries, early Polish socialists were for the most part grouped in a circle in St. Petersburg. At the turn of 1876-77 they extended their activity to the kingdom, and the arrival of Ludwik Waryński (1856–89) in Warsaw marked the beginnings of socialism in Congress Poland. A born tribune of the people, endowed with great energy and oratory gifts, Waryński was supported by such theorists as Aleksander Więckowski (1854-1919) and Stanisław Mendelson (1858-1913). The first Polish socialist brochures appeared, followed in 1879 by the printing in the Geneva-published paper *Równość* (Equality) of the so-called Brussels program. It spoke of class struggle and international solidarity of revolutionaries and only cautiously touched on the question of national aspirations by saying that the triumph of socialist principles was "the necessary condition of a propitious future of the Polish nation."

Arrests in Congress Poland forced Waryński to escape to Galicia and from there, after an unsuccessful attempt to establish a socialist underground, to Switzerland. Around the *Równość* a Socialist group emerged in Geneva in which a former insurgent of 1863, Bolesław Limanowski (1835-1935), figured prominently. The group was soon torn by disputes centering on the question of nationalism versus internationalism. While following Marx in other respects, Waryński and Kazimierz Dłuski (1855-1930) played down his championship of the Polish cause. Dłuski repudiated the old watchword *vive la Pologne* which Marx used in his greetings to the Poles on the fiftieth anniversary of the November Insurrection. Although Marx and Engels had on occasion indicated that once a revolutionary force emerged in Russia Poland's role would become subordinate, they stressed again and again the revolutionary value of the Polish struggle for independence. In 1882 Engels asserted that the Poles "not only have the right but the duty to be nationalistic before they become internationalists."[10] He decried the internationalism of the *Równość* as a deviation.

To Waryński, Dłuski, and their followers, socialism was a loftier idea than patriotism and the latter had to be sacrificed to the former. Only complete internationalist unity between the Polish and the Russian proletariat could lead to the overthrow of tsardom. A struggle for an independent Poland, even if democratic and socialist, could well produce a regime that by invoking national solidarity would sacrifice class interests of the proletariat. Limanowski thought otherwise. Believing in the need for an international revolution, he retained the patriotic and national outlook of the 1863 insurgents. Socialism was to assist Poland in regaining her independence; it was not to make independence a mechanical by-product of a victorious social revolution. Breaking away from his associates in 1881, Limanowski set up an organization called the Polish People (Lud Polski) which openly advocated Poland's independence as its goal. On the question of whether future Poland was to be historic and federalized or ethnic and unitary, the manifesto of the Polish People used a compromise formula which spoke of frontiers determined by "voluntary gravitation"—*libre fédération* in a French translation.

On Waryński's return to Warsaw in 1881 the first Socialist organization, the Proletariat, appeared on native soil. Known later as the Great Proletariat—to distinguish it from its short-lived successor of 1887—the organization formulated its program in 1882. In contrast to earlier, hazy and general formulae, the program of the Proletariat was not only an ideological platform but also a plan of action. Its objective was the overthrow of the tsarist regime, the main obstacle to the emancipation of the working class. It postulated the transfer of land and means of production to the state. The stress was on internationalism, although the program asserted that a victorious social revolution would also end national oppression. The distinctiveness of Polish socialism was implied in an alliance which the Proletariat signed in 1884 with the Russian Narodnaia volia. The agreement—in some ways a veritable international treaty—provided for Polish revolutionary action in Polish lands at a moment chosen by the Narodnaia volia which would simultaneously strike against the tsarist regime in Russia. The Narodnaia volia recognized Polish national rights not on historic or ethnic grounds but because the Polish

10. Engels to Kautsky, cited in Karl Marx and Friedrich Engels, *The Russian Menace To Europe*, edited by Paul W. Blackstock and Bert F. Hoselitz (Glencoe, Ill.: Press Press, 1952), p. 118.

people wanted them, and it provisionally defined the area of Polish activity as the Congress Kingdom "until a different frontier delimitation" took place (a confidential agreement).

Cooperation between the Proletariat and the Narodnaia volia ended with mass arrests by the tsarist police. Waryński and his successor Stanisław Kunicki (1861–86) were arrested and tried. Six of the leading members of Proletariat were hanged; Waryński was imprisoned in Schlüsselburg where he died. The first Socialist organization in the kingdom collapsed, but not so the socialist movement. The latter had simultaneously made progress in other parts of Poland and in the emigration. Regarded as a threat to the established order by some and as a menace to national solidarity by others, Polish socialism was to find its final organizational forms in the following decades. Together with democratic nationalism and populism it radicalized Polish politics and accelerated the evolution of society in the direction of national self-assertion and, eventually, independence.

# CHAPTER 11

# Galician Autonomy and the Kulturkampf in Prussian Poland

I. GALICIA IN THE AGE OF CONSTITUTIONAL REFORMS

IN THE 1860s the Habsburg monarchy went through a period of profound political reorganization which reached its high point with the Austro-Hungarian Compromise *(Ausgleich)* of 1867. This development provided the Polish leaders, gravely shaken by the collapse of the January Insurrection, with the possibility of negotiating and even bargaining with Vienna. In the course of heated discussions a conservative trend prevailed in Galicia which combined loyalism to the Habsburgs with a program of "organic work" *sui generis*. A virtually autonomous regime for Galicia was achieved, which brought genuine political advantages to the Poles. It tended to perpetuate, however, a backward socioeconomic structure and produced no solution of the Polish-Ruthenian controversy. Although the conservatives could claim achievements in the field of education and even some success in social and economic matters—especially toward the end of the period—their primacy was eventually challenged by the rising forces of social radicalism and nationalism, both Polish and Ruthenian (Ukrainian). Still, in spite of all shortcomings Galicia did become the freest of all the parts of partitioned Poland, and signally contributed to Polish civilization and the twentieth-century statehood.

Austrian defeat in the Italian war of 1859 opened the period of constitutional experiments. The former governor of Galicia, Gołuchowski, was largely responsible for the October Diploma of 1860 which sought to federalize the empire by distributing power between the emperor, the state council (Reichsrat), and the provincial diets (Landtäge). The Galician diet expressed its appreciation of this new departure. In an address presented to the emperor, it emphasized the historical rights of the Polish nationality, requested polonization of the administration, and expressed itself in favor of complete equality of the Jews. In 1861, however, a new ministry in Vienna issued the more centralist February Patent which put emphasis on the role of the Reichstrat and limited the role of provincial diets. The legislative powers of the monarchy became vested in the emperor and a two chamber central parliament. Poles and Ruthenians were represented in both chambers: the upper house (Herrenhaus), which consisted of hereditary members, imperial nominees, and church dignitaries, and the lower chamber (Reichsrat), composed of deputies elected by provincial diets. The number of deputies was calculated by taking into account not only the area and the size of the population but also the financial contribution of the province. This last factor accounted for Galicia's relative underrepresentation in the Reichsrat.

The provincial statute of 1861 regulated the composition and the mode of election of the Galician diet as well as the competence of this body. The diet consisted of ex-officio members and of representatives of great landed property, chambers of commerce, towns, and small towns and rural areas. A four curia *(Kurie)* system provided for separate elections in each group. In the first curia (that of great landowners) forty-four deputies, and in the second curia (that of chambers of commerce: Lemberg, Cracow, and Brody) three deputies were elected directly. The voters in the third curia, that of towns, had to qualify on property or educational grounds and elected twenty deputies. Representatives of the fourth curia (seventy-four) were elected by rural communes voting in a two-stage system and by lesser landowners who voted directly. The suffrage was by open ballot. Although the number of fourth curia delegates was higher in Galicia than in other Austrian provinces, the whole electoral system denied proportional representation. Not only was the largest stratum of the population disqualified, but a deputy in the first curia represented 52 electors, in the second 39, in the third 2,264, and in the fourth 8,764.

The competence of the diet was limited to such local affairs as *Landeskultur* (understood at first as agricultural development) as well as public buildings, charities, and communal, ecclesiastical, and educational matters within the framework of general legislation. The diet could deliberate and approve decrees initiated by the government or by the diet itself, but imperial sanction was obligatory and the emperor could dissolve the diet at any time. It could only impose and collect supplementary taxes not exceeding 10 percent of the direct state tax. Thus finances under the diet's control were extremely meager.

The executive organ of the diet, the Provincial Department (Landesausschuss, Wydział Krajowy), was composed of the marshal (speaker) appointed by the emperor and a number of deputies chosen by the diet. It supervised the elected bodies of self-government on the level of the village commune and the district (Bezirk, powiat), but had no administrative apparatus of its own. To implement its decisions the department had to rely on the imperial Galician administration, from the governor down to the smallest railroad, police, or postal official. This dual system, known as the "two track" administration, was characteristic with minor differences for the entire Austrian part of the monarchy. In 1861 Galicia was under the firm control of the imperial administration, and the local institutions of self-government were of little consequence. The diet itself, in which a large number of government-sponsored peasant deputies received their seats, was the scene of constant friction over the "servitudes." In the Reichsrat the intense activity of Polish deputies failed to bring specific concessions to Galicia.

The outbreak of the January Insurrection deeply affected the Galician Poles and eventually involved the local Whites. The Austrians forbade a meeting of the diet and proclaimed a state of emergency. There were even some reprisals against the participants in the insurrection. Consequently, Polish deputies withdrew from the Reichsrat; a general feeling of tension prevailed. The collapse of the insurrection came as a shock and produced far-reaching consequences for subsequent developments in Galicia. The conservatives, who had taken part in the insurrection largely against their better judgement, felt doubly bitter that they had permitted themselves to entertain such hopes and illusions. Now they went all out to condemn not only the last insurrection but also the whole tradition of uprisings and émigré politics. Resorting to biting satire in their publication Stańczyk's Portfolio (Teka Stańczyka)—named after a sixteenth-century court jester—prominent Cracow intellectuals such as the historian of literature Count Stanisław Tarnowski (1837–1917), the editor of Czas, Stanisław Koźmian (1836–1922), the historian Józef Szujski (1835–83), and others engaged in heated polemics with their opponents. The Portfolio angered many people who felt that the tragedy of the insurrection at least deserved respect; the term stańczyk became a current political term to describe the Cracow conservatives.

The program of the conservatives went beyond an attitude of mere negation. Advocating an accommodation with the Habsburg monarchy, the Cracow conservatives based their stand on an analysis of the existing situation as well as on a critical reappraisal of Polish history. They considered that Vienna could always keep Galicia in check by wielding the peasant and Ruthenian weapons. Only loyal cooperation could bring concessions. Furthermore, given the latent Austro-Russian antagonism, the interests of Vienna and of the Poles could coincide. As Koźmian put it in his study of the Insurrection of 1863, the Poles could only recover independence when aided by a great power, and he implied that such a power was Austria. But this was a distant goal, and Koźmian argued that while independence was the most perfect form of national existence it was not the only one. As for hopeless insurrectionary attempts to achieve independence, they were, in fact, endangering national existence.

The Cracow conservatives diagnosed the evils of the insurrectionary tradition by reinterpreting Poland's past. The Cracow historical school attacked Lelewel and his liberal-democratic heritage. In a booklet entitled *A few Truths from our Past (Kilka prawd z dziejów naszych)*, Szujski drew an analogy between the old *liberum veto* and what he called *liberum conspiro* (freedom to conspire). The former had degenerated into an anarchic principle and had contributed to Poland's partitions. The use of the latter, after 1863, could only promote a social revolution advantageous to the partitioning powers but not to the Poles. Regarding the state rather than the nation as the educator in civic virtues, the Cracow conservatives desired to bring up a new generation of Poles which would think in terms of work, social order, and political realism. Galicia's role was not that of a Polish Piedmont, but rather that of a school in which the Poles would serve an apprenticeship in government and administration. The conservatives did not abandon the ultimate goal of Polish independence, nor did they deny the need for an all-Polish national political center. But by rejecting conspiracy they relegated such objectives to a purely moral sphere. As time went on and as their efforts were crowned with some political success, the conservative leaders of Galicia virtually gave up an all-Polish policy and unwittingly strengthened the concept of Triple Loyalism; this was bound to deepen the divisions between the partitioned Polish lands.

The conservative ascendancy in Galicia could not be effectively opposed by the democrats weakened by postinsurrectionary reprisals. Besides, the democrats lacked strength. Although Austrian legislation in the 1860s did establish the legal framework for a liberal middle-class society, Galicia was too backward to profit from this development. As Marxist writers have put it, liberal-bourgeois codification preceded the formation of a bourgeoisie and a proletariat. The towns were too weak to provide the basis for a large democratic party, although the biggest of them, Lemberg, did become a democratic stronghold. In Eastern Galicia, the Ruthenian question served to strengthen the bond between conservatives and democrats, limiting the freedom of action of the latter. To maintain a united Polish front, the democrats belonged to the conservative-dominated Polish Circle (parliamentary club) in the Reichsrat. Gradually, the most outstanding democratic leaders, Smolka and Ziemiałkowski, gravitated to the Right and cooperated with the government. So did the conservative commoner Mikołaj Zyblikiewicz (1823–87), who himself was not a *stańczyk*. While continuing to view Galicia as a Polish Piedmont, while counting on international events to reopen the Polish question, while defending the insurrectionary tradition, the democrats were bound to be drawn more and more into local and Austrian affairs. Although they realized that a democratic federalization of the Habsburg monarchy could bring no real solution for Poland, they actively promoted such a reorganization of the empire and a fully autonomous status for Galicia. Their role in Galician politics, however, was always secondary. The conservatives were the dominant group. Supported by the landed gentry and the Cracow intellectuals, and profiting from the curial system, they were on their way to achieving a near monopoly of power which they retained until the end of the nineteenth century.

The governmental crisis in 1865 forced Vienna to return to a policy of further constitutional changes in the monarchy. With a clear majority of landowners, the new Galician diet was in a position to converse with Vienna. Austria's defeat at Sadova in 1866 only underlined the need for a reconstruction of the empire. Gołuchowski came back to rule Galicia as viceroy (Statthalter, namiestnik), and on December 10, 1866, the Galician diet adopted an important address to the throne. With every word carefully weighed the address envisaged Austria's future through self-government of its provinces. Asserting their faith in Austria's mission of protecting Western civilization—which had been Poland's historic task—the address said that, "without fear of denying our own national idea" the Poles stood and wished to stand by the emperor. Far from being an example of conservative servility, as contemporary and later critics have argued, the address was a political offer of loyal cooperation in exchange for autonomy and support of the Polish question against Russia. It only became an act of unilateral submission to the monarchy when the Austrian side failed to satisfy Polish conditions and the Poles did not draw back from cooperation.

The Austro-Hungarian Compromise of 1867 presented the Galician Poles with a dilemma. Were they to insist on a federalization of the monarchy and make common cause with the Czechs, or should they accept the Compromise in return for limited provincial autonomy? At first, a federalist approach seemed more attractive to conservatives and democrats alike. The diet adopted an address to that effect and withdrew it only after it became known that Vienna would use all available means to curb Galicia. In protracted negotiations conducted by Gołuchowski, a master realist who believed in exploiting opportunities as they arose, and joined by Ziemiałkowski and Zyblikiewicz, the Poles obtained piecemeal concessions. Heated discussions arose in the diet and the Galician press.The conservatives argued that to insist on federalization would antagonize Vienna, help the Czechs to achieve a strong position at Galicia's expense, and amount to an anti-Hungarian position. What is more, Austria might be pushed toward a *rapprochement* with Russia. Consequently, the Poles accepted, although with serious misgivings, the *Ausgleich* and the Constitution of December, 1867, for Cisleithenia.

Under Smolka's leadership the democrats launched a campaign for a comprehensive autonomy for Galicia. After protracted debates and attempts to pressure Vienna—Polish deputies withdrew briefly from the Reichsrat—the diet passed a compromise resolution, the so-called Galician Resolution of 1868, which set the tone for the next four years of constitutional wrangles. The resolution requested a carefully spelled-out home rule *(Selbständige Stellung)*. It involved a separate administration, presided over by the viceroy and responsible to the diet, and self-government in matters of administration, police, justice (with a special supreme court), education, and culture. There would be a Galician chancellor in Vienna, and Polish deputies in the Reichsrat would only take part in debates pertaining to matters common to the entire monarchy. In fact, Galicia would become a Polish Kingdom within Austria, and Gołuchowski, who favored the resolution, told Francis Joseph of his great wish to see the emperor assume one day the Polish crown. For a second time the Poles were openly stating their predilection for an Austro-Polish solution of their national question. Yet, Vienna did not take up the Polish offer. The principal reason was its fear of Russia, which strongly objected to the emergence of a Polish nucleus under Austria. Francis Joseph cancelled his visit to Galicia; Gołuchowski resigned.

Austro-Polish relations then developed along two parallel lines. The Galician Resolution was maintained but could not win the required majority in the Reichsrat. It figured in various combinations, then contemplated in Vienna, including international alignments. At the time of the Franco-Prussian War of 1870, the Poles thought of tying their question to an Austro-French alliance. In 1871 Austria's foreign minister, Andrássy, toyed with the idea of war against Russia and a subsequent reconstruction of Poland. Naturally Bismarck, intent on maintaining the unity of the partitioning powers, would never stand for such a solution. When in 1873 the Reichsrat introduced direct suffrage in place of elections through the provincial diets, it administered a *coup de grâce* to the program of a comprehensive Galician autonomy.

The Galician Resolution, however, affected a second line of development. Equally unwilling to force the Poles into total opposition and to grant them a special status of autonomy, Vienna proceeded to make significant piecemeal concessions to Galicia. By 1867 the administrative subdivision of Galicia, which had always aroused Polish fears of a real division of the province into Polish and Ruthenian parts, came to an end. In 1869 the Polish language was declared the tongue of the province *(Landessprache)*; this had incalculable practical repercussions for Galicia. After the Poles returned to the Reichsrat in 1870, having briefly boycotted it in 1869, higher education was polonized, a learned academy (Akademia Umiejętności) permitted, and a minister without portfolio (a Pole) appointed to deal with Galician affairs. When in 1871 Gołuchowski became viceroy for the third time, Galicia enjoyed a *de facto* autonomy.

## II. AUTONOMOUS GALICIA: LIGHTS AND SHADOWS

The regime that prevailed in Galicia in the last decades of the nineteenth and the first fourteen years of the twentieth century was not based on a comprehensive status or agreement comparable to the *Ausgleich*. The government could withdraw its concessions to the Poles, but since it needed their support this was an unlikely contingency. According to the Constitution of 1867, the competence of the diet—the Polish name "Sejm" is appropriate from that time on—was enlarged to include all matters not expressly reserved to the Reichsrat. The Sejm shared with the government control over the educational system in Galicia, the most important organ of which was the Provincial School Board (Rada Szkolna Krajowa). The crucial language decree of 1869 polonized the administration, the judiciary system, and schools. This concession virtually excluded non-Poles from positions of authority in Galicia, even though the use of Ruthenian was legally safeguarded in the eastern parts of the country and in certain institutions. Given the socioeconomic structure of Galicia and the curial system, the Polish upper classes had all the real power in their hands. Fears of illiterate masses infringing on the government —memories of 1846 still festered—resulted in the exclusion of Polish peasants from the Sejm in the years 1877-89. The Ruthenians had only fourteen deputies in 1867, and the bulk of the Ruthenian masses were disfranchised by the existing electoral law.

The generation of conservative leaders who ruled Galicia after Gołuchowski's death, in 1873, showed an increasingly class-conscious and Catholic clerical attitude. Not that all long-range Polish aspirations were abandoned! During the Balkan crisis of 1875-78, a group of Polish conservatives counting on European Catholic support—these were the years of the *Kulturkampf* in Germany—attempted to create a "national government" in anticipation of a showdown between Austria and Russia. Polish conservatives and democrats alike submitted memoranda to the Berlin Congress in 1878, but without achieving any results. The two groups split, however, on the question of Austrian occupation of Bosnia and Hercegovina, the democrats voting against it in the Reichsrat.

Frustrated in international affairs, Galician Poles concentrated on local matters. The existing regime showed little capacity for change and evolution. The enlightened Cracow conservatives tried to reform the administration so as to eliminate some of the confusion of the "two track" system, especially on the lowest level. They were unsuccessful mainly because of the attitude of their Eastern Galician allies, the so-called *Podolacy* (the Podolians), who opposed changes in the relationship between the manorial demesnes and the predominantly Ruthenian communes. The slogan of the *Podolacy*, as expressed by one of the leaders in Ruthenian, *naj budu jak buwalo*, was the equivalent of "let sleeping dogs lie." This was particularly true for their stand on the crucial Ruthenian question, which demanded a bold and imaginative approach on the part of the Poles.

The historian Szujski termed the Ruthenian issue "a social question with national aspirations," and he advocated the recognition of Ruthenians in the diet, in schools, and in the communes in return for their acceptance of unity with the Poles. Another Cracow conservative, Tarnowski, opined that the nascent Ukrainian movement which stressed the unity of Galician Ruthenians with Russian Ukrainians ought to be protected and encouraged. It was up to the Poles to nurse this movement in Galicia so that it would spread to the Ukraine and eventually lead to a Polish-Ukrainian union. The *Podolacy* opposed such long-range schemes. They found it easier to deal with the conservative Ruthenian clergy, which needed the patronage of the nobility, than with the young Ukrainian nationalists and social radicals. Efforts to achieve some Polish-Ruthenian (Ukrainian) *modus vivendi* in the 1860s and 1870s broke down on the resistance of the Eastern Galician Poles (conservatives and democrats alike). Fear of the Ruthenian masses, which according to the 1880 census made up 43 percent of the entire population of Galicia, paralyzed political reforms.

While the Ruthenian question was both national and social, the Jewish problem was in part a religious and cultural, in part an economic phenomenon. The largely unassimilated Jewish population more than doubled between 1857 and 1890 and reached 11.5 percent of the total population. In eight towns the Jews formed 75 percent of the burghers; in fifty-five, 50-75 percent; and in sixty towns, 25 to 30 percent. In 1881 about 75-80 percent of local trade was in Jewish hands. Jews owned the bulk of such industries as sawmills, tanneries, brick factories, small oil refineries, and leather factories. In 1874 Jewish landowners controlled 16.2 percent of all the estates. The mass of Jewry lived in conditions of great misery, typical for the Galician lower classes.

Austrian Jews enjoyed full equality of rights after 1867, and the Sejm overwhelmingly endorsed this status in 1868. Actual participation of Jews in political and administrative life was proportionately higher than that of the Ruthenians but well below that of the Poles— five deputies in the diet, some city councilors and officials, some members of the chambers of commerce, and a few town mayors, for instance, in Stryj and Brody. One of the reasons for this state of affairs was the low degree of assimilation among the Jews. Advocated by democrats and Cracow conservatives, polonization of Galician Jews made some strides after the local schools became Polish. In the late 1870s and 1880s a pro-Polish trend began to prevail over a pro-German orientation. One of several leaders of the assimilationist movement, the writer and critic Wilhelm Feldman (1868–1919), urged, as a Polish patriot, a total integration of the Jews with the Poles. Indeed, Jewish deputies from Galicia belonged to the Polish Circle in the Reichsrat. But, assimilation processes never encompassed the bulk of the population. Orthodox Jewish leaders opposed it. Increasing economic competition between Christians and Jews contributed to anti-Semitism, which affected even a wing of the Polish democrats. Eastern Galician conservatives, part of the clergy, and the rising populist movement were inimical to the Jews. As a whole, Galician Jewry could not easily be absorbed even under the most advantageous circumstances, but a number of prominent individuals and groups were.

The Poles in Galicia had a great deal of control over the education but less so over the economy of the country. In the former field the record of the conservatives was quite impressive; in the latter they failed to overcome the basic weaknesses of the Galician economy. The outlook of the governing class imposed certain limitations on the nature of educational and economic policies. Illiteracy, which stood at the staggering figure of 95 percent in the 1850s, declined to 67 percent in 1890, but although the principle of free and compulsory elementary education was adopted it could not be realized in practice. Funds were lacking, and, besides, many a reactionary deputy viewed education of peasant children with suspicion. High schools and universities were of a high level, but fears were voiced that the country's economy could not absorb a large number of graduates. The growth of Ruthenian schools was restricted, and for a long time there was only one Ruthenian high school; a university was never created.

Most of Galicia's problems—political, social, national, and educational—were rooted in the backwardness of the country's economy. As late as 1830 some 80 percent of the population lived in the countryside, often in conditions of great poverty. In spite of a high mortality rate the country was becoming rapidly overpopulated. Although the peasants owned about 58 percent of land in 1860 and 61 percent in 1890, they had virtually no pastures or forests— a result of the "servitudes" arrangement following the 1848 emancipation. Constant subdivision of land accounted for the fact that most peasant holdings were of uneconomical size, namely, 2.5 to 12.5 acres. Farming methods remained antiquated. In contrast, about 20 percent of the land belonged to 160 great landowners who had abundant cheap labor and made little effort to invest in machinery and engage in intensive farming. Smaller estates fared less well and often had to seek income from cutting timber in their forests or parceling out their land. Parceling, however, proceeded at a slower pace in Galicia than in other parts of Poland.

After 1867 the Austrian Ministry of Agriculture subsidized farming. In the 1870s and 1880s railroad building, new credit facilities, and developments in other branches of the Galician economy brought some improvements. Following the crisis of 1878, Austria began to construct strategical railroad lines linking Galicia with Hungary; by 1912, 3,447 kilometers of tracks had been added to the existing 673. The new lines facilitated the exportation of Galician agrarian products as well as of salt and crude oil. The stationing of large army corps in the province meant additional consumers. The construction of fortresses stimulated the labor market. In the field of finance, alongside the old Land Credit Association, a peasant credit institution (Zakład kredytowy włościański) was founded in 1863; it survived for the next twenty years. In 1883 the first Polish self-governing banking institution, the Provincial Bank (Bank Krajowy), was established. In spite of the small amount of initial capital the bank greatly affected the economic life of the province. Until 1891 it advanced money to agricultural enterprises; later it also extended loans to industry and commercial institutions. In 1890 cooperative credit associations, so-called Kasy Szefczyka which catered to poorer peasants, came into existence. All these developments helped to eliminate antiquated farming methods and led to increasing cultivation of such crops as sugar beets and tobacco. Industries connected with agriculture, namely, breweries, distilleries, and sugar refineries, registered progress. Yet, Galicia could not compare with an advanced and modern farming region such as Poznania, nor did it have the possibility of becoming one.

The chances of industrializing Galicia and creating a large consumers' market were small. The province could not compete with the Austrian and Czech finished products that flooded the country. Tariffs and railroad freight rates were discriminatory, and it paid to export raw materials and import finished goods. Galicia exported salt, corn, cattle, and crude oil; its balance of trade with the other provinces of the monarchy was constantly unfavorable. In terms of size and population Galicia constituted more than one-fourth of Cisleithania, but it had only 9.2 percent of the industrial enterprises of Austria and only 4 percent of the larger plants. In 1880 the value of total factory and artisan production was calculated at 21 million crowns.

In 1881 Zyblikiewicz put forward a program of industrialization, but a combination of subjective and objective factors militated against progress. Representing vested land interests, the Galician Sejm showed relatively little awareness of the need to industrialize the province. The more conservative landowners were loathe to lose the abundant cheap labor that would have been drawn into industry. They viewed factories as the breeding ground of socialism and radicalism. Only a few of the great landowners went into business. Austrian and English capital pre-dominated in the oil industry, German capital in the relatively small coal mining area.

In absolute figures Galician production increased in several fields. During the period from 1870 to 1890, coal output rose from 197,000 to 609,000 tons, and that of oil, the youngest and most promising branch of industry, increased four times. In the years between 1869 and 1890 the population of Lemberg rose from 70,000 to 120,000, and that of Cracow from 50,000 to 70,000. The remaining small towns grew more slowly. The number of industrial workers reached a hundred thousand only in 1900.

One of the main obstacles to a large investment program was the unresolved question of indemnity to the landlords arising out of the peasant emancipation of 1848. While the monarchy financed payments through loans to Galicia, the increasing indebtedness to Vienna hung like a sword of Damocles over the province. Moreover, the amortization and interest rates of the indemnity bonds took over 50 percent of the supplementary tax, the only income at the disposal of the Galician Provincial Department. Consequently, the budget of the department was totally inadequate and no investments could be undertaken. The situation improved in 1889 and 1890. The state took away the landlords' monopoly of production and sale of spirits, and although the compensation paid was greatly advantageous to the landowners, the income from spirit sales later went to the province. In 1890 the Reichsrat agreed to annul Galicia's debts to the empire and to pay a yearly subsidy toward the completion of the indemnity operation. For the first time since Galicia became virtually autonomous, the budget of the Provincial Department was cleared of debts and the province could seriously approach the question of local investments. But the possibilities for such investments were limited. An indication of Galicia's poverty was its share in the total income of Austria (10-13 percent), and in the monarchy's expenditure (16-18 percent). In both cases the figures were disproportionately lower than Galicia's size and population.

In 1888 a Lemberg democrat, Stanisław Szczepanowski (1846–1900), shocked Polish public opinion by publishing a book entitled *Galician Misery (Nędza Galicyjska)*. His picture of the lowest classes in Galicia was frightening, as was his assertion that fifty thousand people died annually of starvation. Using statistical data, Szczepanowski showed that the food consumption of a citizen of Galicia was one-half that of an average European, and his working capacity was one-fourth. An underfed man could not work more effectively, but unless he did, his position would not improve. It was a vicious circle, and Szczepanowski called for an industrialization of the province.

The conservative ruling circles could be, and were, blamed for the situation that prevailed in autonomous Galicia, but as yet their power was not seriously challenged. Through a central election committee, set up in 1876, and occasional administrative pressures they controlled the elections to the provincial bodies and to the Reichsrat. They claimed to have achieved a privileged position for the Poles not only in Galicia but also in the monarchy. The Polish Circle played a crucial part in the parliamentary life of the state, and without Polish deputies "constitutional government in Austria would have been impracticable."[1] Galician Poles, including Alfred Potocki (1817–89), Gołuchowski, Kazimierz Grocholski (1815–80), Julian Dunajewski (1824–1907), and Kazimierz Badeni (1846–1909), occupied the highest positions in the Viennese cabinet. Did their activity serve long-range Polish interests? Or did it merely exemplify the most successful application of Triple Loyalism?

Polish influences in Vienna did not bring about the realization of an Austro-Polish solution as envisaged in the Galician addresses.

1. Z. A. B. Zeman, *The Break-up of the Habsburg Empire 1914-1918* (London: Oxford University Press, 1961), p. 250.

Involvement in the Balkans lessened Austrian interest in the Polish question. The original patriotism of the Cracow school tended to degenerate into mere loyalty and a defense of the *status quo*. In the process of making Galicia a Polish center, particulary in the cultural sphere, that radiated its influence over other lands, the conservatives increasingly tended to identify their rule over Galicia with Polish patriotism. A political and ideological stagnation set in, in spite of the efforts of such outstanding young conservatives as the historian and politician Michał Bobrzyński (1849-1935) to breathe in new life and instill new ideas. In the 1880s the democrats attacked the conservatives as the "gravediggers of the idea of Polish statehood," but theirs were the voices of the epigoni of the January Insurrection. It fell to the rising movements of populism, socialism, and a little later to National Democrats to relate politics to changing socioeconomic realities and to assault the existing order from the position of social and national radicalism. Demands were raised for universal suffrage and social justice. The old and the new were slowly coming to grips with each other in Galicia as well as throughout the whole Habsburg monarchy.

Influenced in part by the Russian *narodniki*, but mainly a product of specific local conditions, populism arose in Galicia in the 1870s. Peasant grievances over woods and pastures, the spirit monopoly, and vexing remnants of feudal practices were voiced by Poles and Ruthenians alike. Although the enlightened Tarnowski deplored the existence of practices that still smacked of the *corvée*, most landowners, especially in Eastern Galicia, favored a patriarchal approach to the peasantry. In the context of Galician autonomy, the Polish leading class had no need of peasants as political allies. Peasant deputies were successfully kept out of the Sejm for more than a decade, and a phenomenon of "two nations"—peasant and "Polish"—survived until the early twentieth century. In those conditions it fell to the lower clergy and the landless intelligentsia— even if they were of gentry stock—to provide the impetus for an organized peasant movement.

The first Populist movement in Galicia was launched by a dynamic and ambitious priest, Stanisław Stojałowski (1845-1911). With the use of two weeklies, which he bought and edited in a populist spirit, Stojałowski agitated among the peasants, urging them to improve their position through thrift and cooperative farming. He advised them to lessen their dependence on landowners and Jews. Rebuked by the administration and censured by the ecclesiastical hierarchy, Stojałowski became a radical and demagogic tribune of the people. His ambition and fiery temperament led him later to change his position and to end up on the political Right, but he greatly contributed toward activating the peasantry and making a peasant mass movement possible.

The populist creed of another leader, Bolesław Wysłouch (1855-1937), a political émigré from Russian Poland, took different forms. His program was both populist and patriotic. Regarding the peasantry as the backbone of the nation, he sought to achieve for it equality and a proper place in society. A reformer rather than a revolutionary, he advocated in his journal the participation of peasants in politics and fulfillment of their social needs. As for a reborn Poland, he stressed that she ought to be a free federation of all the nationalities of the former commonwealth and not a Poland exclusively dominated by the Poles.

In contrast to populism, which rested on a wide social basis and developed slowly because of the immaturity and poverty of the peasantry, socialism encountered difficulties because of the minuscule industrial proletariat in Galicia. Although the impetus came from Russian Poles—Limanowski and Waryński—the Socialist movement in Galicia assumed a different shape than it did in Russian Poland. Waryński's insistence on conspiracy and revolutionary action contrasted with the more pragmatic and practical tendencies of local Socialists, who also included young Ruthenian radicals such as the poet Ivan Franko (1856-1916) and Mykhailo Pavlyk (1853-1915). In 1878 the first Socialist committee was set up by Limanowski, who the same year was expelled as a troublesome foreigner. A spectacular trial of Socialists took place in 1880; it ended with Waryński's expulsion but the Galician defendants were not punished. Although the conservative *Czas* fulminated against the "wildest theories" of the Socialists, the democratic and liberal press was sympathetic to the accused. The trial brought a good deal of publicity for socialist ideas.

While the "nationalist versus internationalist" controversy raged in the émigré center in Geneva, Galician Socialists attempted to reconcile the two concepts in their program of 1881. Given the conditions in the monarchy and in Galicia, they placed emphasis on universal suffrage and a minimum program of reforms. They also formulated the wish that the "Polish and Ruthenian peoples recover their independent national existence." When the Austrian Social Democratic movement emerged as a party in 1889 they established ties with it. Galician Socialists published the first Polish Socialist paper, *Praca* (Work), and from Galicia came the text of the battle song "The Red Flag." Although they were members of a local movement with specific characteristics and tactics, Galician Socialists thought in terms that transcended the boundaries of the Habsburg monarchy, not only in the internationalist but primarily in the Polish sense. Together with the Populist and the Ruthenian (Ukrainian) radicals, they began to rise as a political force in the traditionally conservative Galician society.

III. PRUSSIAN POLAND ON THE EVE OF THE *KULTURKAMPF*

The twenty-odd years following the January Insurrection can be divided, as far as Prussian Poland is concerned, into three phases, all of which were dominated by Bismarck's personality. During the period 1863-71, Prussia achieved the unification of Germany under her leadership, and in spite of strong Polish protests, Pomerania and Poznania became incorporated first into the North German Confederation (1867) and then into the German Empire (1871). This meant that even Poznania, whose special status had been recognized by the Congress of Vienna, would simply merge into Germany. Henceforth the continuing Polish conflict with the Prussian administration increasingly acquired the characteristics of a struggle between Germandom *(Deutschtum)* and the Polish provinces which were now regarded as the eastern borderlands of the Reich. At the same time, however, the Poles gained a new political forum, the all-German Reichstag, in which their deputies operated within a different party alignment than in the Prussian Landtag.

The second and crucial phase, 1872-85, was dominated by the *Kulturkampf* launched in Germany in order to integrate and centralize the Reich against centrifugal, particularist tendencies of regionalism and Catholicism. In the Catholic Polish provinces the *Kulturkampf* acquired the features of a struggle between nationalities, even though Prussian *raison d'état* rather than German nationalism was its driving force. The *Kulturkampf* contributed to a closing of Polish ranks, under the slogan of national survival, in order to resist governmental pressures. It also resulted in a temporary alliance with the German Catholic Center Party.

The third phase, starting in 1885, marked the beginning of a new Prussian policy toward the Poles. Finally realizing that the Poles could not be divided into the inimical gentry and clergy and a potentially loyal mass of "Polish-speaking Prussians," the government resorted to measures of germanization and colonization that were directed against the entire Polish population.

Political loyalism, practiced with a good deal of success in Galicia, stood little chance in Poznania. Owing to the local conditions, "organic work" proved a much more successful means of resistance to Bismarckian policies. Operating within the frame of German legality—even if that legality did not exclude the pressures of an efficient, ruthless, and incorruptible Prussian administrative apparatus—the Poles were able to strengthen their socioeconomic and cultural positions. Assisted by the prevailing economic and social trends, they even perfected their means of counteraction. The Prussian Pole developed characteristics that distinguished him from his countryman under Austria or Russia. He was better educated; he was disciplined, hard-working, and enjoyed a higher standard of living; he could compete on nearly equal terms with the Germans. An article written in 1872 well expressed the Poznanian concept of "organic work": "If you are a shoemaker make better shoes, if you are a blacksmith do a better job on the cart . . . if you are a Polish housewife make better and cleaner butter, have better vegetables, linen, fruits, and poultry than the Germans have. In this way you will save yourself and Poland. . . . Learning, work, order, and thrift, these are our new weapons."[2]

Around 1864 Poznania and Pomerania offered the picture of a fairly prosperous and developing society. Largely due to German policies that assigned them the role of a "granary" of the Reich, the area continued to be predominantly agrarian. By 1882, 65 percent of Poznania's population was still engaged in agriculture, but it was a prospering agriculture assisted by Germany's policies of protectionism. Large estates predominated, occupying about 60 percent of the land in 1860 and 57 percent thirty years later. Sizable peasant farms prevailed over small and uneconomical holdings. The phenomenon of widely scattered strips, typical in the Russian and Austrian lands, was unknown in Poznania. Consequently, consolidated farms permitted more advanced farming techniques and intensive methods of cultivation. Yields increased rapidly and almost doubled those in Congress Poland; natural and chemical fertilizers were increasingly used; there was a rational forest culture. In the 1880s steam plows came into use as well as machines for threshing grain and processing dairy products. The percentage of farms that used machinery increased in the years 1882-95 from 10.2 to 42.6. Cultivation of sugar beets was profitable to farmers, and their property was enhanced by rising land prices. All these achievements were at least in part connected with the original Prussian land reform which had been realized at the expense of the poorest stratum of the peasantry. The number of landless grew, and because of the insufficient industrialization the landless had to seek employment in western Germany, particularly Westphalia, or they had to emigrate overseas.

During this period the Poles lost a considerable number of landed estates to German Junkers, so that by the 1880s the latter held more

2. Cited in Witold Jakóbczyk, *Studia nad dziejami Wielkopolski w XIX-w.* Prace Komisji Historycznej, vol. 28, issue 3 (Poznań: Poznańskie Towarzystwo Przyjaciół Nauk, Wydział Historii i Nauk Społecznych, 1967), 2:77n.

land than the former. Polish farmers in Poznania, however, still controlled 655,000 hectares as compared to 400,000 owned by Germans. The main exports of Poznania and Pomerania were grains, timber, hogs, hides, and unrefined sugar. The imports were coal, coke, iron, steel, beer and wine, fish, fats, and oils. The balance of trade was favorable.

Most of the industries of Prussian Poland were connected with food-processing or agriculture: spirit refineries, sugar refineries, and machinery works, most of which produced agricultural tools. Only in Danzig and Elbing (Elbląg) were there large enterprises such as naval yards. In Posen Hipolit Cegielski (1815–68) established the first Polish factory that produced machinery, the most important in the province. Sugar works which employed modern methods of production, and in the 1870s operated as large establishments, registered spectacular progress. Their output rose from 7,000 quintals (a quintal equals 220.46 pounds) in 1870 to 1.9 million quintals in 1900.

Otherwise, industrial development was slow. Around 1867 less than 13 percent of the population derived its living from industry (including crafts) in both Poznania and Pomerania. By way of comparison, the figure for the province of Brandenburg was over 30 percent. The percentage increased to roughly 18 for Prussian Poland in 1882 and passed the figure of 20 in 1895. Polish, as opposed to German, participation in industries was proportionately lower. There were hardly any Poles among the greater industrialists, bankers, or traders. While the Poles constituted about 48 percent of the owners of enterprises and 28 percent of the traders, most of the enterprises in Polish hands were small—only ninety-five employed more than fifty workers, and only nineteen had over two hundred workers in 1882. The Jews, who on the whole cooperated with the Germans, dropped to 2.5 percent of Poznania's population by 1890. Many emigrated westward to larger cities and more industrialized areas. Emigration for economic motives also affected the Germans in Prussian Poland. In the years 1861–90 the percentage of German-speaking population dropped in four regencies: from 75.3 percent to 72.12 in Danzig; from 62.5 to 60.9 percent in Marienwerder (Kwidzyń), from 53.4 to 49.86 percent in Bromberg (Bydgoszcz), and from 41.1 to 34.26 percent in Posen.

Communications and transport in Prussian Poland was in much better shape than in Galicia or the Russian-ruled provinces. Railroad construction began early and the network was relatively dense. By 1870 there were 528.1 kilometers of tracks in Poznania alone, roughly 33.3 kilometers per 10,000 inhabitants.[3] By 1900 there were

3. Data based on T. Dohmalowa's doctoral dissertation at Poznań University,

about 2,000 kilometers of tracks. Most of the lines connected the region with the rest of Prussia, thus contributing to commercial exchanges. At first the lines were privately owned and the capital came from German banks. Starting in 1870, the government began to buy them out; in 1883 a decree nationalizing the railroads was passed.

Governmental reprisals against Prussian Poles who had taken part in the January Insurrection did not seriously affect the program of "organic work," but they brought into sharper relief the anti-Polish attitude of the administration. Nearly two thousand Poles were tried; eleven were sentenced to death in absentia, others imprisoned for one or two years. After Prussia's victory over Austria, a general amnesty was declared. As in the past, stern measures were mainly directed against the landowning gentry and the clergy. The archbishop of Gnesen-Posen incurred the wrath of the government for having regarded himself, during the insurrection, as the primate of all Poland. But Bismarck's attempts through the papacy to weaken the archdiocese were not crowned with success. The Iron Chancellor was determined, however, to prevent the Polish question from re-emerging on the international forum, and he viewed with great suspicion any signs of Austro-Polish cooperation. But Bismarck intimated that should the Polish issue ever be used by St. Petersburg or Vienna in a manner endangering Prussian interests, he would make use of the issue himself. As he put it in the 1880s, Poland was like "a hot iron," but "we will grab it to defend ourselves."[4]

Polish political activity in the 1860s was largely restricted to a traditional defense of Polish rights in Poznania. Older Polish leaders, such as Władysław Niegolewski (1819–85) or Kazimierz Kantak (1824-86), did not favor policies of Triple Loyalism, and their views were shared by the politically active clergy. The Polish Circle (parliamentary club) in the Landtag comprised twenty-six deputies, six of whom came from Pomerania (West Prussia). It had a conservative-clerical and a national-liberal wing, but the conflict between the two was really of marginal importance.

Social conflicts naturally existed, but the Polish-German antagonism tended to push them into the background. Poznanian landowners and the clergy were obviously the leading forces in the province. But unlike their counterparts in other Polish lands they participated more fully and jointly with the middle class and the peasantry. The peasantry took the initiative of setting up agricultural societies, and the first one organized in 1862 was the earliest institution of its

"Rozwój transportu w Wielkopolsce 1815–1914," and kindly supplied to this author by Professor Lech Trzeciakowski.
4. Józef Feldman, *Bismarck a Polska* (2nd ed.; Warszawa: Czytelnik, 1947), p. 316.

kind founded in any part of partitioned Poland. The landowners began to join these societies at a fairly early date, and one of them, Maksymilian Jackowski (1815–1905), became their "patron." The societies taught modern farming methods and urged landowners and peasants to keep the land in Polish hands. In the 1870s about thirty agricultural circles operated in Prussian Poland. The clergy played an important part in them.

In towns the gymnastic organization Sokół (Falcon), credit-saving associations (Spółki Zarobkowe), associations of industrialists and artisans, and various social unions existed and flourished. They provided a focus for communal activities, advanced money to their members, and promoted Polish customs and the Polish way of life. In 1862 the Poznanian Industrial Association participated in the Industrial Exhibition in London. In 1865 the Central Economic Association (Centralne Towarzystwo Gospodarcze) was revived under Cegielski's leadership. A land bank and the Agrarian-Industrial Bank (1870) followed. Father Augustyn Szamarzewski (1832–91) was instrumental in uniting the credit associations, of which he became the "patron." In 1886 a bank of the union of these associations (Bank Związku Spółek Zarobkowych), based mainly on local Polish capital, came into being.

Parallel to societies that worked to raise the socioeconomic standards of Poles under Prussia, there operated cultural and educational associations, some of which went back to the 1840s. From its inception in 1841 up to 1890, the Association of Scholarly Aid (Towarzystwo Pomocy Naukowej) assisted through grants and scholarships some three thousand future teachers, doctors, lawyers, and craftsmen. The Association of Popular Education (Towarzystwo Oświaty Ludowej), founded in 1872, organized reading rooms in small towns and made Polish books available to the general public. Suppressed in 1879 during the *Kulturkampf*, it reemerged under the name of the Association of Popular Libraries (Towarzystwo Czytelni Ludowych). Given the fact that illiteracy in Prussian Poland was minimal, cultural and educational associations played an important part in the life of these provinces. Centering in Poznania where they had a mass following, they extended to the more germanized Pomerania. Clerical influences were strong not only because the clergy was active and respected but also because in the process of resisting Protestant Prussia the term Pole and Catholic became virtually synonymous. The part played by the Polish press was particularly important. No wonder that during those years the national consciousness and political maturity of Poles grew and began to extend also to those who had previously become germanized or thought of themselves as Polish-speaking Prussians.

IV. THE *KULTURKAMPF* AND A NEW COURSE

In early 1872 Bismarck wrote his minister of the interior: "I have the feeling that even if today the ground in the territories of our Polish provinces does not yet clearly tremble under our feet, it is so undermined that it could collapse as soon as a Polish-Catholic-Austrian policy is developed."[5] This appraisal of the situation in Prussian Poland was closely connected with Bismarck's launching of the *Kulturkampf* in Germany. The Polish factor figured prominently in the campaign, even if Bismarck did exaggerate it on purpose to mobilize German public opinion against the Poles and thus gain additional support for his policies.

In all-German terms the object of the *Kulturkampf* was to weld together the newly established empire, in the name of a progressive and secular German culture. Catholicism, with its strong hold in many parts of Germany and reinforced by the 1870 decree on papal infallibility and the ultramontane movement, appeared as the principal foe. Its connection with Catholic Austria, only recently expelled from Germany and anxious to retain her influence there, made the church doubly suspicious to Bismarck and the bourgeoisie as represented in the National Liberal Party. The latter sought to complete German unification by breaking the church's influence on education and subordinating it to secular state controls. In a series of decrees passed from 1872 to 1876, the high point being the laws of May, 1873, the state declared war on the church. The Jesuit order was expelled, relations with the papacy broken off, and the Catholic Department of the Prussian Ministry of Culture abolished. Appointments of priests were made conditional on their completion of state high schools and universities, and on their passing of examinations in "culture." The state established control over church estates and declared that henceforth only civil marriages were legal.

Ruthlessly enforced by the administration, which fined and imprisoned recalcitrants, the *Kulturkampf* provoked a major crisis in Germany and had serious repercussions in Europe. It earned Bismarck the wrath of French and Austrian conservatives and the sympathy of Russia and Italy. Domestic opposition was a combination of various elements: Protestants from Hanover, who cherished their own separate traditions, south German Catholics, Alsatians, Danes, and Poles. A large Catholic party, the Zentrum, appeared as a new and significant factor in German politics.

All the elements of the *Kulturkampf*—state versus church, centralism versus autonomy, authorities versus the citizens—appeared with particular sharpness in Prussian Poland. The replacement of

5. Cited in German in Lech Trzeciakowski, *Kulturkampf w zaborze pruskim* (Poznań: Wydawnictwo Poznańskie, 1970), p. 22.

Polish priests as teachers and school inspectors by Prussian state functionaries meant germanization of the educational system. The expulsion of the Jesuits as well as other measures directed against the church endangered one of the pillars of Polish resistance to Germandom. Thus, in Prussian Poland the struggle against the church became an anti-Polish struggle: secularization of education meant germanization; centralism went against the separate identity of Polish provinces. Bismarck himself harped on the national theme to gain the support of the Prussian Junkers, who although mainly Protestant were not anticlerical and did not relish the adoption of bourgeois-liberal policies. By pointing to Polish influences (the Radziwiłłs) in the Catholic Department of the Prussian Ministry of Culture and invoking Polish-Austrian connections, Bismarck spoke of a Polish-Catholic intrigue threatening Prussia and the Reich.

It was somewhat paradoxical that the *Kulturkampf* began at a moment when Prussia had seemingly found a cooperative and accommodating partner in the person of the new archbishop of Posen-Gnesen, Mieczysław Ledóchowski (1822-1902). A cosmopolitan prince of the church, a loyalist highly regarded in Berlin as an ally against democracy, revolution, and Polish nationalism, Ledóchowski tried to keep the church out of politics. Comparing, on one occasion, the Poles to the Burgundians who had not lost anything by becoming Frenchmen, the archbishop was largely responsible for Polish electoral defeats, in the course of which the number of deputies to the Landtag fell from twenty to twelve. He also forbade the saying of masses commemorating national anniversaries and the singing of the hymn "God protect Poland." Enjoying a limited support from the Poznanian ultramontane conservatives, Ledóchowski brought on himself the ire of the Polish liberals and of the people.

At the beginning of the *Kulturkampf*, Ledóchowski was willing to go along with the government on such measures as part of religion classes being taught in German, and an increased germanization of public life. But he adamantly refused to subordinate the church to the state. Imprisoned in 1874 and then expelled from Prussia, he suddenly became a martyr not only of Catholicism but of the Polish cause as well. The overwhelming majority of priests who followed his orders suffered punishment. The suffragan bishops of Posen and Gnesen and over a hundred priests were arrested; ninety parish priests were removed. Out of forty deacons thirty-five were imprisoned. German Catholic bishops in Pomerania who also came in conflict with the state were penalized.

The *Kulturkampf* produced a common front of the Catholic hierarchy of Poznania, Pomerania, and Upper Silesia. In this last province the Polish-speaking masses had not been really hostile to the state, but they now became mobilized for battle under the aegis of the church. German Catholics who made common cause with the Poles were no less alive than Bismarck was to German national interests. But they viewed the germanization of the Poles as a gradual and largely voluntary process which the oppressive *Kulturkampf* could only arrest. Allying itself with the Poles on religious grounds, the Zentrum did not feel that it was betraying the German cause. Polish cooperation with another group hostile to Bismarck's policies, namely, the Social Democrats, was difficult and limited; German Socialists and the socially conservative Catholic Poles hardly spoke the same language.

Polish resistance could not prevent continuing germanization from above. This was particularly true in the field of education. Up to 1870 all children had to learn German, but Polish was the language of instruction in elementary schools and, in a more limited fashion, in Catholic high schools. After 1872 German became the language of instruction in all elementary schools in Poznania. Only religious classes continued to be in part taught in Polish, and Polish also remained one of the subjects in the curriculum. In high schools severe linguistic restrictions were imposed, and in 1874 the use of Polish textbooks was forbidden. Due to the children's low degree of proficiency in German, they were permitted to use Polish as an auxiliary language. In Pomerania, Polish was allowed in religious instruction only in the lower grades, but the study of Polish as a language took place only in the upper grades, that is, after the children were presumably fluent in German.

To force the population to use German in everyday life, a decree that made German the exclusive language of administration and courts was passed in 1876. A customer had to converse in German even at the post office and at the railroad station. Simultaneously, the government sought to efface external signs of the Polish character of Poznania. Polish resistance, "organic work" apart, centered at home, in the press, and in mass meetings. The slogan Home, the Main Bastion of Polishness gained wide currency. The role of the Polish press remained extremely important. In an atmosphere of gloom a few voices were raised exalting Panslavism and appealing for Russia's protection of brother Slavs. Such sentiments played into the hands of the administration, which was ever ready to speak of Polish disloyalty, and were based on ignorance of conditions then prevailing in Russian Poland. Their importance was very limited.

Two political trends emerged in the 1880s: socialism and a new version of conservative loyalism. The former, which such émigrés as Mendelson and Maria Jankowska (1850–1909), a native Poznanian worker Józef K. Janiszewski (1855-98), and a few others attempted to propagate in Poznania in 1881, did not take root. A trial of the Socialist leaders created a stir, but apart from that local conditions militated against the emergence of a Socialist movement. Conservative loyalism was associated with the entrance into politics of representatives of a younger generation whose spokesman was the new president of the Polish Circle, Józef Kościelski (1845-1911). In Bismarckian Prussia the group could claim no successes, nor could it devise a policy that corresponded to the realities.

The abatement of the *Kulturkampf* in Germany brought no relief to the Poles. Although Julius Dinder, Ledóchowski's successor to the archiepiscopal see, was not rabidly anti-Polish, the appointment of a German prelate was an affront to national sentiments. Germanization of schools continued, and in 1887 Polish as a subject was formally abolished. But in the mid-1880s the scene of the German-Polish struggle was shifting from an administrative and educational sphere to an economic and linguistic arena; the old concept of the loyal Polish-speaking Prussians was giving way to slogans of germanization and colonisation of Poznania.

The first sign of this new policy came with orders for the expulsion of around twenty thousand Poles and ten thousand Jews who were not Prussian citizens. This mass expulsion of people, many of whose families had lived in Prussia for generations, shocked German and European public opinion. It also appeared contrary to the interests of Prussian Junkers who needed cheap labor. But it corresponded to the ideas of Bismarck's allies, the National Liberals, who advocated a weakening of the Polish element in the "eastern provinces" and the settlement of these provinces by German colonists. Contemporary writings increasingly drew attention to the German exodus from the east and the move toward western Germany or overseas, and urged measures to reverse this trend. In an article entitled "Retreat of Germandom" *(Rückgang des Deutschtums)* published in 1885, the philosopher Edward Hartmann outlined a program for strengthening the cohesiveness of Germany and germanizing the minorities. He demanded that alien and inimical elements be eliminated *(ausrotten)*. The Polish case was particulary relevant.

In 1886 Bismarck made a major speech in which he raised the question of a compulsory buying out of Polish landed estates. He ironically remarked that the *szlachta* would not find it a great hardship and might even prefer to spend money thus earned in Paris or at roulette in Monte Carlo. A Polish deputy, Father Florian Stablewski (1841-1906), indignantly asked the Reichsrat whether such proposals meant that sheer might was to triumph over the principles of humanity, Christianity, freedom, or even the monarchic idea. While Bismarck's thrust was still directed against the landowning class as distinct from the loyal masses, the National Liberals, who at their 1885 congress took a violently anti-Polish stand, began to view the distinction as obsolete.

The bourgeoisie was willing to contribute financially to a major and systematic program of German colonization of Poznania and Pomerania. Nationalist motives aside, they were interested in creating a German peasant class in the east as a social and political balance to the conservative Junkers. In 1886 Bismarck announced the creation of a Colonization Commission (Ansiedlungs Komission für Westpreussen und Posen) endowed with a fund of one hundred million marks. Its object was to assist the operation of buying land in Poznania and Pomerania and parceling it out among German settlers. It is not absolutely clear to what extent domestic and international reasons combined to make Bismarck adopt this novel policy. Cooperation with the National Liberals would largely explain his domestic motives; changes in foreign policy, notably the forthcoming alliance with Austria-Hungary, may well have strengthened Bismarck's desire to tighten the Prussian hold over the Polish provinces.

The initial successes of German colonization were meager. Instead of the expected 40,000 German settlements only 3,600 were set up, and only 700-odd colonists from outside the region were attracted to Prussian Poland. With land prices rising, German landlords found it profitable to sell land indiscriminately to German settlers and to Poles. The latter quickly organized themselves to cope with the new threat to their position. Still, prior to 1890, the commission was able to buy twelve times more land than were the Poles, most of it having previously belonged to Polish estates.

By 1890, as compared with 1864, the Poles had lost some ground and had been subjected to ever increasing administrative and nationalist German pressures. But they held out in a number of fields and even registered some gains. While the number of Polish deputies to the Landtag was declining, it was increasing in the Reichstag. What is more, attempts were made to elect Poles as deputies from Upper Silesia. Such an expansion of the Polish question beyond the borders of Poznania, which had traditionally been considered by Berlin as the only Polish province properly speaking, was an important development. Under the leadership of a school teacher, Karol Miarka (1825–82), who had established close cooperation with the Zentrum, nationally conscious Poles in Upper Silesia could have their candidates elected. Obviously, at this juncture the Zentrum was the senior partner. The Polish national renascence in Upper Silesia was far from completed; the German clergy and the German upper classes still dominated the province. After the

*Kulturkampf* the need arose to emancipate the Polish movement from the tutelage of the Zentrum, and this led to conflicts with the new nationalistic archbishop of Breslau, George Kopp.

A successful participation of germanized Pomerania in a Polish national movement was not easy. Still, in the Kashubian area (the regions of Wejherowo, Kartuzy, Dirschau [Tczew], and Starogard) people began to elect Polish deputies. This was all the more remarkable because the Germans had always insisted on a distinction between Kashubians and Poles. A local poet and journalist, Hieronim Derdowski (1852-1902), launched the slogan There is no Kashubia without Poland and no Poland without Kashubia, and it proved to be no empty phrase. In the Mazurian area of East Prussia—part of which had belonged to the old commonwealth—there were beginnings of Polish political activity. For the first time, in 1890, a Polish candidate for the Landtag entered the lists in Allenstein (Olsztyn) and received five thousand votes. A Polish national movement, which was all too easily dismissed in Berlin as the work of "Poznanian agitators," was spreading throughout the eastern provinces of Prussia.

CHAPTER 12

# The Lithuanian and
# Ukrainian National Revival

THE January Insurrection of 1863 was the last Polish uprising in which the leaders appealed to the nations of Poland, Lithuania, and Ruś (Ukraine) to struggle for the rebirth of the old commonwealth. It was also the last in which not only Poles but Lithuanian and Belorussian peasants as well fought under the historic banner. Although the insurgent leaders understood the need for the application of federalist principles to these vast areas and agreed to Lithuanian and Ukrainian self-determination, they still thought mainly in terms of prepartition Poland. The collapse of the insurrection, followed by Russian policies of depolonization of the "western guberniias," marked the disintegration of the old historic concept. It may well be that the post-1864 developments merely hastened a natural process of change in the Lithuanian and Ukrainian lands. Native movements expanded, and since the gentry of Lithuania and Ukraine had become Polish, the new forces of national revival had to grow out of the masses of the people. Their leaders repudiated the historic heritage of the commonwealth, which they associated with the rule of the nobility. In their struggle for recognition they opposed both the tsarist regime and the predominantly Polish landowning classes.

To some far-sighted Poles this was an almost inevitable course of events, and they extended a helping hand to Lithuanians and Ukrainians and regarded them as allies against tsardom. To many Poles the national revival in the former western provinces, especially in Lithuania, was a separatist deviation, a misguided and artificial trend which by opposing Polish leadership weakened common resistance against the Russians. They viewed it as socially dangerous and politically unrealistic.

At this stage in history the Ukrainian and especially the Lithuanian revival lacked clear political objectives. Their leaders sought to revive a remote and nearly forgotten national past; they strove to mobilize apathetic masses; they engaged in a cultural-linguistic renascence in an area where the inhabitants were for the most part illiterate, and in the case of Lithuania and Belorussia economically backward. No wonder that prior to 1890 their achievements were limited.

In the decades following the January Insurrection, the Russian government pursued the objective of absorbing the "western guberniias" and integrating them in the empire. The Slavophiles justified these policies on the grounds that Belorussians and "Little Russians" (Ukrainians) were members of the Russian nation and their languages local dialects corrupted by Polish influences. The liberals allegedly wished to protect the peasantry from the Polish landowners. Others invoked the religious argument, namely, the defense of Eastern Orthodoxy against Roman Catholicism, and endorsed the liquidation of the Union of Brest in 1875 and the repressive measures against the Uniates. Finally, Russian politicians justified their measures by invoking the danger of Polish and foreign intrigues to the security of the empire.

Policies of russification were principally directed against the Poles, who were considered the most dangerous element in the "western guberniias," but they affected the entire society. The Polish language was eliminated from all official correspondence, the educational system, and civil registry records. Even Polish shop signs were not tolerated. The Poles were not allowed to buy land, a measure of particular significance for the Lithuanian-Belorussian area which will be discussed later, and they lost a good deal of land through confiscation. Their estates became subject to special heavy taxes and contributions. Yet the ties between the "western guberniias" and Congress Poland were not and could not be completely severed. Cultural contacts continued, and most of the upper and middle classes retained their Polish language and outlook. This was true also for the rising intelligentsia of Lithuania and Belorussia, which knew and commonly used Polish. Clandestine Polish schools operated, and between 1882 and 1883 the tsarist police uncovered one hundred of them. Economic exchanges between Congress Poland and the "western guberniias" remained voluminous. Up the early twentieth century some 60 percent of Congress Poland's textile exports went to the Ukrainian and Lithuanian-Belorussian guberniias. In spite of their small numbers, the Poles continued to own a great deal of land and played an important part in the economic life of these areas.

Largely because of Russian fears of the Polish gentry, the "western guberniias" were denied the privilege of having elected zemstvos and had greatly limited municipal self-government. For the same reason the local peasantry received privileges that the rest of the peasantry in the empire did not enjoy. Under the impact of the January Insurrection the tsarist government issued decrees modifying the provisions of the 1861 emancipation bill. As a result peasant charges were reduced, all labor obligations abolished, relations between the village and the manor severed, and the amount of land allotted to the peasants significantly increased. Consequently, peasants of the "western guberniias" found themselves in a much better position than those in ethnically Russian lands, and they acquired proportionately more land than did the Polish peasantry in the kingdom. Yet several of the measures adopted in Lithuanian, Belorussian, and Ukrainian territories adversely affected the local masses, especially in the linguistic and cultural field.

The position of the Jews, a sizable minority, continued to worsen. In high schools a 10 percent quota was established, and their participation in the legal profession was curtailed. In 1878 a "ritual murder" trial took place. Following the assassination of Alexander II, a wave of pogroms passed through the "western guberniias" with the tacit collusion of the authorities. New restrictions including a prohibition to settle in rural areas were imposed in the mid-1800s. Exceptions continued to be made for the wealthy and the educated Jews who were becoming quickly russified.

Thus, policies of intense russification not only discriminated against the Poles, but were also directed against the Jews, who no longer remained under Polish influences, and affected the local masses. To appreciate the important local differences one needs to treat separately the so-called northwestern land *(severo-zapadnyi krai)*, i.e., the Lithuanian and Belorussian guberniias, and the south-western land *(yugo-zapadnyi krai)*, i.e., the formerly Polish Ukrainian provinces. The Ukrainian picture in turn needs to be completed by an examination of the Ruthenian-Ukrainian movement in Eastern Galicia.

II. "NORTHWESTERN LAND" AND THE LITHUANIAN REVIVAL

According to the imperial census of 1897, the population of the guberniias of Vilna, Vitebsk, Grodno, Kowno, Minsk, and Mohilev consisted of 9,999,811 people who belonged to the following nationalities: Belorussians (55 percent), Jews (14 percent), Lithuanians (13 percent), Poles (5.6 percent), Russians (5 percent), and Latvians and Ukrainians (3 percent each). These figures were almost certainly too low for the Polish and probably the Lithuanian element. They were misleading as regards the Belorussians, many of whom were not nationally conscious and in part remained under Polish cultural and religious influences. Figures given in the 1867 military survey indicated a much higher percentage of Poles, and even these have been contested by Polish scholars. Yet, whatever the exact figures were, the strength of the Polish element in the Lithuanian-Belorussian guberniias did not stem from population percentages but from Polish control of the land. More than 60 percent of the manorial estates in the guberniias of Vilna, Grodno, and Kowno belonged to Polish landowners; Poles owned less than half in the Minsk, Vitebsk, and Mohilev provinces. Although it is virtually impossible to ascertain the exact breakdown of peasant land by nationality, there existed throughout the historic Grand Duchy of Lithuania many Polish villages as well as petty gentry settlements (zaścianki). In 1863 some Russian officials still regarded the majority of the population in the Lithuanian guberniias as Polish, and the minister of the interior had to admonish them by saying that, "we cannot consider anyone as belonging to the Polish tribe except the landowners and part of the burghers."[1]

As a result of a decree in March, 1863, enlarging the emancipation provisions, the Lithuanian and Belorussian peasantry acquired additional land. To mention but two examples, there was an increase of 29.3 percent in the Vilna guberniia and of 46.4 percent in that of Kowno. In spite of this, the percentage of manorial land in the above two guberniias remained high: 44 and 45 percent respectively. The government made efforts to reduce it. In December, 1865, a law was passed forbidding people of "Polish origin" to acquire land in the "northwestern land," except by inheritance. Since in Russian eyes the terms Pole and Catholic were virtually synonymous, the law also affected Lithuanian as well as Belorussian Catholics. Furthermore, in spite of the assumption that only landowners were Polish, the provisions applied also to the peasantry. Not until 1885 were the peasants of "Polish origin" allowed to buy farms not exceeding 60 desiatines (a desiatine equals 2.7 acres). The Polish landowners were hard hit by the imposition of a contribution amounting to 10 and later to 5 percent of their annual income. In 1875 a new land tax was introduced which weighed heavily on the landed gentry *and* on the peasants. Dictated as they were by political considerations, none of these measures were conducive to economic progress of the Lithuanian and Belorussian territories.

The economy of the "northwestern land" for the most part stagnated. Heavily wooded and endowed with good pastures, the area had relatively little land under plow. Yields per acre were low; farming methods, obsolete. Flax for commercial purposes was produced

1. Cited in Jan Kucharzewski, *Od białego caratu do czerwonego* (Warszawa: Kasa J. Mianowskiego, 1925-35), 4:62.

on a small scale, and the few existing industries were mainly connected with agriculture: distilleries, paper mills, and food-processing
industries. There were a few printing plants and metal works. The
value of the industrial production of Vilna guberniia rose from 2.5
million to 4.7 million rubles in the period 1880–90; that of Kowno
reached 5.3 million in 1890. Still, these were not impressive figures.
While the population grew, urbanization was slow. In 1897 the
urban population of the Lithuanian guberniias amounted to only 13
percent of the total. At that time Vilna had 154,000 inhabitants;
Kowno, 70,000. Traditional means of communication—roads, rivers,
canals—were neglected. The Petersburg-Vilna-Warsaw railroad, built
in 1862, and the Libava (Liepaja)-Vilna-Romny line, constructed
from 1871 to 1874, connected Lithuania with Russia, the Baltic
coast, and Poland. Other lines built around 1885 went to Königsberg
(Kaliningrad), Minsk, and south from Vilna to Baranovichi (Baranowicze) and Rovno (Równe, Rivne).

Economic stagnation coupled with the increase in population
eventually led to land hunger and mass emigration. By 1890 about
400,000 people in ethnic Lithuania were landless. According to
various calculations, in the years 1864–1914 nearly one-quarter of the
Lithuanian population emigrated, many of them overseas, especially
to the United States. All this happened despite a low density of
population. As compared with the 110.2 inhabitants per square
kilometer in the Warsaw guberniia, those of Vilna, Kowno, and
Grodno had respectively 37.9, 38.3, and 41.4 inhabitants per square
kilometer. For the Belorussian guberniia of Minsk the figure was
23.5. Although Lithuania underwent a certain industrialization in
the last decade of the nineteenth century her industrial workers
constituted only 0.7 percent of the total population.

Pursuing russification policies, Governor Muraviev came to believe
in 1864 that in a dozen years Russian nationality would establish
itself firmly in the country. Although some of his more extreme
methods were later discontinued, Russian officials and landowners
tried their best to give a Russian veneer to Lithuania. As for Belorussia, a leading Slavophile, Ivan S. Aksakov, admitted that the
Russians forgot that there was a Belorussia at all. The russification
campaign was particularly pronounced in the cultural sphere, and it
affected Poles and Lithuanians alike. In 1864 Russian became the
exclusive language of instruction in schools, and Lithuanian could be
taught as a subject only in a few high schools. Clandestine classes
in Polish and Lithuanian may explain why illiteracy in the Lithuanian
guberniias was proportionately lower than in neighboring Belorussia.
In 1865 a decree of the Ministry of the Interior (not printed in the
official journal) forbade the use of the "Latin-Polish" alphabet in

Lithuanian publications and imposed Cyrillic characters, popularly known as *grazhdanka*. This was an unheard of measure that threatened the very existence of Lithuanian as a written language, and it was far more important than a similar decree that applied to the Belorussian language which generally had been written in Cyrillic script. The Belorussian decree, however, was followed in 1866 by a ban on the use of Belorussian as a written language.

To appreciate fully the Lithuanian reaction and the ensuing struggle against forcible russification, a few words must be said about the Lithuanian cultural and linguistic revival in the decades preceeding the January Insurrection. The impact of Polish romanticism, through the works of such men as Mickiewicz and Lelewel, was strong in Lithuania. Interest in native folklore, ancient Lithuanian history, and the Lithuanian language was characteristic of the period. Encouraged by the bishop of Samogitia (Žemaitija), Józef Giedroyć (1754-1838), such poets as Simanas Stanevičius (1799-1848) and Anatanas Strazdas (Drozdowski, 1763–1833) composed in Lithuanian. A student of Lelewel, Simanas Daukantas (1793–1864), wrote the first history of the Lithuanians and Samogitians *(Darbai senuju Lietuviu ir žemaičiu)*, which was completed around 1830 but not published until the twentieth century. These writers still corresponded with one another in Polish, and their emphasis on Lithuanian distinctiveness had as yet no consciously anti-Polish accents. Written Lithuanian lacked uniform rules in grammar and syntax, and the Samogitian dialect was used as the written language until 1864.

Bishop Maciej Wołonczewski (Valančius, 1801–75) continued to sponsor Lithuanian language and history. Between 1835 and 1841 Teodor Narbutt (1784-1864) wrote a multivolume *History of Lithuania*; although written in Polish the work was imbued with strong nationalist sentiments. The poet Antoni Baranowski (Baranauskas, 1835-1902), who was later a bishop, an admirer of Mickewicz's descriptions of nature, set out to prove that the Lithuanian language was capable of expressing stylistic subtleties. His poem "The Wood of Anykščiai" *(Anykščiu šilèlis)*, written in the late 1850s, is considered a masterly description of a forest. In the years 1846-64 the first periodical publications in Lithuanian, the almanacs, appeared. Written generally in Samogitian, but occasionally in the tongue of Lithuania proper *(Aukštatija)*, they popularized the native printed word. There were as yet no signs of a comparable Belorussian revival although the 1863 insurgents, notably Kalinowski, produced written material for the peasants, especially the *Mužyckaja Prauda*, in which he used Latin characters.

Resistance to the russification of the Lithuanian language took place under the leadership of the clergy, particularly Bishop Wołonczewski. His appeals to boycott the *grazhdanka* were part of a defensive struggle waged against Eastern Orthodoxy—in the decade 1863-73 around 480 Orthodox churches were built by the authorities—and he wished to base Lithuanian resistance on the native peasant culture rather than on the Polish-Lithuanian past. Due to the firm attitude of the people, which was strengthened by sermons in Lithuanian and Polish and by secret schools, only fifty-eight publications using the *grazhdanka* appeared until 1904, when the ban on the Latin alphabet was rescinded. With the exception of a textbook for tailors all were government publications. Genuine Lithuanian writings were printed in East Prussia and smuggled into the country. During these years the Lithuanian language was standardized and modernized, and Czech diacritical marks replaced the traditional Polish-based spelling.

Around 1880, one could discern three cultural and political trends in Lithuania. The weakest was an orientation toward Russia. The second was the traditional Polish-Lithuanian trend, and its adherents comprised not only the gentry and part of the burghers but also some of the peasantry for whom Polish language and culture represented social and cultural advancement. Lithuanian students who went to Warsaw university often returned with a stamp of "Polishness." Historically, Polish-Lithuanian culture had been closely associated with Catholicism and strongly affected the upper clergy, and it is not surprising that Bishop Baranowski, who encouraged the Lithuanian revival, considered himself of Lithuanian race and of Polish nationality *(gente Lithuani natione Poloni)*. The third trend, which may be called "new Lithuanian," was largely based on the lower clergy and the intelligentsia of peasant descent. The latter group while attending Warsaw's Main School (until its closure in 1869) and St. Petersburg and Moscow universities consciously separated itself from the Poles and affirmed its Lithuanian nationality. Yet, even this group was under some Polish literary influences. Mickiewicz's descriptions of Lithuania were eagerly read and translated. In 1881-82, Ignacy Kraszewski's epic poem *Witold's Design (Witoldowy Plan)*, which evoked the Lithuanian medieval past, was translated and enthusiastically received. As mentioned above, even for some of the militant Lithuanian nationalists Polish was the native tongue.

It was actually in the predominantly Lithuanian guberniia of Suwałki, which was part of the Congress Kingdom, that the Lithuanian national revival could more easily develop. The Suwałki high school had Lithuanian students and teachers, and it produced several of the leading figures of the movement. Severely restricted as it was in the Lithuanian guberniias, the national trend was drawing upon reservoirs beyond the borders, in East Prussia and in Congress Poland.

In 1883 there appeared the first issue of the journal *Auszra* (the Dawn) printed in East Prussia. It heralded a turning point in the Lithuanian national revival. Although only some forty issues had appeared by 1886, the importance of this first Lithuanian national paper was considerable. Its chief sponsor, Jonas Basanavičius (1851-1927), earned the name of father of the national renascence. Of peasant stock, a student at the Suwałki school and later at Moscow university, Basanavičius became a physician and lived from 1879 to 1882 in Bulgaria. There he witnessed the rebuilding of a nation that for centuries had been deprived of its own statehood. He was also greatly impressed by the Czech national revival. A liberal and an idealist under the influence of romanticism, Basanavičius gave a particular stamp to *Auszra*. The outlook of the paper, however, was also influenced by another editor, Jonas Šliupas (1861–1945), a radical who had cooperated with the Polish Proletariat and been affected by positivist-progressive trends. Hence, *Auszra* lacked an ideological uniformity, and articles in it reflected clerical and conservative views as well as socially radical attitudes, or more accurately, its emphasis shifted slowly from the former to the latter orientation. Some of its contributors also showed anti-Semitic leanings. Exalting Lithuanian history and language, *Auszra* did not speak of political independence and attempted to steer a loyalist course. Šliupas sought to obtain permission for free circulation of the paper, and in so doing at one point made servile gestures toward Russia and emphasized his anti-Polish attitude. The same Šliupas, however, was among the first to formulate the idea of Lithuanian independence in a booklet published in America in 1886.

Disliked in several quarters, especially among the gentry and some of the clergy, the *Auszra* was criticized as an "ungodly paper." This precipitated its demise. An attempt to replace it with a journal that could reconcile the conservative-clerical and the radical outlook of the intelligentsia failed. In 1889 young members of the intelligentsia grouped in the association Lietuva (Lithuania), organized in Warsaw by Vincas Kudirka (1858–99), began to publish a new journal, *Varpas* (the Bell), which was printed in East Prussia. Subscribing at first to a middle-of-the-road program, *Varpas* moved toward a nationalist and democratic position. With the slogan Lithuania for Lithuanians, the *Varpinkai* became the nucleus of a national democratic movement. By 1890 a Catholic and a social-democratic trend had also begun to crystalize, and Lithuania entered the stage of more clearly delineated political developments.

Relations between the Lithuanian movement and the Poles were important for both sides. In a polemic between the *Auszra* and the *Dziennik Poznański* (Poznań Daily), the latter praised the Lithuanian efforts to preserve their native language but objected to their anti-Polish posture. *Auszra*'s reply was belligerent, and it invoked, without much regard for historical accuracy, examples of Polish domination of Lithuania. The respective positions of Lithuanian and Polish nationalists were understandable. The former repudiated the old commonwealth, which for the peasant-descended intelligentsia was tantamount to an oppressive social order. They argued that the connection with Poland had denationalized Lithuania's upper classes and threatened the very existence of national culture as preserved among the masses. Before a new Lithuanian society could come into existence the balast of the past had to be discarded. The Poles replied that the Lithuanians had entered the wider, European scene—politically, culturally, and economically—through their association on an equal footing with Poland. Polonization of the upper classes had been a voluntary process. While rejecting the charge that they wished to absorb Lithuania, the Poles stressed the lasting value of the old association. Nor did they fail to point out that the survival of the Lithuanian language and historic tradition was at least in part due to the efforts of the polonized upper class which had resisted Russian encroachments.

To a large extent the Lithuanian national movement, which was comparable to that of other nationalities that had lost their statehood long ago and whose upper strata had embraced another culture, meant a break with the past. To overcome this handicap, the rising historiography had to idealize and mythologize the distant past, but the roots of the movement were new. The Lithuanian national renascence was largely made possible by the peasant emancipation that took place between 1861 and 1863 and brought to the fore a new social class. Both for social and linguistic reasons the peasant-born intelligentsia had to be anti-Polish. Tsarist policies of russification, including attempts to spread Eastern Orthodoxy, hardened the movement and strengthened its nationalist outlook. Seen in a wider context, the Lithuanian case conformed to the late nineteenth-century pattern of increasing national and social radicalization of the masses.

III. "SOUTHWESTERN LAND": THE UKRAINIAN REVIVAL

As compared to the Lithuanian-Belorussian provinces, the situation in the three of the formerly Polish guberniias, Volhynia, Podolia, and Kiev (the "southwestern land") showed some similarities as well as important differences. The census of 1897 gave the following nationality figures for Volhynia: Ukrainians, 61.7 percent; Jews, 13.4; Poles, 9.9; and Russians, 2.7. For Podolia the figures were: Ukrainians, 75.1 percent; Jews, 12.3; Poles, 8.8; and Russians, 2.6 percent. In Kiev Ukrainians constituted 78.5 percent of the population; Jews, 12.3; Poles, 2.9; and Russians, 5.4 percent. In comparison with the 1867 survey and other independent calculations, these figures—which included the city of Kiev, outside of the old commonwealth in 1772—tended to lower the real Polish percentages. But there is no doubt that the Poles and even more so the Russians constituted but a small minority in the "southwestern land." Polish strength was derived from extensive land ownership; Poles owned 45 percent of manorial land in Volhynia, 41 percent in Podolia, and 53 percent in the Kiev guberniia, or about a quarter of all land in the three provinces. The Poles produced roughly 40 percent of the total value of agricultural production.

The social structure of the Ukrainian provinces showed a disproportionately large number of Poles among the upper and professional classes. Landowning magnates and gentry apart, the Poles were frequently administrators, even of Russian estates, and tenants. They constituted a sizable proportion of the lawyers, engineers, doctors, bankers, and industrialists. More than half of the intelligentsia was Polish, and it was reinforced by a steady trickle of various specialists from Congress Poland. When one considers that all these figures refer to the last decade of the nineteenth century after some thirty years of russification policies, one can only infer that earlier figures were considerably higher. Thus, it is understandable why immediately after 1863 St. Petersburg was genuinely concerned about the leading position of the Poles and the range of their influences in the Ukrainian guberniias.

The Ukrainian peasantry, like that of Lithuania, benefited from additional and substantial allotments of land in 1863. The fertile Ukrainian soil favored the cultivation of barley and wheat, important and profitable export items, and the country went through several decades of economic growth. The greatest development took place in the cultivation of sugar beets, which assumed immense proportions. The three guberniias produced about 54 percent of the sugar in the entire Russian Empire (Congress Poland excluded). Although the proportion of Polish and Russian capital gradually declined and that of Jewish and Ukrainian capital grew, in 1910 Poles still owned some 40 percent of the sugar industry. Many of the other local industries connected with agriculture, such as flour mills, sawmills, distilleries, and smaller enterprises that produced agricultural machinery, were in Polish hands. On the eve of the First World War, the Poles controlled 54 percent of the private industrial output and paid 34 percent of the taxes. Trade was largely in Jewish hands. The Jews were concentrated in towns and accounted for 40 percent of the urban population of the "southwestern land."

Good waterways facilitated Ukrainian transportation to the Black Sea ports, and the railroads greatly assisted production and trade. In 1865 the Balta-Odessa (Odesa) line connected the Ukraine with the Black Sea. The Kiev-Kursk line opened new connections with the east. In the decades following the January Insurrection, other railroads were built, most of which linked the Ukraine and Russia. As some Ukrainian writers have pointed out, tsarist tariff and freight rate policies did not operate to the advantage of the country. Had the Ukrainians been masters in their own land, the railroad network would have followed a different pattern. Be that as it may, the "southwestern land" fared well economically during these decades. Interestingly enough, its ties with Congress Poland remained close, and Polish textile imports satisfied at least one-half of the needs of the local market.

The relative economic prosperity contrasted with the political and cultural state of affairs. After the Insurrection of 1863, the Russian reaction not only denounced Polish claims to the Ukraine but also accused the Ukrainians and their rising national movement of being the instrument of a "Polish intrigue." Asserting that the Ukrainian language "has not existed and does not exist," but has been an artificial creation formed "especially by Poles," the tsarist minister of the interior imposed in June, 1863, a ban on printing in "Little Russian." Had the Poles really played a decisive role in assisting the Ukrainian movement?

Unlike the situation in Lithuania, the line dividing the Poles from the majority of the population was clearly drawn. The religious barrier between Catholic Poles and Orthodox Ukrainians was very real. Grouped organizationally into two dioceses, Lutsk-Zhitomir and Kamenets Podolsky, Polish Catholics were a group apart. A good illustration of this fact is provided by the *ukaze* of 1865 which forbade people of Polish origin to buy land without special permission from the governor general. As mentioned above, a similar measure in the "northwestern land" also affected the Lithuanians and the Catholic Belorussians. In the Ukraine no such confusion existed. There were few if any Poles of the type *(gente Rutheni, natione Poloni)* who encouraged or influenced native cultural developments like Bishop Baranowski did in Lithuania. Tymko Padura (1801–71), a Pole who composed Ukrainian popular songs, operated on the margins of the Ukrainian revival. Włodzimierz Antonowicz (1834–1908), a member of the Polish gentry of distant Ukrainian ancestry, launched together with a few other squires who were nicknamed *Khlopomani*—peasant lovers—a Populist movement at the end of the fifties and beginning of the sixties. But he abandoned "Polishness" and Catholicism and became a Ukrainian scholar as Volodymyr Antonovych. The sad fate of the youthful Polish democrats who attempted in 1863 to combine popular democracy with the idea of Polish statehood showed the near hopelessness of such ventures. While there were instances of isolated cooperation and mutual appeals for burying the past, united Polish-Ukrainian action was almost impossible.

Polish cultural imprints on the Ukrainian cultural revival were noticeable, as were some Russian influences, but the national movement had to stand largely on its own feet. Only a few land-owners sided with it; the leadership was in the hands of the nascent intelligentsia and part of the declassé gentry.

To survey rapidly the stages of Ukrainian renascence prior to the russification measures of 1863, one needs to stress the impact of romanticism. True, Ivan Kotlyarevsky's travesty of the *Aeneid* (1798) was the first literary work written in the Ukrainian vernacular, but the real revival came in the nineteenth century. Deeply concerned with folklore and history, the romanticists exalted and idealized the common people. The fascinating Ukrainian folklore, its sad ballads and *dumkas*, and the turbulent Cossack past filled with tragedy and hope provided rich sources for poets and romantic historians. The Polish "Ukrainian School," and to some extent its Russian counterpart, influenced the native movement which expressed traditional strivings for freedom. In the 1840s there emerged in Kiev the Brotherhood of St. Cyril and Methodius, in which Mykola Kostomarov (1817–85) was the chief ideologist and Taras Shevchenko (1814–61) the greatest artist. The brotherhood advocated the abolition of serfdom and dreamt of a future federation of equal and free Slav nations. From its circle came *The Books of the Genesis of the Ukrainian People (Knyhy bytiia ukrainskoho narodu)* written by Kostomarov, and inspired in part by Mickiewicz's *Books of the Polish Nation*. The brotherhood was dissolved by the Russian authorities in 1847; its members suffered severe penalties, notably Shevchenko who was exiled to Turkestan.

The leading figures of the Ukrainian renascence, Kostomarov, Shevchenko, Panteleimon Kulish (1817-97), Antonovych, Mykhailo Drahomanov (Drahomaniv and in Russian spelling Dragomanov, 1841–95), and others made a lasting contribution to Ukrainian language, history, political thought, ethnography, and *belles lettres*. Before the total russification of schools in the "southwestern land" some of these leaders taught in the "Sunday schools" for Ukrainian laborers, edited historical songs, collected manuscripts, and wrote original works in Ukrainian which they also defended as the language of education. True, Ukrainian as a vehicle of literary or scholarly expression needed purification and standardization. A congress of scholars held in 1848 in Galicia attempted to introduce a uniform system of spelling, but differences persisted. It was only in the 1860s and 1870s that a literary language based chiefly on the Poltava and Kiev dialects gained full recognition. The writings of Shevchenko and the language of the periodical *Osnova* (Foundation) provided its firm bases. Prevented from further evolution in the Ukraine by a ban on publications, it crystallized in Eastern Galicia where enriched by some local terms it shaped written Ukrainian in that province.

Kostomarov's chief contribution lay in the field of historical writings, although he also attempted to create Ukrainian romantic tragedy and was a poet of some significance. The unsurpassed poet of the Ukraine was Taras Shevchenko. A liberated peasant-serf, Shevchenko, whose vast range of talents included painting, made his debut with the volume of romantic poetry *Kobzar*, published in 1840. The next year saw the appearance of his great poem "Haidamaky," based on the theme of the Ukrainian peasant uprising of 1768. The artistic qualities of Shevchenko's poetry, the beauty of his language, the musicality of the verse akin to native songs, and the force of expression made him the greatest Ukrainian bard. His national message was disguised in romantic symbolism in which "glory" stood for national tradition, "word" for national culture, and "truth" for universal human demands, and it was not always fully understood by his contemporaries.

Given Shevchenko's stature and influence, his attitude toward the Poles deserves brief mention. He met several of them in exile and sent one of his poems to Mickiewicz. Although in some of his works he dwelt on the Ukrainian-Polish struggle, he displayed no national hatred. In a poem addressed to his dead, living, and yet to be born countrymen he warned against the boast of having pulled down the old Poland. "It fell, yes, but it also buried you under its ruins." But while wishing for a reconciliation with the Poles, he insisted on freedom and justice for his beloved Ukraine. In his national political thinking he went beyond the often opportunistic and cautious ideas of his countrymen.

The periodical *Osnova*, edited in St. Petersburg from 1861 to 1862 by Kulish, formed a bridge between the St. Cyril and Methodius group and the Hromady (Societies) of the 1870s. Its program, which Kostomarov had a large part in formulating, professed loyalism to the Russian Empire and rejected complete separation of the Ukraine. It demanded, however, the right for cultural freedom. Kostomarov placed the Ukrainians on the same national level as the Russians and the Poles, and in a letter to Herzen insisted that neither the former nor the latter ought to call the Ukraine their own. The leading figure of the periodical, Kulish contributed a great deal to the Ukrainian cultural renascence. An author of historical novels à la Walter Scott, a remarkable story teller, and at a later stage a poet, he expressed in his writings a romantic vision of history. Kulish was a controversial man who passed through different stages in his long life, and he hurt his popularity by taking extreme and unpopular positions. In his *History of the Unification of Russia (Istoriia wozsoedinenia Russi)* he questioned the historic role of the Cossacks and fulminated against the "robbers" on the Dnieper. He naturally clashed with such historians as Antonovych and others. After the closing of the *Osnova* and the beginning of strict russification policies after 1863, Kulish assisted the Russian government in the Kholm region in Congress Poland. He also introduced the *kulishuvka* spelling in Eastern Galicia. His anti-Polish stand then underwent a change, and in the 1880s he promoted Polish-Ukrainian cooperation in Galicia to the annoyance of his countrymen.

The post-1863 reprisals struck another Ukrainian leader, Drahomanov, who lost his chair of history at Kiev university. A descendant of an ennobled Cossack family from Hadiach (Hadziacz), Drahomanov was one of the most outstanding figures of the national renascence. Highly cultivated and in close contact with Western Europe, he had been active in the "Sunday schools," in the collecting of historical songs, and in historic and ethnographic studies. His political works bore the imprint of Comte's positivism and later Proudhon's socialism. Active in exile—in Sofia and Geneva—he denounced Russian hypocrisy: concern for Balkan Slavs while depriving Ukrainians, Belorussians, and Poles of basic national rights. His radicalism and federalism greatly influenced the younger generation of Ukrainians, especially in Galicia. Perhaps more than any other contemporary figure, Drahomanov directly contributed to the emergence of a clearly politically oriented Ukrainian national movement.

Operating under worsened conditions—a ban on Ukrainian writings and a russification of education which contributed to the 80 percent illiteracy in the Ukraine—the Ukrainians found an outlet for their activities in the Hromady. That of Kiev came into being in 1873 and was prominent in propagandizing the native heritage. Meanwhile ethnographic and folkloristic studies were undertaken within the framework of the southern branch of the Imperial Russian Geographic Society. A Ukrainian opera in Kiev contributed to the national and cultural awakening of the people. Many of these activities could be and were justified on the grounds of regional patriotism of a cultural nature. Nor was such an argument far from the truth.

Few Ukrainians could as yet be called conscious political nationalists or separatists. Russian statehood was not seriously questioned. The younger generation engaged in social protests within all-Russian radical movements. But as Kostomarov had warned, a denial of Ukrainian identity could stir up a rebellious national feeling. In many of these young people, he said, there slumbered a Vyhovsky, Doroshenko, or Mazepa—the heroes of the Cossack struggle for independence.

The Russian government chose to ignore such warnings. Alarmed by Ukrainian activities, Alexander II ordered in 1875 the creation of a commission to investigate the "Ukrainophile danger." The commission concluded in its report that toleration of the Ukrainian "dialect" could in the long run contribute to separatism; it recommended stern measures. Consequently, the ban on publications in the Ukrainian tongue was reimposed, and importation of Ukrainian books from abroad prohibited. Historic documents and old literary productions could appear in Ukrainian, but they had to be printed in Russian Cyrillic characters and follow Russian spelling. The decree of May, 1876, also forbade the printing or even the public rendition of Ukrainian songs. Theatrical performances in Ukrainian were prohibited, the southern branch of the geographical society dissolved, the influential paper *Kievsky Telegraf* closed. The tsarist policy of russification plunged the Ukraine into cultural darkness. Local scientific societies had to publish in Russian under the watchful eye of the censor. Although the Ukrainian theater was revived in the early 1880s, after the authorities permitted the performance of plays picturing Ukrainian folklore no comparable concessions were made to historical writings or *belles lettres*. What is more, St. Petersburg decided to assist financially the pro-Russian (Russophile) trend among the Ukrainians in Eastern Galicia; this was an important move given the crucial role Galicia was assuming in an all-Ukrainian national rebirth.

Driven out of the Ukraine, the national movement sought and found shelter in Galicia. As an outstanding Ukrainian historian and leader put it: "To the oppressed Ukrainians in Russia, Galicia appeared an open window looking out on the free expanse of Ukrainian development and in time of extremity a place of refuge."[2] It was there that the Shevchenko Society (later named the Shevchenko Scientific Society) was founded in 1873 with financial assistance from Russian Ukrainians. The first all-Ukrainian journals such as *Pravda* (the Truth) were printed there. It was in Galicia that the song that later became the national anthem, "The Ukraine has not died yet"

2. M. Hrushevskyi, *A History of the Ukraine* (New Haven: Yale University Press, 1941), p. 501.

*(Shche ne vmerla Ukraina)*, .was first sung. And it was in Lemberg that a chair of Ukrainian history was founded in 1894 and given to the Kiev historian Mykhailo Hrushevsky (1866-1934).

IV. THE UKRAINIAN REVIVAL IN EASTERN GALICIA

Eastern Galicia occupied a special place in the all-Ukrainian revival and in Polish-Ukrainian relations. It was also of considerable interest to Russia. The Poles saw the region as an integral part of historic Poland. The Ruthenian voiedvodship had belonged to the Polish crown since the mid-fourteenth century and was considered distinct from the Ukraine which in a sense transcended Polish statehood. The prepartition borders had already divided the Ukraine along the Dnieper River, and that part of the Ukraine on the left bank was outside the Polish sphere of interest. To the Poles the Ukraine was a living concept; Eastern Galicia was not. The Russians, especially the Slavophiles, regarded Eastern Galicia (Halich) as part of the old Kievan patrimony, hence a Russian land which only awaited unification with the rest of the empire. As for the majority of the local inhabitants who still generally referred to themselves as Ruthenians, the whole issue of Eastern Galicia and its relationship to the Ukraine, Poland, and Russia was a complex and baffling question, to which an answer was being sought in connection with the national revival.

In the early decades of the nineteenth century the dividing lines, religious and linguistic, between the Ruthenians and the Poles were not yet sharply drawn. The Age of Romanticism and Polish national struggles greatly affected the Ruthenian awakening in Eastern Galicia. As Ivan Franko noted, the November Insurrection of 1830 contributed to the rise of a conscious Ruthenian patriotism in the cultural and later in the political sphere. In the early stages linguistic problems came naturally to the foreground. Was Ruthenian to be written in Latin or in some form of the Cyrillic alphabet? Was the future all-Ukrainian literary tongue to be based on one of the local dialects, and if so on which one? Some of the contemporaries favored that of the Kołomyja (Kolomyia) region, half way between the San and the Dnieper rivers. Among the leading figures of the cultural movement were: Markijan Shashkevych or Szaszkiewicz (1811-43), Ivan Vahylovych or Wagilewicz (1811–66), and Jakiv Holovatsky (1814-88), the so-called Ruthenian Romantic Triad. Jointly they authored a collection of folk ballads and poems called *The Dniestr Nymph (Rusalka Dnistrovaia)*, published in 1837. This date is often regarded as marking the birth of modern Ukrainian literature in Galicia.

In a political sense, the national revival was still in search of its own identity. Of the above three poets, only Shashkevych remained a Ruthenian-Ukrainian; Holovatsky and Wagilewicz later identified themselves respectively with Russia and Poland. The revolutionary events of 1848 produced the Ruthenian-Polish clash, discussed earlier in this book, as well as the emergence of a Ukrainian Council (Holovna Rada Ruska). The latter was instrumental in organizing cultural efforts of the Ruthenian intelligentsia, and it founded among other things a "National House" in Lemberg. When faced with the choice of a Russian or an all-Ukrainian orientation, the council chose the latter, but without inner conviction. The language question still created problems, and the conservative Ruthenian leadership—so-called Old Ruthenians—associated with the Uniate hierarchy frowned on the use of the lowly peasant vernacular. Nor were they fully awake to the socioeconomic needs of the peasant masses. The movement was parochial, loyalist toward Vienna, and antagonistic to the Poles. The latter, bent on achieving an autonomous Galicia, necessarily relegated the Ruthenians to a position of inferiority.

From the perspective of Kiev, Eastern Galicia in the 1860s to 1890s may well have appeared an "open window." The *Ausgleich* of 1867, which satisfied only the Hungarians, did not affect the status of Galician Ruthenians. The Uniate church remained unmolested; there was elementary education in the native language, as well as a small number of high schools (the first was established in Lemberg in 1874 and by 1890 two more were added), bilingual teachers' seminaries, and a few chairs at Lemberg university. The Ruthenians could publish their newspapers and books, form cultural and scientific associations, and use their language in the Galician diet, courts, administration, and municipal institutions. A Ukrainian theater in Lemberg performed regularly from 1864 onwards. Indeed, Polish interference notwithstanding, the province could become an all-Ukrainian Piedmont if the local leadership remained united and showed a broad outlook.

The Eastern Galician leaders regarded the problem of polonization as the most immediate and urgent matter, and at times they lost sight of the larger, international aspects of the Ukrainian issue. True, they could point to the fact that the number of Poles in Eastern Galicia had increased between 1880 and 1890 from 28 to 31 percent. In some districts and in several towns the Poles were in a majority, especially as large parts of the German and Jewish population became polonized. They stressed that they had only fourteen deputies in the Sejm, and three as opposed to fifty-seven Polish deputies in the Viennese Reichsrat. In the socioeconomic and educational fields the Ruthenians were clearly the underdogs. While the number of Ruthenian elementary schools was roughly proportionate to the Ruthenian population in the province, they had only half as many grades as Polish schools. A saying attributed to the Austrian premier Friedrich von Beust, that the extent of Ruthenian existence had been left to the discretion of the Galician Sejm, sounded like an ominous disinterest in the fate of the East Galician Ruthenians.

In the prevailing circumstances, the national movement had a choice of three alternatives: survival in cooperation with the Poles; preparation for an eventual merger with Russia; and crystallization of an all-Ukrainian nationality striving for unification and freedom.

A Polish-Ruthenian compromise along the lines proposed by the conservative Cracow historian Szujski—full recognition of the Ruthenians in the diet, schools, and communes in exchange for their acknowlment of an insoluble union with the Poles—stood little chance of acceptance. As mentioned earlier, the Poles, especially the Podolian conservatives and their allies, opposed it, and so did the two wings of the Ruthenian movement, the Old Ruthenians and the rising Ukrainian party. As the prominent radical writer Franko, who had cooperated closely with Polish leftists and Socialists, put it, the Poles "must, once and for all, give up any thought of building a 'historical' Poland in non-Polish lands, and they must accept, as we do, the idea of a purely ethnic Poland."[3] This was a position which few Poles could readily accept, particularly with respect to ethnically mixed Eastern Galicia with its predominantly Polish capital Lemberg. Besides, race played no significant part in the Polish-Ruthenian conflict. Mixed families were common, and within one family one brother could be and often was a Polish patriot and another a Ruthenian patriot.

Rejecting the idea of historic Poland, the Ruthenians could find their identity either in an all-Russian concept or in an all-Ukrainian national movement. In the sixties, seventies, and eighties the line of division ran between the Old Ruthenians and the rising Young Ruthenians, or Populists (narodovci), or as they finally began to call themselves, the Ukrainians. The Compromise of 1867 brought disappointment to Galician Ruthenians, who could but envisage a worsening of their position, especially under the rule of Gołuchowski. No wonder that some of the Old Ruthenian leaders saw in the Austro-Hungarian Ausgleich the beginning of the disintegration of the Habsburg monarchy and looked forward to a future union with Russia. Father Ivan Naumovych (1826–91), who originally considered himself Polish and then Ruthenian-Ukrainian, now predicted the liberation of Eastern Galicia by Russia. Controlling

3. Cited in Ivan L. Rudnytsky, "The Ukrainians in Galicia under Austrian Rule," *Austrian History Yearbook*, vol. 3, pt. 2 (1967), p. 407.

the Uniate metropolitan consistory, the newspaper *Slovo* (the Word), and the representation to the Sejm and the Reichsrat, the Old Ruthenians enjoyed for a while a near monopoly of Ruthenian politics and cultural affairs. Paternalistically inclined toward the peasantry, they found some common ground for a day-to-day *modus vivendi* with the Eastern Galician landowners. But they made no real effort at a political compromise with the Poles, nor were the latter inclined to make any overtures. The Polish administration viewed the Old Ruthenians with suspicion and tried to discredit their Russophilism by alerting Vienna. Eventually such Polish attempts met with some success in the 1880s.

The Old Ruthenians insisted on the Old Slavonic, using in practice a linguistic mixture which their opponents contemptuously referred to as jargon *(jazychie)*. They stubbornly observed the Julian calendar and the Cyrillic script; their deputies made speeches in Russian. Apart from Naumovych their leaders included the writer Bohdan Didytsky (1827–1908) and a number of figures connected with the Uniate hierarchy. Russian funds, which were readily available through the chaplain of the Russian embassy in Vienna, made some of the Old Ruthenians dependent on tsarist aid. While active in politics they also showed a good deal of initiative in assisting extracurricular education, organizing reading rooms, and publishing popular newspapers and books.

The Populists appeared on the stage as early as the 1860s. Inspired by Shevchenko, whose impact on Galicia was great, they declared in their ideological pamphlet of 1867 that they were proud to belong to a Ukrainian nation of fifteen million people. Like the Russian *narodniki* they decided to go to the masses and rejected the conservative clericalism of the Old Ruthenians. Although they counted among their leaders some priests, most of them were members of a rising lay intelligentsia, especially young high school teachers. Influenced by a certain romanticized historical outlook, some of them adopted the Cossack dress and hailed the Cossack tradition. Not yet ready to challenge directly the political position of the Old Ruthenians, they concentrated on educational and cultural work. In 1868 they established an adult educational society, the Prosvita, in the 1870s the Shevchenko Society, and in 1880 the journal *Dilo* (Deed). Among their more radical leaders were such students of Drahomanov as Pavlyk, Franko, and Ostap Terletsky (1850–1902), the author of the first Socialist pamphlets in Ruthenian.

The highly talented Ivan Franko, the author of important novels, stories, and articles dwelling on social issues *(Boa Constrictor, Boryslav Laughs*, and others), worked in the rising Socialist movement in Galicia. Together with Pavlyk and Polish Socialists, he was a defendant in the Cracow trial. But eventually his socialism became subordinate to the Ukrainian national cause. The cause meanwhile was greatly strengthened by reaction to the russification policies in the Ukraine, on the one hand, and by the collapse of the Old Ruthenian movement, compromised by its ties with tsarist Russia, on the other. Drahomanov's final break with Russia and his emergence as a consciously Ukrainian national leader made him the spiritual father of the radical movement in Galicia. The founding of *Pravda* and *Zoria* (Dawn), the first all-Ukrainian journals to which Russian Ukrainians contributed, forged another link between Eastern Galicia and the Ukraine. The former was rapidly gaining the position of a Ukrainian cultural Piedmont, although it was not yet fully prepared to assume such a heavy burden.

In 1882 the Old Ruthenian movement suffered a blow from which it never fully recovered. A number of its leaders including Naumovych were tried for treason; although they were eventually acquitted, they lost their standing and prestige. All the double-faced activities of the Old Ruthenians came to light. They had professed loyalty to Vienna while collaborating with and receiving funds from Russia. They had insisted on their championship of the Uniate church while helping to impose Orthodoxy on the Uniates of Kholm. As a result of public exposure, the metropolitan had to resign and several leaders left the country. By 1890 the Populists had the upper hand; a Ruthenian-Ukrainian Radical Party emerged. What is more, the Populists had largely succeeded in replacing the term "Ruthenian" by the term "Ukrainian," thus promoting the concept of an undivided Ukrainian nation that had been temporarily split by the Russo-Austrian political boundary.

The Eastern Galician Ruthenians had thus found their identity, although the road ahead remained strewn with obstacles and difficulties. While Eastern Galicia had become the center of Ukrainian cultural, scholarly, and educational activities, and while the main works of Ukrainian writers had appeared in the province, it had a long way to go to achieve political, social, and economic advancement. A real merger of the Ukrainians of Galicia with those of the Ukraine proved to be hard even in the twentieth century. A progressive national outlook was still confined to an elite; political opportunism, social conservatism, and clericalism distinguished large and influential circles of Galician Ukrainians. There was still a good deal of passivity among the masses. The more radical Ukrainians, both of the Ukraine and of Galicia found it difficult to discard the heritage of the past. The Polish impact remained strong. Russian influences were on the increase in the "southwestern land" not to mention the left bank of the Ukraine, where russification and the influx of Russians attracted by the developing heavy industries were putting a foreign stamp on the Ukrainian land.

The three decades after 1860 saw an important evolution of Ruthenian-Ukrainian society and prepared the ground for further and more strictly political developments. From the Polish point of view the changes represented—although it was not fully understood or appreciated at the time—a mounting challenge to the concept of the historic commonwealth.

# CHAPTER 13

# The Era of Positivism

During the three decades following the January Insurrection the lands of partitioned Poland began to draw farther apart. Economically, they became more closely knit with the partitioning powers which conditioned the rate and the direction of their development. Political conditions permitted autonomous processes in Galicia, but operated against the Poles under the Prussian and Russian rules. In the former Grand Duchy of Lithuania, in the Ukraine, and in Eastern Galicia native movements challenged the old Polish supremacy. A native Polish revival was taking place in Prussian Upper Silesia and in parts of Eastern Prussia. In Teschen Silesia under Austria, the Polish renascence was making important strides. Polish-language newspapers appeared, thanks in part to the initiative of Andrzej Cienciała (1825–98); a society of scholarly aid was organized in 1872, and a Polish high school set up in 1895. Thus, while Polish culture was losing some ground in the east it was gaining in the west. Policies of accommodation with foreign rule, largely stemming from the 1863 catastrophe, namely, Triple Loyalism, by necessity deepened the differences between Russian, Austrian, and Prussian Poland.

Institutionally, Polish culture was linked with each of the partitioning powers which determined the character and the scope of education, controlled the organization of scholarly life, traced the limits for the use of the native language, and supervised cultural activities. By means of censorship the authorities could determine what appeared in print or on the stage, and tsarist censorship in particular severely limited cultural freedom. Policies of the partitioning governments created the framework for Polish culture, but even through russification and germanization measures the governments could not easily replace that culture with their own. Polish culture and the Polish way of life continued to develop and transcend the political boundaries that divided the old commonwealth. A relative freedom of movement, including the choice of domicile, permitted frequent interaction and exchange between the Russian, German, and Austrian parts. Cultural autonomy in Galicia naturally made this province the center of Polish life radiating over all the former territories of the partitioned country.

Socioeconomic changes—emancipation of the peasantry, a certain modernization of agriculture, industrial revolution, material progress, and rapid population growth—conditioned the general transformation of the country. But the so-called bourgeois culture and civilization of the late nineteenth century took certain specific forms in the Polish lands. In contrast to most of Western Europe, the Polish equivalent of a middle-class culture was still in essence a landowning-gentry civilization, which had been transmitted in part and adapted in part to an urban environment. The intelligentsia and even the rising proletariat were affected by it. Most of the leading figures in cultural life had some links with the gentry, even if they were in open rebellion against the social and cultural values of this group. This was also true for people of Jewish and German background. Thus the Polish cultural élite, with minor exceptions, differed in descent and outlook not only from their Western counterparts but also from the rising Lithuanian or Ukrainian intelligentsia.

The Polish intelligentsia constituted a sociocultural phenomenon largely unknown in the West; it stood close to the Russian intelligentsia but differed from it fundamentally in one important respect. The Russian intelligentsia was largely alienated within its own state because of the tsarist regime; the Polish counterpart, precisely because it had no state of its own, assumed the responsibility for national cultural leadership. In the late nineteenth century its outlook was influenced by a belief in reason, progress, and above all science—the panacea of society. Women played an important role in the intelligentsia, and their emancipation preceded that of women in several Western European countries. In 1871 the first Polish woman became a student at Zurich university in Switzerland; by 1900 there were eighty-one women students at Cracow university.

The Polish nation was completing its transformation into a modern society. While in the industrialized West such a society encompassed mainly two components, the bourgeoisie and the proletariat, in Polish conditions it was mainly a gentry-peasant conglomerate. Its ethnic composition was changing. Some polonized Ukrainians and Lithuanians were leaving it; some germanized Poles were returning to it. An outstanding example of the latter was Wojciech Kętrzyński (1838-1918), who later became a noted Polish historian. A certain group of Jews, especially in Galicia, became assimilated with the Poles, but the movement did not reach mass proportions. The Jewish Haskalah sought to lead the Jews out of their traditional isolation, but it stood for emancipation not for assimilation. In Prussia, Jews increasingly identified themselves with Germandom. As the social basis widened the nation began to be envisaged more in ethnic than in historic terms.

In spite of the modernization that was taking place, living conditions of the masses remained low. The peasantry and the workers were underpaid and undernourished. Although the mortality rate had decreased it was higher than in the West. Warsaw was still the only city in Russian Poland to have a sewage system. Housing remained inadequate, even though the ancient ramparts of Cracow and Warsaw were almost totally demolished and cities were expanding into new quarters. The typical ugly tenant houses, built for profit, were characteristic for Warsaw and other towns. They provided a variety of dwellings, ranging from big and luxurious apartments that faced the street, to small, dark, and crowded rooms that opened out onto numerous inner courtyards. Hygienic conditions were often deplorable, and in spite of medical progress scarlet fever and tuberculosis were on the increase. The period witnessed, however, the beginnings of physical culture and a rising interest in health and bodily fitness. The gymnastic association Sokół (Falcon), brought over from the Czech lands, made its appearance in Galicia in 1867 and thence spread to Prussian Poland. Numerous watering spas discovered at the foot of the Carpathian Mountains in Galicia became popular; in Congress Poland the spa of Ciechocinek gained local fame.

The period from 1863 to 1890 saw the rise, the zenith, and the decline of positivism. The term came from the French philosopher Auguste Comte who defined as "positivist" such values as "real" (in contrast to mysterious and chimerical), "utilitarian," "certain and precise," "relative" (in contrast to absolute), and "positive" (in opposition to negative). In its broadest sense positivism stood for a view of the universe governed by scientific laws, and it rejected earlier religious or metaphysical interpretations. Stressing rational forces of progress, it placed emphasis on scientific education. Polish positivism adopted some of the features of the French model, but it also possessed native characteristics. It shared with French positivism a conviction about the superiority of industrial civilization, and advocated the application of modern technology to industry and agriculture. It rejected revolutions which interrupted natural progress and spread anarchy. Combining the ideas of Comte, John Stuart Mill, and Herbert Spencer, and influenced by Darwin and Buckle, Polish positivism insisted on a rational, utilitarian, and empirical attitude toward life. But, unlike its Western prototype, it was less of a philosophical school and more of a literary, social, and political trend. Rejecting the romantic myth of the chosen nation, it postulated the view that the nation was an organism. It wished to strengthen this organism so that it could withstand the pressures of the occupying powers.

Reinforced by the "organic work" concept, Polish positivism was thus a *Weltanschauung* and a watchword rather than a philosophy. The leading Warsaw positivist Świętochowski, whose temperament and approach were somewhat akin to Voltaire's, castigated the ideals of the past and demanded that European currents ventilate the Polish "stuffy hut." Although Polish positivists were united in their opposition to the romantic tradition of struggle and sacrifice, which had failed to assist the Polish cause, positivism took different forms in Russian, Prussian, and Austrian Poland. In Poznania, the positivists adopted an attitude close to that of the Western liberals. They opposed ultramontanism and policies of collaboration with autocratic Prussia. They stressed "organic work" and national solidarity. There was no Poznanian writer comparable to the iconoclastic Świętochowski. The Cracow positivists contributed to the onslaught on the romantic heritage through their interpretation of Poland's past. But their condemnation of the unruly Polish character, which they held responsible for the partitions, led them to a conservative and loyalist position that was characterized by a strong attachment to Catholicism.

The positivist slogan of Organic Work applied to cultural, social, and economic spheres of life. The leading economist Supiński, who was among the first to use the term, defined it as work that was useful and purposeful for the entire social organism. Just like work in nature "organic work" was the mainspring of the social organism and assured its life and growth. Supiński emphasized rational economic progress and voiced concern lest Poland remain behind the rest of Europe in the process of modernization. The refrain of a contemporary song, "we have no weapons, but Poles; work is our weapon today," expressed the prevailing mood. Foregoing the heroics of soldiers, the positivists extolled the heroism of physicians struggling against sickness or of teachers fighting obscurantism. Engineers, industrialists, and land cultivators, who mastered nature and placed the fruits of their inventions and labors at public disposal, became the new heroes.

Eventually, positivism became identified with the largely futile policies of Triple Loyalism, the materialistic and "bourgeois" *Weltanschauung*, and a virtual abandonment of national ideals. Its emotional appeal was limited, and it engendered new forces that destroyed it. Yet its importance for Polish literature, arts, and learning was incontestable. It reflected and in part shaped the Polish reality of the post-January decades, and contributed some new values and talents to Polish civilization.

The positivist program was popularized through the press and literature. Newspapers and periodical publications grew rapidly in number and gained a position of great social importance. Indeed many authors made their debut in journals. Between 1864 and 1894 the number of periodicals increased from 22 to 92 under the Russian rule, from 15 to 45 under Prussia, and from 28 to 126 in autonomous Galicia. Although the editions remained relatively small—only *Kurjer Warszawski* (Warsaw Courier) had about thirty thousand subscribers and the leading Lemberg and Posen papers about ten thousand—the size of the reading public was naturally much larger. Leading articles in such conservative newspapers as the Cracow *Czas*, the Warsaw *Dziennik Warszawski*, the Poznanian *Kurier Poznański*, and the St. Petersburg *Kraj* gave the appearance of a concerted Polish press activity that transcended political borders. A relative novelty were the Populist papers addressed to the peasantry in Congress Poland, Galicia, and Prussian Poland. In Upper Silesia, Miarka's *Katolik* (the Catholic) was not only a highly influential organ but also served as a rallying point for Polish cultural and political activity in the province. Contemporary papers became highly diversified and catered to an ever widening circle of readers. The *feuilleton*, often written by a prominent author, gained currency. To enhance their attractiveness, newspapers began to publish novels in installments. Some journals offered their subscribers premiums in the form of books.

Periodicals played a great part in the formulation and propagation of the philosophy of Warsaw positivism and of "organic work." Świętochowski developed his program largely through the Warsaw *Przegląd Tygodniowy* (Weekly Review) and *Prawda* (Truth). As a journalist, novelist, and playwright, he typified in many ways the writer of the positivist period. His review condemned class prejudices, criticized the clergy, promoted the emancipation of Jews and of women, and expressed its arguments in a utilitarian and rationalist language.

The characteristic style of Polish literature in the late nineteenth century was realism. True to life descriptions and analyses which often carried a utilitarian message became highly appreciated. Novels and short stories triumphed over poetry and the old-fashioned tale (*gawęda*). Lyrics were demoted unless they sought to awaken the compassion of the reader for the underprivileged and down-trodden. The romantic cult of fantasy and the glorification of tragic love became discredited. The novel or the play tended to idealize the hero of the new epoch and to ridicule and unmask the traditionalist and the obscurantist. Novels dealing with social questions *(powieść obyczajowa)* gained an important place among the genres; the historical novel, however, continued to be recognized and admired. The short story often widened literary horizons by exploring the social problems of small towns and villages.

Among the host of writers who wrote during this period a few reached great artistic heights and exercised a lasting influence on the Polish public. One of them was Bolesław Prus (the pseudonym of Aleksander Głowacki, 1847–1912). A graduate of the Warsaw Main School and later a journalist whose column became a popular chronicle of late nineteenth-century Warsaw, Prus won general recognition through his novels and short stories. In *The Outpost (Placówka)* his main character was a realistically portrayed peasant, a hero *malgré lui*, who struggled for land against the German colonists. The author contrasted him with the noble squire who was losing his *raison d'être* as a national leader in the countryside. Two sociological novels, *The Doll (Lalka)* and *The Emancipationists (Emancypantki)*, were among the first works of fiction to focus on Warsaw's middle class. The second was concerned with the feminist question. With a double theme—the past as seen through the diary of an old shop attendant, and the present—*The Doll* presented a panorama of Warsaw's life. Its hero, a successful businessman, reached a tragic end, caught between stern reality and the romantic heritage. Like Dickens, who influenced his writings, Prus was a convinced positivist and realist. At the same time some of the most attractive characters in his books are those individuals who were out of step with the surrounding reality. In the historical novel *The Pharaoh (Faraon)*, for instance, the reader's sympathy is clearly on the side of the idealistic and impulsive young ruler who fights a losing battle against the learned, ruthless, and politically sophisticated high priests.

The woman novelist Eliza Orzeszkowa (1841–1910) showed in her writings a passionate concern for the victims of obscurantism and intolerance. All her novels took place in the Lithuanian-Belorussian lands whose landscape and nature she depicted with a rare appreciation for beauty. In one of her major novels, *On the Niemen River (Nad Niemnem)*, she contrasted the petty gentry, deeply attached to the land, with the more cosmopolitan and snobbish nobility. Her heroes represented the program of "organic work" combined with the ardent patriotism of the Lithuanian Poles. Orzeszkowa identified herself with the cause of women's emancipation, and female characters played an important role in her books. Becoming closely acquainted with the painful Jewish question, she strongly defended the Jews and advocated their full emancipation. Her principal novel dealing with this question was *Meir Ezofowicz*.

Even though some of her works *(On the Niemen River)* tend to be didactic and moralizing, Orzeszkowa's descriptions of nature have a lasting artistic value. Restricted in her freedom of expression by tsarist censorship—a problem that all Polish authors had to contend with—Orzeszkowa had to resort to symbolism and allegory when touching on such forbidden themes as the January Insurrection.

Perhaps the most popular among the writers of the positivist age, although his great historical Trilogy marked a turning point in the reaction against positivism, was Henryk Sienkiewicz (1846-1916). A product of the Warsaw Main School and at first a journalist, Sienkiewicz traveled more widely than most of his contemporaries and even visited the United States. His early short stories and novels dealt with contemporary society, and he showed a realistic, indeed a pessimistic outlook in his sketches of peasant life. These works fade, however, in comparison with his great historical epics. Turning to the seventeenth century, the period of Poland's greatness and trial, he produced between 1884 and 1888 his famous Trilogy: *With Fire and Sword (Ogniem i mieczem), The Deluge (Potop)*, and *Pan Wołodyjowski*. His work was immensely popular and occasioned a heated and widespread debate in which few people remained neutral. Sienkiewicz was accused of being a conservative and of glorifying the nobility, although his clearly stated purpose was to offer moral comfort to his countrymen living in the post-insurrectionary age. His message was that Poland has lived through great calamities and yet had survived. His appeal, particularly to the younger generation which was beginning to yearn for military action and glory, was immense and had profoundly antipositivist overtones. His influence, in spite of all criticisms on political and literary grounds, proved to be lasting, and several of his characters, notably Zagłoba, the Polish Falstaff, earned him undying fame.

Sienkiewicz was a great narrator and he excelled in dialogues. He succeeded in imposing his vision of the past on the readers by a suggestiveness unsurpassed perhaps by any other Polish historical novelist. His battle scenes resembled monumental canvasses. Some of his characters and their adventures were stereotypes, and his intellectual capabilities were inferior to his talents as a writer, but Sienkiewicz's main books must be largely judged by their political and social impact. Among his other historical novels were *Quo Vadis*, which dealt with ancient Rome and earned him the Nobel Prize, and *The Teutonic Knights (Krzyżacy)*. Both had excellent parts but did not come up to the level of the Trilogy.

French naturalism reached Poland in the 1880s and influenced Gabriela Zapolska (1857–1921), a playwright and novelist remembered among others for her *Kaśka Kariatyda*, a story of a debauched peasant girl. Zapolska tackled subjects that were generally avoided by the positivists, for instance, social aspects of sex and the degradation of women. Although she began to write during this period, she properly belongs to the next phase of Polish literature. Equally influenced by naturalism was Adolf Dygasiński (1839–1902), whose novels and short stories depicted the countryside and the animal world. He departed from the old tradition of "humanizing" animals, and as an enthusiast of science showed them subject to the inexorable laws of nature.

Two poets at least deserve to be mentioned here: Adam Asnyk (1838-97) and Maria Konopnicka (1842-1910). The former, brought up in the 1863 tradition and coming as an émigré to Galicia, embraced the positivist creed. Although he opposed the destruction of "altars of yesterday" he felt that "one must go forward with the living, reach for a new life, and not crown one's head stubbornly with a bunch of withered laurels." His simple and austere sonnets expressed his philosophical intellectualism. Maria Konopnicka was more of a poet of the people; she was deeply concerned with social issues and radical and anticlerical in her outlook. In some ways her interests paralleled those of her friend Orzeszkowa. She is best remembered for her long peasant epic *Mr. Balcer in Brazil (Pan Balcer w Brazylii)*, completed in 1910 and concerned with the fate of Polish emigrants overseas. Her fighting anti-German verse *Rota*, later put to music, became one of the chief Polish patriotic songs of the twentieth century.

Although this period produced hardly any prominent Polish playwrights, the theater played an important role in the cultural life of the country. The government-owned Warsaw theaters were the only places where Polish could be publicly spoken in front of an audience. Despite stringent controls the theater reached high technical levels and had several brilliant actors. Theaters in Cracow and Lemberg were equally good if not better; that of Posen, established in 1875, displayed the motto that the Czech National Theater in Prague adopted a little later—The Nation to Itself. In addition to permanent theaters there existed itinerant troupes and local amateur shows. In one of the traveling companies Helena Modrzejewska (1840–1909), later a famous Shakespearean actress, made her debut. She became well known in the United States where she emigrated and performed under the name of Modjeska.

Fine arts acquired a place of increased importance in Polish cultural life. Sienkiewicz's fame as a national novelist was matched by that of Jan Matejko (1838-93) as the most popular and influential national painter. Matejko was the president of the Cracow School of Fine Arts, the only such institution in Poland after the closing of the

Warsaw academy, although in Warsaw Gerson's atelier served as a private school. Matejko painted huge, mainly historical canvases in a rather academic style. But his realism had a touch of romanticism and his evocation of Poland's past had a great impact on the public. Some of his compositions (*The Sermon of Skarga, Stańczyk, The Sejm of the Partitions*) were educational in the sense of drawing attention to Polish historical failures. Others glorified the achievements of the past. As years went by the evaluation of Matejko on purely artistic grounds became increasingly critical, but there is no doubt that one or two generations of Poles could only visualize their national history through the painter's eyes. The creation of the National Museum in Cracow in 1879 as a center of contemporary art was largely due to his influence.

Other painters never equaled his popularity although several gained appreciation and even admiration from the critics and the public. Among the older artists Rodakowski, who lived chiefly in Paris, still painted during this period, and Juliusz Kossak continued to charm people with his landscapes and horses. Grottger, whose paintings met with such great success, died at the age of thirty only a few years after the January Insurrection. The Gierymski brothers, Aleksander (1849-1901) and Maksymilian (1846-74), originally under Gerson's influence and trained in Munich, painted scenes from everyday life and landscapes. Aleksander was in some ways a precursor of expressionism. Henryk Siemiradzki (1843-1902) was a Cracow artist, and his picture inaugurated the collection at the National Museum. Although Polish painting could not aspire to rival the great contemporary European masterpieces, it influenced, through its historical and native themes, Polish culture and maintained a link with the West—Rome, Paris, Vienna, and Munich.

Except for Antoni Kurzawa (1843-98) and Cyprian Godebski (1835-1909), there were no works of lasting value in sculpture. Nor were there any striking departures in architecture. In music, the only important figure was the virtuoso violinist Henryk Wieniawski (1835-80). The operatic tradition of Moniuszko continued to be very much alive.

While literature and to some extent the visual arts were believed by positivists to have a utilitarian role, education was the major concern of contemporary Poles. On the level of higher learning, the Warsaw Main School performed an important function until its liquidation in 1869, and its scholars and students left a mark on society. Among them were Jakub Natanson (1832–84), a great organic chemist, and the internationally famous linguist Jan Baudouin de Courtenay (1845-1929). Świętochowski, Prus, Orzeszkowa, Sienkiewicz, and Dygasiński were all former students. About four-fifths of the students at the Russian university that replaced the Main School, were Poles, but low academic standards and an atmosphere of oppression were not conducive to studies. In time, most students from Congress Poland went to foreign universities or to the Polish universities in Galicia.

In the last decades of the nineteenth century the Jagiellonian University in Cracow and the university in Lemberg became the real centers of Polish learning. Their professors came from all over Poland, and the size of the student body increased. Although predominantly of upper or middle class background, Galician students began to include also representatives of the peasantry. The Lemberg Politechnika (technical university), founded in 1871, and the Cracow School of Fine Arts became equally all-Polish in their character and composition. The great scientists Zygmunt Wróblewski (1845-88) and Karol Olszewski (1846-1915), who were the first to achieve the liquefaction of oxygen, nitrogen, and carbon monoxide, taught at Cracow. The creation in that city of the Academy of Learning (Polska Akademia Umiejętności) in 1873 was a great event in Polish scholarly and intellectual life. The academy comprised among its hundred members the elite of scholars from all parts of partitioned Poland and served as the focal point of national learning.

The shortage of university teaching positions forced some scholars to go abroad. Others had to teach in high schools. The leading Slavist Aleksander Brückner (1856-1939) accepted a chair at Berlin university; the outstanding biochemist Marceli Nencki (1847-1901) worked outside of the country. The ethnographer Benedykt Dyboski (1833-1930) and the geologist and geographer Jan Czerski (1845-92) greatly contributed to their branches of learning in Siberia.

Among the scholarly disciplines that significantly developed during this period and gained wider influence was history. Keeping in step with current methodological changes and seeking to make history more scientific, Polish historians adopted the seminar system, pioneered in Germany, and devoted great attention to modernizing their discipline. Source materials continued to be edited and published, auxiliary branches of history were perfected, and monographic studies that dealt particularly with the Middle Ages and the sixteenth to eighteenth centuries appeared. The Polish Historical Association was founded in Lemberg in 1886, and the next year it began to publish a historical quarterly *(Kwartalnik Historyczny)*. In keeping with the prevailing spirit of scientific inquiry, historians insisted on exhaustive collection and correlation of facts and largely followed Ranke's approach of writing history "as it really was." Digging into archival sources, scholars engaged in debates concerning Poland's past and sought to explain the causes of the partitions. Members of the Cracow school—Szujski, Walery Kalinka (1826-86), and the youngest and most brilliant of them, Bobrzyński—critically evaluated Polish institutions and put emphasis on the domestic causes of the partitions. Their "pessimistic" interpretation provoked a rebuttal from the "optimistic" Warsaw historians, notably Tadeusz Korzon (1839-1918) and Władysław Smoleński (1851-1926), who came up with new material showing the importance and depth of the Polish revival under Stanislas Augustus. The appearance in 1879 of Bobrzyński's synthesis of Polish history, which stressed the absence of a strong government in the old commonwealth, provoked controversies that transcended the scholarly *milieu*. Irrespective of differing interpretations which stimulated interest in the past, historical research made great strides. The Lemberg historians Ksawery Liske (1838-91), Oswald Balzer (1858-1933), and Tadeusz Wojciechowski (1838-1919) contributed extremely valuable studies on Polish medieval history and on constitutional developments.

As in the case of higher education, the Poles could directly influence the high schools only in Galicia. Between 1861 and 1890 their numbers rose significantly: from sixteen to twenty-seven schools, and from five thousand to fifteen thousand students. Here, as in Russian and in part in Prussian Poland, the emphasis in the curricula was on classical education. High schools in Congress Poland were subjected to russification—both in terms of the language of instruction and the material taught—and developed even more slowly than in Russia proper. They were overcrowded and the students suffered from the chicaneries of the Russian teachers. Secondary education under Prussian rule was of a higher level but it was strictly German. Polish attempts to obtain permission to set up a university in Posen were in vain, and consequently many high school graduates went to the universities of Berlin or Breslau.

Elementary education fared worse under Russia, where the number of schools was far too small and the levels of instruction conspicuously low. The already mentioned mass illiteracy clearly resulted from this state of affairs. In Prussian Poland the reverse was true. The government paid special attention to elementary education as a major instrument for bringing up loyal citizens. Although the school teachers were not outstanding—their training resembled that of skilled artisans—and their educational methods were traditional, there was hardly any illiteracy. By 1890 the process of germanization of elementary schools was close to completion. In Galicia the main effort to improve elementary education and make it more universal came after 1890, but during the first decades of autonomy some progress was noticeable. Between 1871 and 1890 the number of elementary schools rose from 2,374 to 3,814. At the same time a clear-cut distinction between town and village schools remained. The latter often had only one class and the ratio of the number of schools to that of inhabitants was most unsatisfactory.

Even though conditions differed sharply from province to province, some room was left for Polish private initiative in the field of education. The efforts of Poles in Prussian Poland, such as aid to students, popular libraries, adult education, and others, have already been discussed in the preceding chapters. In the Congress Kingdom, such institutions as the Commercial College founded by Kronenberg or the Museum of Industry and Agriculture (1875) were due to private initiative. Among important publications there were the Polish Geographical Dictionary, the Dictionary of the Polish Language, and the Great Illustrated Encyclopedia. The Mianowski Foundation, based on private donations, assisted scholars and institutions in research and publications. Consequently, people who had no university teaching positions were able to pursue important studies. During this period representatives of the older generation, Kolberg and Supiński, continued to work respectively in ethnography and economics. Among the younger men Wacław Nałkowski (1857–1911) rose as a prominent geographer, and the sociologist Ludwik Krzywicki (1859–1941) began to publish extensively.

In addition to old and well-established institutions, such as the Ossolineum in Lemberg and Działyński's Kórnik in Poznania, the Czartoryski Museum was founded in Cracow, thanks to the initiative of Władysław Czartoryski, Prince Adam's son. It contained invaluable collections and archives. Literary and political émigré archives including those bearing on the January Insurrection were deposited in the Rapperswil castle in Switzerland. With respect to private initiative the situation under the tsarist regime was by far the worst, although, as mentioned above, there were impressive achievements. In Congress Poland, cultural, scholarly, and even philanthropic organizations could only be set up with imperial permission. Exhibitions of paintings with national themes were forbidden; libraries and even bookstores were strictly controlled. In Lithuania, deprived of theaters and most cultural and scholarly institutions, the local magnates (the Ogińskis and Tyzenhauzes) were at least able to establish private symphony orchestras and a music school which trained many of the future Lithuanian composers.

Still, Polish culture continued to develop and preserve its all-national character. All-Polish meetings, for instance, of doctors and natural scientists took place. People in one part of the country knew what was being written, read, and exhibited in other parts. Sienkiewicz' Trilogy appeared in simultaneous installments in three conservative papers of Russian, Austrian, and Prussian Poland.

With the popularization of Polish culture and its gradual penetration to the masses, a more integrated national "organic" society was emerging. This society was increasingly conscious as a whole of its separate cultural identity and unity.

*Part Four*

ON THE ROAD TO INDEPENDENCE, 1890-1918

CHAPTER 14

# The Rise of Mass Movements

I. ON THE THRESHOLD OF THE TWENTIETH CENTURY

THE 1890s and the 1900s saw the growth of new social and political forces that seriously challenged the existing order. Their rise was related both to specific Polish conditions and to more general phenomena characteristic of the Age of Imperialism. The rapid pace of economic change including the concentration and export of capital, the growth of trusts and monopolies, and the expansion into new markets, accompanied by the development of political and economic nationalism, had an impact on the lands of the old commonwealth. Naturally, the evolution of the Polish lands was slower than that of the advanced industrial countries, and the scope of problems more limited. Remnants of cottage industry, handicrafts, small trade patterns, and businesses of mixed agricultural-industrial nature survived. The economic life of Austrian and Prussian Poland was largely dependent on German, Austrian, or Czech banks. As more joint stock companies arose, Austrian, German, and even English capital entered into them. In Congress Poland, where local capital played a major role and penetrated Russian lands, it became subordinated to the capital of the rapidly industrializing Russian Empire. Polish businesses participated in all-Russian cartels of coal, sugar, and iron.

Each of the Polish lands was increasingly integrated into the economy of its partitioning power. The protectionist policies of the powers strengthened economic barriers and cut Polish producers off from raw materials across the border. There was still no direct railroad connection between Warsaw and Posen, and a traveler going from Warsaw to Lemberg had to take long detours. The poorly developed railroad system in the western parts of Congress Poland contrasted with the dense network in Prussian Poland. The latter

275

was mainly oriented toward Germany. No wonder that the great bourgeoisie was reluctant to defy, for reasons of Polish patriotism, what seemed the inescapable logic of economic development. Their businesses were related to whatever empire ruled over them. At the other extreme, a leading Socialist thinker, Rosa Luxemburg (1870-1919), seemed to prove in a scholarly fashion that the economic amalgamation of Polish lands with the partitioning powers had inescapable consequences for the working class.

Growth of production as well as structural changes in business and finance did not basically diminish the importance of the agrarian sector. The process of parceling out estates almost came to a halt in the "Vistula Land" but continued in Galicia which, except for the "western guberniias," still had the largest proportion of land in the possession of magnates. Changes in the distribution of land in Poznania became inextricably linked with the German-Polish struggle and were accompanied by a growing cooperative movement. The landowning class continued to represent the real political and economic power in the Ukrainian, Lithuanian-Belorussian, and Galician lands. Although that class had begun to share its power with the big bourgeoisie in Congress Poland, and with the middle class in Poznania, its primacy had not yet been effectively challenged.

The poverty of the masses led to large-scale emigration which at the turn of the century reached its peak. Between 1870 and 1914 about 1.3 million people emigrated from Russian Poland, about 1.2 million from Prussian Poland, and roughly 1.1 million from Galicia. Craftsmen and landless peasants went to the United States, Canada, and Brazil. In the years 1896–1910 over 400,000 Poles, nearly 150,000 Ukrainians, and some 170,000 Jews emigrated from Galicia. Their departure was not always a total loss for the homeland. Some returned with money and new skills; others sent money to their families. In the case of Galicia this aid amounted to $52 million annually.

The established Polish political leadership, largely concentrated in the hands of the upper classes, sought conciliation with Russia and Prussia. Their efforts, unlike those of the Galician conservatives, produced meager results. Accused of servile loyalism to the oppressors, they proved unable to cope with the rising forces within Polish society whose emergence was assisted by a gradual socioeconomic transformation of the country. Socialism, national democracy, and to a lesser extent populism proclaimed their all-Polish character and challenged on political, national, and social grounds the primacy of the conservatives. Confining their activity at first to the preparatory work of awakening and educating the masses, the new movements gradually made political headway and sapped the bases of power of the conservative elite.

Among the Ukrainians and the Lithuanians the cultural national renascence was assuming distinctly political features. Parties invoking popular support and pursuing national goals came into conflict with Polish movements. In this atmosphere of nationalist friction, the Jewish question took on a new coloring. Anti-Semitism became an openly used political and economic weapon, which in turn stimulated the growth of Jewish nationalism. As the bases of social and political life broadened old conflicts acquired new dimensions.

The international situation was changing, too. With Bismarck's fall in 1890, the German-Russian Reinsurance Treaty lapsed, and Germany entered a new course. Between 1891 and 1894 a Russian-French alliance came into being. Europe was on the road to being divided into two rival camps with Poland in opposite blocs. A slim chance for a rebirth of the Polish question appeared.

## II. GALICIA AND CONGRESS POLAND

During the 1890s and 1900s, the rate of economic growth in Galicia increased but not enough to change the basic character of the province. The output of raw materials, especially of petroleum oil and paraffin wax—Galicia had a world monopoly of the latter until 1908—became much larger. By 1905 oil production reached 794,000 tons (5 percent of total world production) and a couple of years later passed the 1 million mark. Most of the capital, however, that controlled refineries and dictated prices was of foreign origin. Coal output nearly tripled between 1890 and 1914. Large sugar refineries (Lubomirski's in Przeworsk) and breweries (Goetz's in Okocim and Archduke Charles Stephen's in Żywiec) were established. Still, only 7 factories in Galicia employed more than 1,000 workers, and only some 60,000 of the total working population of 320,000 in 1912 were industrial workers, properly speaking.

A large number of uneconomical "dwarf farms" plagued the rural economy, and the parceling out of estates proceeded too slowly. But there were improvements in farming methods and increases in yields per acre. The number of cattle and horses grew. Among novel developments in the countryside were cooperatives—Polish, Ukrainian, and Jewish—dealing with credit, technical improvements, and even sales. If the general standard of living remained low, there was at least some progress after decades of stagnation.

In the cultural field the Provincial School Board carried out reforms under the energetic leadership of Bobrzyński. The number of schools and students rose sharply, as did the percentage of peasant students. Cultural freedom in Galicia and local autonomy increasingly made the province a focus of Polish intellectual and even political life.

The central issue of Galician politics was that of democratization of political and socioeconomic conditions in the country. The discrepancy between Galicia's structure and its political representation in Vienna and in the Sejm was glaring, and a Socialist tribune called the province "an estate leased to the Polish *szlachta*."[1] The middle classes, the peasantry, the Ukrainians, and the representatives of the working class were clamoring for a voice in the affairs of the country. Attacks came from both the Left and from the new National Democratic Right. The outstanding and tough conservative viceroy Count Kazimierz Badeni sought a compromise with the Ukrainians and tried to contain social and national radicals. But the arrangement with the Ukrainians, which included bringing the Kiev historian Hrushevsky to teach at Lemberg as well as other educational concessions, proved short-lived. The use of administrative pressure and even fraud during provincial elections antagonized the Ukrainians as well as Polish radical groups. A crisis developed which Galicia shared with the entire monarchy, and Vienna sought to resolve it by electoral concessions.

In 1895 Badeni was called on by the emperor to form a new cabinet, and leaning on Austrian conservatives and Czechs (enticed by linguistic concessions), he introduced the universal fifth curia. All males of age became electors and could vote directly for their representatives, but the number of representatives was severely limited. For Galicia the fifth curia meant the addition of fifteen mandates to the existing fifty-three. The fifteen new deputies, however, represented more voters than the other four curia put together. The Poles accepted the fifth curia with the provision that two-mandate districts would be established in Eastern Galicia in order to protect the Polish minority. Through the widely accepted Austrian practice of "electoral geometry" they also succeeded in setting up smaller districts in the west than in the east.

The objective of the fifth curia was to perpetuate the existing regime while offering a palliative to the masses. Would it act as a safety valve? Or would it stimulate demands for universal suffrage? Elections held in 1897, which were stormier than usual and necessitated the proclamation of martial law in 1898, showed that the latter was likely to be the case. Pressure from the radicals in Vienna led to the overthrow of Badeni, and the slogan of universal suffrage became the battle cry of the Left. For the first time, Polish deputies to the Reichsrat—Populists and Socialists elected in the fifth curia—refused to join the parliamentary Polish Circle.

Faced with a fragmentation of political life in Galicia, where Cracow conservatives, *Podolacy*, Socialists, Democrats, Populists, and National Democrats were all competing with each other, the ruling

1. Ignacy Daszyński, *Pamiętniki* (Kraków: Proletarjat, 1925-26), I, 13.

group attempted to revitalize its movement. The creation of a neoconservative club in 1896, however, could not be a lasting remedy, although it did bolster the party that still controlled the administration and most public positions. Its regime was shaken again in 1902 when a widespread agricultural strike of Ukrainian and Polish farmhands took place in Eastern Galicia. The province was tense and there was no political solution in sight. What is more, Galicia appeared increasingly as a Polish Piedmont in which émigrés from the Congress Kingdom began to establish their editorial and propagandistic bases. Their influence on local politics, especially after 1905, operated against the conservative leadership.

Congress Poland continued to be fairly prosperous, although the industrialization of Russia proper cast a shadow on the Polish economy. After overcoming a period of crisis, agriculture experienced a new boom after 1893. The growth of the population and the concomitant increased consumption necessitated the enlargement of tilled areas and even importation of Ukrainian grain. Prices went up. The parceling out of estates assisted by the Russian Peasant Bank (Bank Włościański), which operated since 1890 in the "Vistula Land," began to slow down perceptibly. By 1900, the value of industrial and artisan production (656 million rubles) surpassed that of agriculture (400 million). Coal output reached 6.8 million tons before the First World War; that of iron ore, 311,000 tons. The production of pig iron more than tripled between 1890 and 1913. During the same period sugar production rose from 73,000 to 216,000 tons. Concentration was taking place in heavy industries and sugar refineries; local and all-Russian cartels arose. Over fifty factories employed one thousand or more workers. Foreign capital continued to be invested in Polish industries, although it also began to shift to the more profitable Ukraine.

The grandiose and ambitious program of industrialization of Russia, launched by Sergei I. Witte in 1892, was bound to create economic difficulties for the kingdom. At the time it was hardly noticeable, and the argument about an insoluble economic connection between Poland and Russia seemed well founded. But there were ominous harbingers of change. Congress Poland had no raw materials, save coal and small iron ore deposits. High Russian duties on raw materials began to hurt the Polish producer, and the textile industry, which sent three-fourths of its exports to Russia, began to encounter competition. Given the big distances and differential freight rates, Polish industry could hardly compete with the heavy industry of the Ukraine once the latter was fully developed. Higher taxes paid by the inhabitants of Congress Poland, less money available for education than in Russia proper, a gradual transfer of foreign investments eastward—all these factors were likely to raise the costs of production in the kingdom and affect its future developments. True, new branches of industry were developing, as for instance, rayon production financed by Italian capital, and the chemical industry. German capital contributed to the emergence of an electrical engineering industry. More advanced sales techniques led to the appearance of the first department stores. The number of industrial workers kept increasing but at a slower rate than before: 244,000 in 1897, and 317,000 in 1913. But if St. Petersburg really decided to discriminate against the Congress Kingdom economically, the future would be bleak. Such prospects furnished the Polish upper classes with an additional argument for a policy of reconciliation with Russia.

The accession of Nicholas II to the throne in 1894 revived Polish hopes. The population wanted reconciliation with Russia, and therefore it believed reconciliation was possible. The urbane manners of the two succeeding governor generals of Warsaw, Count Shuvalov and Prince Imeretinsky, appealed to the Polish aristocracy and to the upper classes. The St. Petersburg-published *Kraj* and Wielopolski welcomed even minor concessions, such as permission to erect Mickiewicz's statue in Warsaw, albeit without any public manifestation of patriotic feelings. During the tsar's visit to Warsaw, Wielopolski assured Nicholas that the Poles "unflinchingly" desired to serve their "beloved monarch." A delegation headed by Wielopolski presented the tsar with a gift of one million rubles which he used to establish a Russian politechnika in Warsaw. But chances of a genuine reconciliation were virtually nil. Polish Socialists stole and published a secret report of Imeretinsky which showed the latter's contempt for the policies of the kingdom's upper classes. In 1897 a huge Eastern Orthodox church was built in the center of Warsaw, a gesture which appeared to the Poles to be a calculated insult and a symbol of Russian domination. Opposition to extreme Russian measures seemed to fare better than subserviency. In 1902 Polish nationalists inspired a school strike protesting the teaching of religion classes in Russian. Since a similar conflict in Poznania had produced such adverse publicity for the Prussian government, Nicholas decided to be accommodating: religious instruction in Polish was permitted throughout the entire kingdom.

Among contemporary issues, the Jewish question became more acute in the 1890s, and the authorities fanned the anti-Jewish sentiments of the population. Following new restrictions in the empire, Jews from the "western guberniias," the so-called Litvaks, began to move into Congress Poland. Often strongly influenced by Russian culture, they regarded the kingdom as merely another part of Russia in which they could settle and work. Their presence produced new debates and strengthened the opponents of assimilation who argued against the possibility of absorbing an increasingly large and alien element. While in 1827 Jews constituted 9.3 percent of the kingdom's population, they had risen to 14.6 percent by 1909. The proportion in towns was much higher. Jews controlled 63.5 percent of the textile trade, and with the rise of a Polish middle class competition became severe. Given a Catholic reaction against positivism, anti-Semitism flourished also on religious grounds. Symptomatic of the changing atmosphere was the fact that the first openly anti-Semitic journal in the kingdom was published by a former advocate of assimilation. Among the Jews, nationalism grew and took the form of Zionism which crystallized around 1895. An all-Russian Zionist conference was held in Minsk in 1902, and Zionists became also active in Galicia where they demanded an independent national Jewish policy.

### III. PRUSSIAN POLAND

Economic progress in Prussian Poland forcibly contrasted with the intensified Polish-German strife which only briefly subsided during an attempt at conciliation by Polish loyalist conservatives. Although industrial establishments in that region were small, and only a few employed more than one thousand workers, their production continued to increase. Breweries in Poznania occupied the first place in the German Empire; the sugar industry was third. Construction industry grew. The number of industrial workers increased from around 30,000 to 162,000 between 1875 and 1907. Technical progress was visible in agriculture, and 80 percent of farms larger than five hectares had some machinery. After 1890 the shortage of farm laborers forced the government to permit again the employment of seasonal workers from Galicia and Russian Poland.

The great issue of the period, political and economic, was the parceling out of Polish estates and the setting up of German farms. Begun with the Colonization Commission in 1886, this process represented a serious danger to the Poles. In principle the commission strove to strengthen the German element in ethnically mixed areas and tried to establish large settlements in predominantly Polish regions so as to prevent polonization of local Germans. In predominantly German areas, it only bought land that threatened to fall into Polish hands. As mentioned in an earlier chapter, the commission succeeded in buying a considerable amount of land, and the Polish riposte was inadequate. A land bank (Bank Ziemski) was set up with local capital, as well as with Polish funds from Galicia and the kingdom, but the founding capital was very small. The bank's director, Teodor Kalkstein (1851–1905), felt that he must first try to assist needy Polish estates which would otherwise have to sell some land to modernize their farming techniques.

Attempts at a *modus vivendi* with Bismarck produced no effects. Because of the Prussian electoral system the Polish delegation to the Landtag was small and hardly counted in politics. Realizing that it could not bargain with the government, the delegation was less conciliatory, except for some aristocrats in the upper house (Herrenhaus), and more openly critical of anti-Polish measures in linguistic and economic spheres than were other groups. In the imperial Reichstag the Poles had a sizable representation, greater possibilities of political maneuvering, and potential allies. But the very fact that in 1890 every tenth Prussian was Polish-speaking or a Pole was more of a political liability than an asset. The size of the Polish population aroused German fears about the future of the eastern provinces and increased German nationalism.

In 1890 the Bismarck era came to an end. The new chancellor, Count Leo von Caprivi, found it useful for domestic and international reasons to offer minor concessions to the Poles in return for their loyal cooperation. In the changing international situation a certain relaxation in Prussian-Polish relations was desirable. Also, the new government had no working majority in the Reichstag and needed the votes of the Polish Circle. Among the Poles, pressure for conciliation came mainly from two political quarters: the conservatives and the Populists. The former, led by Kościelski, felt that a patriotic stand had not prevented anti-Polish measures; they believed that a *détente* was also in the Germans' interest. As Kościelski put it in 1891, "it is not the existence of Poles in the east but the attempt to germanize them that makes for Germany's weakness; give it up and immediately you will have a power at your disposal."[2] A rising Polish Populist movement, centered around the journal *Orędownik*, argued on its side that as loyal citizens of Prussia the Poles ought to be treated on an equal footing with the German-speaking Prussians. The Populists, led by a former Democrat who was a bit of a demagogue, Roman Szymański (1840–1908), drew their support from the middle and lower classes. They contested the leadership of the landowning gentry and represented a new form of nationalism that was more pragmatic and less historically minded.

Exchanges between Caprivi and Kościelski resulted in a compromise. The government would not press germanization and would grant limited concessions to Poznania. These would not extend to Pomerania which Caprivi viewed as the old home of the

2. Cited in Lech Trzeciakowski, *Polityka polskich klas posiadających w Wielkopolsce w erze Capriviego 1890–1894* (Poznań: Państwowe Wydawnictwo Naukowe, 1960), pp. 116–17.

Teutonic Knights. In return, the Polish parliamentary circle led by Kościelski would support the government. Berlin's concessions fell into three categories. First, the government agreed that Father Stablewski become archbishop. Although Stablewski stressed his adherence to policies of conciliation and loyalism, the appointment of a Pole to the archdiocese was a net gain, especially because since 1900 all major bishops in Prussian Poland were Germans. Second, private lessons of Polish in school buildings were authorized and religious classes in Polish tolerated. Futhermore, Polish was permitted as an elective subject in a number of elementary schools. The government was unwilling to go any further and dismissed the argument of liberal German circles that the obligatory use of German as the language of instruction slowed down children's education. The third, and most important, were the economic concessions. Poles could benefit from new Prussian legislation that greatly facilitated state credits to prospective land buyers. This enabled them to compete seriously with the Colonization Commission. Between 1891 and 1894, that is, before the government stepped in again to prevent the system from operating to Polish advantage, the Poles succeeded in launching a systematic campaign of land acquisition. Even if they were only able to buy a fourth as much land as the commission was able to buy, the ratio was improving, and the Poles equaled the Germans in numbers of settlers. Finally, the all-important Polish credit association (Związek Spółek Zarobkowych) received the right to appoint its own auditors; this gave it much greater freedom in credit policies.

For four years the Polish parliamentary circle steadfastly supported the government and voted for expanded military and naval expenditure. Kościelski's opponents nicknamed him "the admiral," and his group a "party of courtiers." Support of German militarism seemed a heavy price to pay for limited concessions, and there were doubts about Berlin's sincerity. From 1890 on, German population censuses introduced a new category for Kashubians and Mazurians; this step was clearly designed to weaken a united Polish front. Although a Kashubian cultural revival followed, the region continued to return Polish deputies to the parliament. The Kościelski group incurred the Poles' criticism for its failure to support Polish national revival in Silesia and for its far too frequent usage of the term "Polish-speaking Prussians." It was also attacked for representing vested interests of the big landowners to the detriment of other classes.

This last accusation was only in part true. Kościelski's speeches against the "Socialist threat" were largely for German consumption and hardly relevant for Poznania where no such threat existed.

When the Polish Circle voted for commercial treaties that favored industrial interests, it was mainly because of loyalist policies and not their own class interests. In the Prussian diet, the Poles favored revision of the electoral system, introduction of the secret ballot, and elimination of the administrative autonomy of the landed estates. These were hardly examples of narrow class considerations.

In 1894 Kościelski failed to persuade the circle to vote for the naval budget and resigned. The flimsiness of reconciliation was quickly exposed. At the Galician provincial exhibition Kościelski himself spoke of a Polish national organism divided by state boundaries. William II made anti-Polish pronouncements. With the dismissal of Caprivi the brief era of reconciliation was over. It brought certain advantages to the Poles; in particular it enabled them to wage a more effective struggle against germanization. At the same time, loyalism brought more confusion to the political life of Prussian Poland.

German reaction against Caprivi's policies reached major proportions. The Junkers criticized the Poles on economic grounds; the National Liberals opposed the dependence of the government on Polish votes in the Reichstag; the rising Pangerman organizations indulged in militant nationalist propaganda. On the initiative of three wealthy landowners, Ferdinand von Hansemann, Hermann Kennemann, and Heinrich von Tiedemann, a society for the promotion of German interests in the east was organized in 1894. Called eventually the Deutscher Ostmark Verein but popularly known as HKT (after its founders' initials), the association had the blessings of the retired Bismarck. The chief aim of HKT was colonization and germanization of the "eastern marches." Although referring to defense against the "aggressiveness of the Poles," "Hakatism" quickly became synonymous with chauvinism. The HKT set up a German land bank, supported the local German peasantry and townspeople, and voiced the slogan Nationality Follows Language. They insisted that German officials should have German wives, be conscious propagators of "Germandom," and subscribe to the principle of "my country right or wrong." According to them the Polish language was not a cultural medium. Hakatist propaganda implied German racial superiority over the Poles, although simultaneously it expressed concern lest the Germans in the eastern provinces succumb to polonization.

The first Hakatist leaders were landowners with close connections to financial circles; they included many politicians, industrialists, and scholars. As time went on, the bulk of the society was increasingly composed of government officials, teachers, army officers, new settlers, and Protestant ministers. Only a small percentage of the Germans living in Prussian Poland belonged to the HKT. There were relatively few typical Junkers, German Catholics, and Jews in the movement, and its chiefly Protestant outlook was quickly exploited by the Poles, who mobilized Catholic forces against it. The importance of the HKT lay not so much in its numbers as in its influence on German attitudes toward Poles. The association became a powerful lobby that pressed for germanization of the eastern provinces and made it a German and not solely a Prussian issue. Some of its slogans had a ring that sounds familiar to those acquainted with the later Nazi ideology of the *Lebensraum*.

Largely thanks to Hakatist pressures, the government intensified its anti-Polish policies. In 1896 the colors of Posen—red and white— were changed to obliterate its Polish past; scores of towns and villages received new German names (for instance, Inowrocław became Hohensalza). Polish language was eliminated from sermons and masses in the Kulm, Ermland (Warmia), and Breslau dioceses. Finally, from 1898 on the government resorted to exceptional laws *(Ausnahmgesetze)* which called into question Prussian legalism and made the Poles second class citizens. Special funds, which by 1907 reached the sum of over two million marks, were granted to the local administration in order to strengthen German nationality in the east. Officials who could prove their nationalist activities received bonuses. Poznania became saturated with officials, Posen being the city with the highest percentage of government employees in the Reich. The government invested heavily in Prussian Poland so as to amalgamate it more effectively with Germany. It built more schools, railroads, libraries, and museums. In the long run these investments proved beneficial to the Poles.

Huge sums—100,000 marks in 1898, 150,000 in 1908, half a million in 1913—were spent on land purchases and settlements. Much of that money became in fact a gigantic relief program for the Junkers, who made their patriotism a highly lucrative business. Aid to the German middle class was also largely wasteful as it lessened their competiveness and efficiency.

From 1901 on, the government began to enforce the exclusive use of German in religion classes; this led to open defiance on the part of Polish children in the little town of Wreschen (Września). Their resistance was crushed by flogging and other penalties, but the affair became a *cause célèbre* which the Poles publicized throughout Europe as an example of German barbarism.

Unable to win the struggle for the land through purely economic means, the government began to use special legislation. In 1904 a law was enacted that made it an offense to construct a house on acquired land if it contravened the spirit of colonization policies. Another public scandal broke out when a Polish peasant, Michał

Drzymała (1857-1937), bypassed the law by bringing a covered circus wagon to his plot and making it his home. The Poles publicized the affair to dramatize the living conditions in Prussia where a Pole had to live in a wagon on his own land. While governmental measures stiffened Polish resistance, Hakatist chauvinism inflamed Polish nationalism. "Organic work" was now combined with slogans of boycotting German shops and associations, as well as German culture.

Polish successes in the struggle for land were largely due to the mobilization of capital—including German capital—during the Caprivi era, and to the adroit organizing and purchasing policies of the Poles. In the years 1896-1904, the Poles registered a net gain of 59,000 hectares over the Colonization Commission, because the bulk of the commission's purchases came from German landed estates. True, around one hundred thousand Germans settled on new plots, but only half of them were immigrants from Germany. The Polish Land Purchase Bank (Bank Parcelacyjny) established in 1897 was able to pay higher dividends and to provide credit on easier terms than were the German banks. An efficient and well organized network of cooperative associations made it possible to register progress even with modest funds. Polish banks in Upper Silesia and East Prussia showed that this dynamic movement was not confined to Poznania. A new form of peasant cooperatives (Rolniki) provided its members, richer peasants and landowners, with fertilizers, seeds, and fodder. Stepping into the place of Jewish merchants —the percentage of Jews in Poznania sank from 2.5 percent to 1.2 percent between 1890 and 1910—the Poles moved into the cattle and grain trade. Old credit institutions and agricultural circles expanded their membership and accumulated new capital. Between 1890 and 1913 the Union of Credit Associations, under its "patron" Father Piotr Wawrzyniak (1849-1910), increased its membership in Poznania, Pomerania, and Upper Silesia from 26,553 to 146,312. Its deposits rose by more than twenty times. The membership of the agricultural circles increased tenfold between 1873 and 1914.

New organizations arose: the Association of Landowners (Związek Ziemian) in 1901 and the Association of Polish Manufacturers (Związek Fabrykantów Polskich) in 1910. A German expert, Ludwig Bernhard, writing around 1910 highly assessed the Polish achievements: " . . . the organization of Poles for struggle under the Prussian rule is and remains a universal model of how a national minority can keep its independent existence and even strengthen it against a far stronger state authority."[3] Whether the Poles could be as successful in the long run, especially if the authorities embarked on a

3. Cited in Witold Jakóbczyk, ed. *Wybitni Wielkopolanie XIX wieku* (Poznań: Wydawnictwo Poznańskie, 1959), p. 28.

policy of unlimited oppression, was a question that worried sober-minded Poles. The Poles were but a small minority in the German Reich, and their means of defense were limited.

Stained with loyalism which produced meager results, Poznanian conservatives were in no position to organize a modern political party. Like the church hierarchy and the Populists, they relied for the most part on numerous economic and social institutions and their press organs. They were in danger of losing contact with the masses as well as with the richer peasantry and the middle class which through the Populists demanded more voice in public affairs of the province. When in 1902 Archbishop Stablewski and a few conciliatory aristocrats decided to take part in welcoming William II in Posen, they ran the danger of becoming completely isolated. Their policy of steering clear of the Silesian issue, for fear of antagonizing the German nation, deprived them of any influence over developments in that region.

Younger members of the intelligentsia and the landowning class who had some connections with the Populists were searching for new policies that would benefit the Polish nation. Rejecting the idea of an armed uprising and critical of Poznanian parochialism, they sought a common platform with their countrymen who lived under Russian and Austrian rule. Eventually, they found it in the Polish League and the nascent National Democratic movement, both of which were all-Polish in character.

The younger representatives of the Poznanian intelligentsia carefully followed the developments in Upper Silesia. The region had become a great industrial center in which most of the Poles were workers and miners. Slowly, there appeared also Polish artisans and merchants—some of them immigrants from Poznania and Pomerania—and a small intelligentsia which was in part of local origin. A situation in which the upper classes were German and the working proletariat Polish theoretically offered ideal conditions for the growth of Polish socialism, and the fact that the Polish national cause rather than socialism became the unifying political factor was due to specific local conditions. On the one hand, the ardent Catholicism of the masses became equated with "Polishness"; on the other, the nationalist tendencies of the German Social Democratic Party dissipated the attractiveness of socialist slogans. In the continuing national evolution of the region, the terms Pole and Upper Silesian no longer seemed contradictory, and the people were moving beyond the stage of defense of their religion and language. This evolution undermined the basis of cooperation between Upper Silesian Poles and the German Zentrum. True, Polish political leadership in Upper Silesia, grouped around the journal *Katolik* and Adam Napieralski (1870–1928), still cooperated with the Zentrum for tactical reasons. But a challenge to these policies would come from the same forces that were arising throughout the Polish lands from the mid-1890s onward.

### IV. NATIONAL DEMOCRACY AND POPULISM

The rise of future mass political parties in the 1890s was the single most important development of this period. It took place in the political, social, and economic context outlined above, and the two major parties were the Socialist and the National Democratic. Populist or peasant parties did not attain the same importance and will be only mentioned briefly.

The National Democratic movement grew out of the Polish League, which was founded in 1887.[4] Rejecting both political passivity and a program of reconciliation with the partitioning powers, the league strove to mobilize the Poles for the cause of national independence. Although its leading figures did not subscribe to a single political trend they shared a belief in the need for an active, democratic, and patriotic policy. In 1893 the character of the league changed as a result of an internal coup within its Warsaw organization. The main person responsible for the coup was Roman Dmowski (1864-1939), who together with Popławski and Balicki became the leader of the movement. The central committee of the league was moved to Warsaw, and the organization renamed the National League. The change indicated an emancipation from émigré tutelage as well as from alleged freemasonic influences. The league's structure was tightened and the central committee assumed wide powers. Largely due to these changes the youth organization Zet ended its formal link with the league and for the next four years assumed an independent status.

The National League entered a path that lead it away from the radical insurrectionist tradition toward integral nationalism. Its founders "took the empirical method from the positivists, they recognized the dictates of organic work, and they complemented them by politics. As for the idea of the nation and the aims of political action, they were the successors of the romanticists."[5] The evolution was gradual, and for several years to come the league denounced reconciliation and the class egoism of the loyalist aristocracy. It took a fairly tolerant view of the Socialists and even saw the possibility of a division of spheres of action, with the Socialists concentrating on the workers.

4. National Democracy was popularly called, especially by its adversaries, *endecja* and its members *endeks*, a term coined from the initials N.D.
5. Stanisław Kozicki, *Historia Ligi Narodowej: Okres 1887–1907* (London: Myśl Polska, 1964), pp. 473–74.

Stressing an all-Polish national character which was its fundamental tenet, the league saw itself as a secret directorate presiding over all manifestations of national life. It early showed a tendency to claim a monopoly on patriotism and the right to determine what was nationally desirable. It sought to guide the nation, to integrate its evolving social structure, to educate the people in a nationalist spirit, and to bring about a complete cohesion of the Polish nation. It concentrated first on educational and cultural work, and up to 1905 it accomplished a great deal in this field.

In 1895 Dmowski, obliged to flee Congress Poland, founded the *Przegląd Wszechpolski* (All-Polish Review) in Galicia. The main watchwords of the paper were: unity and political identity of the Polish nation, regeneration of its political forces through cultural progress, and national awareness and civic integration of the masses. Two years later the league decided to publish the first program of the National Democratic Party in Russian Poland (the party as such could not be organized under existing conditions), which affirmed that for a nation with a living sense of unity and distinct interests the only form of existence was statehood. The test of national policies was whether they could bring the Poles closer to this goal. The Zet now returned to the league, although it continued to retain a somewhat more leftist outlook and did not reject prosocialist tendencies until 1900. In 1899 the National League informed the Polish people of its clandestine existence.

The decision to come out partly into the open resulted from contemporary political trends. The tsar's visit to Warsaw had given hope to the loyalists. The subsequent publication of Imeretinsky's report had exposed the slender bases of reconciliation. The Russian Poles were becoming politically disoriented. The Socialists intensified their activity. Under these circumstances the league felt it necessary to enter the political arena and to announce its program to the public. In keeping with its all-Polish character, the league attempted to penetrate all the lands of the partitioned country. In Congress Poland it founded in 1899 the Society for National Education (Towarzystwo Oświaty Narodowej), which in a short time had three thousand circles. When the Wreschen affair in Poznania threatened to turn the attention of Russian Poles away from similar discriminatory policies in the kingdom, the league encouraged a school strike which brought the earlier mentioned tsarist concessions in 1902. A year later, the league founded a Society for the Protection of the Uniates and spread its influence among the Catholic clergy. All the above societies naturally remained secret, as did the league itself.

In Galicia, the league successfully infiltrated the Association of Elementary Schools (TSL), the Academic Reading Circle, and the

Sokół. In 1902 it purchased a popular daily, *Słowo Polskie* (Polish Word), to spread its ideas. Given the activity of legal Polish parties in the province, a penetration of Galician political life proved more difficult. The league, however, gained influence over the *Podolacy* wing of the conservatives and over some peasant groups. In 1902 the economist Stanisław Głąbiński (1862-1943) became the first representative of the National Democratic trend in the Viennese Reichsrat. Challenging the conservatives, the league successfully used the slogan of being the only truly national Polish movement that transcended social classes and Galician provincialism.

In Poznania, the league gained its first members around 1899. The fact that it was a secret, all-Polish organization made the Poznanian conservatives and Populists wary. They suspected an anti-Prussian intrigue on the part of Russia and were suspicious of conspiratorial activities. Again, the method of infiltrating cultural and social organizations assisted the growth of the league. Its program of defending the interests of the people and of coordinating Polish activities in Poznania, Pomerania, and Upper Silesia appealed to many a Prussian Pole, particularly to those of middle class background. The Leaguers refrained from insisting on the slogan of national independence and skillfully maneuvered between the conservatives and the Populists. As German-Polish relations became increasingly tense, the nationalism of the league fell on fertile ground, which had been already prepared in part by the Populist ideology. Outstanding individuals such as Bernard Chrzanowski (1865-1944), Marian Seyda (1879-1967), and Wojciech Korfanty (1873-1939) from Upper Silesia joined the organization. Zet, particularly its Berlin branch, showed great activity. In 1901 Chrzanowski became the first Leaguer in the Reichstag. Three years later the league won over the Populist Szymański and set up a secret organization called National Defense. Although unable to organize their own party—a program was issued in 1902—the Leaguers' influence grew, and during the 1903 elections a coalition of Populists, progressive gentry, and National Democrats gained a majority.

The league's special interest in Upper Silesia stemmed largely from their tenet that the losses suffered by the Polish element in the east had to be made good in the west. Opposing a dependence on German Catholics, the Leaguers emphasized the all-Polish and populist character of the Silesian movement. The rising local leader Korfanty, an outstanding personality, launched the slogan Away from the Zentrum and engaged in a struggle with the Napieralski group. Imprisoned for a short time, attacked by the clergy, he became the symbol of the young National Democratic movement. Criticizing capitalism and successfully neutralizing Socialist influences, the

Upper Silesian leaders stressed the role of trade unions and spoke not of destroying capitalism but of reforming it. In 1903 Korfanty was elected to the Reichstag; this was a great achievement. Specific Silesian developments, however, gradually led him away from the league and brought about a *rapprochement* with Napieralski. Although the league did not gain control over Upper Silesia, it contributed greatly to its political activism.

A landmark in the ideological evolution of the National League was the appearance in 1902–1903 of important writings by Dmowski and Balicki. Dmowski, who may well be called the father of modern Polish nationalism, came from a poor family of distant gentry background, but he never identified himself with any particular social class. A natural scientist who was impressed with contemporary biological and sociological trends, he excelled in clear and logical formulations of his ideas and a consistency in applying them. Attracted to politics at an early age, he was a theorist in the sense of providing theoretical foundations for his policies, but he was hardly the creator of a doctrine. A hard and occasionally ruthless man with a strong personality, he dominated his associates, including Balicki and Popławski who influenced many of his views. Searching for the mainspring of human and social action, he found it in nationalism, and even if his views were not directly influenced by English or French nationalists—Chamberlain, Déroulède, or Maurras—they were comparable to theirs. Polish nationalism, however, had its own characteristics. Partly a reaction against Pangermanism or Panslavism, it was not a direct outgrowth of the late stages of the industrial revolution. Except to a certain extent in Galicia, it was a nationalism not of the master but of the underdog.

Dmowski exposed his ideas in a collection of articles published in 1903 under the title *The Thoughts of a Modern Pole (Myśli nowoczesnego Polaka)*. The little book became the bible of Polish nationalism, although its author described it as an attempt to stimulate and inspire his countrymen rather than as a finished program or a scholarly treatise. Dmowski harshly criticized his countrymen for their passivity and their fear of struggle. He accused them of clinging to the romantic and messianic heritage and comforting themselves with the thought that subjection was morally superior to lording it over others. Dmowski considered this mentality to be an inheritance from the historic Polish upper class. Poland, he said, fell not because she grew old but because her social evolution was abnormal. The *szlachta* had created hothouse conditions for itself to the detriment of society. The "noble nation" lost all virility and became a "feminine nation." Because the Jews dominated the towns the *szlachta* faced no challenge from the middle class. The masses remained outside society, and consequently the contemporary peasantry "does not remember the commonwealth, the king, or the Sejm—it only remembers the lord." Dmowski denounced some of the most cherished traditions of the old commonwealth: religious toleration, humanity, equality of the Lithuanian and Ruthenian gentry. He saw them mainly as a result of weakness, vested interests, or political immaturity (for instance, involvement in the eastern expansion). But the gentry-dominated society was no more, and the people was now entering the political stage. Since national characteristics were associated with socioeconomic formations, a new Polish nation based on the people *(lud)*, which was "young" but conscious of its nationality, could be moulded in accord with the precepts of modern nationalism. To form this nation and to make it the determining force of Polish society was Dmowski's aim and purpose.

Nationalism, as he saw it, was a new form of patriotism, in which the nation itself was the object of loyalty and veneration. Dmowski defined the nation as a living organism, an integrated social whole. Its individual members were attached to it by innumerable ties. Some of these ties went back to remote times when races emerged. Others were the product of known history. Still others, reinforcing race, tradition, and national character, were now in the process of being made and would become stronger in the future.

Dmowski came close to social Darwinism when he wrote that "struggle is the basis of life" and that "nations that cease to struggle degenerate morally and disintegrate." Drawing his examples from Western imperialism and from Prussia's rise to power, Dmowski attempted to draw a fine distinction between the fact of expansion and a seemingly moral judgment of Prussia's might, which since it was based on injustice could poison the German spirit and ultimately harm Germany herself. The distinction is not very clear, especially since Dmowski also expressed his respect for German and Russian national struggles. One could morally condemn an individual, he said, for harming another person, but one could not condemn nations for struggling with one another. He rather contemptuously dismissed the Polish belief in humanitarianism as an attribute of an advanced civilization. Together with Popławski, he considered this a characteristic not of the masters of civilization but of its lackeys.

Old Polish patriots, Dmowski wrote, viewed the national cause in terms of a fight for freedom and were ready to make concessions to other nationalities: Lithuanians, Ukrainians, and Jews. Not so modern nationalists. The struggle in Prussian Poland was creating a modern type of a Pole. The "magnanimous" Polish policy in eastern Galicia made no sense. The Ukrainians had to be forced either to become Poles or to be toughened in combat to become self-reliant vis-à-vis Poles and Russians. Economic struggle against Jews was a necessity irrespective of whether it was waged by positive means or "accompanied by the whole semiprofessional apparatus of anti-Semitism that appealed to the lower instincts of the masses." Only a small number of Jews fully prepared for assimilation could be absorbed; the rest were dismissed as alien.

At this stage, Dmowski rejected the theory that one ought to concentrate on Polish defenses in the west and dismiss the east. An all-Polish program of struggle applied to all historic or ethnic Polish lands. He simultaneously denounced policies of conciliation and of armed uprising. His aim was to make the nation resistant to the encroachments of the partitioners as well as to Ukrainian or Lithuanian claims. His nationalism could tolerate no movements based on class, caste, or religion. In answer to the charge that his program was essentially that of national egoism and antihumanitarian in nature, he said that surely elevating a nation to the highest level of civilization was a contribution to all humanity. While Dmowski tried in a sense to reconcile nationalism with morality, Balicki in his *National Egoism and Ethics (Egoizm narodowy wobec etyki)*, published in 1902, clearly contrasted individual and social ethics. This was a strikingly new concept in Polish political thought, and both Balicki and Dmowski came under strong attack of conservatives and democrats alike. Dmowski was accused of promoting a Polish version of Hakatism, denying the best national traditions, adopting blatant anti-Semitism, and poisoning Polish relations with Ukrainians and Lithuanians. He was detaching the national cause from humanitarianism, the meeting ground of Polish and European progressive circles.

Dmowski's ideas appealed to the rising middle class competing with the Jews, to the *Podolacy* who liked his anti-Ukrainian stand, and to Prussian Poles ready to turn German methods against the Germans. A part of the younger generation, which did not come under Socialist influence, found Dmowski's criticism of Polish national characteristics convincing. Moreover, his pronouncements were not just views of an isolated political writer, but those of a leader of a powerful group which already claimed substantial accomplishments.

In 1903 there appeared the second program of the National Democratic Party in Russian Poland. Opposing the loyalists as representatives of vested class interests and rejecting armed insurrection, the program omitted national independence as a political goal. Dmowski considered that to announce such a goal might prevent its eventual realization and obscure the reality of everyday struggle.

As he put it, "to believe in future independence and to desire it does not mean . . . having it in one's program."[6] The fact was that the National Democratic movement was adapting its tactics to the current situation and taking the existing division of Poland as the starting point for political activities. With Galicia in mind, the leaders spoke of mobilizing national strength and political elements necessary for assuring "a better future and higher forms of national existence." Undoubtedly Dmowski believed that the movement stood on sufficiently solid ideological grounds to afford tactical changes. While the National League was a small, elitist organization— in 1903 it had 250 members in Congress Poland, 77 in Galicia, 20 in Prussian Poland, 26 in Lithuania, and 6 in the Ukraine—it was firmly in control of a large body of followers and sympathizers. Moreover, since 1895 it had been assured a modest but steady income from the "national treasury" organized by Miłkowski abroad.

To turn now briefly to "populism," in the sense of a strictly peasant movement, it first developed in the poor and overcrowded Galician countryside. The already mentioned populism in Prussian Poland need not be included here since it was really a lower middle class trend with pronounced nationalist overtones. As for Congress Poland, a peasant organization called Polski Związek Ludowy emerged only toward the end of this period, in 1904.

Chronologically, the first Galician peasant party to appear was the Peasant Party Union (Związek Stronnictwa Chłopskiego) in 1893. It was rather locally centered and soon paled in comparison with the Polish Populist Party (Polskie Stronnictwo Ludowe) which was organized two years later. Inspired by the double heritage of Stojałowski—although it competed with his group—and of Wysłouch, the leaders of the new party included the patriotic peasant Jakub Bojko (1857–1945), and a pupil of Wysłouch, the dynamic and realist politician Jan Stapiński (1867–1946). The Populists fought their political battles under difficult conditions. Uneducated, poor, traditionally dominated by the clergy and the landowners, the peasantry had to emerge from its "other world" which was distinct both from the gentry-culture society and from urban civilization. They had to gain education, self-assurance, and political and even national maturity. Seeking to emancipate themselves from the tutelage of the clergy and gentry, the Populists incurred the wrath of ecclesiastical authorities which denounced them as godless Socialists. Only the Democrats and some of the liberal young gentry lent them support.

Preaching political democratization and justice to the peasants, the Populist Party had to define its goals more clearly, and it did

6. Cited in Marian Orzechowski, *Narodowa Demokracja na Górnym Śląsku do 1918 r.* (Wrocław: Ossolineum, 1965), p. 106.

so at the Rzeszów Conference in 1903. The Rzeszów program said that the Populists strove for national, political, economic, and cultural advancement of the people, and formulated some concrete demands. These included secret, universal, equal, and direct ballot, and broader autonomy for Galicia. Economic and social reforms were spelled out less clearly. The middle-of-the-road position taken by the Populist Party largely reflected the complex outlook of the peasantry. As land proprietors—and most active Populists belonged to this group—the peasants tended to be conservative and susceptible to National Democratic influences. As political and social underdogs they inclined toward radicalism, although they mistrusted such Socialist slogans as expropriation or socialization of land. Deeply attached to Catholicism, the younger generation was becoming somewhat anticlerical.

The future of the Populist Party was still uncertain. Since 1895 it had had a few representatives in the Sejm, and since 1897 in the Reichsrat. In the latter body, however, the peasant deputies stayed outside of the Polish Circle. Potentially a powerful movement in an agrarian society, they had as yet little real strength. They lacked allies and sufficient funds. Stapiński, who was a born leader and a master tactician, attempted to remedy both defects, but his maneuvers earned him the reputation of opportunism and eventually contributed to internal splits in the party.

V. SOCIALISM

Around 1890 many Polish Socialists belonging to different groups and scattered through the kingdom, Galicia, Siberian prisons, and the emigration, began to see more clearly an insoluble connection between Socialist revolution and Polish independence. This departure from pure internationalism was due to several factors. A temporary weakening of Russian revolutionary élan led to a critical reassessment of Russia as the center of revolution. The Franco-Russian alliance raised the specter of European war and made several German Socialist leaders feel that the rebuilding of Poland as a dam against tsarist expansion lay in the interest of the European proletariat. In an atmosphere of nationalist tensions it was hard to believe that a social revolution would automatically end nationalist oppression. In his introduction to the Polish edition of the *Communist Manifesto* (1892), Engels wrote that an "independent, strong Poland is a matter that concerns not only the Poles but all of us."[7] Two years earlier he had opined that the population of the "western guberniias" ought to have the right to determine its own fate.

7. *Marks i Engels o Polsce*, ed. by Helena Michnik (Warszawa: Książka i Wiedza, 1960), 2:205.

Events in Poland seemed to confirm this trend. The great strike in Łódź in 1892 was savagely repressed by the Russian authorities and showed that while industrialists were willing to make concessions the authorities were not. Clearly, the Polish proletariat suffered not only from economic exploitation but also from foreign political oppression. Borrowing Lassalle's constitutional thesis, Grabski explained why Polish Socialists had to tear Poland away from Russia. A Russian constitution, he said, reflecting a lower stage of development than that of Poland would afford little protection to the Polish proletariat. Besides, a constitutional Russia could still be nationally oppressive. As for the economic advantages of association with Russia, the empire's industry was potentially stronger than that of the kingdom and the Russian bourgeoisie would grow at the expense of its Polish counterpart. Too great a dependence on the Russian market led to a neglect of domestic needs. A future unification of an independent kingdom with Galicia and Lithuania would more than compensate for the loss of the eastern markets.

In these circumstances it seemed essential for Polish Socialists to go beyond the internationalism of the Second Proletariat—which operated as a small party—and beyond the mainly economic goals of the Association of Polish Workers (Związek Robotników Polskich). The unification of these and other Socialist groups was also a necessity. Outside the kingdom there were Polish Socialists associated with the German and Austrian Social Democratic parties, and there were Socialist circles of young intelligentsia and students in St. Petersburg, Warsaw, and the West. Finally, there were the workers who responded to May 1 celebrations, introduced in 1890, by appearing *en masse* in the streets of Warsaw and of Galician towns.

At the congress of the Second International in Brussels in 1891, several Poles from Galicia, Russian, and Prussian Poland and from the emigration decided to act as a Polish delegation and expressed hopes for a united Socialist party in Poland. Two Socialist journals published abroad, *Przedświt* (Dawn) and *Pobudka* (Clarion), began to agitate in favor of such a party, and the former wrote that a Socialist organization as "the strongest revolutionary party must assume the role of guiding the nation in all its strivings." In January, 1892, Galician Socialists adopted the program of the Austrian Social Democratic Party but constituted themselves into a separate Polish Social Democratic Party of Galicia. They made it clear that they regarded themselves as part of a Polish Socialist movement, struggling for a future workers' Poland.

A single Socialist all-Polish party was, however, hard to achieve. Conditions for Socialist work differed drastically in various Polish lands, and it appeared particularly important to unite the scattered forces of the Socialist underground in the kingdom. Consequently, plans for an all-Polish conference were abandoned, and instead representatives from Congress Poland and the emigration gathered in November, 1892, at a conference in Paris. Presided over by Limanowski, the conference consisted of prominent individuals from various organizations. They were not and could not have been regularly appointed delegates. Not all of them were destined to remain in the Socialist ranks. Mendelson, for instance, shortly thereafter left the Polish Socialist Party, eventually to become a Zionist. Grabski already leaned toward National Democratic tenets to which he later subscribed.

The Paris conference set up an Association of Polish Socialists Abroad (Związek Zagraniczny Socjalistów Polskich). It prepared the outline of a program for a Polish Socialist Party (PPS) which united the existing organizations and was to be set up in Russian Poland. The Paris Program called for: an independent Polish democratic republic based on universal, direct, and secret suffrage; equal rights of nationalities who would join on the principle of voluntary federation; racial and religious equality of all men and women; freedom of press, association, and spoken and written word; free and compulsory education; and a people's militia to replace the standing armies. In the socioeconomic sphere the program called for an eight-hour working day, minimum wages, legislation protecting labor, extensive social insurance, a progressive income tax, and a gradual socialization of land, communication, and means of production.

The stress put on national independence was the most important element of the new platform, and Polish Socialist leaders invoked the views of Marx, Engels, and other contemporary great Socialists to justify their stand. They also developed arguments partly based on the particular Polish situation. Kazimierz Kelles-Krauz (1872-1905), the leading theorist of the new party, argued that a proletarian revolution was not a single, all-inclusive happening, but rather a process with several stages during which the proletariat had to overcome various obstacles. National oppression constituted a major obstacle which had to be removed. By disrupting the Polish market, the partitions had delayed the emergence of full-fledged capitalism out of which socialism would grow. The effects of the partitions had to be undone, and unity based on language and nationality was essential for a rational socialization of means of production. Speaking of stages, Kelles-Krauz anticipated a violent separation from Russia amidst revolutionary conditions and a gradual separation, through autonomy, from Prussia and Austria.

Another leader, Józef Piłsudski (1867–1935), gave examples from everyday life to show that Russian policies of discrimination had worsened the lot of the Polish worker. Higher taxes in the kingdom forced the Polish industrialist to pay his worker less and to raise prices. The worker also suffered because he could not make himself understood in Russian courts and administrative offices. His children, taught in a language they barely understood, had less chance of advancement. Piłsudski emphasized that the Polish worker was thus doubly penalized, and that continued subjugation to a Russia that was lagging in her own socioeconomic and political development was delaying the progress of socialism in Congress Poland.

Polish Socialist leaders were reluctant to place the fate of their movement in the hands of Russian revolutionaries. They argued that the latter ought to be more active, recognize the standpoint of the Poles, and assist them in their strivings. Here the question of the Lithuanian-Belorussian-Ukrainian borderlands played an important role. In a sense, Polish Socialists rejected both the model of the old commonwealth and that of a Poland conceived in purely ethnic terms. They declared that in the "western guberniias" they were ready to work with the local movements, and if such movements failed to materialize to assume leadership themselves. As a participant of the Paris conference later put it: "Carrying socialist propaganda to our brothers in Lithuania and Ruś we are exempt from the charge of imperialism, because we are not concerned with the interests of Polishness, but with the interest of a revolution that will free the peoples. . . . We do not draw thereby the borders of the future Polish republic, because only the victorious revolution will determine them."[8]

The Paris Program became a rallying point for several Socialist groups. In the early summer of 1893, Socialists from Warsaw, Vilna, and St. Petersburg held a secret conference near Vilna which marked the birth of the Polish Socialist Party (PPS). In February, 1894, the second party conference in Warsaw elected the Central Workers' Committee of the Polish Socialist Party. At this early stage a great deal of work was concentrated in the hands of the Association of Polish Socialists Abroad. It represented the PPS, printed party publications which were then smuggled into Poland, maintained contact with other Socialists, and provided a reserve of party activists for the clandestine work at home.

The internationalist wing of Polish socialism reacted unfavorably to the Paris Program. Their publication *Sprawa Robotnicza* (Workers' Cause), which began to appear in the summer of 1893 in Paris, opposed the emerging PPS. Chosing the name of Social Democracy

8. Stanisław Wojciechowski cited in Władysław Pobóg-Malinowski, *Najnowsza historia polityczna Polski 1864–1945* (1st. ed., Paris: Imprimerie de la S. N. I. E., 1953), 1:71n.

of the Kingdom of Poland (SDKP), they held their conference and adopted their party program in the spring of 1894. While recognizing the need to fight national oppression, the program considered the goal of independent Poland a renunciation of effective political struggle and a departure from the immediate as well as the final aims of the proletariat.

This fundamental split in Polish socialism was hastened by the intransigence of both sides. At the 1893 congress of the Second International in Zurich, Ignacy Daszyński (1866-1936), the leading Socialist from Galicia, objected to recognition of the mandates of Rosa Luxemburg and Julian Marchlewski (1866–1925), the two principal internationalists. Three years later at the London congress, Rosa Luxemburg hotly opposed a PPS motion that national independence was a necessity for the Polish as well as for the international proletariat. Eventually, a watered-down resolution that recognized national self-determination in general was adopted.

The chief theorist of the SDKP, Rosa Luxemburg, based her case largely on the thesis of an "organic integration" of Congress Poland into Russia. She developed this thesis in *Die Industrielle Entwicklung Polens* published in 1898. According to it, the Polish nobility was loyalist, the peasants submissive, and the bourgeoisie derived only advantages from an association with Russia. The latter's interest demanded further industrialization of the kingdom and a strengthening of its bourgeoisie. The emergence of a Polish state would thus be contrary to the logic of capitalist development; even if such a Poland did emerge it would be a poor capitalist state opposed to the workers' interests. Only a Socialist revolution could put an end to national oppression, and while Socialists ought to struggle for national autonomy and the preservation of national culture, it was both anachronistic and wrong to strive for Polish independence. As biographers of Rosa Luxemburg have remarked, the Socialist fatherland was as real to her as Poland was to Piłsudski, and indeed the differences between the two corresponded to their different *Weltanschauung*.

Piłsudski and some of his collaborators were little attracted to Marxist economic theories and to the idea of class struggle *per se*. Like the Polish radicals of the 1840s and 1860s who saw an insoluble link between peasant emancipation and the national cause, they regarded the industrial proletariat as a new force that would carry on the old struggle for social justice and national liberation. As Piłsudski put it, the "historical role of socialism in Poland is the role of a defender of the West against reactionary tsardom."[9] And although

9. Józef Piłsudski, *Pisma zbiorowe* (Warszawa: Instytut im. Józefa Piłsudskiego, 1937–38), 1:95.

Piłsudski was less of a genuine Socialist than some of the other leaders, for example, Feliks Perl (1871–1927), his influence on the PPS was profound.

Piłsudski came from ancient but recently impoverished Lithuanian gentry. Brought up in the romantic tradition, greatly admiring Słowacki, faithful to the memories of 1863, he typified the intensely patriotic Poles from the eastern borderlands. Deported to Siberia (1887–92), he returned with an increased hatred of the tsarist prison of nations. By temperament an activist and a conspirator, he had a strong and charismatic personality. A Socialist revolution was to him almost identical with a national insurrection, and as early as the 1890s he assumed that a reborn Poland would at first be a bourgeois regime within which the Socialists would work for the triumph of socialism.

By 1896, the SDKP had virtually disintegrated, and for the next few years the PPS was the sole functioning Socialist party. It had around a thousand members while SDKP had had a couple of hundred; neither could be called a mass organization. The majority of the leadership came from the intelligentsia, in part of gentry, in part of Jewish background. In spite of being in constant financial straits the PPS was very active. In 1902 the Association of Polish Socialists Abroad was moved to Galicia and lost some of its former importance. The greatest achievement of the home organization was the publication of the clandestine *Robotnik* (Worker) edited by Piłsudski. For six years it eluded the vigilance of the tsarist police, but in 1900 it was discovered. Piłsudski was promptly arrested, and although he eventually managed to escape, the blow to the party was great. The PPS was in disarray.

At roughly the same time the young internationalist Feliks Dzierżyński (1877–1926) arrived in Warsaw, together with some comrades from Vilna, and succeeded in reviving the Social Democratic Party. Reorganized in 1900, it added the words "and of Lithuania" to its name—hence the name SDKPiL (Socjaldemokracja Królestwa Polskiego i Litwy). Since three years earlier the Jewish Bund—the League of Jewish Workingmen of Poland, Lithuania, and Russia—had come into existence, the PPS had to compete with two rival movements within the working class. Finally, the Russian Social Democratic Labor Party entered the scene with its first congress at Minsk in 1898, and the SDKPiL and the Bund recognized its primacy.

Frequently on the move since 1901, Piłsudski was well aware of the importance of these developments and felt that the PPS ought to intensify and modify its activities. It had to become an all-Polish party—the adjective was by then a near monopoly of the National Democrats—openly debate issues, try to gain the youth, and generally secure a wider basis even if it meant curtailing purely socialist indoctrination. The halo of mystery that had surrounded the PPS in its early heroic stage and had enhanced its position while concealing its numerical weakness was no longer sufficient. For the new type of activities, possible only in conditions of relative freedom, one had to shift to Galicia and treat it as an important operational base.

Socialism in Galicia was making progress, even if no large party could develop. In Cracow, Daszyński published the first Socialist daily *Naprzód* (Forward), and after the fifth curia reform he entered the Reichsrat where he acquired the reputation of being a fiery orator and a tribune of the people. The Polish Social Democratic Party of Galicia and [Teschen] Silesia (PPSD)—as it called itself finally—stressed repeatedly the fact that in spite of its close association with the Austrian Social Democratic Party it was a distinct Polish party and a sister organization of the PPS. The inclusion of Teschen Silesia in its name was understandable given increased Polish activity and growing socialist agitation in the region. The Duchy of Teschen was by then a highly industrialized area with big coal mines and metallurgical works, and a textile manufacturing center. In 1890 about 40 percent of the population was engaged in mining and industries; by 1902 there were eighty thousand workers. Socialist agitation fell on fertile ground, and local Polish Socialist leaders such as Tadeusz Reger (1872–1938) rose to prominence. Competing with the Czechs and the Germans, the Teschen Poles remained in close contact with Galicia.

Polish Socialists made little headway in Prussian Poland. After the repeal of antisocialist legislation in 1890, German trade unions and the Social Democratic Party became mass movements; in Poznania, however, the best the Social Democrats could do was around a thousand votes at election time. Most of the relatively small trade unions were under Catholic influence. Still, a Socialist paper was printed, first in Berlin, then in Kattowitz (Katowice) in Upper Silesia. In 1893 the Polish Socialist Party (PPS) of Prussian Poland was founded and strove for some freedom of action within the German Socialist movement. It immediately ran into opposition on the part of Rosa Luxemburg, who was prominent in the German party; she accused her Polish comrades of "social patriotism." The growth of the PPS in the difficult Poznanian conditions was thus further impeded by strife with internationalists.

In Congress Poland, the Jewish question and relations with the Russian Social Democratic Party raised particular difficulties for the PPS. Both the SDKPiL and the PPS opposed anti-Semitism, but the PPS tried to draw Jewish workers away from the Bund whose policies it disapproved. The very nature of the Bund affirmed the unity of Russia, including the Polish lands, and was contrary to the independence program of the PPS. In principle it was not Jewish in a nationalistic sense, and indeed it was instrumental in the creation of the Russian Social Democratic Labor Party. At the same time, in view of the more advanced level of Jewish workers and the higher stage of its own organization, the Bund refused simply to dissolve itself in the nascent Russian party. While in 1901 it condemned the policies of the PPS and the goal of Polish independence, it did not see eye to eye with the SDKPiL either, although the relations between these two organization were fairly close. Relations between the PPS and the Russian party were cool. In 1897 the PPS defined the terms on which it could cooperate with Russian Socialists, and these included a recognition of the principle of Polish independence, Russian noninterference with Socialist organizations in the kingdom and Lithuania, and a respect for the right of the non-Russian nationalities to define their attitude toward Russia.

Lenin at first saw dissatisfied nationalities as temporary allies against tsardom, but he was unwilling to commit himself on the issue of national rights. As a centralist he opposed federalist blueprints for the future. In 1903 he agreed to the insertion in the party program of an article saying that a democratic republic ought to safeguard the right of national self-determination. But having recognized self-determination, largely for tactical reasons, he made it clear that this did not mean he supported it in all circumstances. Lenin's flexibility brought him into conflict with the rigid internationalism of Rosa Luxemburg, but in spite of this conflict cooperation between the Russian party and the SDKPiL, which really became a subsidiary of the Russian party, was possible. Such was not the case with the PPS which to Lenin was not a Socialist but rather a petty bourgeois Polish party. The PPS's encouragement of separatism in Russia—in 1903 it decided to support Belorussian Socialists and influence them in the spirit of separation from Russia and cooperation with Poland—was at complete variance with the theories and tactics of Russian Socialists.

The PPS attempted to establish friendly relations with the Russian Socialist Revolutionaries who had emerged as a party and in 1901 recognized the right of the Poles to self-determination. No binding commitments, however, were made on either side. The PPS tried to preserve freedom of action vis-à-vis the Russian movements and continued to explore possibilities of contact and cooperation without establishing any organizational ties.

Toward the end of this period, Polish socialism, national democracy, and to a lesser extent populism had become genuine forces in the context of Polish politics. Contributing toward national self-assertion and class consciousness of the masses, these movements waged a struggle against political passivity and Triple Loyalism. Both the PPS and the National League again raised the standard of Polish independence, although the National Democrats began to adjust their targets to political tactics. The PPS continued the old heritage of the Polish Left; the National Democratic movement, despite its democratic and revolutionary origins, evolved to become a modern representative of the Right. Both stressed the all-Polish character of their programs and activities, and both sought to resolve, although in entirely different ways, the perennial question of the eastern borderlands. Seen in a wider context, Polish Socialists reflected the rising social protest against the established order; National Democrats were a reflection of the radical nationalism then sweeping Europe. The emergence and growth of the two trends had specifically Polish features, but it was not a unique phenomenon. Indeed, the awakening nationalities of the old commonwealth, the Lithuanians and Ukrainians, went through fairly similar developments of their own.

VI. LITHUANIANS, BELORUSSIANS, AND UKRAINIANS

The "northwestern" guberniias continued to live under an oppressive administrative regime, although the governor general of Vilna still deplored the strength of the Polish element and the inability of schools to russify the country. Anti-Catholic policies of the administration led to frequent clashes—one need mention only the notorious incident at Kroże in 1893—which only stiffened Lithuanian resistance. The government, however, was successful in exploiting and fanning Lithuanian antagonism to the Poles. The average Lithuanian thought of a Pole as a lord and a class enemy, but Russian schools propagated hatred of everything Polish. Virtually no political counterpropaganda came from the loyalist Polish aristocracy or from the gentry isolated in their old-type historic patriotism. Within the church, linguistic Polish-Lithuanian friction multiplied as the younger clergy promoted Lithuanian national ideas.

The cultural renascence continued. At the turn of the century the Lithuanian national theater was born, and poetry reached new heights with Maironis (Father Jonas Maciulis, 1862–1932). Kudirka's poem "Lithuania Our Fatherland" later became the country's national anthem. Hundreds of thousands of Lithuanian books were smuggled in from East Prussia, and the book-smuggler became a minor national hero.

In the 1890s the National Democratic, Christian National, and Socialist movements matured. The forerunners of the first group, the *varpinkai*, evolved from a fairly heterogenous grouping in which the leftist elements held the upper hand from 1894 to 1897. Led by Kudirka, Kazys Grinius (1866-1950), Jonas Vileišis (1872-1942), and others, the *varpinkai* strove for national Lithuanian ascendancy in the economic and cultural life of the country. They were not adverse to a Lithuanian-Polish alliance against Russia, but only on the basis of full equality of both partners. In the early twentieth century they spoke of Lithuanian independence as a final goal, to be preceded by reforms in Russia, including autonomy. Both nationalist and democratic trends operated within the party, and their program was not fully clarified until 1905.

The essentially clerical and conservative movement grouped around *Žemaičiu ir Lietuvos Apžvalga* (Lithuanian and Samogitian Review). It criticized the tsarist government for breaking the laws of God and of man, was anti-Semitic and anti-Polish, and vainly tried to regain the polonized aristocracy and gentry. While contributing greatly to national revival, the Christian National movement toned down its original antigovernment slogans and even began to treat the watchword of national independence as unrealistic and foolhardy.

The first Socialist parties in Lithuania were hardly Lithuanian. When the PPS emerged at the conference near Vilna in 1893, local Polish Socialists looked upon themselves as cohosts in the multinational historic Lithuania. The Lithuanian Social Democratic Party (Lietuviu Social-Demokratų Partija) founded in 1896 had a tiny, mostly Polish-speaking membership. Seemingly influenced by PPS ideology, its original program advocated a federation of Poland, Lithuania, and other lands. The party then split into a more national wing and an internationalist Union of Workers. Dzierżyński's attempts to influence the Social Democratic Party in an internationalist direction were not fully successful, but in 1899 and 1900 the emerging SDKPiL took away some members from the two Lithuanian groupings. The Lithuanian Social Democratic Party, led by such people as Augustinas Janulaitis (1878–1950), and Steponas Kairys (1878–1964), competed with the PPS, the union, the SDKPiL, Russian Socialists active in Vilna since 1901, and the Bund. Only the Bund had a large following drawn from the Jewish proletariat. In 1903 the Lithuanian Social Democratic Party was joined by a former *varpinkai* member, Vincas Mickevičius-Kapsukas (1880–1935), who organized its extreme left wing. The Socialist movement in Lithuania was still characterized by internal dissessions and splits; its national and revolutionary goals lacked clarity.

In Belorussia, a cultural national revival began to make timid progress, and Russian authorities viewed it as potentially more dangerous than Polish influences. Radical Belorussians largely relied on the PPS to help them organize the Belorussian Revolutionary (later Socialist) Hromada in 1902–1903, whose program was close to that of the PPS but with local variations. By 1904 the idea appeared of a future federation of Lithuanians, Latvians, and Ukrainians. The national movement was still so weak that an outside observer could hardly see it beneath the Russian and Polish influences which were dominant in agrarian and backward Belorussian society.

The 1890s and early 1900s saw the growth of an all-Ukrainian movement whose outlook differed considerably in Galicia and in the Russian Ukraine. An increasing national maturity of Galician Ukrainians was visible in cultural, economic, and political spheres. The arrival of Hrushevsky, who began to write his monumental history of Ukraine-Rus and raised the Shevchenko Society to the level of an unofficial Ukrainian academy of sciences, deeply influenced Eastern Galicia. A rapid growth of the educational society Prosvita (Enlightenment) and the emergence of private high schools marked continuous cultural progress. The two gymnastic societies, Sokil (Falcon) and Sich, not only provided physical education but also educated their members in a patriotic spirit. The Uniate church gained a new self-assurance with the appointment to the metropolitan see in 1900 of Count Andrei Szeptycki (Sheptytsky, 1865–1944), a member of a thoroughly polonized and patriotic family, who ardently embraced the Ukrainian cause. A man of great character and large vistas, he was not only a religious leader but also a statesman. Promoting liturgical reforms and theological studies, he was interested in the great issue of Eastern Christianity as a whole.

The Ukrainian peasantry, although still desperately poor, began after 1890 to profit from the parceling out of landed estates. This was due to the spectacular rise of credit unions, cooperative stores, and dairies. New organizations, such as The Farmer (Silsky Hospodar), provided agricultural instruction. The big peasant strike of 1902 in Eastern Galicia, which frightened the Polish landowners, was spontaneous and mainly economic, but Ukrainian political movements quickly became involved in it. The political picture was changing. The Polish administration was willing to make cultural concessions and assumed that it would thereby gain the Ukrainians' gratitude. The latter viewed such concessions as a token of more to come. Consequently, they felt deceived, and the Poles became irritated. By 1894 the failure of compromise led to a regrouping of Ukrainian political forces. The Populists were gaining ground over the Russophiles, but their mutual relations were affected by the rise of Polish National Democratic movement. The National Democrats viewed the Russophiles as incapable of challenging Polish supremacy and considered them less dangerous than the Populists.

The Russophiles, in turn, were not adverse to being supported against their Ukrainian rivals and felt that once Eastern Galicia became part of Russia the Polish control of the region would come to an end. This involvement of Polish National Democrats in Ukrainian affairs added considerably to tensions.

The Populist movement was changing, and the bulk of its adherents reorganized in different political groupings or formed new ones. The most important of these were the Radical and the National Democrats. The former, reorganized as the Ukrainian Radical Party, lost most of its nationalist leaders including Franko in 1895; it eventually became a party of agrarian Socialists and anticlericals. The main figures in it were Pavlyk and Lev Bachynsky (1872-1930). The rival, larger, and more influential Ukrainian National Democratic Party, set up in 1899, was largely a coalition of Populists and radicals, and included some rightist Uniate priests. Its emphasis was on nationalism and social reform, and its leaders included Kost Levytsky (1859-1941) and Jevhen Petrushevych (1863-1940). In everyday politics, both parties struggled for proportional representation in the Sejm and for national rights in education, including a Ukrainian university in Lemberg. Eventually they hoped to achieve a separate Ukrainian province within the Habsburg monarchy. The principle of a united and independent Ukrainian nation was the ideal and ultimate goal, although it was conceived in somewhat abstract terms. Even so, its adoption marked a turning point in the evolution of national consciousness and revealed political maturity.

In 1896 Ukrainian Socialists broke away from the Radicals to form their own Social Democratic Party. Led by, among others, Ostap Terletsky (1850-1902) and Mykola Hankevych (1869-1939), it cooperated with Polish Socialists—due in part to the fact that trade unions in Galicia united workers of both nationalities—but was too weak to compete with the National Democrats or the Radicals.

Developments in the Russian Ukraine were slower, as was a national-political awakening of the Ukrainian intelligentsia. As the eastern Galician *Dilo* put it: "The consciousness of a racial affinity between the Ukrainian and Russian nations is an integral part of the national consciousness of Russian Ukrainians."[10] Cultural activity there was, for example, the moving poetry of Lesia Ukrainka (Larysa Kosach, 1871–1913), but it was not until the late 1890s that Ukrainian leaders met in Kiev and Kharkov (Kharkiv) and were instrumental in the emergence of a democratic organization, as well as the Revolutionary Ukrainian Party (RUP). The latter's pamphlet,

10. Cited in Leon Wasilewski, *Ukraina i sprawa ukraińska* (Kraków: Książka, 1911), p. 195.

published in Lemberg and entitled *Independent Ukraine*, spoke of the natural strivings of nationalities toward statehood and of political liberation of Ukrainians. The RUP stood for a united Ukraine between the Don and the San rivers (i.e., including Eastern Galicia), but it was inclined toward autonomy within Russia as a political target. With the party's evolution—socially toward the left and politically toward autonomy—a more nationalist-minded National Ukrainian Party (NUP) emerged in 1902 with the slogan Ukraine for Ukrainians. The efforts of the PPS and Galician Socialists to set up a party in the Ukraine akin to the PPS produced only ephemeral results in 1900. The Ukrainian Social Democratic Union which was organized in 1904 was an extreme leftist splinter of the RUP. None of the above Ukrainian parties was as yet strong enough to lead the masses.

## CHAPTER 15

# From Revolution to World War

I. THE REVOLUTION OF 1905

THE Russo-Japanese War which broke out in February, 1904, shook the tsarist empire. Its effects were quickly felt in Russian Poland. The closing of eastern markets caused a fall in the production of textiles. The kingdom was too remote from the front to receive any orders for its heavy industries. By the end of 1904, overall production had declined by 35 percent; one hundred thousand people became unemployed, and twice that number suffered cuts in pay. News of Russian reverses caused rejoicing which mingled with fear on the part of those eligible for the draft. Polish political circles immediately realized the far-reaching repercussions of the war, but they responded to the new situation in widely divergent ways.

The upper classes and a part of the church hierarchy believed that they might win concessions for the kingdom by manifesting their loyalty to Russia in her hour of distress. At a meeting in Vienna, representatives of this group founded the Party of Realist Politics, officially constituted in 1905, and in a gesture of loyalty offered a "Catholic" (not even Polish) field hospital train for the front. The great landowners of the Vilna guberniia showed their servility by assisting at the unveiling of a statue of Catherine II. While ingratiating themselves, the Realists petitioned the government to grant equal rights to the population of the kingdom. In practice, this meant the introduction of zemstvos and municipal self-government, trial by jury, admission of Poles to the administration, equal taxation, religious toleration, and language concessions in education. It was a moderate program that fell far short of autonomy.

The National League on its side submitted a memorandum that went a little further, notably, by demanding Polish in schools and adminis- tration. It also refrained from any loyalist statements. Anti-Russian

308

and opposed to mobilization of Poles for the eastern front, the National Democrats were critical of what they termed the doctrinaire attitude of the Realists and Socialists. They believed in a wait-and-see policy vis-à-vis St. Petersburg and in a flexible position at home.

The PPS adopted a different stand. It regarded the war which had revealed the weakness of tsarist Russia as a golden opportunity for revolutionary and national activity. In March it inspired an appeal against the war in the Polish, Lithuanian, Latvian, and Belorussian languages, and strove to coordinate its actions with non-Russian Socialists. At the same time it proposed to Russian Social Democrats an interparty conference; the proposal foundered on the opposition of the SDKPiL. In May the PPS proceeded to form its first fighting squad—an insurgent unit designed to oppose the police and to instill greater discipline and self-confidence in the working class so as to strengthen its resistance to mobilization.

The PPS leaders also decided to explore the possibility of cooperation with Japan, and in late May Piłsudski and Tytus Filipowicz (1873–1953) went to Tokyo. There they accidentally met Dmowski, who had come in order to acquaint the Japanese with the Polish situation and to counter any attempts at diversionary action in Congress Poland. Piłsudski and Dmowski presented mutually exclusive programs to the Japanese. The former advocated the creation of a Polish legion in Japan. Its object was to discourage Russia from using Poles at the front, and what was more important, to revive the Polish question and eventually place it on the agenda at the peace conference. Piłsudski was willing to combine a diversion in Poland with some intelligence services for the Japanese general staff, and his aim was a formal Japanese-PPS agreement. In his conversations he stressed the multinational character of the tsarist empire and insisted that the Poles, as its strongest disruptive element, ought to be aided in striking the first blow against Russia.

Dmowski argued that while there was a great deal of inflamatory material in Congress Poland, it was in the Russian interest to ignite it and provoke an uprising. This would be of no advantage to either the Poles or the Japanese. After suppressing such an uprising, Russian troops would be freed for service in the east. Hence peace ought to be maintained in the kingdom, and if Polish extremists were to start large-scale riots, the National Democrats would use all their resources to subdue them.

The Japanese general staff showed interest in Piłsudski's proposals but only to the extent of using Poles for intelligence purposes. This the Socialists could not accept, and the only thing they gained was some Japanese war material smuggled into Poland. The material later came in handy for the fighting squads. As for Dmowski, there is no evidence to show that Tokyo's decision was due to his counsels. Japan was winning the war and probably had no desire anyway to get involved in complex Polish problems.

The stay in Tokyo affected the thinking of both Polish protagonists. Piłsudski's military interests increased. Dmowski was impressed by Japanese patriotism, their devotion to their native tradition, their way of life and their discipline. In his subsequent writings, he put more stress on the inescapable relationship between the individual and the nation. This was a relationship that like the one between nations really lay outside the sphere of Christian ethics and was subject only to "national ethics." Dmowski saw the nation as the necessary moral content of the state. He meant nation *in time*, which signified that the national majority at any given moment need not reflect it. Applying his concept to current Polish problems, Dmowski attacked radicals who were atomizing the nation as well as conservatives who were willing to make a foreign government the guardian of law and order. The principles of national Polish policy, he said, operated in three directions: (1) prevention of tendencies to regulate national affairs from the exclusive viewpoint of individual ethics; (2) acceptance of the idea of the nation as inseparable from the idea of the state, and so a nation, unlike a tribe, could not be satisfied with mere cultural and linguistic distinctiveness; (3) establishment of a government within society. All these conceptions enabled Dmowski to claim that although his movement might occasionally pursue policies similar to those of the Realists it was basically different from theirs. The Realists were merely guided by class interests, had no doctrine, and sought concessions for concessions' sake, but not so the National Democrats.

Meanwhile in the kingdom, the PPS continued its policy of cooperation with revolutionaries as well as with opposition movements in the empire. In October, 1904, it took part in a large conference in Paris together with Russian Constitutional Democrats (Kadets), Socialist Revolutionaries (SRs), and Lithuanian, Belorussian, Finnish, Armenian, and Belorussian representatives. National Democrats were also present at this gathering. Given the wide-ranging composition of the conference, it came up with only general statements about the self-determination of nations. A smaller meeting of the PPS, the SRs, Latvians, and Georgians subsequently agreed on a joint proclamation that spoke of complete national independence "demanded at present by the Poles."

The élan of the PPS, however, was most noticeable at home. In November, 1904, a PPS squad used its arms in a clash with the police and gendarmes on Grzybowski Square in Warsaw. For the first time since 1864, armed Poles battled with Russians. The impression was profound, and the news of the fall of Port Arthur further encouraged Polish workers. The PPS grew rapidly in size, reaching some 55,000 members by 1906. Some of the new adherents as well as the rising "young" leaders differed from the "old" in their admiration for the Russian proletariat, with which they wanted to remain in close touch. The size of SDKPiL also increased to about forty thousand; the Bund numbered some eight thousand in Congress Poland. A Polish Peasant Union, which in ideology was close to the PPS, briefly came into existence. It advocated social liberation and Polish independence.

Another trend, closely related to the reformist movement in Russia, began to manifest itself. Several Polish-Russian meetings in which the Polish liberal Aleksander Lednicki (1866–1934) played a major part took place, and a Polish Progressive-Democratic Union which harked back to the early traditions of liberal positivism arose under the chairmanship of Świętochowski in 1905. Further talks with the Kadets and the SRs followed, and individual Socialists and National Democrats joined in, but their joint resolution spoke only about an autonomy of the kingdom that was compatible with Russian state unity. A definition of autonomy was postponed until a later date; the Russians were reluctant to be explicit.

In the early spring of 1905, events went beyond conferences or reformist manifestations. The Bloody Sunday in St. Petersburg in January, 1905, unleashed all the revolutionary forces; a wave of strikes and terrorism swept Russia. In January the Polish Union of Socialist Youth (ZMS), which remained under the influence of the PPS, the SDKPiL, and the Bund, declared a school strike in Warsaw. The movement spread rapidly, and National Democratic youth organizations joined in. So did teachers' associations. The strike amounted to a boycott of high schools and of Warsaw university, as well as to a campaign to polonize elementary schools. It greatly strengthened national feelings among the younger generation in the country and even beyond the confines of Russian Poland. Peasants rioted in the countryside. It was obvious that previous tsarist policies had not succeeded in winning over the peasantry to Russia's side.

The National League could claim that its educational work among the masses had borne fruit, and it attempted further to influence the peasants. It encroached even on the Socialists' sphere of influence by forming in 1905 the National Workers' Union (Narodowy Związek Robotniczy). The league was on the offensive, and a National Democratic Party was formally set up in Warsaw.

The creation of the Workers' Union was closely connected with current developments in the kingdom. On January 28, the PPS and the SDKPiL proclaimed a general strike which involved some four hundred thousand workers and lasted for a month. Economic concessions were achieved but no political gains. The PPS fighting squads now dominated the working class districts; there were attacks on gendarmes and tsarist officials. The newly appointed governor of Warsaw took refuge in the Ivangorod (Dęblin) fortress. In June, there were barricades in Łódź. All these revolutionary events were stimulated by the news about the defeat of the Russian fleet at Tsushima, the revolt of the battleship *Potemkin*, and upheavals throughout Russia. The government's attempts to divert the revolutionary current by directing it against the Jews—in the spring of 1905 a series of pogroms occurred in Russia—had little success in Congress Poland. Nor were Russian concessions sufficient to calm excited public opinion.

Russian concessions made in mid-1905 were not unimportant. The toleration decree issued in April, 1905, allowed some two hundred thousand former Uniates to return to their faith. The government authorized private teaching of Polish and Lithuanian in schools and permitted Poles to buy land in the "western guberniias." Polish could now be used in communal administration. Realists and National Democrats began seriously to worry about a Socialist-led revolution in Congress Poland. Dmowski argued that even if social unrest and economic chaos in Russia could be said to work to the advantage of the Poles, revolutionary policies in the strongly garrisoned kingdom were suicidal. The league tried to prevent social upheaval by gaining influence among the workers. The National Workers' Union rejected strikes and mass demonstrations and adopted the slogan of autonomy officially endorsed by the league.

With the Workers' Union gaining some sixteen thousand members —it claimed twice that number by 1906—three forces were now operating among the workers. The PPS, with its watchword of independence, demanded a constituent assembly in Warsaw; the SDKPiL wanted to merge the Polish movement in an all-Russian revolution and demanded a constituent assembly in St. Petersburg; the Workers' Union denounced social chaos. In these conditions, clashes between this last group and the first two, particularly the PPS, became unavoidable, and in October, 1905, Łódź was the scene of fratricidal struggles. Dmowski publicly assumed the responsibility for these conflicts by saying that in opposing anarchy it became necessary to shed Polish blood.

In October, 1905, a railroad strike began in Russia, and a Soviet of Workers made its appearance in St. Petersburg. On October 17/30 Premier Witte issued a manifesto announcing a constitutional government in Russia and the calling of a parliament (Duma).

Meanwhile, a new tough governor general of Warsaw, Georgii Skalon, whom many Poles suspected of belonging to the reactionary pro-German camarilla, assumed power. His appointment almost coincided with the encounter between Nicholas II and William II which raised the specter of a German-Russian *rapprochement*. Dmowski felt it imperative to counter these dangers and decided to approach Witte with an offer of cooperation. His belief, however, that one could repeat Wielopolski's experiment of the 1860s was mistaken. In November the government reintroduced martial law in Congress Poland, on the pretext that the Poles wanted to detach themselves from Russia. This was hardly the position of the leading Polish circles. As for the Socialists already excited by the outbreaks in Moscow, the Russian move only provoked them to action. Strongly pressed by the "young" in the party, the PPS called for general struggle against the authorities. Action on this appeal led to the expulsion of some Russian officials, for instance, in Ostrowiec where a short-lived "people's republic" was established; but then the entire movement collapsed.

Dmowski's argument, that only an autonomous regime in the kingdom could end social anarchy and that it was up to the Poles to restore calm, failed to convince Witte. Dmowski's opponents severely criticized him for an alleged offer to massacre Polish Socialists in return for autonomy, and Dmowski indignantly denied this accusation. But he admitted later that the National Democratic Party had made a serious error of judgment in 1905, by underestimating the degree of revolutionization of the urban masses.

The year 1905 in Lithuania witnessed a struggle for national rather than for social liberation. Already in 1904, the government had realized the futility of some of its repressive measures and had permitted the printing of Lithuanian publications in the Latin alphabet. Lithuanian now became one of the compulsory subjects in schools of the Suwałki guberniia, although the Lithuanians complained about the small number of these schools and the absence of a Lithuanian university. For the first time since the January Insurrection, the government allowed a Polish journal to appear in Vilna. A little later a Lithuanian Scientific Society was set up, but its limited cooperation with a Polish counterpart was no indication of a real *rapprochement*—Polish-Lithuanian animosity continued. Clashes multiplied over the language used in churches, and both sides appealed to the Papacy. The Poles in Lithuania rejected the idea that they were merely Polish-speaking Lithuanians. The right-wingers emphasized that they were part of the Polish nation, but they were willing to recognize the distinctiveness of Lithuania. According to them, Lithuania's interests lay in close collaboration with Poland. A liberal such as Michal Römer (Römeris, 1880–1946) argued that politically, economically, and socially local Poles were sons of Lithuania or Belorussia, but culturally they belonged to the Polish nation.

The revolutionary upheaval in Russia immediately affected Lithuania, and in January, 1905, there were strikes in Vilna, Kowno, Szawle (Šiauliai), and Poniewież (Panevežys); these were followed by another wave of strikes in October. While the local SDKPiL, the Bund, and the Russian Social Democrats did not mention Lithuanian national aspirations—except for concessions in schools— Lithuanian Social Democrats advocated a federation of Russia with Lithuania as a separate unit with its own assembly in Vilna. To show that the Social Democratic Party was not discriminating against non-Lithuanian nationalities, its name was changed from "Lithuanian" to "of Lithuania" (LSDP). Within the party whose membership rose to some 2,300—the Bund was still twice that size—two trends appeared. The so-called federalists were inclined toward a future federation with Poland, Belorussia, and Latvia. The autonomists, led among others by Zigmas Aleksa (Angarietis, 1882–1940), favored autonomy within Russia. By 1907 the autonomists won the upper hand, but even so the party did not join the Russian Social Democratic Party. The more nationally oriented wing of the party was led by Mykolas Biržiška (1884–1962).

Lithuanian nationalists followed a course somewhat similar to that of the Polish National Democrats. In November, 1905, Basanavičius submitted a memorandum to Witte demanding wide autonomy which included an assembly in Vilna, as well as Lithuanian schools and administration. By Lithuania the memorandum meant the guberniias of Vilna, Kowno, Grodno, Suwałki, and part of Courland. Basanavičius called for the creation of a national democratic party which would follow a realistic national policy, defend the Lithuanian status quo, and oppose the Poles. Neither the memorandum nor Basanavičius' appeal produced tangible results. The rightists did not succeed in establishing formal parties, and attempts on the part of the clergy, including the initiative of Vilna's bishop to organize a broad Catholic Polish-Lithuanian-Belorussian front, were unsuccessful. The moderate Left fared better. In November, 1905, peasant delegates meeting in Vilna established the Peasant Union of Lithuania. Democrats also organized themselves, although the formal program of the Democratic Party of Lithuania was only adopted in 1906. It defined independence as a long-range goal, the immediate target being a democratic, autonomous regime for ethnic Lithuania with guarantees for its minorities. Vileišis, Mykolas Sleževičius

(1882–1939), and Jurgis Šaulys (1879–1948) were among the leaders. The one successful initiative that came from Basanavičius and his associates was the convocation of a great meeting—the so-called Vilna Sejm—in November and December of 1905. Gathering about two thousand representatives, with Democrats and Socialists exercising the most influence, the meeting adopted a resolution calling for a joint struggle together with the peoples of Russia for autonomy and a legislative assembly. Impressed by this show of solidarity and determination, the governor general of Vilna allowed the use of Lithuanian in elementary schools and in communal administration. Thus, by the end of 1905 the Lithuanians had achieved gains comparable to those of the Poles. Unlike the Poles, they had shown more solidarity but had been unable to organize mass political parties.

Belorussian activity in 1905 was limited in scope. The Hromada succeeded in organizing committees in Vilna and Minsk and appealed to the peasantry to take a stand against the tsar and the lords. Social considerations predominated, but national concern was not completely lacking, and the first Belorussian newspaper was permitted to appear in Vilna in 1906. Modern native poetry and drama found their first representative in Janka Kupala (1882-1942). Still, the Belorussians were at an early stage of national political activity. Lithuanian nationalists considered them "slavicised Lithuanians"; Polish landowners worried about the social implications of Belorussian peasant unrest. The Catholic clergy took hardly any part in the native movement.

The situation in the "southwestern land" was different. In December, 1904, an imperial commission reported that the Ukrainian national movement did not represent "any serious dangers." Consequently cultural concessions were made in 1905. The first periodical, *Chliborob* (Peasant), appeared, and a daily, *Rada* (Council), was printed in Kiev. Ukrainian was introduced into elementary schools and high schools, but this concession was rescinded in 1906. In 1907 the Ukrainian Scientific Society began to function, but no Ukrainian chairs were created by the university. Political developments during the revolution were largely determined by Russian trends, the SRs and the Russian Social Democrats being the real power in the Ukraine. The RUP reorganized itself into the Ukrainian Social Democratic Workers' Party (USDRP) in 1905. In principle it stood for the idea of national independence, but in practice it advocated autonomy and a legislative assembly in Kiev. The Ukrainian Democratic Party (later Democratic Radical, UDRP) cooperated with the Kadets. As for the Ukrainian Social Democratic Union, it moved constantly to the left until in 1908 it affiliated itself with Russian Social Democracy. Thus

Ukrainian political leaders largely looked up to Russia. No genuine cooperation with the local Poles, who were permitted to publish the PPS journal *Hasło* (Watchword), took place.

II. IN THE DUMAS

In October, 1905, Russia officially became a constitutional monarchy, and its parliament, the Duma, was to be elected by universal suffrage. In fact, this constitutionalism was severely restricted. Fundamental laws could only be proposed by the tsar. The Duma could not force the government to resign and had limited budgetary prerogatives. The legislative acts had to be approved by the half-appointed and half-elected State Council as well as by the tsar. Elections were held within four curias: (1) great landed property, (2) urban, (3) peasant, and (4) workers. One vote in the first curia equalled three in the second, fifteen in the third, and forty-five in the fourth. In the last two there were indirect electoral procedures. According to the fundamental laws of April, 1906, the Russian state was "one and indivisible," and autonomy was only contemplated for Finland.

Polish Socialists decided to boycott the elections. The PPS viewed participation in the Duma as an affirmation of Russian rights to the kingdom; the SDKPiL, following the Russian Social Democratic Party, regarded the Duma as counterrevolutionary. Thus, only three groups in Congress Poland took part in the elections: the National Democrats, the Realists, and the Progressive Democrats. The National Democrats agitated under the slogan of autonomy to be achieved through municipal and rural self-government, polonization of schools and administration, and other subsequent measures. They planned to establish a Polish Circle in the Duma, modeled on that in the Austrian Reichsrat. According to National Democratic tactics, the Poles were neither to side with any single Russian group nor link the question of autonomy with a general program of transformation of the empire. The Realists viewed autonomy as a long-range goal and were willing for the moment to be satisfied with linguistic and administrative concessions that included the abolition of exceptional laws in the kingdom. While willing to cooperate with the parties of law and order in the Duma, they felt that only a strictly loyalist attitude toward the government could produce results. They were passively sympathetic to the autonomist strivings of other nationalities in the empire. The Progressive Democrats stood for complete autonomy which the Duma would accept in principle and a constituent assembly in Warsaw could work out in detail. Unlike the preceding two groups, they did not insist on complete solidarity among the members of the Polish Circle regarding all issues to be discussed in the Duma. They favored cooperation with Russian reformist and liberal parties as well as with autonomists of other nationalities.

The elections held in April, 1906, delivered all thirty-four mandates in the kingdom—two were reserved for Lithuanians—to the National Democrats and their sympathizers. In the "western guberniias," Poles captured roughtly one-fourth of all seats. They gained all seven in Vilna, one out of six in Kowno, ten out of twenty-two in the three Belorussian guberniias, and five out of forty-five in the "southwestern land." In addition, three Poles were elected in Russia proper, making the grand total of around fifty-five.[1] Polish hopes for a united circle that would include all the Polish deputies did not materialize. Those from the "western guberniias" argued that they had not been elected by Polish voters alone, and that by joining they might be accused of fomenting Polish separatism in the borderlands. Since many of them were great landowners close to the Realists they did not wish to join a circle dominated by National Democrats. Twelve deputies, however, formed a club of their own which cooperated with the Polish Circle. The seven Lithuanians elected to the Duma and the much larger Ukrainian and Belorussian contingents did not establish their own parliamentary groupings, although the Ukrainians were in the process of organizing one when the Duma was dissolved. The part played by these deputies was of little significance for their respective nations; there was no cooperation between them and the local Polish deputies.

The National Democrats regarded the task of the Polish Circle as largely a political reconnaissance. Dmowski privately admitted that Polish participation in the Duma was contrary to national historical strivings but that it was a tactical necessity. What is more, as the danger of a European conflict became more real, Dmowski believed that the Poles had to become Russia's allies. The circle from which top National Democrats were missing—Dmowski, Balicki, and Popławski having recently returned from Galicia had no voting rights— presented a declaration that favored autonomy, but otherwise engaged in tactical maneuvers. It stood closest to the Kadets, the largest party in the Duma, but also explored contacts with the Trudoviks and Autonomists. In a parliament in which 40 percent of the deputies were non-Russians and more than one-half belonged to the opposition, the circle did not wish to become identified with either category. When in July, 1906, the government dissolved the Duma, the Polish Circle abstained from joining the opposition deputies who issued a ringing antigovernment manifesto from Vyborg (Vipuri).

1. Existing discrepancies in figures for Poles in the first Duma stem largely from the fact that not all of the deputies from the lower curias clearly defined their nationality. The Duma lasted too short a time to permit a satisfactory self-identification.

The balance sheet of Polish participation in the first Duma was unimpressive. Dmowski criticized the circle for courting the Kadets; the Polish Left censured it for its willingness to cooperate with the government. The Realists claimed that the circle had followed their policies even though National Democrats had previously denounced them during the elections. Russian opposition parties were annoyed by the caution of the Poles; the reactionaries doubted Polish sincerity. The minor administrative concessions granted to the kingdom were a far cry from autonomy.

In the elections to the second Duma, held toward the end of 1906, the National Democrats formed an alliance with the Realists and a splinter group from the Progressive Democrats. Together they won a complete victory over their opponents, who included this time the SDKPiL and the Bund. The Polish Circle of thirty-four deputies together with the Western Guberniias Circle of twelve which included a few deputies who belonged to the National League, acted as virtually one body. Dmowski chaired the circle and effectively controlled its activity. Given the division of forces in the Duma between the Left and the Right, the Polish Circle tried to acquire a position comparable to that of the Galician Poles in Vienna. Its project of autonomy submitted in April, 1907, was cautiously formulated, and the circle was willing to achieve first a school bill. To further its objectives and to serve warning to the government, on one occasion it supported the Socialists. Such tactics might have worked in the Reichsrat but not in the Duma. Incensed by the fact that non-Russians could decisively influence state politics, the government dissolved the Duma and introduced a new electoral law designed to weaken both the non-Russians and the leftist opposition. Again the Polish Circle had registered no gains, and there was renewed criticism from both Polish and Russian quarters.

In the third Duma, which opened in November, 1907, non-Russian and lower class representation was cut to a minimum. Entire geographic areas were denied representatives, and only 15 percent of the population retained voting rights. In the borderlands, the Vilna guberniia was now obliged to elect two Russians; that of Kowno, one. The number of Ukrainian, Belorussian, and Lithuanian deputies dwindled. While one deputy from European Russia represented 250,000 electors, his counterpart in Congress Poland represented 750,000. Consequently, only eleven Poles came from the kingdom and seven from the borderlands. The latter constituted themselves into a Polish-Lithuanian-Belorussian Circle.

The Poles now faced the question of whether continued participation in the Duma made any sense at all. Their complaints of being reduced to second-class citizenship were sharply rebuked by

Premier Petr Stolypin, who told them to be proud of being Russian subjects. Determined not to be driven into a policy of mere negation, Dmowski devised new tactics which largely involved the abandonment of autonomy slogans and the substitution of requests for demands. Firmly separating itself from the opposition, the circle attempted to cooperate with the right-center October Party which represented moderate landowners and industrial interests. The circle continued to seek the abolition of discriminatory measures against Poles. It pressed for local government in the kingdom and the "western guberniias," agrarian reforms, equal taxation and expenditure for cultural and educational purposes, as well as for linguistic rights in schools, lower courts, and public institutions. Given the triumph of the reaction in Russia, there was little incentive for the government to accede even to such requests. but Dmowski believed that in the face of an increasing German danger it was possible to influence Russian nationalism in the direction of a Russo-Polish reconciliation. Hence, he emphasized the Russian *raison d'état* which the Poles could recognize, and an all-embracing Slav program within which Polish and Russian interests could be reconciled. This was a significant departure from the original Polish plans connected with the Duma and a shattering of earlier hopes. By 1908 Dmowski and the National Democratic movement had reached the crossroads, but they were not alone in this predicament. Deep-seated crisis had affected the other Polish trends as well. Important changes loomed on the political horizon.

III. CONGRESS POLAND, GALICIA, AND PRUSSIAN POLAND AFTER 1905

The course of events in the kingdom did not inspire confidence in Russia's intentions. The Stolypin reaction was in full swing, and the first year of constitutionalism claimed over two thousand victims, of which nearly four hundred were killed by revolutionaries. Many people were arrested and deported. In June, 1906, the authorities inspired a Jewish pogrom in Białystok, followed a few months later by one in the kingdom at Siedlce. But reprisals were not limited to Polish revolutionary or Jewish quarters. The fast-growing Polish School Organization (Polska Macierz Szkolna), largely a creation of the National League, was disbanded in December, 1907. Around 250 Polish private schools continued to operate but without being able to confer on their graduates the right of admission to universities. In order not to antagonize the government, but also for other reasons, the National Democrats began to withdraw their support from the school strike.

The conciliatory policies of the National Democrats aroused opposition within their own movement and weakened their influence in peasant quarters. A new Populist grouping with clearly defined patriotic and radical social leanings began to emerge around the publication *Zaranie* (Dawn) in 1907. It represented a genuine Populist trend, which was anti-Russian and appealed to the peasantry.

The revolutionary fervor in Congress Poland largely spent itself during 1906, a year which saw nearly half a million people on strike. Trade unions were permitted but given a limited scope of action. Hence, they were reluctant to register with the authorities. Some of them were under the influence of the PPS; others followed the SKDPiL and the National Workers' Union. The PPS was no longer the fairly homogenous party it had once been, and the division between the "old" and the "young" became increasingly marked. Led by Piłsudski, the "old" leaders conceived of the revolution as being an organized, disciplined, and continuous process; they approved of mass terror only insofar as it occupied the Russian troops and weakened their effectiveness. Recognizing a parallelism between Polish and Russian revolutions, the "old" leaders saw the organization of an armed force to be the specifically Polish contribution. The "young" leaders accused them of promoting a national insurrection rather than an international revolution. It was largely under the pressure of the "young" that mass terror and spontaneous revolutionary action continued. At the meeting of the Eighth PPS Congress in Lemberg in 1906, a compromise ideological resolution was adopted. It put the stress on revolution as leading to the fall of tsarism and the creation of a federal republic, but it recognized that revolution also created conditions that in the future would facilitate the realization of national independence.

Piłsudski and the "old" leaders of the PPS controlled the fighting squads, which were now called the Fighting Organization (Organizacja Bojowa), and although they used the organization against tsarist officials—on August 15, 1906, one hundred attempts took place —they preferred different types of action. The organization specialized in attacks on government treasury offices and trains carrying payrolls —for instance, the action at Rogów in November, 1906—to collect much needed funds. Trained in a secret school in Cracow, the Fighting Organization became a semimilitary cadre, a fact that alarmed the "young," who were already suspicious of its autonomous status. Piłsudski, seconded by Daszyński, argued that without strict controls and military discipline, terror and mass demonstrations would degenerate into anarchy and corrupt the fighters. Excesses did in fact occur, which Dmowski promptly denounced as Socialist-inspired crimes and banditry. There was renewed fighting among workers in Łódź, and the local party organization had to be disbanded. At the stormy Ninth Congress of the PPS in Vienna in November,

1906, the predominantly "young" Central Committee accused the Fighting Organization of ignoring the orders of the PPS leadership. Piłsudski and his supporters withdrew taking with them a minority of the rank and file but practically the whole Fighting Organization. They then announced a continuation of the party under the name "PPS Revolutionary Faction (Frakcja)." The majority, after electing a purely "young" committee, later added the adjective "Left" to their party's name. Thus in 1907 the PPS Revolutionary Faction and the PPS Left faced each other.

The PPS Revolutionary Faction which for simplicity's sake will be referred to as PPS, the name it resumed in 1909, held its first congress in March, 1907, and adopted a program drafted in the main by Perl. It stated that while the PPS wished to maintain unity with proletarian revolutionary action, it aimed at an independent democratic Polish republic. The PPS already had some twenty thousand members and gradually increased its numerical lead over the PPS Left. Its outlook was greatly influenced by a reappraisal of the 1905 revolution. Piłsudski and his closest associates, to mention only Leon Wasilewski (1870–1936), considered that the revolution had been a costly failure. Pilsudski opined that "one cannot make uprisings. They depend on circumstances which we are unable to create, but it is necessary that the proletariat and indeed all working people profit from these circumstances" once they arise.[2] With an increased emphasis on the preparation of military cadres for a future revolution or insurrection, the PPS was entering a new stage in its development.

Events in Congress Poland naturally found an echo in Poznania, and the struggle for polonization of Russian schools had its counterpart under Prussian rule. The school strikes that began in 1906 were largely spontaneous and lasted for almost a year. A reaction to new German pressures to teach religion classes in German, they were supported by many segments of Polish society including the clergy, which emphasized their religious character and denied their political implications. This position did not save the conciliatory Archbishop Stablewski from Hakatist attacks, and after his death in 1906, the archiepiscopal see remained vacant until 1914. The National Democrats continued to make strides in Prussian Poland. Controlling, from 1906 on, the influential Poznań *Kurjer*, playing a major role in the Polish Central Electoral Committee which was established in 1904 and encompassed all Polish-speaking lands in the Reich, the league won over such Populist leaders as Szymański, and Wiktor Kulerski (1865–1935) in Pomerania. In the 1907 elections to the Reichstag the Poles gained a record number of seats, including five from Upper Silesia. These successes were countered by new and

2. Cited in Wilhelm Feldman, *Dzieje polskiej myśli politycznej*, 3:195-96.

more menacing pressures from the new government of Prince Bülow.

In 1907 the Prussian ministry submitted the project of a law that permitted expropriation of Polish lands on the "grounds of public good" *(öffentliches Wohl)*. Based on a loose interpretation of constitutional provisions, the project was critized by German conservatives as endangering property rights. The Poles raised an outcry but could not prevent the project from becoming a bill in 1908 and from being implemented in 1912. In 1908 a "muzzle decree" was introduced, enforcing use of the German language in public meetings in all districts where less than 60 percent of the population was Polish. Taken together, these measures offered a new and formidable threat to the national position of Poles under Prussian rule.

In Galicia, the events in Russian Poland not only aroused keen interest but directly affected the political life of the province. The Fighting Organization of the PPS had its secret school in Cracow; party conferences were taking place on Galician soil; the press openly discussed the policies of Socialists, National Democrats, Realists, and Progressive Democrats. The establishment of a National Democratic Party in Galicia was announced in 1905, and its program demanded a separate organization of Galicia within the Habsburg monarchy. The National Democrats strove to win political leadership in the province, and they challenged both the conservatives and the Socialists. They fared best in Eastern Galicia, where even their new trend of reconciliation with Russia found some response among the *Podolacy*. Under the National Democratic aegis a national party appeared in Teschen Silesia.

The Galician Socialist reaction to the events of 1905 was one of nearly revolutionary fervor. Daszyński publicly burnt a portrait of Tsar Nicholas; there were strikes and an impressive growth of trade unions. The Populist Party, under whose influence a peasant party appeared in Teschen in 1906, also manifested great interest in the revolutionary activities in the kingdom and in Russia. Turning to local problems, the Polish Left loudly proclaimed the slogan of universal suffrage, and to further its realization Polish Socialists took part in a general strike organized by Austrian Social Democrats. This mass pressure on the government, connected as it was with revolutionary events across the border, made Franz Joseph approve universal manhood suffrage for the Austrian part of the monarchy. The Polish Circle showed no enthusiasm but went along with the government in exchange for several concessions. These included a number of mandates commensurate with Galicia's population, the retention of two-mandate constituencies in Eastern Galicia and of "electoral geometry," and a certain enlargement of Galician autonomy, particularly in the cultural sphere.

Universal suffrage was a serious threat to the continued dominance of the conservatives. In the 1907 elections, the parties in the Polish Circle fought against both a Socialist-peasant alliance and the National Democrats who, although a party of the circle, put forward a separate list. The conservatives lost heavily. Within the circle they were outnumbered by National Democratic deputies. At the same time the number of Polish deputies who stayed outside of the circle exceeded the number within. Thanks to a hold on the administration and through adroit political maneuvers, the conservatives succeeded in enticing Stapiński, whose Populists had won the largest number of seats of any party, to join the circle. Thus, for the moment they were able to neutralize the National Democrats, but their ascendancy was badly shaken.

The position of the conservatives was also shaken by the continuing Polish-Ukrainian conflict. Violent clashes between Polish and Ukrainian students at Lemberg, mass demonstrations, and occasional bloodshed, made it extremely difficult for the conservatives to work out a *modus vivendi*. Had it not been for the extremist policies of the Polish National Democrats and the *Podolacy* a compromise could perhaps have been found. In late 1907 Polish nationalists and the Russophiles made an electoral deal directed against the Ukrainian parties; a part of the administration apparently favored it. As a result, the Ukrainians suffered a crushing defeat in the election and blamed it on Polish perfidy. Feelings ran so high that when a Ukrainian student assassinated Viceroy Andrzej Potocki in 1908, the Ukrainian press and Ukrainian political representatives refused to condemn the deed.

Thus, around 1908 the Polish nation was in the midst of a deep crisis. In Russian Poland the revolution brought no fundamental changes—Polish policies in the Duma faced an impasse. In Prussian Poland new administrative pressures constituted a serious threat to national survival. In Galicia the incipient breakdown of the conservative rule accompanied by social and Polish-Ukrainian conflicts boded ill for the future. Of the two major political forces, the PPS had split and National Democratic Party was at the crossroads. It was in these circumstances that two trends, symbolized by Dmowski and Piłsudski, crystallized, offering two basically different guidelines to the Poles.

IV. DMOWSKI'S ALTERNATIVE

In early 1908 Dmowski published his *Germany, Russia, and the Polish Question (Niemcy, Rosja i kwestia polska)*. Primarily intended for non-Polish readers, it was quickly translated into Russian and French. The book was really an offer of cooperation with St. Petersburg as well as an attempt to resolve the impasse in the Duma by raising the Polish question to a higher, international level. The gist of Dmowski's thesis could be summarized as follows: The greatest threat to the entire Polish nation came from Prussia. This was so for two reasons: one, Prussian Poland was the cradle and the backbone of the nation and its germanization would lead to a "proletarization" of the Polish people; two, for Berlin the Polish question was really a matter of "to be or not to be." Under Russia and Austria it was an open question which could be resolved locally, but for Germany it was intimately bound up with her eastern expansion. For that reason Germany sought to block Polish advancement under the Habsburgs and wished to cooperate with St. Petersburg against the Poles. Given Germany's drive for world hegemony, the Polish question was thus becoming an international issue that could no longer be ignored by the great powers.

Dmowski spoke cautiously about "the idea of future political unification of the Poles" and likened it to the republican creed of an individual living under a monarchy. Such an individual could still be a loyal citizen. Thus reassuring Russia, he put forward his central idea, namely, that "the key to the solution of the Polish question lay in the Russian state." He made it clear that he spoke only of Congress Poland and raised no claims to the eastern borderlands. Formulating his program of cooperation with Russia against Germany, Dmowski knew that in 1907 and 1908 St. Petersburg was still hesitating between an alignment with England and one with Germany. He wished to facilitate Russian cooperation with the West by removing the traditional Polish obstacle, and he sought to range the Poles behind Neoslavism, which was then on the ascendancy in Russia and arousing interest in Paris. His book was a theoretical justification of reconciliation with Russia and met Russia more than halfway.

Neoslavism had begun to manifest itself around 1906 and was principally anti-German. It aimed, by transforming Austria-Hungary into a federation in which Slavs predominated, to detach her from Berlin and to bring her closer to Russia. Neoslavists emphasized the equality of all Slavs, and it was essential for them that the Russo-Polish conflict be overcome. Dmowski astounded the Russians and bewildered and shocked the Poles by "unconditionally" endorsing Neoslavism. He reasoned that by lifting the Russo-Polish dialogue to an all-Slav level, he would force Russia to treat the Poles as equals and to take the entire Polish nation into account. Yet, the chances of furthering the Polish cause through Neoslavism proved as dim as the renewed Polish efforts in the third Duma. The Slav Congress in Prague in 1908, at which Dmowski affirmed that the Poles thought in terms of Russian statehood, had no real sequel.

At the Duma, the Polish Circle was maneuvered in 1909 into a difficult position. The government linked the question of municipal self-government in the kingdom with a project of detaching the province of Kholm from Congress Poland and placing it under the governor general of Kiev. This encroachment on Kholm, which had long been the scene of attempted russification and struggles against the Uniates, horrified the Poles. Yet, the circle only tried to delay the project and not to denounce it outright. It finally entered in force in March, 1914.

The issue of municipal self-government raised other problems. Reluctant to see city government unduly influenced by the large urban Jewish population, and already committed to anti-Semitism, the circle went along with proposals to restrict Jewish participation. The Realists and Progressives were unhappy about this stand which Russian liberals and Socialists immediately attacked as discriminatory. It also proved futile since the State Council in 1914 rejected the municipal reform altogether. The Poles fared equally badly when the question of zemstvos in the "western guberniias" came up for discussion. Only realized in part, the zemstvos assured Russian predominance and only deepened the antagonism of the Ukrainian and Belorussian peasantry toward Polish landowners. Other developments at the Duma, for instance, the nationalization of the Vienna-Warsaw railroad, which resulted in mass dismissals of Polish personnel, showed that already in 1909 Russia was not responding to Dmowski's persistent efforts at conciliation.

Neoslavism, loyalism toward the Russian state, and the general tenor of Dmowski's policies came under sharp attack at home. Not only Socialists and Progressive Democrats denounced them, but there were also rebellions and secessions in Dmowski's own camp. The National Workers' Union, Zet, and peasant groups out of which the National Peasant Union emerged in 1912 broke with the National League. Between 1907 and 1909, the league lost about 20 percent of its members. Outvoted at a party conference, begged to change the policy of the circle, Dmowski gave up his mandate and said that other men would have to carry out policies of which he disapproved. This was not an admission of political defeat, and Dmowski concentrated on improving the damaged image of the National Democratic movement. From 1910 to 1912, he presided over a phase, called "neoconciliation" by his opponents, which took on strongly anti-Semitic tones. Dmowski and Balicki denounced the Jews as enemies of Russia, who therefore followed a policy harmful to Polish interests. In 1911 Dmowski forced the National League to abandon the policy of school boycott; new secessions followed. In this charged political atmosphere an unknown figure from the PPS Left was put forward to oppose Dmowski at the Warsaw polls in the elections to the fourth Duma in 1912. Dmowski's defeat became a *cause célèbre*, and since it was clear that Warsaw's Jewish voters had largely decided the issue, Dmowski launched the slogan Economic Boycott of Jews.

All these failures notwithstanding, the National Democrats recovered and even improved their position as the leading movement in Congress Poland. Dmowski's arguments that current reverses in the Duma must not obscure the long-range goal of a Russo-Polish alliance against Germany were appreciated. The 1905 revolution had scared the propertied classes, and they saw national democracy as a factor of stability. As for Polish nationalism, it expressed itself more against the Jews and the Ukrainians than against Russia.

In Prussian Poland, the National Democrats continued on the ascendency. Continuous government pressure made some conservatives attempt loyalist overtures that smacked of capitulation, and the National Democrats judged the time ripe to come into the open. In 1909 a Polish Democratic Society, which was later called the National Democratic Society, was founded in Poznania; in 1911, a National Populist Party emerged in Pomerania. The former was kept small—about five hundred members in 1911—the emphasis being on genuine political activism. By 1912 the National Democrats achieved an important position in the Polish Circle, and a year later they cooperated in the creation of the Polish National Council, a representation in a moral sense of Poles in the Reich.

National Democrats were unable to gain such prominence in Galicia. Bobrzyński, who became viceroy in 1908, opposed their strivings and assured a conservative victory in 1911. Yet conservative attempts to enlarge their operational basis were unsuccessful, and in 1913 Stapiński was accused of cooperation with the conservatives and suffered a defeat within the Populist movement. The Polish Populist Party split, and the wing led by Bojko and the most outstanding young Populist leader, Wincenty Witos (1874-1945), formed the Populist Party "Piast." Its party program, adopted in 1914, stood for Poland's independence and populist ideology, but it was not inimical to the National League to which Witos also briefly belonged.

The National Democrats scored heavily in 1913 by contributing to Bobrzyński's fall over the perennial and ever thornier Ukrainian question. In 1913 some documents revealing Ukrainian-German contacts came to light, and the league branded the Ukrainians as tools of Berlin. In fact, the conflict between Bobrzyński and the National Democrats had wider ramifications. The viceroy had subscribed to an Austro-Polish solution, tolerated anti-Russian activities

of the Polish Left in Galicia, and worked for Polish-Ukrainian conciliation to strengthen an anti-Russian front. After his fall, a somewhat
watered-down electoral reform was adopted in 1914 which gave the
Ukrainians a partnership, although only a junior partnership in Galicia.
Coming too late, it was not put into application because of the war.
While the Galician National Democrats could not openly promote
Dmowski's pro-Russian line for fear of being denounced as disloyal
to Austria, they could and did criticize Austria's pro-German orientation and singled out the Ukrainians as the primary enemies of Poland.

V. PIŁSUDSKI'S ALTERNATIVE

Facing the National Democrats was the predominantly Socialist
camp grouped around Piłsudski. Although Piłsudski remained in
the Central Committee of the PPS until 1914, he sought a broader
basis for his program of Polish independence. Heaping scorn on the
"frightened and infantile" Polish society, he said in 1908 that in a
country that knuckles under the whip and does not know how to
fight for its goals, people still have to die for unworthy aims. He
wrote these remarks while personally leading the last major guerilla-
type coup of the Fighting Organization at Bezdany. During his temporary absence from Galicia, his associates organized in the summer
of 1908 the Union of Active Struggle (Związek Walki Czynnej). Its
principle author was Kazimierz Sosnkowski (1885-1969), aided by
Marian Kukiel (1885-1973) and Władysław Sikorski (1881-1943).
Formally subordinated to the PPS, the union postulated the creation
of a non-partisan Polish army which in case of war would march
from Galicia into Russian Poland. To make his plans possible,
Piłsudski had been seeking contacts with Austrian army intelligence
since 1906; in 1909 the general staff showed interest in a movement
that could render significant wartime services to the Habsburg
monarchy.

Tolerated by Vienna, particulary by Viceroy Bobrzyński, the union
sponsored the creation of paramilitary organizations in Galicia,
notably the Riflemen's Union, and operated a school for officers. As
commander of the Union of Active Struggle since 1912, Piłsudski
assumed a role that liberated his masterful personality. Surrounded
by youth who showed blind faith in the commander (Komendant),
Piłsudski saw himself as the leading soldier of Poland. He inspired
his close collaborator Michał Sokolnicki (1880-1967) to publish in
1910 *The Question of a Polish Army*, which lauded military discipline
and martial virtues and criticized political parties, Socialists included.
Piłsudski first thought of organizing an insurrection in Congress
Poland upon the outbreak of international conflict. Then, realizing
that pro-Russian trends fostered there, especially by Realists and

National Democrats, would make it impossible, he decided by 1912-13 on a different tactic. His units upon entering the kingdom would "agitate by means of war," i.e., try to gain the support of Poles having shown them that successes were possible in the course of the regular military operations.

The international crisis of the First Balkan War led to feverish activity in Galicia. A Provisional Commission of Confederated Independence Parties (Tymczasowa Komisja Skonfederowanych Stronnictw Niepodległościowych) arose and included representatives of the PPS, the Galician Social Democrats, the Peasant and National Workers' unions (formerly associated with the National League), and smaller groupings of intelligentsia and Populists from Galicia and Congress Poland. The commission provided a political umbrella for Piłsudski's military activities and named him the commander of Polish armed forces. Declaring that Poland's cause demanded a total defeat of Russia, the commission spoke of reliance on Austria but asserted that, "we shall not lose sight of our own position."

The armed force was growing. By 1913 the Riflemen (Strzelcy) had about seven thousand men, and the Riflemen's Sections (Drużyny) sponsored by the secessionists from the National League had over three thousand. Paramilitary organizations also appeared among the Ukrainians, notably the Sich Riflemen, whom the Union of Active Struggle viewed with some sympathy. In the increasingly exalted and warlike atmosphere the National Democrats could not openly go against the current; they even formed some semimilitary units of their own.

The PPS was involved in this general movement for which it provided leaders and men at the expense of its own program of social revolution. Some leading PPS figures, for example, Perl, voiced criticism of this militarist trend that transcended the party, and organized an ephemeral PPS Opposition. But the practical alternatives for Socialist partisan politics were limited.

Nor were there any real chances of cooperating with Russian Socialists. Such cooperation was possible only for the SDKPiL, and to a lesser extent for the PPS Left, but these two extreme Socialist groups operated on the peripheries of Polish political life. What is more, the SDKPiL split into two rival factions in 1912. There were acrimonius disputes connected with the Menshevik-Bolshevik conflict and controversies between Lenin and Rosa Luxemburg. In 1913 Lenin defined national self-determination "as the right to separate and create an independent state," an elastic formula which he judged necessary to detach the nationalities from the side of reaction and to strike a blow against Great Russian conservative nationalism. His realism contrasted with Rosa Luxemburg's dogmatism, and Lenin accused Luxemburg of the strange error of playing into the hand of the oppressors as a result of her fear of intensifing the "bourgeois nationalism" of oppressed nations. And indeed the extreme Polish Left, by combating nationalism and opposing Polish independence, was eliminating itself from practical politics. Its impact on events was hardly noticeable. The Dmowski and Piłsudski camps dominated the scene.

VI. ON THE EVE OF THE FIRST WORLD WAR

Given the situation in 1914, it was unavoidable that there should be two main Polish orientations, one linking Poland's fate to Russia and the Entente, the other to Austria and the Central Powers. Each possessed inherent weaknesses. The Austro-Polish orientation underestimated Germany's position in the Central Powers' camp. It overestimated Vienna's desire, power, and determination to accomplish the union of Galicia with Congress Poland and to make the Polish nation a partner of the Habsburgs. Dmowski's trend overemphasized the value of the Polish question for the West as well as the possibility of a genuine Russo-Polish reconciliation. It minimized the likely loss of Eastern Galicia to Russia and over-optimistically assumed that a unification of Polish lands under Russia would ultimately lead to independence. Dmowski, however, was aware of the fact that the war *per se* would not necessarily solve the Polish question. It could end with Austria's defeat at Russian hands and with France's defeat on the western front. Should this happen, the Polish question would be at the tender mercies of Berlin and St. Petersburg. To guard against such a development, it was imperative to commit Russia to Poland and do everything possible to assure a Russian victory over Germany. Hence, a pro-Russian stand on the part of the Poles was essential so as to prevent a German-Russian deal at their expense. Dmowski felt that there was no alternative policy, and he argued this point in memoranda submitted to a conference of Polish politicians in Cracow in 1912, and at meetings of the National League Council in Berlin in 1913 and in Vienna in 1914. The Polish slogan was Unification; demands for independence were withheld until later.

Piłsudski's policy was superficially similar to the Austro-Polish program and insisted on independence which could only be achieved with a total collapse of tsarist Russia. Only then would the Polish question be internationalized. In a lecture given in Paris in January, 1914, he opined that in the forthcoming war Russia would succumb to the Central Powers, which in turn would be defeated by the West. His collaborator, Witold Jodko-Narkiewicz (1864–1924), told the SR leader Victor Chernov that in the first phase of the war the Poles (meaning Piłsudski's camp) would go against Russia; later they would turn against the Germans. Yet, Piłsudski was not the type of man to be solely guided by such optimistic prognostics. True to his pragmatism, he explored, along with the possibility of an Austro-Polish solution, cooperation with Berlin. He strongly believed, however, that the war would exhaust the three partitioning powers and create circumstances in East Central Europe that even a small but determined Polish armed force could influence. Hence, in a sense both Piłsudski and Dmowski believed that at some stage the Poles could decisively influence their own destiny. This could be done mainly by diplomacy, according to Dmowski; mainly by force of arms according to Piłsudski. That tsarist Russia might collapse as a result of a revolution was not considered by Dmowski. There is some evidence that Piłsudski did include this possibility in his calculations.

While the Polish political leaders prepared for the coming conflict by taking definite and calculated, albeit mutually exclusive positions, the average man in the street hardly thought in such terms. As a result of the long-lasting *status quo* it was difficult for him to imagine a drastic change in the existing state of affairs. Separated from each other for over a hundred years, by 1914 the Polish lands had a different profile and character. Economically and culturally, Prussian Poland was in the lead, with a per capita income of $113, a favorable balance of trade, 1 kilometer of tracks for 8.5 square kilometers, 1 student for 5 inhabitants. Congress Poland had a per capital income of $63, a favorable balance of trade, 1 kilometer of tracks for 36.5 square kilometers, 1 student per 28 inhabitants. In Galicia the per capita income stood at $38, the balance of trade was unfavorable, there was 1 kilometer of tracks for 19.5 square kilometers, and 1 student for 6 inhabitants.

Long years of foreign domination had left their mark on the outlook and mentality of Polish citizens of Russia, Austria, and Germany. Overawed by the might of the three empires, an average Pole could not readily see how he could affect his own and his nation's fate. In Russian Poland, Dmowski's influence as well as a certain inertia dictated a pro-Russian stand. Autonomous Galicia was mainly for Austria. Tightly controlled Prussian Poland kept largely silent. Could the Poles under these conditions show enough imagination, vitality, and solidarity to make the best out of a war that was about to be fought on their territories? Days of hope, deception, effort, and struggle lay ahead. The course toward eventual independence led through unchartered waters.

# CHAPTER 16

# The First World War
# and the Rebirth of Poland

I. 1914: THE NKN, THE LEGIONS, AND THE RUSSIAN MANIFESTO

On August 1, 1914, Germany declared war on Russia, and six days later Austria-Hungary followed suit. The three partitioning powers were now locked in a struggle that could revive the Polish question and bring it into the open. But the immediate prospects filled many Poles with anxiety and fear. As subjects of the three empires, they were drafted into their respective armies to fight and kill their countrymen in foreign uniforms. Polish towns and villages were facing all the horrors of war and occupation. No wonder an average Pole caught in a struggle between giants felt insignificant and considered the slogan of Polish independence merely a beautiful dream. Mobilization in the lands of partitioned Poland proceeded smoothly. In the Congress Kingdom, the populace acclaimed even the Cossack regiments; in Galicia, war against Russia evoked enthusiasm.

The handful of Poles who had definite political goals and were active in promoting national interests responded immediately to the new situation. Already in the early hours of August 6, the first detachment of Riflemen crossed the Galician border and advanced into Congress Poland. Ordered by Piłsudski, the move was condoned by Austria on the grounds that an anti-Russian uprising in the kingdom would greatly assist her war effort. Piłsudski and his close collaborators knew that a spontaneous revolution in Russian Poland was unlikely. But they believed that by "agitating by means of war" they could establish a base in the kingdom and become an important political and even military factor. Above all, Piłsudski wanted to show that far from being a pawn in the hands of the great powers, the Poles were an active element and were determined to fight for their national goals. Desirous of being as free an agent of Poland as circumstances permitted, Piłsudski issued a fictitious proclamation from a nonexistent clandestine Polish National Government in Warsaw, which appointed him supreme commander and called on the Poles to rise. Such a stratagem freed him from the predominantly leftist Commission of Confederated Parties. It may well be that as an avid student of the Insurrection of 1863, Piłsudski wanted to place himself above the modern version of the Reds—the Socialists—and the Whites— the National Democrats. He addressed the first unit of the Riflemen as the "advance column of the Polish army setting out to fight for the liberation of the Fatherland" and as "the cadre from which the future Polish army would grow."

The march of the Riflemen's company, which was shortly followed by that of five batallions, struck the established Galician leaders as political folly based on military wishful thinking. A handful of youthful fanatics, supported by the commission which had recognized the "government" in Warsaw and declared itself the representative of that "government" in Galicia, was starting its own war against Russia. Russian strategists no longer envisaged an evacuation of the kingdom up to the Vistula; hence, there was no chance of following the retreating Russian troops, raising volunteers, and racing against the Central Powers' armies toward Warsaw. Nor was the reception of the Riflemen encouraging. People were afraid of being compromised by associating with rebels, and the gentry viewed Piłsudski's soldiers as Socialists and revolutionaries. Barred from the Dąbrowa mining region by the Germans, the Riflemen were entering an area that had no PPS organization ready to give them support. Moreover, news about German destruction of the town of Kalisz incensed the Russian Poles, and made them doubly inimical to Piłsudski, who was represented as an agent of the Central Powers.

Piłsudski's lonely venture hung in a vacuum, but it forced Polish and Austrian politicians to clarify their stand with regard to the Polish question. The National Democratic leaders warned Vienna not to expect a Polish uprising against Russia, and advised agreement with Berlin about the creation of a Polish state to be associated with Austria. Only after such an agreement could a Polish army be formed on the side of the Central Powers. On August 5, the National Democrats and their allies established a Central National Committee in Lemberg as a counterweight to the leftist commission. They declared that the Poles would fulfill more than their duty to the monarchy, if assured that Austrian war aims included Poland's independence. Since such a far-reaching Austrian commitment was unlikely at this moment, the National Democrats were clearly bidding for time. Their real aim was to prevent an uprising in Congress Poland.

In the meantime, the conservatives were busy trying to resolve both the larger political issue—the Austro-Polish plan—and the more immediate question raised by Piłsudski's initiative. The former foresaw a Polish state comprising Congress Poland and Galicia and linked with the Habsburg monarchy by ties similar to those existing between Hungary and Austria. Franz Joseph and his chief ministers favored the plan. Berlin voiced no objections, and steps were taken to draft an imperial manifesto. As for Piłsudski's venture, one could not ignore his badly armed units, which had been denied the status of combatants and had already been glorified as freedom fighters by the Galician Left. After consultation with the government and the high command, the chairman of the Polish Circle returned to Cracow with a scheme for saving Piłsudski's Riflemen. They were to be transformed into a Polish legion recognized by Austria and politically subordinated to a representative organization of the Galician political parties. Time was pressing, because Austrian intelligence had already penetrated the fiction of the Warsaw "government" and had reported about the Riflemen's failure to arouse Russian Poles. Annoyed with and suspicious of Piłsudski, the Austrian high command told him on August 13 that it would no longer tolerate his independent action. It gave him the alternative of either dissolving the Riflemen and confining his activity to supervised intelligence work, or joining along with his men the Austrian Landwehr. In either case he would lose his command and his units would cease to exist as Polish troops.

Feverish talks between Polish politicians resulted in the creation, on August 16, of a Supreme National Committee (Naczelny Komitet Narodowy, abbreviated to NKN) to act as "the highest organ of military, financial, and political organization of Polish armed forces" in Galicia. Though its creation was accompanied by a certain patriotic euphoria, the NKN did not mean a sudden reconciliation of divergent Polish political trends. Perhaps only the Cracow conservatives and Democrats entered it without second thoughts. The National Democrats merged their committee with the NKN at the price of limiting the whole undertaking to Galicia and making sure that it could only extend to Congress Poland after an understanding with a comparable representative body there. Thus, they gained control over future activities in Russian Poland. The Socialists, who sought to neutralize the National Democrats, were glad to involve them in a political and military operation originated by Piłsudski, even if it now became subject to the NKN and Vienna. Furthermore, the NKN agreement allowed Piłsudski to retain command over his troops although not over all the legions to be formed. Piłsudski accepted the NKN as a necessary evil, although he realized that "it had saved my existence." He was determined to use it only to the extent it would suit him; he had no intention of abandoning his own independent policy. Hence, each party to the NKN agreement continued to pursue its own aims; friction and splits lay ahead.

On August 27, the Austrian high command created two Polish legions, a western and an eastern one, commanded by Austrian generals of Polish descent. The Riflemen became the First Regiment (later the First Brigade) of the Western Legion and swore an oath of allegiance to Austria modeled on the *Landsturm* formula. Piłsudski regarded it as pure formality. The Eastern Legion, formed on the eve of the invasion of eastern Galicia by the Russians, was dissolved amidst confusion to which the National Democrats who did not favor the undertaking contributed. Only a fraction led by Captain (later Colonel) Józef Haller (1873-1960) eventually grew to become the Second Brigade. For a year it was separated from the first and fought in the Carpathian passes.

The Austro-Hungarian foreign minister welcomed the legions as having put an end to the Polish "national independence movement" started by "radical and socialist parties." But this was only one aspect of the question. The NKN and the legions made sense only as a visible part of the Austro-Polish program. The imperial manifesto that was to announce the program foundered, however, on the rocks of German and Hungarian opposition. Berlin felt that it would preclude a negotiated peace with Russia; the Hungarian premier, Tisza, opined that it would destroy the monarchy's dualism. Could a solution be found in the formation of a virtually independent Poland attached to Austria by dynastic and possibly economic ties? The answer to this question hinged on Berlin's attitude.

German plans regarding Poland were hazy. William II assured the loyalist Count Bogdan Hutten-Czapski (1851-1937) that as a result of the war a Polish state would be restored. The German chief of staff reported about plans of an insurrection in Russian Poland, doubtlessly referring to Piłsudski's initiative as understood by the Austrian high command. Chancellor Bethmann Hollweg briefly explored the possibility of a large Polish state linked with Austria, which would include parts of the Grodno and Kowno guberniias and extend to the Baltic through Courland. In September, however, the chancellor began to consider the possibility of an economic association of Central Europe—*Mitteleuropa*—in which Poland would figure as a separate member. There was talk about improving German strategic boundaries in the east by the annexation of a border strip *(Grenzstreifen)* carved out of Congress Poland. All these plans were fairly nebulous, and Berlin did not wish to burn its bridges to Russia. In 1914 Berlin considered the Polish question purely from a military angle and was mainly interested in the Poles as a pawn against Russia.

Still, German policy demanded better treatment of Prussian Poles, even though no radical changes were contemplated, and some of the German memoranda mentioned eventual transfers of the Polish population from Poznania to a future Polish state. With the outbreak of the war, the emperor recommended Bishop Edward Likowski (1836-1915) to the long vacant archdiocese of Posen-Gnesen and promised concessions regarding the colonization decree of 1904. On August 9, the new archbishop issued a loyalist statement which had a certain impact on Prussian Poles, who voted for the war budget and fulfilled their military obligations. But only a handful of leaders, including Napieralski and Kulerski, seriously thought that Germany might assist the Polish cause. On the whole, the population was careful not to antagonize the government—such were also the instructions of the National Democratic leadership—but in no way did it identify with Germany against Russia. It was symptomatic that when in 1915 a voluntary collection for the German Red Cross took place, Germans from Poznania contributed nine hundred thousand marks while Poles gave only seventeen thousand. Although in subsequent years Korfanty and Wojciech Trąmpczyński (1860-1953) more openly demanded the abolition of the extraordinary laws and insisted on the use of Polish in schools, in the early months of the war Prussian Poles silently awaited the course of events.

In contrast to the Central Powers, whose only public pronouncement was a vague and ineffectual appeal by the military commanders to the population of the Congress Kingdom, Russia came out early with a manifesto to the Poles. Although signed by the commander in chief, Grand Duke Nikolai Nikolaevich, and not by the tsar, the manifesto of August 14 was a well-written and eloquent document. "May the boundaries vanish that have cut asunder the Polish people!" it said. "May it [the Polish people] once again be united under the scepter of the Russian Emperor." Carrying a promise of unification, it spoke also of autonomy and religious and linguistic freedoms. The manifesto was designed as a gesture of reconciliation as well as an attempt to create a bond between the Poles and the tsarist empire. It also strove to counter the attractiveness of the Austro-Polish idea. Dmowski, who had returned to St. Petersburg from abroad on August 12, found the manifesto a basis for cooperation with Russia. He also endorsed *post factum* the dignified but loyalist stand taken by the Polish spokesmen in the Duma.

The manifesto evoked criticism from influential Russians who thought it premature. They feared that once the Polish lands were unified, albeit under the tsar's scepter, the Poles might demand full independence. Dmowski, in fact, looked upon unification and autonomy as steps leading to genuine self-government, but he assumed that sincere Russo-Polish cooperation could be built on the slender basis of common wartime interests. The Russian government proceeded with caution. In a conversation with allied ambassadors, Foreign Minister Sazonov mentioned among Russian war aims the annexation of Eastern Galicia and of the lower course of the Niemen River. Only western Galicia, Poznania, and Silesia would be unified with Congress Kingdom. On August 18, the Grand Duke Nikolai promised, in a less-publicized manifesto, a union of Galician Ukrainians with Russia. All this meant that St. Petersburg's program of unification of Polish lands fell short of Polish goals. The future "unified" Poland was not to be great enough to force the empire to grant it real home rule. Finally, the autonomy mentioned in the grand ducal manifesto was not to apply immediately to Congress Poland but only to the conquered lands.

Dmowski was not blind to all these dangers, but he thought that the Poles must try to ward off the greatest threat, namely, a separate German-Russian peace. Here his views coincided with those of Britain and France: both countries greeted Nikolai Nikolaevich's manifesto as proof of Russia's determination to fight Germany to the bitter end. As Dmowski put it, he strove to commit Russia to Poland and to link the Polish issue with the cause of the Franco-Russian alliance.

In the struggle for Polish public support, Dmowski enjoyed a certain advantage over his political opponents. Piłsudski's independent movement had been curbed by Vienna, and the alternative to a pro-Entente policy was the ill-defined Austro-Polish idea symbolized by the NKN in Cracow. In late August and early September, 1914, National Democrats, Realists and Progressives in the kingdom publicly condemned the NKN and the legions and called on them to stop their activity which was harmful to the Polish cause. In order to create a visible counterweight to the NKN, a Polish National Committee was set up in Warsaw in November. It comprised National Democrats, Realists, and a few nonpartisan figures, but no representatives from the Progressives or smaller centrist groups. The clandestine circle of Piłsudski's followers naturally opposed the committee which, in spite of its limited character, represented the most influential political groups in the kingdom.

Dmowski's cooperation with Russia did not prove easy. There were no concessions in the kingdom. Attempts to create a Polish armed unit, the so-called Puławy Legion, ran into difficulties. It was only a year later that remnants of the legion were organized into the Polish Rifles Brigade, out of which a division and, in 1917, the Polish Army Corps emerged. Russian insistence that the Polish question was a purely domestic affair prevented France from effectively supporting Dmowski's policy. The National Committee received less encouragement from Russia than did the citizens' committees in the kingdom, which concerned themselves with social aid. The policy of the Russian occupation authorities in Eastern Galicia produced the worst possible impression. Regarded as a Russian province restored to the fatherland, Eastern Galicia became the object of intense russification directed against both the Poles and the Ukrainian nationalists. Conciliatory and loyalist efforts of a National Democratic Galician leader, Stanisław Grabski (1871–1949), were to no avail. The gap between the hopes aroused by Nikolai Nikolaevich's manifesto and stark reality was widening.

Political trends and developments in the early months of the war must be seen against the background of strategic and military operations. The Central Powers' plan foresaw a lightning offensive in the west, designed to crush France within a few weeks. During this period Austrian armies, supported by German troops, were to attack Russia, but the main blow of the Central Powers' war machine was to come only after the victory in the west. Russia on her side threw over 60 percent of her armies against Austria, and fewer troops than foreseen in the Franco-Russian military planning against Germany. At first, the Austro-Hungarian armies that advanced against Congress Poland registered successes in the Lublin and Kholm areas. The Germans also advanced along their sector of the front. Then a major Russian offensive drove deep into Galicia and forced the Austrians to retreat from that province as well as from the Congress Kingdom. On September 3, the Russians entered Lemberg and moved forward. In response, however, to urgent French appeals to relieve the pressure on the western front, Russian armies began an ill-prepared offensive in East Prussia and suffered defeats at the hands of Hindenburg and Ludendorff. German armies then moved eastward while the Austrians advanced from the south. In October, Warsaw seemed on the eve of falling into the hands of the Central Powers. When winter came the front became stabilized. The German-Austrian armies were in control of a part of Congress Poland; the Russians occupied seven-eights of Galicia, including all of Eastern Galicia. While the German armies had been successful, the forces of the Habsburg monarchy had suffered numerous defeats and had lost a good deal of prestige in the eyes of their German partners. The Austrian high command was bitter about the loss of Galicia, and some of its annoyance turned against the Poles, both the National Democrats and Piłsudski. The former became politically suspect, the latter appeared too independent.

While profiting from Austrian support and appearing to cooperate with the NKN politicians and the high command, Piłsudski persevered in maintaining the national character of the First Brigade. His soldiers were contemptuous of the Austrians; they refused to wear the yellow and black arm bands, retained their own version of salute and their own uniform, and following the tradition of Dąbrowski's legion, addressed each other as "citizen." With a sizable proportion of intelligentsia in the ranks, the First Brigade was an ideologically motivated unit. The words of their marching tune, although written later, well expressed their feeling that they were lonely fighters surrounded by popular misunderstanding and intensely dedicated to their cause and to the leader who "was with us." If Piłsudski believed himself the true representative of fighting Poland and an incarnation of his nation, this did not stem from sheer megalomania. If his moves were often unorthodox, it was because he operated in highly unorthodox circumstances. Simultaneously an insurrectionist national leader and a mere brigadier of the Austrian-sponsored legions, he used others as instruments of his policy and knew how to be ruthless. Brought up in a conspiratorial school he believed in secrecy or semisecrecy. He knew that his means were limited and that he had to bluff and to take risks. By nature he seemed to enjoy doing both.

Forced by the NKN agreement to disband his political "war commissariats" in occupied parts of Congress Poland, he quickly replaced them with the Polish National Organization. The organization, while seemingly representative of various political trends in the kingdom, was in fact controlled by his men. He ordered his followers in Russian-held Poland to organize the secret Polish Military Organization (Polska Organizacja Wojskowa, abbreviated to POW). Nor did he neglect contacts with the West where he sent representatives to explain that his war effort was purely a Polish undertaking and was in no way directed against the Western Allies.

In October Piłsudski used the Polish National Organization to establish relations with the German army. He inspired an agreement, in a manner somewhat reminiscent of his early dealings with the Austrians. According to it the Poles promised sabotage and diversion behind the Russian lines, and the Germans agreed to allow part of Piłsudski's brigade to participate in the march on Warsaw and to be stationed there after the seizure of the capital. Although the Poles hardly had the means of keeping their part of the bargain, the risk seemed worth taking if it meant getting to Warsaw and weakening

Piłsudski's dependence on the NKN and Vienna. The offensive on Warsaw, however, broke down, and German friendliness toward the Poles turned to rancor. The episode was over, and Piłsudski fell back on cooperation with the NKN.

His prestige did not suffer. The First Brigade was fighting with distinction, for instance, at the battle of Łowczówek (Christmas Eve, 1914), and Piłsudski's military talents gained recognition. Politically, his position grew stronger as the NKN became torn by recriminations between the Left and the National Democrats. The latter, accused of disloyalty and ambiguous behavior in Russian-occupied Galicia, left the NKN. The weakened committee needed Piłsudski more than the "commander" needed them. The fact that the Polish National Organization was admitted to the NKN indicated the committee's increasing willingness to become involved in the affairs of the occupied parts of Congress Poland. For one thing, the legions needed more men and these could only be recruited in the kingdom.

Austro-Polish, Russo-Polish, and Ukrainian-Polish relations were gravely affected by the Russian occupation of Eastern Galicia. Russification policies there included the closing of Polish schools, and proselytizing activities of the imported Eastern Orthodox clergy among the Ukrainians. Metropolitan Szeptycki was deported to Russia; "Old Ruthenian" organizations gained the upper hand. The impact of these developments on the relations between the National Democrats, on the one hand, and St. Petersburg and Vienna, on the other, has already been mentioned. As for the Ukrainians, they blamed the Polish administration and intensified their political campaigns in Vienna and even in Berlin.

The Ukrainian National Council had defined its national objectives as early as August 3, 1914. In a manifesto signed among others by Kost Levytsky and Pavlyk, the Ukrainians spoke of the approaching hour of liberation and identified their victory with that of Austro-Hungary. The manifesto spoke of a transformation of Eastern Galicia (together with Bukovina) into a separate crownland and advocated the creation of a Ukrainian state composed of lands under Russia's rule. Ukrainian Sich Riflemen saw action in September and suffered severe losses which could not easily be replaced after the occupation of Eastern Galicia. Still, their military effort made some impression in Vienna. The Austrian government gave support to the Union for the Liberation of the Ukraine, a group composed mainly of leftist émigrés from the Russian Ukraine, which concentrated its efforts on the "southwestern land." The union also sought to interest Germany, and in Berlin, where the headquarters were moved in 1915, it agitated for the cause of an independent and democratic state. Although registering little success, the group was not ignored by the German government which subsidized its activity. German and Austrian Catholic politicians and the Catholic hierarchy listened with interest to plans, which were identified with Metropolitan Szeptycki, for an eventual union of Uniate and Eastern Orthodox Ukrainians. But, as in the case of Poland, the Central Powers still maintained a cautious and noncommittal attitude. The time for new political and military departures would come in 1915.

II. FROM THE AUSTRO-GERMAN OCCUPATION OF CONGRESS POLAND
   TO THE TWO EMPERORS' MANIFESTO

In May, 1915, a joint German-Austrian offensive broke through the Russian front at Gorlice. On August 5, Warsaw was taken, and by September the Russians had evacuated the entire Congress Kingdom and Lithuania. All of ethnic Poland was now under the control of the Central Powers. The major part of the kingdom (6.5 million inhabitants out of 9.4 million) including Warsaw fell to the Germans and was placed under Governor General Hans Hartwig von Beseler. Directly responsible to the emperor, Beseler headed all military and civilian authorities, much to the annoyance of the Eastern Army Command, the Oberost. The latter had under its jurisdiction the Lithuanian and Belorussian lands and two areas detached from the kingdom—Suwałki and part of Podlachia. Beseler was a professional soldier descended from an intellectual north German family, and while Poland was a new terrain for him, he took his "viceroyalty" seriously. Determined to enforce "law and order," he was ready to undo the hundred years of Russian misrule. He was not inimical to the Poles, but he found them politically immature. At first he assumed that the Congress Kingdom would be returned to Russia; only slowly did he begin to see the advantages of its permanent association with the Central Powers.

The Germans quickly curbed the Russian-sponsored citizens' committees but permitted a Central Welfare Council (RGO) to act as an intermediary between the population and the occupation authorities. They assumed control over courts and schools—divided into Polish-language and German-language institutions—and allowed the opening of a Polish university and a politechnika in Warsaw. In 1916 they permitted elections to town councils and established district diets. Political parties could function openly. On the whole, in spite of strict political controls and censorship, the Poles had more freedom than under the tsarist regime.

In the economic field everything was subordinated to German war needs, and the kingdom was greatly exploited. By mid-1916, the Germans had taken about 70 percent of the land's raw materials for their own industries. They dismantled factories, virtually destroying the textile industry, and took machinery—even church bells—to the Reich. German need of timber led to serious deforestation of the country. The number of employed workers dropped to 22 percent in 1916; the unemployed were recruited for work in Germany. No wonder that many Poles felt that Germany was aiming to reduce the kingdom to the level of a colony. Discontent was rampant, and the masses had little use for the German occupants.

The Austrian occupation zone, which eventually included the Kholm region, was ruled from Lublin by military governors who were quite familiar with the Polish scene. Polish civilian officials from Galicia had at first only an advisory role, but after mid-1916 a predominantly Polish civilian administration took over. Schools and courts were largely in Polish hands, and Galician models were introduced. Compulsory deliveries of foodstuffs were less onerous and labor recruiting centers less ruthless than in the German zone. On the other hand, Austrian authorities took longer than Beseler in allowing the creation of municipal and rural self-government.

The occupation of Congress Poland raised the whole Polish issue to a higher political level of discussion. Bethmann Hollweg saw three alternative solutions: (1) the return of the kingdom to Russia, minus a strategic frontier strip; (2) the creation of an autonomous kingdom closely associated with one of the Central Powers; (3) the union of Congress Poland with Galicia, Germany being compensated by larger border rectifications. He concluded: " . . . an advantageous and satisfactory solution of the Polish problem does not exist for us at all."[1] The first alternative made sense only in case of a separate peace with Russia, but the prospects of such a peace were slim. Hence, the second and third variants became the object of endless secret Austro-German exchanges. Vienna naturally favored the third alternative but balked at the cession of a borderstrip—which in some of the German plans amounted to an area with nearly two million people—and worried about other German demands.

Austro-German negotiations went through several phases. In mid-August, 1915, Vienna was under the impression that Berlin consented to the Austro-Polish solution. On August 19, however, Bethmann Hollweg spoke for the first time publicly about the Polish question, but after mentioning Poland's liberation "from the Russian yoke," he indulged in generalities and said nothing about the future of the country. During the autumn and winter of 1915, the Polish question became linked with the vast *Mitteleuropa* scheme. The concept meant different things to different people. The German high command saw in it a consolidated base for the German war effort. In later

1. Cited in Werner Conze, *Polnische Nation und deutsche Politik im ersten Weltkrieg* (Köln, Graz: Böhlau Verlag, 1958), p. 80.

years it subordinated *Mitteleuropa* to an undisguisedly expansionist *Osteuropa* idea. The writer Friedrich Naumann, whose book published in late 1915 popularized *Mitteleuropa*, envisaged it as a solution to Central European economic and social problems. Although he took Germany's leading role for granted, he did not lack a certain idealism and had a vision of the future. To some Austrian writers, *Mitteleuropa* was a device for preserving and reconstructing the Habsburg monarchy.

As an American historian aptly put it, "the way to *Mitteleuropa* led over Poland."[2] Poland could become a bridge linking the two Germanic states, and although views regarding Poland varied in Berlin, William II and the Foreign Affairs Ministry came to believe that a modified Austro-Polish arrangement might best fit the entire scheme. The kingdom united with Galicia would be associated with Austria (subdualism), while Germany would be assured economic and military advantages. After a conference in November, the Austrians began to feel that what Germany really proposed was to burden Austria with the political and social problems connected with the assumption of sovereignty, while reserving to herself a hold over the kingdom's economy and the borderstrip. In such circumstances it was hardly worthwhile for Vienna to take the Congress Kingdom at all.

By February, 1916, Berlin started to think seriously about a Poland closely linked with Germany, and in mid-April Bethmann Hollweg rejected the Austro-Polish solution. The only pro-Austrian gesture he contemplated was to invite Archduke Karl Stefan Habsburg to mount the Polish throne. In a major speech on April 5, the German chancellor merely said that Germany and Austria-Hungary would bring a solution to the Polish question which had not been raised by the Central Powers but arose as a result of the war. After such a cataclysm, he said, a return to the *status quo* was unthinkable and Germany could not remain exposed to a Russian threat from the east. To people aware of the secret exchanges it was clear that the speech meant that a closer association of Poland with Germany was Berlin's *raison d'état*. The ever present question of a separate peace with Russia, however, did not disappear, and in May there were new feelers to the tsarist empire.

The Russian attitude toward the kingdom was obviously of crucial importance. The tsarist government had shown a profound reluctance to go beyond the Nikolai Nikolaevich manifesto of August, 1914. As a Russian minister candidly admitted, "our aim is not to satisfy the

2. P. R. Sweet, "Germany, Austria and Mitteleuropa August 1915–April 1916," Hugo Hantsch and Alexander Novotny, eds., *Festschrift für Heinrich Benedikt* (Vienna: Notrig, 1957), p. 206.

Poles but to keep them from separating."³ Dmowski's and Zygmunt
Wielopolski's (1863–1919) efforts to persuade St. Petersburg (Petrograd since 1914) to grant genuine autonomy to the kingdom were
unsuccessful, except for the introduction of municipal self-government
on March 30, 1915. When a few weeks later the Russian front collapsed at Gorlice, the government belatedly decided to make concessions. On the eve of the evacuation of Lemberg, a Russo-Polish
commission was set up to discuss the question of autonomy; but in
spite of a most conciliatory stand on the part of the Poles, agreement was nowhere in sight. When the fall of Warsaw became imminent,
Premier Goremykin declared that the tsar had ordered the preparation of laws that, while preserving the unity of the state, would give
the Poles the right to organize freely their national, cultural, and
economic life on the basis of autonomy. In late February, 1916, Premier
Stürmer and Foreign Minister Sazonov reiterated Russia's intention to
unify the Polish lands. They denounced the Central Powers which
had divided the kingdom and sought to ensnare the Poles by such
concessions as the opening of Warsaw university and promises of a
Polish army. The opposition in the Duma did not fail to point out
that the government was only reacting to events and was still unwilling
to be specific about autonomy. What is more, it tried to ignore all
the long-range developments that were slowly making the Polish
question an international issue.

In November, 1915, Dmowski went to the West. His departure
resulted in part from his being cut off from Congress Poland, in part
from his realization that the Polish cause could be more effectively
promoted in the West. Providing him with a diplomatic passport,
the Russians hoped that he would neutralize other Polish trends in
the Allied countries, which were inimical to Russia.

Indeed, a number of prominent Poles were active in the West,
particularly in Switzerland: Sienkiewicz, the historians Szymon
Askenazy (1867–1935) and Jan Kucharzewski (1866–1952), the
scientist Gabriel Narutowicz (1865–1922), the Realist politician
Piltz, and others. Ignacy Paderewski (1860–1941) spent a good deal
of his time there. Several Polish organizations sprang up in Switzerland, France, England, and the United States, ranging from non-
partisan humanitarian institutions to information, propaganda, and
political agencies. Most of them were designed to further the Polish
cause in the Entente countries. National Democrats, Realists,
supporters of the Austro-Polish solution, and Piłsudski's followers

3. Cited in Alexander Dallin, "The Future of Poland," Russian Institute, Occasional Papers, Columbia University, *Russian Diplomacy and Eastern Europe 1914-
1917* (New York: King's Crown Press, 1963), p. 14.

were active in them; at times they even cooperated or maintained secret contact. Among the most influential organizations in Switzerland was the Central Polish Agency, which came increasingly under the domination of the Dmowski-Piltz supporters. In London, representatives of the National Democrats and Realists on the one hand, and August Zaleski (1883–1972)—originally sent by Piłsudski—on the other, strove to influence the British government. It may seem paradoxical that the West tolerated the diplomatic and propagandistic activity of Austro-Polish supporters, but one must not forget that neither London nor Paris had as yet lost interest in the Habsburg monarchy. Both regarded it as a counterweight to Germany.

Dmowski's objective was to create a veritable Polish representation in the West, which would follow his political line and be recognized as Poland's spokesman in the Allied camp. Establishing himself in London, he presented on March 2, 1916, a memorandum to the Russian ambassador in Paris, Izvolsky, in which, as in a preceeding talk, he mentioned for the first time Polish independence. The memorandum was really destined for the Western Allies, and Dmowski pressed for an Allied declaration in favor of a unified and independent Kingdom of Poland linked to Russia by ties essential for common defense and mutual economic interests. Petrograd was greatly dissatisfied. It reiterated to its envoys in the Western capitals that the Polish question was a domestic Russian issue. France was cautious and while favorable to the Poles had no desire to endanger her relations with Russia. In Britain, Foreign Secretary Sir Edward Grey wished to stay clear of the Polish question; his successor, Balfour, had serious doubts about the wisdom of creating an independent Polish state separating Russia and Germany. He argued that it would create new trouble as well as deprive France of effective Russian support. The British prime minister in turn made only general public statements about Allied concern for the independent status and free development of the weaker countries.

Sazonov realized that the longer the war lasted the more complex the Polish question would become. If the Central Powers succeeded in winning over the Poles and formed a sizable army in the kingdom, London and Paris might put pressure on Russia to make concessions. Sazonov wished to forestall such developments, and he urged the tsar to issue a manifesto granting far-reaching autonomy. The empress and the premier opposed such concessions, and they viewed even the most loyalist Poles as suspects. In July, 1916, Sazonov was dismissed from office. Petrograd continued to adhere to its policy of trying to evade rather than to resolve the Polish question.

Internal developments in the Polish lands between mid-1915 and mid-1916 were affected both by the international situation and by local trends. After Congress Poland became free of the Russians, it was expected that Warsaw would speak out; but the kingdom was politically cautious and noncommital. Undoubtedly the brutal behavior of the German and Austrian military had discouraged many people. In Eastern Galicia the march on the Austrian troops had been marked by the gallows of alleged Russian spies, mass arrests, burning, and looting. For the first time since the mid-nineteenth century an Austrian became viceroy of Galicia, and the Ukrainians, who had urged it all along, demanded that the Poles be deprived of their leading position in the province. The kingdom had suffered severe hardships during the Russian retreat which involved forced mass evacuation of its civilian population and attempts at scorched-earth tactics. It seemed that there was not much to choose between the occupants.

The National Democrats, Realists, and some Progressives adopted a policy that quickly earned them the name "Passivists." United in the Interparty Political Circle (Międzypartyjne Koło Polityczne) set up in 1915, they shunned political cooperation with the Central Powers and opposed the NKN. They were willing, however, to participate in economic and local government affairs. The so-called Activists represented a whole range of trends and opinions. Those who leaned toward an Austro-Polish solution were grouped in the League for Polish Statehood; those who believed that Poland's future depended on Germany gathered in the small but vocal Club of Polish Statehood under Władysław Studnicki (1867–1953). Two larger groupings— Union and Confederation—comprising the PPS, the National Workers' Union, the National Peasant Party, the Polish Peasant Party "Wyzwolenie," and other progressive intelligentsia parties, set up a Union of Independence Parties (Zjednoczenie Stronnictw Niepodleg-łościowych). The union resembled somewhat the prewar leftist commission in Galicia, which had backed Piłsudski. Given the passivity of the most influential parties in Congress Poland and the great fragmentation of political life, it fell to the Polish leaders operating from Galicia to try to shape the outlook of the kingdom.

Fearing the possibility of a permanent division of Congress Poland between Germany and Austria, the chairman of the NKN issued on August 8, 1915, a declaration urging unification of the entire kingdom with Galicia. He stated that the question of the relationship between such a state and the Habsburg monarchy could surely be resolved. His move, based on a belief that Berlin would go along, appeared as an attempt to force Vienna's hand. To strengthen its position, the NKN and in particular its Military Department, presided over by Colonel Władysław Sikorski, began a recruitment campaign in Congress Poland. The results were meager. Between August 21 and

September 11, 1915, only twenty-six hundred volunteers enlisted. Shortly thereafter the German command forbade further recruitment to the legions.

This weak response on the part of the population stemmed not only from its passivity, but also from Piłsudski's stand against recruitment, which he expressed through the Union of Independence Parties. Such an attitude on Piłsudski's part, while constituting a reversal of his earlier position, was not as paradoxical as it might appear. In fact, it was fairly consistent with his general line of thought. Piłsudski reasoned that the kingdom was a card that had not yet been shown, and that it must be used as a trump in the intricate game being played with the Central Powers. In essence, Piłsudski wanted to bluff Berlin and Vienna by concealing the actual strength or weakness of Congress Poland. If recruitment produced results, it might be taken to mean that the Poles could be bought at a cheap price. If it failed, it would show that the kingdom was less of a military and political asset than the Central Powers had imagined. Wishing to preserve a Sphinx-like image of the kingdom, Piłsudski fulminated against the "silly policy of Austria and the NKN."

When Piłsudski came to Warsaw on August 15 and was promptly asked to leave by the German authorities, he spent two days in nearby Otwock, where he outlined his strategy. He favored pursuing simultaneously several lines of activity. While defying the NKN, he did not wish to break with the Cracow conservatives, and he intimated to them his willingness to travel for a while the common road of an Austro-Polish policy. He made strenuous efforts to bring about a political consolidation of the kingdom and made repeated but vain overtures to the Passivists to set up a truly representative national council. Finally, he resorted to his "secret weapon"—the POW (Polish Military Organization). While forbidding recruitment to the legions, he encouraged volunteers to join the POW. Like the Riflemen before them, the well-disciplined POW members were a military and political instrument entirely in Piłsudski's hands. Given their underground character, they were a good illustration of Piłsudski's point about the Sphinx-like character of Congress Poland.

Piłsudski's opposition to the Austrian-sponsored recruitment exposed Vienna's undecided policy toward Poland—although Vienna did not have a free hand—and was firmly grounded in reality. Germany was against strengthening the legions, and there was little likelihood of mass volunteering on the part of former Russian Poles. When the Union of Independence Parties stated that it would support recruitment provided the legions came under Piłsudski's command and received the status of an independent Polish force responsible to a representative Polish body, it was putting forward unacceptable demands. But such demands strengthened Piłsudski's hand.

A conflict between Vienna and the NKN on the one hand and Piłsudski on the other was unavoidable, and the "commander" sought a showdown. In late 1915 the legionary brigades were brought together, and Piłsudski's units came in direct contact with the high command. The latter professed an Austro-Polish outlook and clashed with Piłsudski's stand. The "commander" complained that the legions were in danger of losing their Polish character, and he spoke of resigning and dissolving the First Brigade. The conflict was eventually patched up by Austria, and Piłsudski's national stature was enhanced. In turn, the bravery and military skill the legions showed in the campaigns of late 1915 and early 1916 raised their value. The German high command began to show a growing interest in these units.

As mentioned earlier, in April, 1916, Berlin rejected the Austro-Polish solution, and Beseler started to advocate a close association of the kingdom with Germany. A German-conducted population census revealed that the kingdom had nearly 1.5 million men of military age, a fact that could not be easily ignored in the third year of the war. The creation of a Polish army under German command, however, was not the only reason for Beseler's stand. He argued in favor of a solution of the Polish question in the frame of *Mitteleuropa* and considered that it was up to Germany to assume the leadership. The Poles had neither trained administrators nor professional officers. On May 3, 1916, gigantic manifestations commemorating the anniversary of the 1791 constitution took place in the kingdom. Even such former Passivists as Archbishop Aleksander Kakowski (1862-1938) and the mayor of Warsaw, Prince Zdzisław Lubomirski (1865-1941), took part in them. Beseler viewed the moment to be psychologically ripe for some moves concerning the Polish question. Acting on his own, he allowed elections to municipal councils; 75 percent of those eligible went to the polls. He also made his own views known to the Poles. He told them that politics was the art of the possible, and that nations had to subordinate their more ambitious aims to cooperation with larger powers or groupings of states. In private he said that a large Poland extending to the prepartition borders in the east was not feasible. His reference to the touchy problem of the eastern borderlands becomes clearer if one examines the contemporary situation in Lithuania and Belorussia.

German troops occupied Kowno in August, 1915, and a month later they entered Vilna. A large number of people, perhaps as many as four hundred thousand, left the country with the retreating Russians. The military occupation regime of the Oberost was set up in November, and it controlled Courland and the Kowno, Vilna, Suwałki, and Białystok provinces. Unlike the Beseler regime, the Oberost permitted no political activities in the country. At first, the Germans showed no awareness of the Lithuanians, and they viewed the area as historically Polish, witness General Pfeil's order that referred to Vilna as "the pearl of the glorious Polish kingdom." But no concessions to the Poles followed. Vilna university was not opened, and only two Polish high schools were allowed to function. The country became the object of ruthless economic exploitation. High quotas were set for compulsory grain and potato deliveries. Cattle were requisitioned, and workers recruited for labor in the Reich.

The rise of the *Mitteleuropa* idea produced no attempts to engage Poles or Lithuanians in a political dialogue. The local Baltic Germans seemed a reliable pillar of any future combinations. When Bethmann Hollweg said that Germany would not return the Lithuanians to Russia, he had no plans for organizing a Lithuanian organism comparable to the Congress Kingdom. High quarters in Berlin thought of a simple annexation of Lithuania and Courland, and there were even projects for future German colonization and transfers of Poles from Lithuania into Congress Poland. The Oberost frowned on the "Polonophile" policies of Beseler and eyed suspiciously the Catholic hierarchy in Lithuania as an instrument of Polish influence in the country. It was largely to weaken the Poles that the Oberost extended some protection to Lithuanians and Belorussians and allowed the creation of a social welfare organization, the Lithuanian Committee, directed by Antanas Smetona (1874–1944).

In the early months of the war three principal trends had developed among the Lithuanians. A pro-Russian orientation, based on clerical, nationalist, and some progressive groups, was represented by the Duma deputy Martinas Yčas (1885–1941). The second, the Autonomists, were led by Democratic, Social Democratic, and nationalist leaders such as Kairys, Smetona, Vileišis, and Jurgis Šaulys. Finally, there was the extreme Left which declared that only a proletarian revolution could end the war and bring freedom to the toiling masses. The first group voiced its loyalty to tsarist Russia, and after the manifesto of Grand Duke Nikolai Nikolaevich of August, 1914, to the Poles, expressed hopes for an autonomous, ethnic Lithuania (including the northern part of East Prussia) under the Romanovs. After the occupation of Lithuania, contacts between Yčas and the leaders at home were interrupted, and the pro-Russian group lost some of its importance. Simultaneously Lithuanian activity in the West and at home became more intense.

One of the main centers in the West was in Switzerland, where Juozas Gabrys (really Paršaitis, 1880-1951) edited *Pro Lithuania* and engaged in propagandistic activity. Seeking potential allies, he cooperated both with French and American intelligence and with Germany. At first, Lithuanians living abroad spoke of national autonomy, as for instance in the Chicago diet in September, 1914, and at the Bern and Stockholm meetings a year later. At conferences held in early 1916 in Bern, the Hague, and Lausanne, they raised demands for national independence. At the Lausanne meeting they denounced the German occupation regime and appealed to world public opinion to defend their national rights. In June, 1916, a conference of oppressed nationalities of Russia recognized Lithuania's right to independence. Efforts at home had to be more circumscribed. In June, 1916, Lithuanian politicians addressed a memorandum to the Oberost describing Lithuanian national development and aspirations which included ultimate independence of the country. The Germans gave no reply, but they allowed Smetona, Šaulys, and Kairys to travel to a meeting abroad and to stop in Berlin where they established contact with ranking German politicians. Prominent Lithuanians agreed not to link their activity with that of the Poles, and at the Bern meeting in 1916 rejected the idea of reviving the Polish-Lithuanian union. But the Polish aspects of the Lithuanian question could not be simply ignored. Nor could one forget that demands for a large Lithuania also raised the Belorussian question.

Lithuanian Poles held divergent views concerning Lithuania's independence. A democratic group, largely composed of intellectuals and known as *krajowcy* (from *kraj*, or homeland), tried to reconcile their divided loyalties to Poland and Lithuania by advocating a Polish-Lithuanian federation. Among their leaders were such "Polono-Lithuanians" as Michał Römer, Ludwik Abramowicz (1879-1938), and Stanisław Narutowicz (Narutavicius, 1862-1932), and the Lithuanian Mykolas Biržiška. A clandestine Polish Democratic Bloc for Independence in Lithuania and Belorussia declared in September, 1915, for a federation. The Polish Committee in Vilna gradually came to prefer simple merger. In Poland, Piłsudski and his supporters advocated federation; the rightist Interparty Circle spoke in general terms about close unity. The German census of 1916 revealed a Polish majority in the city of Vilna and in those parts of the guberniia it had included. Did not this fact justify a different treatment of the province as contrasted with ethnically Lithuanian or Belorussian lands? Many Poles definitely thought so.

As for the Belorussians, their political possibilities were extremely limited. Ethnic Belorussia was cut in two by the front, and at first the German authorities noticed only the Polish upper class. Quickly realizing that local Poles pursued an independent policy favoring the recreation of the historic union, the Germans sought to oppose them by supporting the Belorussians and the Jews. From early 1916, the Belorussian langugage was placed on a level of equality with other tongues. Elementary Belorussian schools were set up and courses for teachers opened, since almost no native teachers were available. The Germans permitted a Belorussian newspaper, the *Homan* (Voice), to appear; it spoke in friendly terms of the Lithuanians and considered future ties with the Ukraine. Its activity as well as the emergence of an organization called the Confederation of the Great Duchy of Lithuania had anti-Polish overtones. A small Belorussian group which was opposed to the treatment of the Lithuanian-Belorussian lands as a unit aimed at a future severance of all ties with Lithuania. But given the strict regime of the Oberost none of these groups could really come into the open or appeal to wider circles. The future of Lithuania, either conceived in the narrower, ethnic sense or in the broader, historic sense, was highly uncertain in the summer of 1916.

During the summer, severe fighting took place on the eastern front. The great Brusilov offensive rolled westward and was stopped only with German military assistance to the Austrians. The Polish legions fought well. "The Pole is a good soldier," Ludendorff commented, and both Vienna and Berlin recognized the need for more Polish troops. In mid-August the Central Powers reached a compromise regarding Congress Poland. It took the form of an agreement to proclaim a self-governing *(selbständig)* Polish hereditary and constitutional kingdom, bound through a military convention with Austria and Germany, and placed economically under Austro-German condominium. Its eventual territorial cessions to Germany would be made up by gains in the east, possibly in the Vilna area. Berlin obviously wished to limit Austrian participation in Polish affairs to a bare minimum, but it could not ignore the fact that the legions and one part of the kingdom were under direct Austrian control. The actual establishment of a Polish state would take place after the end of the war, and nothing concrete was said about its boundaries. The main motives for reaching a decision at this point were: rumors of an impending Russian declaration on Poland (possibly in connection with the unsuccessful attempts of Sazonov), dwindling chances of a separate peace with Russia, and last but not least, changes in the German high command. In August, 1916, Hindenburg and Ludendorff took over the army, and they both believed that the outcome of the war would be decided in the east. Striking a tactical alliance with Beseler, they prevailed upon Bethmann Hollweg and those German politicians who felt that any decisive move on the Polish question would slam the door to future negotiations with Russia to go along.

The German high command was principally interested in new troops. Vienna felt that too obvious a connection between political promises to the Poles and demands for volunteers would produce bad results. The Austrians did not wish to merge their own zone, which was an important bargaining asset, with the German-occupied part and hoped that a revival of the Austro-Polish idea was still possible. They courted the Poles by such measures as attaching the Kholm region to their zone and establishing a predominantly Polish civilian administration. Toward the end of October, 1916, a Polish delegation was encouraged to visit Berlin and Vienna. Composed of Activists, it formulated Polish requests for: (1) a regent (opposed by Berlin but not by Vienna); (2) a merger of the two zones (Berlin was for this, Vienna against); (3) the creation of a provisional state council (approved by both Central Powers provided it were a purely advisory body); (4) a Polish military department and the use of the legions as the cadre of a Polish army (Vienna favored this with some reservations, while Berlin was opposed); (5) the proclamation of a king, and the tracing of frontiers at the peace conference (Vienna and Berlin thought this a premature demand).

At that moment Piłsudski was no longer in the legions. During the summer he had insisted that Polish soldiers could only fight for Poland's independence, and he was backed by senior legion officers. The Austrians tried to neutralize him by offering him the command of all the legions and by suggesting that he organize a political representation in the Austrian zone of the kingdom. Piłsudski refused and resigned his brigadiership; his resignation was accepted on September 26. Many officers and men, following his lead, demanded to be released from the legions. On the verge of mutiny, the troops were withdrawn from the front and sent to Baranowicze in the German zone.

On November 5, 1916, the governors in Warsaw and Lublin, acting on behalf of the German and Austrian emperors, issued a manifesto to the Poles announcing a self-governing Polish Kingdom composed of former Russian territories with frontiers to be delimited at a later date. In its close association with the Central Powers, the manifesto said, the kingdom would find necessary guarantees for a free development of its forces. Its army would be organized following a common agreement.

The Two Emperors' Manifesto had far-reaching domestic and international repercussions. Although it was a statement of intentions rather than an act establishing a Polish state, it created great commotion among the Poles. Long-forgotten words such as "Polish state," "Polish army," and "self-government" could not but move the people. But the initial enthusiasm quickly wore off. Only four days later, Beseler, pressed by Hindenburg and Ludendorff, appealed for Polish volunteers. This produced the impression that the manifesto was merely bait to draw in Polish cannon fodder for the Central Powers. Subsequent declarations promising a provisional state council could not easily efface this impression. Vienna, in particular, found itself in an embarrassing position because Galicia was to remain outside of the Polish Kingdom. The emperor's announcement of a special status for the province, to be elaborated by the Polish Circle in the Reichsrat, met with a cool reception. The Left took a negative stand, and only the conservatives, hoping for a revival of the Austro-Polish solution, reacted favorably. Their political standing in Galicia consequently declined.

The November manifesto, as the French Chamber of Deputies quickly recognized, "stamped the Polish question with an international" character. This greatly perturbed Russia which on November 15 protested against this violation of international law and recalled Russian pledges for a unified Poland. Asked to join the protest, Paris and London publicly thanked the Russian government for its positive approach to the Polish question. The Italian premier seconded them. The Allied move showed that the Polish issue could no longer be regarded as a purely Russian affair. Realizing this, Petrograd pursued a double policy. Officially, it stressed its commitment to a free Poland; secretly, it negotiated with France to retain a free hand in the Polish question. The first approach was illustrated by Premier Trepov's speech, and particularly by the tsar's Christmas Day order, which enumerated among Russia's war aims "the creation of a free Poland from all three of her until now separated provinces." Communicated with Allied endorsement to the president of the United States, this statement taken together with the Two Emperors' Manifesto enabled Woodrow Wilson to single out Poland in his message to the Senate on January 22, 1917. Invoking the principle of government by consent of the governed, Wilson said that "statesmen everywhere are agreed that there should be a united, independent, and autonomous Poland." In contrast of official pronouncements, the Russian government simultaneously opposed granting real freedom to Poland. In a secret accord reached with France in March, 1917, it obtained a free hand in fixing Russia's western borders. Paris thus agreed to subordinate Poland's future to the wishes of Petrograd.

Given the lukewarm attitude of the West and the ambivalent position of Russia, many Poles tried to make the best of the Two Emperors' Manifesto. In spite of all limitations the kingdom did become a "school of fresh political life." Although it was destined to be a phantom state with a phantom government it provided some scope for national activity.

On December, 1, 1916, Beseler welcomed the Polish legions (some twenty thousand men) into Warsaw. Would these troops become a genuine Polish force or merely an instrument of the Central Powers? The POW quickly put up posters in Warsaw with the slogan No Army without a Government. Piłsudski and his followers began to raise the ante in the new round of political poker being played with Beseler and the Central Powers. The first step in the direction of self-government was the creation of the Provisional State Council (Tymczasowa Rada Stanu) which began its sessions in mid-January, 1917. With purely advisory functions, it comprised departments of Finance, Political Affairs, Interior, Education and Religion, and a Military Commission. Composed of twenty-five delegates (from both zones) who were chosen by the occupation authorities after some consultation with the major Polish parties, the council had a majority of rightist and center Activists. The Interparty Political Council had only been willing to participate on its own terms; this Beseler and the Activists found unacceptable. Hence it was not represented at all. The PPS, the Peasant Party, and the National Workers' Party had four members in all. Piłsudski entered as a nonparty member—he had formally withdrawn from the PPS in 1916—and received the chairmanship of the Military Commission.

In a gesture that the council greatly appreciated, the POW placed itself under the council's orders. This was meant to show Beseler that Piłsudski's soldiers would only serve a Polish authority. The German governor and Piłsudski had a long conversation, in the course of which the former tried to convince the latter that an army could only be organized by the qualified and experienced German command. He warned the Pole against premature demands in the military and administrative spheres. If one accepts Beseler's premise of a Poland intimately associated with a victorious Germany, he was correct. But Piłsudski sought to advance the Polish cause by rapid improvisation so as to have a rudimentary Polish state and an army when the war ended with the collapse of the Central Powers. To Beseler, the Poles were "political children" and Piłsudski a "military dilettante and demagogue" who could not command a modern army. Piłsudski's position bordered on treason, especially since, as Beseler observed, he was gifted and had a charismatic influence over his followers. A Beseler-Piłsudski collaboration was not possible. Piłsudski's proposals of a national government and army were not acceptable, and he made them so as to place his views on record. Unlike the real Activists, who tried to achieve the feasible in cooperation with Berlin, Piłsudski went through the motions of chairing his commission and harped on the theme that Beseler's and the Central Powers' policy could not bring any results for Poland.

German disappointment with the meager results of recruitment to an army whose national status was still not clarified found its expression in a stiffening of the German high command. Ludendorff pressed the Reich's chancellor to secure Austrian agreement to a merging of the two zones and the introduction of stricter controls. A draft constitution for the kingdom, prepared by German officials, was to be phrased in such a way as to avoid mentioning dependence of the kingdom on the Reich; the stress was put on economic ties, "the only sure chain" by which Poland would be "permanently" attached to Germany. No tariffs were foreseen to protect Polish industries, and the whole area was to become a vast agricultural *Hinterland*. What is more, the high command again insisted on a broad frontier strip as well as on a corridor running from Lithuania to Brest-Litovsk. This last-named city was to be a "Prussian provincial town." Vilna, Grodno, and Minsk would go to Lithuania. The truncated kingdom, hemmed in on the east and the west, was destined to be a vassal of the Reich. Berlin hoped to gain Austrian assent by proposing that Romania come under Habsburg rule, and the new emperor, Charles, showed interest. Vienna was prepared to make concessions to Germany in Poland in order to make Berlin more amenable in the West and make peace possible.

III. THE FATEFUL YEAR:
AMERICA IN THE WAR AND THE RUSSIAN REVOLUTIONS

The character of the First World War changed dramatically in 1917. In April the United States declared war on Germany, and in December on Austria-Hungary. In Russia, the February Revolution (old style calendar) swept away the tsarist regime in March. In November the Bolsheviks triumphed in the October Revolution. The entry of the United States proved decisive in breaking the military stalemate in the west and assuring Allied victory. It also brought to the fore the ideological element—the slogan A War to End All Wars, the struggle of democracy against authoritarianism. The two revolutions in Russia resulted in the country leaving the war, thus considerably weakening the Entente. The Bolshevik Revolution offered a challenge to the existing political and socioeconomic order of Europe. Its slogan Peace without Annexations and Indemnities and its championship of self-determination of peoples struck a responsive chord in the war-weary masses. It also put fear in the heart of the defenders of the established regime. The war had reached its ideological-revolutionary stage, but its outcome still remained an open question. Could the Central

Powers, victorious in the east, defeat Britain and France before the vast resources of America were thrown into the balance? Would the war end through a proletarian revolution in Europe? Was a compromise peace a possibility? No one had a ready answer, but these momentous questions influenced greatly the developments in 1917 and constituted the broad framework within which one must examine the vicissitudes of the Polish question.

On March 12, the tsarist regime fell. A Provisional Government based on the liberal and democratic parties took over; it was soon to be challenged by the Soviet of Workers' and Soldiers' Deputies. The Poles enthusiastically welcomed the revolution as a victory of freedom over hated tsardom. Those active in Russia concentrated their efforts on gaining assurances from the new regime. Largely due to their efforts, the Petrograd Soviet issued on March 28 an appeal to the Poles recognizing their rights to "national self-determination" and to "complete independence in national and international affairs." The Provisional Government followed suit two days later. Denouncing the false promises of the tsarist government and warning against the duplicity of the Central Powers, its manifesto said that "the creation of an independent Polish state, comprised of all the lands in which the Polish people constitute a majority of the population, would be a reliable guarantee for lasting peace in the new Europe of the future." At the same time the manifesto made it clear that Poland would be united with Russia by "a free military alliance." The document also spoke of "a new fraternal alliance," a "union of our hearts and feelings," and a "future union of our states." Borders between Poland and Russia would be delimited with the consent of a Russian constituent assembly. The Provisional Government appointed a mixed Russo-Polish Liquidation Commission, presided over by Lednicki, and a little later agreed to the formation of a Polish army in Russia.

This was great progress indeed, but numerous Polish politicians, particularly of the Activist group, clearly perceived the limitations of Russian promises. As the historian Askenazy put it, the new Russia had not yet liberated Poland from either the Austro-Germans or from herself, and already she was speaking of four kinds of alliances with Poland and reserving for herself the decision on future borders. After dismissing much of the manifesto as verbiage, Lenin said that the proposed alliance between a "small Poland and a huge Russia amounts to a complete military subjugation of Poland." The Provisional State Council in Warsaw criticized the manifesto for trying to prejudge military and territorial issues and for emphasizing the purely ethnic nature of future Poland. The PPS reminded the council that it could not speak as a government of a free nation, but it voiced similar criticism and invoked the principle of national self-determination of Lithuania, Belorussia, and the Ukraine. The Socialists hoped that the first two peoples would find it advantageous to establish close ties with Poland. Virtually all the Polish political parties signed a declaration favoring a future Polish-Lithuanian union. Even the Interparty Circle voiced reservations about the Russian manifesto.

Piłsudski viewed the Russian Revolution as a turning point, after which the Central Powers rather than Russia would become the main obstacle to the realization of Poland's independence. The State Council had been vainly urging Berlin and Vienna to resolve the question of the Polish army, and in April its wishes were disregarded when the legions were handed over to Beseler. Piłsudski's repeated pleas, that the council resign in protest and publicly list all Polish demands, did not sway the majority of the council. In their opinion the Russian Revolution, by weakening the Entente, was likely to increase the chances of the Central Powers' victory. The conservative upper classes and the church hierarchy worried about the social implications of the Russian Revolution and feared lest a republican and radical trend prevail in Poland. The council pressed Vienna and Berlin to give it control over education and courts; it demanded a regent and a right to send diplomatic representation abroad. But it was unwilling to provoke a breach over military affairs. In the autumn education and justice were indeed handed over to the council, but not any political or military matters.

Piłsudski now had really more in common with the Interparty Circle than with the Activists; in May the PPS, the Populists, and other democratic groups came closer to the circle. They drew away a little later because of ideological incompatibility. Piłsudski considered the Provisional State Council a lost cause that existed in a vacuum, and he pointed to the virtual death of the Austro-Polish solution. Even conservative and democratic adherents to such a solution had to associate themselves with a resolution adopted in May, 1917, by the Polish Circle in Vienna, which demanded a united and independent Poland with access to the sea. Prussian Poles could not openly formulate such demands, but Korfanty was clashing with the Prussian ministers in the parliament, and Berlin was obliged to suspend some of the exceptional laws in Poznania. It was five minutes to twelve, Piłsudski warned. The Congress Kingdom was not yet in danger of a revolution, he said, alluding to the strikes and social unrest sweeping the hungry and improverished country. But a conservative policy of the Wielopolski type could precipitate one.

After unsuccessful negotiations concerning the person of a regent, the council suspended its activities on May 15 but dared not provoke a crisis. Piłsudski and his supporters were pushing toward one, and they chose as the main issue the question of the oath to be sworn by the German-directed Polish Army (Polnische Wehrmacht). When the council agreed to the proposed formula, Piłsudski and his followers resigned. The First and most of the Third Brigade refused to take the oath. Officers and soldiers who were natives of Congress Poland were arrested and interned. Austrian subjects were grouped in the Polish Auxiliary Corps—whose formation had been foreseen as early as the autumn of 1916. It was small, as was Beseler's Polnische Wehrmacht, which had only 139 officers and 2,600 men at the turn of 1917–18. As for Piłsudski, he contemplated various actions, among them an attempt to cross into Russia and assume the command of Polish troops there. But on the night of July 21–22, both he and his chief of staff, Sosnkowski, were arrested, taken to Germany, and eventually imprisoned in the fortress of Magdeburg. The crippled Provisional State Council disappeared on August 25, to make room for other institutions then prepared by the Central Powers.

A decree, dated October 12 and issued on behalf of the two emperors, established: a Regency Council, to be named by the occupation authorities; a State Council, whose character was to be defined later; and a Council of Ministers. The Regency Council was vested with executive powers, and it shared its legislative powers with the new (no longer provisional) State Council. In practice, the regency could only control educational and judicial matters, and the Austrian and German governors were entitled to veto all legislation. The three regents, installed on October 27, were Warsaw's mayor, Lubomirski, the wealthy landowner Józef Ostrowski (1850-1924), and Archbishop Kakowski. They represented upper class conservatism and leaned toward the Austro-Polish solution. The premiership went to Kucharzewski, who returned from abroad and formed his cabinet in early December.[4] The State Council, which was mainly elected, came into existence in June, 1918. Most of its members had once been Passivists and stood close to the political Right. The entire regime had a narrow social base, and much of its policy tended to preserve the ephemeral Polish statehood. The might of the Central Powers impressed them more than the far-off prospects of an eventual victory of the Western powers.

The Polish Left in the kingdom continued to voice demands for a genuine Polish government, parliament, and army. It periodically demanded Piłsudski's release. Prior to his imprisonment, Piłsudski had striven to create some form of cooperation between the Left and the Right. The former created a secret organization (Konwent) of

4. The cabinet had the following ministries: Interior, Justice, Army, Politics, Education, Treasury, Agriculture, Industry and Commerce, Public Works and Social Welfare, and Food.

so-called A parties. The Socialist Jędrzej Moraczewski (1870–1944) and the ranking colonel of the First Brigade, Edward Rydz-Śmigły (1886–1941), played a leading part in the organization. Rydz-Śmigły also commanded its military arm, the POW, which went through an extensive territorial and numerical growth. A corresponding organization of rightist parties, cooperating within a united front of major political parties, never materialized.

The PPS Left and the SDKPiL continued to operate largely on the margins of Polish political life. Split since 1912 into two factions, the SDKPiL regrouped itself and somewhat uneasily cooperated with the PPS Left and the Jewish Bund. Its political effectiveness was seriously impaired by a dogmatic and arrogant rejection of national Polish ideals of unity and independence. Deprived of its most important leaders—Rosa Luxemburg, Marchlewski, and Karl Radek—who were active outside of Poland, the SDKPiL lacked real vision and a sense of tactics. It fared badly in municipal elections in 1916, and it dismissed the Regency Council as merely a "native Polish whip *(knut)*." Given such policies, the Polish Social Democrats could hardly become the spearhead of a revolution in the kingdom.

In the spring and summer of 1917, the Austrians increasingly came to realize that they could not continue the war. Peace based on a return to 1914 would be most desirable, and to gain peace Vienna was even willing to make concessions to Germany in Poland, possibly in Galicia, provided Berlin would make concessions to France. The Germans were hardly enthusiastic. Besides, in early October William II and the foreign ministry became interested in Romania and were inclined to revive the Austro-Polish solution. The high command was willing to go along provided a large frontier strip were carved out of Poland, Austria gave up its part of Silesia, and Germany maintained real economic control over the kingdom.

In all these combinations, Lithuania occupied an important place in the thinking of Berlin. The Two Emperors' Manifesto had encouraged the Lithuanians to work more forcefully for independence. The February Revolution enabled the Lithuanian groups in Russia to be more active, and in March, 1917, a fairly representative Lithuanian National Council came into existence. The united front, however, was short-lived. The Left and the Right split over the question of whether the Lithuanians should declare independence at once or leave the issue of independence, autonomy, or federation with Russia to the decision of the people. In June a Lithuanian "diet" in Petrograd adopted the first position, and the Left withdrew.

Meanwhile developments in occupied Lithuania indicated possibilities of a dialogue with the Germans. In February, 1917, the

German chancellor and the high command permitted the formation of a Lithuanian representative body, and a committee led among others by Smetona and Šaulys emerged in Vilna. It soon learned from Berlin that Lithuania was facing two alternatives. It could either side with Germany and accept a military convention, a customs union, and coownership of strategic railroads, or it was likely to be eventually partitioned between Germany and Russia. In reality, after the Russian Revolution and Wilson's pronouncements, Berlin felt that Lithuania and Courland could not be simply annexed to the Reich. In mid-March the Kowno and Vilna regions were joined to form a militarily administered Lithuania (Militärverwaltung Litauen), and Berlin sought proper external forms to disguise Lithuania's total dependence on Germany.

On September 18, 1917, a Lithuanian conference, composed of over two hundred delegates—mainly intelligentsia, priests, and wealthier peasants—took place with German approval in Vilna. Representatives of other nationalities inhabiting Lithuania were not invited. The conference declared in favor of an independent, democratic, ethnic Lithuania, and left the decision on ties with neighboring countries to a future constituent assembly. It elected a council, Taryba, whose twenty members ranged from conservatives to centrists and nationalists. Only two Social Democrats and one "Polono-Lithuanian" were included. Non-Lithuanian nationalities, whose delegates were to be coopted later, refused to participate. Polish parties in Lithuania immediately denied the Taryba the right to speak in the name of the whole country and the Belorussians took a critical position.

Germany recognized the Taryba as a consultative body which should not venture into real politics, but rather act as a rubber stamp for German decisions. Comparable in some respects to the Polish Provisional State Council, the Taryba did not wish to be a mere tool of Berlin. Many Lithuanians abroad recognized it as the highest national organ, and it made early attempts to win concessions from the Germans. Obviously its bargaining powers were minimal. Desirous of German recognition of Vilna as Lithuania's capital, the Taryba took an anti-Polish stand which the high command exploited for the purposes of a *divide et impera* policy in the east. In November, 1917, the new chancellor, Hertling, acting under the pressure of the Reichstag, recognized the right of self-determination of the ex-Russian nationalities. The Taryba immediately proposed to declare national independence and then enter into a perpetual alliance with Germany. Berlin wished to reverse the order or at least to have the Taryba announce both things simultaneously. The Taryba gave in. On December 11, it declared Lithuania independent, with Vilna as its capital, and placed the state under German protection. The declaration spoke of a perpetual association with the Reich in the form of a military alliance and a customs and monetary union. Former ties to other states—meaning Poland and Russia—were denounced. Berlin was satisfied but did not officially acknowledge the declaration. Lithuanian Socialists protested and unsuccessfully called on their representatives to leave the Taryba.

The Russian February Revolution had greatly affected the diplomacy of the Entente, making it easier for France and for Dmowski to bring the Polish question into the open. The threat of a large German-sponsored Polish army worried Paris and London, and Dmowski exaggerated this threat to obtain some pronouncements on Poland. He was only moderately successful. On June 4, 1917, the French president issued a decree authorizing the creation of a Polish army in France. This move, which caught Dmowski unaware, stemmed largely from Russian concern lest the Polish question be taken up by the United States. There were rumors of a Polish army or even a Polish government on American soil, and Petrograd preferred France to handle the delicate Polish issue in the spirit of the Franco-Russian alliance. The Provisional Government had not abandoned any of the war aims of its predecessor and expected the Western allies to respect Russian interests. On August 15, Dmowski was able to establish the Polish National Committee in Lausanne and a week later moved it to Paris. Although composed largely of National Democrats and Realists, it could claim to represent an important section of Polish public opinion. It maintained contact with the Interparty Circle in Congress Poland and in Russia, as well as with political supporters in Galicia and with the secret Polish Committee in Poznania. In September France recognized it as Poland's spokesman in the Allied camp; between October and December Britain, Italy, and the United States followed suit. After the Bolshevik Revolution, the Committee gradually assumed control over the Polish army in France (agreements of February 22 and September 28, 1918), and in October it named the newly arrived General Haller commander in chief.

Dmowski's political objectives were expressed in a long memorandum entitled *Problems of Central and Eastern Europe*, privately printed in English and French in some five hundred copies. He argued for a complete reconstruction of East Central Europe on the basis of nationality. Advocating the destruction of Austria-Hungary, he supported the creation of an independent Czechoslovakia and the enlargement of other countries, successors to the Habsburg monarchy. As for Poland, Dmowski insisted on a large state, transcending purely ethnic boundaries and including western fringes of the borderlands. The proposed border with Russia, later known as the Dmowski Line although the authorship was Grabski's, corresponded roughly to the line of the second partition. Dmowski's championship of Poland, however, still encountered serious obstacles. Neither Britian nor France, then engaged in secret exchanges with Vienna, wanted to commit themselves to the destruction of Austria-Hungary. The Allies were also unwilling to take on any binding engagements regarding Poznania and Pomerania. Dmowski's argument, that the secret Franco-Russian deal—now publicized by the Bolsheviks—created the worse possible impression among the Poles and had to be countered by a joint Allied statement on Poland, carried little weight. The Inter-Allied Conference of November 29–December 1, 1917, made no reference to Poland; but Premier Orlando of Italy and French Foreign Minister Stephen Pichon did speak of Polish independence in their addresses of December 12 and 27. The situation changed in early 1918, mainly because of current developments in the east, to wit the Central Powers' peace negotiations with the Bolsheviks.

IV. THE YEAR OF INDEPENDENCE

The Conference of Brest-Litovsk (December 22, 1917–March 3, 1918) provided the Bolsheviks with an international platform for peace and national self-determination propaganda. To counter its effectiveness and trying to prevent a separate peace on the eastern front, the West had to clarify its ideology and war objectives. Wilson was emerging as the Western champion, but Lloyd George also wished to place his views on record. On January 5, 1918, he delivered a major speech in which he said that "an independent Poland, comprising all those genuinely Polish elements who desire to form part of it, is an urgent necessity for the stability of Western Europe." Five days later came the Fourteen Points of Wilson, and Point Thirteen stated that "an independent Polish State should be erected which should include the territories inhabited by indisputably Polish populations, which should be assured a free and secure access to the sea, and whose political and economic independence and territorial integrity should be guaranteed by international covenant." Wilson's pronouncements made him a hero in the eyes of the Poles, even if, as Dmowski discovered in Washington, "access to the sea" could be understood to mean internationalization of the Vistula River and not recovery of Pomerania. Still, Wilson's pronouncement, for which Colonel House, who in turn was influenced by Paderewski, bears much credit, was the most important and decisive statement yet to come from the West.

To appreciate fully the tenor of Allied diplomacy, one must go back and examine the impact of the October Revolution on Polish and related questions. After seizing power, the Bolsheviks issued a Decree on Peace and a Declaration of the Rights of the Peoples of Russia. The decree urged peace without annexations and contributions, and defined the former as forcible incorporation of a nationality irrespective of when and where it occurred. The declaration granted all former nationalities of Russia the right to self-determination including secession and formation of national states. But Moscow was not inclined to preside over a decomposition of the former Russian Empire; both domestic events and the peace negotiations at Brest-Litovsk indicated that clearly.

The Bolsheviks demanded German evacuation of all occupied territories not because of the inviolability of historic Russian frontiers —"formed by acts of violence against peoples, especially the Polish people"—but because of the right of concerned nationalities to determine their own fate. They rejected the German argument that the Poles had already determined their fate in Congress Poland. They pointed to the real conditions there and said that Berlin and Vienna had not even allowed the Kucharzewski government to be represented at Brest-Litovsk. This was true, and Kucharzewski informed the Central Powers that the Polish nation could not recognize decisions taken in its absence. The Bolsheviks viewed the Regency Council as a German puppet, but they declared repeatedly that they would recognize a Polish delegation representing the people. The Bolshevik stand at Brest-Litovsk contrasted strangely with their activities at home. They forcibly dissolved a Belorussian congress in Minsk which in late December tried to take over Belorussia. They invaded the Ukraine, where the Central Council (Rada) had announced the formation of a republic in November, 1917, and declared full independence on January 22, 1918.

With the Ukrainians denouncing Bolshevik violations and two delegates of the SKDPiL bitterly attacking German policies in Poland, the conference became an arena for verbal fencing. On the whole, the Bolsheviks were scoring, and Polish Socialists and leftist Democrats regarded Lenin as a friend of the Polish cause. The Taryba in turn, emboldened by Russian demands that the Germans produce the evidence of Lithuanian self-determination, decided on February 16 to repeat its statement about independence without any mention of ties with Germany. Berlin objected and hard bargaining followed. There were even some contacts between Lithuanians and Poles, and later, in June, there was an abortive agreement on cooperation. The agreement had no future. The Poles objected to the Taryba as such; the Lithuanians wished to preserve it as a convenient instrument. On February 16, 1918, the Taryba declared Lithuania's independence. Berlin was furious, and after the signing of the Treaty of Brest-

Litovsk forced the Lithuanians to return to its original declaration of December, 1917. Germany recognized Lithuanian independence but made it conditional on future links with the Reich. In June, the Taryba transformed itself into a State Council of Lithuania (Lietuvos Valstybas Taryba) and announced the creation of a constitutional monarchy under Prince Wilhelm Urach. Berlin did not acknowledge the change and made no promises concerning Urach and Lithuania's constitutional regime. Given this state of affairs, the Socialists resigned from the Taryba, and Gabrys, after failing to persuade Smetona to set up a Lithuanian representation on the Allied side, denounced the Taryba as a reactionary tool of the Germans. The future of Lithuania appeared dark and uncertain.

Brest-Litovsk greatly affected the Ukraine and to some extent Belorussia. After the signing of the treaty, the executive committee of the previously dispersed Belorussian congress, which had constituted itself into a government in February, proclaimed a Belorussian People's Republic on March 25. The Germans ignored it; the Bolsheviks were busy preparing a Communist takeover. The Ukrainian situation was very different. On February 9, 1918, the Central Powers signed a peace treaty with the Ukrainian Rada at Brest-Litovsk, although the Rada had lost most of the country to the Bolsheviks. In March, German troops entered Kiev and restored the Rada, which, however, did not prove to be a docile instrument. Consequently it was deposed, and the conservative regime of Hetman Skoropadsky installed in its place. Berlin, and especially Vienna, looked on the treaty of February 9 as a "bread peace" which opened the economic riches of the Ukraine to the Central Powers, but there were also important political aspects. The new Ukraine, even more than Lithuania, was to curb Polish ambitions and activities. The formerly Polish borderlands were "liberated" only to form a chain of vassal states that hemmed in Poland and were dependent on Berlin.

The Ukrainian treaty provided for a transfer of the Kholm region to the Ukraine. It also contained a secret promise of separation of Eastern Galicia and the creation of a Ukrainian crownland in the Habsburg monarchy. Foreign Minister Czernin, who was unfriendly to the Poles, was willing to take the risk of antagonizing them, and Vienna apparently miscalculated the extent of their opposition. When a crisis developed, the Austrian government sought to assure the Poles that their interests would not be injured. The harm, however, was done, and the treaty dealt a death blow to the Austro-Polish solution. News about the projected cession of Kholm and rumors about Eastern Galicia raised outcries of a "fourth partition of Poland." The Kucharzewski cabinet resigned in protest, and so did the governor of the Austrian zone, General Stanisław Szeptycki (1867–1946). The

Regency Council declared that Brest-Litovsk had undermined the basis of the Two Emperor's Manifesto; after fifty years of cooperation with the government, the Polish Circle in Vienna joined the opposition. Mass manifestations of all kinds occurred. The Polish Auxiliary Corps reacted vehemently, and a number of its units led by General Haller broke through the Austrian lines and marched into the Ukraine. Vienna was incensed, and trials of Poles began and quickly became a *cause célèbre*.

Haller's aim was to join the Polish formations that existed in Russia. Created during the chaotic days of the Provisional Government and affected by internal Polish dissensions, these troops consisted of three army corps. The first, commanded by a former tsarist general, Józef Dowbór-Muśnicki (1867–1937), operated in Belorussia; the other two were stationed in the Ukraine. After the Bolshevik Revolution, these troops became the object of agitation on the part of the SKDPiL which controlled the Polish Commissariat set up by the Bolsheviks. Consequently, some Polish Red Army detachments emerged and were later organized in the Western Rifles Division. Dowbór-Muśnicki attempted to maintain neutrality in the developing civil war in Russia, but eventually he found himself in open warfare against the Bolsheviks. The other two corps, largely engaged in defending Polish property against the revolutionary peasantry, also became involved in hostilities. Emissaries of the POW, acting in some contact with the Interparty Circle, sought to extricate the Polish troops from Russia and bring them in touch with the Entente. Dowbór-Muśnicki saw the salvation of his troops in placing them under the protection of the powerless Regency Council and in negotiating with the Germans. In May, 1918, he had to capitulate to the latter. Haller's troops in the Ukraine offered resistance to the Germans but were defeated in the battle of Kaniev. Only small Polish units that were cooperating with the intervening Entente remained in Murmansk, Odessa, or Siberia. Individual officers and soldiers escaped to the West, and among them was Haller himself.

In the summer of 1918, confusion prevailed in Congress Poland, Galicia, and the eastern borderlands. A new government of the Regency Council proposed to Berlin on April 29 to negotiate a concrete settlement for the kingdom allied with the Central Powers. This move, dictated in part by a belief in German invincibility and in part by fears of a social revolution, made little sense. The Interparty Circle, which had a strong representation in the State Council, opposed any concessions to Germany. So did the POW, which in late 1918 stepped up its activities. The PPS opposed the Central Powers, and its fighting squads began to harass the Germans. In Prussian Poland, the election of a new chairman of the Polish Circle marked the crystallization of an unequivocally anti-German stand. Efforts of the new Austrian foreign minister, Burián, to undo the effects of Czernin's policy—by revising the Kholm deal and canceling the Eastern Galician protocol—came too late to breathe any life into the moribund Austro-Polish idea.

Official pronouncements from the West and from Russia assisted the Polish cause. On June 3, 1918, the Inter-Allied Conference of Versailles described the creation of a united, independent Poland, with free access to the sea, as one of the conditions of a just and lasting peace. In secret Franco-Austrian negotiations there was still mention of a historic Poland associated with Austria, but such schemes lacked reality. In late August, Russia signed supplementary treaties with the Central Powers and took this occasion to invalidate a number of old conventions between the tsarist regime and the Germanic states. The third paragraph of the Soviet decree formally denounced the partition treaties "as contrary to the principle of national self-determination and to the sense of revolutionary legality of the Russian people." The precise meaning of this clause, often called mistakenly *the* decree on partitions, is controversial. The Russians did not intend to say that they were now recognizing the *status quo* of 1772, although some Poles interpreted this decree to mean precisely that. Nor could the Russians legally invalidate multilateral treaties. At best, the clause could mean that Russia no longer considered herself legally bound to uphold German and Austrian rights to Polish lands acquired through the partitions.

In September the Regents in Warsaw dismissed the cabinet which had been compromised by its overtures to Berlin. A month later, seeking to efface the stigma of German nominees, they issued a proclamation to the nation announcing a united and independent Poland, the dissolution of the State Council, a promise of a truly representative cabinet, and preparations of an electoral law. The Populist and Socialist leaders, Daszyński and Witos, refused, however, to participate in a Regency cabinet, and the PPS declared a one-day strike demanding social reforms and a constituent assembly. Thus, the new cabinet had a National Democratic coloring, but in order to placate the Left, the imprisoned Piłsudski was named minister of war. By October, the Regency Council took over the administration and the Polnische Wehrmacht, whose size increased significantly.

The Poles were rapidly advancing toward independence. Emperor Charles' manifesto of October 16, which sought to save the Habsburg monarchy by transforming it into a federation, enjoyed the support of only the Cracow conservatives. As a last concession to them, the word "also" was added to a Galician-Polish statement that said that the Poles considered themselves "also" citizens of a Polish state.

The Liquidation Commission, set up in Cracow on October 29, comprised only Socialists, National Democrats, and "Piast" Populists. It proceeded to sever ties with the monarchy and to organize a Polish administration. In Teschen Silesia, a Polish National Council emerged which proclaimed incorporation into Poland. In order to avoid conflict with the Czechs, it agreed to draw a temporary demarcation line that cut Teschen into two parts. Preparing to take over control in Eastern Galicia, the Liquidation Commission was confronted with the proclamation of a West Ukrainian Republic in Lemberg and with the Ukrainian attempt to seize the city; the Poles were shocked and surprised, although they should have known better. Already after the Austro-German conquest of Congress Poland in 1915, the Ukrainian National Council had demanded the fulfillment of Ukrainian aspirations in Kholm and Volhynia, and the creation of a large state allied with Germany and Austria-Hungary. After the Two Emperors' Manifesto, the Ukrainians demanded that should Galicia receive a new status, its eastern part be separated and endowed with its own diet. At the time of the proclamation of the Ukrainian Republic in Kiev in November, 1917, conferences of political leaders held in Lemberg reiterated the demand for separation of Eastern Galicia.

Brest-Litovsk seemed to have satisfied Ukrainian aspirations, but in practice great difficulties remained. Concessions were shelved, and the Ukrainians were unable to make effective use of their Sich Riflemen under Archduke Wilhelm ("Vasyl Vishyvanyi"), a potential candidate for the Ukrainian throne. A Ukrainian Constitutent Assembly—comprising the National Council, members of the Reichsrat, as well as members of the diets of Galicia and Bukovina, and three delegates of major political parties—met in Lemberg on October 18 and 19. Invoking Charles' manifesto, it resolved to constitute a Ukrainian state. Although there was a tendency to lean on Vienna, the precise links with Austria were not determined. Nor did the assembly decree a union with the Ukrainian Republic, given the uncertainty of the Skoropadsky regime. On October 20, a West Ukrainian Republic was formally declared in a statement read in front of the Uniate St. George's Cathedral in Lemberg. The method of actual takeover in Eastern Galicia was unresolved. After feverish exchanges with Vienna, the Ukrainians were told that the government would consider the matter on October 31. Fearing that the Polish Liquidation Commission would assert its authority in the meantime, the Ukrainians decided on a *fait accompli*.

In the early morning of November 1, Ukrainian flags were hoisted on public buildings in Lemberg. The Austrian governor was interned; he refused to sanction the coup, but at the same time he delegated his powers to the Ukrainian deputy mayor. In turn, the Austrian military commander ordered the demobilization of non-Ukrainian units, which produced chaos that did not prove beneficial to the Ukrainians. Led by the POW, local Poles offered stubborn resistance and heavy fighting began. While hostilities went on in Lemberg, the Ukrainians succeeded in gaining control of the countryside.

A few days after the Ukrainian coup, the Lithuanian Taryba instructed Augustinas Voldemaras (1883–1946) to form an independent government for the country. The Taryba, however, faced a challenge from two directions. The Lithuanian Poles quickly organized themselves into self-defense units in Vilna; the Lithuanian Bolsheviks led by Mickevičius-Kapsukas and Angarietis prepared to seize power in cooperation with the Red Army. Lemberg in the south and Vilna in the north became two symbols of a showdown between an emerging Poland and the nations that had once been part of the commonwealth.

Meanwhile under Prussian rule, where already in October the Poles had declared for an independent and united Poland with access to the sea, a Supreme People's Council and a provincial diet appeared in Posen. But instead of creating *faits accomplis* in the revolution-torn Germany, the Prussian Poles decided to await the decision of the future peace conference. In Warsaw the cabinet tried to break publicly with the Regency Council, whose unpopularity had prevented the creation of a coalition ministry, but the Regents succeeded in forcing its resignation. The Left then took the initiative. Preferring a democratic coalition to either broad Right-Left cooperation or a revolutionary front advocated by the extreme Left, Socialists, "Wyzwolenie" Populists, and radical intelligentsia groups in Lublin proclaimed on November 7 the Provisional Government of the Polish People's Republic. Daszyński assumed the premiership and Rydz-Śmigły took charge of military affairs. Witos, whose name appeared among the ministers, denied his adherence. This meant that "Piast" Populists were keeping their options open.

The new government's Lublin Manifesto abolished the Regency Council and declared Poland a republic. It announced elections to a constituent sejm on the basis of universal, direct, secret, proportional, and equal suffrage. It decreed such social reforms as an eight-hour working day, nationalization of entailed estates and forests, and the creation of a people's militia. It reserved for the constituent sejm the decision on expropriation of large estates, nationalization of mines, the oil industry, and transportation, as well as on introduction of social welfare and the establishment of compulsory and free education. The manifesto called on Lithuanian Poles to recreate, in harmony with Lithuanians and Belorussians, the historic Lithuanian state. Poles in Galicia and the Ukraine were asked to seek a peaceful solution of existing conflicts. The manifesto said that the nations of Lithuania, Belorussia, Ukraine, Bohemia, Slovakia, and Poland should assist each other in the task of creating an association of free and equal nations.

The Polish Right saw the Lublin Manifesto as a quasi-Communist statement. The extreme Left regarded it as a clever move to sabotage a proletarian revolution. Workers' councils were arising in parts of Congress Poland, and the chaotic conditions accompanying the collapse of Germany produced strikes, unrest, and outbreaks in the countryside. Although most of the leaders of the Lublin government belonged to the Konwent of Leftist organizations and seemingly executed Piłsudski's old directives, their action was in keeping with the PPS program of a democratic coalition. Whatever the motives of the coalition, the short-lived government accomplished one thing: it asserted the importance of a social program and of a republican and democratic form of government.

On November 10, 1918, Piłsudski, who had been released from Magdeburg in the midst of the German revolutionary upheaval, arrived in Warsaw. The Regents greeted him as a man who could avert a social revolution. The POW and the Left welcomed him as their hero. Even the National Democrats did not openly oppose him. His credentials as a national leader who had fought against all the partitioning powers seemed impeccable. Nor was there any rival in Poland who could successfully challenge him. On November 11, the day of the armistice in the West, the Regents handed over the army to Piłsudski. The commanders in Warsaw, Cracow, and Lublin recognized his authority. Three days later the Regency Council transferred civilian power to Piłsudski and dissolved itself. The resignation of the Lublin government followed. Piłsudski was virtual dictator of Poland.

But what was the Poland that had reemerged after 123 years of being partitioned? Although a successor to the old commonwealth, Warsaw-controlled Poland comprised at this point only the Congress Kingdom and Western Galicia, that is, only a part of the lands that were ethnically Polish. Although Piłsudski successfully arranged an orderly German evacuation of the kingdom, German troops remained, in accord with Article 12 of the Armistice, in the borderlands and the Baltic countries. Their value as a dam against the Bolshevik westward drive was problematic, and they pursued their own aims in the Baltic region and Lithuania. While the Polish army was tiny and ill-equipped, it constituted a real asset in the chaotic conditions that accompanied Poland's rebirth. The Polnische Wehrmarcht had some five thousand men; the POW, about twenty thousand. In addition, there were semimilitary formations of various kinds. This army had to suffice for the time being to carry on the struggle in

Eastern Galicia, and a little later against the Czechs and the Bolshe- viks. The modern army of Haller was not destined to return to the country for several months, and its return was linked with the broader question of relations between Piłsudski's government and the French- sponsored National Committee of Dmowski in Paris. In political and military terms Poland was reemerging amidst untold difficulties. The economic picture was scarcely any brighter.

The lands that eventually made up postwar Poland were in a sorry state. War operations, forced evacuations of the civilian population, removal of workers, compulsory deliveries of raw materials, and dismantling of entire industries left deep scars on the Polish economy and society. Over 40 percent of the larger bridges, 63 percent of the railroad stations, and 48 percent of the rolling-stock mills were destroyed. Nearly half of the Congress Kingdom's industrial plants had been closed as early as 1916. By 1918, only 15 percent of the industrial workers in Congress Poland were still actively employed. The country regressed toward an agrarian economy, but agriculture had also been severely hit. The amount of land under cultivation dropped to 25 percent of the prewar total in the Austrian part of Poland, to 37 percent in the German part, and to 55 percent in the Russian part. Galicia and the Congress Kingdom lost around 30–40 percent of their horses and around 20–30 percent of their cattle. After the devastation of some 1.5 million acres of woods, there was a serious problem of deforestation. On the whole, villages and small towns suffered more through burning and wanton destruction than did big cities. Peasant farms fared worse than did landed estates.

The demographic picture was affected by a dislocation of the population and high mortality rates. Out of the millions of Poles who had fought in the partitioning armies, 450,000 were killed and 900,000 wounded. Some 700,000 people moved east as a result of the Russian forced evacuation. Large numbers of workers had been sent to Germany and Austria. The "Spanish influenza" epidemic claimed numerous victims. The Poland that reemerged in 1918 was a ruined country with an impoverished and hungry population. Cur- rency confusion and inflation led to black markets, speculation, and disorder. That such a country avoided revolution, became integrated, and survived large scale struggles which lasted until 1920 was short of miraculous.

The debate over the factors that proved decisive for Poland's recovery has been going on for years. Was Piłsudski or Dmowski the savior? Was Wilson or the Bolshevik Revolution mainly responsible for the country's rebirth? As in the case of every great historical event, multiple factors combined to bring about Poland's resuscita- tion. The war and the complex sociopolitical upheavals that accompanied it, the collapse of the partitioning powers, the Russian revolutions, and the emergence of a new diplomacy—each had its share in the final outcome. And yet, all the favorable circumstances notwithstanding, Poland might not have reappeared on the map of Europe had it not been for the stamina, patriotism, and determination of the Polish nation, which had never fully accepted the verdict of the partitions.

# The Era of "Young Poland"

AT THE turn of the nineteenth and twentieth centuries Polish cultural and intellectual life underwent important changes. Its stimuli were provided by the socioeconomic evolution in the Polish lands, even if the pace of that evolution was not rapid. Material progress continued, although significant differences between the more advanced Prussian Poland and the more backward Austrian and Russian parts remained. On the whole, changes were more striking in the towns than in the countryside. The gap between the richer and the poorer strata of society was not essentially narrowed. In Congress Poland, only four cities had adequate sewage systems and running water. But electric power was coming into wider use, and Warsaw and several other cities in the kingdom had power plants, as did twenty-five towns in Galicia. Between 1894 and 1904, the electric streetcar made its appearance in Warsaw, Lemberg, and Cracow. The telephone network in Warsaw had around twenty thousand subscribers. A few automobiles owned by rich sportsmen, aristocrats, and financiers could be seen around the country. Cinematography made its debut. Interest in physical education and sports gained wider circles. Soccer became popular, and the old gymnastic societies gained new impetus with the appearance of boy scouting which came to the country from England around 1910. The "discovery" of the Tatra Mountains made the village of Zakopane a favorite resort and a meeting place for Poles, not only from Galicia but from other parts of Poland as well.

During the decades preceding World War I, the popular press made important strides. Newspapers such as *Wiek Nowy* (New Age) and *Illustrowany Kurjer Codzienny* (Illustrated Daily Courier) became a new mass cultural media. Sizes of editions continued to increase. The Pomeranian *Gazeta Grudziądzka* (Grudziądz Gazette) exceeded 120,000 copies by 1914; the Jewish-language paper *Hejret* in Warsaw was even larger. Party newspapers in Galicia, for instance, the Socialist *Naprzód* (Forward) in Cracow, attested to a politicization of the masses. Still, this point should not be overstressed. The dominant outlook of the period continued to be gentry-bourgeois in character, although this view was being assailed by socialism, populism, and modern nationalism.

In literature, the positivist-bourgeois trend came under attack when modernism swept most of Europe at the turn of the century. In a way this phenomenon was comparable to the onslaught of romanticism on classicism at the beginning of the century—a struggle of the young against the old. Germany (das Junge Deutschland) and Scandinavia, and especially such figures as Nietzsche, Schopenhauer, Wagner, and Hamsun, had a tremendous impact on the Polish movement which was given the name "Young Poland." Reacting against objective realism, social utilitarianism, and the cult of science, the adherents of this movement at first took up the then current slogan Art for Art's Sake. Rejecting the "philistine-bourgeois" outlook, they stressed aestheticism, pure form, and art as an absolute. In search of the inner being, the "naked soul," the artist regarded himself as standing above materialistically inclined mortals. Proclaiming their new truths, the members of "Young Poland" proudly espoused the style of bohemia and defied accepted conventions.

The movement began around two reviews: *Życie* (Life), published in Cracow, and *Chimera*, edited by Zenon Przesmycki ("Miriam," 1861–1944) in Warsaw. In 1898 the term "Young Poland" was used in *Życie* and began to gain currency. It was paradoxical and perhaps inevitable that the strongly conservative and traditional city of Cracow should become the center of "Young Poland's" activity. The arrival of Stanisław Przybyszewski (1868–1927) from Germany, where he had gained repute as an author of German-language manifestoes, novels, and dramas, gave a real impetus and much publicity to the movement. Przybyszewski elevated modernism, or, as its opponents called it, decadentism, to a new sacred dogma. Preoccupied with sexual passion as the most powerful and elemental manifestation of human beings, Przybyszewski was not unlike Strindberg in his portrayal of the struggle between lust and conscience. He and his followers shocked Cracow's elite, for whom the bohemian artists, who flaunted their rejection of social morality, assumed almost demoniac qualities. The erotic poetry, symbolism, and the use of an artificially archaic language seemed to be not only a challenge to the accepted and recognized artistic canons, but also an attack on the Polish way of life as understood by the Cracow conservatives.

"Young Poland" quickly acquired specific features which distinguished it from late European modernism. "Art for art's sake" was virtually impossible to cultivate in a partitioned country whose intellectual elite had always been in the forefront of the national struggle. While "art for art's sake" broadened the horizons of Polish literature and visual arts by bringing in Scandinavian or even Japanese elements, it was bound to succumb to a preoccupation with national and social themes. The neoromanticism of "Young Poland" led to a cult of Słowacki and a discovery of Norwid, whose national and democratic message fell on fertile soil. The most outstanding writers of the period used their new artistic forms and ideas with reference to the perennial Polish question. Wyspiański brought the national elements to the foreground; Orkan's main concern was with social problems; in Żeromski the national and the social merged. Perhaps the most characteristic and lasting achievements of "Young Poland" were in the field of drama. But, since most of the representatives of the movement used a variety of artistic media, the impact of "Young Poland" was evident in prose, poetry, literary criticism, visual arts, and music.

Stanisław Wyspiański (1869–1907) was most representative of "Young Poland" and almost epitomized its best qualities. His death at the age of thirty-eight strikes one as a dramatic reminder of the youthful and the tragic elements of the movement. Wyspiański was a symbolist who had experimented with virtually all the visual arts, and he was a poet; but above all he was a playwright and a man of the theater. To the theater he brought his fantastic imagination and his concept of drama seen in theatrical terms. He was both a playwright and a director with his own vision of stagecraft. A precursor of an autonomous "art of the theater," he was a unique phenomenon even on an all-European scale. Wyspiański towered over his contemporaries, and his influence reached the greatest Polish political figures— Dmowski and Piłsudski. His language alone had myth-creating qualities; many phrases from his masterpiece *The Wedding (Wesele)* became proverbial in Polish.

In Wyspiański's plays one finds a combination of elements characteristic for the period (for instance, a fascination with ancient tragedy), together with specifically Polish components. A neoromanticist, he rejected the romantic myth whose phraseology and lofty dreaming became a substitute for action. He opposed messianism and the attitude of nostalgic resignation. He expressed his own convictions in a great number of plays written during one decade. In *Acropolis*, the actors are figures from tapestries and tombstones in Wawel Castle and Cathedral; while the national message is there, the play also reflects Wyspiański's preoccupation with death and his inner struggles. In *November Night (Noc Listopadowa)*, Greek goddesses of victory mingle with youthful insurgents, and the words "all that is to live must die" seemed highly relevant to young Polish conspirators and legionnaires of the 1914–18 period. The most striking of Wyspiański's plays, *The Wedding*, has been called a national misterium and was a traumatic experience for contemporaries. Wyspiański turned a portrait of an actual wedding in a village near Cracow into a symbol of deep national significance. The drama is both a satire on facile nationalist poses, and an attempt to shake national consciousness out of lethargy. Using suggestive expressions and occasional biting irony, the author shows the inner strength of the peasantry; but he also exposes the superficial belief, then current among the propeasant intelligentsia, in the maturity and leadership of the peasant masses. *The Wedding* was at once recognized as a major literary and national event.

Wyspiański's influence and appeal survived him, but even during his lifetime the impact he made on his contemporaries was of political and social significance. Contemporary Polish patriots recognized the meaning of such words as "she who has died claims her own" *(upomina się o swoje umarła)* and saw in them a call for national action.

The influence exercised by Wyspiański is comparable to that of his contemporary, who, however, lived for nearly two decades longer, Stefan Żeromski (1864–1925). A prose writer, although his prose resembles at times blank verse, Żeromski had lyrical and romantic inclinations. In his writings he combined pessimism and a naturalistic approach with lyrical outbursts and a fine appreciation of nature and of moods. He also had a feeling for the beauty of language. While Wyspiański uttered bitter truths about his nation and his fellow men, Zeromski engaged in agonizing national soul searching. Fearing for the future of his nation, he insisted that "its wounds be kept open lest they heal in ignominy." He spoke of his country as being caught between two millstones (Germany and Russia) and said that Poland had to harden to granite in order to escape destruction.

A writer close to the PPS, although never an actual member, Żeromski exercised a great sway over the radical youth of the early twentieth century. Preoccupied with national problems, he violently reacted against social injustice. His great historical novel *Ashes (Popioły)*, which has at times been compared to Tolstoy's *War and Peace*, is concerned with Polish efforts during the Napoleonic wars. Had these efforts all turned to ashes, or is the last scene in the book, of the invasion of Russia in 1812, meant to point to another great war which would bring deliverance to Poland? *The Faithful River (Wierna Rzeka)* deals with the January Insurrection, and its pervading pessimism can also be found in novels with a predominantly social content: *Sisyphean Labors (Syzyfowe Prace)* and *Homeless People (Ludzie Bezdomni)*.

A writer slightly younger than Żeromski, Władysław S. Reymont (1867–1925), can be regarded as a "Young Poland" modernist only in a special sense. His is a realist style, and his great novel *The Peasants (Chłopi)* has hardly any symbolistic or romantic overtones, although it has certain "Young Polish" stylizations. *The Peasants,* which won Reymont a Nobel Prize in 1924, is a superbly narrated story that has pathos but no sentimentality. The peasant is shown as subject to a relentless struggle for existence against nature and his neighbors. He is neither idolized nor patronized, and Reymont makes him speak his own dialect. One of his lesser novels, *The Promised Land (Ziemia Obiecana),* has some social importance insofar as it deals with the seamy side of life in the industrial town of Łódź.

The period of "Young Poland" produced a score of authors of talent and distinction, although not all of them were part of the new movement. Władysław Orkan (1875–1930), already mentioned for his concern with social problems, stands out as a novelist and a playwright. Greatly attached to his native Tatra highlands, he described their savage beauty and the misery of their inhabitants. Important are the novels of Wacław Berent (1873–1940) and Wacław Sieroszewski (1858–1945), the dramas of Karol H. Rostworowski (1877–1938), and the works of several others. Józef Weyssenhoff (1860–1932), who strongly opposed "Young Poland," also deserves to be mentioned.

Three poets stand out as heralds of "Young Poland": Tetmajer, Kasprowicz, and Staff. Kazimierz Przerwa-Tetmajer (1865–1940), a lyrical poet, is best remembered for his introduction of the highlanders' *(górale)* folklore into Polish literature. The elemental in the highlanders' life appealed greatly to this typical child of the *fin de siècle,* whose early poetry was "decadent" and pessimistic. Tetmajer's lyricism is reflected even in his stories written in prose (and in the highland dialect), *In the Rocky Highlands (Na Skalnym Podhalu),* although these stories have epic qualities as well.

Jan Kasprowicz (1860–1926), a lyrical poet, resembles somewhat in his sweep Whitman. His lyricism was profoundly philosophical, and he was more universalist in outlook than was Tetmajer. Concerned first with social injustice, particularly peasant misery, he later became engrossed in religious and philosophical themes. Protesting human suffering, he explored the theme of struggle between the heroic human spirit and the power of God. Symbolist in his expression, pessimist in his *Weltanschauung,* he characterized well the inner conflict of most of the "young Poland" writers. At times he rejected the concept of beauty of form to achieve a more dramatic effect, but he retained in his descriptions of nature a striking lyrical beauty.

Leopold Staff (1878–1957) differed both from the "modernist" Tetmajer and the "promethean" Kasprowicz. Greatly influenced by

Nietzsche in his early writings, Staff moved in the direction of a refined, polished, and reflective lyricism expressed with superb craftsmanship. Over the years his sadness, which at times bordered on despair, became tempered by a strong belief in truth and love.

Almost all the "Young Poland" writers came from the Austrian and Russian parts of the country, but Przybyszewski and Kasprowicz belied the theory of intellectual barrenness of Prussian Poland. The 1905 Revolution and the impending world war made Polish literature increasingly political. Zeromski's *Ashes* revived the cult of national struggle, and the January Insurrection became a subject of several novels and short stories. In addition to *Faithful River*, Żeromski contributed *Echoes of the Woods (Echa Leśne)*; Orzeszkowa wrote *Gloria Victis*, and a young participant of the 1905 Revolution, Andrzej Strug (Gałecki, 1871–1937), made his debut with *Our Fathers (Nasi Ojcowie)*. Strug's *History of One Bullet (Historia Jednego Pocisku)* —meant for the Russian governor general—was directly relevant for the political situation. Equally relevant were several studies in military history, mentioned elsewhere in this volume, which appeared in Galicia on the eve of the First World War.

Artistic and literary criticism rose to prominence in the cultural milieu of the early twentieth century, with important social and political consequences. The writings of Stanisław Witkiewicz (1851-1915), an outstanding art critic, need to be mentioned, and of even greater note were the contributions of Wilhelm Feldman, an important proponent of Jewish assimilation. Feldman edited the progressive journal *Krytyka*, which subscribed to the goal of national independence and embodied the political aspirations of "Young Poland." The most important and tragic figure among the critics—somewhat reminiscent of Mochnacki—was Stanisław Brzozowski (1878–1911). A Socialist who was expelled from his party on the basis of accusations which were never proved, Brzozowski was a radical who saw literature as an instrument of political action. He attacked the concept of "art for art's sake" and criticized both the romantic and the neoromantic outlook for weakening the individual and national determination to act. His *Legend of Young Poland (Legenda Młodej Polski)*, a pessimistic verdict on contemporary literature, was his largest and best remembered work.

The theater, on which Wyspiański's impact has already been mentioned, rose to new heights. Theaters appeared in Łódź and Vilna, and the Teatr Polski, housed in a new building, achieved great importance. A novel type of a political-literary cabaret appeared in Cracow. It gained wide renown, especially for the satirical verses of Boy (Tadeusz Żeleński, 1874–1941), who was later famous as a writer, critic, and translator of French literature.

In architecture, trends corresponding to Vienna's "seccessionist" style temporarily gained the upper hand. "Secession" was a revolt against classical forms and symmetry and often favored pretentious stylization. The great contribution of "Young Poland" was in the domain of applied art—graphic arts, decorative arts, and artistic crafts—with frequent borrowing of highland motives. Here again the contributions and the ideas of Wyspiański, as well as Witkiewicz's, deserve to be mentioned.

In painting, the period saw the gradual ascendancy of impressionism, although other styles coexisted. The symbolistic and allegorical compositions of Wyspiański, Jacek Malczewski (1854–1929), and Józef Mehoffer (1869–1946) well reflected the artistic outlook of "Young Poland." While Jan Stanisławski (1860–1907), Józef Pankiewicz (1866–1940), and Leon Wyczółkowski (1852–1936) were mainly creating in the homeland, the cubist Tadeusz Makowski (1882–1932) and Olga Boznańska (1865–1940) lived chiefly abroad and identified themselves with the *Ecole de Paris*. The wide public was only slowly accepting the novel forms. It preferred the traditionally and realistically painted lancers and horses of Kossak, and admired the huge panoramic painting of the battle of Racławice installed in a specially constructed rotunda in Lemberg. Among sculptors, the name of Ksawery Dunikowski (1875–1964) began to attract great attention.

Contemporary music derived much of its inspiration from Wagner, Tchaikovsky, Skriabin, and Richard Strauss. Prominent among the "Young Poland" composers were: Mieczysław Karłowicz (1876–1909), whose works were mainly symphonic poems, and Ludomir Różycki (1884–1953) who wrote operas and neoromantic symphonic pieces. This period saw the rise of probably the most gifted and original Polish composer of the first half of the twentieth century, Karol Szymanowski (1882–1937). The internationally famous virtuoso, Ignacy Jan Paderewski (1860–1941), was spreading the fame of Polish music abroad.

As throughout most of the nineteenth century, Polish arts and learning continued to transcend the political borders that separated the partitioned lands. The five-hundredth anniversary of the founding of the Jagiellonian University (or rather its reopening in 1400) drew huge crowds from all the Polish lands to Cracow. The burial of Mickiewicz's remains, brought from France, in Wawel Castle became an all-Polish event. Paderewski's gift of a monument commemorating the Polish victory over the Teutonic Knights at Grunwald in 1410—a reply to German policies that were current in Poznania—was yet another national manifestation. Polish intellectuals moved from one part of the partitioned country to another; Galicia continued to be the center of virtually unrestricted cultural activities. After the 1905

Revolution, many Russian Poles came to study in Galicia and abroad.

Scholarly and academic life reached new dimensions and achievements. Thanks to additional endowments the Polish Academy of Learning in Cracow became financially independent. In Warsaw, the year 1907 saw the founding of a learned society (Towarzystwo Naukowe Warszawskie). Twelve years earlier a private engineering college, the Wawelberg and Rotwand Academy, had been opened in Congress Poland. In Galicia, new departments and chairs were added at Cracow and Lemberg universities, and an agricultural academy appeared in Dublany. After 1906 a Polish Society of Friends of Learning existed for a time in Vilna. Elementary and high school education expanded in all three parts of partitioned Poland, but while Galicia made important strides, Congress Poland remained backward. Between 1904 and 1914 the number of elementary school pupils increased in Congress Poland from 281,000 to 461,000; in Galicia, from 718,000 to 1,336,000; in Prussian Poland, from 1,427,000 to 1,643,000.[1] In relation to the number of inhabitants, one school corresponded in 1914 to 1,900 people in Congress Poland, to 1,400 in Galicia, and to 700 in Poznania. Illiteracy figures around 1900 were: 69 percent in Congress Poland, 56 percent in Galicia, and virtually zero in Prussian Poland. The situation in the Lithuanian, Belorussian, and Ukrainian guberniias was worse than in Congress Poland.

In 1912 and 1913, high school students amounted to sixty-seven thousand in Congress Poland (more than a twofold increase from the years 1903 and 1904), forty-two thousand in Galicia (about 30 percent increase), and thirteen thousand in Poznania. These figures became more meaningful if one realizes that Congress Poland had a large number of private schools patronized mainly by wealthier parents, with Polish as the language of instruction. In Galicia, the number of peasant children who went to high schools and then to universities was on the increase. As regards girls' schools, the Congress Kingdom had the largest number. During the First World War the educational picture in Congress Poland changed drastically. When the German and Austrian occupation authorities handed over education to the Poles, there was a threefold increase in the number of students and schools (both elementary and high schools) between 1915 and 1917. Warsaw university and the Warsaw Politechnika began to function as Polish schools of higher learning. Finally, adult education, which is not included in the above figures and percentages, registered great progress during the period, particularly in Congress Poland and Galicia.

As was the case throughout Central Europe and even in parts of Western Europe, Polish high schools and universities had an elitist

1. The last two figures refer to the period 1901–14.

character. Their scholastic levels were high. Most of the great Polish scholars of these decades were products of these institutions, although many also studied abroad. Among those who became prominent and were the successors or contemporaries of the Polish men of learning mentioned in this volume were natural scientists, humanists, and social scientists. Marian Smoluchowski (1872–1917) who taught at Cracow and Lemberg was a theoretical physicist with great achievements in the field of thermodynamics. Józef Babiński (1857–1932) is considered as one of the founders of neurosurgery; Ludwik Hirschfeld (1884–1954) was a great bacteriologist, who is best remembered for his study of blood groups. In biochemistry, the name of Kazimierz Funk (b. 1884) became internationally known. Maria Skłodowska (1867–1934) achieved world fame in Paris, where together with her husband Pierre Curie she discovered radioactivity. She received first a joint and then an individual Nobel Prize for her work. Kazimierz Fajans (b. 1887) became a pioneer of radiology in the United States. The chemist Ignacy Mościcki (1867–1946) and the cofounder of Swiss hydrotechnology, Gabriel Narutowicz (1865–1922), taught in Switzerland. Both would later become presidents of the Polish Republic. The list of outstanding Polish scientists in the homeland and abroad is long indeed.

In the humanities, the Cracow philosopher Wincenty Lutosławski (1865–1954) symbolized the break with positivism, but his neo-platonism and messianism led him to extremes that affected both his philosophy and his way of life. The philosopher-sociologist Edward Abramowski (1868–1918) was important and influential as a popularizer and social worker. In linguistics, Jan Rozwadowski (1867–1929) and Kazimierz Nitsch (1874–1958) came to rival their famous older Polish colleagues—even the greatest of them, Baudouin de Courtenay.

As always, the role of history was particularly great, and Polish historiography became significantly enriched by the contributions of Szymon Askenazy (1867–1935). A professor of history at Lemberg university, a prolific writer, and a most influential teacher, Askenazy formed his own school in which research in Polish history of the postpartition period constituted a great novelty. His great biographical studies of Łukasiński and Józef Poniatowski had an impact which went beyond academic circles. In contrast to the "pessimistic" Cracow school, Askenazy pointed to the heroism of national struggles, stressed Poland's greatness, and appealed to the young independence-oriented Polish activists. Ideologically, he stood close to the Piłsudski camp, and so did—although with important differences—such younger historians as Wacław Tokarz (1873–1937), Michał Sokolnicki (1880–1967), Marian Kukiel (1885–1973), and the historian of culture

Stanisław Kot (b. 1885). The importance of the nineteenth century was universally recognized, and even political leaders such as Piłsudski, Grabski, and Marchlewski wrote on recent historical subjects.

Rich in controversy, Polish historiography provided an important link in the cultural chain that bound together all parts of partitioned Poland. It greatly affected the Polish intelligentsia which had played a crucial part in preserving the national heritage during the hundred-odd years of partition. When the great challenge came in 1914–18 many of those mentioned in the preceding pages eagerly responded to it by actively promoting the cause of Poland's independence. Largely divorced from vested class interests, the intelligentsia as a group assumed the burden of leadership in recreating the Polish state.

# Bibliographical Essay

THE criteria for the selection of the works cited below require a brief explanation. First of all, most of the relevant studies in English and West European languages are included on the assumption that they would be more accessible to the reader. Second, very few publications in Lithuanian, Ukrainian, or Russian are listed. Third, because of lack of space comments are reduced to a bare minimum, but the reader's attention ought to be drawn to different historiographical trends and especially to the new interpretations of the post–1945 "Marxist school." Within the latter, a distinction must be made between studies written during the Stalinist period, i.e., roughly from 1950 to 1956—which are characterized by rigid dogmatism and even distortions—and later works. Furthermore, studies bearing on contemporary issues, for instance, socialism or relations with Russia, tend to be less reliable than those treating less touchy problems. Two articles by Elizabeth Valkenier, "Soviet Impact on Polish Postwar Historiography" and "Sovietization and Liberalization in Polish Postwar Historiography," *Journal of Central European Affairs* 11 (January, 1952): 372-96, and 19 (July, 1959): 149-73 are illuminating in that respect. Among older historiographical studies, Władysław Smoleński, *Szkoły historyczne w Polsce* (reprint, Wrocław: Ossolineum, 1952) is a classic; and Bronisław Dębiński, Oskar Halecki, and Marceli Handelsman, *L'Historiographie polonaise du XIXème et du XXème siècle* (Warszawa: Société Polonaise d'Histoire, 1937) is a valuable survey. So are two articles by Marian H. Serejski and Andrzej F. Grabski respectively on the Cracow and Warsaw historical schools in *Acta Poloniae Historica* 26 (1972): 127-51 and 153-69. The second author's book on historical thought in Poland is somewhat confusing. For the postwar period, see Stefan Kieniewicz, "Historiografia lat 1795–1914 w dorobku dwudziestolecia," *Kwartalnik Historyczny* 72 (1965): 9-27.

Numerous topics in nineteenth-century Polish history have provoked discussions and controversies. Only a few can be mentioned here as examples. Appraisals of the role of Adam Czartoryski differ considerably, and Handelsman and Kukiel belong to his staunchest supporters. Among younger historians Halicz and Skowronek disagree not only with previous interpretations but also between themselves about the prince's ideas and policies. Was Alexander I or Napoleon the father of the Duchy of Warsaw? Older Russian historians as well as the Pole Loret incline to the former view; Handelsman and recently Halicz, to the latter. Was the November Insurrection of 1830 a logical outcome of the preceding fifteen years? Askenazy and the authors of the postwar *Historia Polski* consider that it was; Bobrzyński, Kukiel, and Leslie tend to ascribe its outbreak to carbonari inspirations. Dutkiewicz in turn questions Kukiel's opinion. Drucki-Lubecki's policies of industrialization were glorified by Smolka and treated more critically by Ajzen. The whole problem of industrialization divides contemporary historians, and Jedlicki especially has questioned the theory of accumulated growth. The VIIIth Conference of Polish Historians in 1958 has devoted a good deal of its discussion to the beginning date of the industrial revolution in Poland. Grodek's thesis that capital accumulation and a capitalist *folwark* occurred only at the very end of the nineteenth century is largely rejected by Kula, Kieniewicz, Halicz, and others.

The January Insurrection of 1863 is still the subject of heated debates. Some of the issues that divide historians have been well brought out in a brief article by Henryk Wereszycki, "Spór o powstanie styczniowe," *Odra*, no. 5/27 (May, 1963): 33-40. A good deal of data is to be found in Stefan Kieniewicz, "A propos du centenaire de l'insurrection de 1863–1864," *Acta Poloniae Historica* 8 (1963): 31-53. Stankiewicz's bibliographical essay in his monograph on Wielopolski gives a good idea of the changing views about the margrave. Naturally, there has been a great deal of disagreement concerning the main political parties, Dmowski, Piłsudski, factors responsible for Poland's rebirth in 1918, and so forth. The origins of socialism, histories of working class movements, and the 1846 peasant uprising are among the sensitive topics of current Polish historiography.

There are several bibliographies of Polish history. The old standard bibliography is that of Ludwik Finkel, reprinted in 1955. It covers the period up to 1815. The postwar *Bibliografia historii Polski* covers, in volume 2, parts 1 and 2, the postpartition era up to 1918. A special bibliography of nineteenth-century Polish history edited by Stanisław Płoski remains uncompleted; the second volume published in 1972 brings it up to 1864. A yearly, or nearly yearly *Bibliografia historii polskiej* prepared by different editors lists current publications. The *Bibliographie zur Geschichte der polnischen Frage bis 1919* published in Stuttgart in 1940 as part of the Weltkriegsbücherei series, numbers 26-28, is a useful selection. The historical biographical dictionary *(Polski Słownik Biograficzny)*, still in progress, is an indispensable aid. The periodical *Acta Poloniae Historica* published in Warsaw is unique in the sense that it prints articles and reviews in Western European languages. Many articles concerned with nineteenth-century Polish history appear frequently in such English language periodicals in the United States, Canada, and England as the *Slavic Review*, the *Eastern European Quarterly* (which in a sense continues the *Journal of Central European Affairs*), *The Polish Review*, *Canadian Slavonic Papers*, and the *Slavonic and East European Review*. Feliks Tych, "Les publications polonaises de sources de l'histoire des XIXe et XXe siècles" in *La Pologne au XIIe Congrès International des sciences historiques à Vienne* (Warszawa: P.A.N., 1965) may be profitable consulted.

GENERAL WORKS

Two principal histories in English are: the *Cambridge History of Poland*, edited by William F. Reddaway (Cambridge: Cambridge University Press, 1941–50), and *History of Poland*, edited by Stefan Kieniewicz (Warszawa: Polish Scientific Publishers, 1968). The major syntheses in Polish are: the prewar *Polska, jej dzieje i kultura od czasów najdawniejszych do chwili obecnej* (Warszawa: Trzaska, Ewert i Michalski, 1927–32) and the staunchly Marxist *Historia Polski* (Warszawa: Polska Akademia Nauk, Instytut Historii, Państwowe Wydawnictwo Naukowe, 1958). A thought-provoking synthesis and interpretation came from the pen of the Cracow conservative historian and politician Michał Bobrzyński, *Dzieje Polski w zarysie* (4th ed., Warszawa: Gebethner i Wolff, 1927–31). Georg v. Manteuffel-Szoege, *Geschichte des polnischen Volkes während seiner Unfreiheit 1772–1914* (Berlin: Duncker and Humblot, 1950), is also of interest.

The period from the last partition to Poland's rebirth in 1918 is treated in three major surveys: Marian Kukiel, *Dzieje Polski porozbiorowe 1795–1921* (London: B. Świderski, 1961); Stefan Kieniewicz, *Historia Polski 1795–1918* (Warszawa: Państwowe Wydawnictwo Naukowe, 1968); and Krzysztof Groniewski and Jerzy Skowronek, *Historia Polski 1795–1914* (Państwowe Zakłady Wydawnictw Szkolnych: Warszawa, 1971). The author of the first work is a prominent Polish scholar recently deceased in London; the second is a learned and prolific Marxist historian. The early decades are the object of a stimulating, semisociological study by Tadeusz Łepkowski, *Polska:*

*Narodziny nowoczesnego narodu: 1762–1870* (Warszawa: Państwowe Wydawnictwo Naukowe, 1967). The post-1863 period has been treated by Henryk Wereszycki, *Historia polityczna Polski w dobie popowstaniowej: 1864–1918* (Warszawa: Instytut Pamięci Narodowej, 1948) and by Władysław Pobóg-Malinowski, *Najnowsza historia polityczna Polski 1864–1945*, mainly the first volume in a revised edition (London: Gryf Printers, 1963), a somewhat one-sided and opinionated study. The theme of modern nationalism is pursued by Łepkowski in "La formation de la nation polonaise moderne dans les conditions d'un pays démembré," *Acta Poloniae Historica* 19 (1968): 18-36, and by Stefan Kieniewicz, "Le développement de la conscience nationale polonaise au XIXe siècle," *ibid.*, 37-48. A valuable essay is that by Peter Brock, "Polish Nationalism" in *Nationalism in Eastern Europe*, edited by Peter F. Sugar and Ivo J. Lederer (Seattle: University of Washington Press, 1969). Stephen P. Mizwa edited a useful collection of biographical essays entitled *Great Men and Women of Poland* (New York: Macmillan, 1942) and concerned mainly with the nineteenth century. Two broad and controversial themes of the period are treated by: Henryk Wereszycki, "Polish Insurrections as a Controversial Problem in Polish Historiography," *Canadian Slavonic Papers* 9 (Spring, 1967): 98-121—a most valuable contribution— and Stanislaus B. Blejwas, "The Origins and Practice of 'Organic Work' in Poland 1795-1863," *The Polish Review* 15, no. 4 (Autumn, 1970), pp. 23-54. A brief survey on another important topic is Günther Weber, *Die polnische Emigration im neunzenthen Jahrhundert* (Essen: Essener Verlagsanstalt, 1937).

ECONOMIC AND SOCIAL PROBLEMS: There is no economic history of Poland in English. Jerzy Jedlicki, "Industrial State Economy of Poland in the 19th century," *Acta Poloniae Historica* 18 (1968): 221-37 is a most stimulating contribution. The crucial peasant question is well covered by the lucid study of Stefan Kieniewicz, *The Emancipation of the Polish Peasantry* (Chicago: University of Chicago Press, 1969). On demography one can still refer to Zofia Daszyńska-Golińska, "L'Accroissement de la population en Pologne à l'époque des partages 1816–1914" in *La Pologne au VIIe Congrès des Sciences Historiques* (Warszawa: 1930), 1:115-25. The most extensive synthesis of Polish economic history is Jan Rutkowski's pioneer work, *Historia gospodarcza Polski* (Poznań: Księgarnia Akademicka, 1947–50). The French translation covers only the prepartition period. Among recent general surveys are Władysław Rusiński, *Rozwój gospodarczy ziem polskich w zarysie* (2nd ed., Warszawa: Książka i Wiedza 1969) and Benedykt Zientara et al., *Dzieje gospodarcze Polski do 1939 r* (Warszawa: Wiedza Powszechna, 1965). An older work still of use is Stanisław A. Kempner, *Rozwój gospodarczy Polski od rozbiorów do*

*niepodległości* (Warszawa: Biblioteka Polska, 1924). Agriculture is
covered in Polska Akademia Nauk, *Histoire de l'economie rurale en
Pologne jusqu'à 1864* (Wrocław: Ossolineum, 1965). A sociological
article by Aleksander Gella, "The Life and Death of the Old Polish
Intelligentsia," *Slavic Review* 30 (March, 1971): 1-27 is important for
bibliographical indications and for presenting the main issues in a
nutshell. Nineteenth- and twentieth-century economic history is
surveyed by I. Kostrowicka, Z. Landau, and J. Tomaszewski, *Historia
gospodarcza Polski XIX i XX wieku* (Warszawa: Książka i Wiedza,
1966); the post-1863 decades are dealt with by Witold Kula in
*Historia gospodarcza Polski popowstaniowej* (Warszawa: Instytut
Pamięci Narodowej, 1948). Industrialization is discussed by Natalia
Gąsiorowska, "Les Origines de la grande industrie polonaise au
XIXe siècle" in *La Pologne au VIe Congrès International des Sciences
Historiques* (Warszawa and Lwów: 1930), and more recently in a
general outline by Andrzej Jezierski and Stanisław M. Zawadzki,
*Dwa wieki przemysłu w Polsce: zarys dziejów* (Warszawa: Wiedza
Powszechna, 1966). Irena Pietrzak-Pawłowska edited *Uprzemysło-
wienie ziem polskich w 19 i 20 wieku: studia i materiały* (Wrocław:
Ossolineum, 1970) which contains a wealth of material including
statistics. Natalia Gąsiorowska, *Polska na przełomie życia gospod-
arczego 1764-1830* (Warszawa: Wiedza, 1947) is useful; Karol Bajer,
*Przemysł włókienniczy na ziemiach polskich od początku XIX w. do
1939 r.* (Łódź: Łódzkie Towarzystwo Naukowe, 1958) surveys the
all-important Polish textile industry. The story of factory workers is
told in a popular outline—an attempted synthesis—by Elżbieta
Kaczyńska, *Dzieje robotników przemysłowych w Polsce pod zaborami*
(Warszawa: Państwowe Wydawnictwo Naukowe, 1970). Of great
importance is the controversial and stimulating study by Jerzy Jedlicki,
*Nieudana próba kapitalistycznej industrializacji: analiza państwo-
wego gospodarstwa przemysłowego w Królestwie Polskim XIX w.*
(Warszawa: Książka i Wiedza, 1964). The above author's English
article, which summarizes his ideas, has been already mentioned. The
history of the Polish peasantry has been attempted by Aleksander
Świętochowski, *Historia chłopów polskich w zarysie* (Lwów and
Poznań: Wydawnictwo Polskie, 1928), an old-fashioned, uneven but
interesting study. Stanisław Śreniowski has recently discussed the
emancipation question in *Uwłaszczenie chłopów w Polsce* (Warszawa: Państwowe Wydawnictwo Naukowe, 1956). The early use of
machinery in agriculture has been described by Julian Bartyś,
*Początki mechanizacji rolnictwa polskiego* (Wrocław: Ossolineum,
1966).

CONSTITUTIONAL, LEGAL, AND IDEOLOGICAL QUESTIONS: The main
textbook on Polish constitutional history after the partitions is still

the old Stanisław Kutrzeba, *Historia ustroju Polski w zarysie* (Lwów and Warszawa: B. Połoniecki, 1920–49). The German translation *Grundriss der polnischen Verfassungsgeschichte* (Berlin: Puttkammer and Mühlbrecht, 1912) is a partial translation of an early edition. Very useful is Bohdan Winiarski, *Les institutions politiques en Pologne au XIXe siècle* (Paris: Picart, 1924), a translation from the Polish. A recent work edited by W. J. Wagner, *Polish Law throughout the Ages* (Stanford, Calif.: Hoover Institution Publication, 1970), has a good chapter by Wacław Soroka on the postpartition period. There is no comprehensive up-to-date history of Polish political thought. The sketchy Wilhelm Feldman, *Geschichte der politischen Ideen in Polen seit dessen Teilungen* (reprint, Osnabrück: O. Zeller, 1964) and the much larger Polish version, *Dzieje polskiej myśli politycznej w okresia porozbiorowym*, remain the standard work on the period after 1795. Marceli Handelsman, *Les idées françaises et la mentalité politique de la Pologne au XIXe siècle* (Paris: F. Alcan, 1927) was later expanded into a larger study of the topic in Polish. Bolesław Limanowski, *Historia demokracji polskiej w epoce porozbiorowej* (4th ed., Warszawa: Książka i Wiedza, 1957) is a classic. William J. Rose, *The Rise of Polish Democracy* (London: G. Bell & Sons, 1946) cannot quite rival it. Bohdan Suchodolski, *Polskie tradycje demokratyczne* (Kraków and Wrocław: M. Arct, 1946) briefly introduces some of the leading Polish democrats. Lidia and Adam Ciołkosz, *Zarys dziejów socializmu polskiego* (London: Gryf Publication, 1966) paint on a broad international canvas the story of Polish socialism throughout the nineteenth century. The second volume published in 1972 brings it up to the 1870s. A large volume by Marian Żychowski, *Polska, myśl socjalistyczna XIX i XX wieku do roku 1918* (Warszawa: Państwowe Wydawnictwo Naukowe, 1972) is a new synthesis written in Poland. Adam Bromke, *Poland's Politics: Idealism versus Realism* (Cambridge, Mass.: Harvard University Press, 1967) has interesting although controversial formulations concerning Polish political thinking. George Krzywicki-Herburt, "Polish Philosophy" in *The Encyclopedia of Philosophy*, edited by Paul Edwards (New York: Macmillan, 1967) may well serve as an introduction to the subject.

CULTURAL HISTORY: There are few general surveys in English. Manfred Kridl, *A Survey of Polish Literature and Culture* (S'Gravenhage: Brill, 1956) is useful. Marian Dobrowolski, *Polish Scholars: Their Contribution to World Science* (Warszawa: Polonia Publishing House, 1960) is quite informative, although badly organized and superficial. The recent book by Czeslaw Milosz, *The History of Polish Literature* (New York: Macmillan, 1969) is very readable, although one has to remember the likes and dislikes of the author. The old monumental works of Aleksander Brückner, *Tysiąc lat kultury polskiej* (reprint, Paris: Księgarnia Polska, 1954–56) and *Dzieje kultury polskiej* (Warszawa: J. Przeworski, 1939–46) have retained their value and importance.

MILITARY HISTORY: Virtually no studies in English exist. Marian Kukiel, "Problèmes des guerres d'insurrection au XIXe siècle," *Antemurale* 2 (1955): 70-79 is pertinent. The same author's *Zarys dziejów historii wojskowości w Polsce* (Kraków: Krakowska Spółka Wydawnicza, 1929) is still valuable, as is Tadeusz Korzon's larger work, *Dzieje wojen i wojskowości w Polsce* (Lwów: Ossolineum, 1923). The most recent and yet unfinished collective study is: Wojskowy Instytut Historyczny, *Zarys dziejów wojskowości polskiej* (Warszawa: Ministerstwo Obrony Narodowej, 1966). A collective survey in French, *Histoire militaire de la Pologne: problèmes choisis, dissertations, études, esquisses* (Warszawa: Ministerstwo Obrony Narodowej, 1970), has two relevent chapters.

THE JEWS: There is need for a balanced history since the classic by Semen M. Dubnov, *History of the Jews in Russia and Poland* (Philadelphia: Jewish Publications of America, 1920) tends to be one-sided. A good relevant chapter can be found in I. Schiper, A. Tartakower, and A. Hafftka, *Żydzi w Polsce odrodzonej* (Warszawa: Wydawnictwo, 1932–33). Also very useful is Majer Bałaban, *Dzieje Żydów w Galicji i w Rzeczpospolitej krakowskiej 1772–1868* (Lwów: B. Połoniecki, 1916). Two recent additions deserve mention: Artur Eisenbach, *Kwestia równouprawnienia Żydów w Królestwie Polskim* (Warszawa: Książka i Wiedza, 1972), and Dawid Fajnhauz, "Ludność żydowska na ziemiach dawnego Wielkiego Księstwa Litewskiego," *Pamiętnik Wileński* (London: Polska Fundacja Kulturalna, 1972), pp. 351–70.

PRUSSIAN POLAND: A good outline is Martin Broszat, *Zweihundert Jahre deutsche Polenpolitik* (Munich: Ehrenwirth, 1963). A thoughtful analysis of the period after the formation of the German Empire is provided by Hans-Ulrich Wehler, "Die Polenpolitik im deutschen Kaiserreich 1871-1918," in *Politische Ideologien und National-staatliche Ordnung: Studien zur Geschichte des 19 und 20 Jahrhunderts, Festschrift für Theodor Schieder*, edited by K. Klux and W. J. Mommsen (München: Oldenburg, 1968). In contrast Manfred Laubert, *Die preussische Polenpolitik von 1772–1914* (Krakau: Burg-Verlag, 1944) while informative, is written from a strongly nationalist position. The most recent study concentrating on "organic work" in Poznania is Witold Jakóbczyk, *Studia nad dziejami Wielkopolski* (Poznań: Prace Komisji Historycznej), vol. 16, no. 2 (1951); vol. 18, no. 3 (1959); and vol. 21, no. 3 (1967). It covers the period from 1815 to 1914. The author has contributed numerous other works, for example a useful collection of essays on the leading figures in Poznania—

*Wybitni Wielkopolanie XIX wieku* (Poznań: Wydawnictwo Poznań-skie, 1959). A useful English treatment is William W. Hagen, "National Solidarity and Organic Work in Prussian Poland 1815-1914," *Journal of Modern History*, vol. 44, no. 1 (March, 1972), pp. 38-64. Among older studies are: Kazimierz Rakowski, *Dzieje Wielkiego Księstwa Poznańskiego w zarysie: 1815-1900* (Kraków: Gebethner, 1904); Stanisław Karwowski, *Historya Wielkiego Ksiestwa Poznańskiego* (Poznań: J. Winiewicz, 1918-31); and Józef Buzek, *Historia polityki narodowościowej rządu pruskiego wobec Polaków od traktatów wiedeńskich do ustaw wyjątkowych 1908 r.* (Lwów: H. Altenberg, 1909). Useful are the mainly descriptive but heavily documented works of Ludwik Żychliński, *Historya sejmów Wielkiego Księstwa Poznańskiego do r. 1847* (Poznań: L. Merzbach, 1867) and Roman Komierowski, 2 vols. *Koła polskie w Berlinie* (Poznań: Dziennik Poznański, 1905 and 1910), covering respectively the 1875-1900 and the 1844-60 periods. Czesław Łuczak has written extensively on Poznanian industries and crafts, notably the two-volume *Przemysł wielkopolski* (Warszawa: Państwowe Wydawnictwo Naukowe, 1959, and Poznań: Wydawnictwo Poznańskie, 1960) which treat the 1815-1914 era. The emancipation of the peasantry has been dealt with by Marian Kniat, *Dzieje uwłaszczenia włościan w Wielkim Księstwie Poznańskim* (Poznań: Towarzystwo Przyjaciół Nauk, 1939-49), and more recently in a shorter form by Jakóbczyk. There are large collective works published periodically on Pomerania and Poznania; an interesting study in English on the Kashubians is Friedrich Lorentz, Adam Fischer, and Tadeusz Lehr-Spławiński, *The Cassubian Civilization* (London: Faber and Faber, 1935). Bolesław Limanowski, *Mazowsze pruskie* (Kraków: Księgarnia Robotnicza, 1925) is useful.

AUSTRIAN POLAND: For a short survey and analysis see: Henryk Wereszycki, "The Poles as an Integrating and Disintegrating Factor," Piotr S. Wandycz, "The Poles in the Habsburg Monarchy," and Ivan L. Rudnytsky, "The Ukrainians in Galicia under Austrian Rule," *Austrian History Yearbook*, vol. 3, pt. 2 (1967), pp. 261-86, 287-13, and 394-429. Among the older and larger studies Franciszek Bujak, *Galicja* (Lwów: H. Altenberg, 1908-10) deserves to be singled out. For constitutional issues see Stanisław Grodziski, *Historia ustroju społeczno-politycznego Galicji, 1772-1845* Prace Komisji Nauk Historycznych, no. 28 (Wrocław, Warszawa, Kraków, Gdańsk: Ossolineum, P.A.N. w Krakowie, 1971) and Konstanty Grzybowski, *Galicja 1848-1914: Historia ustroju politycznego na tle historii ustroju Austrii* (Warszawa and Wrocław: Ossolineum, 1959). Political trends are not always interpreted objectively by Wilhelm Feldman, *Stronnictwa i programy polityczne w Galicji 1846-1906* (Kraków: "Książka," 1907). Cracow's independent existence is surveyed by Stefan

Kieniewicz in "The Free State of Cracow 1815–1846," *Slavonic and East European Review* 26 (1947-48): 64-89.
RUSSIAN POLAND (CONGRESS KINGDOM): Szymon Askenazy's brief *Sto lat zarządu w Królestwie Polskim 1800–1900* (2nd ed., Lwów: H. Altenberg, 1903) provides a good summary of the tsarist rule in the kingdom. Hedwig Fleischhacker, *Russische Antworten auf die polnische Frage 1795–1917* (München: R. Oldenburg, 1941) is popular but informative. Recently many publications have appeared dealing with economic issues. The more general in scope are: Natalia Gąsiorowska, Z *dziejów przemysłu w Królestwie Polskim 1815–1918* (Warszawa: Państwowe Wydawnictwo Naukowe, 1965); Andrzej Jezierski, *Handel zagraniczny Królestwa Polskiego 1815–1914* (Warszawa: Państwowe Wydawnictwo Naukowe, 1967); and the collective works edited by Witold Kula, *Społeczeństwo Królestwa Polskiego: Studia o uwarstwowieniu i ruchliwości społecznej* (Warszawa: Państwowe Wydawnictwo Naukowe, 1965–66). More specialized are the detailed studies of the beginnings of Łódź textile industry: Gryzelda Missalowa, *Studia nad powstaniem łódzkiego ośrodka przemysłowego* (Łódź: Wydawnictwo Łódzkie, 1964); Tadeusz Sobczak, *Przełom w konsumpcji spożywczej w Królestwie Polskim w XIX wieku* (Wrocław: Ossolineum, 1968); and the older, pioneering work of Hipolit Grynwaser, *Kwestia agrarna i ruch włościan w Królestwie Polskim w pierwszej połowie XIX w.* (Warszawa: Kasa Mianowskiego, 1935). The question of Polish eastern borderlands, generally a touchy subject for contemporary historiography, is interestingly presented by Adam Zoltowski, *A Border of Europe: A Study of the Polish Eastern Provinces* (London: Hollis and Carter, 1950). The old and detailed work by Louis Lescoeur, *L'Eglise catholique en Pologne sous le gouvernement russe 1772–1875* (Paris: E. Plon, 1876) has not been superseded by more recent studies.
LITHUANIA: There is no satisfactory history of Lithuania in English. The best general histories are: Adolfas Sapoka, ed., *Lietuvos Istorija* (Kaunas: Svietimo Ministerijos Knygn, 1936), and Jerzy Ochmański, *Historia Litwy* (Wrocław: Ossolineum, 1967). The latter is particularly valuable for Polish-Lithuanian relations and has achieved a good degree of impartiality. On the Lithuanian national awakening see: Jerzy Ochmański, *Litewski ruch narodowo-kulturalny w XIX w* (Białystok: Białostockie Towarzystwo Naukowe, 1965); and Manfred Hellmann, "Die litauische Nationalbewegung im 19 und 20 Jahrhundert," *Zeitschrift für Ostforschung*, 2, no. 1 (1953): 66-106. Alfred E. Senn, *The Emergence of Modern Lithuania* (New York: Columbia University Press, 1959) is important. The only other book in English, Jack J. Stukas, *Awakening Lithuania: A Study on the Rise of Modern Lithuanian Nationalism* (Madison, N.J.: Florham Park Press, 1966)

is very popular and hardly scholarly. The brief essay by M. Birżyszka, *Skrót dziejów piśmiennictwa litewskiego* (Wilno: "Głos Litwy," 1919) contains some useful material. For Polish-Lithuanian relations, Władysław Wielhorski, *Polska a Litwa: stosunki wzajemne w biegu dziejów* (London: Polish Research Centre, 1947) is illuminating. Leon Wasilewski, *Litwa i Białoruś* (Kraków: J. Mortkowicz, 1925) is very valuable and interesting; Nicholas P. Vakar, *Belorussia: The Making of a Nation* (Cambridge, Mass.: Harvard University Press, 1956) is disappointing, although it has a good bibliography. Peter Scheibert, *Die weissrusschiche politische Gedanke bis 1919* (special reprint from *Jomsburg*, 1938) is very useful. So are several chapters in *Pamiętnik Wileński* (London: Polska Fundacja Kulturalna, 1972), notably by Kazimierz Okulicz, Bohdan Podoski, Wacław Panucewicz, and Wiesław Lasocki.

UKRAINE: Extensive bibliographical data as well as a general picture of the Ukrainian evolution in the nineteenth century can best be obtained from *Ukraine: A Concise Encyclopedia*, edited by Volodymyr Kubijovyč (Toronto: University of Toronto Press, 1963). Among several brief histories in English the best are: Mykhailo Hrushevsky, *A History of the Ukraine* (New Haven: Yale University Press, 1941) and William E. D. Allen, *The Ukraine: A History* (New York: Russell and Russell, 1963). Nicholas Czubatyj, "The Modern Ukrainian Nationalist Movement," *Journal of Central European Affairs* 4 (October, 1944): 281-305, gives a brief summary of the salient points. There is some interesting material in the otherwise tendentious Henryk Jabłoński, "Zarys dziejów Ukrainy radzieckiej" in *Sesja naukowa w trzechsetną rocznicę zjednoczenia Ukrainy z Rosją 1654–1954* (Warszawa: Polska Akademia Nauk and Instytut Polsko-Radziecki, 1956). Particularly informative is Leon Wasilewski, *Ukraińska sprawa narodowa w jej rozwoju historycznym* (Warszawa: J. Mortkowicz, 1925). Brief and valuable is Władysław Wielhorski, *Ziemie ukrainne Rzeczypospolitej: zarys dziejów* (London: Koło Lwowian, 1959).

SOURCES: Collections of sources for the postpartition period have been appearing in an unsystematic fashion. The projected and monumental *Źródła do dziejów Polski porozbiorowej* resulted in relatively few volumes which will be listed later. Leonard Chodźko (Comte d'Angeberg), *Recueil des traités, conventions et actes diplomatiques concernant la Pologne* (Paris: Amyot, 1862) is still most valuable. A selection of documents edited by Karol Lutostański, *Les partages de la Pologne et la lutte pour l'independence* (Paris-Lausanne: Commité National Polonais, 1918) is useful. Manfred Kridl, Władysław Malinowski, and Józef Wittlin, eds., *"For Your Freedom and Ours": Polish Progressive Spirit Through the Centuries* (New York: F. Ungar, 1943) contains some well-chosen documents.

The Polish version published in 1945 in London is more comprehensive. A selection of documents on legal-political relations between Russia and the Congress Kingdom was compiled by Maciej Radziwiłł and Bohdan Winiarski, *Materyały do sprawy polskiej, Królestwo Polskie: dokumenty historyczne, dotyczące prawno-politycznego stosunku Królestwa Polskiego do Carstwa Rosyjskiego* (Warszawa: Gebethner i Wolff, 1915). The protocols of the kingdom's Administrative Council were recently published: *Sumariusz protokołów Rady Administracyjnej Królestwa Polskiego 1815-1867* (Warszawa: Państwowe Wydawnictwo Naukowe, 1958-62).

Several sourcebooks designed primarily for university students have appeared in Poland in the last few decades. Stefan Kieniewicz, Tadeusz Mencel, and Władysław Rostocki edited *Wybór tekstów źródłowych z historii Polski w latach 1795-1864* (Warszawa: Państwowe Wydawnictwo Naukowe, 1956). Similar collections of documentary excerpts were edited for Galicia by Stefan Kieniewicz and Marian Tyrowicz, for the Cracow Republic by Janina Bieniarzówna, for Prussian Poland by Witold Jakóbczyk, for Pomerania by Andrzej Bukowski, and for Masurian and Warmia (Ermland) regions by Władysław Chojnacki.

PART ONE, 1795-1830. MONOGRAPHS AND SOURCES

Among several biographies of leading Polish figures, particularly important are: Szymon Askenazy, *Le Prince Joseph Poniatowski* (Paris: Plon-Nourit, 1921), a classic available also in Polish, and Poniatowski's biography by Adam Skałkowski; the multivolume Marceli Handelsman, *Adam Czartoryski* (Warszawa: Towarzystwo Naukowe Warszawskie, 1948-50) and Marian Kukiel, *Czartoryski and European Unity 1770-1861* (Princeton: Princeton University Press, 1955); Gabriel Zych, *Jan Henryk Dąbrowski* (Warszawa: Ministerstwo Obrony Narodowej, 1964) which in part replaces the older studies by Władysław Smoleński, Wacław Tokarz, and Marian Kukiel; Jadwiga Lechicka, *Józef Wybicki* (Toruń: Towarzystwo Naukowe w Toruniu, 1962); and Barbara Szacka, *Stanisław Staszic: portret mieszczanina* (Warszawa: Państwowy Instytut Wydawniczy, 1966) which is a more popular presentation although based on original sources. There is no fully satisfactory biography of Lelewel, but William J. Rose, "Lelewel as Historian," *The Slavonic Review* 15 (1937):649-62, provides an introduction for the English reader. The old classic by Nikolai K. Schilder, *Imperator Aleksandr Pervyi* (St. Petersburg: A. S. Suvorin, 1897-98) is still important. Polish military efforts are well presented in the general summary of Marian Kukiel, *Dzieje wojska polskiego w dobie napoleońskiej* (rev. ed., Warszawa: E. Wende, 1918-20). Important for cultural history is Bohdan Suchodolski, *Rola Towarzystwa*

*Przyjaciół Nauk w rozwoju kultury umysłowej w Polsce* (Warszawa: Towarzystwo Naukowe Warszawskie, 1951), an interpretative essay which complements the old multivolume descriptive work of Aleksander Kraushar. A stimulating study is Hipolit Grynwaser, *Demokracja szlachecka: studium historycznokrytyczne 1795–1831* (Warszawa: Państwowy Instytut Wydawniczy, 1948), later reprinted in Grynwaser's collected writings *(Pisma)*. For eastern Polish lands annexed by Russia see Henryk Mościcki, *Pod berłem carów* (Warszawa: Biblioteka Polska, 1924).

POSTPARTITION YEARS TO 1807: There has been no definitive monograph on the Polish legions, but Janusz Pachoński is in the process of writing a multivolume one entitled *Legiony polskie 1794–1807: prawda i legenda*. So far volumes 1 and 3 have appeared (Warszawa: Ministerstwo Obrony Narodowej, 1969, 1971). Volume 3 covers the period up to 1797. Among the studies written early in the twentieth century Adam Skałkowski's books on the legions and Marian Kukiel's on insurrectionary attempts are important. Szymon Askenazy, *Napoléon et la Pologne* (Paris: E. Leroux, 1925), particularly in its much larger Polish version, stands out as a classic. The early phases of the Austrian rule in Galicia are discussed by Henryk Lepucki and Wacław Tokarz; the Prussian occupation, by Władysław Smoleński and more recently by Jan Wąsicki; the Russian provinces, by Henryk Mościcki and in German by Uno L. Lehtonen. The early years and policies of Czartoryski have been recently examined by Patricia K. Grimstead, *The Foreign Ministers of Alexander I* (Berkeley: University of California Press, 1969), and by Jerzy Skowronek, "Le Programme européen du prince Adam Jerzy Czartoryski en 1803–1805," *Acta Poloniae Historica* 17 (1968):137-59 as well as in his book *Antynapoleońskie koncepcje Czartoryskiego* (Warszawa: Państwowe Wydawnictwo Naukowe, 1969). Educational problems in the Wilno district are interestingly discussed by Stefan Truchim, *Współpraca polsko-rosyjska nad organizacją szkolnictwa rosyjskiego w początkach XIX wieku* (Łódź: Łódzkie Towarzystwo Naukowe, 1960).

DUCHY OF WARSAW: Although there is no monograph on the duchy, and only one old, general work, Fryderyk Skarbek, *Dzieje Xięstwa Warszawskiego* (2nd ed., Poznań: J. K. Zupański, 1976), books on various aspects of the period abound. The origins were discussed by Marceli Handelsman, and especially by Maciej Loret, *Między Jeną a Tylżą 1806-1970*, Monografie w zakresie dziejów nowożytnych (Warszawa: Laskauert, Ska. 1920). Recently Emanuel Halicz returned to the subject in "La Question polonaise à Tilsit," *Acta Poloniae Historica* 12 (1965):44-64 and in his larger *Geneza Księstwa Warszawskiego* (Warszawa: Ministerstwo Obrony Narodowej, 1962). Very valuable are the two different studies by Marceli Handelsman,

*Napoléon et la Pologne 1806–1807* (Paris: F. Alcan, 1909) and *Napoleon a Polska* (Warszawa: E. Wende, 1911). Juliusz Willaume has ably discussed the Saxon ruler, *Fryderyk August jako książę warszawski* (Poznań: Towarzystwo Przyjaciół Nauk, 1939), and Tadeusz Mencel contributed *Feliks Łubieński: minister sprawiedliwości Księstwa Warszawskiego 1758–1848* (Warszawa: Towarzystwo Naukowe Warszawskie, 1952). Military history including the 1809 campaign had been the subject of older studies by Bronisław Gembarzewski, *Wojsko polskie: Księstwo Warszawskie 1807–1814* (2nd ed., Warszawa: Gebethner i Wolff, 1912), and by Bronisław Pawłowski, Emil Kipa, and more recently Janusz Staszewski and Gabriel Zych. The only work in a Western language is the popular Jan Chelminski and A. Malibran, *L'Armée du Duché de Varsovie* (Paris: J. Leroy, 1913). The war of 1812 is discussed in detail by Marian Kukiel, *Wojna 1812 roku* (Kraków: Polska Akademia Umiejętności, 1937); various aspects are treated by Abel Mansuy, *Jérôme Napoléon et la Pologne en 1812* (Paris: F. Alcan, 1931); Janusz Iwaszkiewicz, *Litwa w 1812 roku*, Monografie w zakresie dziejów nowożytnych (Kraków and Warszawa: Laskauer & Ska., 1912); and Bronius Dundulis, *Napoléon et la Lithuanie en 1812* (Paris: Alcan, Presses Universitaires de France, 1940). Marceli Handelsman, *Rezydenci napoleońscy w Warszawie 1807–1813* (Kraków: Akademia Umiejętności, 1915) has not been superseded. Russian rule in the Tarnopol district has been examined by Jan Leszczyński.

Constitutional and legal problems are well surveyed by Władysław Sobociński, *Historia ustroju i prawa Ksiestwa Warszawskiego* (Toruń: Toruńskie Towarzystwo Naukowe, 1964), and there are several other more detailed studies. The old article by Hipolit Grynwaser, "Le Code Napoléon dans le Duché de Varsovie," *Revue des Études Napoléoniennes* 12 (1917): 129-70, and the recent study by Jerzy Jedlicki, "Bilan social du Duché de Varsovie," *Acta Poloniae Historica* 14 (1966):93-104 are valuable. New light on the economic development of the duchy is thrown by Barbara Grochulska, *Handel zagraniczny Księstwa Warszawskiego* (Warszawa: Państwowe Wydawnictwo Naukowe, 1967)—who also authored a brief, popular history of the duchy—and on legal-economic problems by Monika Senkowska-Gluck, "Les majorats français dans le Duché de Varsovie," *Annales Historiques de la Revolution Française*, no. spécial (July-September, 1964), pp. 373-86. The latter author developed her thesis in *Donacje napoleońskie w Księstwie Warszawskim: studium historyczno-prawne*, Zakład Historii Państwa i Prawa, Studia (Wrocław and Warszawa: Polska Akademia Nauk, 1968). Educational matters had been discussed in an older study by Wincenty Gorzycki.

CONGRESS KINGDOM: The only general synthesis is the old "Poland

and the Polish Revolution" by Szymon Askenazy in *Cambridge Modern History* (Cambridge: The University Press, 1907), 10:445-74, expanded in Polish in book form. The opening phases are examined by Józef Bojasiński, *Rządy tymczasowe w Królestwie Polskiem 1813-1815*, Monografie w zakresie dziejów nowożytnych (Warszawa: Laskauer & Ska., 1902), and Kazimierz Bartoszewicz, *Utworzenie Królestwa Polskiego* (Kraków: Wydawnictwo NKN, 1916). Eugeniusz Wawrzkowicz, *Anglia a sprawa polska 1813-1815*, Monografie w zakresie dziejów nowożytnych (Warszawa: Laskauer & Ska., 1919) discussed the British attitudes toward Poland. The classic by Szymon Askenazy, *Łukasiński* (2nd ed., Warszawa: E. Wende, 1929) is more than a biographical study and deals with the Patriotic Society as a whole. The latter is also the subject of an important new work by Hanna Dylągowa, *Towarzystwo Patriotyczne i Sąd Sejmowy 1821–1829* (Warszawa: Państwowe Wydawnictwo Naukowe, 1970). The Polish liberals are discussed by Helena Więckowska, *Opozycja liberalna w Królestwie Kongresowym* (Warszawa: Towarzystwo Naukowe Warszawskie, 1925). There are several studies of the Decembrists and their relations with the Poles, notably those by Leon Baumgarten and Henryk Batowski. A useful introduction to the topic in English is Franklin A. Walker, "Poland in the Decembrists' Strategy of Revolution," *The Polish Review* 15 (Spring, 1970): 43-53. Maria Manteufflowa, *J. K. Szaniawski: ideologia i działalność 1815-1830* (Warszawa: Towarzystwo Naukowe Warszawskie, 1936) deserves to be mentioned. The important diet of 1825 is discussed by Ryszard Przelaskowski, *Sejm warszawski roku 1825* (Warszawa: Towarzystwo Naukowe Warszawskie, 1929). The army is the subject of a study by Wacław Tokarz, *Armia Królestwa Polskiego 1815–1830* (Piotrków: Dept. Wojsk. N.K.N., 1917).

Economic and social problems are discussed in two important works on Drucki-Lubecki: Stanisław Smolka, *Polityka Lubeckiego przed powstaniem listopadowem* (Kraków: Akademia Umiejętności, 1907) and Mieczysław Ajzen, *Polityka gospodarcza Lubeckiego 1821–1830* (Warszawa: Towarzystwo Naukowe Warszawskie, 1932). The latter is more critical of Drucki-Lubecki than the former. Czesław Strzeszewski, *Handel zagraniczny Królestwa Kongresowego 1815-1830* (Lublin: Towarzystwo Naukowe, K.U.L., 1937) and Natalia Gąsiorowska, *Górnictwo i hutnictwo w Królestwie Polskim 1815–1830* (Warszawa and Kraków: Biblioteka Wyższej Szkoły Handlowej, 1923) deal respectively with trade and heavy industry. Władysław Sobociński, "Quelques observations sur le bilan social de la Pologne en 1815," *Acta Poloniae Historica* 15 (1966): 105-16, is an inquiry into social problems. Jerzy Jedlicki, *Klejnot i bariery społeczne: przeobrażenia szlachectwa polskiego w schyłkowym okresie feudal-*

*izmu* (Warszawa: Państwowe Wydawnictwo Naukowe, 1968) is a stimulating analysis of the changing status of the nobility.

SOURCES: Protocols of the State Council of the Duchy of Warsaw as well as instructions and dispatches of French residents in Warsaw have been published respectively by Bronisław Pawłowski and Marceli Handelsman, Handelsman also began the compilation of the proceedings of the diet but only those of 1807 have been published. Adam Skałkowski has published Poniatowski's correspondence with the French and excerpts of Kościuszko's correspondence, as well as the important Wybicki archive. Documents of the Governing Commission of 1807 were compiled by Michał Rostworowski. Czartoryski's correspondence with Alexander I had been partly published by Władysław Czartoryski. Two French diplomats in Warsaw, Bignon and de Pradt, had their memoirs published; Bignon's is of particular importance. Julian Ursyn Niemcewicz's memoirs are also of considerable value.

For the period 1815–30, particularly important is the correspondence of Drucki-Lubecki with the secretary of state, published by Stanisław Smolka. Leon Sapieha's memoirs, which go up to 1863, are important for this as well as for the next period, and the same is true for the important memoirs of Władysław Zamoyski. A sourcebook edited by Stefan Kieniewicz gives the student a selection of documents on social and economic changes in the kingdom from 1815 to 1830.

PART TWO, 1830-64. MONOGRAPHS AND SOURCES

THE NOVEMBER INSURRECTION OF 1830 AND ITS AFTERMATH: The only treatment of the insurrection as a whole in English is R. F. Leslie, *Polish Politics and the Revolution of November 1830* (London: University of London, 1956), an important book somewhat marred by one-sided interpretations. A comprehensive and up-to-date monograph of the November Insurrection remains yet to be written. Its origins have been examined by among others: Wacław Tokarz, *Sprzysiężenie Wysockiego i noc listopadowa* (Warszawa: Gebethner i Wolff, 1925); Juliusz Harbut, *Noc listopadowa w świetle i cieniach historii i procesu przed najwyższym sądem kryminalnym* (2nd ed., Warszawa: Książnica Atlas, 1930); and in Marian Kukiel's article in *Teki Historyczne* 9 (1958): 40-62. Czesław Bloch's article about French inspirations appeared in *Kwartalnik Historyczny* 71 (1964): 27-44. Relations with France are the subject of Józef Dutkiewicz, *Francja a Polska w 1831 r.* (Łódź: Łódzkie Towarzystwo Naukowe, 1950), a valuable study, and of an article by S. Wędkiewicz in French in the *Bulletin de l'Academie Politique des Sciences et des Lettres* no. 12 (1954): 17-45. Dutkiewicz also contributed the important *Austria wobec powstania listopadowego* (Kraków: Gebethner i Wolff, 1933).

I. A. Betley, *Belgium and Poland in International Relations 1830–31* (S'-Gravenhage: Mouton, 1960) is useful, and for a general picture so is Charles Morley, "The European Significance of the November Uprising," *Journal of Central European Affairs* 11 (January, 1952): 407-16. Marian Kukiel, "La Révolution de 1830 et la Pologne," *Revue Internationale d'Histoire Politique et Constitutionelle* 11 (1953): 235-48 is an attempt at synthesis. Four recent books dealing with internal problems of the insurrection deserve special mention: Władysław Rostocki, *Władza wodzów naczelnych w powstaniu listopadowym*, Studium Historyczno-prawne (Wrocław: Ossolineum, 1955); Zdzisław Gołba, *Rozwój władz Królestwa polskiego w okresie powstania listopadowego* (Wrocław: Ossolineum, 1971); Władysław Bortnowski, *Walka o cele rewolucji listopadowej* (Łódź and Wrocław: Ossolineum, 1969); and Władysław Zajewski, *Walki wewnętrzne ugrupowań politycznych w powstaniu listopadowym 1830–1831* (Gdańsk: Gdańskie Towarzystwo Naukowe, 1967). Jerzy Łojek, *Szanse powstania listopadowego* (Warszawa: Pax, 1966) contributes stimulating although not always convincing reflections about the chances of the insurrection.

In addition to the biographies mentioned earlier, Jan Kucharzewski and Artur Śliwiński wrote on Mochnacki, and Śliwiński contributed a study of Lelewel. Juliusz Harbut and Stanisław Szenic produced biographies of Chłopicki, and Bolesław Limanowski one of Worcell. All of these works were written between 1910 and 1930. A recent biography of Bem by Eligiusz Kozłowski is valuable but controversial. The peasant question is the object of Maksymilian Meloch, *Sprawa włościańska w powstaniu listopadowym* (3rd ed., Warszawa: Państwowy Instytut Wydawniczy, 1953); it is hardly the last word on the subject. Edmund Oppman discussed the Patriotic Society in *Warszawskie 'Towarzystwo Patriotyczne' 1830–31* (Warszawa: Towarzystwo Miłośników Historii, 1937). Tadeusz Łepkowski dealt with the city of Warsaw during the insurrection in *Warszawa w powstaniu listopadowym* (Warszawa: Wiedza Powszechna, 1957). Łepkowski is also the author of the illuminating article "Społeczne i narodowe aspekty powstania 1831 na Ukrainie," *Kwartalnik Historyczny* 64 (1957): 41-65. Stanisław Dangel, *Rok 1831 w Mińszczyźnie* (Warszawa: Instytut Badania ziem wschodnich Rzeczpospolitej, 1925) concerns the insurrection in Belorussia.

The Polish-Russian war is the object of several studies. Wacław Tokarz, *Wojna polsko-rosyjska 1830 i 1831 r.* (Warszawa: Wojskowy Instytut Naukowo-Wydawniczy, 1930) is a classic. Michał Sokolnicki contributed a shorter study. Aleksandr K. Puzyrevsky, *Polsko-russkaia voina 1831 g.* (St. Petersburg: Tipografia shtaba voisk gvardii, 1866) is important and has been translated into French, German, and Polish. There are older studies in German by W. Willisen and H. Kunz. Several histories of the insurrection and of the military operations were written shortly after the events by participants. They fall halfway between secondary works and sources. Stanisław Barzykowski, *Historia powstania listopadowego* (Poznań: J. K. Żupański, 1883-84) is voluminous and pro-Czartoryski. Maurycy Mochnacki, *Powstanie narodu polskiego w roku 1830 i 1831*, Dzieła, vol. 2 (Poznań: K. Żupański, 1862) gives the other side of the story. Ludwik Mierosławski's *Powstanie narodu polskiego w roku 1830 i 1831* (Paris: Bourgogne et Martinet, 1845), intended as a continuation of Mochnacki, is more polemical. The short *Czterej ostatni wodzowie polscy przed sądem historii* (Kraków: NKN, 1916) by Ignacy Prądzyński includes an evaluation of Chłopicki and Skrzynecki by a prominent general of the insurrection.

There is no exhaustive study of the Great Emigration. Lubomir Gadon, *Wielka emigracja w pierwszych latach po powstaniu listopadowym* (2nd ed., Paris: Księgarnia Polska, 1960) was written by a participant close to the Czartoryski camp. Michał Sokolnicki, *Les Origines de l'émigration polonaise en France 1831–32* (Paris: F. Alcan, 1910) is useful. A *vue d'ensemble* of the cultural contribution can be found in Witold Łukaszewicz, "Wielka emigracja 1831–1862," *Prace Polonistyczne*, Series 9 (Wrocław, 1951): 147-82. The democratic camp is surveyed by one of its leaders Wiktor Heltman; his *Demokracja polska na emigracji* (Warszawa: Książka i Wiedza, 1965) is a memoir rather than a study. Historical works include: Sławomir Kalembka, *Towarzystwo Demokratyczne Polskie w latach 1832–1846* (Toruń: Państwowe Wydawnictwo Naukowe, 1966); Bronisław Baczko, *Poglądy społeczno-polityczne i filozoficzne Towarzystwa Demokratycznego Polskiego* (Warszawa: Książka i Wiedza, 1955), which is seriously marred by "Stalinist" ideas and jargon; and Peter Brock, "The Political Program of the Polish Democratic Society," *Polish Review* 14 (Spring and Summer, 1969): 89-105 and 5-24. The last article has an excellent bibliographical note. Brock also contributed several articles germane to the subject in the *Journal of Central European Affairs* (1953), the *Slavic and East European Review* (1961), etc. Pertinent is the first volume of Lidia and Adam Ciołkosz, mentioned earlier among general works.

In addition to the biographies mentioned above, Witold Łukaszewicz contributed studies of Krępowiecki and Szymon Konarski, and Helena Łuczakówna wrote on Wiktor Heltman.

Jan Kucharzewski examined the domestic scene in the Congress Kingdom in *Epoka paskiewiczowska: dzieje oświaty* (Warszawa and

Kraków: Gebethner & Wolff, 1914); Eugeniusz Boss concentrated on
the workers: *Sprawa robotnicza w Królestwie Polskim w okresie
paskiewiczowskim 1831–1855* (Warszawa: Towarzystwo Naukowe
Warszawskie, 1931); Natalia Gąsiorowska discussed "Commercialisa-
tion, concentration et mécanisation de l'industrie minière et
métallurgique d'État dans le Royaume de Pologne pendant la
pèriode de l'administration de la Banque de Pologne" in *La Pologne
au VIIe Congrès International des Sciences Historiques* (Warszawa:
1933). Conspiracies in Galicia are dealt with by Stefan Kieniewicz,
*Konspiracje galicyjskie 1831–1845* (Warszawa: Książka i Wiedza,
1950). Dembowski's philosophical ideas are discussed by Jerzy
Ładyka, *Dembowski* (Warszawa: Wiedza Powszechna, 1968). The
beginnings of positivism are the subject of the interesting study by
Barbara Skarga, *Narodziny pozytywizmu polskiego 1831–64* (Warszawa: Państwowe Wydawnictwo Naukowe, 1964).

THE DECADE 1846–56: The central theme of agrarian reform is dealt
with by Krzysztof Groniowski, *Problem rewolucji agrarnej w ideologii
obozów politycznych 1846–1870* (Warszawa: Państwowe Wydawnictwo Naukowe, 1957), a work that is marred by "Stalinist" terminology and interpretations. There is no fully satisfactory study of the
1846 revolution and the Galician *jacquerie*, although numerous
authors have discussed both. Bolesław Łoziński, Kazimierz Ostaszew-
ski-Barański, and Stanisław Schnür-Pepłowski denounce Austrian
machinations. The Austrian point of view is defended by M. von
Sala. Bolesław Limanowski attempted to understand rather than to
condemn the *jacquerie*, and Michał Janik indicated new approaches.
Post-World War II Marxist historiography placed an increasing emphasis on the progressive nature of the peasant class struggle. Stefan
Kieniewicz, *Ruch chłopski w Galicji 1846 r.* (Wrocław: Ossolineum,
1951) is scholarly in his approach, while Czesław Wycech's, Marian
Żychowski's, and Roman Werfel's books verge on political tracts.
There is an older study by Marian Tyrowicz, *Jan Tyssowski: dyktator
krakowski* (Warszawa: Kasa Mianowskiego, 1930).

The Spring of Nations in Polish lands was ably discussed by
Józef Feldman, *Sprawa polska 1848 r* (Kraków: Polska Akademia
Umiejętności, 1933). The monumental *W stulecie wiosny ludów
1848–1948* edited by Natalia Gąsiorowska (Warszawa: Państwowe
Wydawnictwo Naukowe, 1948-53) devotes the first, fourth, and fifth
volume to Polish problems. The work becomes increasingly ideologically motivated in the later parts. Stefan Kieniewicz, "The Social
Image of Poland in 1848," *Slavonic and East European Review* 27
(1948): 91-105 is very useful. Marceli Handelsman's *Czartoryski,
Nicholas Ier et la question du Proche Orient* (Paris: A. Pedone,
1934), and his *Ukraińska polityka Adama Czartoryskiego przed*

*wojnę krymską, Rozwój narodowości współczesnej*, vol. 3 (Warszawa: Ukraiński Instytut Naukowy, 1937) give an excellent insight into Czartoryski's diplomacy. Karol Widman contributed a biography of Smolka, and Władyslaw T. Wisłocki one of Jerzy Lubomirski; Wisłocki also examined the Prague Congress in his *Kongres słowiański 1848 r. i sprawa polska* (Lwów: Ossolineum, 1927). Bronisław Łoziński discussed the early period of Gołuchowski. More recent biographies include Marian Żychowski, *Generał klęski: Ludwik Mierosławski* (Warszawa: Państwowe Wydawnictwo, "Iskry," 1965) and Witold Jakóbczyk, *Karol Marcinkowski 1800–1846* (Poznań: Wydawnictwo Poznańskie, 1966).

The 1848 revolution in Poznania is the subject—apart from an old study by Kazimierz Rakowski—of Stefan Kieniewicz, *Społeczeństwo polskie w powstaniu poznańskim 1848 r.* (New rev. ed., Warszawa: Państwowe Wydawnictwo Naukowe, 1960); Zdzisław Grot, *Działalność posłów polskich w sejmie pruskim, 1848–1850* (Poznań: Wydawnictwo Poznańskie, 1961); C. E. Black, "Poznan and Europe in 1848," *Journal of Central European Affairs* 8 (July, 1948): 191-206; Georg Wolfgang Hallgarten, *Studien über die deutsche Polenfreundschaft in der Periode der Märzrevolution* (Munich: R. Oldenbourg, 1928); Jan Kucharzewski, "The Polish Cause in the Frankfurt Parliament of 1848," *Bulletin of the Polish Institute of Arts and Sciences in America* 1 (October, 1942–July, 1943), 42-73.

There is interesting material in Anna Minkowska, *Organizacja spiskowa 1848 roku w Królestwie Polskiem* (Warszawa: Towarzystwo Naukowe Warszawskie, 1923), and Dawid Fajnhauz, *Ruch konspiracyjny na Litwie i Białorusi, 1846–1848* (Warszawa: Państwowe Wydawnictwo Naukowe, 1965). A recent Soviet publication is Evdokia M. Kossachevskaia, *Vostochnaia Galitsiia nakanune i v period revoliutsii 1848 r* (Lvov: Izd. Lvovskogo Universiteta, 1965).

THE JANUARY INSURRECTION OF 1863: The historical literature is extremely rich and many sources have been published. The most recent is the monumental synthesis of Stefan Kieniewicz, *Powstanie styczniowe* (Warszawa: Państwowe Wydawnictwo Naukowe, 1972). R. F. Leslie, *Reform and Insurrection in Russian Poland 1856–1865* (London: University of London, 1963) is not very satisfactory. A wealth of information is to be found in the multivolume, detailed study written shortly after the events: Walery Przyborowski, *Historia dwóch lat. 1861–1862*, 5 vols. (Kraków: W. L. Anczyc, 1892–96); *Dzieje 1863 roku*, 5 vols. (Kraków: W. L. Anczyc, 1897-1919); and *Ostatnie chwile powstania styczniowego*, 3 vols. (Poznań: J. K. Żupański, 1887–88). Agaton Giller's history is largely a valuable account of a leading participant. Józef Dąbrowski (Józef Grabiec), *Rok 1863* (3rd ed., Poznań: K. Rzepecki, 1929) is valuable. Stanisław Koźmian,

*Rzecz o roku 1863* (Kraków: Księgarnia Spółki Wydawniczej Polskiej, 1894–95) is more important for the views of Cracow conservatives than for the insurrection itself. Popular histories ranging from Bolesław Limanowski's and Artur Śliwiński's to the more recent book by Stanisław Strumph Wojtkiewicz indicate the changing views and controversies. For the background particularly important are Stefan Kieniewicz, *Między ugodą a rewolucją: Andrzej Zamoyski w latach 1861–1862* (Warszawa: Państwowe Wydawnictwo Naukowe, 1962) and Henryk Wereszycki, "Hotel Lambert i obóz Białych przed wybuchem powstania styczniowego," *Przegląd Historyczny* 50 (1959): 514-44, 651-60. A useful study in English is Irena M. Rosevare, "Wielopolski's Reforms and their Failure before the Uprising of 1863," *Antemurale* 15 (1971): 87-214. Valuable especially for its rich documentation is Irena Koberdowa, *Wielki Książę Konstanty w Warszawie 1862–1863* (Warszawa: Państwowe Wydawnictwo Naukowe, 1962). Henryk Lisicki's biography of Wielopolski in French and Adam Skałkowski's in Polish are inadequate. The recent work of Zbigniew Stankiewicz, *Dzieje wielkości i upadku Aleksandra Wielopolskiego* (Warszawa: Wiedza Powszechna, 1967) is most interesting and has a good bibliographical essay. Władysław Grabski wrote the classical *Historya Towarzystwa Rolniczego* (Warszawa: Gebethner i Wolff, 1904). Its social ideas were recently examined by Ryszarda Czepulis.

The all-important peasant question and the emancipation reform is the subject of Stefan Kieniewicz, *Sprawa włościańska w powstaniu styczniowym* (Wrocław: Ossolineum, 1953); Emanuel Halicz, *Kwestia chłopska w Królestwie Polskim w dobie powstania styczniowego* (Warszawa: Książka i Wiedza, 1955); and Ivan I. Kostiuchko, *Krestianskaia reforma 1864 g v tsarstve polskom* (Moscow: Akademia Nauk SSSR, 1962). Interesting is W. Bruce Lincoln, "The Making of a New Polish Policy: N. A. Milyutin and the Polish Question 1861-1863," *The Polish Review* 15 (Winter, 1970): 54-66. Zbigniew Ćwiek, *Przywódcy powstania styczniowego: Sześć sylwetek* (Warszawa: Wiedza Powszechna, 1963) is a good introductory sketch of six leaders. Among numerous biographies, Władysław Karbowski wrote on Padlewski, Henryk Jabłoński on Waszkowski, Zbigniew Marciniak and A. F. Smirnov (the latter in Russian) on Sierakowski, Wiktor Kordowicz and Smirnov on Kalinowski, Walentyna Rudzka on Majewski, S. Myśliborski-Wołowski and Helena Rządkowska on Langiewicz. A satisfactory biography of Traugutt is lacking. Good introductions in English to major issues are: Marian Kukiel, "Military Aspects of the Polish Insurrection of 1863–64" and Walentyna Rudzka, "Studies on the Polish Insurrectionary Government in 1863–64," *Antemurale*,

7-8 (1963): 363-396, 397-473. See also the old, extremely detailed Stanisław Zieliński, *Bitwy i potyczki 1863–1864* (Rapperswyl: Muzeum Narodowe, 1913) based on sources that have since been destroyed, and the recent Leonard Ratajczyk, *Polska wojna partyzancka 1863–1864* (Warszawa: Ministerstwo Obrony Narodowej, 1966).

A great deal has been written about the international aspects of the insurrection. The major collection of sources edited by Adam Lewak contains a series of good introductory surveys. Important works are: Józef Feldman, *Mocarstwa wobec powstania styczniowego* (Kraków: Krakowska Spółka Wydawnicza, 1929); Vladimir G. Revunenkov, *Polskoe vosstanie 1863 g. i evropeiskaia diplomatiia* (Leningrad: Univ. im. A.A. Zhdanova, 1957); Stanisław Bóbr-Tylingo, "Napoléon III, l'Europe et la Pologne en 1863—64," *Antemurale*, 7-8 (1963): 1-362 and several articles by the same author; Henryk Wereszycki, *Austria a powstanie styczniowe* (Lwów: Ossolineum, 1930) and his *Anglia a Polska w latach 1860–65* (Lwów: Archiwum Towarzystwa Naukowego, 1934). Václav Žáček and Endre Kovacs are among those who discuss the echoes of the insurrection in Bohemia and Hungary. Its impact on Prussian Poland is dealt with by Zdzisław Grot and Andrzej Bukowski in Polish, and by Felix H. Gentzen in German. There is an old study by Franciszek Rawita-Gawroński, *Powstanie 1863 na Rusi* (Lwów: H. Altenberg, 1902–1903), and a recent Soviet work, which is one-sided and rather unsatisfactory, Grigorii I. Marakhov, *Polskoe vosstanie 1863 na pravoberezhnoi Ukraine* (Kiev: Kievsky Universitet, 1967). Vasyl Lutsiv, *Ukrainians and the Polish Revolt of 1863* (New Haven: Slavia Library, 1961) is quite useful. A. J. Liaskovsky, *Litva i Belorussiia v vosstanii 1863 g* (Berlin: Arzamas, 1939) and Ona Maksimaitiené, *Lietuvos sukiliu kovos 1863–1864* (Vilnius: Mintis, 1969) are among major Belorussian and Lithuanian publications.

SOURCES: The amount of published documentation for the period from 1831 to 1864, especially for the 1860s, is impressive. Bronisław Pawłowski edited documents pertaining to the Russo-Polish war; Michał Rostworowski, the proceedings of the 1830–31 Sejm. The correspondence between Tsar Nicholas and Grand Duke Constantine and Diebitsch was published respectively in *Sbornik Russkogo Istoricheskogo Obshchestva* (1910-11) and in *Russkaia Starina* (1882). The important memoirs of General Prądzyński were published by Bronisław Gembarzewski. Karolina and Władysław Rostocki edited the memoirs of Antoni Ostrowski. Zamoyski's and Sapieha's memoirs, mentioned in the preceding section, are very important for this period. Participants' accounts in Lithuania in 1831 were compiled by

Henryk Mościcki; those of Galician conspirators, by Karol Lewicki. Józef Dutkiewicz compiled a selection of sources pertaining to the November Insurrection as a whole.

For the events in Galicia in 1846, a selection of sources by Józef Sieradzki and Czesław Wycech is somewhat one-sided. Bronisław Baczko's documents on the Democratic Society were also published during the "Stalinist" period. Stefan Kieniewicz edited selected source material of the 1846 and 1848 revolutions in Poland. Anna Rynkowska edited Darasz's diary, an interesting testimony of a leftist émigré. Franciszek Smolka's diary is important, and so are the protocols of the Polish parliamentary circle in Berlin edited by Zdzisław Grot. A series in Polish and Russian *(Vosstanie 1863 goda: materialy i dokumenty)* published by the Polish and Russian academies of science, mainly under the editorship of Stefan Kieniewicz and I. Miller, comprises several volumes of documents: correspondence of the viceroys and governors, documents of the Central Committee and the National Government, testimony from trials, material on Polish-Russian revolutionary cooperation, the underground press, peasant affairs, and revolutionary activity in the provinces. Most of these volumes appeared from 1960 to 1968 in connection with the centennial of the insurrection. Emanuel Halicz compiled the proceedings of the trial of Traugutt and his associates; Irena Koberdowa, the political reports of French consuls in Warsaw (this volume is complemented by reports published by Stanisław Bóbr-Tylingo in *Antemurale* in 1969 and 1971). A separate publication of the Jewish Historical Institute in Warsaw concerns the Jews and the January Insurrection. Very important are the letters of Leopold Kronenberg edited by Stefan Kieniewicz, and the diary of Władysław Czartoryski, including protocols of the meetings in Hôtel Lambert, edited by Henryk Wereszycki. The collections of documents on Polish diplomatic activity in 1863-64, edited by Adam Lewak, appeared in part before the war, in part after. It is a very important source. A selection of sources on Polish democrats during the insurrection was prepared by Emanuel Halicz. Several publications, which also include sources, concentrate on Russian-Polish revolutionary cooperation, notably, the works of Vladimir A. Diakov, Svetlana M. Falkovich, and volumes of the Soviet-Polish Institute. Józef Jarzębowski, *Traugutt: dokumenty* (London: Veritas, 1970) is useful.

Of the numerous memoirs one need mention only those of Agaton Giller, Marian Dubiecki, and Jakub Gieysztor. Gieysztor's is very valuable for Lithuania. Karl Marx, *Manuskripte über die polnische Frage 1863–1864* has been edited by Werner Conze and Dieter Hertz-Echenrode. A new and rival edition has been published recently in Soviet Russia, Poland, and East Germany.

PART THREE, 1864–90. MONOGRAPHS AND SOURCES

The major general studies on post-1863 history are the books by Wereszycki, Kula, and Pobóg-Malinowski, mentioned at the beginning of this essay. The most recent survey of the origins of socialism in the Polish lands is Józef Buszko, *Narodziny ruchu socjalistycznego na ziemiach polskich* (Kraków: Wydawnictwo Literackie, 1967). A general work on the peasant movement, Tadeusz Rek, *Ruch ludowy w Polsce* (Łódź: Wydawnictwo Ludowe, 1947), also covers the early phase. The Polish League is briefly discussed in Stanisław Kozicki, *Historia Ligi Narodowej* (London: "Myśl Polska," 1964). The old work of Aleksandr L. Pogodin, *Glavnyia techeniia polskoi politicheskoi mysli 1863–1907* (St. Petersburg: Prosveshchenie, 1908) remains very valuable. So is D. Ryazanoff (David B. Goldenbach), "Karl Marx und Friedrich Engels über die Polenfrage," *Archiv für die Geschichte des Sozialismus und der Arbeiterbewegung* 6 (1916): 175-221. For the international context see Henryk Wereszycki, *Sojusz trzech cesarzy: Geneza 1866–1872* (Warszawa: Państwowe Wydawnictwo Naukowe, 1965) and the sequel, *Walka o pokój europejski 1872–1878* (Warszawa: Państwowe Wydawnictwo Naukowe, 1971). The third volume is in preparation. Also relevant is Jerzy Zdrada, *Zmierzch Czartoryskich* (Warszawa: Polskie Wydawnictwo Naukowe, 1969).

RUSSIAN POLAND:  In addition to the studies listed above, particularly in the section on economics, Juliusz Łukasiewicz, *Przewrót techniczny w przemyśle Królestwa Polskiego* (Warszawa: Państwowe Wydawnictwo Naukowe, 1963), Janina Leśkiewicz, *Warszawa i jej inteligencja po powstaniu styczniowym 1864–1870* (Warszawa: Państwowe Wydawnictwo Naukowe, 1961), and Krzysztof Groniowski, *Kwestia agrarna w Królestwie Polskim 1871–1914* (Warszawa: Państwowe Wydawnictwo Naukowe, 1966) are among the best recent works on socioeconomic problems. On the rise of socialism in Russian Poland, the classic study is Res (Feliks Perl), *Dzieje ruchu socjalistycznego w zaborze rosyjskim do powstania PPS* (Reprint, Warszawa: Książka i Wiedza, 1958). See also Leon Baumgarten, *Dzieje Wielkiego Proletariatu* (Warszawa: Książka i Wiedza, 1965), and in Western European languages: Lucjan Blit, *The Origins of Polish Socialism: The History and Ideas of the First Polish Socialist Party 1878–1886* (London and New York: Cambridge University Press, 1971), and Ulrich Haustein, "Sozialismus und nationale Frage in Kongresspolen bis zur Gründung der PPS," *Jahrbücher für Geschichte Osteuropas*, no. 4 (1962): 513-62, and his *Sozialismus und Nationale Frage in Polen* (Köln: Böhlau, 1969). On the post-January 1863 emigration see Jerzy Borejsza, *Emigracja polska po powstaniu*

*styczniowym* (Warszawa: Państwowe Wydawnictwo Naukowe, 1966).
GALICIA AND PRUSSIAN POLAND: Particularly relevant for Galicia in
the age of autonomy are the biographies by Stefan Kieniewicz,
*Adam Sapieha* (Lwów: Ossolineum, 1939) and Irena Homola-Dzi-
kowska, *Mikołaj Zyblikiewicz 1823–1887* (Kraków: Ossolineum, 1964).
Michał Bobrzyński, Władysław Leopold Jaworski, and Józef Milewski,
*Z dziejów odrodzenia politycznego Galicji 1859–1873* (Warszawa:
Gebethner i Wolff, 1905) is very informative. Emil Haecker, *Historia
socjalizmu w Galicji i na Śląsku Cieszyńskim* (Kraków: Towarzys-
two Uniwersytetów Robotniczych, 1933) is valuable. In English,
Peter Brock, "Boleslaw Wyslouch, Founder of the Polish Peasant
Party," *Slavonic and East European Review* 30 (1951): 139-63 is to
be recommended.

For Prussian Poland, Józef Feldman, *Bismarck a Polska* (2nd ed.,
Warszawa: Czytelnik, 1966) is still important. The most recent studies
are Lech Trzeciakowski, *Kulturkampf w zaborze pruskim* (Poznań:
Wydawnictwo Poznańskie, 1970), a well-written and documented
study, and from the German point of view, Günther Dettmer, *Die Ost-
und westpreussischen Verwaltungsbehörden in Kulturkampf* (Heidel-
berg: Quelle & Meyer, 1958). Narrower in scope but very detailed is
Zygmunt Zieliński, "Kulturkampf: Wykonanie ustawy sejmu pruskiego . . . na terenie archidiecezji gnieźnieńskiej i poznańskiej
1873–1887," *Studia Historica* 2 (1968): 7-172. A good survey is Lech
Trzeciakowski, "The Prussian State and the Catholic Church in Prussian Poland 1871–1914," *Slavic Review* 26 (December, 1967): 618-
37, as well as his "Polskie ugrupowania polityczne zaboru pruskiego
wobec Niemiec 1871–1918," *Dzieje Najnowsze* 4 (1972): 25-44.
The expulsion of Poles by Bismarck is discussed by Andrzej Brożek,
*Wysiedlenia Polaków z Górnego Śląska przez Bismarcka 1885-1887*
(Katowice: Śląsk, 1963); from a German point of view, by Helmut
Neubach, *Die Ausweisungen von Polen und Juden aus Preussen
1885–86* (Wiesbaden: Harrassowitz, 1967); and in a somewhat dogmatic Marxist spirit by Joachim Mai, *Die preussisch-deutsche Polenpolitik 1885–1887* (Berlin: Rütten und Leoning, 1962). On the origins
of socialism see Stanisław Kubiak, *Ruch socjalistyczny w Poznańskiem 1872–1890* (Poznań: Wydawnictwo Poznańskie, 1961). Works
pertaining to Prussian colonization policies will be discussed in
another section.
LITHUANIAN AND UKRAINIAN NATIONAL REVIVAL: In addition to studies
listed in the general section under Lithuania and the Ukraine, the
following are particularly pertinent: Leon Wasilewski, "Stosunki
polsko-litewskie w dobie popowstaniowej," *Niepodległość* 1 (October,
1929-March, 1930): 30-59; Leonas Sabaliunas, "Social Democracy in
Tsarist Lithuania 1893-1904," *Slavic Review* 31 (June, 1972): 323-42;

Ivan L. Rudnytsky, "Mykhailo Drahomanov and the Problems of Ukrainian-Jewish Relations," *Canadian Slavonic Papers* 11 (Summer, 1969): 182-98; Dmytro Doroshenko, "Mykhailo Dragomanov and the Ukrainian National Movement," *Slavonic and East European Review* 16 (July, 1937-April, 1938): 654-66; Elżbieta Hornowa, *Ukraiński obóz postępowy i jego współpraca z polską lewicą społeczną w Galicji 1876-1895* (Wrocław: Ossolineum, 1968); and Fedir Savchenko, *Zaborona Ukrainstva 1876 r* (Reprint of 1930 Kiev edition, München: W. Fink, 1970).

SOURCES: There are relatively fewer published sources for this period. Materials bearing on the Great Proletariat have been published in Moscow by Henryk Bicz. Felicja Romaniukowa edited a selection of writings and documents pertaining to the radical democrats during the period 1863-75. Materials concerning the Polish question in the First International have appeared under the general editorship of Henryk Katz. Helena Michnik compiled a two-volume selection of Marx and Engels' utterings on Poland. A compilation of sources on Polish Communism by Strobel cited in the last section of this essay is also relevant for this period.

Documents on the emancipation of the peasantry in Congress Poland were edited by Krystyna and Stanisław Śreniowski. Among memoirs those of Florian Ziemiałkowski are of interest, as well as the English translation by William J. Rose, *From Serfdom to Self-Government: Memoirs of a Polish Village Mayor 1842–1927* (London: Minerva Publ. Co., 1941).

PART FOUR, 1890–1918. MONOGRAPHS AND SOURCES

Demographic changes from the late nineteenth to the early twentieth century are discussed with much data by Włodzimierz Wakar, *Rozwój terytorialny narodowości polskiej* (Warszawa: Kasa Mianowskiego; Kielce: Wydawnictwa Biura Pracy Społecznej, 1917-18). A good deal of statistical material on the Ukrainian lands can be found in Aleksander Weryha-Darowski, *Kresy ruskie Rzeczpospolitej* (Warszawa: Koło Polaków Ziem Ruskich, 1919).

MASS MOVEMENTS AND EVENTS TO 1904: On National Democracy the most important studies, in addition to the earlier mentioned Stanisław Kozicki's essential work on the National League, are: Ellinor von Puttkamer, *Die polnische Nationaldemokratie* (Krakau: Institut für deutsche Ostarbeit, 1944); Tadeusz Bielecki, *W szkole Dmowskiego: szkice i wspomnienia* (London: Polska Fundacja Kulturalna, 1968) by a leading National Democrat; Władysław Pobóg-Malinowski, *Narodowa demokracja 1887–1918: fakty i dokumenty* (Warszawa: "Zjednoczona Polska," 1933), an attack from a Piłsudskiite position; as well as two Marxist interpretations by Jerzy Marczewski, *Narodowa*

*demokracja w Poznańskiem 1900–1914* (Warszawa: Państwowe
Wydawnictwo Naukowe, 1967) and Marian Orzechowski, *Narodowa
demokracja na Górnym Śląsku* (Wrocław: Ossolineum, 1965). A new
contribution is the stimulating essay by Andrzej Micewski, *Roman
Dmowski* (Warszawa: Verum, 1971). Also valuable is Jerzy J.
Terej, *Idee, mity, realia—szkice do dziejów Narodowej Demokracji* (Warszawa: Wiedza Powszechna, 1970). On Piłsudski the most detailed
work is Władysław Pobóg-Malinowski, *Józef Piłsudski* (London:
Komitet Wydawniczy, 1964) and the most interesting Anatol Muhl-
stein, *Le Maréchal Piłsudski 1867–1919* (Paris: Plon, 1939). A useful
although controversial introduction for the English reader is Marian
Kamil Dziewanowski, "Joseph Piłsudski 1867–1967," *East European
Quarterly* 2 (January, 1969): 359-83. See also the opening chapters
of his *Joseph Piłsudski a European Federalist 1918–1922* (Stan-
ford: Hoover Institution Press, 1969). W. F. Reddaway, *Marshal
Piłsudski* (London: G. Routledge & Sons, 1939), Rom Landau,
*Piłsudski: Hero of Poland* (London: Jarrolds, 1930), and Alexandra
Piłsudska, *Józef Piłsudski: A Biography by his Wife* (New York:
Dodd, Meade & Co., 1941) belong to the better biographies available
in English.

Among studies on Polish socialism, important are: Adam Próchnik,
*Studia z dziejów polskiego ruchu robotniczego* (Warszawa: Książka
i Wiedza, 1958); Wiesław Bieńkowski, *Kazimierz Kelles-Krauz: życie
i dzieło* (Kraków: Ossolineum, 1969); Marian Żychowski, *Bolesław
Limanowski* (Warszawa: Książka i Wiedza, 1971); Bolesław Danilczuk,
*Działalność SPD i PPS zaboru pruskiego w Poznańskiem w latach
1891–1914* (Toruń: Toruńskie Towarzystwo Naukowe, 1962); and
Józef Buszko, *Ruch socjalistyczny w Krakowie 1890–1914* (Kraków:
Wydawnictwo Literackie, 1961). Free from "official" interpretations,
although not always as well documented as publications published
in Poland, are the early sections of Marian Kamil Dziewanowski,
*The Communist Party of Poland* (Cambridge, Mass.: Harvard Uni-
versity Press, 1959); J. P. Nettl, *Rosa Luxemburg* (New York: Oxford
University Press, 1966); and the interesting polemical essay by Adam
Ciołkosz, *Róża Luksemburg a rewolucja rosyjska* (Paris: Instytut
Literacki, 1961). For the Populist movement, Peter Brock, "The Early
Years of the Polish Peasant Party 1895–1907," *Journal of Central
European Affairs* 14 (October, 1954): 219-35 is valuable. Informative
are the two studies by Krzysztof Dunin-Wąsowicz, *Dzieje stronnictwa
ludowego w Galicji* (Warszawa: Ludowa Spółdzielnia Wydawnicza,
1956) and *Jan Stapiński: trybun ludu wiejskiego* (Warszawa: Książka
i Wiedza, 1969).

There is a large number of publications on Prussian Poland. Apart
from the old study of Prussian colonization policies by Wiktor Sukien-

nicki, the following are of considerable importance: Adam Galos, Felix-Heinrich Gentzen, and Witold Jakóbczyk, *Die Hakatisten: der deutsche Ostmarkverein 1894–1934* (Berlin: Deutscher Verlag der Wissenschaften, 1966), which has been translated into Polish; Richard Tims, *Germanizing Prussian Poland . . . 1894–1919* (New York: Columbia University Press, 1941); Rudolf Korth, *Die preussische Schulpolitik und die polnischen Schulstreiks* (Würzburg: Holzner Verglag, 1963); Marian Pirko, *Bülow a sprawa polska* (Warszawa: Wojskowa Akademia Polityczna, 1963); and two studies by Lech Trzeciakowski, *Walka o polskość miast Poznańskiego na przełomie XIX i XX w.* (Poznań: Wydawnictwo Poznańskie, 1964) and *Polityka polskich klas posiadających w Wielkopolsce w erze Capriviego 1890-1894* (Poznań: Państwowe Wydawnictwo Naukowe, 1960). For Galicia, Jerzy Myśliński, *Grupy polityczne Królestwa Polskiego w zachodniej Galicji 1895–1904* (Warszawa: Książka i Wiedza, 1967) contains much interesting information. Useful is Ezra Mendelsohn, "Jewish Assimilation in Lvov: the Case of Wilhelm Feldman," *Slavic Review* 28 (December, 1969): 577-90. For Congress Poland, Irena Pietrzak-Pawłowska, *Królestwo Polskie w początkach imperializmu 1890–1905* (Warszawa: Państwowe Wydawnictwo Naukowe, 1955) is a fairly typical product of the 1950s. Adam Próchnik, *Bunt łódzki w roku 1892* (Warszawa: Książka i Wiedza, 1950) is an interesting treatment of a narrow subject. Revealing, although one-sided, is Wacław Lednicki, "Rosyjsko-polska Entente Cordiale: jej początki i fundamenty 1903–1905," *Zeszyty Historyczne* 10 (1966): 9-138.

FROM THE 1905 REVOLUTION TO WORLD WAR I: The revolution still awaits a comprehensive and balanced monographic treatment. The most extensive although controversial coverage of it can be found in Stanisław Kalabiński and Feliks Tych, *Czwarte powstanie czy pierwsza rewolucja: lata 1905–07 na ziemiach polskich* (Warszawa: Wiedza Powszechna, 1969). Stanisław Kalabiński, *Antynarodowa polityka endecji w rewolucji 1905–1907* (Warszawa: Państwowe Wydawnictwo Naukowe, 1955) is more concerned with a thesis than with objectivity. Józef Buszko and Henryk Dobrowolski, *Udział Galicji w rewolucji 1905–1907* (Kraków: Wydawnictwo Literackie, 1957) contains some useful data. Buszko's *Sejmowa reforma w Galicji 1905-1914* (Warszawa: Państwowe Wydawnictwo Naukowe, 1956) is somewhat rigid in its interpretations. Peasant problems in the kingdom are analysed by Wiesław Piątkowski, *Dzieje ruchu zaraniarskiego* (Warszawa: Ludowa Spółdzielnia Wydawnicza, 1956) and by Zenon Kmiecik, *Ruch oświatowy na wsi: Królestwo Polskie 1905–1914* (Warszawa: Ludowa Spółdzielnia Wydawnicza, 1963). The split within PPS is discussed by Anna Żarnowska, *Geneza rozłamu w Polskiej Partii Socjalistycznej 1904–1906* (Warszawa: Państwowe

Wydawnictwo Naukowe, 1965), and the author's sympathies clearly lie with the "Young." The Revolutionary Faction is discussed in a similar spirit by Teodor Ładyka, *Polska Partia Socjalistyczna (Frakcja Rewolucyjna) w latach 1906–1914* (Warszawa: Książka i Wiedza, 1972). Polish participation in the Duma is the subject of Edward Chmielewski, *The Polish Question in the Russian State Duma* (Knoxville: University of Tennessee Press, 1970), a useful but not an inspiring book; Zygmunt Łukawski, *Koło polskie w rosyjskiej Dumie państwowej w latach 1906–1909* (Wrocław: Ossolineum, 1967); and Mirosław Wierzchowski, *Sprawy polskie w III i IV Dumie państwowej* (Warszawa: Państwowe Wydawnictwo Naukowe, 1965). Wierzchowski strongly stresses class aspects. For Prussian Poland, Michał Pirko, *Niemiecka polityka wywłaszczeniowa na ziemiach polskich w latach 1907–1908* (Warszawa: Ministerstwo Obrony Narodowej, 1963) contains a wealth of material; Zygmunt Hemmerling, *Posłowie polscy w parlamencie Rzeszy niemieckiej i sejmie pruskim 1907–1914* (Warszawa: Ludowa Spółdzielnia Wydawnicza, 1968) is valuable. Prewar Polish political trends are illuminated by Stanisław Biegański, "Idee państwowe w ruchu niepodległościowym w latach 1908–1914," *Niepodległość*, n.s. 5 (1955): 60-116, and by the more controversial Kurt G. Hausmann, "Dmowskis Stellung zu Deutschland vor dem Ersten Weltkriege," *Zeitschrift für Ostforschung* 13, nos. 1/2 (1964): 56-91. On Polish military preparations see Andrzej Garlicki, *Geneza legionów: zarys dziejów Komisji Tymczasowej Skonfederowanych Stronnictw Niepodległościowych* (Warszawa: Książka i Wiedza, 1964), a very detailed study ably criticized by Jan Ciałowicz, "O genezie Legionów," *Najnowsze Dzieje Polski: Materiały i Studia z Okresu 1914–1939* 10 (1966): 187-206. Very informative is Henryk Bagiński, *U podstaw organizacji wojska polskiego 1908–1914* (Warszawa: Sekcja historyczna "Zarzewie," 1935). Władysław Sikorski's role is briefly discussed in the opening chapters of Marian Kukiel, *Generał Sikorski* (London: Instytut Polski i Museum im. Gen. Sikorskiego, 1970).

THE FIRST WORLD WAR:  A great deal has been written on this subject, beginning with studies that came out shortly after the event—for instance, Stanisław Kutrzeba, *Polska odrodzona 1914–1921* (Kraków: Gebethner i Wolff, 1921)—until the present. In English the most exhaustive coverage of the international aspects is Tytus Komarnicki, *The Rebirth of the Polish Republic 1914–1920* (London: Heinemann, 1957). See also the opening chapter of Hans Roos, *A History of Modern Poland* (New York: A. Knopf, 1966). An older but still valuable study is Joseph Blociszewski, *La restauration de la Pologne et la diplomatie européenne* (Paris: A. Pedone, 1927). On the military aspect see Wacław Lipiński, *Walka zbrojna o niepodległość Polski*

*1905–1918* (Warszawa: Instytut Badania Najnowszej Historii Polski,
1931). Old and still valuable is Marceli Handelsman, *La Pologne,
sa vie économique et sociale pendant la guerre* (Paris: Les Presses
Universitaires de France, 1933). Among recent syntheses very useful
is Jerzy Holzer and Jan Molenda, *Polska w pierwszej wojnie światowej*
(Warszawa: Wiedza Powszechna, 1963). The book has a most valuable little dictionary of Polish organizations and institutions and some
good statistics. Several studies dealing with the First World War and
written in Poland in the 1950s are so blatantly propagandistic and
biased that despite occasional valuable parts they hardly merit being
included in a serious bibliography. As an example one can mention
Stefan Arski's book on the First Brigade, some of the works of Leon
Grosfeld, and some publications of the Party Institute. Limited space
prevents, on the other hand, the listing of numerous valuable articles
scattered throughout Polish periodicals. On the Polish question and
the Entente powers particularly important are: Janusz Pajewski,
*Wokół sprawy polskiej: Paryż, Lozanna, Londyn* (Poznań: Wydawnictwo Poznańskie, 1970)—an original and stimulating study—and
Remigiusz Bierzanek, *Państwo polskie w politycznych koncepcjach
mocarstw zachodnich 1917–1919* (Warszawa: Polski Instytut Spraw
Międzynarodowych, 1964). On the Central Powers there is Pajewski's
article in *Roczniki Historyczne* (Poznań, 1962), and a monograph by
Leon Grosfeld, *Polityka państw centralnych wobec sprawy polskiej
1914–1918* (Warszawa: Państwowe Wydawnictwo Naukowe, 1962).
For the *Mitteleuropa* question, discussed by Pajewski and others,
a good introduction is P. R. Sweet, "Germany, Austria and Mitteleuropa, Aug. 1915-April 1916," *Festschrift für Heinrich Benedikt*,
edited by Hugo Hantsch and Alexander Novotny (Vienna: Notrig,
1957), pp. 180-212. The pioneering although controversial work of
Fritz Fischer, *Germany's Aims in the First World War* (New York:
W. W. Norton, 1967) contains a wealth of valuable material on German
policies toward Poland and the eastern borderlands. On German-
Polish relations valuable are: Werner Conze, *Polnische Nation und
deutsche Politik im ersten Weltkrieg* (Köln: Böhlau, 1958) and Imanuel
Geiss, *Der polnische Grenzstreifen 1914-1918* (Lübeck and Ham-
burg: Mathiesen Verlag, 1960). On Germany and the eastern border-
lands see Hans J. Beyer, *Die Mittelmächte und die Ukraine* (Munich:
Isar, 1956) and Oleh S. Fedyshyn, *Germany's Drive to the East and
the Ukrainian Revolution 1917–1918* (New Brunswick, N.J.: Rutgers
University Press, 1971). On Lithuania see Gerd Linde, *Die deutsche
Politik in Litauen im ersten Weltkrieg* (Wiesbaden: Harrassowitz,
1965). An excellent appraisal of Russian policies toward Poland is in
Alexander Dallin, "The Future of Poland," *Russian Diplomacy and
Eastern Europe 1914–1917*, Russian Institute Occasional Papers,

Columbia University (New York: King's Crown Press, 1963), pp. 1-77. See also the opening chapters of Piotr S. Wandycz, *Soviet-Polish Relations 1917–1921* (Cambridge, Mass.: Harvard University Press, 1969). On the first phase of the war particularly noteworthy are: Konstanty Srokowski, *NKN: Zarys historii Naczelnego Komitetu Narodowego* (Kraków: Krakowska Spółka Wydawnicza, 1923) written by a participant who was also a critical and sharp observer; Michał Sokolnicki, *Rok Czternasty* (London: Gryf Publication Ltd., 1961) the work of a Piłsudski partisan and historian. Of great interest are Szymon Askenazy, *Uwagi* (Warszawa: E. Wende, 1924) which provides good insights and Władysław Baranowski, *Rozmowy z Piłsudskim 1916–1931* (Warszawa: Biblioteka Polska, 1938) which records private conservations with the future marshal of Poland. Also see: Casimir Smogorzewski, *Joseph Piłsudski et les activistes polonais pendant la guerre* (Paris: Gebethner, 1930–31); and Jan Rzepecki, *Sprawa legionu wschodniego 1914 roku* (Warszawa: Państwowe Wydawnictwo Naukowe, 1966). For the Dmowski orientation see especially Marian Leczyk, *Komitet Narodowy Polski a Ententa i Stany Zjednoczone 1917–1919* (Warszawa: Państwowe Wydawnictwo Naukowe, 1966), and Czesław Kozłowski, *Działalność polityczna Koła Międzypartyjnego w latach 1915–1918* (Warszawa: Książka i Wiedza, 1967). On Polish troops in Russia compare Henryk Bagiński, *Wojsko polskie na wschodzie 1914–1920* (Warszawa: Wojskowy Instytut Naukowo-Wydawniczy, 1921) and Mieczysław Wrzosek, *Polskie korpusy wojskowe w Rosji w latach 1917–1918* (Warszawa: Z Pola Walki, 1969). Useful is Stefan W. Wojstomski, *Traktat Brzeski a Polska* (London: Polska Fundacja Kulturalna, 1969). On Lenin and Poland as well as on Bolshevik-Polish relations the recent literature in Poland is immense, and such events as the hundredth anniversary of Lenin's birth produced a new avalanche of writings. Some of the more important items up to 1968 are listed in this author's book on Soviet-Polish relations. A good deal has also been written—although it has not always been divorced from present-day political considerations—on political life in Poland during the war. Henryk Jabłoński wrote on the PPS; Jan Molenda, on the Polish Peasant Party; Feliks Tych, on the PPS Left; Felicja Figowa, on the "bourgeois" parties. For a more general survey of the leftist parties see *Ruch robotniczy i ludowy w Polsce w latach 1914–1923* (2nd ed.; Warszawa: Książka i Wiedza, 1961).

SOURCES: Documents on the SDKPiL were published by O. B. Schmidt in Moscow. A useful collection is also Georg W. Strobel (ed.), *Quellen zur Geschichte des Kommunismus in Polen, 1878–1918: Programme und Statuten* (Köln: Wissenschaft and Politik, 1968). Selected documents illustrating the revolutionary ferment in Congress

Poland, and the struggle of tsardom and the propertied classes against the Revolution of 1905 were edited respectively by Herman Rappaport and Stanisław Kalabiński. Reports of the tsarist chiefs of police in Warsaw for the years 1895–1913 were edited by Helena Kiepurska and Zbigniew Pustula. Stefan Arski and Józef Chudek published documentation designed to prove Piłsudski's dependence on Austrian intelligence in their *Galicyjska działalność wojskowa Piłsudskiego* (Warszawa: Państwowe Wydawnictwo Naukowe, 1967). NKN (Naczelny Komitet Narodowy) published a collection of its documents covering the 1914–17 period. Stanisław Lato and Witold Stankiewicz compiled political programs of the Populists' parties with many useful annexes. The United Peasant Party *(Zjednoczone Stronnictwo Ludowe)* published sources on the history of the peasant movement. The first volume covers the period up to 1918. Stanisław Filasiewicz, ed., *La Question Polonaise pendant la guerre mondiale: recueil des actes diplomatiques, traités et documents concernant la Pologne* (Paris: Comité National Polonais, 1920) is still extremely useful. Theofil Hornykiewicz edited documents from the Austrian archives bearing on the Ukrainian question during the First World War. Collected works of Piłsudski were published in the 1930s and there exists a selection edited by D. R. Gillie, *Joseph Piłsudski: The Memoirs of a Polish Revolutionary and Soldier* (London: Faber and Faber, 1931); those of Dmowski were not completed, and the reader has to look for several of Dmowski's writings elsewhere. The publication of a most helpful collection of Dmowski's letters, reminiscences, and other material began in London in 1968 under the editorship of Marian Kułakowski. There is an abundance of memoirs of uneven importance and credibility. Bobrzyński's memoirs were published by Adam Galos in the 1950s, and they are revealing. Also important are those of Leon Biliński and Stanisław Głąbiński. Among the socialist leaders both Limanowski and Daszyński published their memoirs. Those of Stapiński appeared a little over a decade ago. Witos' memoirs were published in Paris in the 1960s. General Haller dictated his in London and they are unreliable and disappointing. The reminiscences of Hutten-Czapski are important for German-Polish relations. A systematic publication of sources for the first two decades of the twentieth century is not yet far advanced.

# Index

Abramowicz, Ludwik, 349
Abramowski, Edward, 379
Academic Reading Circle, 289
Academy of Learning, 220, 269, 378
"Activists," 345, 351
Administration: of commonwealth, 4; in Galicia, 12, 216, 220, 257; in Prussian Poland, 14, 179; in "western guberniias," 18, 83, 127, 155; in partitioned Poland, 20; in Duchy of Warsaw, 40, 64; in Poznania, 68; in Congress Kingdom, 122, 125, 156, 168, 171, 195-96, 198; "two-track," 216, 221
Administrative Council, 75, 78, 88-89, 90, 107, 122, 195
Agency (Agencja), 26, 28-29, 30, 32
Agrarian democracy, 117
Agrarian-Industrial Bank, 232
Agricultural Academy, Dublany, 378
Agricultural Institute, 184
Agricultural societies, 231-32, 286
Agricultural Society (Towarzystwo Rolnicze), 156, 159, 161-62, 163, 165
Agriculture: in commonwealth, 6-7, 9, 21; in Prussian Poland, 15-16, 70-71, 229, 281; three-field system, 16, 71, 124, 200; crop rotation, 16, 124; in Galicia, 71, 223-24; in Congress Kingdom, 79, 82, 124, 158-59; increase in production, 200-1; in "northwestern lands," 242-43; in "southwestern lands," 248; postwar, 369. See also Estates; Folwark; Gentry; Land; Magnates; Peasants; Serfdom
Akademia Umiejętności. See Academy of Learning
Aksakov, Ivan S., 243
Albedynsky, P. P., 195
Aleksa (Angarietis), Zigmas, 314, 367
Alexander I, Tsar: and Czartoryski, 33-34; and "western guberniias," 35; and Polish radicalism, 39; and Polish question, 40-41, 77, 82; and Tilsit agreement, 41; at Erfurt, 52; and France, 54, 56; and Lithuanian

magnates, 55; and Congress of Vienna, 61-62; and provisional government, 61; and constitution of Congress Kingdom, 84; and Freemasonry, 85; and secret societies, 86; death of, 87; and educational reforms, 95
Alexander II, Tsar, 155-56, 161, 168, 178, 194, 196, 207, 241, 253
Alexander III, Tsar, 208
Allenstein (Olsztyn), 238
*Allgemeines Landrecht*, 14
Alvensleben Convention, 173
Amis de la Verité, 85
Amnesty, 44, 152, 156, 231
Andrássy, Gyula, 219
Angarietis. See Aleksa, Zigmas
Anglo-Austrian Coalition, 62
Anti-Semitism, 207, 222, 246, 277, 280, 281, 293, 302, 325
Antonowicz, Włodzimierz (Antonovych, Volodymyr), 249, 250, 252
Apukhtin, Aleksandr, 208
Architecture, 10, 97, 188-89, 268, 377
Area: of commonwealth, 3; of Prussian Poland, 14; of Duchy of Warsaw, 43; of Congress Kingdom, 65, 74; of Grand Duchy of Posen, 68; of Galicia, 71; of Cracow Republic, 72
Aristocracy, 20, 21, 23, 25, 39, 93. See also Magnates; Nobility
Army: of commonwealth, 4, 13; peasant obligations to, 13, 19, 21, 47, 78; foreign, conscription of Poles in, 31; budget, opposition to, 55-56; Lithuanian, 59; Prussian, and "Polish movement," 141. See also Legions; Lithuanian Army Corps —Polish: in Italy, 28-29; size of, 39-40, 112; in Duchy of Warsaw, 48, 61, 63; Corps, 51, 337; in Congress Kingdom, 75, 78, 124; in November Insurrection, 105, 106; formed in Russia, 355; Auxiliary Corps, 357, 368; formed in France, 360
Arsenevich, I. A., 17

413

428																Index

Sich Riflemen, 328, 339, 366
Sicily, 137
Siedlce, 45
Siemiradzki, Henryk, 268
Sienkiewicz, Henryk, 266, 268, 271, 343
Sierakowski, Zygmunt, 160, 175
Sieroszewski, Wacław, 375
Sikorski, Władysław, 327, 345
Silesia, 41, 149, 186, 283. See also Teschen
Silesia; Upper Silesia
Skalon, Georgii, 315
Skarbek, Fryderyk, 93
Skłodowska, Maria (Marie Curie), 379
Skoropadsky, Pavel, 363, 366
Skrzynecki, Jan, 114, 115-16
Slav Congress of 1848, 145, 146, 149; of
1908, 324
Slavism, 120, 121
Slavophilism, 101-2, 195, 240
Šleževičius, Mykolas, 316
Šliupas, Jonas, 246
Słowacki, Juliusz, 132, 182-83, 184, 300,
373
Smetona, Antanas, 348, 349, 359, 363
Smith, Adam, 93
Smoleński, Wladyslaw, 270
Smolka, Franciszek, 142, 147, 218, 219
Smoluchowski, Marian, 379
Smuglewicz, Franciszek, 97
Śniadecki, Jan, 93, 95, 101
Śniadecki, Jędrzej, 93
Social Darwinism, 292
Social Democracy of the Kingdom of
Poland (SDKP), 298-99, 300
Social Democracy of the Kingdom of
Poland and Lithuania (SDKPiL), 300, 302,
304, 311-12, 314, 316, 320, 328, 358
Social Democratic movement, Austrian, 227
Social Democratic Party, Ukrainian, 306
Social Democratic Party of Lithuania, 314
Socialism: forerunners of, 119; rise of, 193-
94, 210, 211; Jewish, 207; early Polish,
211-13; Galician, 226, 227-28, 278, 296,
322; Poznanian, 235-36; Eastern Galician,
257-58; German, 295; Belorussian, 302;
growth of, 303, 304; Russian, 304; Ukrai-
nian, 306-7; Lithuania, 360. See also
Polish Socialist Party; Social Democracy
of the Kingdom of Poland and Lithuania
Socialist International, First, 209; Second,
296, 299
Society for National Education, 289
Society for the Protection of the Uniates,
289
Society of Educational Aid, 128
Society of Friends of Learning, 92-93, 94,
122, 184-85, 378
Society of Plebeians, 132
Society of Polish Republicans, 27-28, 30, 32
Society of Scythemen, 69
Sokół (Falcon), 232, 262, 290, 305
Sokolnicki, Michał, 327, 379
Somosierra, 56
Sorel, Albert, 11

Sosnkowski, Kazimierz, 327, 357
Southern Prussia, 14
"Southwestern land," 248-53
Soviet of Workers, 312
Soviet of Workers' and Soldiers' Deputies,
355
Spasowicz, Włodzimierz, 209
Spencer, Herbert, 262
Spielberg (Špilberk), 128
Spinning, 81, 205
Spirits, 82, 127, 197, 225, 230
Sports, 371
Stablewski, Florian, 236, 283, 287, 321
Stadion, Franz, 142, 143, 144
Staff, Leopold, 375-77
Stańczyk's Portfolio, 216
Stanevičius, Simanas, 244
Stanislaus Augustus, King, 10, 97, 98, 270
Stanisławski, Jan, 377
Stapiński, Jan, 294, 295, 323, 326
Starogard, 238
Staszic, Stanisław, 10, 35, 44, 79-80, 92, 93,
101, 102
State Council, 50, 53, 122, 165, 316, 357,
364, 365
State Council of Lithuania, 363
State: nationality, 5; and nation, 22
Steam engine, 73, 81, 82, 90, 123, 158, 202
Steel, 204, 206
Stein, Baron Karl von, 37
Stern, Abraham, 92
Stoczek: battle of, 114
Stojałowski, Stanisław, 226-27, 294
Stolypin, Petr, 319
Strazdas (Drozdowski), Anatanas, 244
Strikes: in Congress Poland, 207, 356;
school, 246, 289, 311, 319, 321; agricultu-
ral, 279; at Łódź, 296; peasant, 305;
general, 311-12, 320, 368; railroad, 312; in
Lithuania, 314; in Warsaw, 365
Stroganov, Pavel, 33
Strug (Gałecki), Andrzej, 376
Stryj, 222
Students, 73, 74, 89, 95, 159-61, 330. See
also Education; Schools; Universities
Studnicki, Władysław, 345
Stürmer (Premier), 343
Sugar beets, 71, 82, 124, 158, 202, 204, 206,
223, 229, 230, 277, 279, 281
Sukhozanet, Nikolai, 167
Sukowski, Józef, 28
"Sunday Schools," 250, 252
Supiński, Józef, 185, 263, 271
Supreme National Committee (NKN), 333,
336, 338, 339, 345, 346
Supreme People's Council, 367
Surgical-Medical Academy, 185
Suvorov, Aleksander, 21, 32
Suwałki, 245-46, 340
Šwarce, Bronisław, 170
Świętochowski, Aleksander, 208, 209, 263,
264, 268, 311
Syrokomla, Władysław (Ludwik Kondra-
towicz), 187